AMERICAN LIVES, AMERICAN ISSUES

AMERICAN LIVES, AMERICAN ISSUES

Robert S. Newman

State University of New York at Buffalo

Prentice
Hall

Upper Saddle River, New Jersey

Library of Congress Cataloging-in-Publication Data

Newman, Robert S. 1935–
    American lives, American issues / Robert S. Newman.
      p. cm.
    Includes bibliographical references and index.
    ISBN 0-13-085134-5 (alk. paper)
      1. Pluralism (Social sciences)—United States. 2. United States—Ethnic relations. 3.
    United States—Race relations. 4. United States—Social conditions—1980– 5.
    Minorities—United States—Social conditions. 6. Minorities—United States—Biography.
    I. Title.
    E184.A1 .N49 2001
    305.8′00973—dc21

                                   2001044798

Editor-in-Chief: Leah Jewell
Acquisitions Editor: Corey Good
Editorial Assistant: John Ragozzine
VP, Director of Production and Manufacturing: Barbara Kittle
Senior Managing Editor: Mary Rottino
Production Editor: Randy Pettit
Prepress and Manufacturing Manager: Nick Sklitsis
Prepress and Manufacturing Buyer: Mary Ann Gloriande
Director of Marketing: Beth Gillett Mejia
Senior Marketing Manager: Brandy Dawson
Cover Design Director: Jayne Conte
Cover Art: Robert Neubecker/Stock Illustration Source
Director, Image Resources: Melinda Lee Reo
Image Specialist: Beth Boyd-Benzel
Photo Researcher: Anthony Arabia
Manager, Rights and Permissions: Kay Dellosa

For permission to use copyrighted material, grateful acknowledgment is made to
the copyright holders listed on pages 559–562, which is considered an extension
of this copyright page.

This book was set in 10/12 Bembo by Publications Development Company of Texas
and printed and bound by Courier-Stoughton. The cover was printed by Phoenix.

Printed in the United States of America
10 9 8 7 6 5 4 3 2 1

ISBN 0-13-085134-5

Pearson Education LTD., London
Pearson Education Australia Pty, Limited, Sydney
Pearson Education North Asia Ltd, Hong Kong
Pearson Education Canada, Ltd, Toronto
Pearson Education de Mexico, S.A. de C.V.
Pearson Education - Japan, Tokyo
Pearson Education Malaysia, Pte. Ltd
Pearson Education, Upper Saddle River, New Jersey

CONTENTS

4 AMERICAN PLURALISM 211

5 THE AMERICAN DREAM: CLASS IN AMERICA   295

8 CHANGE IN AMERICA 490

PREFACE

This anthology of readings in American pluralism is designed for use in freshman composition courses or in courses devoted explicitly to pluralism and diversity. It consists of two kinds of writings—essays about individual lives (autobiographical, journalistic) and argumentative or analytic essays, often arranged in terms of opposing viewpoints. The combination is a familiar one in American literature, from Benjamin Franklin's *Autobiography,* postulating Franklin himself as the model new American, to the *Autobiography of Malcolm X,* arguing for the transformation of black rage and white silence through the example of Malcolm's own conversions. *American Lives, American Issues* thus suggests that life-stories often raise argumentative issues for both readers and writers. Conversely, argumentative issues, to be truly understood, must be illustrated and tested by particular life-stories.

The distinctiveness of *American Lives, American Issues* lies in two areas: (1) the insistence on oppositional viewpoints even in the sensitive arena of multiculturalism and (2) the emphasis on *linking* of personal and argumentative writings rather than on their *separation.*

───── OPPOSING VIEWPOINTS IN MULTICULTURALISM ─────

In the argumentative sections of this anthology, essays exhibiting opposing viewpoints about multiculturalism have been chosen because most anthologies on these subjects no longer exhibit the new complexities of the pluralism "primes" (race, class, gender) that figure in current discussions. (Indeed, we can now speak of "multicultural conservatism," as Angela D. Dillard does in *Guess Who's Coming to Dinner New? Multicultural Conservatism in America;* see her recent essay "Multicultural Conservatism: What It Is, Why It Matters," a sympathetic but ultimately skeptical account, in *The Chronicle of Higher Education,* March 2, 2001).

In an earlier era, it was necessary to shock readers into awareness of the ways in which the actualities of American life belied the high hopes of the American Dream (to choose a convenient symbol). We needed to know that assumptions from a white middle-class male perspective about the nature of social reality did not meet the experience of large numbers of other groups in American life. In one way or another, however, that task has been accomplished: laws have changed, attitudes have changed, TV commercials have changed. While some would argue that such changes are not enough—women still don't make the kind of money men do, racial discrimination may still persist, millions of Americans still face constrained lives and lowered life-chances; others would say that with artificial bars gone, it's up to individuals to improve their lot: government should not do more. The key term nowadays is individual "responsibility," the key philosophy of the moment is in some respects the libertarian one (consider Doug Bandow's piquant essay "Private Prejudice, Private Remedy" or Roger Pilon's provocative "The Right to Do Wrong," a defense of both flag-burning and private discrimination!).

Regardless of whether you believe that much has or has not been done to remove the straitjackets of discrimination in their manifold forms (Manning Marable, page 281, is not so sure), the new challenges of an individualistic ethic and a zigzagging stock market will force both defenders and critics of the American Dream to reexamine their cases. Although Gregory Mantsios (page 304) for example argues that income mobility—the American Dream—is nothing but a "myth" perpetuated by a cynical media, Michael Cox and Richard Alm say its Mantsios's hypothesis that is the real myth about the rich and the poor and that the American Dream is alive and well (stop whining, they seem to be saying). In turn however, defenders of the Dream will themselves have to answer renewed objections from the next generation of critics. Thus when the conservative American Enterprise Institute explains that women really make 98 cents to the male dollar, contra the older feminist arguments of 74 cents, Ellen Bravo in *Ms.* magazine says that's just so much nonsense: the higher figure applies only to unmarried professional women and the rest do not benefit.

A superb example of what happens when you ignore the opposition can be seen in recent criticism of one of the greats of American liberal philosophy, Richard Rorty (whose essay "What's Wrong with Rights Talk" concludes this volume). Writing in *The Partisan Review,* a mainstay of Left-liberalism since the 1930s, Robert Sidowsky faults Rorty for refusing to even consider conservative arguments about class, the American Dream, or the nature of human nature. Rorty's analysis Sidowsky charges, "avoids any reference to the contrary theory, familiar evidence or argument that alternative strategies of free market competition may generate rates of economic growth resulting in improvement for the masses of society." Rorty's image of American "chauvinistic militarism" as depicted by John Wayne is nonsense, Sidowsky says, and is belied by the contrary image held by most Americans "of the United States as a country which provides equality before the law or multiple opportunities so that the poor achieve the good life, if not for themselves, then for the next generation."

The stunning thing about Sidowsky's criticism is that it is angry not simply at Rorty's actual positions but at Rorty's failure to realize that there are new people on the block, new thinking about race, class, and gender, and that conservatives, neoliberals, and even liberals now offer analyses of social ailments in the body politic that cannot simply be ignored outright.

In this respect, *American Lives, American Issues* aims to present as much as possible of both sides of current issues in American pluralism. Indeed, for the reasons that Sidowsky outlines, refusal to engage with the opposition means a fallacious assumption that what has been achieved in America to date is inadequate, that "socialist" critiques of America ignore the nature of human nature and its dark side, or finally that conservatives have developed alternative evidences and arguments that counter those of the socialist Left.

LIVES AND ISSUES

Along with the insistence on oppositional viewpoints, *American Lives, American Issues* emphasizes the connection between life-writing and argumentation. But as Irene L. Clark notes in *Writing About Diversity,* this linkage has often been criticized:

> Most textbooks . . . present argumentation as a completely different genre [from personal forms of writing], a sophisticated "second semester" concept unrelated to the less formal, more personal writing that students often engage in during their first semester.

In particular, personal forms of writing have been criticized as either too easy or too hard (to write well) and as logically useless. On the first point, the personal essays included here have proven to be useful models in classroom settings, producing solid essays by the students who work from them. As to the second point, autobiographically based essays accomplish crucial argumentative functions: they help crystallize complex social phenomena; they make us realize the difference between what we say and what we do; they reveal the power of individual choice despite adverse social forces; and, finally, they impel us to investigate those crucial factors that distinguish one person's account from another's. As Irene Clark observes,

> writing about any issue originates with the self and it is difficult for students to formulate an opinion, develop a thesis, and provide a convincing argument about a topic unless they first explore their own perspective on it.

Suzanne Pharr's provocative essay "A Match Made in Heaven, Lesbian Leftie Chats with a Promise Keeper" (Chapter 8) offers a superb example of just how lives and issues intersect. A lesbian activist writing

in the liberal magazine *The Progressive,* Pharr tells how she met up
with a Christian Promise Keeper on a plane and shared an unexpectedly engaging exchange with him. In terms of conventional stereotypes of either a "lesbian leftie" or a Christian Promise Keeper
(dedicated, as one source has it, "to keeping men as the spiritual
headship of the family") you wouldn't expect any meeting of the
minds whatsoever, but Pharr discovered that although she and her
opposite number disagreed about feminism and religion—notably
whether wives must ultimately accept a husbands' "headship"—they
actually agreed on others and shared family experiences that helped
them understand each other's values.

The issue that Pharr's story raises is whether people from opposite ideological camps can even talk with each other let alone understand each other's principles. The answer Pharr gives is most
certainly a yes, especially when you talk to the foot-soldiers of the
movement, not the leadership. She and her fellow passenger ex-
changed long-distance phone calls weeks after their trip. We ourselves can read Pharr's essay and identify with either or both Pharr
and the Promise Keeper, and we can also be happy about the connection, limited but fruitful, that the two of them made. Here, the
events in Pharr's account illuminate a broad issue involving communication and narrower issues of theology and organizational loyalty.

───────── WHAT IS AN AMERICAN? ─────────

American Lives, American Issues has the word *American* twice in its
title, partly because it's intriguing and quasi-alliterative, partly because it touches on a key idea, that there is something arguably
unique about the American experience. In the Preface to *Americans,*
the historian Edward Countryman puts it in terms of simple personal
experience:

> One result of my long stay among the British [Countryman
> writes] was to learn that I never would be one of them, how-
> ever great my taste for "real ale" and fish and chips doused in
> salt and vinegar, however adept I am at driving on the left.

But what does "American" mean in more positive and scholarly terms
to Countryman? Good historian that he is, Countryman rehearses the
many different and "colliding" histories that make up American history at large (e.g., African enslavement, white colonization and the
fight for independence, Tejano "lost possibilities," and so on) and
then insists on a return to the spirit underlying all of them, that of
Jefferson and the Declaration of Independence:

all the stories [he writes] circle around the mixture of hope and disappointment of Thomas Jefferson's proclamation that "all men are created equal." All the people in all the stories have found themselves living in a world of disruption and transformation. All of them have tried to form meaningful ties with other people in the same plight so they could establish patterns that would give their lives sense and cohesion.

Thus, says Countryman,

If I, a white American, would understand what shaped me, if I would not be a stranger to myself, I must understand people who may not look like me but whose history is fundamentally, inextricably, and forever intertwined with my own.

As Countryman implicitly recognizes, there is a historical factor to American identity because the idea of being "American" has changed with the times, both in the long history of the past, from the eighteenth century to the present (melting pot assimilation, pluralism or acculturation, and racial separatism for example) and in the most recent present, where immigrants (legal and illegal) and refugees from many different lands have complicated the racial/ethnic/national mixture of Americanness, and where subgroups within once seemingly monolithic groups (Asian, African, Hispanic) now complicate a once simple picture of black versus white racial identity and make us realize the more complex situation created by many different and specific groups—Chinese, Japanese, Indonesian, Pakistani, Indian, Cuban, Tejano, Chicano, just to name a few.

(An opposing viewpoint warning: from the position of conservatives like John O'Sullivan in the *National Review* or talk show host Don Feder, speaking to the Christian Coalition, or even the liberal historian Arthur Schlesinger, Jr., in *The Disuniting of America, Reflections on a Multicultural Society,* such "hyphenated" Americanness—such extreme "multiculturalism"—is suspect, a denial of the "unum" in our country's motto—"Out of many, one"—"E pluribus unum." What do you think?)

In the matter of "lives and issues," it thus becomes possible to ask where *you* fit in within the rubric of "American"? What has been your experience? Unambiguous or complicated? Hope fulfilled or disappointment realized? Where do you fit in terms of "assimilation"? Do you side more with those who want more "pluribus" or more "unum"? Is there a difference between you and your family on any of these issues? You and your friends? You and your home neighborhood and your new neighborhood of college or university? You will want to read the essays in this anthology and write your own analyses of them, to see if they accord with your experience or not and to determine whether or not the authors's generalizations need modifying in the light of your own understanding of American culture or society.

──────── ORGANIZATION OF THIS ANTHOLOGY ────────

People write best when they write from their own experience or when they face conflicting views and must sort out why they prefer one view over another. These are the motivating principles behind *American Lives, American Issues*. However, writing from experience isn't as simple as it sounds, because it depends on how good an observer and meditator the writer is. These difficulties can be overcome by using good models of personal writing and by reseeing one's experience from alternative viewpoints. Therefore, the text is arranged in terms of a broadening progression from individuals writing about what happened to them to journalists and scholars concerned with interpreting individual experience from larger social and theoretical viewpoints.

Chapters 1 and 2 offer models of writing about specific incidents (Chapter 1) and geographical locales (Chapter 2): the focus is on producing well-told stories about specific cultural encounters. The model that has been used is Marianna DeMarco Torgovnick's "On Being White, Female, and Born in Bensonhurst" with its twin encounters at the center—the death of a black youth in the Italian section of Brooklyn and Torgovnick's own defiance of gender taboos in the Italian old men's club—a pairing of anecdotes that usually produce a rich crop of essays about discrimination encountered and (sometimes) discrimination overcome. From those students who don't take up the issue of discrimination, thoughtful essays about family and home matters, usually generational, reveal many of the same fault lines as the racial/gender encounters can be created.

Chapter 2 on place and geographical locale is designed to enlarge students' perceptions and writing opportunities from the directly personal to the more objective possibilities that writing about a place encourages. What can be said about our neighborhood, city, or rural area is often easier to write about than writing directly about our feelings or conflicts with others. Students, responding to the challenge of such essays as Dorothy Blew's account of life on a rural dairy farm in the 1950s, Esmeralda Santiago's account of being transported from rural Puerto Rico to multicultural New York, or Lucy Lippard's intriguing invitation to provide *from within* a story about "the lure of the local" have produced richly detailed and thought-provoking accounts of key positive or negative moments in their earlier lives.

Later chapters (3 through 8) provide larger-than-individual viewpoints from which to reconsider the initial drafts of essays of the first two chapters or to start afresh, from a different viewpoint, on comparable material. Since student essays modeled on the essays of Chapters 1 and 2 often deal with discrimination and groups in conflict, Chapter 3 takes up theories of prejudice and discrimination, especially two basic approaches to these problematic areas of experience—i.e., the idea of racism per se and the idea of group identity. In particular, readings encourage students to reexamine their actual experience with prejudice and discrimination in order to see to what extent either theories of racism or of group identity help them understand what they have experienced.

Following up on the material in Chapter 3, Chapter 4 enlarges our understanding of prejudice and discrimination by linking it to different versions of American history and the "theory of America"— Nathan Glazer's view (in "The American Ethnic Pattern") that America, give or take some bad patches, is a land of inclusion, dedicated to the progressive realization of "liberty and justice for all" and Ronald Takaki's point-for-point rebuttal of Glazer that, give or take some good patches, America has until only recently become a land of inclusion, especially from the viewpoint of racial if not ethnic minorities. (Is the glass half full, as Glazer might have it, or half empty, as Takaki would see it?) Here students can place their own immediate experience in the context of two rival versions of American history and identity: has their experience been good or bad, and how does it intersect with rival views of larger historical forces? Chapter 4 then asks students to take a long and hard view of their own and their families's lives by placing them in the context of variant views of what it means to be an "American."

Chapters 5 through 8 take up particular areas of recent concern that may help students to examine anew material they've written about in previous chapters or, taking a cue from the readings themselves, try their hand at new pieces dealing with specific aspects of American identity—the ideal of the American Dream (Chapter 5), gender questions (Chapter 6), and religious issues (Chapter 7). Finally, Chapter 8 offers varied essays on the possibilities of change, including some which argue that changes already underway are negative, not positive.

THE BOOK'S PROGRESSION ILLUSTRATED

The move from the particular to the general that *American Lives, American Issues* offers can be illustrated by one of my favorite essays, Torgovnick's "Bensonhurst," and what might be done with it. Students

should begin their rereading of the essay by jumping to the concluding anecdote, a one-page narrative of Torgovnick's experience in trying to find—just before returning to her job in North Carolina—a
cremolata, a kind of ice. She can't get one at the bakery because it's
too early in the morning, but eventually she remembers that it's available in the Italian old men's club. However, women aren't allowed in
the club during the day (and at night only in the company of a man),
but Torgovnick wants that cremolata desperately, so she goes into the
club no matter what the taboos are. And once in it she is treated to a
chorus of hisses and epithets (*strega,* whore). She has violated the
neighborhood rules and she knows it. But she also knows that unlike
the violation of the racial taboos by the black youths in the pizza parlor incident, she won't die for her transgression.

This final anecdote alone is worth almost the whole essay and student writers can and do find all sorts of ways to imitate Torgovnick's
narrative practice and ethical sensibility (despite the fact that the
essay as a whole is a very complex and sophisticated performance).
The key anecdote here is crystal clear—a superb model of narration
for students to emulate and a pointed message (in one or two sentences) about the larger significance of taboo-busting behavior.

But Torgovnick's anecdote, and various generalizations, assertions, and casual cause-effect analyses throughout the essay—like any
student performance—also profits from being reseen through the
lens of different theoretical viewpoints. Thus in dealing with the
murder of the black youths by a white mob in her own old neighborhood, Torgovnick offers a number of informal explanations of why
this happened. In one case, for example, she suggests that economic
pressures in a transitional neighborhood produce anxiety and hence
racist behavior. By turning to Chapter 3 of *American Lives, American
Issues,* one can read more complex versions of such an explanation—
McLemore on "Group Gains" and "Situational Pressures"—and thus
get a new way to look at issues similar to those Torgovnick raises. Or,
from Chapter 1, one can consider Torgovnick's discussions about Italian-American ethnic identity and resee those discussions in the light
of either Glazer's optimistic or Takaki's pessimistic understanding of
the "American ethnic pattern." And finally, perhaps, in view of Torgovnick's references to gender issues, one can read Patricia Ireland's
essay in Chapter 6 about her feminist awakenings or Judith Lorber's
essay on the social construction of sexuality and gender in order to
see how one might place (and replace) the men's club view of women
more exactly than a personal essay allows.

Writing is rewriting and seeing is reseeing (old American transcen-
dalist ideas going back at least to Thoreau and Emerson). Although
Allen Ginsberg is reputed to have said: "First draft, best draft," this anthology is based on a different principle, that one's initial observations

can be fruitfully revised in subsequent drafts and by applying new critical viewpoints or, alternatively, that one's initial observations can be forgotten and something new and better written on the same subject, under the stimulus of new frameworks and opposing voices.

ACKNOWLEDGMENTS

In the preparation of this text, I have received invaluable help and encouragement from many people. My colleagues in the English Department offered much appreciated suggestions and support (Barbara Bono, Mili Clark, Art Efron, Stefan Fleischer, Ann Keefer, Arabella Lyon, Josh Lukin, Howard Wolfe); Alf Walle of SUNY/Geneseo and Cathy Colucci of Prentice-Hall gave me practical advice very early on; the secretarial staff of the English Department helped me continuously with faxing, Xeroxing and trouble-shooting (Dawn Becker, Linda Bogdan, Tricia Darstein, Marilyn Dunlap, Barbara Pajda); and Buffalo's Lockwood Memorial Library helped me many times with obscure references and overdue books. I appreciate the work of reviewers of early drafts, who took the time to tell me what they thought did and didn't work. (David L. Ison, Fort Hays State University; Joan B. Karbach, Tri-State University; Stefan Fleischer, SUNY/Buffalo; Alison Piepmeier, Vanderbilt University; and Philip Nel, Kansas State University.) I owe special thanks to my wife Milda Newman, whose understanding of identity has taught me most of what I know and to my son Richard Newman, whose advice on early American and civil rights history has been invaluable. Eric and Ruth Newman cheerfully answered niggling questions about which essays to put in and which to take out.

Special thanks go to my editor, Vivian Garcia, for her patience in helping me focus on the important selections and issues; to the production editor Randy Pettit and to the marketing editor, Brandy Dawson for coping with the transformation of a manuscript into a book. I would especially like to thank Prentice-Hall's copy editor, Patricia Cabeza, who helped immeasurably in clarifying both ideas and style in the original manuscript.

Above all, I'd like to thank the many students over the years whose autobiographical and research essays have been a joy to read and ponder; they have given me the hope that a multicultural America is a current reality, warts and all, and will continue to be one in the future even when we argue about what its assumptions and dimensions actually involve.

—ROBERT S. NEWMAN

1

PERSONAL NARRATIVE: THE INDIVIDUAL VIEW

Concrete, particularized stories help us feel the emotional weight of the world's troubles without so burdening us that we despair of ever being able to change things. As the philosopher Richard Rorty reminds us, the best way to promote compassion and solidarity is not by appealing to some general notion of goodness, but by encouraging people to respond to specific human lives. Responsibility in this view is not an abstract principle but a way of being. It exists only in the doing.

—*Paul Rogat Loeb,* Soul of a Citizen,
Living with Conviction in a Cynical Time

Like Marianna deMarco Torgovnick's keynote essay "On Being White, Female, and Born in Bensonhurst" (pages 3–14), the autobiographical essays in this chapter all combine personal narrations with analysis or argument; they are meant to engage the reader with affecting stories but also to send that reader a message—that the experience was not only interesting but also raises, however tantalizingly brief, a crucial problem or issue.

As narratives these essays are meant to put you in the writer's place so you can in some way feel what the writer felt. Kenneth Burke speaks of this as *identification,* a more powerful communicative act than simple *persuasion.* The cliché still holds: unless you've walked in someone else's shoes, you may not really appreciate what they are saying. Take Torgovnick's "Bensonhurst" for example (pages 3–14). Torgovnick concludes her essay with an extended anecdote about walking into an Italian-American men's club in her old Brooklyn neighborhood, in search of a dessert delicacy, a *cremolata.* She explains that the bakery she normally would have gotten it from is not making it yet and she wants one now. She knows from having grown up in the neighborhood that the club is off-limits to women. But she wants the *cremolata* and she is, after all, a grown woman, living in modern times and of some stature (a professor). So she defies convention and goes into the

1

club and asks for a *cremolata.* And indeed she is served. But the old men have been watching her resentfully and they express their resentment in choice Italian epithets—*strega* (whore). No matter, Torgovnick has gotten what she wants and has successfully defied the rules of the old men's game. But, as she adds at the very last, such ignoring of the "rules" didn't turn out so happily for the blacks who came into a pizza parlor a few months earlier and were assaulted by a mob of whites; for them, breaking the rules was a killing matter, literally.

We can identify with Torgovnick as she tells the anecdote. We can "empathize" with her: she thirsted after a *cremolata,* she knew that the only place at this time of day to get one was the old men's club, and she figured that as an adult she could brave their scorn and go get what she wanted.

But there is also an aesthetic aspect to Torgovnick's story. The concluding anecdote is a perfect miniature story or drama, with a succinctly described situation, an interesting narrator, other characters, dramatic conflict, suspense, and even an ironic twist at the end. The point of thinking about writing in terms of the well-told tale is that such telling gets the reader interested in what you have to say in a way that a bald summary or message statement would not.

The other essays in this chapter, like Torgovnick's, are excellent examples of well-told tales, fixed precisely in time and space. Glenn Loury remembers a shameful episode of betrayal in his adolescence; Malcolm X recounts the moment his high school teacher told him to think of what he could do with his hands, not with his head; Charles McBride evokes the puzzles his mixed Jewish-black background created, as when he would ask what race he was and his mother would tell him to remember that God "is the color of water"; Andrew Sullivan thinks back to early schooling when a girl asked him why he wasn't out there on the rugby field playing with the other boys; Chang-Rae Lee uses his mother's difficulties with English to suggest how one might be oddly sympathetic to Korean-only signs in one's neighborhood; Abu-Jaber's essay on "difference" answers a question all of us have been asked at one time or another: Why are we interested in something "foreign"?

In all the accounts in this chapter, writers make their ideas felt through dramatic and detailed stories that ultimately lead readers to identify with the writer's situation and his or her later speculations about its meaning and significance. That combination is always imitable.

Marianna deMarco Torgovnick

In her essay, Torgovnick asks rhetorically,

What has Bensonhurst to do with what I teach today and write? Why did I need to write about this killing in Bensonhurst, but not in the manner of a news account or a statistical sociological analysis?

Now a Professor of English at Duke University, Maria DeMarco Torgovnick was born in 1949 in Bensonhurst, an Italian-American section of Brooklyn. Her often-reprinted essay shows how a life experience can prompt thoughtful re-examination of heretofore unsuspected issues. The essay took shape, Torgovnick says, after she read about the killing of a black man and the injuring of two others by a mob of whites in the community she grew up in and the one in which her parents still live—Bensonhurst. "Within days of hearing the news," she writes, "I began to plan this essay to tell the world what I knew, though I stopped midway, worried that my parents or their neighbors would hear about it." This last reflects a key ambivalence in Torgovnick's attitude: she is horrified at the racial violence itself and at the clannish defensiveness of her family associated with it, but she also understands, as someone born and raised in the neighborhood, how her parents and former neighbors might view the situation quite differently than she does. "I detested the racial killing," she says, "but I also understood it."

On Being White, Female, and Born in Bensonhurst[*]

The Mafia protects the neighborhood, our fathers say, with that peculiar satisfied pride with which law-abiding Italian Americans refer to the Mafia: the Mafia protects the neighborhood from "the coloreds." In the fifties and sixties, I heard that information repeated, in whispers, in neighborhood parks and in the yard at school in Bensonhurst. The same information probably passes today in the parks (the word now "blacks," not "coloreds") but perhaps no longer in the schoolyards. From buses each morning, from neighborhoods outside Bensonhurst, spill children of all colors and backgrounds—American black, West Indian black, Hispanic, and Asian. But the blacks are the only ones especially marked for notice. Bensonhurst is no longer

---

[*] In this memoir, some names and circumstances have been altered slightly.

entirely protected from "the coloreds." But in a deeper sense, at least for Italian Americans, Bensonhurst never changes.

Italian-American life continues pretty much as I remember it. Families with young children live side by side with older couples whose children are long gone to the suburbs. Many of those families live "down the block" from the last generation or, sometimes still, live together with parents or grandparents. When a young family leaves, as sometimes happens, for Long Island or New Jersey or (very common now) for Staten Island, another arrives, without any special effort being required, from Italy or a poorer neighborhood in New York. They fill the neat but anonymous houses that make up the mostly tree-lined streets: two-, three-, or four-family houses for the most part (this is a working, lower to middle-middle class area, and people need rents to pay mortgages), with a few single family or small apartment houses tossed in at random. Tomato plants, fig trees, and plaster madonnas often decorate small but well-tended yards which face out onto the street; the grassy front lawn, like the grassy back yard, is relatively uncommon.

Crisscrossing the neighborhood and marking out ethnic zones— Italian, Irish, and Jewish, for the most part, though there are some Asian Americans and some people (usually Protestants) called simply Americans—are the great shopping streets: Eighty-sixth Street, Kings Highway, Bay Parkway, Eighteenth Avenue, each with its own distinctive character. On Eighty-sixth Street, crowds bustle along sidewalks lined with ample, packed fruit stands. Women wheeling shopping carts or baby strollers check the fruit carefully, piece by piece, and often bargain with the dealer, cajoling for a better price or letting him know that the vegetables, this time, aren't up to snuff. A few blocks down, the fruit stands are gone and the streets are lined with clothing and record shops, mobbed by teenagers. Occasionally, the el rumbles overhead, a few stops out of Coney Island on its way to the city, a trip of around one hour.

On summer nights, neighbors congregate on stoops which during the day serve as play yards for children. Air conditioning exists everywhere in Bensonhurst, but people still sit outside in the summer—to supervise children, to gossip, to stare at strangers. *"Buona sera,"* I say, or *"Buona notte,"* as I am ritually presented to Sal and Lily and Louie, the neighbors sitting on the stoop. *"Grazie,"* I say when they praise my children or my appearance. It's the only time I use Italian, which I learned at high school, although my parents (both second-generation Italian Americans, my father Sicilian, my mother Calabrian) speak it at home to each other but never to me or my brother. My accent is the Tuscan accent taught at school, not the southern Italian accents of my parents and the neighbors.

It's important to greet and please the neighbors; any break in this decorum would seriously offend and aggrieve my parents. For the neighbors are the stern arbiters of conduct in Bensonhurst. Does Mary keep a clean house? Did Gina wear black long enough after her mother's death? Was the food good at Tony's wedding? The neighbors know and pass judgment. Any news of family scandal (my brother's divorce, for example) provokes from my mother the agonized words: "But what will I *tell* people?" I sometimes collaborate in devising a plausible script.

A large sign on the church I attended as a child sums up for me the ethos of Bensonhurst. The sign urges contributions to the church building fund with the message, in huge letters: EACH YEAR ST. SIMON AND JUDE SAVES THIS NEIGHBORHOOD ONE MILLION DOLLARS IN TAXES." Passing the church on the way from largely Jewish and middle-class Sheepshead Bay (where my in-laws live) to Bensonhurst, year after year, my husband and I look for the sign and laugh at the crass level of its pitch, its utter lack of attention to things spiritual. But we also understand exactly the values it represents.

In the summer of 1989, my parents were visiting me at my house in Durham, North Carolina, from the apartment in Bensonhurst where they have lived since 1942: three small rooms, rent-controlled, floor clean enough to eat off, every corner and crevice known and organized. My parents' longevity in a single apartment is unusual even for Bensonhurst, but not that unusual; many people live for decades in the same place or move within a ten-block radius. When I lived in this apartment, there were four rooms; one has since been ceded to a demanding landlord, one of the various landlords who have haunted my parents' life and must always be appeased lest the ultimate threat—removal from the rent-controlled apartment—be brought into play. That summer, during their visit, on August 23 (my younger daughter's birthday) a shocking, disturbing, news report issued from the neighborhood: it had become another Howard Beach.

Three black men, walking casually through the streets at night, were attacked by a group of whites. One was shot dead, mistaken, as it turned out, for another black youth who was dating a white, although part-Hispanic, girl in the neighborhood. It all made sense: the crudely protective men, expecting to see a black arriving at the girl's house and overreacting; the rebellious girl dating the outsider boy; the black dead as a sacrifice to the feelings of the neighborhood.

I might have felt outrage, I might have felt guilt or shame, I might have despised the people among whom I grew up. In a way I felt all four emotions when I heard the news. I expect that there were many people in Bensonhurst who felt the same rush of emotions. But mostly I felt that, given the set-up, this was the only way things could have happened. I detested the racial killing, but I also understood it. Those streets, which should be public property available to all, belong to the neighborhood. All the people sitting on the stoops on August 23 knew that as well as they knew their own names. The black men walking through probably knew it too—though their casual walk sought to deny the fact that, for the neighbors, even the simple act of blacks walking through the neighborhood would be seen as invasion.

Italian Americans in Bensonhurst are notable for their cohesiveness and provinciality; the slightest pressure turns those qualities into prejudice and racism. Their cohesiveness is based on the stable economic and ethical level that links generation to generation, keeping Italian Americans in Bensonhurst and the Italian-American community alive as the Jewish-American community of my youth is no longer alive. (Its young people routinely moved to the suburbs or beyond and were never replaced, so that Jews in Bensonhurst today are almost all very old people.) Their provinciality results from the Italian Americans' devotion to jealous distinctions and discriminations. Jews are suspect, but (the old Italian women admit) "they make good husbands." The Irish are okay, fellow Catholics, but not really "like us"; they make bad husbands because they drink and gamble. Even Italians come in varieties, by region (Sicilian, Calabrian, Neapolitan, very rarely any region further north) and by history in this country (the newly arrived and ridiculed "gaffoon" versus the second or third generation).

Bensonhurst is a neighborhood dedicated to believing that its values are the only values; it tends toward certain forms of inertia. When my parents visit me in Durham, they routinely take chairs from the kitchen and sit out on the lawn in front of the house, not on the chairs on the back deck; then they complain that the streets are too quiet. When they walk around my neighborhood (these De Marcos who have friends named Travaglianti and Occhipinti), they look at the mailboxes and report that my neighbors have strange names. Prices at my local supermarket are compared, in unbelievable detail, with prices on Eighty-sixth Street. Any rearrangement of my kitchen since their last visits is registered and criticized. Difference is not only unwelcome, it is unacceptable. One of the most characteristic things my mother ever said was in response to my plans for renovating my house in Durham. When she heard my plans, she looked around, crossed her arms, and said, "If it was me, I wouldn't change nothing." My father once asked me to level with him about a Jewish boyfriend who lived in a different part of the neighborhood, reacting to his Jewishness, but even more to the fact that he often wore Bermuda shorts: "Tell me something, Marianna. Is he a Communist?" Such are the standards of normality and political thinking in Bensonhurst.

I often think that one important difference between Italian Americans in New York neighborhoods like Bensonhurst and Italian

Americans elsewhere is that the others moved on—to upstate New York, to Pennsylvania, to the Midwest. Though they frequently settled in communities of fellow Italians, they did move on. Bensonhurst Italian Americans seem to have felt that one large move, over the ocean, was enough. Future moves could be only local: from the Lower East Side, for example, to Brooklyn, or from one part of Brooklyn to another. Bensonhurst was for many of these people the summa of expectations. If their America were to be drawn as a *New Yorker* cover, Manhattan itself would be tiny in proportion to Bensonhurst and to its satellites, Staten Island, New Jersey, and Long Island.

"Oh, no," my father says when he hears the news about the shooting. Though he still refers to blacks as "coloreds," he's not really a racist and is upset that this innocent youth was shot in his neighborhood. He has no trouble acknowledging the wrongness of the death. But then, like all the news accounts, he turns to the fact, repeated over and over, that the blacks had been on their way to look at a used car when they encountered the hostile mob of whites. The explanation is right before him but, "Yeah," he says, still shaking his head, "yeah, but what were they *doing* there? They didn't belong."

Over the next few days, the television news is even more disturbing. Rows of screaming Italians lining the streets, most of them looking like my relatives. I focus especially on one woman who resembles almost completely my mother: stocky but not fat, mid-seventies but well preserved, full face showing only minimal wrinkles, ample steel-gray hair neatly if rigidly coiffed in a modified beehive hairdo left over from the sixties. She shakes her fist at the camera, protesting the arrest of the Italian-American youths in the neighborhood, protesting the shooting. I look a little nervously at my mother (the parent I resemble), but she has not even noticed the woman and stares impassively at the television.

What has Bensonhurst to do with what I teach today and write? Why did I need to write about this killing in Bensonhurst, but not in the manner of a news account or a statistical sociological analysis? Within days of hearing the news, I began to plan this essay, to tell the world what I knew, even though I was aware that I could publish the piece only someplace my parents or their neighbors would never see or hear about it. I sometimes think that I looked around from my baby carriage and decided that someday, the sooner the better, I would get out of Bensonhurst. Now, much to my surprise, Bensonhurst—the antipode of the intellectual life I sought, the least interesting of places—had become a respectable intellectual topic. People would be willing to hear about Bensonhurst—and all by the dubious virtue of a racial killing in the streets.

The story as I would have to tell it would be to some extent a class narrative: about the difference between working class and upper middle class, dependence and a profession, Bensonhurst and a posh suburb. But I need to make it clear that I do not imagine myself as writing from a position of enormous self-satisfaction, or even enormous distance. You can take the girl out of Bensonhurst (that much is clear), but you may not be able to take Bensonhurst out of the girl. And upward mobility is not the essence of the story, though it is an important marker and symbol.

In Durham today, I live in a twelve-room house surrounded by an acre of trees. When I sit on my back deck on summer evenings, no houses are visible through the trees. I have a guaranteed income, teaching English at an excellent university, removed by my years of education from the fundamental economic and social conditions of Bensonhurst. The one time my mother ever expressed pleasure at my work was when I got tenure, what my father still calls, with no irony intended, "ten years." "What does that mean?" my mother asked when she heard the news. Then she reached back into her experience as a garment worker, subject to periodic layoffs. "Does it mean they can't fire you just for nothing and can't lay you off?" When I said that was exactly what it means, she said, "Very good. Congratulations. That's *wonderful.*" I was free from the *padrones,* from the network of petty anxieties that had formed, in large part, her very existence. Of course, I wasn't really free of petty anxieties: would my salary increase keep pace with my colleagues', how would my office compare, would this essay be accepted for publication, am I happy? The line between these workers and my mothers' is the line between the working class and the upper middle class.

But getting out of Bensonhurst never meant to me a big house, or nice clothes, or a large income. And it never meant feeling good about looking down on what I left behind or hiding my background. Getting out of Bensonhurst meant freedom—to experiment, to grow, to change. It also meant knowledge in some grand, abstract way. All the material possessions I have acquired, I acquired simply along the way—and for the first twelve years after I left Bensonhurst, I chose to acquire almost nothing at all. Now, as I write about the neighborhood, I recognize that although I've come far in physical and material distance, the emotional distance is harder to gauge. Bensonhurst has everything to do with who I am and even with what I write. Occasionally I get reminded of my roots, of their simultaneously choking and nutritive power.

Scene one: It's after a lecture at Duke, given by a visiting professor from a major university. The lecture was long and a little dull and—bad luck—I had agreed to be one of the people having dinner with the lecturer afterward. We settle into our table at the restaurant: this man, me, the head of the comparative literature program (also a professor of German), and a couple I like who teach French, the husband at my university, the wife at one nearby. The conversation is sluggish, as it often is when a stranger, like the visiting professor, has to be assimilated into a group, so I ask the visitor a question to personalize things a bit. "How did you get involved in what you do? What made you become a professor of German?" The man gets going and begins talking about how it was really unlikely that he, a nice Jewish boy from Bensonhurst, would have chosen, in the mid-fifties, to study German. Unlikely indeed.

I remember seeing *Judgment at Nuremberg* in a local movie theater and having a woman in the row in back of me get hysterical when some clips of a concentration camp were shown. "My God," she screamed in a European accent, "look at what they did. Murderers, MURDERERS!"—and she had to be supported out by her family. I couldn't see, in the dark, whether her arm bore the neatly tattooed numbers that the arms of some of my classmates' parents did—and that always affected me with a thrill of horror. Ten years older than me, this man had lived more directly through those feelings, lived with and *among* those feelings. The first chance he got, he raced to study German. I myself have twice chosen not to visit Germany, but I understand his impulse.

At the dinner, the memory about the movie pops into my mind but I pick up instead on the Bensonhurst—I'm also from there, but Italian American. Like a flash, he asks something I haven't been asked in years: Where did I go to high school and (a more common question) what was my maiden name? I went to Lafayette High School, I say, and my name was De Marco. Everything changes: his facial expression, his posture, his accent, his voice. "Soo, Dee Mawko," he says, "dun anything wrong at school today—got enny pink slips? Wanna meet me later at the park or maybe bye the Baye?" When I laugh, recognizing the stereotype that Italians get pink slips for misconduct at school and the notorious chemistry between Italian women and Jewish men, he says, back in his elegant voice: "My God, for a minute I felt like I was turning into a werewolf."

It's odd that although I can remember almost nothing else about this man—his face, his body type, even his name—I remember this lapse into his "real self" with enormous vividness. I am especially struck by how easily he was able to slip into the old, generic Brooklyn accent. I myself have no memory of ever speaking in that accent, though I also have no memory of trying not to speak it, except for teaching myself, carefully, to say "oil" rather than "earl."

But the surprises aren't over. The female French professor, whom I have known for at least five years, reveals for the first time that she is also from the neighborhood, though she lived across the other side of Kings Highway, went to a different, more elite high school, and was Irish American. Three of six professors, sitting at an eclectic vegetarian restaurant in Durham, all from Bensonhurst—a neighborhood where (I swear) you couldn't get the *New York Times* at any of the local stores.

Scene two: I still live in Bensonhurst. I'm waiting for my parents to return from a conference at my school, where they've been summoned to discuss my transition from elementary to junior high school. I am already a full year younger than any of my classmates, having skipped a grade, a not uncommon occurrence for "gifted" youngsters. Now the school is worried about putting me in an accelerated track through junior high, since that would make me two years younger. A compromise was reached: I would be put in a special program for gifted children, but one that took three, not two, years. It sounds okay.

Three years later, another wait. My parents have gone to school this time to make another decision. Lafayette High School has three tracks: academic, for potentially college-bound kids; secretarial, mostly for Italian-American girls or girls with low aptitude-test scores (the high school is de facto segregated, so none of the tracks is as yet racially coded, though they are coded by ethnic group and gender); and vocational, mostly for boys with the same attributes, ethnic or intellectual. Although my scores are superb, the guidance counselor has recommended the secretarial track; when I protested, the conference with my parents was arranged. My mother's preference is clear: the secretarial track—college is for boys; I will need to make a "good living" until I marry and have children. My father also prefers the secretarial track, but he wavers, half proud of my aberrantly high scores, half worried. I press the attack, saying that if I were Jewish I would have been placed, without question, in the academic track. I tell him I have sneaked a peak at my files and know that my IQ is at genius level. I am allowed to insist on the change into the academic track.

What I did, and I was ashamed of it even then, was to play upon my father's competitive feelings with Jews: his daughter could and should be as good as theirs. In the bank where he was a messenger, and at the insurance company where he worked in the mailroom, my father worked with Jews, who were almost always his immediate supervisors. Several times, my father was offered the supervisory job but turned it down after long conversations with my mother about the dangers of making a change, the difficulty of giving orders to friends. After her work in a local garment shop, after cooking dinner and washing the floor each night, my mother often did piecework making bows; sometimes I would help her for fun, but it *wasn't* fun, and I was free to stop while she continued for long, tedious hours to increase the family income. Once a week, her part-time boss, Dave, would come by to pick up the boxes of bows. Short, round, with his shirttails sloppily tucked into his pants and a cigar almost always dangling from his lips, Dave was a stereotyped Jew but also, my parents always said, a nice guy, a decent man.

Years after, similar choices come up, and I show the same assertiveness I showed with my father, the same ability to deal for survival, but tinged with Bensonhurst caution. Where will I go to college? Not to Brooklyn College, the flagship of the city system—I know that, but don't press the invitations I have received to apply to prestigious schools outside of New York. The choice comes down to two: Barnard, which gives me a full scholarship, minus five hundred dollars a year that all scholarship students are expected to contribute from summer earnings, or New York University, which offers me one thousand dollars above tuition as a bribe. I waver. My parents stand firm: they are already losing money by letting me go to college; I owe it to the family to contribute the extra thousand dollars plus my summer earnings. Besides, my mother adds, harping on a favorite theme, there are no boys at Barnard; at NYU I'm more likely to meet someone to marry. I go to NYU and do marry in my senior year, but he is someone I didn't meet at college. I was secretly relieved, I now think (though at the time I thought I was just placating my parents' conventionality), to be out of the marriage sweepstakes.

The first boy who ever asked me for a date was Robert Lubitz, in eighth grade: tall and skinny to my average height and teenage chubbiness. I turned him down, thinking we would make a ridiculous couple. Day after day, I cast my eyes at stylish Juliano, the class cutup; day after day, I captivated Robert Lubitz. Occasionally, one of my brother's Italian-American friends would ask me out, and I would go, often to ROTC dances. My specialty was making political remarks so shocking that the guys rarely asked me again. After a while I recognized destiny: the Jewish man was a passport out of Bensonhurst. I of course did marry a Jewish man, who gave me my freedom and, very important, helped remove me from the expectations of Bensonhurst. Though raised in a largely Jewish section of Brooklyn, he had gone to college in Ohio and knew how important it was, as he put it, "to get past the Brooklyn Bridge." We met on neutral ground, in Central Park, at a performance of Shakespeare. The Jewish-Italian marriage is a common enough catastrophe in Bensonhurst for my parents to have accepted, even welcomed, mine—though my parents continued to treat my husband like an outsider for the first twenty years ("Now Marianna. Here's what's going on with you brother. But don't tell-a you husband").

Along the way I make other choices, more fully marked by Bensonhurst cautiousness. I am attracted to journalism or the arts as careers, but the prospects for income seem iffy. I choose instead to imagine myself as a teacher. Only the availability of NDEA fellowships when I graduate, with their generous terms, propels me from high school teaching (a thought I never much relished) to college teaching (which seems like a brave new world). Within the college teaching profession, I choose offbeat specializations: the novel, interdisciplinary approaches (not something clear and clubby like Milton or the eighteenth century). Eventually I write the book I like best about primitive others as they figure within Western obsessions: my identification with "the Other," my sense of being "Other," surfaces at last. I avoid all mentoring structures for a long time but accept aid when it comes to me on the basis of what I perceive to be merit. I'm still, deep down, Italian-American Bensonhurst, though by the time I'm a lot of other things as well.

Scene three: In the summer of 1988, a little more than a year before the shooting in Bensonhurst, my father woke up trembling and in what appeared to be a fit. Hospitalization revealed that he had a pocket of blood on his brain, a frequent consequence of falls for older people. About a year earlier, I had stayed home, using my children as an excuse, when my aunt, my father's much loved sister, died, missing her funeral; only now does my mother tell me how much my father resented my taking his suggestion that I stay home. Now, confronted with what is described as brain surgery but turns out to be less dramatic than it sounds, I fly home immediately.

My brother drives three hours back and forth from New Jersey every day to chauffeur me and my mother to the hospital: he is being a fine Italian-American son. For the first time in years, we have long conversations alone. He is two years older than I am, a chemical engineer who has also left the neighborhood but has remained closer to its values, with a suburban, Republican inflection. He talks a lot about New York, saying that (except for neighborhoods like Bensonhurst) it's a "third-world city now." It's the summer of the Tawana Brawley incident, when Brawley accused white men of abducting her and smearing racial slurs on her body with her own excrement. My brother is filled with dislike for Al Sharpton and Brawley's other vocal supporters in the black community—not because they're black, he says, but because they're troublemakers, stirring things up. The city is drenched in racial hatred that makes itself felt in the halls of the hospital: Italians and Jews in the beds and as doctors; blacks as nurses and orderlies.

This is the first time since I left New York in 1975 that I have visited Brooklyn without once getting into Manhattan. It's the first time

I have spent several days alone with my mother, living in her apartment in Bensonhurst. My every move is scrutinized and commented on. I feel like I am going to go crazy.

Finally, it's clear that my father is going to be fine, and I can go home. She insists on accompanying me to the travel agent to get my ticket for home, even though I really want to be alone. The agency (a Mafia front?) has no one who knows how to ticket me for the exotic destination of North Carolina and no computer for doing so. The one person who can perform this feat by hand is out. I have to kill time for an hour and suggest to my mother that she go home, to be there for my brother when he arrives from Jersey. We stop in a Pork Store, where I buy a stash of cheeses, sausages, and other delicacies unavailable in Durham. My mother walks home with the shopping bags, and I'm on my own.

More than anything I want a kind of *sorbetto* or ice I remember from my childhood, a *cremolata,* almond-vanilla-flavored with large chunks of nuts. I pop into the local bakery (at the unlikely hour of 11 A.M.) and ask for a *cremolata,* usually eaten after dinner. The woman—a younger version of my mother—refuses: they haven't made a fresh ice yet, and what's left from the day before is too icy, no good. I explain that I'm about to get on a plane for North Carolina and want that ice, good or not. But she has her standards and holds her ground, even though North Carolina has about the same status in her mind as Timbuktoo and she knows I will be banished, perhaps forever, from the land of *cremolata.*

Then, while I'm taking a walk, enjoying my solitude, I have another idea. On the block behind my parents' house, there's a club for men, for men from a particular town or region in Italy: six or seven tables, some on the sidewalk beneath a garish red, green, and white sign; no women allowed or welcome unless they're with men, and no women at all during the day when the real business of the club—a game of cards for old men—is in progress. Still, I know that inside the club would be coffee and a *cremolata* ice. I'm thirty-eight, well-dressed, very respectable looking; I know what I want. I also know I'm not supposed to enter that club. I enter anyway, asking the teenage boy behind the counter firmly, in my most professional tones, for a *cremolata* ice. Dazzled, he complies immediately. The old men at the card table have been staring at this scene, unable to place me exactly, though my facial type is familiar. Finally, a few old men's hisses pierce the air. *"Strega,"* I hear as I leave, *"mala strega"*—"witch," or "brazen whore." I have been in Bensonhurst less than a week, but I have managed to reproduce, on my final day there for this visit, the conditions of my youth. Knowing the rules, I have broken them. I shake hands with my discreetly rebellious past, still an outsider walking through the neighborhood, marked and in-sulted—though unlikely to be shot.

Analysis

1. "Bensonhurst is no longer entirely protected from 'the coloreds.'" Things are changing in Bensonhurst (ethnic succession is what the so-ciologists might speak of—Jews move out, Puerto Ricans move in). What indeed are the changing racial aspects of the neighborhood as Torgovnick sees them? What "zones"—ethnic and otherwise—mark Bensonhurst, according to Torgovnick?

2. Using a puzzling hypothetical attitude in her voice, "I might have felt outrage. I might have felt guilt or shame. . . . ", Torgovnick observes "I detested the racial killing but I also understood it." Is this a rationali-zation or a painful truth of the conflict between "insider" and "out-sider" perspectives?

3. "Italian Americans are notable for their cohesiveness and provinciality; the slightest pressure turns those qualities into prejudice and racism." Torgovnick advances a sophisticated theory of prejudice here: group self-interest, not racism, is the source of prejudice and of racism itself, and that such self-interest can become morally blind. Does she illus-trate this notion of "pressure" in the essay? Do you agree with her conjectures?

Writing Possibilities

1. Take a conflictful incident you have lived through yourself and recount it with the same attention that Torgovnick displays to drama and char-acterization (as in the old men's club story), drawing whatever gener-alizations seem relevant at the conclusion. If you revise it, consider whether your original account reflects your latest views.

2. What zones (ethnic, racial, generational, etc.) "crisscross" the neighbor-hood you live in? How does it feel to go from one to the other of such zones or spaces? Is there conflict or harmony in or between these "eth-nic zones"? Why is there either one or the other, so far as you can tell?

3. Do the gender-ethnic conflicts Torgovnick records ("My parents stand firm: They are already losing money by letting me go to college. . . . ") have any resonance in your own experience? If so, what was the upshot?

Glenn C. Loury

A noted African American economist, Glen Loury recounts a shameful moment in his adolescence when he turned his back on an African American friend who, though he looked white, was not passing. Using this incident as the nucleus for further meditation in the present, Loury examines the issues of false racial solidarity, identity, and group pressure. In the final section of the essay (not reprinted here), Loury reflects on how identity is socially constructed and hence how it can fruitfully change over time.

Free at Last? A Personal Perspective on Race and Identity in America

Then Peter opened his mouth and said, Of a truth I perceive that God is no respecter of persons: But in every nation he that feareth him, and worketh righteousness, is accepted with him.

—Acts 10:34–35

A formative experience of my growing up on the South Side of Chicago in the 1960s occurred during one of those heated, earnest political rallies so typical of the period. I was about eighteen at the time; Woody, who had been my best friend since Little League, suggested that we attend. Being political neophytes, neither of us knew many of the participants. The rally was called to galvanize our community's response to some pending infringement by the white power structure, the exact nature of which I no longer remember. But I can still vividly recall how very agitated about it we all were, determined to fight the good fight, even to the point of being arrested if it came to that. Judging by his demeanor, Woody was among the most zealous of those present.

Despite this zeal, it took courage for Woody to attend that meeting. Though he often proclaimed his blackness, and though he had a Negro grandparent on each side of his family, he nevertheless looked to all the world like your typical white boy. Everyone, on first meeting him, assumed as much. I did, too, when we began to play stickball together nearly a decade earlier, just after I had moved into the middle-class neighborhood (called Park Manor) where Woody's family had been living for some time.

There were a number of white families on our block when we first arrived; within a couple of years they had all been replaced by aspiring black families like our own. I often wondered why Woody's parents never moved. Then I overheard his mother declare to one of her new neighbors, "We just wouldn't run from our own kind," a comment that befuddled me at the time. Somewhat later, while we were watching the movie "Imitation of Life" on television, my mother explained how someone could be black, though they looked white. She told me about people like that in our own family—second cousins living in a fashionable suburb on whom we would never dare simply to drop in, because they were "passing for white." This was my earliest glimpse of the truth that racial identity in America is inherently a social and cultural construct, not simply a biological one— that it necessarily involves an irreducible element of choice.

From the moment I learned of it, I was at once intrigued and troubled by this idea of "passing." I enjoyed imagining my racial brethren surreptitiously infiltrating the citadels of white exclusivity. It allowed me to believe that, despite appearances and the white man's best efforts to the contrary, we blacks were nevertheless present, if unannounced, *everywhere* in American society. But I was disturbed by an evident implication of the practice of passing—that denial of one's genuine self is a necessary concomitant of a black person making it in this society. What passing seemed to say about the world was that if one were both black and ambitious, it was necessary to choose between racial authenticity and personal success. Also, it seemed grossly unfair to my adolescent mind that however problematic it might be, this passing option was, because of my relatively dark complexion, not available to me!

It dawned on me after the conversation with my mother that Woody's parents must have been passing for white in preintegration Park Manor. The neighborhood's changing racial composition had confronted them with a moment of truth. They had elected to stay and to raise their children among "their own kind." This was a fateful decision for Woody, who, as he matured, became determined not simply to live among blacks but, perhaps in atonement for his parents' sins, unambiguously to become one. The young men in the neighborhood did not make this easy. Many delighted in picking fights with him, teasing him about being a "white boy" and refusing to credit his insistent, often-repeated claim: "I'm a brother, too!"

The fact that some of his relatives were passing made Woody's racial identity claims more urgent for him, but less compelling to others. He desperately wanted to be black, but his peers in the neighborhood would not let him. Because he had the option to be white—an option he radically rejected at the time—those without the option could not accept his claim to a shared racial experience. I knew Woody well. We became good friends, and I wanted to accept him on his own terms. But even I found myself doubting that he fully grasped the pain, frustration, anger, and self-doubt many of us felt upon encountering the intractability of American racism. However much he sympathized with our plight, he seemed to experience it only vicariously.

So there we were, at this boisterous, angry political rally. A critical moment came when the leaders interrupted their speech making to solicit input from "the people." Woody had an idea, and enthusiastically raised his voice above the murmur to be heard. He was cut short before finishing his first sentence by one of the dashiki-clad brothers-in-charge, who demanded to know how a "white boy" got the authority to have an opinion about what black people should be doing. That was one of our problems, the brother said; we were always letting white people "peep our hole card," while we were never privy to their deliberations in the same way.

A silence then fell over the room. The indignant brother asked if anyone could "vouch for this white boy." More excruciating silence ensued. Now was *my* moment of truth; Woody turned plaintively toward me, but I would not meet his eyes. To my eternal disgrace, I refused to speak up for him. He was asked to leave the meeting, and he did so without uttering a word in his own defense. Subsequently, neither of us could bear to discuss the incident. I offered no apology or explanation, and he asked for none. Though we continued to be friendly, however, our relationship was forever changed. I was never again to hear Woody exclaim, "I'm a brother, too."

I recall this story about Woody because his dilemma, and mine, tell us something important about race and personal identity in American society. His situation was made so difficult by the fact that he embraced a self-definition dramatically inconsistent with the identity reflexively and stubbornly imputed to him by others. This lack of social confirmation for his subjective sense of self left him uncertain, at a deep level, about who he really was. Ultimately there seemed to be no way for him to avoid living fraudulently—either as a black passing for white, or a white trying too hard to be black. As his close friend and frequent companion, I had become familiar with, and occasionally shared in, the pitfalls of this situation. People would assume when they saw us together both that he was white, and that I was "the kind of Negro who hangs out with white boys." I resented that assumption.

Since then, as a black intellectual making my living in the academic establishment during a period of growing racial conflict in our society, I have often experienced this dissonance between my self-concept and the socially imputed definition of who I am supposed to be. I have had to confront the problem of balancing my desire not to disappoint the expectations of others—both whites and blacks, but more especially blacks—with my conviction that one should strive to live life with integrity. This does not make me a heroic figure; I eschew the libertarian ideologue's rhetoric about the glorious individual

who, though put upon by society, blazes his own path. I acknowledge that this opposition between individual and society is ambiguous, in view of the fact that the self is inevitably shaped by the
objective world, and by other selves. I know that what one is being
faithful to when resisting the temptation to conform to others' expectations by "living life with integrity" is always a socially determined,
if subjectively experienced, vision of the self.

Still, I see this incident of a quarter century ago as a kind of private metaphor for the ongoing problem of living in good faith, particularly as it relates to my personal identity as a black American. I have
since lost contact with Woody. I suspect that, having tired of his
struggle against society's presumptions about him, he is now passing.
But that moment of truth in that South Side church basement, and my
failure in the face of it, have helped me understand the depth of
my own need to be seen by others as "black enough."

Upon reflection, my refusal to stand up for Woody exposed the
tenuous quality of my personal sense of racial authenticity. The fact
is, I willingly betrayed someone I had known for a decade, a person
whom I loved and who loved me, in order to avoid the risk of being
rejected by strangers. In a way, at that moment and often again later in
my life, I was "passing" too—hoping to be mistaken for something I
was not. I had feared that to proclaim before the black radicals in the
audience that this "white boy" at my side was in fact our "brother"
would have compromised my own chance of being received among
them as a genuine colleague. Who, after all, was there to vouch for
me if I had been dismissed as an "Uncle Tom"?

This was not an unfounded concern, for at that meeting, as at so
many others of the period, people with insufficiently militant views
were berated as self-hating, shuffle-along, "house nigger" types, com-
plicit with whites in the perpetuation of racial oppression. Then, as
now, blacks who befriended (or, heaven forbid, married) whites, who
dressed or talked or wrote or wore their hair a certain way, who listened to certain kinds of music, read certain books, or expressed certain opinions, were laughed at, ostracized, and generally demeaned as
inauthentic by other, more (self-)righteous blacks. The indignant
brother who challenged Woody's right to speak at that rally was not
merely imposing a racial test ("Only blacks are welcome here"), he
was applying a loyalty test ("Are you truly with us or against us?"),
and this was a test that anyone present could fail through a lack of
conformity to the collective definition of what it meant to be genuinely black. I feared that speaking up for Woody would have marked
me as a disloyal "Tom" among the blacker-than-thou crowd. In those
years, this was a fate the thought of which I could not bear.

I now understand how this desire to be regarded as genuinely
black, to be seen as a "regular brother," has dramatically altered my

life. It narrowed the range of my earliest intellectual pursuits, distorted my relationships with other people, censored my political thought and expression, informed the way I dressed and spoke, and shaped my cultural interests. Some of this was inevitable, and not all of it was bad, but in my experience the need to be affirmed by one's racial peers can take on a pathological dimension. Growing into intellectual maturity has been, for me, largely a process of becoming free of the need to have my choices validated by "the brothers." After many years I have come to understand that until I became willing to risk the derision of the crowd, I had no chance to discover the most important truths about myself or about life—to know and accept my calling, to perceive what I really value and what goals are most worth striving toward. In a perverse extension of the lesson from "Imitation of Life," I have learned that one does not have to live surreptitiously as a Negro among whites in order to be engaged in a denial of one's genuine self for the sake of gaining social acceptance. This is a price that blacks often demand of each other as well.

ANALYSIS

1. What is a dashiki?
2. What does Loury mean by the phrase "plays our hole card"?
3. Loury points to the issue which the memory of this incident relates— the "dissonance between my self-concept and the socially imputed definition of who I am supposed to be." What does Loury mean here? Do you agree with him that it is a problem?

WRITING POSSIBILITIES

Loury's essay illustrates how thinking about a life-incident can lead to an awareness of larger issues and possible generalizations about them. Take some moment of conflict in your own experience—a choice you had to make like Loury's, for example—and develop the circumstances of that moment, explaining why you chose to act as you did. Concentrate on the drama of the situation and the build-up to it first; then develop your generalizations as they flow from both memories and present reflections (note Loury's questioning of why Woody's parents never moved, his trouble at the idea of passing, his doubts even about Woody's sensitivity to racism). Note particularly how well, but briefly, Loury describes the actual moment of Woody's banishment ("So there we were . . . ," "A silence fell over the room. . . . "

Mike Rose

The essay usually reprinted from Rose's book Lives on the Boundary *is "I Just Want to be Average," a plea from a high school friend who, unable to cope with tough academic reading, just gave up the struggle. In this essay, Rose focuses on how he, unlike his friend, didn't give up the struggle and instead, with the aid of helpful teachers, learned how to master difficult reading. Rose also argues that the ultimate source of his reading difficulties lay in the intricacies of social class: the expectations of blue-collar youth, he suggests, are simply different from those of the middle class; when a working-class kid like Rose comes face to face with a world of books dealing with such things as the "metaphysical foundations" of modern science, he collapses—unless someone takes the time and energy to help him understand how to cope.*

Entering the Conversation

If you walked out the back door of 9116 South Vermont and across our narrow yard, you would run smack into those four single-room rentals and, alongside them, an old wooden house trailer. The trailer had belonged to Mrs. Jolly, the woman who sold us the property. It was locked and empty, and its tires were flat and fused into the asphalt driveway. Rusted dairy cases had been wedged in along its sides and four corners to keep it balanced. Two of its eight windows were broken, the frames were warped, and the door stuck. I was getting way too old to continue sharing a room with my mother, so I began to eye that trailer. I decided to refurbish it. It was time to have a room of my own.

Lou Minton had, by now, moved in with us, and he and I fixed the windows and realigned the door. I painted the inside by combining what I could find in our old shed with what I could afford to buy: The ceiling became orange, the walls yellow, the rim along the windows flat black. Lou redid the wiring and put in three new sockets. I got an old record player from the secondhand store for five dollars. I had Roy Herweck, the illustrator of our high school annual, draw women in mesh stockings and other objets d'redneck art on the yellow walls, and I put empty Smirnoff and Canadian Club bottles on the ledges above the windows. I turned the old trailer into the kind of bachelor digs a seventeen-year-old in South L.A. would fancy. My friends from high school began congregating there. When she could, my mother would make us a pot of spaghetti or pasta fasul'. And there was a clerk across the street at Marty's Liquor who would sell to us: We would run back across Vermont Avenue laughing and clutching our bags and seal ourselves up in the trailer. We spun fantasies about the waitress at the Mexican restaurant and mimicked our teachers and caught touchdown passes and, in general, dreamed our way through adolescence. It was a terrible time for rock 'n' roll—Connie Francis and Bobby Rydell were headliners in 1961—so we found rhythm and blues on L.A.'s one black station, played the backroom ballads of troubadour Oscar Brand, and discovered Delta and Chicago blues on Pacifica's KPFK:

I'm a man
I'm a full-grown man

As I fell increasingly under Mr. MacFarland's spell, books began replacing the liquor bottles above the windows: *The Trial* and *Waiting for Godot* and *No Exit* and *The Stranger.* Roy sketched a copy of the back cover of *Exile and the Kingdom,* and so the pensive face of Albert Camus now looked down from that patch of wall on which a cartoon had once pressed her crossed legs. My mother found a quilt that my grandmother had sewn from my father's fabric samples. It was dark and heavy, and I would lie under it and read Rimbaud and not understand him and feel very connected to the life I imagined Jack MacFarland's life to be: a subterranean ramble through Bebop and breathless poetry and back-alley revelations.

In 1962, John Connor moved into dank, old Apartment 1. John had also grown up in South L.A., and he and I had become best friends. His parents moved to Oregon, and John—who was a good black-top basketball player and an excellent student—wanted to stay in Los Angeles and go to college. So he rented an apartment for forty dollars a month, and we established a community of two. Some nights, John and I and Roy the artist and a wild kid named Gaspo would drive into downtown L.A.—down to where my mother had waited fearfully for a bus years before—and roam the streets and feel the excitement of the tenderloin: the flashing arrows, the blue-and-orange beer neon, the burlesque houses, the faded stairwell of Roseland—which we would inch up and then run down—brushing past the photos of taxi dancers, glossy and smiling in a glass display. Cops would tell us to go home, and that intensified this bohemian romance all the more.

About four months after John moved in, we both entered Loyola University. Loyola is now coeducational; its student center houses an Asian Pacific Students Association, Black Student Alliance, and Chicano Resource Center; and its radio station, KXLU, plays the most untamed rock 'n' roll in Los Angeles. But in the early sixties, Loyola was pretty much a school for white males from the middle and upper middle class. It was a sleepy little campus—its undergraduate enrollment was under two thousand—and it prided itself on providing spiritual as well as intellectual guidance for its students: Religion and Christian philosophy courses were a required part of the curriculum.

It defined itself as a Catholic intellectual community—promotional brochures relied on phrases like "the social, intellectual, and spiritual aspects of our students"—and made available to its charges small classes, a campus ministry, and thirty-six clubs (the Chess Club, Economics Society, Fine Arts Circle, Debate Squad, and more). There were also six fraternities and a sports program that included basketball, baseball, volleyball, rugby, soccer, and crew. Loyola men, it was assumed, shared a fairly common set of social and religious values, and the university provided multiple opportunities for them to develop their minds, their spirits, and their social networks. I imagine that parents sent their boys to Loyola with a sigh of relief: God and man strolled together out of St. Robert Bellarmine Hall and veered left to Sacred Heart Chapel. There was an occasional wild party at one of the off-campus fraternity houses, but, well, a pair of panties in the koi pond was not on a par with crises of faith and violence against the state.

John and I rattled to college in his '53 Plymouth. Loyola Boulevard was lined with elms and maples, and as we entered the campus we could see the chapel tower rising in the distance. The chapel and all the early buildings had been constructed in the 1920s and were white and separated by broad sweeps of very green grass. Palm trees and stone pines grew in rows and clumps close to the buildings, and long concrete walkways curved and angled and crossed to connect everything, proving that God, as Plato suspected, is always doing geometry.

Most freshman courses were required, and I took most of mine in St. Robert Bellarmine Hall. Saint Robert was a father of the church who wrote on papal power and censored Galileo: The ceiling in his hallway was high, and dim lights hung down from it. The walls were beige up to about waist level, then turned off-white. The wood trim was dark and worn. The floor combined brown linoleum with brown and black tile. Even with a rush of students, the building maintained its dignity. We moved through it, and its old, clanking radiators warmed us as we did, but it was not a warmth that got to the bone. I remember a dream in which I climbed up beyond the third floor—up thin, narrow stairs to a bell tower that held a small, dusky room in which a priest was playing church music to a class of shadows.

My first semester classes included the obligatory theology and ROTC and a series of requirements: biology, psychology, speech, logic, and a language. I went to class and usually met John for lunch: We'd bring sandwiches to his car and play the radio while we ate. Then it was back to class, or the library, or the student union for a Coke. This was the next step in Jack MacFarland's plan for me—and I did okay for a while. I had learned enough routines in high school to act like a fairly typical student, but—except for the historical sketch I received in Senior English—there wasn't a solid center of knowledge and assurance to all this. When I look back through notes and papers and various photographs and memorabilia, I begin to remember what a disengaged, half-awake time it really was. I'll describe two of the notebooks I found. The one from English is a small book, eight by seven, and only eleven pages of it are filled. The notes I did write consist of book titles, dates of publication, names of characters, pointless summaries of books that were not on our syllabus and that I had never read ("*The Alexandria Quartet:* 5 or 6 characters seen by different people in different stages of life"), and quotations from the teacher ("Perception can bring sorrow.") The notes are a series of separate entries. I can't see any coherence. My biology lab notes are written on green-tint quadrille. They, too, are sparse. There is an occasional poorly executed sketch of a tiny organism or of a bone and muscle structure. Some of the formulas and molecular models sit isolated on the page, bare of any explanatory discussion. The lecture notes are fragmented; a fair number of sentences remain incomplete.

By the end of the second semester my grades were close to dipping below a C average, and since I had been admitted provisionally, that would have been that. Jack MacFarland had oriented me to Western intellectual history and had helped me develop my writing, but he had worked with me for only a year, and I needed more than twelve months of his kind of instruction. Speech and Introductory Psychology presented no big problems. General Biology had midterm and final examinations that required a good deal of memorizing, and I could do that, but the textbook—particularly the chapters covered in the second semester—was much, much harder than what I read in high school, and I was so ill-adept in the laboratory that I failed that portion of the class. We had to set up and pursue biological problems, not just memorize—and at the first sign of doing rather than memorizing, I would automatically assume the problem was beyond me and distance myself from it. Logic, another requirement, spooked me with its syllogisms and Venn diagrams—they were just a step away from more formal mathematics—so I memorized what I could and squirmed around the rest. Theology was god-awful; ROTC was worse. And Latin, the language I elected on the strength of Jack Mac-Farland's one piece of bad advice, had me suffocating under the dust of a dead civilization. Freshman English was taught by a frustrated novelist with glittering eyes who had us, among other things, describing the consumption of our last evening's meal using the images of the battlefield.

I was out of my league.

Faculty would announce office hours. If I had had the sense, I would have gone, but they struck me as aloof and somber men, and I felt stupid telling them I was . . . well—stupid. I drifted through the required courses, thinking that as soon as these requirements were over,

I'd never have to face anything even vaguely quantitative again. Or anything to do with foreign languages. Or ROTC. I fortified myself with defiance: I worked up an imitation of the old priest who was my Latin teacher, and I kept my ROTC uniform crumpled in the greasy trunk of John's Plymouth.

Many of my classmates came from and lived in a world very different from my own. The campus literary magazine would publish excerpts from the journals of upperclassmen traveling across Europe, standing before the Berlin Wall or hiking through olive groves toward Delphi. With the exception of one train trip back to Altoona, I had never been out of Southern California, and this translated, for me, into some personal inadequacy. Fraternities seemed exclusive and a little strange. I'm not sure why I didn't join any of Loyola's three dozen societies and clubs, though I do know that things like the Debate Squad were way too competitive. Posters and flyers and squibs in the campus newspaper gave testament to a lot of connecting activity, but John and I pretty much kept to ourselves, ragging on the "Loyola man," reading the literary magazine aloud with a French accent, simultaneously feeling contempt for and exclusion from a social life that seemed to work with the mystery and enclosure of the clockwork in a music box.

It is an unfortunate fact of our psychic lives that the images that surround us as we grow up—no matter how much we may scorn them later—give shape to our deepest needs and longings. Every year Loyola men elected a homecoming queen. The queen and her princesses were students at the Catholic sister schools: Marymount, Mount St. Mary's, St. Vincent's. They had names like Corinne and Cathy, and they came from the Sullivan family or the Mitchells or the Ryans. They were taught to stand with toe to heel, their smiles were inviting, and the photographer's flash illuminated their eyes. Loyola men met them at fraternity parties and mixers and "CoEd Day," met them according to rules of manner and affiliation and parental connection as elaborate as a Balinese dance. John and I drew mustaches on their photographs, but something about them reached far back into my life.

Growing up in South L.A. was certainly not a conscious misery. My neighborhood had its diversions and its mysteries, and I felt loved and needed at home. But all in all there was a dreary impotence to the years, and isolation, and a deep sadness about my father. I protected myself from the harsher side of it all through a life of the mind. And while that interior life included spaceships and pink chemicals and music and the planetary moons, it also held the myriad television images of the good life that were piped into my home: Robert Young sitting down to dinner, Ozzie Nelson tossing the football with his sons, the blond in a Prell commercial turning toward the camera. The images couldn't have been more trivial—all sentimental phosphorescence—but as a child tucked away on South Vermont, they were just about the only images I had of what life would be without illness and dead ends. I didn't realize how completely their message had seeped into my being, what loneliness and sorrow was being held at bay—didn't realize it until I found myself in the middle of Loyola's social life without a guidebook, feeling just beyond the superficial touch of the queen and her princesses, those smiling incarnations of a television promise. I scorned the whole silly show and ached to be embraced by one of these mythic females under the muted light of a paper moon.

So I went to school and sat in class and memorized more than understood and whistled past the academic graveyard. I vacillated between the false potency of scorn and feelings of ineptitude. John and I would get in his car and enjoy the warmth of each other and laugh and head down the long strip of Manchester Boulevard, away from Loyola, away from the palms and green, green lawns, back to South L.A. We'd throw the ball in the alley or lag pennies on Vermont or hit Marty's Liquor. We'd leave much later for a movie or a football game at Mercy High or the terrible safety of downtown Los Angeles. Walking, then, past the *discotecas* and pawnshops, past the windows full of fried chicken and yellow lamps, past the New Follies, walking through hustlers and lost drunks and prostitutes and transvestites with rouge the color of bacon—stopping, finally, before the musty opening of a bar where two silhouettes moved around a pool table as though they were underwater.

I don't know what I would have found if the flow of events hadn't changed dramatically. Two things happened. Jack MacFarland privately influenced my course of study at Loyola, and death once again ripped through our small family.

The coterie of MacFarland's students—Art Mitz, Mark Dever, and me—were still visiting our rumpled mentor. We would stop by his office or his apartment to mock our classes and the teachers and all that "Loyola man' bullshit." Nobody had more appreciation for burlesque than Jack MacFarland, but I suppose he saw beneath our caustic performances and knew we were headed for trouble. Without telling us, he started making phone calls to some of his old teachers at Loyola—primarily to Dr. Frank Carothers, the chairman of the English Department—and, I guess, explained that these kids needed to be slapped alongside the head with a good novel. Dr. Carothers volunteered to look out for us and agreed to some special studies courses that we could substitute for a few of the more traditional requirements, courses that would enable us to read and write a lot under the close supervision of a faculty member. In fact, what he promised were tutorials—and that was exceptional, even for a small college. All this would start up when we returned from summer vacation. Our sopho-more year, Jack MacFarland finally revealed, would be different.

When Lou Minton rewired the trailer, he rigged a phone line from the front house: A few digits and we could call each other. One night during the summer after my freshman year, the phone rang while I was reading. It was my mother and she was screaming. I ran into the house to find her standing in the kitchen hysterical—both hands pressed to her face—and all I could make out was Lou's name. I didn't see him in the front of the house, so I ran back through the kitchen to the bedroom. He had fallen back across the bed, a hole right at his sideburn, his jaw still quivering. They had a fight, and some ugly depth of pain convulsed within him. He left the table and walked to the bedroom. My mother heard the light slam of a .22. Nothing more.

That summer seems vague and distant. I can't remember any specifics, though I had to take care of my mother and handle the af-fairs of the house. I probably made do by blunting a good deal of what I saw and navigating with intuitive quadrants. But though I can-not remember details, I do recall feelings and recognitions: Lou's sui-cide came to represent the sadness and dead time I had protected myself against, the personal as well as public oppressiveness of life in South Los Angeles. I began to see that my escape to the trailer and my isolationist fantasies of the demimonde would yield another kind of death, a surrender to the culture's lost core. An alternative was some-how starting to take shape around school and knowledge. Knowledge seemed . . . was it empowering? No, that's a word I would use now. Then I felt freed, as if I were untying fetters. There simply were times when the pain and confusion of that summer would give way to some-thing I felt more than I knew: a lightness to my body, an ease in breathing. Three or four months later I took an art history course, and one day during a slide show on Gothic architecture I felt myself rising up within the interior light of Mont-Saint-Michel. I wanted to be re-leased from the despair that surrounded me on South Vermont and from my own troubled sense of exclusion.

Jack MacFarland had saved me at one juncture—caught my fancy and revitalized my mind—what I felt now was something further, some tentative recognition that an engagement with ideas could foster competence and lead me out into the world. But all this was very new and fragile, and given what I know now, I realize how easily it could have been crushed. My mother, for as long as I can remember, always added onto any statement of intention—her or others—the phrase *se vuol Dio,* if God wants it. The fulfillment of desire, no matter how trivial, required the blessing of the gods, for the world was filled with threat. "I'll plant the seeds this weekend," I might say. "Se vuol Dio," she would add. *Se vuol Dio.* The phrase expressed several lifetimes of ravaged hope: my grandfather's lost leg, the failure of the Rose

Spaghetti House, my father laid low, Lou Minton, the landscapes of South L.A. *Se vuol Dio.* For those who live their lives on South Vermont, tomorrow doesn't beckon to be defined from a benign future. It's up to the gods, not you, if any old thing turns out right. I carried within me no history of assurances that what I was feeling would lead to anything.

Because of its size and because of the kind of teacher who is drawn to small liberal arts colleges, Loyola would turn out to be a very good place for me. For even with MacFarland's yearlong tour through ideas and language, I was unprepared. English prose written before the twentieth century was difficult, sometimes impossible, for me to comprehend. The kind of reasoning I found in logic was very foreign. My writing was okay, but I couldn't hold a candle to Art Mitz or Mark Dever or to those boys who came from good schools. And my fears about science and mathematics prevailed: Pereira Hall, the Math and Engineering Building, was only forty to fifty yards from the rear entrance to the English Department but seemed an unfriendly mirage, a malevolent castle floating in the haze of a mescaline dream.

We live, in America, with so many platitudes about motivation and self-reliance and individualism—and myths spun from them, like those of Horatio Alger—that we find it hard to accept the fact that they are serious nonsense. To live your early life on the streets of South L.A.—or Homewood or Spanish Harlem or Chicago's South Side or any one of hundreds of other depressed communities—and to journey up through the top levels of the American educational system will call for support and guidance at many, many points along the way. You'll need people to guide you into conversations that seem foreign and threatening. You'll need models, lots of them, to show you how to get at what you don't know. You'll need people to help you center yourself in your own developing ideas. You'll need people to watch out for you. There is much talk these days about the value of a classical humanistic education, a call for an immersion in the humanities, a return to the great books. These appeals raise lots of suspicions, for such curricula have traditionally served to exclude working-class people from the classroom. It doesn't, of necessity, have to be that way. The teachers that fate and Jack MacFarland's crisis intervention sent my way worked at making the humanities truly human. What transpired between us was the essence of humane liberal education, and it enabled me to move far beyond the cognitive charade of my freshman year.

From the midpoint of their freshman year, Loyola students had to take one philosophy course per semester: Logic, Philosophy of Nature, Philosophy of Man, General Ethics, Natural Theology, and so on. Logic was the first in the series, and I had barely gotten a C. The rest of the courses looked like a book fair of medieval scholasticism with the mold scraped off the bindings, and I dreaded their advent. But I was beginning my sophomore year at a time when the best and brightest of the Jesuit community were calling for an intellectually panoramic, socially progressive Catholicism, and while this lasted, I reaped the benefits. Sections of the next three courses I had to take would be taught by a young man who was studying for the priesthood and who was, himself, attempting to develop a personal philosophy that incorporated the mind and the body as well as the spirit.

Mr. Johnson could have strolled off a Wheaties box. Still in his twenties and a casting director's vision of those good looks thought to be all-American, Don Johnson had committed his very considerable intelligence to the study and teaching of philosophy. Jack MacFarland had introduced me to the Greeks, to Christian scholasticism, eighteenth-century deism, and French existentialism, but it was truly an introduction, a curtsy to that realm of the heavens where the philosophers dwell. Mr. Johnson provided a fuller course. He was methodical and spoke with vibrance and made connections between ancients and moderns with care. He did for philosophy what Mr. MacFarland had done for literary history: He gave me a directory of key names and notions.

We started in a traditional way with the Greek philosophers who preceded Socrates—Thales, Heraclitus, Empedocles—and worked our way down to Kant and Hegel. We read a little Aquinas, but we also read E. A. Burtt's *The Metaphysical Foundations of Modern Science,* and that gave me entry to Kepler, Copernicus, Galileo (which I was then spelling *Galelao*), and Newton. As he laid out his history of ideas, Mr. Johnson would consider aloud the particular philosophical issue involved, so we didn't, for example, simply get an outline of what Hegel believed, but we watched and listened as Don Johnson reasoned like Hegel and then raised his own questions about the Hegelian scheme. He was a working philosopher, and he was thinking out loud in front of us.

The Metaphysical Foundations of Modern Science was very tough going. It assumed not only a familiarity with Western thought but, as well, a sophistication in reading a theoretically rich argument. It was, in other words, the kind of book you encounter with increased frequency as you move through college. It combined the history of mathematics and science with philosophical investigation, and when I tried to read it, I'd end up rescanning the same sentences over and over, not understanding them, and, finally, slamming the book down on the desk—swearing at this golden boy Johnson and angry with myself. Here's a typical passage, one of the many I marked as being hopeless:

> We begin now to glimpse the tremendous significance of what these fathers of modern science were doing, but let us

continue with our questions. What further specific metaphysical doctrines was Kepler led to adopt as a consequence of this notion of what constitutes the real world? For one thing, it led him to appropriate in his own way the distinction between primary and secondary qualities, which had been noted in the ancient world by the atomist and skeptical schools, and which was being revived in the sixteenth century in varied form by such miscellaneous thinkers as Vives, Sanchez, Montaigne, and Campanella. Knowledge as it is immediately offered the mind through the senses is obscure, confused, contradictory, and hence untrustworthy; only those features of the world in terms of which we get certain and consistent knowledge open before us what is indubitably and permanently real. Other qualities are not real qualities of things, but only signs of them. For Kepler, of course, the real qualities are those caught up in this mathematical harmony underlying the world of the senses, and which, therefore, have a causal relation to the latter. *The real world is a world of quantitative characteristics only; its differences are differences of number alone.*

I couldn't get the distinction that was being made between primary and secondary qualities, and I certainly didn't have the background that would enable me to make sense of Burtt's brief historical survey: from "atomist and skeptical schools [to] . . . Campanella." It is clear from the author's italics that the last sentence of the passage is important, so I underlined it, but because Burtt's discussion is built on a rich intellectual history that I didn't know, I was reading words but not understanding text. I was the human incarnation of language-recognition computer programs: able to record the dictionary meanings of individual words but unable to generate any meaning out of them.

"What," I asked in class, "are primary and secondary qualities? I don't get it." And here Don Johnson was very good. "The answer," he said, "can be found in the passage itself. I'll go back through it with you. Let's start with primary and secondary qualities. If some qualities are primary and others secondary, which do you think would be most important?"

"Primary?"

"Right. Primary qualities. Whatever they are. Now let's turn to Kepler, since Kepler's the subject of this passage. What is it that's more important to Kepler?"

I pause and say tentatively, "Math." Another student speaks up, reading from the book: "Quantitative characteristics."

"All right. So primary qualities, for Kepler, are mathematical, quantitative. But we still don't know what this primary and secondary opposition really refers to, do we? Look right in the middle of the paragraph. Burtt is comparing mathematical knowledge to the immediate knowledge provided by—what?"

My light bulb goes on: "The senses."

"There it is. The primary-secondary opposition is the opposition between knowledge gained by pure mathematical reasoning versus knowledge gained through our five senses."

We worked with *The Metaphysical Foundations of Modern Science* for some time, and I made my way slowly through it. Mr. Johnson was helping me develop an ability to read difficult texts—I was learning how to reread critically, how to tease out definitions and basic arguments. And I was also gaining confidence that if I stayed with material long enough and kept asking questions, I would get it. That assurance proved to be more valuable than any particular body of knowledge I learned that year.

For my second semester, I had to take Philosophy of Man, and it was during that course that Mr. Johnson delivered his second gift. We read Gabriel Marcel and Erich Fromm, learning about phenomenology and social criticism. We considered the human animal from an anthropological as well as philosophical perspective. And we read humanistic psychologist Abraham Maslow's *Toward a Psychology of Being.* Maslow wrote about "the 'will to health,' the urge to grow, the pressure of self-actualization, the quest for one's identity." The book had a profound effect on me. Six months before, Lou Minton's jaw quivered as if to speak the race's deepest sorrow, and through the rest of that summer I could only feel in my legs and chest some fleeting assurance that the world wasn't a thin mask stretched over nothingness. Now I was reading an articulation of that vague, hopeful feeling. Maslow was giving voice to some delicate possibility within me, and I was powerfully drawn to it. Every person is, in part, "'his own project' and makes himself." I had to know more, so I called Mr. Johnson up and asked if I could visit with him. "Sure," he said, and invited me to campus. So one Saturday morning I took a series of early buses and headed west.

Mr. Johnson and the other initiates to the priesthood lived in an old white residence hall on the grassy east edge of campus, and the long walk up Loyola Boulevard was quiet and meditative: Birds were flying tree to tree and a light breeze was coming in off Playa del Rey. I walked up around the gym, back behind Math-Engineering to his quarters, a simple one-story building with those Spanish curves that seem simultaneously thick and weightless. The sun had warmed the stucco. A window by the door was open, and a curtain had fluttered out. I rang the bell and heard steps on a hardwood floor. Mr. Johnson opened the door and stepped out. He was smiling and his eyes were attentive in the light . . . present . . . there. They said, "Come, let's talk." . . .

When I was learning my craft at Jack MacFarland's knee, I continually misused words and wrote fragments and run-on sentences and had trouble making my pronouns agree with whatever it was that preceded them. I also produced sentences like these:

> Some of these modern-day Ramses are inherent of their wealth, others are self-made.

> An exhibition of will on the part of the protagonist enables him to accomplish a subjective good (which is an element of tragedy, namely: the protagonist does not fully realize the objective wrong that he is doing. He feels objectively justified if not completely right.)

I was struggling to express increasingly complex ideas, and I couldn't get the language straight: Words, as in my second sentence on tragedy, piled up like cars in a serial wreck. I was encountering a new language—the language of the academy—and was trying to find my way around in it. I have some more examples, written during my first year and a half at Loyola. There was inflated vocabulary:

> I conjectured that he was the same individual who had arrested my attention earlier.

> In his famed speech, "The American Scholar," Ralph Waldo Emerson posed several problems that are particularly germane to the position of the young author.

There were cliches and mixed and awkward metaphors:

> In 1517, when Luther nailed his 95 theses to the door of Wittenburg Cathedral, he unknowingly started a snowball rolling that was to grow to tremendous reprocussions.

And there was academic melodrama:

> The vast realm of the cosmos or the depths of a man's soul hold questions that reason flounders upon, but which can be probed by the peculiar private insight of the seer.

Pop grammarians and unhappy English teachers get a little strange around sentences like these. But such sentences can be seen as marking a stage in linguistic growth. Appropriating a style and making it your own is difficult, and you'll miss the mark a thousand times along the way. The botched performances, though, are part of it all, and developing writers will grow through them if they are able to write for people who care about language, people who are willing to sit with them and help them as they struggle to write about difficult things. That is what Ted Erlandson did for me.

Dr. Erlandson was one of the people who agreed to teach me and my Mercy High companions a seminar—a close, intensive course that would substitute for a larger, standard offering like Introduction to Prose Literature. He was tall and lanky and had a long reddish brown beard and lectured in a voice that was basso and happy. He was a strong lecturer and possessed the best memory for fictional detail I'd ever witnessed. And he cared about prose. The teachers I had during my last three years at Loyola assigned a tremendous amount of writing. But it was Ted Erlandson who got in there with his pencil and worked on my style. He would sit me down next to him at his big desk, sweep books and pencils across the scratched veneer, and go back over the sentences he wanted me to revise.

He always began by reading the sentence out loud: "Camus ascented to a richer vision of life that was to characterize the entirety of his work." Then he would fiddle with the sentence, talking and looking up at me intermittently to comment or ask questions: "'Ascent'. That sounds like 'assent', I know, but look it up, Mike." He'd wait while I fluttered the dictionary. "Now, 'the entirety of his work' . . . try this instead: 'his entire work.' Let's read it. 'Camus assented to a richer vision of life that would characterize his entire work.' Sounds better, doesn't it?"

And another sentence. "'Irregardless of the disastrous ending of *Bread and Wine,* it must be seen as an affirmative work.' 'Irregardless' . . . people use it all the time, but 'regardless' will do just fine. Now, I think this next part sounds a little awkward; listen: 'Regardless of the disastrous ending of *Bread and Wine,* it . . .' Hear that? Let's try removing the 'of' and the 'it': 'Regardless of the disastrous ending, *Bread and Wine* must be seen as an affirmative work.' Hmmm. Better, I think."

And so it would go. He rarely used grammatical terms, and he never got technical. He dealt with specific bits of language: "Try this here" or "Here's another way to say it." He worked as a craftsman works, with particulars, and he shuttled back and forth continually between print and voice, making me breathe my prose, making me hear the language I'd generated in silence. Perhaps he was more directive than some would like, but, to be truthful, direction was what I needed. I was easily frustrated, and it didn't take a lot to make me doubt myself. When teachers would write "no" or "awkward" or "rewrite" alongside the sentences I had worked so hard to produce, I would be peeved and disappointed. "Well, what the hell *do* they want?" I'd grumble to no one in particular. So Ted Erlandson's linguistic parenting felt just right: a modeling of grace until it all slowly, slowly began to work itself into the way I shaped language.

——— ANALYSIS ———

1. Does it matter to you that Rose rattles off many concepts (e.g., "Christian scholasticism") and the names of seemingly important figures from the ancient or modern world ("Hegel")? Do you think Rose expects his readers to recognize these concepts and names?
2. Rose remarks "We live, in America, with so many platitudes about motivation and self-reliance and individualism—that we find it hard to accept the fact that they are serious nonsense." How does Rose develop and support this point? Do you agree with it or not? Why?
3. What is the function of speaking of reading as "entering the conversation"? What are the connotations, especially, of "conversation" here?
4. Rose speaks of the "profound effect" that Abraham Maslow's *Toward a Psychology of Being* had on him and later Maslow's idea that every person "is his own project." What are Maslow's themes? What might the idea of a person as a "project" suggest?

——— WRITING POSSIBILITIES ———

1. What problems of joining a "conversation" in the academic sense have you experienced? Try to pin them down by specifics. For example, in a puzzling passage from a text or a lecture, did you get beyond the difficulties? In what ways? How do you look back on the situation now?
2. How would you describe the possibilities and/or limitations of a neighborhood you have grown up in? What connections might be made between the world of that neighborhood and the world of the college or university you now inhabit?
3. Rose attacks the Horatio Alger myth of success in America, the "platitudes about motivation and self-reliance and individualism. . . ." Does your experience support Rose's conclusion that these ideas are "serious nonsense"?
4. How does the passage (20) compare with the following demographic analysis from Rose's first chapter?

[My family moved] to 9116 South Vermont Avenue, a house about one and one-half miles northwest of Watts. The neighborhood was poor, and it was in transition. Some old white folks had lived there for decades and were retired. Younger black families newly arrived from the South and the Midwest. Immigrant Mexican families were coming in from Baja. Any such demographic mix is potentially volatile, and as the fifties wore on, the neighborhood would be marked by outbursts of violence.

Andrew Sullivan

An editor of The New Republic *and a practicing Catholic, Andrew Sullivan explains how he discovered that he was different from other boys—that although he found girls interesting intellectually, he didn't think of them in a romantic or sexual way. Sullivan got an inkling of what he will eventually call homosexuality when a girl asks him why he isn't playing football with the other boys; when he says he doesn't like to, she asks if there might not be a girl hidden somewhere inside him. Though some homosexuals might bridle at this notion, Sullivan remembers the exchange as the one that started him thinking about the difference between himself and other boys. He makes clear that a homosexual orientation is a deeply ingrained probably biological matter and not an environmental one—a cleaving to one's mother as against one's father for example (his two siblings had the same upbringing but neither are gay). Homosexuality simply is a condition, almost innate, of nature and this being so, Sullivan argues, homosexuals must be accepted for what they are.*

What Is a Homosexual?

from Virtually Normal

Thinking, according to the analogy of the *Theaetetus,* is a process of catching not wild birds, not what is outside experience, but tame birds already within the cage of the mind.

—*Michael Oakeshott*

One can only *describe* here and say: this is what human life is like.

—*Ludwig Wittgenstein*

I remember the first time it dawned on me that I might be a homosexual. I was around the age of ten and had succeeded in avoiding the weekly soccer practice in my elementary school. I don't remember exactly how—maybe I had feigned a cold, or an injury, and claimed that because it was raining (it always seemed to be raining), I should be given the afternoon inside. I loathed soccer, partly because I wasn't very good at it and partly because I felt I didn't quite belong in the communal milieu in which it unfolded. The way it's played in English junior schools puts all the emphasis on team playing, and even back then this didn't appeal much to my nascent sense of *amour-propre.* But that lucky afternoon, I found myself sequestered with the girls, who habitually spent that time period doing sewing, knitting, and other appropriately feminine things. None of this, I remember, interested me much either; and I was happily engaged reading. Then a girl sitting next to me looked at me with a mixture of curiosity and disgust. "Why aren't you out with the boys playing football?" she asked. "Because I hate it," I replied. "Are you sure you're not really a girl under there?" she asked, with the suspicion of a sneer. "Yeah, of course," I replied, stung, and somewhat shaken.

It was the first time the fundamental homosexual dilemma had been put to me so starkly. It resonated so much with my own internal fears that I remember it vividly two decades later. Before then, most of what I now see as homosexual emotions had not been forced into one or the other gender category. I didn't feel as a boy or a girl; I felt as me. I remember vividly—perhaps I was five or six—being seated in the back of a car with my second cousin, a tousle-headed, wide-grinned kid a few years older, and being suddenly, unwittingly entranced by him. It was a feeling I had never felt before, the first inkling of a yearning that was only to grow stronger as the years went by. I remember too that around the age of eight, I joined a gang of four boys—modeled perhaps on the ubiquitous, vaguely homo-erotic male pop groups common at the time—and developed a crush on one of them. He was handsome and effortlessly athletic, and in my difficult attempt to cement both a companionship and a premature love affair, I felt the first strains of the homosexual hurt that is the accompaniment of most homosexual lives. It was not so much the rejection; it was the combination of acceptance and rejection. It was feeling that that part of the male-male bond that worked—the part that works with most heterosexual male-male friendships—was also the part that destroyed the possibility of another, as yet opaque but far more complete longing that for me, but not for him, was inextricable from the relationship. It was a sense that longing was based on a structural lack of reciprocity; that love was about being accepted on the condition that you suppressed what you really felt.

Looking back, this inchoate ache was all that I knew of the homosexual experience. But I knew also, because of the absence of any mention of the subject, because of the lack of any tangible visible reflections of it in the world around me, that there was something wrong with it. So when that afternoon, I was abruptly asked whether I was actually a girl, I blanched and stammered. Had my friend seen something I thought was hidden? She had, of course, merely accused me of being a sissy—something all young geeks, whatever their fledgling sexual orientation, were well used to. But I wondered whether she hadn't detected something else, something deeper. How had she known? And what, anyway, was it? By the age of ten, the only answer I had been given was that I was simply the wrong gender, something that any brief perusal of my body would discount.

Maybe I should be clearer here. The longing was not sexual. I was too young to feel any explicit sexual desire. I had no idea what an expression of sexual love might be. So far as I can remember it, it was a desire to unite with another: not to possess, but to join in some way; not to lose myself, but to be given dimension. At the time, I also had fantasies of being part of some boys' gang, or a rock group—some institution that could legitimately incorporate the half-understood, half-felt emotions that were filtering through my system. Nowhere else in the world did I see relationships that incorporated this desire. There were many that intimated it—the soccer team, my father and his friends, the male atmosphere of the local pub or the rugby club—but all these, I divined even then, were somehow premised on a denial of the acknowledged intimacy I had begun to crave. They were a simulacrum of acceptance. Because of their proximity to the very things I felt I wanted, they had developed a visceral hostility to the very thing that I was. So I had to be careful, in case they found out.

The secret, then, began when I was young. I hardly dared mention it to anyone; and the complete absence of any note of the subject in my family or in school, in television, newspapers, or even such books as I could get ahold of, made the secret that much more mystifying. I wondered whether there was any physical manifestation of this unmentionable fact. I was circumcised, unlike many other English boys: had that done it? I remember looking up physical descriptions of men and women in the local library to see if my own body corresponded to the shape of the male (I was, I determined, not broad-shouldered enough). When I was a little late going through puberty, I wondered whether that might be related, and half imagined that my voice might not break, and reveal my difference. Eventually, I succumbed to panic and mentioned it before God. I was in the communion line at my local parish church, Our Lady and Saint Peter's, the church that was linked to my elementary school. Please, I remember asking of the Almighty almost offhandedly as I walked up the aisle to receive communion from the mild-mannered Father Simmons for the umpteenth time, please, help me with *that*.

When people ask me whether homosexuality is a choice or not, I can only refer them to these experiences. They're the only thing I know for sure. Dozens of surveys have been written, countless questionnaires filled out, endless theories elaborated upon; but in most of these purportedly objective studies, opaque and troubling emotions are being reduced to statistics in front of strangers. I distrust them. But I don't fully distrust my own experience, or the experience of so many homosexuals I have met over the years. This experience is filtered, as all experience is, through the prism of reflection and self-reflection: it is not some raw datum in the empirical, verifiable world which I am presenting for review. But it is as honest a sketch as I can provide of the experience of finding oneself a homosexual.

Not that this was yet a truly sexual condition. In some sense, physical contact had, in a somewhat comic way, implanted itself in my mind. But it was still intensely abstract. I remember when I was around seven or eight seeing a bare-chested man on television one night and feeling such an intense longing for him that I determined to become a doctor. That way, I figured, I could render the man unconscious and lie on top of him when no one else was in the room. But then, I quickly realized, I would be found out and get into trouble. I spent most of the night awake, working out this scenario, and ending up as confused and as overcome by desire as when I began. But already I had divined that the expression of any kind of longing would have to take devious and subterranean forms. I would have to be an outlaw in order to be complete. I also remember making a joke in a debate competition at the age of twelve, at the time of a homosexual scandal involving the leader of the British Liberal Party. I joked that life was better under the Conservatives—or behind the Liberals, for that matter. It achieved a raucous response, but I had no idea what the analogy meant. Perhaps my schoolboy audience hadn't, either. We had learned the social levers of hostility to homosexuality before we had even the foggiest clue what they referred to.

My attraction to the same sex was not a desire as natural as sneezing, or eating, or sleeping, as some people claim. It was a secondary part of my psychological and emotional makeup; it operated in that confused and confusing part of my mind that was a fusion of involuntary desire and conscious aspiration. My first explicit sexual fondlings were with girls; but they were play, and carried no threat of emotional intimacy. Looking back, I realize I had no deep emotional ties to girls at all; they were friends, sometimes companions, sometimes soul mates. At elementary school, where I was academically ahead of my class, my closest colleagues were precocious girls. Their intellect I respected. But I had no longing to unite with them, and, looking back, didn't even want to talk with them much. I preferred hanging out with boys, traipsing through the neighboring woods with them, forming secret clubs, cycling around nearby lanes, playing childhood chase games (and in much of this, I guess I was indistinguishable from any other boy). But looking back, I also remember a nascent sense of a deeper, more intuitive, more emotional longing. I have always enjoyed the company of women, sustained many deep, strong friendships, had countless, endless conversations; but I have never longed for a woman in the way that I have longed for a man, never yearned for her physical embrace or her emotional solidarity.

I was, in other words, virtually normal. Like many homosexuals, I have spent some time looking back and trying to decipher what might have caused my apparent aberration. One explanation does make some sort of sense. I had a very close relationship with my mother and a somewhat distant one with my father. My father provided very basic physical and practical support—when I had asthmatic attacks as a child, it was my father who picked me up in the middle of the night and calmed me down to help me breathe. He made my birthday cakes, picked me up from school, and provided a solid, if undemonstrative, base of emotional support. But it was my mother who filled my head with the possibilities of the world, who conversed with me as an adult, who helped me believe in my ability to do things in the wider world. It was her values that shaped and encouraged me; and my father who sought to ground me in reality, and to keep my inflated ego in some sort of check. In my adolescence I warred with my father and sided with my mother in the family fights that took place. And in all of this, I suppose, I follow a typical pattern of homosexual development.

But then so do many heterosexuals. Both my brother and sister grew up in the same atmosphere, and neither of them turned out to be homosexual. Many heterosexual boys have intense bonds with their mothers, and seek to recreate them in the women they eventually love. Many heterosexual boys fight with their fathers and loathe organized sports. And some homosexual boys may sense in their fathers—especially those who cast an extremely heterosexual image—a rejection that they then intensify and internalize. Because the son feels he cannot be what his father wants, he seeks refuge in the understanding of a perhaps more sympathetic mother, who can temporarily shield her gay son from the disappointment and latent suspicions of his father. In other words, homosexuality may actually cause a young boy to be distant from his father and close to his mother, rather than be caused by it.

But whatever its origins, by puberty, my nascent homosexual emotional makeup interacted with my burgeoning hormones to create the beginnings of a sexual implosion. Something like this, of course, happens to gay and straight kids alike; but gay children have a particularly weird time of it. It was then that the scope of my entire situation began to click into place in my head. My longings became so intense that I found myself drawing sketches of the men I desired; I cut out male models from glossy magazines and made catalogues of them; I moved from crushes to sexual obsessions. I could no longer hide from this explicit desire: there it was on paper, in my brain, before my eyes—an undeniable and powerful attraction to other boys and men. And of course, with all of this came an exquisite and inextricable sense of exhilaration as well as disgust. It was like getting on a plane for the first time, being exhilarated by its ascent, gazing with wonder out of the window, seeing the clouds bob beneath you, but then suddenly realizing that you are on the wrong flight, going to a destination which terrifies you, surrounded by people who inwardly appall you. And you cannot get off. You are filled with a lurching panic. You are one of them.

It is probably true that many teenagers experience something of this panic. Although there is an understandable desire to divide the world starkly into heterosexual desire and its opposite, most of us, I'd guess, have confronted the possibility at some time in our lives of the possibility of our own homosexuality. There is something of both attractions in all of us, to begin with. For the majority, it is resolved quite early; our society forces such a resolution. Except for a few who seem to retain throughout their lives a capacity for attraction to both sexes, for most of us the issue is largely resolved before the teenage years set in. On this, both experience and empirical study agree. It is not always—perhaps never—easy, for either the homosexual or the heterosexual. Sometimes, the strength of the other attraction requires such a forceful suppression that it resonates much later in life. How else to explain the sometimes violent fear and hostility to homosexuals that a few heterosexual males feel? And how else to account for the sense of distance and betrayal that haunts some homosexuals? In this early, panicked resolution—one way or another—are the roots of many subsequent pathologies, pathologies that are not always pervious to reason.

But before the teenage years, panic is intermixed with pre-adult ambiguity. Many pubescent children play at sex with members of the same gender, before graduating on to the real thing. Many homosexuals do the exact opposite. For my part, my feelings were too strong and too terrifying to do anything but submerge them completely. There were, of course, moments when they took you unawares. Gay adolescents are offered what every heterosexual teenager longs for: to be invisible in the girls' locker room. But you are invisible in the boys' locker room, your desire as unavoidable as its object. In that moment, you learn the first homosexual lesson: that your survival depends upon self-concealment. I remember specifically coming back to high school after a long summer when I was fifteen and getting changed in the locker room for the first time again with a guy I had long had a crush on. But since the vacation, he had developed enormously: suddenly he had hair on his chest, his body had grown and strengthened, he was—clearly—no longer a boy. In front of me, he took off his shirt, and unknowingly, slowly, erotically stripped. I became literally breathless, overcome by the proximity of my desire. The gay teenager learns in that kind of event a form of control and sublimation, of deception and self-contempt, that never leaves his consciousness. He learns that that which would most give him meaning is most likely to destroy him in the eyes of others; that the condition of his friendships is the subjugation of himself.

In the development of any human being, these are powerful emotions. They form a person. The homosexual learns to make distinctions between his sexual desire and his emotional longings—not because he is particularly prone to objectification of the flesh, but because he needs to survive as a social and sexual being. The society separates these two entities, and for a long time the homosexual has no option but to keep them separate. He learns certain rules; and, as with a child learning grammar, they are hard, later on in life, to unlearn.

It's possible, I think, that whatever society teaches or doesn't teach about homosexuality, this fact will always be the case. No homosexual child, surrounded overwhelmingly by heterosexuals, will feel at home in his sexual and emotional world, even in the most tolerant of cultures. And every homosexual child will learn the rituals of deceit, impersonation, and appearance. Anyone who believes political, social, or even cultural revolution will change this fundamentally is denying reality. This isolation will always hold. It is definitional of homosexual development. And children are particularly cruel. At the age of eleven, no one wants to be the odd one out; and in the arena of dating and hormones, the exclusion is inevitably a traumatic one.

It's also likely to be forlorn. Most people are liable to meet emotional rejection by sheer force of circumstance; but for a homosexual, the odds are simply far, far higher. My own experience suggests that somewhere between two and five percent of the population have involuntarily strong emotional and sexual attractions to the same sex. Which means that the pool of possible partners *starts* at one in twenty to one in fifty. It's no wonder, perhaps, that male homosexual culture has developed an ethic more of anonymous or promiscuous sex than of committed relationships. It's as if the hard lessons of adolescence lower permanently—by the sheer dint of the odds—the aspiration for anything more.

Did I know what I was? Somewhere, maybe. But it was much easier to know what I wasn't. I wasn't going to be able to enter into the world of dating girls; I wasn't going to be able to feel fully comfortable among the heterosexual climate of the male teenager. So I decided, consciously or subconsciously, to construct a trajectory of my life that would remove me from their company; give me an excuse, provide a dignified way out. In Anglo-Saxon culture, the wonk has such an option: he's too nerdy or intellectual to be absorbed by girls. And there is something masculine and respected in the discipline of the arts and especially the sciences. You can gain respect and still be different.

So I threw myself into my schoolwork, into (more dubiously) plays, into creative writing, into science fiction. Other homosexuals I have subsequently met pursued other strategies: some paradoxically threw themselves into sports, out-jocking the jocks, gaining ever greater proximity, seeking respect, while knowing all the time that they were doomed to rejection. Others withdrew into isolation and despair. Others still, sensing their difference, flaunted it. At my high school, an older boy insisted on wearing full makeup to class; and he was accepted in a patronizing kind of way, his brazen otherness putting others at ease. They knew where they were with him; and he felt at least comfortable with their stable contempt. The rest of us who lived in a netherworld of sexual insecurity were not so lucky.

Most by then had a far more acute sense of appearances than those who did not need to hide anything; and our sense of irony, and of aesthetics, assumed a precociously arch form, and drew us subtly together. Looking back, I realize that many of my best friends in my teen years were probably homosexual; and that somewhere in our coded, embarrassed dialogue we admitted it. Many of us also embraced those ideologies that seemed most alien to what we feared we might be: of the sports jock, of the altar boy, of the young conservative. They were the ultimate disguises. And our recognition of ourselves in the other only confirmed our desire to keep it quiet.

I should add that many young lesbians and homosexuals seem to have had a much easier time of it. For many, the question of sexual identity was not a critical factor in their life choices or vocation, or even a factor at all. Perhaps because of a less repressive upbringing or because of some natural ease in the world, they affected a simple comfort with their fate, and a desire to embrace it. These people alarmed me: their very ease was the sternest rebuke to my own anxiety, because it rendered it irrelevant. But later in life, I came to marvel at the naturalness of their self-confidence, in the face of such concerted communal pressure, and to envy it. I had the more common self-dramatizing urge of the tortured homosexual, trapped between feeling wicked and feeling ridiculous. It's shameful to admit it, but I was more traumatized by the latter than by the former: my pride was more formidable a force than my guilt.

When people ask the simple question What is a homosexual? I can only answer with stories like these. I could go on, but too many stories have already been told. Ask any lesbian or homosexual, and they will often provide a similar account. I was once asked at a conservative think tank what evidence I had that homosexuality was far more of an orientation than a choice, and I was forced to reply quite simply: my life. It's true that I have met a handful of lesbians and gay men over the years who have honestly told me that they genuinely had a choice in the matter (and a few heterosexuals who claim they too chose their orientation). I believe them; but they are the exception and not the rule. As homosexual lives go, my own was somewhat banal and typical.

This is not, of course, the end of the matter. Human experience begins with such facts, it doesn't end with them. There's a lamentable tendency to try to find some definitive solution to permanent human predicaments—in a string of DNA, in a conclusive psychological survey, in an analysis of hypothalami, in a verse of the Bible—in order to cut the argument short. Or to insist on the emotional veracity of a certain experience and expect it to trump any other argument on the table. But none of these things can replace the political and moral argument about how a society should deal with the presence of homosexuals in its midst. I relate my experience here not to impress or to shock or to gain sympathy, but merely to convey what the homosexual experience is actually like. You cannot discuss something until you know roughly what it is.

It is also true, I think, that the lesbian experience is somewhat different than the homosexual male experience. Many lesbians argue that homosexuality is more often a choice for women than for men; that it involves a communal longing as much as an individual one; that it is far more rooted in moral and political choice than in ineradicable emotional or sexual orientation. Nevertheless, many lesbians also relate similar experiences to the one I have just related. Because girls and women can be less defensive about emotions and sexuality than boys and men, the sense of beleaguerment may be less profound than it is for boys, and the sense of self-contradiction less intense. But the coming to terms with something one already is, the slow unfolding of a self-realization around a basic emotional reality, is the same. In many, and probably most, cases, they cannot help it either.

The homosexual experience may be deemed an illness, a disorder, a privilege, or a curse; it may be deemed worthy of a "cure," rectified, embraced, or endured. *But it exists.* And it exists in something like the form I have just described. It occurs independently of the forms of its expression; it is bound up in that mysterious and unstable area where sexual desire and emotional longing meet; it reaches into the core of what makes a human being who he or she is. The origins of homosexuality are remarkably mysterious, and probably are due to a mixture of some genetic factors and very early childhood development (before the ages of five or six). But these arguments are largely irrelevant for the discussion that follows. The truth is that, for the overwhelming majority of adults, the condition of homosexuality is as involuntary as heterosexuality is for heterosexuals. Such an orientation is evident from the very beginning of the formation of a person's emotional identity. These are the only unavoidable premises of the arguments that follow.

Given a choice, many homosexuals along the way would have preferred this were not so, which is about as good a piece of evidence that it is. Men married happily for years eventually crack and reveal the truth about themselves; people dedicated to extirpating homosexuality from the face of the earth have succumbed to the realization that they too are homosexual; individuals intent on ridding it from their systems have ended in defeat and sometimes despair; countless thousands have killed themselves in order not to face up to it, or often because they *have* finally faced up to it. They were not fleeing a chimera or chasing a deception; they were experiencing something real, whatever it was.

This is not a book about how a person deals with his or her sexuality. It is a book about how we as a society deal with that small minority of us which is homosexual. By "homosexual," I mean simply someone who can tell a similar story to my own; someone who has found in his or her life that he or she is drawn emotionally and sexually to the same gender, someone who, practically speaking, has had no fundamental choice in the matter. Every society in human history has devised some way to account for this phenomenon, and to accommodate it. As I write, Western society is in the middle of a tense and often fevered attempt to find its own way on the matter. Amid a cacophony of passion and reason, propaganda and statistics, self-disclosures and bouts of hysteria, the subject is being ineluctably discussed. This book is an attempt to think through the arguments on all sides as carefully and honestly as possible; to take the unalterable experience of all of us, heterosexual and homosexual, and try to make some social and political sense of it.

ANALYSIS

1. What does Sullivan mean by the title of his book, *Virtually Normal?* Why "virtually"?
2. Sullivan says, "When people ask me whether homosexuality is a choice or not, I can only refer them to these experiences. . . . Dozens of surveys have been written . . . opaque and troubling emotions are being reduced to statistics. . . . I distrust them. But I don't fully distrust my own experience. . . . " Does Sullivan convince you that his personal testimony is worth crediting?
3. In Chapter 1 of *Virtually Normal* (not reprinted here), Sullivan lays out the ground rules for reasoned discussion of religion and sexuality:

> . . . when the bigot seeks to explain his feeling [Sullivan writes] and when the religious citizen seeks to provide a civil reason that is rooted in his religious belief, then the argument can begin. And such religiously based civil reasons are an essential part of any liberal polity.

What does Sullivan mean by "explain" or "civil reason" when talking about the connection between feelings and argument? What is the meaning of "liberal polity" in the context of this essay?

Writing Possibilities

---

1. In this prologue to his book, Sullivan hopes his personal account of dawning homosexuality will convince (heterosexual) readers that it is not a choice but something "almost innate." In what ways does Sullivan's tone and style throughout this essay help draw the reader's assent to his basic point?

2. Have you ever faced the need to not simply reveal your feelings but to "explain" them? What were the circumstances? How did you provide something like Sullivan's "civil reason" (see the quote above) for your feelings? How did reasoned "argument" take place (assuming it did!)?

Malcolm X and Alex Haley

Malcolm X was born Malcolm Little in 1925. He was shot to death in 1965—most likely by embittered black nationalists—after predicting at the end of his Autobiography *that he would soon be dead.*

"Mascot" is an almost perfect demonstration of how to tell a story of a "major turning point" in one's life (Malcolm's own words). Malcolm describes how, in the eighth grade (about 1939) he was asked by his English teacher Mr. Ostrowski (Richard Kaminska actually) what he planned to do with himself, and Malcolm replied that he hoped to be a lawyer. Ostrowski/Kaminska tells Malcolm to be more "realistic" and think instead of doing something with his "hands," for example being a carpenter. This advice so embitters Malcolm that he turns away from whites, education, and the straight-and-narrow path generally, to a life on the margins; engaging in low-level crime, he eventually winds up in prison. In subsequent chapters of the Autobiography, *Malcolm details his progress from prisoner to black nationalist spokesman, founder of his own black nationalist group, and finally as rival to Martin Luther King, Jr. Malcolm X pleaded the separatist cause of black nationalism as a temporary solution to prejudice and discrimination.*

MASCOT

from The Autobiography of Malcolm X

That summer of 1940, in Lansing, I caught the Greyhound bus for Boston with my cardboard suitcase, and wearing my green suit. If someone had hung a sign, "HICK," around my neck, I couldn't have looked much more obvious. They didn't have the turnpikes then; the bus stopped at what seemed every corner and cowpatch. From my seat in—you guessed it—the back of the bus, I gawked out of the window at white man's America rolling past for what seemed a month, but must have been only a day and a half.

When we finally arrived, Ella met me at the terminal and took me home. The house was on Waumbeck Street in the Sugar Hill section of Roxbury, the Harlem of Boston. I met Ella's second husband, Frank, who was now a soldier; and her brother Earl, the singer who called himself Jimmy Carleton; and Mary, who was very different from her older sister. It's funny how I seemed to think of Mary as Ella's sister, instead of her being, just as Ella is, my own half-sister. It's probably because Ella and I always were much closer as basic types; we're dominant people, and Mary has always been mild and quiet, almost shy.

Ella was busily involved in dozens of things. She belonged to I don't know how many different clubs; she was a leading light of local so-called "black society." I saw and met a hundred black people there whose big-city talk and ways left my mouth hanging open.

I couldn't have feigned indifference if I had tried to. People talked casually about Chicago, Detroit, New York. I didn't know the world contained as many Negroes as I saw thronging downtown Roxbury at night, especially on Saturdays. Neon lights, nightclubs, poolhalls, bars, the cars they drove! Restaurants made the streets smell—rich, greasy, down-home black cooking! Jukeboxes blared Erskine Hawkins, Duke Ellington, Cootie Williams, dozens of others. If somebody had told me then that some day I'd know them all personally, I'd have found it hard to believe. The biggest bands, like these, played at the Roseland State Ballroom, on Boston's Massachusetts Avenue—one night for Negroes, the next night for whites.

I saw for the first time occasional black-white couples strolling around arm in arm. And on Sundays, when Ella, Mary, or somebody took me to church, I saw churches for black people such as I had never seen. They were many times finer than the white church I had attended back in Mason, Michigan. There, the white people just sat and worshiped with words; but the Boston Negroes, like all other Negroes I had ever seen at church, threw their souls and bodies wholly into worship.

Two or three times, I wrote letters to Wilfred intended for everybody back in Lansing. I said I'd try to describe it when I got back.

But I found I couldn't.

My restlessness with Mason—and for the first time in my life a restlessness with being around white people—began as soon as I got back home and entered eighth grade.

I continued to think constantly about all that I had seen in Boston, and about the way I had felt there. I know now that it was the sense of being a real part of a mass of my own kind, for the first time.

The white people—classmates, the Swerlins, the people at the restaurant where I worked—noticed the change. They said, "You're acting so strange. You don't seem like yourself, Malcolm. What's the matter?"

I kept close to the top of the class, though. The topmost scholastic standing, I remember, kept shifting between me, a girl named Audrey Slaugh, and a boy named Jimmy Cotton.

It went on that way, as I became increasingly restless and disturbed through the first semester. And then one day, just about when those of us who had passed were about to move up to 8-A, from which we would enter high school the next year, something happened which was to become the first major turning point of my life.

Somehow, I happened to be alone in the classroom with Mr. Ostrowski, my English teacher. He was a tall, rather reddish white man and he had a thick mustache. I had gotten some of my best marks under him, and he had always made me feel that he liked me. He was, as I have mentioned, a natural-born "advisor," about what you ought to read, to do, or think—about any and everything. We used to make unkind jokes about him: why was he teaching in Mason instead of somewhere else, getting for himself some of the "success in life" that he kept telling us how to get?

I know that he probably meant well in what he happened to advise me that day. I doubt that he meant any harm. It was just in his nature as an American white man. I was one of his top students, one of the school's top students—but all he could see for me was the kind of future "in your place" that almost all white people see for black people.

He told me, "Malcolm, you ought to be thinking about a career. Have you been giving it thought?"

The truth is, I hadn't. I never have figured out why I told him, "Well, yes, sir, I've been thinking I'd like to be a lawyer." Lansing certainly had no Negro lawyers—or doctors either—in those days, to hold up an image I might have aspired to. All I really knew for certain was that a lawyer didn't wash dishes, as I was doing.

Mr. Ostrowski looked surprised, I remember, and leaned back in his chair and clasped his hands behind his head. He kind of half-smiled and said, "Malcolm, one of life's first needs is for us to be realistic. Don't misunderstand me, now. We all here like you, you know that. But you've got to be realistic about being a nigger. A lawyer—that's no realistic goal for a nigger. You need to think about something you *can* be. You're good with your hands—making things. Everybody admires your carpentry shop work. Why don't you plan on carpentry? People like you as a person—you'd get all kinds of work."

The more I thought afterwards about what he said, the more uneasy it made me. It just kept treading around in my mind.

What made it really begin to disturb me was Mr. Ostrowski's advice to others in my class—all of them white. Most of them had told him they were planning to become farmers. But those who wanted to strike out on their own, to try something new, he had encouraged. Some, mostly girls, wanted to be teachers. A few wanted other professions, such as one boy who wanted to become a county agent; another, a veterinarian; and one girl wanted to be a nurse. They all reported that Mr. Ostrowski had encouraged what they had wanted. Yet nearly none of them had earned marks equal to mine.

It was a surprising thing that I had never thought of it that way before, but I realized that whatever I wasn't, I *was* smarter than nearly all of those white kids. But apparently I was still not intelligent enough, in their eyes, to become whatever *I* wanted to be.

It was then that I began to change—inside.

I drew away from white people. I came to class, and I answered when called upon. It became a physical strain simply to sit in Mr. Ostrowski's class.

Where "nigger" had slipped off my back before, wherever I heard it now, I stopped and looked at whoever said it. And they looked surprised that I did.

I quit hearing so much "nigger" and "What's wrong?"—which was the way I wanted it. Nobody, including the teachers, could decide what had come over me. I knew I was being discussed.

In a few more weeks, it was that way, too, at the restaurant where I worked washing dishes, and at the Swerlins'.

One day soon after, Mrs. Swerlin called me into the living room, and there was the state man, Maynard Allen. I knew from their faces that something was about to happen. She told me that none of them could understand why—after I had done so well in school, and on my job, and living with them, and after everyone in Mason had come to like me—I had lately begun to make them all feel that I wasn't happy there anymore.

She said she felt there was no need for me to stay at the detention home any longer, and that arrangements had been made for me to go and live with the Lyons family, who liked me so much.

She stood up and put out her hand. "I guess I've asked you a hundred times, Malcolm—do you want to tell me what's wrong?"

I shook her hand, and said, "Nothing, Mrs. Swerlin." Then I went and got my things, and came back down. At the livingroom door I saw her wiping her eyes. I felt very bad. I thanked her and went out in front to Mr. Allen, who took me over to the Lyons'.

Mr. and Mrs. Lyons, and their children, during the two months I lived with them—while finishing eighth grade—also tried to get me to tell them what was wrong. But somehow I couldn't tell them, either.

I went every Saturday to see my brothers and sisters in Lansing, and almost every other day I wrote to Ella in Boston. Not saying why, I told Ella that I wanted to come there and live.

I don't know how she did it, but she arranged for official custody of me to be transferred from Michigan to Massachusetts, and the very week I finished the eighth grade, I again boarded the Greyhound bus for Boston.

I've thought about that time a lot since then. No physical move in my life has been more pivotal or profound in its repercussions.

If I had stayed on in Michigan, I would probably have married one of those Negro girls I knew and liked in Lansing. I might have become one of those state capitol building shoeshine boys, or a Lansing Country Club waiter, or gotten one of the other menial jobs which, in those days, among Lansing Negroes, would have been considered "successful"—or even become a carpenter.

Whatever I have done since then, I have driven myself to become a success at it. I've often thought that if Mr. Ostrowski had encouraged me to become a lawyer, I would today probably be among some city's professional black bourgeoisie, sipping cocktails and palming myself off as a community spokesman for and leader of the suffering black masses, while my primary concern would be to grab a few more crumbs from the groaning board of the two-faced whites with whom they're begging to "integrate."

All praise is due to Allah that I went to Boston when I did. If I hadn't, I'd probably still be a brainwashed black Christian.

ANALYSIS

1. Why does Malcolm title this episode "Mascot"?
2. How does Malcolm's experience in Boston prepare us for his angry reaction to Ostrowski's suggestion?
3. Does it make a difference in your evaluation of this story that progressive educators of the 1920s and 1930s (the formative years for Mr. Kaminska) counseled work with their "hands" for minority groups as the most practical solution for the problems of racial minorities?

WRITING POSSIBILITIES

1. Can we see in the telling of the story Alex Haley's own middle-of-the-road style (Haley after all wrote for popular magazines like the *Reader's Digest* and the *Saturday Evening Post*)? Who is Haley/Malcolm's audience here? How does Haley's *rhetoric*—his adjustment of language, tone, and attitude to audience (black and/or white)—help us appreciate Malcolm's attitude?
2. Using the "Mascot" incident as a model, tell the story of any "turning point" you have encountered so far, in which someone else gave you advice which you either found useful or had to reject. Focus on specific moment, place, and motivations as Malcolm does.

James McBride

"As a boy," McBride explains, "I never knew where my mother was from—where she was born, who her parents were. When I asked she'd say, "God made me." When I asked if she was white, she'd say, "I'm light-skinned," and change the subject. "She raised twelve black children and sent us all to college and in most cases graduate school. Her children became doctors, professors, chemists, teachers—yet none of us even knew her maiden name until we were grown. It took me fourteen years to unearth her remarkable story—the daughter of an Orthodox Jewish rabbi, she married a black man in 1942—and she revealed it more as a favor to me than out of any desire to revisit her past. Here is her life as she told it to me, and betwixt and between the pages of her life you will find mine as well."

A professional jazz musician, McBride is a former staff writer for the Boston Globe, People *magazine, and the* Washington Post. *The title of McBride's book,* The Color of Water, *comes from one of the many replies his mother made to questions about race. "What color is God's spirit," McBride asks one day, pursuing his Jewish mother's evasions; "It doesn't have a color," his mother tells him; "God is the color of water. Water doesn't have a color." The lesson sinks in: "I could buy that," McBride remembers saying.*

McBride's chapter-essays are excellent examples of narrative point of view—*the vantage point, physical or mental, from which we tell or record our experiences. McBride's story shows us how an individual born of* mixed *racial origins views experience from a point of view different from that of someone born into* one *group. (During the throes of the Black Power era of the 1960s, McBride remembers being terrified that it could mean "the end of my mother.")*

SCHOOL

from Color of Water

Back in the 1960s, when she had money, which was hardly ever, Mommy would take us down on Delancey Street on Manhattan's Lower East Side to shop for school clothes. "You have to go where the deals are," she said. "They won't come to you."

"Where are the deals?" we asked.

"The Jews have the deals."

I thought Jews were something that was in the Bible. I'd heard about them in Sunday school, through Jesus and such. I told Ma I didn't know they were still around.

"Oh, they're around," she said. She had a funny look on her face.

The Hasidic Jewish merchants in their black *yarmulkes* would stare in shock as Mommy walked in, trailed by five or six of us. When they recovered enough to make money, she would drive them to the wall, haggling them to death, lapsing into Yiddish when the going got tough. "I know what's happening here! I know what's happening!" she snapped when the merchants lapsed into Yiddish amongst themselves during negotiations over a pair of shoes. She angrily whipped off some gibberish and the merchants gawked even more. We were awed.

The first time it happened, we asked, "Ma, how'd you learn to talk like that?"

"Mind your own business," she said. "Never ask questions or your mind will end up like a rock. Some of these Jews can't stand you."

Looking back, I realize that I never felt any kinetic relationship to Jews. We were insulated from their world and any other world but our own. Yet there was a part of me that recognized Jews as slightly different from other white folks, partly through information gleaned from Mommy, who consciously and unconsciously sought many things Jewish, and partly through my elder siblings. My sister Rosetta's college education at the all-black Howard University was completely paid for—tuition, books, even school clothes—by the Joseph L. Fisher Foundation, which was run out of the Stephen Wise Free Synagogue of Manhattan. In addition, my oldest brother, Dennis, guru of wisdom and source of much of our worldly news in the 1960s, came home from college with respect for Jewish friends he'd met. "They support the civil rights movement," he reported. Mommy was for anything involving the improvement of our education and condition, and while she would be quick to point out that "some Jews can't stand you," she also, in her crazy contradictory way, communicated the sense to us that if we were lucky enough to come across the right Jew in our travels—a teacher, a cop, a merchant—he would be kinder than other white folks. She never spoke about Jewish people as white. She spoke about them as Jews, which made them somehow different. It was a feeling every single one of us took into adulthood, that Jews were different from white people somehow. Later as an adult when I heard folks talk of the love/hate relationship between blacks and Jews I understood it to the bone not because of any outside sociological study, but because of my own experience with Jewish teachers and classmates—some who were truly kind, genuine, and sensitive, others who could not hide their distaste for my black face—people I'd met during my own contacts with the Jewish world, which Mommy tacitly arranged by forcing every one of us to go to predominantly Jewish public schools.

It was in her sense of education, more than any other, that Mommy conveyed her Jewishness to us. She admired the way Jewish parents raised their children to be scholastic standouts, insulating them from a potentially harmful and dangerous public school system by clustering together within certain communities, to attend certain schools, to be taught by certain teachers who enforced discipline and encouraged learning, and she followed their lead. During the school year she gave us careful instructions to bring home every single paper that the teachers handed out at school, especially in January, and failure to follow these instructions resulted in severe beatings. When we dutifully arrived with the papers, she would pore over them carefully, searching—"Okay . . . okay . . . here it is!"—grabbing the little form and filling it out. Every year the mighty bureaucratic dinosaur known as the New York City Public School System would belch forth a tiny diamond: they slipped a little notice to parents giving them the opportunity to have their kids bused to different school districts if they wanted; but there was a limited time to enroll, a short window of opportunity that lasted only a few days. Mommy stood poised over that option like a hawk. She invariably chose predominantly Jewish public schools: P.S. 138 in Rosedale, J.H.S. 231 in Springfield Gardens, Benjamin Cardozo, Francis Lewis, Forest Hills, Music and Art. Every morning we hit the door at six-thirty, fanning out across the city like soldiers, armed with books, T squares, musical instruments, an "S" bus pass that allowed you to ride the bus and subway for a nickel, and a free-school-lunch coupon in our pocket. Even the tiniest of us knew the subway and local city bus schedules and routes by heart. *The number 3 bus lets you off at the corner, but the 3A turns, so you have to get off . . .* By age twelve, I was traveling an hour and a half one way to junior high school by myself, taking two buses each direction every day. My homeroom teacher, Miss Allison, a young white woman with glasses who generally ignored me, would shrug as I walked in ten minutes late, apologizing about a delayed bus. The white kids stared at me in the cafeteria as I gobbled down the horrible school lunch. Who cared. It was all I had to eat.

In this pre-busing era, my siblings and I were unlike most other kids in our neighborhood, traveling miles and miles to largely white, Jewish communities to attend school while our friends walked to the neighborhood school. We grew accustomed to being the only black, or "Negro," in school and were standout students, neat and well-mannered, despite the racist attitudes of many of our teachers, who were happy to knock our 95 test scores down to 85's and 80's over the most trivial mistakes. Being the token Negro was something I was never entirely comfortable with. I was the only black kid in my fifth-grade class at P.S. 138 in the then all-white enclave of Rosedale, Queens, and one afternoon as the teacher dutifully read aloud from our history book's one page on "Negro history," someone in the back of the class whispered, "James is a nigger!" followed by a ripple of tittering and giggling across the room. The teacher shushed him and glared, but the damage had been done. I felt the blood rush to my face and sank low in my chair, seething inside, yet I did nothing. I imagined what my siblings would have done. They would have gone wild. They would have found that punk and bum-rushed him. They never would've allowed anyone to call them a nigger. But I was not them. I was shy and passive and quiet, and only later did the anger come bursting out of me, roaring out of me with such blast-furnace force that I would wonder who that person was and where it all came from.

Music arrived in my life around that time, and books. I would disappear inside whole worlds comprised of *Gulliver's Travels, Shane,* and books by Beverly Cleary. I took piano and clarinet lessons in school, often squirreling myself away in some corner with my clarinet to practice, wandering away in Tchaikovsky or John Philip Sousa, trying to improvise like jazz saxophonist James Moody, only to blink back to reality an hour or two later. To further escape from painful reality, I created an imaginary world for myself. I believed my true self was a boy who lived in the mirror. I'd lock myself in the bathroom and spend long hours playing with him. He looked just like me. I'd stare at him. Kiss him. Make faces at him and order him around. Unlike my siblings, he had no opinions. He would listen to me. "If I'm here and you're me, how can *you* be there at the same time?" I'd ask. He'd shrug and smile. I'd shout at him, abuse him verbally. "Give me an answer!" I'd snarl. I would turn to leave, but when I wheeled around he was always there, waiting for me. I had an ache inside, a longing, but I didn't know where it came from or why I had it. The boy in the mirror, he didn't seem to have an ache. He was free. He was never hungry, he had his own bed probably, and his mother wasn't white. I hated him. "Go away!" I'd shout. "Hurry up! Get on out!" but he'd never leave. My siblings would hold their ears to the bathroom door and laugh as I talked to myself. "What a doofus you are," my brother Richie snickered.

Even though my siblings called me "Big Head" because I had a big head and a skinny body, to the outer world I was probably on the "most likely to succeed" list. I was a smart kid. I read a lot. I played music well. I went to church. I had what black folks called "good" hair, because it was curly as opposed to nappy. I was light-skinned or brown-skinned, and girls thought I was cute despite my shyness. Yet I myself had no idea who I was. I loved my mother yet looked nothing like her. Neither did I look like the role models in my life—my stepfather, my godparents, other relatives—all of whom were black. And *they* looked nothing like the other heroes I saw, the guys in the movies, white men like Steve McQueen and Paul Newman who beat the bad guys and in the end got the pretty girl—who, incidentally, was always white.

One afternoon I came home from school and cornered Mommy while she was cooking dinner. "Ma, what's a tragic mulatto?" I asked.

Anger flashed across her face like lightning and her nose, which tends to redden and swell in anger, blew up like a balloon. "Where'd you hear that?" she asked.

"I read it in a book."

"For God's sake, you're no tragic mul—What book is this?"

"Just a book I read."

"Don't read that book anymore." She sucked her teeth. "Tragic mulatto. What a stupid thing to call somebody! Somebody called you that?"

"No."

"Don't ever ever use that term."

"Am I black or white?"

"You're a human being," she snapped. "Educate yourself or you'll be a nobody!"

"Will I be a black nobody or just a nobody?"

"If you're a nobody," she said dryly, "it doesn't matter what color you are."

"That doesn't make sense," I said.

She sighed and sat down. "I bet you never heard the joke the teacher and the beans," she said. I shook my head. "The teacher says to the class, 'Tell us about different kinds of beans.'

"The first little boy says, 'There's pinto beans.'

"'Correct,' says the teacher.

"Another boy raises his hand. 'There's lima beans.'

"'Very good,' says the teacher.

"Then a little girl in the back raises her hand and says, 'We're all *human* beans!' "

She laughed. "That's what you are, a *human* bean! And a *fart-buster* to boot!" She got up and went back to cooking, while I wandered away, bewildered.

Perplexed to the point of bursting, I took the question to my elder siblings. Although each had drawn from the same bowl of crazy logic Mommy served up, none seemed to share my own confusion. "Are we black or white?" I asked my brother David one day.

"*I'm* black," said David, sporting his freshly grown Afro the size of Milwaukee. "But *you* may be a Negro. You better check with Billy upstairs."

I approached Billy, but before I could open my mouth, he asked, "Want to see something?"

"Sure," I said.

He led me through our house, past Mommy, who was absorbed in changing diapers, past a pile of upended chairs, books, music stands, and musical instruments that constituted the living room, up the stairs into the boys' bedroom, and over to a closet which was filled, literally, from floor to ceiling, with junk. He stuck his head inside, pointed to the back, and said, "Look at this." When I stuck my head in, he shoved me in from behind and slammed the door, holding it shut. "Hey, man! It's dark in here!" I shouted, banging at the door and trying to keep the fear out of my voice. Suddenly, in the darkness, I felt hands grabbing me and heard a monster roar. My panic zoomed into high-level terror and I frantically pounded on the door with all my might, screaming in a high-pitched, fervent squawk, "BILLLLYYYYYYYY!" He released the door and I tore out of the closet, my brother David tumbling out behind me. My two brothers fell to the floor laughing, while I ran around the house crying for Ma, zooming from room to room, my circuits blown.

The question of race was like the power of the moon in my house. It's what made the river flow, the ocean swell, and the tide rise, but it was a silent power, intractable, indomitable, indisputable, and thus completely ignorable. Mommy kept us at a frantic living pace that left no time for the problem. We thrived on thought, books, music, and art, which she fed to us instead of food. At every opportunity she loaded five or six of us onto the subway, paying one fare and pushing the rest of us through the turnstiles while the token-booth clerks frowned and subway riders stared, parading us to every free event New York City offered: festivals, zoos, parades, block parties, libraries, concerts. We walked for hours through the city, long meandering walks that took in whole neighborhoods which we would pass through without buying a thing or speaking to anyone. Twice a year she marched us to the Guggenheim dental clinic in Manhattan for free care, where foreign dental students wearing tunics and armed with drills, picks, and no novocaine, manned a row of dental chairs and reduced each of us to a screaming mass of tears while the others waited in line, watching, horrified. They pulled teeth like maniacs, barking at us in whatever their native tongues were while they yanked our heads back and forth like rag dolls'. They once pulled my brother Billy's tooth and then sent him out to Ma in the waiting room, whereupon she looked into the mouth full of gauze and blood and discovered they had yanked the wrong tooth. She marched back in and went wild. In summer she was the Pied Piper, leading the whole pack of us to public swimming pools, stripping down to her one-piece swimming suit and plunging into the water like a walrus, the rest of us following her like seals, splashing and gurgling in terror behind her as Mommy flailed along, seemingly barely able to swim herself until one of us coughed and sputtered, at which time she whipped through the water and grabbed the offending child, pulling him out and slapping him on the back, laughing. We did not consider ourselves poor or deprived, or depressed, for the rules of the outside world seemed meaningless to us as children. But as we grew up and fanned out into the world as teenagers and college students, we brought the outside world home with us, and the world that Mommy had so painstakingly created began to fall apart.

The sixties roared through my house like a tidal wave. My sister Helen's decision to drop out of school and run off at age fifteen, though she returned home five years later with a nursing degree and a baby girl, was the first sign of impending doom. Now the others began to act out, and the sense of justice and desire for equal rights that Mommy and my father had imparted to us began to backfire. Kind, gentle, Sunday school children who had been taught to say proudly, "I am a Negro," and recite the deeds of Jackie Robinson and Paul Robeson now turned to Malcolm X and H. Rap Brown and Martin Luther King for inspiration. Mommy was the wrong color for black pride and black power, which nearly rent my house in two.

One by one, my elder siblings broke with her rules, coming home bearing fruits of their own confusion, which we jokingly called their "revolution." An elder brother disappeared to Europe. Another sister had an affair at college and came home with a love child, fairly big news in 1967. My brother Richie got married at eighteen over Mommy's objections, divorced, then entered college, and was home on summer break when he got stopped by two cops while walking down the street with a friend. A group of boys who were walking about ten yards in front of Richie and his friend had ditched what appeared to be a bag of heroin as the cop car approached. The cops grouped the boys together, lined them up against a fence, and demanded to know which of them had jettisoned the bag, which later turned out to be filled with quinine, not heroin. All denied it, so the cops searched them all and found ninety dollars of Richie's college-bank-loan money in his pocket. When the policeman asked him where he got the money from, Richie told him it was his college money and he'd forgotten he'd had it. If you knew Richie, you'd nod and say, "Uh-huh," because it was perfectly in character for him to forget he was carrying around ninety precious dollars, which was a huge sum in those days. We used to call him "the Mad Scientist" when he was little. His science experiments would nearly blow up the house because whatever he created, he'd leave it bubbling and boiling while he went to search for food, forgetting it completely. He could remember the toughest calculus formulas and had nearly perfect pitch as a musician, but he literally could not remember to put his pants on. He would play John Coltrane-type solos on his sax for hours and be dressed in a winter jacket and gym shorts the whole time. He was that kind of kid, absentminded, and very smart, and later in life he became a chemist.

But to the cops, he was just another black perpetrator with a story, and he was arrested and jailed.

Mommy paced the house all night when she got the news. She showed up early at Richie's arraignment the next day and took a seat right behind the defense table. When they brought him out in handcuffs and she saw him cuffed and dirty after being in the holding pen all night, she could not contain her grief and began muttering like a crazy woman, wringing her hands. Through her reverie of mumbo jumbo she heard the court-appointed lawyer lean over to Richie and offer two words of legal advice: "Plead guilty." She jumped up and screamed, "Wait!" She charged past the court officers, shouting to the judge that it was a mistake, that none of her kids had ever been in trouble with the law before, that her son was a college student, and so forth. The white judge, who had noticed Mommy sitting in the largely black courtroom, released Richie to her custody and the charges were later dropped.

But that experience made Mommy bear down on the younger ones like me even more. She was, in retrospect, quite brilliant when it came to manipulating us. She depended heavily on the "king/queen system" which she established in our house long before I was born: the eldest sibling was the king or queen and you could not defy him or her, because you were a slave. When the eldest left for college, the next ascended to the throne. The king/queen system gave us a sense of order, rank, and self. It gave the older ones the sense that they were in charge, when in actuality it was Mommy who ruled the world. It also harked back to her own traditional Orthodox upbringing where the home was run by one dominating figure with strict rules and regulations. Despite the orchestrated chaos of our home, we always ate meals at a certain time, always did homework at a certain time, and always went to bed at a certain time. Mommy also aligned herself with any relative or friend who had any interest in any of her children and would send us off to stay with whatever relative promised to straighten us out, and many did. The extended black family was Mommy's hole card, and she played it as often as the times demanded because her family was not available to her. As I grew older, it occurred to me at some point that we had some relatives we had never seen. "How come we don't have any aunts and uncles on your side?" I asked her one day.

"I had a brother who died and my sister . . . I don't know where she is," she said.

"Why not?"

"We got separated."

"How's that?"

"I'm removed from my family."

"Removed?"

"Removed. Dead."

"Who's dead?"

"I'm dead. They're dead too by now probably. What's the difference? They didn't want me to marry on the black side."

"But if you're black already, how can they be mad at you?"

Boom. I had her. But she ignored it. "Don't ask me any more questions."

My stepfather, a potential source of information about her background, was not helpful. "Oh, your mama, you mind her," he grunted when I asked him. He loved her. He seemed to have no problem with her being white, which I found odd, since she was clearly so different from him. Whereas he was largely easygoing and open-minded about most worldly matters, she was suspicious, strict, and inaccessible. Whenever she stepped out of the house with us, she went into a sort of mental zone where her attention span went no farther than the five kids trailing her and the tightly balled fist in which she held her small bit of money, which she always counted to the last penny. She had absolutely no interest in a world that seemed incredibly agitated by our presence. The stares and remarks, the glances and cackles that we heard as we walked about the world went right over her head, but not over mine. By age ten, I was coming into my own feelings about myself and my own impending manhood, and going out with Mommy, which had been a privilege and an honor at age five, had become a dreaded event. I had reached a point where I was ashamed of her and didn't want the world to see my white mother. When I went out with my friends, I'd avoid telling her where we were playing because I didn't want her coming to the park to fetch me. I grew secretive, cautious, passive, angry, and fearful, always afraid that the baddest cat on the block would call her a "honky," in which case I'd have to respond and get my ass kicked. "Come and let's walk to the store," she said one afternoon.

"I can go by myself," I said. The intent was to hide my white mom and go it alone.

"Okay," she said. She didn't seem bothered by my newfound independence. Relieved, I set off to a neighborhood grocery store. The store owner was a gruff white man who, like many of the whites in St. Albans, was on his way out as we blacks began to move in. He did not seem to like black children and he certainly took no particular liking to or interest in me. When I got home, Mommy placed the quart of milk he sold me on the table, opened it up, and the smell of sour milk filled the room. She closed the carton and handed it to me. "Take it back and get my money back."

"Do I have to?"

"Take it back." It was an order. I was a Little Kid in my house, not a Big Kid who could voice opinions and sway the master. I had to take orders.

I dragged myself back to the store, dreading the showdown I knew was coming. The owner glared at me when I walked in. "I have to return this," I said.

"Not here," he said. "The milk is opened. I'm not taking it back."

I returned home. Ten minutes later Mommy marched into the store, doing her "madwalk," the bowlegged strut that meant thunder and lightning was coming—body pitched forward, jaw jutted out, hands balled into tight fists, nose red, stomping like Cab Calloway with the Billy Eckstein band blowing full blast behind him. I followed her sheepishly, my plan to go it alone and hide my white mother now completely awash, backfired in the worst way.

She angrily placed the milk on the counter. The merchant looked at her, then at me. Then back at her. Then at me again. The surprise written on his face changed to anger and disgust, and it took me completely by surprise. I thought the man would see Ma, think they had something in common, then give her the dough and we'd be off. "That milk is sold," he said.

"Smell it," Ma said. "It's spoiled."

"I don't smell milk. I sell milk."

Right away they were at each other, I mean really going at it. A crowd of black kids gathered, watching my white mother arguing with this white man. I wanted to sink into the floor and disappear. "It's okay, Ma . . . " I said. She ignored me. In matters of money, of which she had so little, I knew it was useless. She was going full blast—". . . fool . . . think you are . . . idiot!"—her words flying together like gibberish, while the neighborhood kids howled, woofing like dogs and enjoying the show.

After a while it was clear the man was not going to return her money, so she grabbed my hand and was heading toward the door, when he made another remark, something that I missed, something he murmured beneath his breath so softly that I couldn't hear, but it made the crowd murmur "Ooohhhh." Ma stiffened. Still holding the milk in her right hand, she turned around and flung it at him like a football. He ducked and the milk missed him, smashing into the cigarette cabinet behind him and sending milk and cigarettes splattering everywhere.

I could not understand such anger. I could not understand why she didn't just give up the milk. Why cause a fuss? I thought. My own embarrassment overrode all other feelings. As I walked home, holding Mommy's hand while she fumed, I thought it would be easier if we were just one color, black or white. I didn't want to be white. My siblings had already instilled the notion of black pride in me. I would have preferred that Mommy were black. Now, as a grown man, I feel privileged to have come from two worlds. My view of the world is not merely that of a black man but that of a black man with something of a Jewish soul. I don't consider myself Jewish, but when I look at Holocaust photographs of Jewish women whose children have been wrenched from them by Nazi soldiers, the women look like my own mother and I think to myself, *There but for the grace of God goes my own mother—and by extension, myself.* When I see two little Jewish old ladies giggling over coffee at a Manhattan diner, it makes me smile, because I hear my own mother's laughter beneath theirs. Conversely, when I hear black "leaders" talking about "Jewish slave owners" I feel angry and disgusted, knowing that they're inflaming people with lies and twisted history, as if all seven of the Jewish slave owners in the antebellum South, or however few there were, are responsible for the problems of African-Americans now. Those leaders are no better than their Jewish counterparts who spin statistics in marvelous ways to make African-Americans look like savages, criminals, drags on society, and "animals" (a word quite popular when used to describe blacks these days). I don't belong to any of those groups. I belong to the world of one God, one people. But as a kid, I preferred the black side, and often wished that Mommy had sent me to black schools like my friends. Instead I was stuck at that white school, P.S. 138, with white classmates who were convinced I could dance like James Brown. They constantly badgered me to do the "James Brown" for them, a squiggling of the feet made famous by the "Godfather of Soul" himself, who back in the sixties was bigger than life. I tried to explain to them that I couldn't dance. I have always been one of the worst dancers that God has ever put upon this earth. My sisters would spend hours at home trying out new dances to Archie Bell and the Drells, Martha Reeves, King Curtis, Curtis Mayfield, Aretha Franklin, and the Spinners. "Come on and dance!" they'd shout, boogying across the room. Even Ma would join in, sashaying across the floor, but when I joined in I looked so odd and stupid they fell to the floor laughing. "Give it up," they said. "You can't dance."

The white kids in school did not believe me, and after weeks of encouragement I found myself standing in front of the classroom on talent day, wearing my brother's good shoes and hitching up my pants, soul-singer-style like one of the Temptations, as someone dropped the needle on a James Brown record. I slid around the way I'd seen him do, shouting "Owww–shabba-na!" They were delighted. Even the teacher was amused. They really believed I could dance! I had them fooled. They screamed for more and I obliged, squiggling my feet and slip-sliding across the wooden floor, jumping into the air and landing in a near split by the blackboard, shouting "Eeeee-yowwww!" They went wild, but even as I sat down with their applause ringing in my ears, with laughter on my face, happy to feel accepted, to be part of them, knowing I had pleased them, I saw the derision on their faces, the clever smiles, laughing at the oddity of it, and I felt the same ache I felt when I gazed at the boy in the mirror. I remembered him, and how free he was, and I hated him even more.

ANALYSIS

1. How do McBride's metaphors at key moments suggest his emotional state—e.g., "The question of race was like the power of the moon. . . ."?
2. How does McBride uses dialogue to recreate moments in the discovery of his identity?
3. How would you characterize McBride's attitude towards the prejudice he experienced both as a child initially and later as an adult, looking back on those instances?
4. How does McBride's dual viewpoint allow him to see more acutely into matters that affect both traditions rather than if he had come from only one group? Look at his examination of how black leaders talk about Jewish slaveowners; why the quotes around "leaders"? What is the effect to "Jewish counterparts"?

WRITING POSSIBILITIES

1. How do McBride's anecdotes about race and Jewishness establish his understanding of both? In an essay, describe McBride's dawning sense of what it meant to come from a mixed background? To what extent do you come from a mixed background (ethnic as well as racial)? Do you favor one side or the other? Does this depend on who you are with at the time?
2. Using McBride's model, describe how you have coped (or failed to cope) with prejudice or discrimination. Be on the alert for bits of dialogue to establish the significance of those instances.
3. McBride says of the arrival of black power, "Mommy was the wrong color for black pride and black power, which nearly rent my house in two." What is (or was) McBride's attitude towards his internal conflict between black power and his mother's beliefs?

Chang-Rae Lee

Lee is a Korean-American novelist, the author of Native Speaker *(1995) and* Gesture Life *(1999). In this essay, he explains what it is like for immigrant parents who must learn to cope with a new linguistic world. He sympathizes—up to a point—with the dominant English-speaking world and its "frustrations" with new immigrants who don't, seemingly, want to learn English.*

MUTE IN AN ENGLISH-ONLY WORLD

EUGENE, ORE.

When I read of the troubles in Palisades Park, N.J., over the proliferation of Korean-language signs along its main commercial strip, I unexpectedly sympathized with the frustrations, resentments and fears of the longtime residents. They clearly felt alienated and even unwelcome in a vital part of their community. The town, like seven others in New Jersey, has passed laws requiring that half of any commercial sign in a foreign language be in English.

Now I certainly would never tolerate any exclusionary ideas about who could rightfully settle and belong in the town. But having been raised in a Korean immigrant family, I saw every day the exacting price and power of language, especially with my mother, who was an outsider in an English-only world.

In the first years we lived in America, my mother could speak only the most basic English, and she often encountered great difficulty whenever she went out.

We lived in New Rochelle, N.Y., in the early 70's; and most of the local businesses were run by the descendants of immigrants who, generations ago, had come to the suburbs from New York City. Proudly dotting Main Street and North Avenue were Italian pastry and cheese shops, Jewish tailors and cleaners and Polish and German butchers and bakers. If my mother's marketing couldn't wait until the weekend, when my father had free time, she would often hold off until I came home from school to buy the groceries.

Though I was only 6 or 7 years old, she insisted that I go out shopping with her and my younger sister. I mostly loathed the task, partly because it meant I couldn't spend the afternoon playing catch with my friends but also because I knew our errands would inevitably lead to an awkward scene, and that I would have to speak up to help my mother.

I was just learning the language myself, but I was a quick study, as children are with new tongues. I had spent kindergarten in almost complete silence, hearing only the high nasality of my teacher and comprehending little but the cranky wails and cries of my classmates. But soon, seemingly mere months later, I had already become a terrible ham and mimic, and I would crack up my father with impressions of teachers, his friends and even himself. My mother scolded me for aping his speech, and the one time I attempted to make light of hers I rated a round-house smack on my bottom.

For her, the English language was not very funny. It usually meant trouble and a good dose of shame, and sometimes real hurt. Although she had a good reading knowledge of the language from university classes in South Korea, she had never practiced actual conversation. So in America, she used English flashcards and phrase books and watched television with us kids. And she faithfully carried a pocket workbook illustrated with stick-figure people and compound sentences to be filled in.

But none of it seemed to do her much good. Staying mostly at home to care for us, she didn't have many chances to try out sundry words and phrases. When she did, say, at the window of the post office, her readied speech would stall, freeze, sometimes altogether collapse.

One day was unusually harrowing. We ventured downtown in the new Ford Country Squire my father had bought her, an enormous station wagon that seemed as long—and deft—as an ocean liner. We were shopping for a special meal for guests visiting that weekend, and my mother had heard that a particular butcher carried fresh oxtails, which she needed for a traditional soup.

We'd never been inside the shop, but my mother would pause before its window, which was always lined with whole hams, crown roasts and ropes of plump handmade sausages. She greatly esteemed the bounty with her eyes, and my sister and I did also, but despite our desirous cries she'd turn us away and instead buy the packaged links at the Finast supermarket, where she felt comfortable looking them over and could easily spot the price. And, of course, not have to talk.

But that day she was resolved. The butcher store was crowded, and as we stepped inside the door jingled a welcome. No one seemed to notice. We waited for some time, and people who entered after us were now being served. Finally, an old woman nudged my mother and waved a little ticket, which we hadn't taken. We patiently waited again, until one of the beefy men behind the glass display hollered our number.

My mother pulled us forward and began searching the cases, but the oxtails were nowhere to be found. The man, his big arms crossed, sharply said, "Come on, lady, whaddya want?" This unnerved her, and she somehow blurted the Korean word for oxtail, soggori.

The butcher looked as if my mother had put something sour in his mouth, and he glanced back at the lighted board and called the next number.

Before I knew it, she had rushed us outside and back in the wagon, which she had double-parked because of the crowd. She was furious, almost vibrating with fear and grief, and I could see she was about to cry.

She wanted to go back inside, but now the driver of the car we were blocking wanted to pull out. She was shooing us away. My mother, who had just earned her driver's license, started furiously working the pedals. But in her haste she must have flooded the engine, for it wouldn't turn over. The driver started honking and then another car began honking as well, and soon it seemed the entire street was shrieking at us.

In the following years, my mother grew steadily more comfortable with English. In Korean, she could be fiery, stern, deeply funny and ironic; in English, just slightly less so. If she was never quite fluent, she gained enough confidence to make herself clearly known to anyone, and particularly to me.

Five years ago, she died of cancer, and some months after we buried her I found myself in the driveway of my father's house, washing her sedan. I liked taking care of her things; it made me feel close to her. While I was cleaning out the glove compartment, I found her pocket English workbook, the one with the silly illustrations. I hadn't seen it in nearly 20 years. The yellowed pages were brittle and dog-eared. She had fashioned a plain-paper wrapping for it, and I wondered whether she meant to protect the book or hide it.

I don't doubt that she would have appreciated doing the family shopping on the new Broad Avenue of Palisades Park. But I like to think, too, that she would have understood those who now complain about the Korean-only signs.

I wonder what these same people would have done if they had seen my mother studying her English workbook—or lost in a store. Would they have nodded gently at her? Would they have lent a kind word?

ANALYSIS

1. Why is it that Lee "unexpectedly" begins to sympathize with the long-time residents of Palisades Park?
2. What does Lee mean by "exclusionary ideas"?
3. How does Lee prepare us to understand his mother's hopes and feelings before the climactic moment in which she blurts out, mistakenly, the Korean word for "oxtail"?
4. Why is Lee's title forceful?

WRITING POSSIBILITIES
---

1. If you are yourself an immigrant or refugee, or the son or daughter of parents who are, have you ever experienced the kind of language conflicts that Lee describes? Can you pin these down with specific incidents of the sort that forms the core of Lee's essay? What generalizations would you offer about your experience? Your parents'?

2. Lee's essay illustrates perfectly the combination of dramatic incident and (implied) generalizations about and from the events. But what might happen if Lee had chosen to write a straightforward argumentative essay rather than a dramatic and personal one? Try your hand at reversing Lee's procedures about some event comparable to the ones Lee describes.

Diana Abu-Jaber

An essayist, novelist, and English professor, Diana Abu-Jaber is of Arab American extraction and has lived in both Jordan and America. This short statement invokes the key word of pluralistic philosophy, difference, *and does so mindful of the contemporary understanding of that term, that difference is not necessarily a matter of superior and inferior, good and bad. An older racism argued that difference was indeed hierarchical: some races, it maintained, were better than others—not merely different. Abu-Jaber's point is quite the contrary: ". . . the other, the foreign, the different, is us."*

ON READING DIFFERENCE
from Ploughshares

The question I am asked, as a teacher and writer, is: Why do you read Native American literature? What is your justification or rationale for studying the thought and cultures of American native peoples?

Not merely enjoying or appreciating, but actually *studying,* immersing yourself in it?

Likewise, you might wonder, how much of the Plains or the Southwest is really in, say, an author who spent much of her life in New York City? What is the justification in beginning a work centered on the Plains, like *My Antonia,* from the perspective of someone displaced, recently arrived from Virginia?

Victorians, Medievalists, Modernists, lovers of Proust and Dostoyevsky, of Plato and Dante, ask me about these odd choices.

Because, you see, they say that precision of language, grace of thinking, and humanity of prose are circumscribed by the boundary waters of country and language and their attendant traditions.

Because translation, especially the translation of blood, eye, hair, and skin color, or suffering and revenge-lust, is an illusion: it is not to be achieved. Thus the chapter is closed between Heidegger and his Japanese philosopher colleague. Lord Krishna closes his violet eyes upon the West.

How many Arabian generations descend to myself and my sisters? There is Palestinian blood in my ancestry: their memory is one part of my inheritance, as are the swords of the Muslim nation.

So I study the words of Arabs, it's true, and celebrate their lives as cousins, brothers, aunts, and uncles. I'm concerned with their achievements and disappointments. But even here there is translation, or its illusion, shimmering sleight of hand, house of mirrors. The gesture is passed from surface to surface, from Jordan to America, into my eyes.

I'm here, in America. A creation of its creation. I look straight into its reflection, nothing else: birthplace, place of beginnings, schooling, of private child's warfare, of maturation. No sleight of hand; what emerges from my viscera comes from what I see.

I feel from the heart of the displaced and dispossessed. I mourn for a generation of loss, and in that state, the spirits of the displaced and dispossessed *around me* raise their voices and speak as clearly as parents. The spirit of the survivors of the Holocaust said, Never again. Never again the unspeakable, never again the bloodletting, the animal, the empty bodies, hearts of murderers. The spirit of Mormons, Puritans, of all the persecuted, said, Never again.

The necessity and the holiness of coexisting resides in utter, conscientious respect, in the endeavor, the physical striving for and after human respect. I know this as a woman, an Arab, an American, in all the ways I may be vulnerable, the methods by which someone may wish me evil, might hunt me in the ways I have seen those around me hunted down.

The question is: Can the leopard change its spots? The outer markings of the leopard betray its "nature," that of predator, merciless, ruthless, and, not least, animal. Its identity is immutable and cannot be altered by environment or the guileless curl upon its feline lips. We, the prey, the observers of the gullet, confer this identity, knowing so well how irresistible this fate to prey upon things is.

As prey and predator, the identities oscillate within each personal orbit and are, in turn, projected out, so often inverse to whatever we truly suppose ourselves to be. The animal class is a valuable one, as it appears to offer the possibility of certitude. If my neighbor, who looks and sounds and behaves differently from myself, is unpredictable and angry, I may call him an animal and treat him as such. I am forgiven my duties of difficult, that is to say, relentless interaction, forgiven the terrible experience of hearing what the leopard may have to say about his spots or, even, his sabre teeth, because I already know the leopard never has anything new to say about himself.

So annihilation occurs in the blackness of the spot, on the tip of the tooth, annihilation occurs as the leopard disappears into the dilated pupil of the prey. If a man appears in the jungle with his gun and proceeds to destroy the leopard, may we then expect the same behavior every time he meets a leopard, indeed, every time he meets an "animal" with his gun?

My white students tucked away in Iowa sometimes ask, Why should we care about riots in Florida, about voter registration in Chicago? Why should we read the works of foreign people?

I say, Because the foreign, the other, the different, is us.

Let us read the words of difference.

Analysis

1. What kinds of difference does Abu-Jaber catalogue in her essay? What kinds of similarities?
2. What is the function of the extended passage on the leopard and its spots?

Writing Possibilities

1. The "bad" version of difference—Abu-Jaber's critics might say—is "moral relativism" (or just plain relativism); i.e., if everything "other" is just "us," then how do you make distinctions (moral, political)? Explain what you think Abu-Jaber might say to this charge. What would you say?
2. In a very practical spirit, Abu-Jaber cites a frequently asked question: "Why should we care about riots in Florida, about voter registration in Chicago?" Discuss the likely response to similar specific "foreign" situations of both Abu-Jaber's and yourself.
3. Have you ever encountered, like Abu-Jaber, the question of why you are interested in something "foreign"? Explain what the circumstances were and why you were interested.
4. If you have different ethnic, racial, or national identities in your makeup, explain how you see these converging or diverging.

2

AMERICAN PLACES

The essays in this chapter focus on external place and geographical landscape as more-or-less objective ways to get at subjective feelings and states of mind—often an easier task than focusing directly on what is going on inside our minds. Also, such essays introduce us to varied American locales which we might otherwise not recognize. Mary Clearman Blew's "The Apostate in the Attic" (pages 69–75) reveals what it was like to grow up on a farm in the 1950s—an experience very few Americans now have. By contrast, Lalo Alcaraz' "L.A. Cucaracha" depicts the conflicting urban landscape of Los Angeles, in which the minority (Chicano) has given up on protest (except for the new "Pocho" challenge of the cartoonist's generation itself!) and while the majority (Anglo) culture continues to hold stereotypes of the minority, it appropriates that minority culture. Esmeralda Santiago's essay from *When I Was Puerto Rican* tell what it is like to cross borders, to come from rural Puerto Rico where everyone in town is black to polyglot Harlem where the Puerto Ricans differ in color. Leslie Marmon Silko's essay, one of two often anthologized (the other being the confrontative "The Border Patrol State"), shows us a Native-American landscape where centuries of habitation have invested the land with profound stories and meaning. Gloria Anzaldua's *"La conscienca de la mestiaza*/Towards a New Consciousness," from *Borderlands,* suggests how physical borders among groups and nations are tied up with monocultural mental borders—Anzaldua argues powerfully for the opposite, for mixture or a "mestiza" consciousness (where the feminine "a" ending indicates a challenge to male macho culture as well). Gerda Lerner's "No place to go back to", from *Why History Matters* and Monk Phen Anonthasy's "East/West Values" reveal the effect of a new world enjoyed and/or suffered by refugees who come to America in search of freedom and equality. And finally, Lucy Lippard's "Lure of the Local" shows how a sophisticated art critic explains her own Maine seacoast life (on the top of the book-page) in relation to theoretical ideas of a "multicentered" culture (on the bottom of the page).

Practically speaking, these essays suggest how writers use details of outward physical place to probe difficult inner feelings, ambivalent attitudes, and complicated statements of value. Finally, these essays raise, by implication, a question about the connection or disconnection between American culture and American landscape: Are there ways in which these writers from different physical places or regions in America *all* assume some common American identity? And if so (with the *if* a big one), where does that commonalty lie?

Mary Clearman Blew

A college teacher and writer, Mary Clearman Blew reveals in "The Apostate in the Attic" what it was like to grow up on a Montana dairy farm in the 1950s, disabusing us of the romanticized image of farming and the American frontier. Eventually Blew notes the sheer difficulty of a farming life—how the very obstinacy of the animals, the fierce winters, the competition from dairies as far away as Washington State— meant the end of her father's dream. The "Apostate" of her title stems from Blew's retreat into her own semiprivate world of books and reading, triggered by the discovery of old books from the earlier inhabitants of the farmhouse; it is these that saved her in more ways than one, she suggests. Rhetorically, Blew's essay shows how a writer balances both gritty realism and appropriate nostalgia in her appreciation of a particular place and time in her past.

THE APOSTATE IN THE ATTIC
from Bone Deep in Landscape

I was twelve when my father sold the ranch where he had been born and bought another, in the foothills of the Snowy Mountains, near Lewistown, Montana, so that my younger sisters and I could live at home when we were ready for high school. Other rural children might be boarded in town during their high school years, as he him-self had been, or they and their mothers might live in rented houses during the week and come home on weekends. But my father would make any other sacrifice, even the sale of the home ranch, before he would let us go.

It was not a move any of us wanted to make, and even the weather seemed enraged by it. Blizzards swept across Montana the December that we moved. The pastures and roads were buried in snow, and the temperature dropped below zero and stayed there. When I cried, my mother told me that, if I felt bad, to think of how my grandmother must feel, who had lived so much of her life near Spring Creek, in the lap of the South Moccasin Mountains, and now would be moving with us.

My father and mother visited the new ranch once, before we made the move, and I went along. From Lewistown we turned south toward the Snowies, and soon the old truck was howling and grind-ing through the drifts on an unploughed road that wound deeper and deeper into pine-covered hills. The frozen stream at the bottom of the ravine was Casino Creek, which flowed down from Sawmill Gulch. We would be living only seven miles from town, I had been told, but the road seemed endless to me as it twisted and wound under the heavily snow-laden pines. Every new turn was unfamiliar, but finally the road broke out of deep timber and stopped at a pole gate. In the deep cleft between two forested ridges squatted a huge unpainted barn, some log sheds, and a square stone house with an unpainted lean-to sagging off its back door. . . .

My father had started a dairy. He poured a concrete floor in the old barn and installed milking stanchions, built a springhouse, and bought big, lumbering cows with heavy udders, mottled black-and-white Holsteins for the most part, with a few rangy Brown Swiss and the occasional doe-eyed Guernsey. At least the days of hand milking were long past. Three Surge milking machines chugged away, powered by an electrical line he had run in from the utility pole, but each milking still took two hours. He was up at five in the morning, seven days a week, winter and summer, to feed the cows and finish milking by eight. At five in the afternoons he started all over again, feeding and milking. In between he drove his daughters to school and delivered milk to the creamery in ten-gallon cans, cleaned the barns, attended to the unending ranch chores. In the summer there was seeding and haying and harvesting.

To get everything done in twenty-four hours, we all helped. My father washed udders and milked, but my grandmother laid the grain in the stanchions and then worked in the springhouse, washing equipment and straining the milk through filters and pouring it into the cans, which she set to chill in a tank of springwater. And either my mother or I carried every bucket of milk the fifty yards down from the barn to the springhouse, back and forth.

Milk-carrying was a monotonous, heavy, endless task. Out of the cold and into the barn, where my glasses immediately fogged up from the body heat of thirty milk cows munching the feed in their stanchions and occasionally lifting their tails and dropping a steaming green pile into the gutter. The reek of manure blended with the smell of warm milk as my father, crouched under a flank, wiped off an udder with a rag wrung out in warm water and attached the suction cups to the teats with a little hiss that turned into the rhythmic chug, chug of the milking machine. By that time, one of the other machines would be ready to be emptied. Full of milk, it would weigh nearly forty pounds. My father would unclip it from the surcingle that held it suspended under the cow's belly, take off the top, and step across the gutter where I waited for my buckets to be filled with the white, fragrant foam. Then he was off to attach the machine to another cow, and I was off with my buckets for another trip down to the springhouse. I was sulky about it, of course. I would rather have been doing anything else.

Frustrations, fatigue. The unrelenting routine took its toll. In the winter, the stars would be out long before we finished milking. And some of the cows were touchy about being milked, especially the Brown Swiss. With their heads locked in the stanchions, they couldn't get away, but they would wrench and struggle and try to kick. My father sometimes snapped a pair of metal kickers on their hocks, but more often he would loop a piece of half-inch rope around a cow's foot and lash her to one of the metal support posts that ran down the middle of the barn. While the cow rolled back her eyes, trying to see what he was doing, he'd make the perfunctory swipe with the rag wrung out in warm water and snap the suction cups on her teats.

Why he hadn't tied up that Brown Swiss on one particular night, I don't know. He stepped up to her with his pail of warm water and the milking machine, and she picked up that big cloven hind hoof and drove it right into his eye.

I was waiting with my buckets in that split second of absolute suspended time. The cow, the kick, my father's head reeling back. Then time resumed its normal speed, and my father reached for the old oak wheel-spoke that he kept handy, and he laid the wheel-spoke across the cow's flanks and back and sides in hard repeated blows, one two three four five six seven eight nine, and I lost count as the cow reared against her stanchion with her bell jangling, cringing as more blows thundered down on her, crashing when she lost her footing on the manure-smeared cement. Fifteen sixteen seventeen eighteen blows, and every cow in the barn was rearing back, thirty cows fighting their stanchions while their cowbells clanged.

He stopped when his arm wore out. The cow found her footing and stood trembling in every muscle while welts rose in a grid across her creamy brown hide. The confusion of cowbells up and down the barn gradually died. He turned, and he saw me, and I saw that half his face was imprinted by mud and manure and blood in the shape of that cloven hoof, while under that foul layer the flesh swelled and purpled around the single bloodshot eye.

During the spring and summer, the milk cows were turned out to pasture on the pine slopes, and my task was to ride out on horseback, morning and afternoon, and bring them in for milking. It might take me twenty minutes or two hours, depending on how deep into the underbrush they'd gone for grass or hiding from flies. I liked wrangling better than carrying milk. Mornings could be pleasant, with the alarm going off in the not quite daylight, my sisters still asleep in the opposite bed, my bare feet on the cool linoleum as I reached for my blue jeans. Silence from the other bedroom. My getting up for the morning wrangling meant that my father could get an extra hour or two of sleep.

Often I didn't bother with shoes, but slipped downstairs in the quiet of the stone house, pushing my hair back from my face and buttoning my shirt. Stars would be fading over the points of the firs by the picket fence, and I would close the gate behind me and pad the hundred yards to the barn, wincing if it was too early in the spring for my bare feet to have grown calluses. The little buckskin chore horse would be waiting for me in the corral.

I would slide a bridle over her head, mount her bareback, and ride up the hill to the night pasture with my fingers wound in her mane. At this hour, even the wind was usually still, even the owls gone home, and I would be listening for the faintest tinkle of cowbells. At least the night pasture was smaller than the day pasture, less choked with underbrush for cows to hide in, and sometimes I would find them right away, their big warm bodies looming up like mottled black-and-white boulders out of the grass where they had made their beds. As the days grew longer and the light broke earlier and earlier, they might already be grazing with their bells clanking, and I would count them—was I lucky, were they all here? Twenty-five, twenty-six, twenty-seven. Grace wasn't here, Verna wasn't here, Baby wasn't here—and Grace and Verna and Baby were the ramblers, likely to have climbed the ridge beyond this one, looking for grass, or maybe they were grazing on the slope in the opposite direction, and I would have to ride another loop, hunting and listening for the sound of their bells.

"How can you tell which is which?" asked one of my cousins from town. "They all look alike."

"No they don't," I said, although one of the first lessons I had learned in town school was that not everybody saw the world with the eyes I had been trained to see with, and I felt as though I was constantly shifting focus, from close to distant. "They all look different."

"They're all black and white."

"But they all look different." . . .

My parents slept in the upstairs room with the square hole in the floor that let heat rise from the stove downstairs. My sisters and I slept in the other room, and my grandmother had a bed in the hall. With no plumbing, a nighttime urge meant either a cold walk under the stars to the outhouse or else the sneak through the hall to the chamber pot behind the curtain in the room which might have been meant for a bathroom but which my mother had filled with boxes of odds and ends that took on ominous shapes in the dark. No sound was a secret, not the snores and twitches, not the creaks and heavy breathing from the bedroom next door, not the stealthy pad of footsteps in the hall or the fizz of a hot stream being released into the pot. Trying not to listen made every fart and groan more intense.

I had begun to mature after the move to the stone house, and my mother had provided me with an elastic belt and safety pins and bulky pads, which I tried to change without being watched by curious little sisters. I cringed at the way my shirts rubbed against my sore nipples, hated the way my breasts bounced and ached when I rode horseback. A woman's body was nothing I had ever wanted, and nothing my mother had ever wanted for me, either, I could tell by her new watchfulness, her face halfway between anger and derision.

"What do you want to take a bath so often for?" everybody asked me. "What have you been working so hard at, that you think you're dirty?"

The physical education teacher at school had lectured all the girls on personal hygiene. The daily bath, the shaved legs and armpits, the antiperspirant. Envying the girls from town for the way they seemed to flaunt their hips and breasts and yet disengage themselves from bodily nastiness, I dragged out the galvanized tub every night, set it up in the kitchen, and filled it with hot water from a bucket, sat in soap scum with my knees under my chin, and worried about my flaws. Picked at the beaded rows of scabs along the fresh thorn scratches, licked the white lines of old scars and wondered if they would ever fade. Were my feet too big? I stuck a leg out of the tub, tried the rotating exercise that some book in the home economics room at school said would make my ankles more slender.

Everyone would have gone to bed except my father, who sat reading at the kitchen table and trying not to look at me. When had my father ever been embarrassed by my naked body? What had happened, since the move to the stone house, to change us all? I wished I knew a way, like putting my glasses back on, that would bring us all back into a familiar focus.

In my search for privacy, I tried the attic. It must have been deep summer, because I remember the stale heat in my face when I lifted the trapdoor, not for the first time, of course, but the other times I had been chased off by the bats. But now the bats were gone, killed off, perhaps, by the D-Con my mother had put down to poison the mice. I hoisted myself through the square hole in the ceiling and found myself in a closed space of rafters and shadows, illuminated by a single dirty window.

I couldn't take a step without crunching on the mouse droppings—or bat droppings—that littered the floorboards. And what was there to see? Through the little dormer window, an expanse of shingled roof and the tops of the firs, oddly foreshortened when seen from above. Behind me on a nail hung the fiddle that had been my grandfather's, its bow and strings lost long ago, its soundboard chewed by mice.

If my grandfather's fiddle had been stored there, the attic must also have held other family odds and ends, stowed away after the move from the home place. And yet I remember seeing none of these things. No boxes of canning jars, no boxes of old clothing or odd dishes—what else would there have been? Sometimes it seems to me that there was a trunk—but maybe that is because, along with an old fiddle, every attic is expected to hold a trunk, and memory is only too likely to retain its expectations.

What one corner of the attic held—and this I am certain of, because I possess them today—were three very old books, nibbled at their corners and swollen as if from moisture that had long dried. Curious, with no premonition, I lifted them out of the dust and flyspecks and examined them. After all, I was always looking for something to read. The first book was red, or had once been red. Stamped in gold on its cover was *Junior Latin Reader: Sanford and Scott.* Also in gold on the cover was an emblem like a torch, stamped mysteriously with the initials SPQR. On its endpapers was a map, labeled Imperium Romanum, and a penciled price, 1$\frac{50}{}$. I turned another page and found, also written in pencil, notes on the use of the dative case with verbs meaning to favor, help, please, trust, believe, persuade, command, obey, serve, resist, envy, threaten, pardon & spare.

Latin was still taught at that time in my high school, but usually not to girls from the country, who were thought to have more practical aims than a filigreed, college-bound diploma. As I held that book in my hands, I felt as though I were opening another window, too dirty to see through clearly, but offering a limitless expanse.

The second book was brown, stamped in black with *Arnold's Latin Prose Composition* and a border of acanthus leaves. Its price had been 1$\frac{80}{}$, and it held another clue—"Fran" Ruckman, written in spidery ink. So! A daughter of this very house. (Or could "Fran" have been a son? A daughter, I decided, emphatically.)

The third book was in the worst condition, its maroon cover mottled pink with waterspots. From the label inside, it had once been the property of the University of Montana library. Its pages were stained and speckled, but it was the first of these books that I could read. Its title was *Julian: Philosopher and Emperor and the Last Struggle of Paganism against Christianity,* by Alice Gardner, Lecturer and Associate of Newnham College, Cambridge, Author of "Synesius of Cyrene," published in 1906.

Below me in the hall, my sisters had set up a dollhouse and were having a fight between the dolls. Their quarreling voices rose to the attic, but I deliberately shut my ears. Squatting in the dust, in the fecal heat under the eaves, by gold light sifted through an encrusted window, I began to read about an apostate emperor who had been raised a Christian but, loving classical letters and learning, had ascended to the throne of the Holy Roman Empire in A.D. 355, turned his back on the cross, and set the pagan gods back in their pantheon. It was the first time I had ever come across the word *apostate.*

"Fran Ruckman," said my Latin teacher, thoughtfully, at the University of Montana a few years later. "She must have been a student of mine."

I have never heard Fran Ruckman's name spoken since then, although I still possess her books. Whether, from the ragbag of her adolescence, out of shadowy scraps of motives and urges, conscious choices and half-conscious responses, Fran Ruckman pieced together the reasons why she attended the University of Montana in the early years of the twentieth century, whether she supposed that she was running away from hard work and responsibilities, or whether she thought she was running after her mind and taking her body with her, I have no way of knowing. Did Fran Ruckman wear glasses? When she bought a book written in 1906 by a woman scholar, did she think of herself as an apostate? Did her dreams drift as far and remote as the spires of Newnham College, Cambridge?

Did Fran Ruckman ever learn anything about double vision, about the shapes of individual blades of grass an inch from her nose, and how she lost sight of those shapes when she put her glasses back on to look at the horizon? Did she imagine that she had to choose between a close focus and the longer view?

Did she intend never to come home again, and if so, how did her old Latin textbooks happen to be stored for years in the attic of the old Ruckman house? After wandering the far corridors of sleepless nights, did she find herself again and again in that attic, under that encrusted window in the odor of bats and mice? Sifting dust, endlessly, compulsively, trying to understand.

ANALYSIS

1. What details of physical setting does Blew provide that bring alive for non-Montanans what rural life was like for her and her family?
2. Why does Blew give us the account of her father's horrific beating of the recalcitrant cow? How does Blew peer into her father's consciousness with her own personal speculations as to his motivations?
3. What leads Blew to suggest that "not everybody saw the world with the eyes I had been trained to see"?
4. What role is played by the books and magazines Blew finds in the farmhouse attic?

—————————— **WRITING POSSIBILITIES** ——————————

1. Farm life is not generally a subject for diversity or multiculturalism; after all, only a very small percentage of Americans nowadays live on farms (especially family farms) and work them. Indeed, as TV specials sometimes show, such family farms are exceedingly difficult to run profitably. What then might be the usefulness of reading Blew's account of growing up on a dairy farm? Are there, for example, values that are needlessly being lost? (Thomas Jefferson believed that American democracy itself would be secure only in the hands of small farmers.) Or, per contra, is this the end of a way of life that no longer makes sense? Explain how Blew views the matter?

2. If you come from a farm background, what for you is important (rightly or wrongly) about Blew's account? Does she get things about right? Or does she miss by a country mile? Has your own experience given you variations on Blew's concerns that need to be explained and developed for nonfarm audiences?

3. Farm life, even if it segues into town life, is often that of a world of homogeneity, where everyone around you is like you and your family. Coming to a big city or to a big state university one may experience the shock of recognition: Who are all these different kinds of people? And who am I? Is this your experience?

4. Have you ever been rescued, like Blew, by chance finds of books and magazines? Explain.

Lalo Alcaraz

Lalo Alcaraz's cartoons have appeared in L.A. Weekly *and other magazines in the United States and abroad. Alcaraz drew editorial cartoons for his college newspaper the* Daily Aztec *at San Diego State University in 1984, earned an M.A. in architecture from University of California at Berkeley and has been a staff writer for the Fox TV show* Culture Club.

L.A. CUCARACHA URBAN SKETCH JOURNAL
from Urban Latino Cultures, La Vida Latina en L.A.

The landscape of Los Angeles has long served as a generous muse in my editorial cartoon work. She may not always be pretty, but she's always willing to inspire a 'toon, or stand back and let me scribble on her as a backdrop to the ironies and foibles of the Latino culture and political landscape. My strip began to run in the *L.A. Weekly* in June of 1992, just weeks after the infamous Los Angeles riotous uprising of April. The first panel was #1, "White Men Can't Run the System," a parody of the film *White Men Can't Jump* and a commentary on the lack of control and leadership from the local and national power structure.

#2, "(Help the Authorities) Find Cuco Now," casts the main character in my strip, Cuco Rocha, a disaffected Chicano cockroach, as the object of a "Where's Waldo?" parody. The setting is recast as somewhere in bustling Boyle Heights and restates the Rodney King beating with a mostly Chicano cast.

#3, "Malti-Cultural," comments on some of the reasons L.A.'s inner city may have been so quick to go up in flames—cheap liquor targeted at minority imbibers.

©2001 Lalo Alcaraz www.cartoonista.com

#15, "Café Attitudo." Living on the east side of L.A.'s vast metropolitan sprawl, I don't usually venture all that far into West L.A., but when I do, I often have odd encounters with the strange foreign culture of the more affluent and chronically snide Westside. This fellow actually "happened" to me and a few Chicano friends at one of your snootier establishments.

#16, "Wacky Wilson's Welfare Warehouse." California Governor Pete Wilson, in addition to scapegoating immigrant Latinos and adding to their stress and paranoia, also turned his aim at the poor in general. Los Angeles County bore the brunt of Wilson's political scheme to further disempower minority poor.

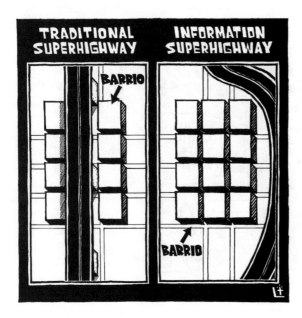

#17, "Infosuper-highway." Free-ways in Los Angeles tend to run right through the middle of many Chicano/Latino neighbor-hoods, but the new information superhighway seems to be tak-ing pains to avoid disturbing any lower-income barrios.

ANALYSIS

1. Alcaraz says his work satirizes "the ironies and foibles of the Latino cultural and political landscape"; Alcaraz's explanatory comments on each of the panels helps us understand what in particular he is mocking. What is the connection between the style of the cartoons and Alcaraz's satire? How, in other words, does he embody in cartoon languages the attack on "ironies and foibles"?

2. If you're familiar with either the Los Angeles scene that Alcaraz satirizes or comparable scenes elsewhere in the country, do you agree with his satire—e.g., the LAPD's notorious beating of Rodney King, the "vote-grabbing politicians" guilty of the "demonization of Latino children"?

WRITING POSSIBILITIES

1. Explain the power of Alcaraz's caricatures and parodies. How does he parody mainstream forms (e.g., "Where's Waldo?") to make his satiric point? How would you describe the visual effects that Alcaraz achieves through drawing and imagery?

2. In an essay "Generation Mex," in *Next,* edited by Eric Liu, Lalo Lopez Alcaraz (Alcaraz's full name) highlights the conflict *L.A. Cucaracha* aroused in an older generation of Mexican Americans: "While the older *Raza* called themselves Mexican American, the sixties and seventies rads were *Chicanos,* a term that made the older generations recoil in

disgust. . . . We in turn declare its successor, the once-loathed term of *Pocho,* to be the righteous cultural and political force that will shape the "New World Borders." Pochismo is Chicanoism with a sick sense of humor." What generational conflicts do you find within your own group? Is there, as with Lopez and Alcaraz, a difference of opinion about protest and dissent, or does it work along similar lines? Explain.

3. Of his own comic-strip for *L.A. Cucaracha,* Alcaraz explains why he satirized the Mexican land-liberator Emiliano Zapata as a complacent figure in an easy chair "holding his sombrero in one hand and the remote control in another . . . staring zombielike at a TV just the way most of the people in our community do every night after their hard day at work, or after their 'stimulating' day at college. My point was to show that activism needs to get up off the couch and turn that tube off." Do Alcaraz's comments here shed light on the satire in *L.A. Cucaracha?*

Esmeralda Santiago

Santiago was born in Puerto Rico and came to the mainland as a thirteen-year-old. She won a place in the School for the Performing Arts in New York City and went on to become a film producer. When I Was Puerto Rican *(1993), is the first volume of her autobiography, and* Almost a Woman *(1999), the second, explain how vibrant the world of Puerto Rico that she came from was; although her family was poor and the environment marred by conflicts between her father and mother, she also received devoted attention and encouragement from both parents and felt the warm and enchanting presence of the Puerto Rican landscape and culture surrounding her. In this chapter from* When I Was Puerto Rican, *Santiago describes her first encounters with New York City. The description is noteworthy for its cool tone and the way Santiago records truthfully and realistically the tensions and conflicts that she sees around her between Puerto Ricans and Jews and between Puerto Ricans and blacks.*

ANGELS ON THE CEILING
from When I Was Puerto Rican

There were angels on the ceiling. Four fat naked cherubs danced in a circle, their hands holding ivy garlands, their round buttocks half covered by a cloth swirling around their legs. Next to me, Mami snored softly. At the foot of the bed, Edna and Raymond slept curled away from each other, their backs against my legs. The bedroom had very high ceilings with braided molding all the way around, ending in a circle surrounded by more braid above the huge window across from the bed. The shade was down, but bright sunlight streaked in at the edges. The cherubs looked down on us, smiling mysteriously, and I wondered how many people they had seen come in and out of this room. Slowly I crawled over Mami, out of bed.

"Where are you going?" she mumbled, half asleep.

"To the bathroom," I whispered.

The bed was pressed into the corner against the wall across from the window, next to a wide doorway that led into the next room. A long dresser stretched from the doorway to the window wall, leaving an aisle just wide enough to open the drawers halfway out.

It was six in the morning of my first day in Brooklyn. Our apartment, on the second floor, was the fanciest place I'd ever lived in. The stairs coming up from Tata's room on the first floor were marble, with a landing in between, and a colored glass window with bunches of grapes and twirling vines. The door to our apartment was carved with more bunches of grapes and leaves. From the two windows in the main room we could look out on the courtyard we had come through the night before. A tree with broad brown leaves grew from the middle of what looked like a well, circled with the same stones that lined the ground. Scraggly grass poked out between the cracks and in the brown dirt around the tree. The building across from ours was three stories high, crisscrossed by iron stairs with narrow landings on which people grew tomatoes and geraniums in clay pots. Our building was only two stories high, although it was almost as tall as the one across the courtyard. We, too, had an iron balcony with a straight ladder suspended halfway to the ground. It made me a little dizzy to look down.

The main room of our apartment was large and sunny and decorated with more braided molding. The whole apartment was painted pale yellow, except for the ceilings, which were smoky gray. The floor was covered with a flat rug whose fringes had worn away into frayed edges where they met the wood floor. A fireplace had been blocked up with a metal sheet. More cherubs, grapes, and vines decorated the mantel. One of the cherubs was missing a nose; another had lost both hands and a foot. Next to the fireplace there was a small stove with four burners close together, a narrow counter with shelves underneath, and a deep sink. A door next to the sink led to the toilet, which was flushed by pulling a chain attached to a wooden box on the wall above the seat. On the other side of the toilet room door, on the wall opposite the windows, there was a huge, claw-foot bathtub covered by a metal sheet. In the middle of the room was a formica table and four chairs with plastic seats and backs that matched the tabletop. A lopsided couch and lumpy chair covered in a scratchy blue fabric faced the tub as if bathing were a special event to which spectators were invited.

The windows and door were locked, and Mami had warned the night before that I was not to leave the apartment without telling her. There was no place to go anyway. I had no idea where I was, only that it was very far away from where I'd been. Brooklyn, Mami had said, was not New York. I wished I had a map so that I could place myself in relation to Puerto Rico. But everything we owned was packed and stacked against the yellow walls. Not that there was a map in there, either.

There was nothing to do, nowhere to go, no one to talk to. The apartment was stifling. Inside the closed rooms, the air was still. Not even dust motes in the sunlight. Outside the windows, a steady roar was interrupted by sharp sirens or the insistent crash and clang of garbage cans, the whining motors of cars, and the faint sound of babies crying.

La marketa took up a whole block. It was much bigger and more confusing than the plaza in Bayamón, although it carried pretty much the same types of things. It was a red brick building with skylights in the high ceiling, so that whatever sun made it in lit up the dusty beams and long fluorescent light fixtures suspended from them. The floor was a gritty cement and gravel mix, sticky in places, spotted with what looked like oil slicks. Stalls were arranged along aisles, the merchandise on deep shelves that slanted down.

On the way to *la marketa* we had passed two men dressed in long black coats, their faces bearded. Ringlets hung from under their hats alongside their faces.

"Don't stare," Mami pulled on my hand.

"Why are they dressed so strange?"

"They're Jewish. They don't eat pork."

"Why not?"

"I don't know. They all live in the same neighborhood and only buy food from each other."

In *la marketa* almost all the vendors were Jewish, only they didn't wear their coats and hats. They wore white shirts and little round doilies on their heads. Many of them spoke Spanish, which made it easy for Mami to negotiate the price of everything.

"You never pay the first price they tell you," she instructed. "They like to bargain."

We went from stall to stall, arguing about every item we picked out. The vendors always made it seem as if we were cheating them, even though Mami said everything was overpriced.

"Don't ever pay full price for anything," Mami told me. "It's always cheaper somewhere else."

It was a game: the vendors wanting more money than Mami was willing to spend, but both of them knowing that eventually, she would part with her dollars and they would get them. It made no sense to me. It took most of the day to buy the stuff we needed for our apartment. Had she spent less time shopping around, she might have bought more. As it was, she only had half the things we needed, and we were exhausted and irritable by the time we got home. I had spent my entire first day in New York hunting for bargains.

The second day was no different. "We have to buy your school clothes, and a coat," Mami said.

Winter would be coming soon, Tata said, and with it, chilly winds, snowstorms, and short days.

"The first winter is always the worst," Don Julio explained, "because your blood is still thin from living in Puerto Rico." I imagined my blood thickening into syrup but didn't know how that could make me warmer.

"I can't wait to see snow," Edna chirped.

"Me neither," said Raymond.

Two days in Brooklyn, and they already loved everything about it. Tata cared for them while Mami and I shopped. She sat them down in front of a black-and-white television set, gave each a chocolate bar, and they spent the entire day watching cartoons, while Tata smoked and drank beer.

"What good kids they are," she complimented Mami when we came back. "Not a peep out of them all day."

Graham Avenue in Williamsburg was the broadest street I'd ever seen. It was flanked by three- and four-story apartment buildings, the first floors of which contained stores where you could buy anything. Most of these stores were also run by Jewish people, but they didn't speak Spanish like the ones in *la marketa*. They were less friendly, too, unwilling to negotiate prices. On Graham Avenue there were special restaurants where Mami said Jewish people ate. They were called delis, and there were foreign symbols in the windows, and underneath them the word *kosher*. I knew Mami wouldn't know what it meant, so I didn't bother asking. I imagined it was a delicacy that only Jewish people ate, which is why their restaurants so prominently let them know you could get it there. We didn't go into the delis because, Mami said, they didn't like Puerto Ricans in there. Instead, she took me to eat pizza.

"It's Italian," she said.

"Do Italians like Puerto Ricans?" I asked as I bit into hot cheese and tomato sauce that burned the tip of my tongue.

"They're more like us than Jewish people are," she said, which wasn't an answer.

In Puerto Rico the only foreigners I'd been aware of were *Americanos*. In two days in Brooklyn I had already encountered Jewish people, and now Italians. There was another group of people Mami had pointed out to me. *Morenos.* But they weren't foreigners, because they were American. They were black, but they didn't look like Puerto Rican *negros.* They dressed like *Americanos* but walked with a jaunty hop that made them look as if they were dancing down the street, only their hips were not as loose as Puerto Rican men's were. According to Mami, they too lived in their own neighborhoods, frequented their own restaurants, and didn't like Puerto Ricans.

"How come?" I wondered, since in Puerto Rico, all of the people I'd ever met were either black or had a black relative somewhere in their family. I would have thought *morenos* would like us, since so many of us looked like them.

"They think we're taking their jobs."

"Are we?"

"There's enough work in the United States for everybody," Mami said, "but some people think some work is beneath them. Me, if I have to crawl on all fours to earn a living, I'll do it. I'm not proud that way."

I couldn't imagine what kind of work required crawling on all fours, although I remembered Mami scrubbing the floor that way, so that it seemed she was talking about housework. Although, according to her, she wouldn't be too proud to clean other people's houses, I hoped she wouldn't have to do it. It would be too embarrassing to come all the way from Puerto Rico so she could be somebody's maid.

The first day of school Mami walked me to a stone building that loomed over Graham Avenue, its concrete yard enclosed by an iron fence with spikes at the top. The front steps were wide but shallow and led up to a set of heavy double doors that slammed shut behind us as we walked down the shiny corridor. I clutched my eighth-grade report card filled with A's and B's, and Mami had my birth certificate. At the front office we were met by Mr. Grant, a droopy gentleman with thick glasses and a kind smile who spoke no Spanish. He gave Mami a form to fill out. I knew most of the words in the squares we were to fill in: NAME, ADDRESS (CITY, STATE), and OCCUPATION. We gave it to Mr. Grant, who reviewed it, looked at my birth certificate, studied my report card, then wrote on the top of the form "7–18."

Don Julio had told me that if students didn't speak English, the schools in Brooklyn would keep them back one grade until they learned it.

"Seven gray?" I asked Mr. Grant, pointing at his big numbers, and he nodded.

"I no guan seven gray. I eight gray. I teeneyer."

"You don't speak English," he said. "You have to go to seventh grade while you're learning."

"I have A's in school Puerto Rico. I lern good. I no seven gray girl."

Mami stared at me, not understanding but knowing I was being rude to an adult.

"What's going on?" she asked me in Spanish. I told her they wanted to send me back one grade and I would not have it. This was probably the first rebellious act she had seen from me outside my usual mouthiness within the family.

"Negi, leave it alone. Those are the rules," she said, a warning in her voice.

"I don't care what their rules say," I answered. "I'm not going back to seventh grade. I can do the work. I'm not stupid."

Mami looked at Mr. Grant, who stared at her as if expecting her to do something about me. She smiled and shrugged her shoulders.

"Meester Grant," I said, seizing the moment, "I go eight gray six mons. Eef I no lern inglish, I go seven gray. Okay?"

"That's not the way we do things here," he said, hesitating.

"I good studen. I lern queek. You see notes." I pointed to the A's in my report card. "I pass seven gray."

So we made a deal.

"You have until Christmas," he said. "I'll be checking on your progress." He scratched out "7–18" and wrote in "8–23." He wrote something on a piece of paper, sealed it inside an envelope, and gave it to me. "Your teacher is Miss Brown. Take this note upstairs to her. Your mother can go," he said and disappeared into his office.

"Wow!" Mami said, "you can speak English!"

I was so proud of myself, I almost burst. In Puerto Rico if I'd been that pushy, I would have been called *mal educada* by the Mr. Grant equivalent and sent home with a note to my mother. But here it was my teacher who was getting the note, I got what I wanted, and my mother was sent home.

"I can find my way after school," I said to Mami. "You don't have to come get me."

"Are you sure?"

"Don't worry," I said. "I'll be all right."

I walked down the black-tiled hallway, past many doors that were half glass, each one labelled with a room number in neat black lettering. Other students stared at me, tried to get my attention, or pointedly ignored me. I kept walking as if I knew where I was going, heading for the sign that said STAIRS with an arrow pointing up. When I reached the end of the hall and looked back, Mami was still standing at the front door watching me, a worried expression on her face. I waved, and she waved back. I started up the stairs, my stomach churning into tight knots. All of a sudden, I was afraid that I was about to make a fool of myself and end up in seventh grade in the middle of the school year. Having to fall back would be worse than just accepting my fate now and hopping forward if I proved to be as good a student as I had convinced Mr. Grant I was. "What have I done?" I kicked myself with the back of my right shoe, much to the surprise of the fellow walking behind me, who laughed uproariously, as if I had meant it as a joke.

Miss Brown's was the learning disabled class, where the administration sent kids with all sorts of problems, none of which, from what I could see, had anything to do with their ability to learn but more with their willingness to do so. They were an unruly group. Those who came to class, anyway. Half of them never showed up, or, when they did, they slept through the lesson or nodded off in the middle of Miss Brown's carefully parsed sentences.

We were outcasts in a school where the smartest eighth graders were in the 8–1 homeroom, each subsequent drop in number indicating one notch less smarts. If your class was in the low double digits, (8–10 for instance), you were smart, but not a pinhead. Once you got into the teens, your intelligence was in question, especially as the numbers rose to the high teens. And there were the twenties. I was in 8–23, where the dumbest, most undesirable people were placed. My class was, in some ways, the equivalent of seventh grade, perhaps even sixth or fifth.

Miss Brown, the homeroom teacher, who also taught English composition, was a young black woman who wore sweat pads under her arms. The strings holding them in place sometimes slipped outside the short sleeves of her well-pressed white shirts, and she had to turn her back to us in order to adjust them. She was very pretty, with almond eyes and a hairdo that was flat and straight at the top of her head then dipped into tight curls at the ends. Her fingers were well manicured, the nails painted pale pink with white tips. She taught English composition as if everyone cared about it, which I found appealing.

After the first week she moved me from the back of the room to the front seat by her desk, and after that, it felt as if she were teaching me alone. We never spoke, except when I went up to the blackboard.

"Esmeralda," she called in a musical voice, "would you please come up and mark the prepositional phrase?"

In her class, I learned to recognize the structure of the English language, and to draft the parts of a sentence by the position of words relative to pronouns and prepositions without knowing exactly what the whole thing meant.

The school was huge and noisy. There was a social order that, at first, I didn't understand but kept bumping into. Girls and boys who wore matching cardigans walked down the halls hand in hand, sometimes stopping behind lockers to kiss and fondle each other. They were *Americanos* and belonged in the homerooms in the low numbers.

Another group of girls wore heavy makeup, hitched their skirts above their knees, opened one extra button on their blouses, and teased their hair into enormous bouffants held solid with spray. In the morning, they took over the girls' bathroom, where they dragged on cigarettes as they did their hair until the air was unbreathable, thick with smoke and hair spray. The one time I entered the bathroom before classes they chased me out with insults and rough shoves.

Those bold girls with hair and makeup and short skirts, I soon found out, were Italian. The Italians all sat together on one side of the cafeteria, the blacks on another. The two groups hated each other more than they hated Puerto Ricans. At least once a week there was a fight between an Italian and a *moreno*, either in the bathroom, in the school yard, or in an abandoned lot near the school, a no-man's-land that divided their neighborhoods and kept them apart on weekends.

The black girls had their own style. Not for them the big, pouffy hair of the Italians. Their hair was straightened, curled at the tips like Miss Brown's, or pulled up into a twist at the back with wispy curls and straw straight bangs over Cleopatra eyes. Their skirts were also short, except it didn't look like they hitched them up when their mothers weren't looking. They came that way. They had strong, shapely legs and wore knee socks with heavy lace-up shoes that became lethal weapons in fights.

It was rumored that the Italians carried knives, even the girls, and that the *morenos* had brass knuckles in their pockets and steel toes in their heavy shoes. I stayed away from both groups, afraid that if I befriended an Italian, I'd get beat up by a *morena*, or vice versa.

There were two kinds of Puerto Ricans in school: the newly arrived, like myself, and the ones born in Brooklyn of Puerto Rican parents. The two types didn't mix. The Brooklyn Puerto Ricans spoke English, and often no Spanish at all. To them, Puerto Rico was the place where their grandparents lived, a place they visited on school and summer vacations, a place which they complained was backward and mosquito-ridden. Those of us for whom Puerto Rico was still a recent memory were also split into two groups: the ones who longed for the island and the ones who wanted to forget it as soon as possible.

I felt disloyal for wanting to learn English, for liking pizza, for studying the girls with big hair and trying out their styles at home, locked in the bathroom where no one could watch. I practiced walking with the peculiar little hop of the *morenas*, but felt as if I were limping.

I didn't feel comfortable with the newly arrived Puerto Ricans who stuck together in suspicious little groups, criticizing everyone, afraid of everything. And I was not accepted by the Brooklyn Puerto Ricans, who held the secret of coolness. They walked the halls between the Italians and the *morenos*, neither one nor the other, but looking and acting like a combination of both, depending on the texture of their hair, the shade of their skin, their makeup, and the way they walked down the hall.

ANALYSIS

1. What are the threatening and unpleasant elements in the New York City world that Santiago encounters? What are the comforting ones?
2. What are the lines of ethnic and racial conflict that Santiago reveals here? What is her attitude towards these conflicts?
3. What does Santiago's "jaunty hop" suggest about her attitude towards blacks in New York (*morenos*)?
4. Santiago takes on the role of the naive (adolescent) narrator: as a stranger, she describes things in New York ways that a native would not. But her descriptions, precisely because they are unadorned with customary perception, may help us focus more on reality. Find examples of this naive perception and its possible effects. (E.g., " It would be too embarrassing to come all the way from Puerto Rico so she [Mami] could be somebody's maid.")

WRITING POSSIBILITIES

1. Have you ever been in Santiago's situation, transported from your original home or homeland to a new and strange place? What was uncomfortable for you in this situation? How did you cope with it?
2. Santiago spends a good deal of time on her educational progress, beginning with her rebelliousness at being placed in a grade-level beneath what she considered to be her proper one. What is the value of her rebelliousness? Have you faced such a situation in a new environment? How did things work out for you?
3. Santiago comments on the "social order" of the school, which at first she didn't understand—the Italian and black girls' differing styles of dress, the two kinds of Puerto Ricans ("[T]he two types didn't mix"), the feelings of disloyalty on her part in wanting to learn English, the discomfort with "the newly arrived Puerto Ricans who stuck together. . . . ", etc. What do you gather about what Santiago eventually learned about the "social order" of the school? Point to the specific terms that reveal what she learned.

Gloria Anzaldua

Gloriz Anzaldua reminds us that a borderland "consciousness" involves a mental as well as physical habitation between cultures (Mexican, Anglo, male and female among others) rather than solely on one habitat or another.

Anzaldua was born in Southwest Texas in 1942 into a Mexican American farm-owning family. She adopts a term which in earlier contexts was denigratory but is now worn proudly—mestiza, mixed—and makes a case for change based on the personal discovery that she does in fact belong to more than one group, shares in multiple rather than single identities, and lives on a borderland between cultures rather than in any one culture. The change required, she argues, is the "new consciousness" of accepting this borderland situation and relishing its multiple values and languages. More, she might say, is better.

LA CONCIENCIA DE LA MESTIZA
TOWARDS A NEW CONSCIOUSNESS
from Borderlands

> Por la mujer de mi raza
> hablará el espíritu.

Jose Vascocelos, Mexican philosopher, envisaged *una raza mestiza, una mezcla de razas afines, una raza de color—la primera raza síntesis del globo*. He called it a cosmic race, *la raza cósmica,* a fifth race embracing the four major races of the world. Opposite to the theory of the pure Aryan, and to the policy of racial purity that white America practices, his theory is one of inclusivity. As the confluence of two or more genetic streams, with chromosomes constantly "crossing over," this mixture of races, rather than resulting in an inferior being, provides hybrid progeny, a mutable, more malleable species with a rich gene pool. From this racial, ideological, cultural and biological cross-pollinization, an "alien" consciousness is presently in the making—a new *mestiza* consciousness, *una conciencia de mujer*. It is a consciousness of the Borderlands.

Una lucha de fronteras / A Struggle of Borders

> Because I, a *mestiza,*
> continually walk out of one culture
> and into another,
> because I am in all cultures at the same time,

alma entre dos mundos, tres, cuatro,
me zumba la cabeza con lo contradictorio.
Estoy norteada por todas las voces que me hablan
simultáneamente.

The ambivalence from the clash of voices results in mental and emotional states of perplexity. Internal strife results in insecurity and indecisiveness. The *mestiza*'s dual or multiple personality is plagued by psychic restlessness.

In a constant state of mental nepantilism, an Aztec word meaning torn between ways, *la mestiza* is a product of the transfer of the cultural and spiritual values of one group to another. Being tricultural, monolingual, bilingual, or multilingual, speaking a patois, and in a state of perpetual transition, the *mestiza* faces the dilemma of the mixed breed: which collectivity does the daughter of a darkskinned mother listen to?

El choque de un alma atrapado entre el mundo del espíritu y el mundo de la técnica a veces la deja entullada. Cradled in one culture, sandwiched between two cultures, straddling all three cultures and their value systems, *la mestiza* undergoes a struggle of flesh, a struggle of borders, an inner war. Like all people, we perceive the version of reality that our culture communicates. Like others having or living in more than one culture, we get multiple, often opposing messages. The coming together of two self-consistent but habitually incompatible frames of reference causes *un choque,* a cultural collision.

Within us and within *la cultura chicana,* commonly held beliefs of the white culture attack commonly held beliefs of the Mexican culture, and both attack commonly held beliefs of the indigenous culture. Subconsciously, we see an attack on ourselves and our beliefs as a threat and we attempt to block with a counterstance.

But it is not enough to stand on the opposite river bank, shouting questions, challenging patriarchal, white conventions. A counterstance locks one into a duel of oppressor and oppressed; locked in mortal combat, like the cop and the criminal, both are reduced to a common denominator of violence. The counterstance refutes the dominant culture's views and beliefs, and, for this, it is proudly defiant. All reaction is limited by, and dependent on, what it is reacting against. Because the counterstance stems from a problem with authority—outer as well as inner—it's a step towards liberation from cultural domination. But it is not a way of life. At some point, on our way to a new consciousness, we will have to leave the opposite bank, the split between the two mortal combatants somehow healed so that we are on both shores at once and, at once, see through serpent and eagle eyes. Or perhaps we will decide to disengage from the dominant culture, write if off altogether as a lost cause, and cross the border into a wholly new and separate territory. Or we might go another route. The possibilities are numerous once we decide to act and not react.

A TOLERANCE FOR AMBIGUITY

These numerous possibilities leave *la mestiza* floundering in uncharted seas. In perceiving conflicting information and points of view, she is subjected to a swamping of her psychological borders. She has discovered that she can't hold concepts or ideas in rigid boundaries. The borders and walls that are supposed to keep the undesirable ideas out are entrenched habits and patterns of behavior; these habits and patterns are the enemy within. Rigidity means death. Only by remaining flexible is she able to stretch the psyche horizontally and vertically. *La mestiza* constantly has to shift out of habitual formations; from convergent thinking, analytical reasoning that tends to use rationality to move toward a single goal (a Western mode), to divergent thinking, characterized by movement away from set patterns and goals and toward a more whole perspective, one that includes rather than excludes.

The new *mestiza* copes by developing a tolerance for contradictions, a tolerance for ambiguity. She learns to be an Indian in Mexican culture, to be Mexican from an Anglo point of view. She learns to juggle cultures. She has a plural personality, she operates in a pluralistic mode—nothing is thrust out, the good the bad and the ugly, nothing rejected, nothing abandoned. Not only does she sustain contradictions, she turns the ambivalence into something else.

She can be jarred out of ambivalence by an intense, and often painful, emotional event which inverts or resolves the ambivalence. I'm not sure exactly how. The work takes place underground—subconsciously. It is work that the soul performs. That focal point or fulcrum, that juncture where the *mestiza* stands, is where phenomena tend to collide. It is where the possibility of uniting all that is separate occurs. This assembly is not one where severed or separated pieces merely come together. Nor is it a balancing of opposing powers. In attempting to work out a synthesis, the self has added a third element which is greater than the sum of its severed parts. That third element is a new consciousness—a *mestiza* consciousness—and though it is a source of intense pain, its energy comes from continual creative motion that keeps breaking down the unitary aspect of each new paradigm.

En unas pocas centurias, the future will belong to the *mestiza.* Because the future depends on the breaking down of paradigms, it depends on the straddling of two or more cultures. By creating a new mythos—that is, a change in the way we perceive reality, the way we see ourselves, and the ways we behave—*la mestiza* creates a new consciousness.

The work of *mestiza* consciousness is to break down the subject-object duality that keeps her a prisoner and to show in the flesh and through the images in her work how duality is transcended. The answer to the problem between the white race and the colored, between males and females, lies in healing the split that originates in the very foundation of our lives, our culture, our languages, our thoughts. A massive uprooting of dualistic thinking in the individual and collective consciousness is the beginning of a long struggle, but one that could, in our best hopes, bring us to the end of rape, of violence, of war.

La encrucijada / The Crossroads

A chicken is being sacrificed
at a crossroads, a simple mound of earth
a mud shrine for *Eshu,*
Yoruba god of indeterminacy,
who blesses her choice of path.
She begins her journey.

Su cuerpo es una bocacalle. La mestiza has gone from being the sacrificial goat to becoming the officiating priestess at the crossroads.

As a *mestiza* I have no country, my homeland cast me out; yet all countries are mine because I am every woman's sister or potential lover. (As a lesbian I have no race, my own people disclaim me; but I am all races because there is the queer of me in all races.) I am cultureless because, as a feminist, I challenge the collective cultural/religious male-derived beliefs of Indo-Hispanics and Anglos; yet I am cultured because I am participating in the creation of yet another culture, a new story to explain the world and our participation in it, a new value system with images and symbols that connect us to each other and to the planet. *Soy un amasamiento,* I am an act of kneading, of uniting and joining that not only has produced both a creature of darkness and a creature of light, but also a creature that questions the definitions of light and dark and gives them new meanings.

We are the people who leap in the dark, we are the people on the knees of the gods. In our very flesh, (r)evolution works out the clash of cultures. It makes us crazy constantly, but if the center holds, we've made some kind of evolutionary step forward. *Nuestra alma el trabajo,* the opus, the great alchemical work; spiritual *mestizaje,* a "morphogenesis," an inevitable unfolding. We have become the quickening serpent movement.

Indigenous like corn, like corn, the *mestiza* is a product of crossbreeding, designed for preservation under a variety of conditions. Like an ear of corn—a female seed-bearing organ—the *mestiza* is tenacious, tightly wrapped in the husks of her culture. Like kernels she clings to the cob; with thick stalks and strong brace roots, she holds tight to the earth—she will survive the crossroads.

Lavando y remojando el maíz en agua de cal, despojando el pellejo. Moliendo, mixteando, amasando, haciendo tortillas de masa. She steeps the corn in lime, it swells, softens. With stone roller on *metate,* she grinds the corn, then grinds again. She kneads and moulds the dough, pats the round balls into *tortillas.*

> We are the porous rock in the stone *metate*
> squatting on the ground.
> We are the rolling pin, *el maíz y agua,*
> *la masa harina. Somos el amasijo.*
> *Somos lo molido en el metate.*
> We are the *comal* sizzling hot,
> the hot *tortilla,* the hungry mouth.
> We are the coarse rock.
> We are the grinding motion,
> the mixed potion, *somos el molcajete.*
> We are the pestle, the *comino, ajo, pimienta,*
> We are the *chile colorado,*
> the green shoot that cracks the rock.
> We will abide.

El camino de la mestiza / The Mestiza Way

Caught between the sudden contraction, the breath sucked in and the endless space, the brown woman stands still, looks at the sky. She decides to go down, digging her way along the roots of trees. Sifting through the bones, she shakes them to see if there is any marrow in them. Then, touching the dirt to her forehead, to her tongue, she takes a few bones, leaves the rest in their burial place.

She goes through her backpack, keeps her journal and address book, throws away the muni-bart metromaps. The coins are heavy and they go next, then the greenbacks flutter through the air. She keeps her knife, can opener and eyebrow pencil. She puts bones, pieces of bark, *hierbas,* eagle feather, snakeskin, tape recorder, the rattle and drum in her pack and she sets out to become the complete *tolteca.*

Her first step is to take inventory. *Despojando, desgranando, quitando paja.* Just what did she inherit from her ancestors? This weight on her back—which is the baggage from the Indian mother, which the baggage from the Spanish father, which the baggage from the Anglo?

Pero es difícil differentiating between *lo heredado, lo adquirido, lo impuesto.* She puts history through a sieve, winnows out the lies, looks at the forces that we as a race, as women, have been a part of. *Luego bota lo que no vale, los desmientos, los desencuentos, el embrutecimiento. Aguarda el juicio, hondo y enraízado, de la gente antigua.* This step is a conscious rupture with all oppressive traditions of all cultures and religions. She communicates that rupture, documents the struggle. She reinterprets history and, using new symbols, she shapes new myths. She adopts new perspectives toward the darkskinned, women and queers. She strengthens her tolerance (and intolerance) for ambiguity. She is willing to share, to make herself vulnerable to foreign ways of seeing and thinking. She surrenders all notions of safety, of the familiar. Deconstruct, construct. She becomes a *nahual,* able to transform herself into a tree, a coyote, into another person. She learns to transform the small "I" into the total Self. *Se hace moldeadora de su alma. Según la concepción que tiene de sí misma, así será.*

Que no se nos olvide los hombres

"Tú no sirves pa' nada—
you're good for nothing.
Eres pura vieja."

"You're nothing but a woman" means you are defective. Its opposite is to be *un macho.* The modern meaning of the word "machismo," as well as the concept, is actually an Anglo invention. For men like my father, being "macho" meant being strong enough to protect and support my mother and us, yet being able to show love. Today's macho has doubts about his ability to feed and protect his family. His "machismo" is an adaptation to oppression and poverty and low self-esteem. It is the result of hierarchical male dominance. The Anglo, feeling inadequate and inferior and powerless, displaces or transfers these feelings to the Chicano by shaming him. In the Gringo world, the Chicano suffers from excessive humility and self-effacement, shame of self and self-deprecation. Around Latinos he suffers from a sense of language inadequacy and its accompanying discomfort; with Native Americans he suffers from a racial amnesia which ignores our common blood, and from guilt because the Spanish part of him took their land and oppressed them. He has an excessive compensatory hubris when around Mexicans from the other side. It overlays a deep sense of racial shame.

The loss of a sense of dignity and respect in the macho breeds a false machismo which leads him to put down women and even to brutalize them. Coexisting with his sexist behavior is a love for the mother which takes precedence over that of all others. Devoted son, macho pig. To wash down the shame of his acts, of his very being, and to handle the brute in the mirror, he takes to the bottle, the snort, the needle, and the fist.

Though we "understand" the root causes of male hatred and fear, and the subsequent wounding of women, we do not excuse, we do not condone, and we will no longer put up with it. From the men of our race, we demand the admission/acknowledgment/disclosure/testimony that they wound us, violate us, are afraid of us and of our power. We need them to say they will begin to eliminate their hurtful put-down ways. But more than the words, we demand acts. We say to them: We will develop equal power with you and those who have shamed us.

It is imperative that *mestiza* support each other in changing the sexist elements in the Mexican-Indian culture. As long as woman is put down, the Indian and the Black in all of us is put down. The struggle of the *mestiza* is above all a feminist one. As long as *los hombres* think they have to *chingar mujeres* and each other to be men, as long as men are taught that they are superior and therefore culturally favored over *la mujer*, as long as to be a *vieja* is a thing of derision, there can be no real healing of our psyches. We're halfway there—we have such love of the Mother, the good mother. The first step is to unlearn the *puta/virgen* dichotomy and to see *Coatlapopeuh-Coatlicue* in the Mother, *Guadalupe*.

Tenderness, a sign of vulnerability, is so feared that it is showered on women with verbal abuse and blows. Men, even more than women, are fettered to gender roles. Women at least have had the guts to break out of bondage. Only gay men have had the courage to expose themselves to the woman inside them and to challenge the current masculinity. I've encountered a few scattered and isolated gentle straight men, the beginnings of a new breed, but they are confused, and entangled with sexist behaviors that they have not been able to eradicate. We need a new masculinity and the new man needs a movement.

Lumping the males who deviate from the general norm with man, the oppressor, is a gross injustice. *Asombra pensar que nos hemos quedado en ese pozo oscuro donde el mundo encierra a las lesbianas. Asombra pensar que hemos, como femenistas y lesbianas, cerrado nuestros corazónes a los hombres, a nuestros hermanos los jotos, desheredados y marginales como nosotros.* Being the supreme crossers of cultures, homosexuals have strong bonds with the queer white, Black, Asian, Native American, Latino, and with the queer in Italy, Australia and the rest of the planet. We come from all colors, all classes, all races, all time periods. Our role is to link people with each other—the Blacks with Jews with Indians with Asians with whites with extraterrestrials. It is to transfer ideas and information from one culture to another. Colored homosexuals have more knowledge of other cultures; have always been at the forefront (although sometimes in the closet) of all liberation struggles in this country; have suffered more injustices and have survived them despite all odds. Chicanos need to acknowledge the political and artistic contributions of their queer. People, listen to what your *jotería* is saying.

The *mestizo* and the queer exist at this time and point on the evolutionary continuum for a purpose. We are a blending that proves that all blood is intricately woven together, and that we are spawned out of similar souls.

Somos una gente

Hay tantísimas fronteras
que dividen a la gente,
pero por cada frontera
existe también un puente.
—*Gina Valdés*

Divided Loyalties

Many women and men of color do not want to have any dealings with white people. It takes too much time and energy to explain to the downwardly mobile, white middle-class women that it's okay for us to want to own "possessions," never having had any nice furniture on our dirt floors or "luxuries" like washing machines. Many feel that whites should help their own people rid themselves of race hatred and fear first. I, for one, choose to use some of my energy to serve as mediator. I think we need to allow whites to be our allies. Through our literature, art, *corridos,* and folktales we must share our history with them so when they set up committees to help Big Mountain Navajos or the Chicano farmworkers or *los Nicaragüenses* they won't turn people away because of their racial fears and ignorances. They will come to see that they are not helping us but following our lead.

Individually, but also as a racial entity, we need to voice our needs. We need to say to white society: We need you to accept the fact that Chicanos are different, to acknowledge your rejection and negation of us. We need you to own the fact that you looked upon us as less than human, that you stole our lands, our personhood, our self-respect. We need you to make public restitution: to say that, to compensate for your own sense of defectiveness, you strive for power over us, you erase our history and our experience because it makes you feel guilty—you'd rather forget your brutish acts. To say you've split yourself from minority groups, that you disown us, that your dual consciousness splits off parts of yourself, transferring the "negative" parts onto us. (Where there is persecution of minorities, there is shadow projection. Where there is violence and war, there is repression of shadow.) To say that you are afraid of us, that to put distance between us, you wear the mask of contempt. Admit that Mexico is your double, that she exists in the shadow of this country, that we are irrevocably tied to her. Gringo, accept the doppelganger in your psyche. By taking back your collective shadow the intracultural split will heal. And finally, tell us what you need from us.

By Your True Faces We Will Know You

I am visible—see this Indian face—yet I am invisible. I both blind them with my beak nose and am their blind spot. But I exist, we exist. They'd like to think I have melted in the pot. But I haven't, we haven't.

The dominant white culture is killing us slowly with its ignorance. By taking away our self-determination, it has made us weak and empty. As a people we have resisted and we have taken expedient positions, but we have never been allowed to develop unencumbered—we have never been allowed to be fully ourselves. The whites in power want us people of color to barricade ourselves behind our separate tribal walls so they can pick us off one at a time with their hidden weapons; so they can whitewash and distort history. Ignorance splits people, creates prejudices. A misinformed people is a subjugated people.

Before the Chicano and the undocumented worker and the Mexican from the other side can come together, before the Chicano can have unity with Native Americans and other groups, we need to know the history of their struggle and they need to know ours. Our mothers, our sisters and brothers, the guys who hang out on street corners, the children in the playgrounds, each of us must know our Indian lineage, our afro-*mestisaje,* our history of resistance.

To the immigrant *mexicano* and the recent arrivals we must teach our history. The 80 million *mexicanos* and the Latinos from Central and South America must know of our struggles. Each one of us must know basic facts about Nicaragua, Chile and the rest of Latin America. The Latinoist movement (Chicanos, Puerto Ricans, Cubans and other Spanish-speaking people working together to combat racial discrimination in the market place) is good but it is not enough. Other than a common culture we will have nothing to hold us together. We need to meet on a broader communal ground.

The struggle is inner: Chicano, *indio,* American Indian, *mojado, mexicano,* immigrant Latino, Anglo in power, working class Anglo, Black, Asian—our psyches resemble the bordertowns and are populated by the same people. The struggle has always been inner, and is played out in the outer terrains. Awareness of our situation must come before inner changes, which in turn come before changes in society. Nothing happens in the "real" world unless it first happens in the images in our heads.

El día de la Chicana

I will not be shamed again
Nor will I shame myself.

I am possessed by a vision: that we Chicanas and Chicanos have taken back or uncovered our true faces, our dignity and self-respect. It's a validation vision.

Seeing the Chicana anew in light of her history, I seek an exoneration, a seeing through the fictions of white supremacy, a seeing of ourselves in our true guises and not as the false racial personality that has been given to us and that we have given to ourselves. I seek our woman's face, our true features, the positive and the negative seen clearly, free of the tainted biases of male dominance. I seek new images of identity, new beliefs about ourselves, our humanity and worth no longer in question.

Estamos viviendo en la noche de la Raza, un tiempo cuando el trabajo se hace a lo quieto, en el oscuro. El día cuando aceptamos tal y como somos y para en donde vamos y porque—ese día será el día de la Raza. Yo tengo el conpromiso de expresar mi visión, mi sensibilidad, mi percepción de la revalidación de la gente mexicana, su mérito, estimación, honra, aprecio, y validez.

On December 2nd when my sun goes into my first house, I celebrate *el día de la Chicana y el Chicano.* On that day I clean my altars, light my *Coatlalopeuh* candle, burn sage and copal, take *el baño para espantar basura,* sweep my house. On that day I bare my soul, make myself vulnerable to friends and family by expressing my feelings. On that day I affirm who we are.

On that day I look inside our conflicts and our basic introverted racial temperament. I identify our needs, voice them. I acknowledge that the self and the race have been wounded. I recognize the need to take care of our personhood, of our racial self. On that day I gather the splintered and disowned parts of *la gente mexicana* and hold them in my arms. *Todas las partes de nosotros valen.*

On that day I say, Yes, all you people wound us when you reject us. Rejection strips us of self-worth; our vulnerability exposes us to shame. It is our innate identity you find wanting. We are ashamed that we need your good opinion, that we need your acceptance. We can no longer camouflage our needs, can no longer let defenses and fences sprout around us. We can no longer withdraw. To rage and look upon you with contempt is to rage and be contemptuous of ourselves. We can no longer blame you, nor disown the white parts, the male parts, the pathological parts, the queer parts, the vulnerable parts. Here we are weaponless with open arms, with only our magic. Let's try it our way, the *mestiza* way, the Chicana way, the woman way.

On that day, I search for our essential dignity as a people, a people with a sense of purpose—to belong and contribute to something greater than our *pueblo*. On that day I seek to recover and reshape my spiritual identity: *¡Anímate! Raza, a celebrar el día de la Chicana.*

El retorno

All movements are accomplished in six stages,
and the seventh brings return.
                                        —*I Ching*

Tanto tiempo sin verte casa mía,
mi cuna, mi hondo nido de la huerta.
                                        —"Soledad"

I stand at the river, watch the curving, twisting serpent, a serpent nailed to the fence where the mouth of the Rio Grande empties into the Gulf.

I have come back. *Tanto dolor me costó el alejamiento.* I shade my eyes and look up. The bone beak of a hawk slowly circling over me, checking me out as potential carrion. In its wake a little bird flickering its wings, swimming sporadically like a fish. In the distance the expressway and the slough of traffic like an irritated sow. The sudden pull in my gut, *la tierra, los aguaceros.* My land, *el viento soplandó la arena, el lagartijo debajo de un nopalito. Me acuerdo como era antes. Una región desértica de vasta llanuras, costeras de baja altura, de escasa lluvia, de chaparrales formados por mesquites y huizaches.* If I look real hard I can almost see the Spanish fathers who were called "the cavalry of Christ" enter this valley riding their burros, see the clash of cultures commence.

Tierra natal. This is home, the small towns in the Valley, *los pueblitos* with chicken pens and goats picketed to mesquite shrubs. *En las colonias* on the other side of the tracks, junk cars line the front yards of hot pink and lavender-trimmed houses—Chicano architecture we call it, self-consciously. I have missed the TV shows where hosts speak in half and half, and where awards are given in the category of Tex-Mex music. I have missed the Mexican cemeteries blooming with artificial flowers, the fields of aloe vera and red pepper, rows of sugar cane, of corn hanging on the stalks, the cloud of *polvareda* in the dirt roads behind a speeding pickup truck, *el sabor de tamales de rez y venado.* I have missed *la yegua colorada* gnawing the wooden gate of her stall, the smell of horse flesh from Carito's corrals. *He hecho menos las noches calientes sin aire, noches de linternas y lechuzas* making holes in the night.

I still feel the old despair when I look at the unpainted, dilapidated, scrap lumber houses consisting mostly of corrugated aluminum. Some of the poorest people in the U.S. live in the Lower Rio Grande Valley, an arid and semi-arid land of irrigated farming, intense sunlight and heat, citrus groves next to chaparral and cactus. I walk through the elementary school I attended so long ago, that remained segregated until recently. I remember how the white teachers used to punish us for being Mexican.

How I love this tragic valley of South Texas, as Ricardo Sánchez calls it; this borderland between the Nueces and the Rio Grande. This land has survived possession and ill-use by five countries: Spain, Mexico, the Republic of Texas, the U.S., the Confederacy, and the U.S. again. It has survived Anglo-Mexican blood feuds, lynchings, burnings, rapes, pillage.

Today I see the Valley still struggling to survive. Whether it does or not, it will never be as I remember it. The borderlands depression that was set off by the 1982 peso devaluation in Mexico resulted in the closure of hundreds of Valley businesses. Many people lost their homes, cars, land. Prior to 1982, U.S. store owners thrived on retail sales to Mexicans who came across the border for groceries and clothes and appliances. While goods on the U.S. side have become 10, 100, 1000 times more expensive for Mexican buyers, goods on the Mexican side have become 10, 100, 1000 times cheaper for Americans. Because the Valley is heavily dependent on agriculture and Mexican retail trade, it has the highest unemployment rates along the entire border region; it is the Valley that has been hardest hit.

"It's been a bad year for corn," my brother, Nune, says. As he talks, I remember my father scanning the sky for a rain that would end the drought, looking up into the sky, day after day, while the corn withered on its stalk. My father has been dead for 29 years, having worked himself to death. This life span of a Mexican farm laborer is 56—he lived to be 38. It shocks me that I am older than he. I, too, search the sky for rain. Like the ancients, I worship the rain god and the maize goddess, but unlike my father I have recovered their names. Now for rain (irrigation) one offers not a sacrifice of blood, but of money.

"Farming is in a bad way," my brother says. "Two to three thousand small and big farmers went bankrupt in this country last year. Six years ago the price of corn was $8.00 per hundred pounds," he goes on. "This year it is $3.90 per hundred pounds." And, I think to myself, after taking inflation into account, not planting anything puts you ahead.

I walk out to the back yard, stare at *los rosales de mamá*. She wants me to help her prune the rose bushes, dig out the carpet grass that is choking them. *Mamagrande Ramona también tenía rosales.* Here every Mexican grows flowers. If they don't have a piece of dirt, they use car tires, jars, cans, shoe boxes. Roses are the Mexican's favorite flower. I think, how symbolic—thorns and all.

Yes, the Chicano and Chicana have always taken care of growing things and the land. Again I see the four of us kids getting off the school bus, changing into our work clothes, walking into the field with Papí and Mamí, all six of us bending to the ground. Below our feet, under the earth lie the watermelon seeds. We cover them with paper plates, putting *terremotes* on top of the plates to keep them from being blown away by the wind. The paper plates keep the freeze away. Next day or the next, we remove the plates, bare the tiny green shoots to the elements. They survive and grow, give fruit hundreds of times the size of the seed. We water them and hoe them. We harvest them. The vines dry, rot, are plowed under. Growth, death, decay, birth. The soil prepared again and again, impregnated, worked on. A constant changing of forms, *renacimientos de la tierra madre.*

> This land was Mexican once
>   was Indian always
>   and is.
>   And will be again.

ANALYSIS

1. How does Anzaldua see the relationship between Mexican and white communities?

2. How does this essay exhibit Anzaldua's refusal to accept what for her is the traditional limiting role for females that Chicano culture offers?

3. Anzaldua says that it's no use simply locking oneself into a "counter-stance," where you "refuse . . . the dominant culture's views." Why does Anzaldua believe that a counterstance alone is of no use?

4. Anzaldua analyzes the concept of "machismo" as an "Anglo" invention. How does she argue for this derivation? For example, what to Anzaldua distinguishes true *macho* from falsely derived *machismo?*
5. What does Anzaldua mean by saying "the struggle is inner"?

─────── WRITING POSSIBILITIES ───────

1. To what extent does Anzaldua's analysis of being "sandwiched between two cultures" apply to other groups besides Mexican Americans? Would it apply to groups that are part of your experience? Do you see the need for change that Anzaldua does?
2. Anzaldua speaks of "a tolerance for ambiguity" because on the borderland, one receives "conflicting information and points of view. . . . The borders and walls that are supposed to keep the undesirable ideas out are entrenched habits and patterns of behavior." But don't borders and boundaries also define identities? How can one, according to Anzaldua's view or on your own, differentiate between those "habits and patterns of behavior" that are desirable, vis-à-vis those that are "undesirable"? Also: would not "ambiguity" leave you anxious and tense? Or not? Using your own experience as a focal point, discuss Anzaldua's idea of "a tolerance for ambiguity" or the values and disvalues of "borders."
3. Anzaldua writes in a lyrical and often abstract style; did this intrigue you or put you off? Did her switching between English and Spanish annoy you or give you some pleasure? Are there passages in *"La conciencia de la mestiza"* that you don't agree with? Quote enough of one or two such passages to give the reader a good idea of what you find and then comment on how you view it.
4. Where are the more autobiographical and realistic aspects of the essay? How does Anzaldua move back and forth between them and the more abstract parts? Would she have written more persuasively in your view had she started with the realistic and autobiographical elements?
5. A key element of change that Anzaldua insists on is the feminist one— *mestizas* must stand up to men and their (false) *machismo*. What difficulties stand in the way of such defiance, either for a *mestiza* or for anyone?

Gerda Lerner

In this brief excerpt from Why History Matters, *historian Gerda Lerner explains how her particular situation—a Jewish refugee from Nazi Germany who survived the Holocaust—illuminates typically American ideas of assimilation, cultural separatism and acculturation, the latter being Lerner's preferred term for that combination of accepting an overall national framework within which particular groups (racial and ethnic) can enjoy their own cultural identity. The term approximates what is often meant by* cultural pluralism *or* multiculturalism *(or the metaphors of the "mosaic" or the "salad bowl") and thus deserves comparison with the essays in Chapter 4 by Glazer and Takaki on American patterns of multiculturalism and diversity.*

NO PLACE TO GO BACK TO
from Why History Matters

On March 11, 1938, German troops, meeting no resistance, occupied Austria and were greeted enthusiastically by millions of wildly cheering Austrians. The *Anschluss* was quickly followed by outbursts of violence against Jews that exceeded anything that had been inflicted in Germany since 1933. Gangs of armed Nazis terrorized Jewish pedestrians. Jewish men and women were forced to scrub the streets, walls and toilets in police barracks with their bare hands or with toothbrushes to the amusement of crowds of bystanders. Raids on homes and businesses, followed by theft of property by Nazi gangs, were commonplace despite their illegality. In the streets and Jewish communities of Vienna there was open season on Jews for anyone with a Nazi insignia on his lapel. Jewish businesses were forced to close their doors; Jews were dismissed from their jobs and official positions; the University was closed to Jewish students and faculty within six weeks of the *Anschluss*. The legal and administrative regulations to legalize these excesses were soon enacted.

Violent antisemitism came naturally to Austrians, who had a long history of antisemitic political parties and movements. The Germans has to be led into violent antisemitism; in Austrians it erupted spontaneously. Within weeks of the *Anschluss* the situation of Jews in Austria was worse than that of Jews in Germany six years after the Nazi takeover.

Right from the start, a reign of terror was instituted. Prominent Jewish leaders and businessmen, the heads of various Jewish organizations, doctors and university professors, journalists and politicians were arrested without any charges against them and held for weeks and months in jail or in the Dachau concentration camp. Jewish play-wrights, actors and directors were barred from the stage, and many prominent writers and actors were arrested. A Jewish orphanage was closed, the orphans thrown out and the building turned into a Nazi barracks. SA troops forced their way into the biggest Jewish syna-gogue during evening services, arrested all present and desecrated the premises by singing the Horst-Wessel song. All government em-ployees were forced to take a loyalty oath to Hitler; those unwilling to do so were summarily dismissed. By the end of April a decree of the Education Department assured that all school and university ses-sions would open and close with students and faculty giving the Hilter salute. Everywhere, former Nazi sympathizers and "illegal" Nazis* now emerged proudly with new power and status. In the pri-vate school I attended, which had many Jewish teachers and a Jewish director, a number of the teachers turned out to have been under-ground members of the Nazi party. The Jewish director was replaced by one of these illegal Nazis before the end of the school term.

My father fled the country after being warned by a "friendly" Nazi that his name was on a list of people to be arrested. He thought of course his absence would be temporary, but it proved permanent. A few weeks after my father's flight, twelve fully armed stormtroopers raided our apartment, put a gun at my twelve-year-old sister's chest, demanding to know where my father was, tore up the furniture with bayonets and generally terrorized us for hours while they pretended to search the apartment for hidden gold. In the end they took me and my mother to jail. We were taken to regular prison, separated from each other, and for six weeks we were forgotten, not accused, not indicted, not tried. We were, in fact, held as hostages for my father and were re-leased only after he finally signed away all his property and his busi-ness. We were then forced to sign our own deportation orders.

I lived for another six months in Nazi Austria after that, because we could not get the various permits necessary to leave. Each week we had to report to the police, who threatened to throw us in a con-centration camp if by the next week we were still here. During these months, the persecution and daily harassment of Jews increased. Destitute families doubled up in apartments, and many people never left their homes for fear of arrest during the random street raids that were a daily occurrence. The number of Jewish suicides increased from five in January to more than a hundred during each month of that summer. In our circle, each family had its own horror stories; ev-eryone had heard of some acquaintance who had committed suicide rather than be taken to jail. This was long before the "final solution,"

---

*From 1939 on, ever since the assassination of the Austrian Chancellor by Austrian Nazis, the Nazi party was illegal in Austria.

long before any of these persecutions were cloaked in the mantle of legality. The Austrian treatment of Jews was improvised on the spot; its versatility, ingenuity and brutality were then unprecedented.

Legally and theoretically, it was then still possible for Jews to leave the country. In actuality, all borders in Europe and most other countries of the world were closed against refugees from Nazi persecution and only a lucky few had the connections or money to escape. Since by newly enacted legislation, Jews leaving Austria were permitted to take only the equivalent of $10—in cash and their household goods and clothing—money or connections were essential for survival abroad. In April approximately 25,000 Viennese Jews applied to the U.S. consulate for immigration visas; at the time the quota for immigrants from Austria was fixed at 1413 per year.

With the aid of "Aryan" lawyers and by signing over all our property and assets, finally, one week before *Kristallnacht,* my mother, my sister and I secured all the necessary papers and were able to join my father in Liechtenstein, a tiny country on the Austrian border. We had residence permits for Liechtenstein because my father had established a business there in 1934. This fact saved his and our lives. He was also able to rescue his mother and adopted sister, while most of our relatives remained in the death trap.

An emigrant now, awaiting my U.S. immigration visa, I had become virtually a stateless person. With a German passport which marked me as a Jew, return to Germany meant certain death. Being stateless, a Jew and destitute change one's view of what it means to be part of an establishment: my outsider status from then on was firmly fixed. Even after coming to America, I never felt secure in front of anyone connected with an establishment—bureaucrat, policeman, soldier or lawyer.

During World War II the U.S. government forced me and other Jewish immigrants like me to register once a month at the post office as "enemy aliens." Still, I did eventually become an American citizen. Insofar as I now had citizen's rights I could trust, this fact changed my outsider status. But I was different, marked by my experience; I was carrying my "Otherness" within me.

A few years after the end of the war, when the full extent of the horror in which some of my family members had perished had become known, the sense of the difference of my own experience became sharper. My mother had died at age fifty, a death hastened by the hardships of emigration. Still, I was among the very fortunate; most of my close relatives had survived. But the personal loss was dwarfed by the enormity of the loss of a people, of communities, of one's own past.

Sometimes, when you walk up a mountain, the views of the valley below are clear and sharp. Then the weather changes, a cloud of

fog settles into the valley and the view vanishes. There is nothing beneath one's feet except gray mist. It is eerie, like the terror of night-
mares, one is cut off and cast off and the very place from which one
came, what once was home, has vanished. When this happens, on the
mountain, one can console oneself in the knowledge that the place in
the valley is still there; it is as it always was and one will see it when
the fog lifts. But for the refugee such consolation does not exist. The
city in which I had grown up, the circle in which I moved during the
years of my childhood no longer existed. Of the 176,000 Jews of Vienna, over 9 percent of its total population in 1934, only 4746 survived in 1944, a few months before the liberation of the city. More
than 65,000 Austrian Jews died in the ghettoes and concentration
camps of Nazi Europe. The others, who had been deported or forced
to emigrate survived scattered all over the world. I have visited Vienna six times in the past fifty years. The buildings are restored,
some of them are more beautiful than they ever were. But what I notice most, as I walk through the streets of the city is the absence of
Jews, an absence I think only a survivor could notice. For me, there is
no one left to go back to; there is no place to go back to except a
place of hatred and bad memories. There is only one life-line left—
memory, personal and historical. After the Holocaust, history for me
was no longer something outside myself, which I needed to comprehend and use to illuminate my own life and times. Those of us who
survived carried a charge to keep memory alive in order to resist the
total destruction of our people. History had become an obligation.

Like all immigrants, I did not think this through or find such fancy
words for it. I had to struggle for existence and survival and if I gave
any thought to the matter at the time, it was how to become a good
American. I tried to erase whatever I could of my foreign characteristics. I worked hard at acquiring as pure an English as I possibly could.
I shed my indestructible European clothes, as soon as I could afford to
replace them with throw-away American fashions. I tried to make
friends with Americans and be accepted by them. It is no accident that
decades later when I began to prepare for an academic career I chose
the field of American history, not European. I still wanted, as I had in
Austria, to be a "normal" person. Yet, from the start I chose a deviant
field, in fact, a then non-existing field, that of Women's History.
My "Otherness" was obvious from the moment I entered graduate
school—too old (over forty), a foreign-born woman, a Jew, insisting
on specializing in a field of history my professors considered "exotic"
and weird. I will skip over the years of struggling for the legitimation
of this new field of inquiry. It was only when I came to Madison, by
then a well-established historian of fairly advanced age, that for the
first time I began to feel accepted, an insider. The University gave me
recognition, honors, support for my work and clear signs of their

appreciation. The advances made in my embattled field—Women's History—had brought some measure of respectability and, while some colleagues still considered me a deviant sort and not quite up to their measure, my general experience was of having finally made it. I was now an insider and began to worry about being corrupted by that unaccustomed state. Then, a few years ago in April, there was a swastika smeared on a poster on my office door. In August there were forty-one antisemitic incidents in Madison and one, not reported and thus not included in that number, a threatening antisemitic phone message left on my answering machine. Back to square one. The Jew remains "the Other."

My story illustrates quite well the effect on Jews of being designated a deviant out-group. There are essentially three major response patterns: cultural separatism, denial through assimilation, and acculturation.

Cultural separatism means affirming one's "Otherness" as a positive good. We are the chosen people, smarter, better, morally superior and somehow purified by our history of suffering. We prefer to live in self-selected ghettoes, confine our social contact to people like ourselves and cultivate our separate institutions.

Denial through assimilation is an effort to fuse with the majority and ultimately to give up all distinctiveness. For many Jews of the generation between the wars in both Central Europe and in America this took the form of adopting a philosophy of modernism, of anti-nationalism and internationalism, of a desire to find a new form of community which would embrace different cultures, religions and nationalities. This was my mother's philosophy and for a long time it was mine. We abhorred all nationalism and all theories of hierarchy and dominance. Tolerance and a "new humanism" would take the place of the old separations, hatreds and differences.

I married a second-generation American. My husband's family represented another response, in its *shtetl* culture in the Jewish ghetto of Philadelphia. His parents were immigrants from Russia who had come to the U.S. to escape the infamous Kishinev pogroms. They were working-class people who spoke Yiddish and were proudly affiliated with their synagogue, their *Landsmannschaft* and their Yiddish culture. They were as unassimilated as Americans as one can be and they were wonderful, loving people who took me in as their own, even though at first glance I seemed to them to be a *shikse*. Living in solid, tightly knit networks of families, they were mutually supportive, but resisted the tendency of the younger generation—the first-generation Americans— to partake of the general culture, to accommodate to the values of tolerance, multi-culturalism and internationalism. To this younger generation, the old folks seemed hopelessly limited and limiting. The horizontal mobility of first-generation Americans—out of the ethnic working-class ghettoes—into ethnic suburban ghettoes—illustrates this process of "Americanization."

The third response, "acculturation," is both more adaptive and more realistic than the other two. It embraces the demand for integration in regard to rights and opportunities—one wants to be an Austrian or an American with full equality—yet one does not want to lose one's group identity. Integration *and* difference is the goal. Jews with that stance will privatize their Jewishness and separate its communal function within their group from their public roles. Jews would adopt the external behavior and standards of the dominant culture but retain their emotional, psychological affinities to their own group. They might, as in America in the third generation, move into integrated upper-class neighborhoods, attend elite colleges and vote not on the basis of ethnicity but of class, yet their social life would be within a like-minded circle of Jews. My father represented that stance in its European version.

The irony of these choices is that antisemitism would not recognize any difference between the separatist, the assimilated, the acculturated Jew. Hitler's Nuremberg laws defined Jews by "genetic" inheritance into the third generation, and lifestyle choices meant nothing. Similarly, the person who put a swastika on my door in Madison, Wisconsin, fifty years later cared not one bit as to what kind of a Jew I was or I am. I was a Jew, that was sufficient.

Each of us has over a lifetime struggled with choices representing these different positions. And as we choose, we take on ourselves the guilt over our existence. If we choose right, we and the people will be spared. If we get all A's, we will be among the saved. If we choose wrong, the holocaust is our fault. It is a cruel bind, which blames the victim and obscures the actuality of the situation in which he or she exists. What it obscures is that it is not difference, but the designation of difference as inferiority which has created the evil.

The psychological effect on Jews, as on other out-groups designated as deviant, is that they internalize guilt for their being "different" and spend their lives choosing between various forms of adaptations to the constraints placed upon them. But what is really oppressing us is not our choice of adaptation or our nature as a group designated as "different," it is having our definition of self made not by ourselves but by others.

To be a Jew means to live in history. The history of the Jews is a history of one holocaust after another with short intervals of peaceful assimilation and acculturation. Most of us never study this long and bitter history and yet we live with it and it shapes our lives. We live from pogrom to pogrom, one of my friends recently said. What it means to be a Jew—having to look over your shoulder and have your bags packed.

It is only in the light of this history that we can understand the significance of the existence of the state of Israel and even the idiosyncratic behavior of the leaders of the state. It is not always a sign of paranoia to think that one is surrounded by enemies. For many religious Jews, Eretz Yisroel, the land of Israel, means the fulfillment of biblical promise and the re-establishment of their rightful place in a land from which they were driven. But for millions of nonreligious and secular Jews the state of Israel, means that for the first time in two thousand years Jews no longer will allow themselves to be defined by others and scapegoated by them. I think that this particular meaning should be important as well to every non-Jew who believes in the right of people to self-determination and freedom.

It was this understanding of the problem of "Otherness" and of the denial of self-definition which led me to the study of the history of women. For women have, for longer than any other human group, been defined by others and have been defined as "the Other." Women have, for longer than any other group, been deprived of a knowledge of their own history. I have, for the past thirty-five years, tried to comprehend analytically what I experienced and learned as a prototypical outsider—a woman, a Jew, an exile.

ANALYSIS

1. What is the force of Lerner's remark that she has "no place to go back to"? How might this characterize the difference between a refugee (like Lerner) and an immigrant?
2. The title of Lerner's book is *Why History Matters;* on the basis of your own or your family's history, how would you answer Lerner's implied question?

WRITING POSSIBILITIES

1. Compare Lerner's account of "acculturation" with Nathan Glazer's description of "The Emergence of an American Ethnic Pattern," (pages 219–234). To what extent are the two concepts similar?
2. Moving from one place to another triggers awareness in many different areas. If you or your family has moved from one neighborhood, place, or country to another, comment on the applicability of Lerner's terms ("separatism," "assimilation," "acculturation") to yours or your family's situation.
3. How would you compare Lerner's account of Nazi Germany with that of the figures in William Finnegan's "The Unwanted," (pages 130–131)? What is present in Lerner's speaker that's missing from the youth in Finnegan's essay?

Monk Phen Anonthasy

Refugees are not immigrants—that's one immediate lesson to be learned from Phen Anonthasy's oral account of life in Laos and in Oakland, California. As editor John Tenula notes, a refugee under U.S. law is a person "outside his country, and having fled it, fears persecution if forced to return to that country. Refugees are immigrants," Tenula continues, "but not all immigrants are refugees."

Monk Phen Anonathasy was seventy years old when this account was transcribed by oral historian Tenula in 1985. Anonthasy makes two points—one, that life as a Buddhist under the Communists was unendurable:

They took us—all of the monks—and they placed us in a camp. It was a prison and I was afraid they would kill us.

Second, life in America occasions mixed feelings because the value systems between America and Laos are so different.

East / West Values
from Voices from Southeast Asia

He has kept me waiting for almost an hour, sitting on a metal folding chair in some anteroom, adjacent to his office. The temple itself is in an industrial section of Oakland. The building was most likely a garage, and you can still see the original lines of the structure. The heavy smell of incense is hanging in the air.

He must be over seventy years of age, and he is bent over as he approaches. He leads me to his office, then inside the temple. There is a feeling of quiet about this man who seems unconcerned about where he is—be it Laos or Oakland. He remains in a perfect lotus position on the hard floor and never moves. His eyes are fixed on my eyes and I felt that he has your undivided attention. A baby cries close by—but he seems not to even hear the cries.

I left Laos for Thailand in 1976 and stayed there for four years before coming to the United States. I was needed to help my people in the camps. I left Laos because Buddhism and Marxist thought cannot live together. They cannot. It is impossible! For the Communists there can be no alternatives and there can be no compromise; Communism and

Buddhism could not continue in Laos, so I left. This is a political side to life that my people cannot accept. They took us—all of the monks—and they placed us in a camp. It was a prison and I was afraid they would kill us. I am here now. For me, Oakland [California] or Vientiane or Bangkok—it is the same thing. I don't even look out of the window anymore—see, it is all covered! The spirit is with you and a person is still the same person only in a different place. I do not leave the temple; for me, this is my world.

WHAT ARE THE DIFFERENCES YOU SEE BETWEEN THE EAST AND WEST?

I would say the biggest differences between East and West are three. First, we have a different system of values as taught to us through Buddhism. It is a system of thought that affects the way we think—all of our daily activities. You never separated the spiritual from the real. It surrounds the family, the role of each member in that family, and how the family continues to reinforce those values.

Second is the day-to-day existence, the patterns of living. The housing and the places our people live in are very different here from Laos. This affects your life every day. Just look at this room. Do you think I belong here? Look, don't I look lost? Oh, but inside I'm not lost. We live close to our family members and the village system is one where you are aware of who your neighbor is and what he does. Here everything is respect for your privacy and you do not know who your neighbor is or anything about him. You see, we believe that the place of one's birth and the residence of our ancestors is very important for the continuation of our life. Land is important; it is your history, your heritage, your being. If you remove land, you remove spirit. But is this not what the American Indians believed, too? Was not land their soul?

Third, the relationship between parent and child changes too much here. This means children stop obeying parents and they leave home too quickly; also, family life has it that everyone works and you leave early in the morning and return late in the evening. Your time with your children is very short. Children should have more respect for older people. It is terrible what happens between children and older people when they come to America.

I know my people have many problems here. They come to me for discussions and advice and just to be in the temple. They come to reflect. Yesterday, a woman had a car crash and came for advice—she thought she had bad spirits, that she did something wrong. You see, she believed that she was being punished. To her, the car crash said that she was a bad woman. Buddha gives advice on all troubles. You go to Buddha for everything you need. So much discomfort has to do with the work and the language here. Materialism is the need for everyone to work for money; Lao people find it hard and they go in different directions. Capitalism does very strange things to a person's system of values. Too many material goods are here to tempt and confuse you. Money can cause so much unhappiness.

WHAT HAPPENS TO THE LAO FAMILY IN AMERICA?

Work forces women into a new relationship with their husbands and children. I see more women who leave their husbands, and the husbands get depressed with problems because they cannot carry on their roles within the family. Many use welfare but that is not enough money to live on, and when a person does not work, he gets depressed. It is like the air he breathes is being taken away. Work is terribly important for one's self-respect and dignity. I try to help. Buddha teaches control of oneself and to deal with the changes in life. What the Laotian communities in the United States really need are more monks; in all of San Francisco there are no monks.

And there is crime. Yes, there is much crime in Oakland. Many women tell me of rape and robbery. I try to listen to them and to help them. I suppose there is crime everywhere but I do not notice it. I spend most of my days here in the temple. I pray a lot.

--- **ANALYSIS** ---

1. According to Anonthasy, how is day-to-day living in America different from his life in Laos?

--- **WRITING POSSIBILITIES** ---

1. Monk Phen Anonthasy is from Laos; other refugees from Southeast Asia, Africa, the Balkans, Central America would have had somewhat different experiences depending on where they came from and whether they were first, second, or even third generation refugees. In addition, refugees (like immigrants) have experienced economic and social discrimination from their American brethren. If you are from a refugee background or know someone who is, explain how you, your friends, siblings, or parents feel about assimilation in America. You may find it helpful to read the short account by Gerda Lerner (pages 104–110) that distinguishes among assimilation, separatism, and acculturation.

Lucy Lippard

Reprinted here are two pages exactly as they appear in Lucy Lippard's
The Lure of the Local. *They are reprinted in this way to show you how
a book's page-design can mimic some aspects of multicultural
experience: what Lippard (a noted art critic) provides throughout the
book is, above the line-rule, a running autobiographical account of her
life on the Maine seacoast, and, below the line-rule, theoretical insights
into the significance of landscape in a "multicentered" world. Her
above-and-below the line accounts can be used profitably by anyone
who wants to provide readers with a more complex account of their
experience than might be done by a traditional one-way page layout.*

ALL OVER THE PLACE
from The Lure of the Local

Most educated people say where is it written? Our people say
where is it lived?

—*Steve Gonzalez*

We are in the epoch of simultaneity; we are in the epoch of
juxtaposition, the epoch of the near and far, of the side-by-
side, of the dispersed.

—*Michel Foucault*

Place for me is the locus of desire. Places have influenced my life as
much as, perhaps more than, people. I fall for (or into) places faster
and less conditionally than I do for people. I can drive through a
landscape and vividly picture myself in that disintegrating mining
cabin, that saltwater farm, that little porched house in the barrio. (My
taste runs to humble dwellings nestled in cozy spaces or vulnerable in
vast spaces.) I can walk through a neighborhood and picture interi-
ors, unseen back yards. I can feel kinesthetically how it would be to
hike for hours through a vast "empty" landscape that I'm dashing
through in a car—the underfoot textures, the rising dust, the way
muscles tighten on a hill, the rhythms of walking, the feeling of sun
or mist on the back of my neck. In the late seventies, I lived on an
idyllic farm in England for a year. While there, I wrote a weird short
story about a woman who fell erotically in love with the place and
was literally absorbed by it. I missed Ashwell Farm terribly when I returned to New York, then I found I could continue to take my daily
walks in a kind of out-of-body form—step by step, weather, texture,
views, seasons, flowers, wildlife encounters.

We drive over the Piscataqua from Portsmouth, New Hampshire, and we're in Maine! Already it smells different. The air is fresh with salt and anticipation. An hour and a half later we pass Portland, a first whiff of real sea, sharper if the tide is out and the mudflats are breathing. For years, when the papermills upstream felt free to indundate the river with waste, there was a foul smell of rotting cabbages as we crossed the Presumpscot.

Through Brunswick, home of Bowdoin College, and its grove of towering old growth pines, and then—on Witch Spring Hill just outside of Bath—the first glimpse

---

Since childhood I've done the same with the shoreline of a little peninsula on Georgetown Island jutting into the Atlantic Ocean at the mouth of the Kennebec River in Maine, which remains the bedrock place in my life. I first arrived there in 1937, at the age of three months, as a basket case on the boat from Boston. I've returned every summer for sixty years. Although I will always be perceived as "from away," Kennebec Point is for me, as for many of my contemporaries there, my soul's home. When I realized that a book about the local couldn't be approached only with general ideas, Georgetown was the logical point of departure. The "vein of Maine" that runs through this book like a vein of granite or quartz through schist is offered as an antidote to all the tentative concepts surrounding it, an anchor line for my driftings. I have trolled for years in many disciplines and adhere to no particular theory. However out of fashion romanticism and nostalgia may be, I can't write about places without occasionally sinking into their seductive embrace. As I follow the labyrinthine diversity of personal geography, lived experience grounded in nature, culture and history, forming landscape and place, I have to dream a little, as well as listen for the political wake-up calls.

> Everything written in the "objective style" of 1950s social sciences or "New Criticism," and everything written in the opaque style of post-structural discourses, now risks being read as a kind of political cover-up, hidden complicity, and intrigue on either the right or left. Interestingly, the one path that still leads in the direction of scholarly objectivity, detachment, and neutrality is exactly the one originally thought to lead away from these classic virtues: that is, an openly autobiographical style in which the subjective position of the author, especially on political matters, is presented in a clear and straightforward fashion. At least this enables the reader to review his or her own position to make the adjustments necessary for dialogue.
>
> —*Dean MacCannell*

I have chosen to weave myself and my own experiences into this book from time to time because lived experience is central to my

of the green towers of the Carlton Bridge. (As a kid I got a penny if I saw it first.) We cross the broad Kennebec, opening the windows to receive its blessing, passing the huge crane of the Bath Iron Works and the lurking gray destroyers in various stages of construction lined up along the shore. In Woolwich for only a minute or so, we take an abrupt right at the Dairy Queen and cross the Sasanoa on another high bridge, heading south. Past the old Arrowsic Town Hall, Sewall Pond, the front-yard can-

---

writing and to the subject of place. While the North American continent is my hazy focus here, my notions of place are inextricable from all the places I've lived and been, and from accounts of other localities that have moved me. I know I have been lured to the subject of the local by its absence or rather by the absence of value attached to specific place in contemporary cultural life, in the "art world," and in postmodern paradoxes and paradigms. Other threads in this textual fabric are information gathered from decades of scholarship on the subject and the contributions of contemporary artists.

I've spent a lot of my life looking, as a writer on visual arts, but less of it looking around, or around *here.* I was drawn to this particular intersection of land, history, and culture—at once rotary and crossroad—from separate paths and directions, through my previous books on prehistory *(Overlay),* the crosscultural process *(Mixed Blessings),* and the historical representation of Native North Americans *(Partial Recall).* I've spent my adult life not as an art historian but as a witness to the absolutely contemporary—what's happening or should happen in progressive, mostly North American art right *now.* But in the last few years I've found myself mired in history: history of native/white contact in this hemisphere through national organizing to counter the dominant versions of 1492/1992; history of family since the deaths of my parents; and the local histories of places, especially those of Georgetown and a rural *Hispano* village in northern New Mexico I first saw eleven years ago. Combined with a long-standing commitment to grassroots politics and to an art that is part of lived experience, as well as to a feminist fascination with the processes of everyday life, the lure of the local has been a visceral pull for many years now.

Yet this book is also a personal irony characteristic of late twentieth-century life. When I began to write about the lure of the local, I was living in four different states, each of which had its own deep visual and emotional attraction. Although I've now narrowed it down to two, I will continue to be an emotional nomad and a radical (the root of which means "root"), playing the relatively conservative values of permanence and rootedness off against restlessness and a constructed "multicenteredness."

The notion of multicenteredness is an extension of the often-abused notion of multiculturalism. Most of us move around a lot, but when we move we often come into contact with those who haven't non . . . getting closer. Finally the car roars over the "buzzy bridge" between Arrowsic and Georgetown. Almost home.

Past Gene and Claire Reynolds' antler-bedecked garage and gravel pits, past the road to Robinhood, past what was once Allan and Agnes Wells's "Seguin Post" store (later a small pottery, now for sale), past the old Heald (or Heal) roadside cemetery belonging to painter Jason Schoener and his ecologically outspoken wife Virginia. . . .

---

moved around, or have come from different places. This should give us a better understanding of difference (though it will always be impossible to understand everything about difference). Each time we enter a new place, we become one of the ingredients of an existing hybridity, which is really what all "local places" consist of. By entering that hybrid, we change it; and in each situation we may play a different role. A white middle-class art type without much money will have a different affect and effect on a mostly Latino community with less money than on a mostly white upper-class suburb with more money. She/he remains the same person, and may remain an outsider in both cases, but reciprocal identity is inevitably altered by the place, by the relationship to the place itself and the people who are already there. Sometimes the place, or "nature," will provide nourishment that social life cannot.

Another personal paradox is the fact that despite my passion for the hybrid, my own family is terrifyingly monocultural, at least as far as I know. (I once did a performance that began, "I'm 100 per cent WASP and no longer ashamed of it.") My roots are in England, Ireland, Canada, and New England. Some of my ancestors were in Ohio and New York State. Two pairs of my great grandparents went west, but they spent only two generations wandering there, then kept wandering elsewhere. One pair of my grandparents immigrated from London's East End and Nova Scotia in the late nineteenth century. Nevertheless, my own *culture*—the habits, ethics, memories that form me—is decidedly New England on both sides. This despite the fact that I was born in New York City, raised in New York, New Orleans, and Charlottesville, Virginia, studied in Massachusetts, France, and New York, lived part-time in Boulder, Colorado, and sojourned in Mexico, Spain, Italy, and England. As a nomad with a serially monogamous passion for place, I often wonder if this inconsistency constitutes hopeless fragmentation or hopeful integration.

ANALYSIS

1. What does Lippard mean by the key phrase "lure of the local"? How does it help her play off the "conservative values of permanence" and the "restlessness . . . of multicenteredness"?

2. What mileage does Lippard get by speaking of "multicenteredness" rather than "multicultural"? Why do you think Lippard characterizes the latter term as an "often-abused notion"?

3. What does Lippard mean by suggesting that all "local places" are in reality forms of "an existing hybridity"? By saying that individuals change that hybridity by entering it? How do Lippard's examples make clear what she is talking about?

4. How does Lippard engage the reader by raising the question of whether her "inconsistency constitutes hopeless fragmentation or hopeful integration"? As you read Lippard's excerpts, what strikes you most—a sense of "fragmentation" or "integration"?

WRITING POSSIBILITIES

1. In your own native locale (or one of them, if there are more than one), how have the values of the local and the national played off against one another? What for you is the "lure of the local"? Or do you find yourself saying the opposite, that you don't want to have anything more to do with the "local"?

2. Speaking of "multicenteredness," Lippard explains that "when we move . . . we come in contact with those who haven't moved" and this in turn, she suggests, "should give us a better understanding of difference." As you have moved from place to place, have you come to a "better understanding of difference"?

3. Can you verify from your own experience Lippard's idea that "each time we enter a new place . . . we change it . . . and . . . may play a different role"?

4. Can you duplicate from your experience the kind of examples Lippard supplies—e.g., that a "white middle-class type" will have a different "affect and effect" on a Latino suburb vs. on a white "upper-class suburb"? Would you agree or not with Lippard's generalizations here? What reasons would you offer in either case?

5. Lippard says her own family was "terrifyingly monocultural"? Can you characterize your own family's cultural heritage in this way? Or is it the opposite? What details, examples and illustrations might convey the point to an audience of strangers?

6. Try your hand at writing an essay from both above the line-rule and below it. You can do this all at once, adopting, for example, a personal approach above the line and an objective approach below. Or, you might take an earlier essay on one side of a vertical line-rule and write a later essay from a different point of view on the other side. (Computer work makes the importing of an earlier text, plus columnization, an easy task.)

3

THEORETICAL INTERLUDE: PREJUDICE AND DISCRIMINATION

The personal essays of Chapters 1 and 2 have already touched on the role of prejudice and discrimination in the lives of individual writers. But what helps us account for these phenomena? One way to look at the problem is by first reading William Finnegan's "The Unwanted" (pages 121–135), a fascinating journalistic account of "Skinheads" and "Sharps" in the Antelope Valley Section of Los Angeles (Skinheads, imported from Great Britain, are the racists, Sharps are the home-grown antiracists).

Finnegan grew up not far from Antelope Valley not long before the youths he views with both sympathy and puzzlement: Mindy Turner, who while offering a principled rejection of racism admits that she loves Adolf Hitler and Charles Manson; Tim Malone, who says "Now ain't nothing I hate more than a wigger," and Chris Runge of the Nazi Low Riders who declares "[W]hite supremacism just comes from seeing what's happening in society." . . . "We're going down."

Finnegan has his own journalistically informal explanations for such racist attitudes and the killing that resulted from them—downward economic pressures, ignorance, and miseducation in the schools, cartoonish media, inept and frazzled parents, demographic changes (as blacks and Latinos flood into the formerly white Valley) and, perhaps especially, a longing for "identification" in an area changing so fast that kids can't get their bearings straight. (Better for "Nazi Mindy" to identify with psychotic killer Charles Manson than with wishy-washy liberals: at least, says Mindy, "Manson speaks his mind!")

In a more formal vein, S. Dale McLemore summarizes the role of social, psychological, and cultural theories of prejudice (beliefs) and discrimination (actions); in the chart on page 137, of his *Racial and Ethnic Relations in America* McLemore provides a not-to-be ignored visual demonstration of the psychologist Gordon Allport's point that "all" theories of prejudice and discrimination are needed to explain the beliefs and behaviors that Finnegan's Skinheads exhibit. "Key Ideas" (page 137) summarizes theories of prejudice but emphasizes the role of group identity, group gains, and situational pressures in fomenting prejudice, discrimination, and racism (the most virulent form of prejudice and discrimination.)

The other selections in this chapter break down into two basic views of prejudice, discrimination, and racism—those that stress individual causes and those that emphasize societal. For the former, there are essays by Shelby Steele and Roger Pilon (see also Justice Thomas, in Chapter 5, and Doug Bandow in Chapter 8). This viewpoint maintains that prejudice and discrimination are individual matters and hence, given the elimination of state-sponsored segregation (laws mandating separate watercoolers for "whites" and "colored" for example), no further government action is required. Individuals need only do the voluntary and moral thing. (Bandow is especially good on this, see Chapter 8) and nothing else in the way of governmental action should be required.

Countering the individual-causation view is the argument that sociocultural forces acting through the family, education (or miseducation) and media foster stereotyping and often-virulent beliefs about the superiority or inferiority of groups other than one's own. Also, according to some scholars, organizational and structural discrimination persist and requires various forms of social intervention—not individual, voluntary or "moral" action—up to and including "affirmative action" by government, if such syndromes are to be eradicated. This is the argument of: S. Dale McLemore on group identity and group gains, sociologists Michael Omi and Howard Winant on "racial formations," psychologist Beverly Tatum on racism and identity, Native American filmmaker Sherman Alexie, and Korean American journalist Elaine Kim on media stereotyping.

Although S. Dale McLemore (echoing Allport) does say that "all" theories of prejudice and discrimination are needed, he does ultimately award the prize to "sociocultural" theories: family, education, and media are the primary forces that shape our beliefs, stereotypes, and assumptions about other groups, peoples, and nations. Other writers differ, however—as you may yourself may—and insist that it's not society so much that shapes individuals as individuals who (for better or worse) shape society. You will want to consider this conflicting set of views as you read the following individual essays, testing them against such accounts as Finnegan's "The Unwanted" and your own experience of prejudice, discrimination, and racism.

William Finnegan

The obvious question Finnegan's essay poses is: Why do these intelligent kids from a fairly affluent suburb of Los Angeles (and even from liberal, well-educated anthropologist parents!) become racists and skinheads? Why the violence of their behavior or of people they dote on (Mindy Turner and a man she says she loves even though he's in prison for killing two blacks in South Carolina)? Do these young people represent something at large in the culture or simply disturbances peculiar and restricted to the special climate of Southern California? Finnegan has some tentative answers to these questions. You may have others.

THE UNWANTED

In a Los Angeles suburb where schools and parents faltered, the American Dream was replaced by drugs, neo-Nazism, and despair. The hardest hit were Mindy Turner and her friends.

Film companies used to come to the Antelope Valley, in northern Los Angeles County, to shoot high-desert scenes. It was empty country, a good backdrop for Westerns. Now they come when they need to burn down or blow up a housing tract. In 1992, for the fiery climax of "Lethal Weapon 3," Warner Bros. used a development called the Legends, at Avenue J and Thirtieth Street West, in the city of Lancaster. The Legends had become available after its financing failed, leaving unfinished forty-eight large, Spanish-style homes, each named after a legendary American (Babe Ruth, Marilyn Monroe). Mel Gibson and Danny Glover went on a memorable rampage through the tract. When I drove through its curving streets last year, I found a wasteland (tumbleweeds, shopping carts, graffiti-covered sofas) surrounded by a high brown wall.

The transformation of the Antelope Valley from rural desert into modern suburbia—with neighborhoods, literally, to burn—was very sudden, a historical jump cut. In 1980, the combined population of Lancaster and Palmdale, the Valley's two main cities, was sixty thousand. By 1994, their combined population was two hundred and twenty-two thousand, and today estimates of the Valley's total population range as high as four hundred thousand. This hyper-expansion was first sparked by housing prices in Los Angeles and its nearer suburbs, which soared during the nineteen-eighties, and by white flight from an increasingly Latino and Asian city. The Antelope Valley had been considered too remote for commuters, but the completion of the Antelope Valley Freeway, snaking over the San Gabriel Mountains, helped change that. In the Antelope Valley, one could buy for two hundred thousand dollars a new house that might cost four hundred thousand in the San Fernando Valley. What was more, the air was cleaner and the streets were safer. The commute to jobs in the city was longer—an hour longer, at least, each way—but that was the trade-off. And so it was that the desert brought forth swimming pools and convenience stores beyond number, and wide empty streets as far as the eye could see.

Then, in 1990, the Southern California economy, staggered by cutbacks in the aerospace and defense industries, fell into a deep recession. Los Angeles County alone lost more than half a million jobs, and property values throughout the region collapsed. In the Antelope Valley, abandoned housing tracts began to dot the subdivided desert. Boarded-up shopping centers and bankrupt school districts followed, along with a wave of personal financial disasters so severe that *USA Today* dubbed Palmdale "the foreclosure capital of California."

And yet the Antelope Valley's population has continued to grow. Between 1990 and 1994, Palmdale was the second-fastest-growing city in the United States, Lancaster the sixth-fastest. As a rule, the Valley's newest residents are poorer and darker than their predecessors, live in more crowded lodgings, and are more likely to rent. Still, the Valley remains, in a county where whites are a minority, overwhelmingly white (sixty-eight per cent), homeowning, and politically dominated by conservative Republicans of the pro-growth, antitax stripe. And the reasons most people give for moving out from the city—less crime, less smog, cheaper housing—have not changed. The Valley remains particularly attractive to families with children. Indeed, it has been called "the last great breeding ground of Southern California."

For anyone who has spent time there lately, this is a scary thought—if only because growing up these days in the Antelope Valley seems to be, for many kids, a pretty harrowing, dispiriting affair. This may be true today of growing up in America generally, but the Valley's supersonic growth has led to overcrowded, often chaotic schools; according to the high-school district's superintendent, nearly forty-five per cent of the entering students do not finish with their class. The teen-pregnancy rate is also alarmingly high. Juvenile crime is a major problem, usually attributed to "unsupervised children"—to, that is, the huge number of kids whose parents can't afford after-school care and often don't return from their epic commutes until long after dark. With neighborhoods devoid of adults from early morning to night, the most popular youth crime is, naturally, burglary. A sheriff's-department spokesman in Lancaster estimated that fully half the Valley's children are unsupervised after school. He also said that there are now, not coincidentally, more than two hundred youth gangs represented in the Valley.

I grew up, a generation ago, in Woodland Hills, then an outer suburb of L.A., and when I started spending time with teen-agers in the Antelope Valley I figured I had a head start on understanding their world. As it turned out, my youth might as well have been spent in Kathmandu for all the clues it gave me in this new realm. There was a street war raging in Lancaster between a white-supremacist skinhead gang known as the Nazi Low Riders and a rival gang of antiracist skinheads who called themselves Sharps. This obscure, semi-doctrinal conflict fascinated me long before it escalated to homicide, as it eventually did. And yet no adult, I discovered, could shed any real light on it. I needed a native guide, and I found one in Mindy Turner, who, at seventeen, was already well embarked on the kind of casually terrifying existence I was starting to regard as common.

She was living with her mother, her younger brother, and an older half brother in a four-bedroom white stucco ranch-style house in Lancaster. Her mother, Debbie, worked behind the counter at Thrifty Drugs; she had bought the house with the settlement she got after her husband, a crane operator, was electrocuted on the job in 1989, when Mindy was in elementary school. Mindy recalled, "They came to get me at school and said, 'Your dad's gone to be with your dog and your grandpa in Heaven.' I've never gotten over it. Whenever I get sad, I start thinking about it and just cry."

Debbie remembered Mindy being deeply troubled by the idea that her dad had never been baptized, and thought that that was probably why Mindy later became a Mormon—because she wanted to be baptized herself. Actually, before Mindy became a Mormon she had wanted to become Jewish. But that had turned out to be too much work. Becoming a Mormon was relatively easy. All this was before Mindy got addicted to crystal methamphetamine and became a Nazi, in the ninth grade.

Mindy and her mother shared blond good looks, but Debbie was hearty and outgoing, while Mindy was pale, fashionably thin, moody, intense. Her manner oscillated with unnerving speed—from jaded worldliness to girlish enthusiasm, from precocious grace to gawkiness, from thuggish cynicism to tender vulnerability. She spoke in quick, fluid bursts, as if she had to express each thought before she changed her mind.

In her mother's day, Mindy's looks might have made her a homecoming queen. But Mindy stopped going to school while she was in the tenth grade. "I'm not a people person," she told me. "I didn't like all the little gossip circles that went on there."

Mindy had always been a good student, earning B's, but had slipped academically in junior high (as a disturbingly high number of American girls do). In the seventh and eighth grades, she became first a "hesher"—into heavy-metal music and smoking marijuana—

and then a "hippie," into reggae and smoking marijuana. She also became sexually active. Her lovers were mostly older; some were much older. "I was kind of looking for a father," she told me.

Mindy's Nazi period had various sources. Spike Lee had helped get her into it, she said. She and a friend had gone to see "Malcolm X." They found they were the only whites in the audience, and a black guy had asked them sarcastically if they were in the right theatre. "That's why I hate Spike Lee," she told me. "Because he's a racist. And that's when I started thinking, If the black kids can wear 'X' caps, and Malcolm is calling us all 'white devils,' what's wrong with being down with white power?"

Her real political inspiration, though, was methamphetamine, which is also known as crank, crystal, ice, or simply speed. The leading illegal drug in the Valley, methamphetamine is a powerful addictive stimulant whose longtime consumers tend to suffer from paranoia, depression, hallucinations, and violent rages. The Nazi Low Riders were one of Mindy's speed connections. "They're all tweakers," she told me. (Tweakers are speed addicts.) "Speed is just so cheap here. And it makes you feel so powerful, so alert."

The N.L.R.s' hangout was the Malone household, in a run-down neighborhood in downtown Lancaster. Andrea Malone, a single parent, had three teen-age boys, all white-supremacist skinheads, and she worked long hours, giving the kids the run of the house. Mindy, who had grown bored with Mormonism, became a regular there, snorting speed, smoking dope, and becoming fast friends with the N.L.R.s. They called her a "skin bitch," but she refused to shave her head. "My dad always said he loved my long blond hair, so I wouldn't cut it off," she told me. She and the other N.L.R. girls ("They called us Property of the N.L.R.s, not members. It's this weird thing") fought with girls from rival gangs, including Sharps. But Mindy claimed she'd never taken part in random attacks on black people—something that N.L.R.s specialized in. "I just used to sit in the car and watch, while they'd get out and be, like 'Go back to Africa, nigger,' and beat people up."

At first, Mindy's mother had no idea what was going on. "I talked to Mrs. Malone on the phone a few times," Debbie told me. "She seemed really nice. I used to drive Mindy over there, and the Malone kids and some of the others used to come over here. I knew they were prejudiced, but as long as they acted civilized they were welcome. I even took them roller-skating."

The N.L.R.s were into tattoos: swastikas, skulls, Iron Crosses, lightning bolts—though lightning bolts were permitted to be worn only by those who had killed a black person. Mindy got a big swastika on one hip. ("My mom got really mad when she saw it.") Her skinhead friends were also into guns. In early 1995, one of her boyfriends, Jaxon Stines, drove with a group of N.L.R.s by the house of another boy whom Mindy had been seeing, and fired shots through a bedroom window, aiming for the other boy's bed. No one was hurt, but Mindy was picked up by the police for questioning, and Jaxon pleaded guilty to attempted murder.

Debbie was by then deeply alarmed about the company her daughter was keeping. Mindy was severely strung out—a full-tilt tweaker, with a daily habit. She had lost a lot of weight. She rarely slept. Finally, she became so dehydrated that she had to be hospitalized.

While she detoxed, with her mother keeping her skinhead friends away, Mindy seemed to snap out of her gang-girl trance. "I just realized I didn't hate black people," she told me. "Also, I'm totally infatuated with Alicia Silverstone, and she's Jewish. I've seen 'Clueless' like eleven times. So how could I be a Nazi?"

But the N.L.R.s did not take apostasy lightly. "They started calling my house, saying they were going to kick my ass. They started driving by here, throwing bottles at the house." Two N.L.R. girls, Heather Michaels and Angela Jackson, were particularly incensed. "Angela said she was coming over here to kill me. I was scared, but I told her, 'Fine, come over, whatever.' But she never came. Heather, especially, is really, really mad at me. They all say I'm a race traitor."

Debbie Turner took measures. She had an electronic security system installed around the house. "It got really bad after Jaxon went to jail," she told me. "They started coming by here. I was afraid they were going to shoot at the house. It was very scary." Debbie was also paying for a series of painful, expensive laser procedures to remove Mindy's swastika tattoo. The final cost for erasing the tattoo would come to four thousand dollars.

And that was how Debbie and I talked about Mindy's tour with the N.L.R.s during my first visits to the Turners' house—as a nasty accident whose scars were now being, not without cost, erased. Mindy was even back in school, through an independent-study program.

At the same time, we all knew that things were more complicated. For one thing, Jaxon had been released, after just six months in jail, and he and Mindy were seeing each other again. "Me and Jaxon have been through so much together," she told me. For example, a few weeks after her seventeenth birthday, she had had an abortion. "I wanted to keep it," Mindy said. "Because I knew that if Jaxon and I ever broke up I would still have some communication with him, because we would have a kid together. But then we decided we just weren't mentally ready for it. We fight all the time. And I was afraid that if we had a kid and Jaxon stayed friends with those people the kid would be brought up around all that hate."

Jaxon's gang status was actually ambiguous. He hung out with the N.L.R.s, and they considered him one of them, but he didn't publicly "claim" N.L.R. In any event, his association with the N.L.R.s extended no automatic protection to Mindy. She had therefore turned to the antiracist Sharps, her erstwhile enemies, for protection. The Sharps, however, were in no particular hurry to help her—leaving her in an even more vulnerable position.

She and Jaxon did indeed fight all the time, about almost anything. Raves, for example. Mindy indicated a poster on the wall in her bedroom, advertising something called the Insomniac Rave. "That was so great," she said. "It was the first real rave I went to. Dang! It was in Hollywood. Raves are like big parties, with all different races dancing. I took Ecstasy at the Insomniac Rave, and I danced all night." She sighed. "Jaxon can't stand it that I go to raves," she said. "He says I don't act white. But what is acting white? Me and him have been getting drunk almost every night lately, and I ask him, 'What do you think black people do that's so different from whites? They just sit around getting drunk and listening to music. Drive around in cars. Just like us.' "

Kicking around teen-age Lancaster, I sometimes felt as if I had fallen in with a thousand little cultural commissars, young suburban ideologues whose darkest pronouncement on another kid—a kid deviating from, say, the hard-core-punk-anarchist line on some band or arcane point of dress—was, inevitably, "He's confused."

Mindy's own "beliefs," as she called them, were eclectic. Her brave and principled rejection of racism, even her devotion to Alicia Silverstone, did not mean she had embraced enlightened liberalism in all matters. She still had a soft spot for Adolf Hitler—she claimed she was the only N.L.R. to actually study "Mein Kampf"—and her all-time-favorite "leader" was still Charles Manson. "My mom thinks I'm sick, but I think he's cute," she told me. "In a weird, gross way, I think he's attractive. He has the real fuck-you blood. He acts as his own lawyer. He talks for himself. I've read some of 'Helter Skelter.' I wouldn't, like, buy a poster of him and put it up. My mom wouldn't let me do it if I tried. But I don't think it would fit my room, anyway, with all my nice John Lennon and Beatles stuff."

The walls in Mindy's room were indeed adorned with Beatles posters. Her father, she said, had been a big John Lennon fan. But she also loved Trent Reznor, of Nine Inch Nails, whose best-known lyric was "I wanna fuck you like an animal!" I asked about a framed photograph, set next to her bed, of a shirtless, tattooed young man. The picture was obviously taken in prison.

"That's Madness," she said. "He's twenty-three. He says he's in love with me, but he knows I can't get over Jaxon. He's in for armed robbery. I didn't know him too well before he went to jail, but then we started writing letters. He's S.F.V. Peckerwood."

The Peckerwoods are a white gang, known mainly for mindless violence and methamphetamine dealing. They're big in the Antelope Valley but, some say, they're bigger in the San Fernando Valley, or S.F.V. They're biggest of all in prison. "Madness has his beliefs," Mindy said. "He believes whites are better than blacks. But he knows I don't think like that, so we don't talk about it."

Mindy was by no means the only girl I had met in the Valley who had a prisoner boyfriend. I asked her what it was about guys in jail.

"It's sick, I guess," she said. "But I just find it really attractive. I guess it means they're capable of doing something really spontaneous, without regard for the consequences."

"Like shooting somebody."

"Yeah. They're adventurous. And they're tough, usually. There's nothing else to do in there but work out."

Mindy invited me to go with her and some friends to a rave in Hollywood a few days later. "Maybe Darius can come, too," she said. Darius was Darius Houston, one of the Sharps to whom Mindy had turned for protection. Darius is half black, half white, and was probably the N.L.R.s' least favorite skinhead. "I don't think Darius really likes me," Mindy said. "Because when I hung out with the boneheads"—this is a generic term for racist skinheads—"I used to call him a nigger. All the Sharps have good reason to hate me."

I asked Mindy if she might be hoping to become a Sharp herself.

She shook her head, and said, "Most people here say, 'Mindy Turner? Oh, you mean Nazi Mindy.' So I don't want to start being Sharp Mindy. I want to be just Mindy. If somebody asks me what I am now, I just tell them I'm Free Unity. That's not a gang. It's just what I believe."

"Sharp" stands for "skinheads against racial prejudice." It is not, as I first thought, a local Antelope Valley sect. Skinheads claim Sharp throughout the United States, in Europe, and even, reportedly, in Japan. There is no formal organization—just an antiracist ideology, a street-fighting tradition, and a few widely recognized logos, usually worn on jacket patches. Sharp's raison d'être is its evil twin, the better-known white-supremacist and neo-Nazi skinhead movement.

All the Antelope Valley Sharps, I found, were amateur social historians, determined to rescue the skinhead movement—or simply "skinhead," as they call it—from disrepute. In their version, which seemed broadly accurate, the original skinheads emerged in England in the mid-sixties out of other youth cultures—notably the "hard mods" and the Rude Boys, stylish Jamaicans who wore porkpie hats and listened to reggae and ska. Skinheads were clean-cut, working-class, nonracist ("two-tone"), and tough. They loathed hippies, for reasons of both class and hygiene, loved soccer and beer, fighting and ska, scooters and Fred Perry tennis shirts. For a detailed history of skinhead, the Antelope Valley Sharps all urged on me a book, published in 1991, in Scotland, called "Spirit of '69: A Skinhead Bible."

By the seventies, the movement had been hijacked, according to the Sharps, by the anti-immigrant National Front in England. And it was the second wave of British skinhead that crossed over to the United States, in the late seventies, as part of the great punk-rock cultural exchange; by then neo-Nazism and white supremacism were definitely in the mix, and a host of unholy alliances have since been formed between racist skinheads and old-line extremist organizations like the Aryan Nations, White Aryan Resistance, the Church of the Creator, and the Ku Klux Klan. After a decade of hate crimes and racist violence, white-power skinheads have become increasingly familiar figures in the American social landscape, particularly among teen-agers, who tend to know much more about them and their apocalyptic views than adults do.

"The boneheads are looking forward to a race war."

"They're all on some harsh drug."

"Somebody's got to stand up to these guys," Darius Houston said.

Six or seven Sharps were sitting around Jacob Kroeger's mother's house. Jacob, a sardonic eighteen-year-old, still had his hair, but he was about to shave it off and become a full-fledged Sharp—a "fresh cut." His mother was often away with a boyfriend, leaving the house— a modest ranch-style bungalow in a seedy older tract—to become, at least for a while, the Sharps' main hangout. They were a picturesque lot, in boots and braces, extra-short ('flooded") jeans, and Andy Capp-type "snap caps." But the mood that evening was rather grim and besieged. It seemed that a girl from the N.L.R.s had called Christina Fava, Darius's girlfriend, who is white, a "nigger lover" in a hallway at Antelope Valley High School. A black student named Todd Jordan had become involved on Christina's side, and the next day a half-dozen N.L.R.s had jumped Todd on a deserted athletic field, stabbing him five times with a screwdriver. Todd was now in the hospital. Christina, for her part, was transferring to a new school.

Somehow, I said, being a Sharp seemed to mean, more than anything else, a lot of fighting with white-power skinheads.

I was wrong, I was assured.

"It's the music, the fashions, the friendships, the whole life style."

"It's like a big fuckin' family."

"Everybody's got everybody else's back."

"It's all about working class."

This curious, almost un-American class consciousness among the Antelope Valley Sharps turned out, upon examination, to be a very American miscellany. The kids themselves came from a wide range of backgrounds—everything from two-parent middle-class families to drug-addled welfare mothers who had dumped them on the streets as adolescents. For some, "working class" meant simply having a job—any job—as opposed to being a "bum." For others, it was synonymous with "blue collar," and it distinguished them from richer kids, who might decide to be skinheads and buy all the gear but weren't really streetwise and so might just have to be relieved of their new twelve-hole Doc Martens.

There was, in fact, much more to the Sharps than rumbling with the boneheads. For Darius, in particular, Sharp was a godsend. An orphan since his mother died, when he was thirteen, he had been a skateboarder and punk rocker before discovering skinhead. As a half-black kid in a largely white town, being reared by various white relatives, he had always been something of an outsider. Skinhead, as he understood it, was a complete, ready-made aesthetic and way of life. Darius identified, he told me, with its underground energy and its music—he was soon playing bass in a multiracial ska band called the Leisures. Because the idea of a black skinhead drove neo-Nazi skinheads wild, Darius had been fighting on a regular basis for years. He was a skilled fighter, but the backup that the other Sharps provided was still, for Darius, a lifesaver. Going to school had become too dangerous, so he was on independent study. After graduating, he said, he planned to join the Navy and become a medical technician. (Christina, for one, didn't think he was serious.) He was eighteen, beefy, soft-spoken, watchful, with skin the color of light mahogany. When we met, he was homeless and was sleeping on a couch in Jacob's mother's house.

In every gang, the crucial question about any member is "How down is he?" Among the Sharps, one of the most indisputably down was Johnny Suttle. Twenty years old, half Mexican and half Anglo, he was diminutive but superaggressive. He worked graveyard shifts at a Taco Bell, took classes at the local community college, and, I found, had a great deal to say about skinhead. Skinhead was about loyalty—to your class, home town, soccer team, and nationality, according to Johnny. Thus, if a Japanese or a Chinese skinhead decided to beat up a foreigner, it was O.K. "Because they're just defending their country, and that's good," he said. "The thing is, America is not a white man's country, never mind what the boneheads say. It's a melting pot. And we're about defending that."

Johnny always seemed ready to weigh the moral dimensions of violence. I once heard him deliberate one of the timeless questions: Was it ethically permissible to drop bonehead chicks before taking on the boneheads? The answer, ultimately, was yes. While it was not right to hit females, bonehead chicks were simply too dangerous to leave standing while you fought their boyfriends. They would probably stick a knife in your back. Ergo, they had to be dropped at the outset. Q.E.D.

The Nazi Low Riders, while dedicated skinheads, were not skinhead-history buffs. They were, however, keen on Nazi history. "We believe in Hitler's ways," Tim Malone, a leading member, told me. "But that don't mean we worship him. He was smart, but he was a homosexual. I think what he did with the Jews was right, mainly. They was coming into Germany, buying up the businesses, treating the Germans like slaves."

Chris Runge, another N.L.R., who explained to me that Hitler had actually been working with the Vatican, seemed to be the theorist of the Lancaster clique. He was nineteen, hairless, blue-eyed, pale-skinned, with a worried seriousness that was occasionally interrupted by a big, goofy smile. "I'm basically what you call a political Nazi," he said. "A lot of these Nazis out here are unorganized. They're mostly street skins, doing the dirty work. I want to start getting them organized. Democracy doesn't work. As you can see right now, it's falling apart. But Nazism is about a society with no upper class, no lower class. We'd have equality. We wouldn't have homelessness—because we keep the factories going and everybody has a place. With a Nazi government, we'd just take out all the unwanted and start over again—even whites, if they're doing the same thing as the niggers are." Chris gave me one of his big, blue-eyed smiles.

He grew serious again. "White supremacism just comes from seeing what's happening in society," he said. "We're going down." Though Chris's mother was, by all accounts, a serious tweaker, his grandfather, he said, was an executive with the Xerox Corporation—a point of reference, perhaps, for his bitter assessment. Chris himself had dropped out of school in the tenth grade and had been convicted for participating in the same drive-by shooting that sent Jaxon Stines, who was his best friend, to jail. And Chris had "found the Lord" in his cell, he said—an experience that may have softened some of his judgments. Of Mindy, for instance, Chris merely said, "She's confused. She's young." This was notably gentler than the pronouncements of other N.L.R.s on the subject. Chris even showed some self-awareness when he talked about his life. He told me that his mother's ex-husband used to beat her so badly when he was drunk that she would come lie in bed with Chris in the hope that it would make him stop. It didn't. "And that's a lot of the hate I got inside me now," Chris said quietly.

Though I stopped by the Malones house many times, I never saw Andrea there. She worked in a plastics factory in Pasadena, more than an hour's drive away, and, according to Tim, she left the house at dawn and got home only late in the evening. When I first met Tim, who was seventeen, he had just spent two months in jail: he had been locked up as an accessory in the Todd Jordan stabbing, but had been released for lack of evidence. He was wiry and well built, with close-cropped dark hair and, tattooed on the back of his neck, an Iron Cross. He described himself as "more of the Gestapo Storm Trooper type than a political Nazi—the type that's ready to go to war over things. There's gonna be a race war around the year 2000."

Tim's father had been a Hell's Angel, he said, so, he told me, his Nazism "was kind of inherited." His dad drank, did speed, and abused his mother—that was why his parents broke up. The family had lived in a predominantly black neighborhood in Montclair, east of Los Angeles, where Tim, at the age of ten, joined a local Crips set for self-protection. He was the middle brother of three, and his joining a black gang did not please his brothers. "Both my brothers was punk rockers, into speed metal, and they used to beat me up, trying to teach me a lesson," he said. "I thank them for it now. You gotta stick with your own race. Now ain't nothing I hate more than a wigger"—white nigger.

Tim and his brothers, Jeff and Steve, became skinheads after moving to the Antelope Valley four years ago and meeting the local neo-Nazis. They were soon a warm little nest of vipers. "We're all family," Tim said. "Even the little kids. Trouble's son, who's only, like, nine months old, already knows how to *Sieg heil.*" Tim imitated an infant giving a Nazi salute, and laughed. (Trouble was the street name of Robert Jones, one of three N.L.R.s charged with firing into a parked car full of black people in Lancaster in 1995. He was recently sentenced to twelve years.)

Among the many kids who were usually around the Malones' house were some who could not have been more than ten. I wondered if their parents had any notion what kinds of things their children were seeing and hearing there. The attractions of the place as a hangout were not mysterious. It was like a child's idea of a pirates' den: scruffy and run by tattooed brigands. I even got the feeling sometimes that a rough, retrograde, neo-communal sort of social experiment was being conducted. A boy would be opening a can of beans to heat up on the stove. Someone would bellow, "Only bitches cook in this house!" The boy would drop the can, while onlookers guffawed. Angela Jackson, one of Mindy's tormentors, would tear herself away from the TV and finish opening the can, declaring herself "a skin bitch, a Featherwood." This giddy, Pleasure Island atmosphere darkened, I thought, after the feud with the Sharps produced its first dead youth. . . .

Jaxon [Stines] was right: his mother didn't agree with him. A political liberal with a degree in anthropology, she lived with her second husband and her two sons in a big, cathedral-ceilinged house in a gated community. "I don't know why Jaxon holds those racial views," she told me. "I keep hoping it's just a teen-age rebellion, and he'll grow out of it—that it's not how he *is*." Other parents I visited in the Antelope Valley seemed equally mystified by their kids' passionate "beliefs."

Schools failed to provide most parents and children with any common cultural ground. Sheldon Epstein, a high-school principal in Lancaster, who had a cheerleader daughter, told me, "My wife and I are big-time supporters of our daughter's school. But most of the kids are just not bonded with their schools, so for them that school-spirit piece is missing. It's the parents who have school spirit now, not the kids."

The fact was, however, that among the tens of thousands of parents who worked over the mountains, relatively few had the time or energy to involve themselves in their children's schools (or any other community activity). And then there were all those too consumed by their own troubles even to rear their children. I found, that is, a startling number of kids in the Valley being reared not by their parents but by their grandparents. Various explanations were offered for this phenomenon, the commonest being methamphetamine addiction among parents, and particularly mothers. The situation was starkly reminiscent of the better-known syndrome that has left so many African-American grandmothers rearing the children of their crack-addled daughters in the nation's inner cities. In the Antelope Valley, it was white families falling into poverty who were being hit hardest by speed.

Between 1970 and 1995, the poverty rate for children and adolescents in California more than doubled—it is now twenty-eight per cent. And just as crime rates tend to track closely with poverty rates, vast amounts of the state's public spending have been diverted during this period to law enforcement and the penal system. The California prison budget in 1975 was two hundred million dollars. By the year 2000, it will approach five billion dollars. The money for all these jails and prisons has come more or less directly out of the state's higher-education budget. When I graduated from high school, in 1970, California had what was often described as the finest public-university system in the world. That was then. Between 1991 and 1994, the state's higher-education system lost two thousand professors and two hundred thousand students to budget cuts. Meanwhile, University of California tuition in 1995 was, in constant dollars, nearly five times what it was thirty years before. The situation in the schools is no better. When I was in junior high, the state's public schools enjoyed the seventh-highest per-pupil spending in the country; by 1995, California's per-pupil spending ranked forty-seventh nationally.

Nancy Kelso, a middle-aged lawyer in Palmdale who has many juvenile clients, rejects the view, which she says is common among her peers and colleagues, that they grew up in a Golden Age, when children obeyed their parents and ordinary people felt safe and God was in his Heaven. "I remember the Red Scare," she told me. "I remember suffocating pressure to conform. I remember a lot of bad things." She also remembers, however, a radically different opportunity structure. "When I graduated from high school, in 1962, it was like a deal—a contract—between the adults and me," she said. "All I had to do was get a B average and halfway behave myself and I was guaranteed a free education at a top public university, like Berkeley. My four siblings and I all took advantage of it. Our dad was a five-dollar-an-hour nonunion machinist in Los Angeles. We all became productive, responsible citizens. I tell you, I would have a lot more anxiety about what was going to become of me if I were growing up now."

In 1996, Palmdale High School, out of a graduating class of about four hundred, sent exactly six students into the University of California system. Less than ten per cent of the class went on to any four-year college at all.

Listening to Nancy Kelso, I kept thinking of Chris Runge grumbling about "the unwanted." He and his friends look forward to a "Nazi government" whisking this surplus population from sight. Of course, he and his friends undoubtedly feel that they themselves are the real "unwanted." And they are not wrong. But one of the ironies of their predicament is that the withdrawal of resources from education and other social services is fundamentally racist—that is, it is primarily a withdrawal by older whites from the support of those aspects of public welfare, including public education, which seem to benefit a large number of nonwhites. And yet the collapse of educational opportunity caused by this withdrawal is suffered by all nonaffluent children and families. "Affirmative action" is merely the name that many whites give to their sense of disfranchisement.

Issues of race and opportunity are particularly loaded in the Antelope Valley. Esther Gillies, the director of a center for abused children in Lancaster, put it bluntly: "Black families who move to the Valley are often moving up. White families who move to the Valley couldn't make it down below." While I heard many whites complain about lower-class blacks and Latinos settling in the Valley, I often sensed that they were really more concerned about middle-class minority families. Todd Jordon's family lived in a grander house than any of the white-power kids who stabbed him did. I talked with black parents who pronounced themselves delighted with their new, racially integrated neighborhoods (the Valley has developed so fast that the insidious patterns of residential segregation have not taken root), but even they expressed wariness about staying on once their children reach high-school age. In the words of one well-educated black mother of three, "That's when the white-supremacist thing seems to kick in." . . .

So families flee the city for far-flung suburbs, but the evils they hope to escape—drugs, gangs, violent crime—flourish wherever they land.

Why? I kept recalling Mindy's grandmother's remark about how kids were being left to raise themselves. If most parents must work outside the home, the obvious institution to take up the caretaking slack is the school. There are American communities that have begun to reckon with this imperative, but they are a small minority and the Antelope Valley is decidely not among them. Beverley Louw's attempt at Lancaster High to replace the baroque array of "fragmented subcultures" that students tend to join with an old-fashioned, school-based culture was the exception. And her frustrations arose from more than just her students' academic deficits.

Everything is in such flux, which unsettles kids," she told me one afternoon in her office. "The *homelessness* among kids here is just enormous. It's invisible to outsiders, because they don't live on the streets, but they move from place to place, living with friends or relatives or whatever. And lack of supervision is the key, I believe, to most of their problems." Ms. Louw looked out a window onto a wind-blown parking lot, then went on. "I had a straight-A student commit suicide when I was principal of the continuation school. The kids said she did it on a dare. Her father came to the funeral in a yellow leather suit. I couldn't believe it. *A yellow leather suit.*"

Martha Wengert, a sociologist at Antelope Valley College, said, "This area has grown so fast that neighborhoods are not yet communities. Kids are left with this intense longing for identification." Gangs, race nationalism, and all manner of "beliefs" arose from this longing. I thought of Debbie Turner's inability to comprehend Mindy's enthusiasm for the likes of Charles Manson and Adolf Hitler. "The kids reach out to these historical figures," Dr. Wengert said. "But it's through TV, through comic books, through word-of-mouth. There are no books at home, no ideas, no sense of history." One thing the Valley's young people knew, however, Dr. Wengert said, was that the economic downturn of the nineteen-nineties was not cyclical, that the Cold War was over and the aerospace and defense jobs were not coming back.

ANALYSIS
---

1. Finnegan prefaces his essay (which originally appeared in the *New Yorker* magazine) with an account of economic and social change in the Antelope Valley, some 60 miles from Los Angeles. How does this account set the stage for the depiction of Skinhead racism as the essay develops?

2. What is the history of the Skinheads? The SHARPS? Who are the N.L.R.'s?

3. Mindy Turner is a central figure in Finnegan's account, because she seems to be a mixture of liberal and wildly ignorant, even racist,

attitudes. What indications are there as to Finnegan's own attitude towards her? How do you see her?

4. Chris Runge feels that 'whites are going down'? How does Finnegan's
analysis offer a different account of class, racial and demographic
change?

5. Jaxon Stines says he's no Nazi, that even some blacks and Mexicans
are "cool." But still, he tells Finnegan, "the majority . . . are just wel-
fare-mooching scumballs." Is this classic scapegoating? Jaxon's mother,
a liberal with a degree in anthropology, says she doesn't know why
her son holds such views. Why do you think he does? What does
Finnegan suggest here?

6. Why does Finnegan say the SHARP'S idea of "working-class" reveals
an almost "un-American consciousness"? What in fact is their idea of
"working-class," according to Finnegan? Is it your idea? Would you use
the term?

7. Finnegan's basic rhetorical approach is to report almost deadpan
whatever these youths say, only intervening occasionally to offer editorial comments on his own part. A good example would be Mindy
Turner's appreciation of Charles Manson (who murdered pregnant actress Sharon Tate and several companions in a bloody 1969 massacre)
and Chris Runge's history of the Nazi's. What advantages does such an
approach offer? Disadvantages? Look up any standard history of Nazi
Germany—e.g., Ian Kershaw's biography of Hitler or a book on the
Sharon Tate murders—and compare the account with either Turner's
or Runge's.

WRITING POSSIBILITIES

1. How might S. Dale McLemore's theories (below, pp. 138) of group identity, group gains, and situational sources of prejudice help us understand the Southern California youth Finnegan describes? Summarize
what for you might be the crucial aspects of any one of McLemore's discussions and then see to what extent you can connect those aspects
with the particulars of Finnegan's essay.

2. In the full book version of this essay *Cold New World* (1998), Finnegan
emphasizes a number of explanatory possibilities: class structure (he
cites Benjamin DeMott's "double truth," "that within our borders an
opportunity society and a caste society coexist," xv), "abdication of
parental roles and family obligations by adults who themselves never
quite grew up" (xvii), neglect by society of schools (kids know schools
"suck," diplomas are worthless, etc. xviii), a "shortage of historical understanding" (xviii), a "backlash . . . a society-wide . . . movement away
from the movement toward racial equality" xix (not just "racist fringe
movements"), "a social universe in which traditional categories are becoming ever more fluid" (xix), and a "mismatch" between personal experience and "mass media simulacra" (xxi). Which of these would be
your best explanation? Why?

3. Finnegan explains interest in Nazi history and Skinhead ideology by saying that it provided what in his college days represented an "analysis." Such groups, he writes,

> offer more than just companionship and structure—they also offer what was called in my student days an analysis. . . . Kids form and join groups . . . because these groups help explain to them their place in the larger scheme of things. That place often includes class and ethnicity, often very precisely defined. Nearly all of these niche-subculture are "prepolitical" . . . and very few place much emphasis on a critical reading of history. Still, they represent the means, the framework, through which a great many young Americans encounter the world. They connect private and public life. To the extent that young Americans have ever been interested in society as a whole, these groups' diverse, overdetermined interpretation of events have largely replaced traditional political understanding. (349)

4. In the essay, what kind of 'analyses' are presented? What makes them seem cogent and significant? Do you find in your own experience that one or another 'analysis' has helped you understand your place in the world? How does your own understanding of 'place' in this sense compare or contrast with that of your peers? Of your parents?

5. The Nazi Low Riders (Chris Runge) say that what Hitler did "with the Jews was right, they were coming into Germany, treating Germans like slaves." Read Gerda Lerner's account above (Ch. 2) or consult any recent book about the Nazi era and compare its account of the Holocaust and the place of Jews in Nazi Germany with Runge's.

6. Finnegan's portraits and interspersed 'analyses' offer obvious comparisons to material in the rest of this chapter, especially the excerpts from McLemore's *Race and Ethnic Relations in America.* Which of these seems most helpful to you in dealing with the youths of "The Unwanted"? Why?

S. Dale McLemore

Taken from his well-known textbook, Racial and Ethnic Relation in Americans *4th ed., McLemore's ingenious chart illustrates the contention that all theories of prejudice and discrimination need to be considered if we are to fully understand these phenomena (and the associated, aggravated, phenomenon of racism). After the chart you will find McLemore's summary of "Key Ideas" from the chapter on Prejudice and Discrimination, emphasizing group identity aspects—usually ignored— of prejudice and discrimination. These ideas run counter to analyses like those of Michael Omi and Howard Winant (pages 140–152) which emphasize the idea of racism and "racial formations" rather than (as with McLemore) group identity and group gains.*

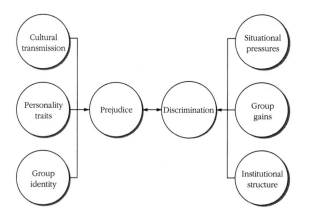

Major Direct and Indirect Causes of Prejudice and Discrimination (arrows indicate the presumed direction of causation)

Key Ideas
from Prejudice and Discrimination

1. Although prejudice (a negative attitude) is usually thought to precede and be the cause of discrimination (a negative action), discrimination may also precede prejudice and be a cause of it. Moreover, a person may be prejudiced but not discriminate and discriminate without with prejudiced.
2. Prejudice arises from several sources. Among the most important of these are:
a. The transmission of specific attitudes and beliefs from one generation to the next—Children learn their group's stereotypes of

different out-groups. They also learn which groups are to be admired and which should be held at a great social distance. In the United States, people from countries of the old immigration are socially least distant from the majority, while nonwhites are the most distant.

b. The effort to manage the personal frustrations and problems of life—People frequently exhibit an exaggerated, seemingly "irrational" hostility toward members of out-groups. Such prejudices appear to have more to do with people's inner tensions and conflicts than with the characteristics of the members of the hated group(s).

c. The sense of group identity, belongingness, and loyalty that people ordinarily develop toward their own group's members and culture—Pride in one's own group may easily shade into or stimulate prejudice toward others' groups.

3. Discrimination arises from several important sources, some of which do not directly involve prejudice:

a. The social pressures that are exerted to ensure people's conformity to the norms of their group—Even when people do not personally desire to ostracize or harm the members of an out-group, they may be expected to do so by the other members of their own group. Those who violate the in-group norms may themselves be ostracized by the in-group members.

b. The material and psychic gains that accompany social dominance—Whether or not it is owing to prejudice, discrimination confers advantages on at least some members of the dominant group. Dominant group members generally enjoy higher incomes, more desirable jobs, less unemployment, and more social deference than the members of subordinate groups.

c. The normal operations of the society's institutions—Equal opportunity and fair play within a given institutional sector (e.g., the economy) may not lead to equal results. The lingering effects of past discrimination or the existence of discrimination in a related institution (e.g., education) may lead to the disproportionate disqualification of the members of minority groups. The rules of organizations may automatically discriminate.

4. Prejudice and discrimination are related to one another in an incomplete and circular fashion. Discrimination may be reduced by attacks on prejudice, and prejudice may be reduced by attacks on discrimination; however, declines in prejudice are not necessarily translated into reductions in discrimination, and vice versa.

ANALYSIS

1. **Prejudice and Discrimination: "Key Ideas," 1, 3a, b, c.** McLemore's chart and discussion in "Key Ideas" tantalizingly suggests that "a person may be prejudiced but not discriminate and discriminate without being prejudiced." Can you see how either or both of these phenomena might be true? Explain.

2. **Prejudice: Cultural Transmission, "Key Ideas," 2a.** On McLemore's view, *stereotypes* operate to transmit cultural attitudes, especially those of the in-group about the out-group. How might this apply to the analyses of Finnegan, Tatum, or Kim in this chapter? What stereotypes do they report on in their discussions? What stereotypes are you familiar with as regards your own group? Some other group?

3. **Personality Theories: "Key Ideas," 2b.** In parts of his text not reprinted here, McLemore vindicates the familiar frustration-aggression theory as a source of prejudice and discrimination: i.e., when individuals are frustrated, they may take out their anger by aggressing against a convenient *scapegoat.* How might this theory apply to Jaxon Stines in Finnegan's "The Unwanted"?

4. **Group Identity: "Key Ideas," 2c.** According to McLemore, drawing boundaries around one's own group (and characterizing others as "out-groups") is a means of group self-definition and survival (though not all such boundary-drawing is legitimate). In what ways might such a theory help us understand ethnic neighborhoods (Mariana DeMarco Torgovnick's "White, Female, and Born in Bensonhurst" (see Chapter 1), Skinheads and Sharps ("The Unwanted," pages 121–134), and blacks in the cafeteria (Beverly Tatum's "Why Are All the Black Kids Sitting Together in the Cafeteria?" pages 154–164)?

5. **Discrimination: Situational Pressures, "Key Ideas," 3a.** As McLemore suggests, people sometimes discriminate and sometimes, surprisingly, they don't. Glen Loury's "Free at Last?" (Chapter 1) illustrates this idea aptly. In your own experience, are there moments when you did something you did not want to do? Or contrariwise?

6. **Group Gains, "Key Ideas," 3b.** Here is another aspect of discrimination which McLemore emphasizes and other theorists do not. How might this theory be applied to the economic pressures argument that Torgovnick makes about her neighborhood, in "White, Female, and Born in Bensonhurst"? If the "gains" argument is operating more so than prejudice per se, how might such fears be answered? Or, on the contrary, are such fears merely covers for prejudice and discrimination?

7. **Institutional Structure, "Key Ideas," 3c.** Read McLemore's summary of "Institutional Structure" in connection with the essays by Beverly Tatum (pages 154–164) and William Julius Wilson (Chapter 5): how do these essays amplify McLemore's overview? Do you have any reservations about the idea of institutional (or organizational) discrimination, either as presented by McLemore or by any of the writers immediately above? Have you had any experiences of your own that would validate some aspect of the institutional idea of discrimination (and not necessarily a racial one, at that)?

──────────────── **Writing Possibilities** ────────────────

1. Which of McLemore's theories (as summarized in the "Key Ideas" section) seem most pertinent to you in explaining the attitudes and behaviors of the youths in Finnegan's "The Unwanted"? Focus on one or
two individuals, cite relevant portions of Finnegan's characterizations
of them, and link Finnegan's discussions to your sense of McLemore's
analyses. Or try your hand at linking some situation you have been
faced with McLemore's Key Ideas discussions. (In both cases, the aim
is to exercise your thinking and intuitive sense of what McLemore is
pointing to—the summaries of key ideas is too brief to make concentrated use of them, so the more you exercise your wits and ingenuity
here, the better off you will be!)

Michael Omi and Howard Winant

*Omi and Winant's essay raises an important question: why abandon the
time-honored terms* prejudice *and* discrimination *in favor of such terms
as* racism *or* racial formation? *Actually, Omi and Winant don't abandon
the term* discrimination *but they do place it in a new context, arguing
that discrimination has been and remains so "pervasive," "cumulative"
and indeed even "permanent" in its effects that a new terminology is
needed:*

> Discriminatory actions by individuals and organizations [they
> say] are not only pervasive, occurring in every sector of soci-
> ety, but also cumulative with effects limited neither to the
> time nor the particular structural area in which they occur.
> This process of discrimination, therefore, extends across gen-
> erations, across organizations, and across social structures in
> self-reinforcing cycles, passing the disadvantages incurred by
> one generation in one area to future generations in many re-
> lated areas.

Furthermore, say Omi and Winant, racial formation *as a term
represents more adequately than* prejudice *or* discrimination *the fact
that those in power—whites in this country—seek to protect their
economic and political gains by creating a system of racial hierarchy in
which whites are at the top and other groups, in varying degrees, remain
on the bottom.*

Omi and Winant's preference for terms like racism *and* racial
formation *stands in contrast to the emphasis on* group *identity,
exemplified by S. Dale McLemore's summary of group identity theories
(page 138). In McLemore's view, prejudice, discrimination, and
interethnic strife generally are the distorted outcomes of the human*

need to find individual identity within the shelter of a group. That need in turn leads to distinctions between groups—"in-groups," for example ("our group," jocks, Gothics, etc.) and "out-groups" (as seen by the in-groups: nerds, geeks, wusses, and so on). Under situational pressures, so this theory goes, such group-thinking can become discriminatory or worse.

The contrast between the way Omi and Winant talk about the sources of discrimination and the way McLemore talks about it is in fact an illuminating one that involves historical and social analysis and the issue of rhetorical forcefulness. To what extent, we can ask, is group identity a "natural" part of human folkways (the term pioneered by the early anthropologist William Graham Sumner) and to what extent is it, rather, the all-pervasive impetus for domination politically and economically (as in Omi and Winant's view)?

Similarly, we can ask about the rhetorical force of these differing terminologies: which of them seems most persuasive and to which groups of people? Opinions on both the societal analysis and the rhetorical one will differ,and it is up to you to say which accords most with your own experience, knowledge, and sense of logic.

Racial Formations
from Racial Formation in the United States

In 1982–83, Susie Guillory Phipps unsuccessfully sued the Louisiana Bureau of Vital Records to change her racial classification from black to white. The descendant of an eighteenth-century white planter and a black slave, Phipps was designated "black" in her birth certificate in accordance with a 1970 state law which declared anyone with at least one-thirty-second "Negro blood" to be black. The legal battle raised intriguing questions about the concept of race, its meaning in contemporary society, and its use (and abuse) in public policy. Assistant Attorney General Ron Davis defended the law by pointing out that some type of racial classification was necessary to comply with federal record-keeping requirements and to facilitate programs for the prevention of genetic diseases. Phipps's attorney, Brian Begue, argued that the assignment of racial categories on birth certificates was unconstitutional and that the one-thirty-second designation was inaccurate. He called on a retired Tulane University professor who cited research indicating that most whites have one-twentieth "Negro" ancestry. In the end, Phipps lost. The court upheld a state law which quantified racial identity, and in so doing affirmed the legality of assigning individuals to specific racial groupings.[1]

The Phipps case illustrates the continuing dilemma of defining race and establishing its meaning in institutional life. Today, to assert that variations in human physiognomy are racially based is to enter a constant and intense debate. *Scientific* interpretations of race have not been alone in sparking heated controversy; *religious* perspectives have done so as well.[2] Most centrally, of course, race has been a matter of *political* contention. This has been particularly true in the United States, where the concept of race has varied enormously over time without ever leaving the center stage of U.S. history.

WHAT IS RACE?

Race consciousness, and its articulation in theories of race, is largely a modern phenomenon. When European explorers in the New World "discovered" people who looked different than themselves, these "natives" challenged then existing conceptions of the origins of the human species, and raised disturbing questions as to whether *all* could be considered in the same "family of man."[3] Religious debates flared over the attempt to reconcile the Bible with the existence of "racially distinct" people. Arguments took place over creation itself, as theories of polygenesis questioned whether God had made only one species of humanity ("monogenesis"). Europeans wondered if the natives of the New World were indeed human beings with redeemable souls. At stake were not only the prospects for conversion, but the types of treatment to be accorded them. The expropriation of property, the denial of political rights, the introduction of slavery and other forms of coercive labor, as well as outright extermination, all presupposed a worldview which distinguished Europeans—children of God, human beings, etc.—from "others." Such a worldview was needed to explain why some should be "free" and others enslaved, why some had rights to land and property while others did not. Race, and the interpretation of racial differences, was a central factor in that worldview.

In the colonial epoch science was no less a field of controversy than religion in attempts to comprehend the concept of race and its meaning. Spurred on by the classificatory scheme of living organisms devised by Linnaeus in *Systema Naturae,* many scholars in the eighteenth and nineteenth centuries dedicated themselves to the identification and ranking of variations in humankind. Race was thought of as a *biological* concept, yet its precise definition was the subject of debates which, as we have noted, continue to rage today. Despite efforts ranging from Dr. Samuel Morton's studies of cranial capacity[4] to contemporary attempts to base racial classification on shared gene pools,[5] the concept of race has defied biological definition. . . .

Attempts to discern the *scientific meaning* of race continue to the present day. Although most physical anthropologists and biologists have abandoned the quest for a scientific basis to determine racial categories, controversies have recently flared in the area of genetics and educational psychology. For instance, an essay by Arthur Jensen which argued that hereditary factors shape intelligence not only revived the "nature or nurture" controversy, but raised highly volatile questions about racial equality itself.[6] Clearly the attempt to establish a *biological* basis of race has not been swept into the dustbin of history, but is being resurrected in various scientific arenas. All such attempts seek to remove the concept of race from fundamental social, political, or economic determination. They suggest instead that the truth of race lies in the terrain of innate characteristics, of which skin color and other physical attributes provide only the most obvious, and in some respects most superficial, indicators.

RACE AS A SOCIAL CONCEPT

The social sciences have come to reject biologistic notions of race in favor of an approach which regards race as a *social* concept. Beginning in the eighteenth century, this trend has been slow and uneven, but its direction clear. In the nineteenth century Max Weber discounted biological explanations for racial conflict and instead highlighted the social and political factors which engendered such conflict.[7] The work of pioneering cultural anthropologist Franz Boas was crucial in refuting the scientific racism of the early twentieth century by rejecting the connection between race and culture, and the assumption of a continuum of "higher" and "lower" cultural groups. Within the contemporary social science literature, race is assumed to be a variable which is shaped by broader societal forces.

Race is indeed a pre-eminently *sociohistorical* concept. Racial categories and the meaning of race are given concrete expression by the specific social relations and historical context in which they are embedded. Racial meanings have varied tremendously over time and between different societies.

In the United States, the black/white color line has historically been rigidly defined and enforced. White is seen as a "pure" category. Any racial intermixture makes one "nonwhite." In the movie *Raintree County,* Elizabeth Taylor describes the worst of fates to befall whites as "havin' a little Negra blood in ya—just one little teeny drop and a person's all Negra."[8] This thinking flows from what Marvin Harris has characterized as the principle of *hypo-descent:*

> By what ingenious computation is the genetic tracery of a million years of evolution unraveled and each man [sic] assigned his proper social box? In the United States, the mechanism

employed is the rule of hypo-descent. This descent rule requires Americans to believe that anyone who is known to have had a Negro ancestor is a Negro. We admit nothing in between. . . . "Hypo-descent" means affiliation with the subordinate rather than the superordinate group in order to avoid the ambiguity of intermediate identity. . . . The rule of hypo-descent is, therefore, an invention, which we in the United States have made in order to keep biological facts from intruding into our collective racist fantasies.[9]

The Susie Guillory Phipps case merely represents the contemporary expression of this racial logic.

By contrast, a striking feature of race relations in the lowland areas of Latin America since the abolition of slavery has been the relative absence of sharply defined racial groupings. No such rigid descent rule characterizes racial identity in many Latin American societies. Brazil, for example, has historically had less rigid conceptions of race, and thus a variety of "intermediate" racial categories exist. Indeed, as Harris notes, "One of the most striking consequences of the Brazilian system of racial identification is that parents and children and even brothers and sisters are frequently accepted as representatives of quite opposite racial types."[10] Such a possibility is incomprehensible within the logic of racial categories in the U.S.

To suggest another example: the notion of "passing" takes on new meaning if we compare various American cultures' means of assigning racial identity. In the United States, individuals who are actually "black" by the logic of hypo-descent have attempted to skirt the discriminatory barriers imposed by law and custom by attempting to "pass" for white.[11] Ironically, these same individuals would not be able to pass for "black" in many Latin American societies.

Consideration of the term "black" illustrates the diversity of racial meanings which can be found among different societies and historically within a given society. In contemporary British politics the term "black" is used to refer to all nonwhites. Interestingly this designation has not arisen through the racist discourse of groups such as the National Front. Rather, in political and cultural movements, Asian as well as Afro-Caribbean youth are adopting the terms as an expression of self-identity.[12] The wide-ranging meanings of "black" illustrate the manner in which racial categories are shaped politically.[13]

The meaning of race is defined and contested throughout society, in both collective action and personal practice. In the process, racial categories themselves are formed, transformed, destroyed and reformed. We use the term *racial formation* to refer to the process by which social, economic and political forces determine the content and importance of racial categories, and by which they are in turn shaped by racial meanings. Crucial to this formulation is the treatment of race as a *central axis* of social relations which cannot be subsumed under or reduced to some broader category or conception.

Racial Ideology and Racial Identity

The seemingly obvious, "natural" and "common sense" qualities which the existing racial order exhibits themselves testify to the effectiveness of the racial formation process in constructing racial meanings and racial identities.

One of the first things we notice about people when we meet them (along with their sex) is their race. We utilize race to provide clues about *who* a person is. This fact is made painfully obvious when we encounter someone whom we cannot conveniently racially categorize—someone who is, for example, racially "mixed" or of an ethnic racial group with which we are not familiar. Such an encounter becomes a source of discomfort and momentarily a crisis of racial meaning. Without a racial identity, one is in danger of having no identity.

Our compass for navigating race relations depends on preconceived notions of what each specific racial group looks like. Comments such as, "Funny, you don't look black," betray an underlying image of what black should be. We also become disoriented when people do not act "black," "Latino," or indeed "white." The content of such stereotypes reveals a series of unsubstantiated beliefs about who these groups are and what "they" are like.[14]

In US society, then, a kind of "racial etiquette" exists, a set of interpretative codes and racial meanings which operate in the interactions of daily life. Rules shaped by our perception of race in a comprehensively racial society determine the "presentation of self,"[15] distinctions of status, and appropriate modes of conduct. "Etiquette" is not mere universal adherence to the dominant group's rules, but a more dynamic combination of these rules with the values and beliefs of subordinated groupings. This racial "subjection" is quintessentially ideological. Everybody learns some combination, some version, of the rules of racial classification, and of their own racial identity, often without obvious teaching or conscious inculcation. Race becomes "common sense"—a way of comprehending, explaining and acting in the world.

Racial beliefs operate as an "amateur biology," a way of explaining the variations in "human nature."[16] Differences in skin color and other obvious physical characteristics supposedly provide visible clues to differences lurking underneath. Temperament, sexuality, intelligence, athletic ability, aesthetic preferences and so on are presumed to be fixed and discernible from the palpable mark of race. Such diverse questions as our confidence and trust in others (for example, clerks or salespeople, media figures, neighbors), our sexual preferences and romantic images, our tastes in music, films, dance, or sports, and our very ways of talking, walking, eating and dreaming are ineluctably shaped by notions of race. Skin color "differences" are thought to explain perceived differences in intellectual, physical and artistic temperaments, and to justify distinct treatment of racially identified individuals and groups.

The continuing persistence of racial ideology suggests that these racial myths and stereotypes cannot be exposed as such in the popular imagination. They are, we think, too essential, too integral, to the maintenance of the U.S. social order. Of course, particular meanings, stereotypes and myths can change, but the presence of a *system* of racial meanings and stereotypes, of racial ideology, seems to be a permanent feature of U.S. culture.

Film and television, for example, have been notorious in disseminating images of racial minorities which establish for audiences what people from these groups look like, how they behave, and "who they are."[17] The power of the media lies not only in their ability to reflect the dominant racial ideology, but in their capacity to shape that ideology in the first place. D. W. Griffith's epic *Birth of a Nation,* a sympathetic treatment of the rise of the Ku Klux Klan during Reconstruction, helped to generate, consolidate and "nationalize" images of blacks which had been more disparate (more regionally specific, for example) prior to the film's appearance.[18] In U.S. television, the necessity to define characters in the briefest and most condensed manner has led to the perpetuation of racial caricatures, as racial stereotypes serve as shorthand for scriptwriters, directors and actors, in commercials, etc. Television's tendency to address the "lowest common denominator" in order to render programs "familiar" to an enormous and diverse audience leads it regularly to assign and reassign racial characteristics to particular groups, both minority and majority.

These and innumerable other examples show that we tend to view race as something fixed and immutable—something rooted in "nature." Thus we mask the historical construction of racial categories, the shifting meaning of race, and the crucial role of politics and ideology in shaping race relations. Races do not emerge full-blown. They are the results of diverse historical practices and are continually subject to challenge over their definition and meaning.

RACIALIZATION: THE HISTORICAL DEVELOPMENT OF RACE

In the United States, the racial category of "black" evolved with the consolidation of racial slavery. By the end of the seventeenth century, Africans whose specific identity was Ibo, Yoruba, Fulani, etc. were rendered "black" by an ideology of exploitation based on racial logic—the establishment and maintenance of a "color line." This of course did not occur overnight. A period of indentured servitude which was not rooted in racial logic preceded the consolidation of racial slavery. With slavery, however, a racially based understanding of society was set in motion which resulted in the shaping of a specific *racial* identity not only for the slaves but for the European settlers as well. Winthrop Jordan has observed: "From the initially common term *Christian,* at mid-century there was a marked shift toward the terms *English* and *free.* After about 1680, taking the colonies as a whole, a new term of self-identification appeared—*white.*"[19]

We employ the term *racialization* to signify the extension of racial meaning to a previously racially unclassified relationship, social practice or group. Racialization is an ideological process, an historically specific one. Racial ideology is constructed from pre-existing conceptual (or, if one prefers, "discursive") elements and emerges from the struggles of competing political projects and ideas seeking to articulate similar elements differently. An account of racialization processes that avoids the pitfalls of U.S. ethnic history[20] remains to be written.

Particularly during the nineteenth century, the category of "white" was subject to challenges brought about by the influx of diverse groups who were not of the same Anglo-Saxon stock as the founding immigrants. In the nineteenth century, political and ideological struggles emerged over the classification of Southern Europeans, the Irish and Jews, among other "non-white" categories.[21] Nativism was only effectively curbed by the institutionalization of a racial order that drew the color line *around,* rather than *within,* Europe.

By stopping short of racializing immigrants from Europe after the Civil War, and by subsequently allowing their assimilation, the American racial order was reconsolidated in the wake of the tremendous challenge placed before it by the abolition of racial slavery.[22] With the end of Reconstruction in 1877, an effective program for limiting the emergent class struggles of the later nineteenth century was forged: the definition of the working class *in racial terms*—as "white." This was not accomplished by any legislative decree or capitalist maneuvering to divide the working class, but rather by white workers themselves. Many of them were recent immigrants, who organized on racial lines as much as on traditionally defined class lines.[23] The Irish on the West Coast, for example, engaged in vicious anti-Chinese race-baiting and committed many pogrom-type assaults on Chinese in the course of consolidating the trade union movement in California.

Thus the very political organization of the working class was in important ways a racial project. The legacy of racial conflicts and arrangements shaped the definition of interests and in turn led to the consolidation of institutional patterns (e.g., segregated unions, dual labor markets, exclusionary legislation) which perpetuated the color line *within* the working class. Selig Perlman, whose study of the development of the labor movement is fairly sympathetic to this process, notes that:

> The political issue after 1877 was racial, not financial, and the weapon was not merely the ballot, but also "direct action"—violence. The anti-Chinese agitation in California, culminating as it did in the Exclusion Law passed by Congress in 1882, was doubtless the most important single factor in the history of American labor, for without it the entire country might have been overrun by Mongolian [sic] labor and *the labor movement might have become a conflict of races instead of one of classes.*[24]

More recent economic transformations in the US have also altered interpretations of racial identities and meanings. The automation of southern agriculture and the augmented labor demand of the postwar boom transformed blacks from a largely rural, impoverished labor force to a largely urban, working-class group by 1970.[25] When boom became bust and liberal welfare statism moved rightwards, the majority of blacks came to be seen, increasingly, as part of the "underclass," as state "dependents." Thus the particularly deleterious effects on blacks of global and national economic shifts (generally rising unemployment rates, changes in the employment structure away from reliance on labor intensive work, etc.) were explained once again in the late 1970s and 1980s (as they had been in the 1940s and mid-1960s) as the result of defective black cultural norms, of familial disorganization, etc.[26] In this way new racial attributions, new racial myths are affixed to "blacks."[27] Similar changes in racial identity are presently affecting Asians and Latinos, as such economic forces as increasing Third World impoverishment and indebtedness fuel immigration and high interest rates, Japanese competition spurs resentments, and U.S. jobs seem to fly away to Korea and Singapore.[28]

Once we understand that race overflows the boundaries of skin color, superexploitation, social stratification, discrimination and prejudice, cultural domination and cultural resistance, state policy (or of any other particular social relationship we list), once we recognize the racial dimension present to some degree in *every* identity, institution and social practice in the United States—once we have done this, it becomes possible to speak of *racial formation*. This recognition is hard-won; there is a continuous temptation to think of race as an *essence,* as something fixed, concrete and objective, as (for example) one of the categories just enumerated. And there is also an opposite temptation: to see it as a mere illusion, which an ideal social order would eliminate.

In our view it is crucial to break with these habits of thought. The effort must be made to understand race as *an unstable and "decentered" complex of social meanings constantly being transformed by political struggle.* . . .

NOTES

1. *San Francisco Chronicle,* 14 September 1982, 19 May 1983. Ironically, the 1970 Louisiana law was enacted to supersede an old Jim Crow statute which relied on the idea of "common report" in determining an infant's race. Following Phipps's unsuccessful attempt to change her classification and have the law declared unconstitutional, a legislative effort arose which culminated in the repeal of the law. See *San Francisco Chronicle,* 23 June 1983.

2. The Mormon church, for example, has been heavily criticized for its doctrine of black inferiority.

3. Thomas F. Gossett notes:

Race theory . . . had up until fairly modern times no firm hold on European thought. On the other hand, race theory and race prejudice were by no means unknown at the time when the English colonists came to North America. Undoubtedly, the age of exploration led many to speculate on race differences at a period when neither Europeans nor Englishmen were prepared to make allowances for vast cultural diversities. Even though race theories had not then secured wide acceptance or even sophisticated formulation, the first contacts of the Spanish with the Indians in the Americas can now be recognized as the beginning of a struggle between conceptions of the nature of primitive peoples which has not yet been wholly settled. (Thomas F. Gossett, *Race: The History of an Idea in America* [New York: Schocken Books, 1965], p. 16).

Winthrop Jordan provides a detailed account of early European colonialists' attitudes about color and race in *White Over Black: American Attitudes Toward the Negro, 1550–1812* (New York: Norton, 1977 [1968]), pp. 3–43.

4. Pro-slavery physician Samuel George Morton (1799–1851) compiled a collection of 800 crania from all parts of the world which formed the sample for his studies of race. Assuming that the larger the size of the cranium translated into greater intelligence, Morton established a relationship between race and skull capacity. Gossett reports that:

In 1849, one of his studies included the following results: The English skulls in his collection proved to be the largest, with an average cranial capacity of 96 cubic inches. The Americans and Germans were rather poor seconds, both with cranial capacities of 90 cubic inches. At the bottom of the list were the Negroes with 83 cubic inches, the Chinese with 82, and the Indians with 79. (Ibid., p. 74).

On Morton's methods, see Stephen J. Gould, "The Finagle Factor," *Human Nature* (July 1978).

5. Definitions of race founded upon a common pool of genes have not help up when confronted by scientific research which suggests that the differences *within* a given human population are greater than those *between* populations. See L. L. Cavalli-Sforza, "The Genetics of Human Populations," *Scientific American* (September 1974), pp. 81–9.

6. Arthur Jensen, "How Much Can We Boost IQ and Scholastic Achievement?", *Harvard Educational Review,* vol. 39 (1969), pp. 1–123.

7. Ernst Moritz Manasse, "Max Weber on Race," *Social Research,* vol. 14 (1947), pp. 191–221.

8. Quoted in Edward D.C. Campbell, Jr, *The Celluloid South: Hollywood and the Southern Myth* (Knoxville: University of Tennessee Press, 1981), pp. 168–70.

9. Marvin Harris, *Patterns of Race in the Americas* (New York: Norton, 1964), p. 56.

10. Ibid., p. 57.

11. After James Meredith had been admitted as the first black student at the University of Mississippi, Harry S. Murphy announced that he, and not Meredith, was the first black student to attend "Ole Miss." Murphy described himself as black but was able to pass for white and spent nine months at the institution without attracting any notice (ibid., p. 56).

12. A. Sivanandan, "From Resistance to Rebellion: Asian and Afro-Caribbean Struggles in Britain," *Race and Class,* vol. 23, nos. 2–3 (Autumn–Winter 1981).

13. Consider the contradictions in racial status which abound in the country with the most rigidly defined racial categories—South Africa. There a race classification agency is employed to adjudicate claims for upgrading of official racial identity. This is particularly necessary for the "coloured" category. The apartheid system considers Chinese as "Asians" while the Japanese are accorded the status of "honorary whites." This logic nearly detaches race from any grounding in skin color and other physical attributes and nakedly exposes race as a juridicial category subject to economic, social and political influences. (We are indebted to Steve Talbot for clarification of some of these points.)

14. Gordon W. Allport, *The Nature of Prejudice* (Garden City, New York: Doubleday, 1958), pp. 184–200.

15. We wish to use this phrase loosely, without committing ourselves to a particular position on such social psychological approaches as symbolic interactionism, which are outside the scope of this study. An interesting study on this subject is S.M. Lyman and W.A. Douglass, "Ethnicity: Strategies of Individual and Collective Impression Management," *Social Research,* vol. 40, no. 2 (1973).

16. Michael Billig, "Patterns of Racism: Interviews with National Front Members," *Race and Class,* vol. 20, no. 2 (Autumn 1978), pp. 161–79.

17. "Miss San Antonio U.S.A. Lisa Fernandez and other Hispanics auditioning for a role in a television soap opera did not fit the Hollywood image of real Mexicans and had to darken their faces before filming." Model Aurora Garza said that their faces were bronzed with powder because they looked too white. "'I'm a real Mexican [Garza said] and very dark anyway. I'm even darker right now because I have a tan. But they kept wanting me to make my face darker and darker'" (*San Francisco Chronicle,* 21 September 1984). A similar dilemma faces Asian American actors who feel that Asian character lead roles inevitably go to white actors who make themselves up to be Asian. Scores of Charlie Chan films, for example, have been made with white leads (the last one was the 1981 *Charlie Chan and the Curse of the Dragon Queen*). Roland Winters, who played in six Chan features, was asked by playwright Frank Chin to explain the logic of casting a white man in the role of Charlie Chan: "'The only thing I can think of is, if you want to cast a homosexual in a show, and you get a homosexual, it'll be awful. It won't be funny . . . and maybe there's something there . . .'" (Frank Chin, "Confessions of the Chinatown Cowboy," *Bulletin of Concerned Asian Scholars,* vol. 4, no. 3 (Fall 1972)).

18. Melanie Martindale-Sikes, "Nationalizing 'Nigger' Imagery Through 'Birth of a Nation'," paper prepared for the 73rd Annual Meeting of the American Sociological Association, 4–8 September 1978, in San Francisco.

19. Winthrop D. Jordon, op. cit., p. 95; emphasis added.

20. Historical focus has been placed either on particular racially defined groups or on immigration and the "incorporation" of ethnic groups. In the former case the characteristic ethnicity theory pitfalls and apologetics such as functionalism and cultural pluralism may be avoided, but only by sacrificing much of the focus on race. In the latter case, race is considered a manifestation of ethnicity.

21. The degree of antipathy for these groups should not be minimized. A northern commentator observed in the 1850s: "An Irish Catholic seldom attempts to rise to a higher condition than that in which he is placed, while the Negro often makes the attempt with success." Quoted in Gossett, op. cit., p. 288.

22. This analysis, as will perhaps be obvious, is essentially DuBoisian. Its main source will be found in the monumental (and still largely unappreciated) *Black Reconstruction in the United States, 1860–1880* (New York: Atheneum, 1977 [1935]).

23. Alexander Saxton argues that:

> North Americans of European background have experienced three great racial confrontations: with the Indian, with the African, and with the Oriental. Central to each transaction has been a totally one-sided preponderance of power, exerted for the exploitation of nonwhites by the dominant white society. In each case (but especially in the two that began with systems of enforced labor), white workingmen have played a crucial, yet ambivalent, role. They have been both exploited and exploiters. On the one hand, thrown into competition with nonwhites as enslaved or "cheap" labor, they suffered economically; on the other hand, being white, they benefited by that very exploitation which was compelling the nonwhites to work for low wages or for nothing. Ideologically they were drawn in opposite directions. *Racial identification cut at right angles to class consciousness.* (Alexander Saxton, *The Indispensable Enemy: Labor and the Anti-Chinese Movement in California* (Berkeley and Los Angeles: University of California Press, 1971), p. 1, emphasis added.)

24. Selig Perlman, *The History of Trade Unionism in the United States* (New York: Augustus Kelley, 1950), p. 52; emphasis added.

25. Whether southern blacks were "peasants" or rural workers is unimportant in this context. Sometime during the 1960s blacks attained a higher degree of urbanization than whites. Before World War II most blacks had been rural dwellers and nearly 80 percent lived in the South.

26. See George Gilder, *Wealth and Poverty* (New York: Basic Books, 1981); Charles Murray, *Losing Ground* (New York: Basic Books, 1984).

27. A brilliant study of the racialization process in Britain, focused on the rise of "mugging" as a popular fear in the 1970s, is Stuart Hall *et al., Policing the Crisis* (London: Macmillan, 1978).

28. The case of Vincent Chin, a Chinese American man beaten to death in 1982 by a laid-off Detroit auto worker and his stepson who mistook him for Japanese and blamed him for the loss of their jobs, has been widely publicized in Asian American communities. On immigration conflicts and pressures, see Michael Omi, "New Wave Dread: Immigration and Intra–Third World Conflict," *Socialist Review,* no. 60 (November–December 1981).

ANALYSIS
---

1. What support do Omi and Winant offer for the assertion that "the concept of race has defied biological definition"? What do they mean by saying later that "Racial beliefs operate as an 'amateur biology'"?
2. What do Omi and Winant mean by saying that race is "a pre-eminently *sociohistorical* concept"?
3. Omi and Winant speak of "preconceived notions" about racial groups as our way of "navigating race relations"; how does this concept relate to the idea of *stereotyping* and *prejudice?*
4. How do Omi and Winant use the term *racialization* to explain historical developments in nineteenth century America, in particular regarding the treatment of immigrants after the Civil War?
5. What is the force of the term *racial formation* as Omi and Winant use it in the second to last paragraph of this selection?
6. What do Omi and Winant mean by saying that we must understand race as "unstable"? As a "'decentered' complex of social meanings"? What is the role of "political struggle"?

WRITING POSSIBILITIES
---

1. According to Omi and Winant, "Film and television . . . have been notorious in disseminating images of racial minorities which establish for audiences what people from these groups look like, how they behave, and 'who they are'." After a period of representative viewings (at least two or three separate instances), explain in an essay to what extent you agree or disagree with Omi and Winant's generalization, support your own generalizations and distinctions by referring to visual and verbal specifics (take some careful notes about what you're watching).
2. Allowing for rhetorical exaggeration for deliberate effect, consider Omi and Winant's argument that "the racial dimension [is] present to some degree in *every* identity, institution and social practice in the United States. . . . " Pick an institution or social practice of your own choosing and (1) examine it from Omi and Winant's point of view and (2) from a contrary point of view. Is it possible to find evidence both for and against Omi and Winant's contention?
3. After reading S. Dale McLemore's summary of group identity and group gains theories, sections 2C, 3B (page 138), compare and contrast McLemore's discussion with Omi and Winant's. In your view, who presents the better support for their analysis? Why? What has been your experience in regard to the issues all three scholars raise? Which formulation—Omi and Winant's or McLemore's—do you find more persuasive? Why?
4. While Omi and Winant speak of "racial formation" as "pervasive" in every area of social life, McLemore, section 3A (page 138) speaks of situational pressures, i.e., the contrast between "creed" and "deed" ("talking" versus "walking"). Which in your view (or experience) helps most to explain prejudice and discrimination?

Beverly Tatum

Inspired by real-life questions from her students, Tatum's essay is both an interesting application of the idea of identity to racial problems (derived from Erik Erikson) and also a good example of how a thoughtful writer offers both a sympathetic and critical analysis of a problematic situation: that is, she shows how understandable it is that black students would congregate in one particular spot in the cafeteria and also why that can be a negative factor in terms of academic interchanges in a college or university.

IDENTITY DEVELOPMENT IN ADOLESCENCE

from Why Are All the Black Kids Sitting Together in the Cafeteria?

Walk into any racially mixed high school cafeteria at lunch time and you will instantly notice that in the sea of adolescent faces, there is an identifiable group of Black students sitting together. Conversely, it could be pointed out that there are many groups of White students sitting together as well, though people rarely comment about that. The question on the tip of everyone's tongue is "Why are the Black kids sitting together?" Principals want to know, teachers want to know, White students want to know, the Black students who aren't sitting at the table want to know.

How does it happen that so many Black teenagers end up at the same cafeteria table? They don't start out there. If you walk into racially mixed elementary schools, you will often see young children of diverse racial backgrounds playing with one another, sitting at the snack table together, crossing racial boundaries with an ease uncommon in adolescence. Moving from elementary school to middle school (often at sixth or seventh grade) means interacting with new children from different neighborhoods than before, and a certain degree of clustering by race might therefore be expected, presuming that children who are familiar with one another would form groups. But even in schools where the same children stay together from kindergarten through eighth grade, racial grouping begins by the sixth or seventh grade. What happens?

One thing that happens is puberty. As children enter adolescence, they begin to explore the question of identity, asking "Who am I? Who can I be?" in ways they have not done before. For Black youth, asking "Who am I?" includes thinking about "Who am I ethically and/ or racially? What does it mean to be Black?"

As I write this, I can hear the voice of a White woman who asked me, "Well, all adolescents struggle with questions of identity. They all become more self-conscious about their appearance and more concerned about what their peers think. So what is so different for Black kids?" Of course, she is right that all adolescents look at themselves in new ways, but not all adolescents think about themselves in racial terms.

The search for personal identity that intensifies in adolescence can involve several dimensions of an adolescent's life: vocational plans, religious beliefs, values and preferences, political affiliations and beliefs, gender roles, and ethnic identities. The process of exploration may vary across these identity domains. James Marcia described four identity "statuses" to characterize the variation in the identity search process: (1) *diffuse,* a state in which there has been little exploration or active consideration of a particular domain, and no psychological commitment; (2) *foreclosed,* a state in which a commitment has been made to particular roles or belief systems, often those selected by parents, without actively considering alternatives; (3) *moratorium,* a state of active exploration of roles and beliefs in which no commitment has yet been made; and (4) *achieved,* a state of strong personal commitment to a particular dimension of identity following a period of high exploration.

An individual is not likely to explore all identity domains at once, therefore it is not unusual for an adolescent to be actively exploring one dimension while another remains relatively unexamined. Given the impact of dominant and subordinate status, it is not surprising that researchers have found that adolescents of color are more likely to be actively engaged in an exploration of their racial or ethnic identity than are White adolescents.

Why do Black youths, in particular, think about themselves in terms of race? Because that is how the rest of the world thinks of them. Our self-perceptions are shaped by the messages that we receive from those around us, and when young Black men and women enter adolescence, the racial content of those messages intensifies. A case in point: If you were to ask my ten-year-old son, David, to describe himself, he would tell you many things: that he is smart, that he likes to play computer games, that he has an older brother. Near the top of his list, he would likely mention that he is tall for his age. He would probably not mention that he is Black, though he certainly knows that he is. Why would he mention his height and not his racial group membership? When David meets new adults, one of the first questions they ask is "How old are you?" When David states his age, the inevitable reply is "Gee, you're tall for your age!" It happens so frequently that I once overheard David say to someone, "Don't say it, I know. I'm tall for my age." Height is salient for David because it is salient for others.

When David meets new adults, they don't say, "Gee, you're Black for your age!" If you are saying to yourself, of course they don't, think again. Imagine David at fifteen, six-foot-two, wearing the adolescent attire of the day, passing adults he doesn't know on the sidewalk. Do the women hold their purses a little tighter, maybe even cross the street to avoid him? Does he hear the sound of the automatic door locks on cars as he passes by? Is he being followed around by the security guards at the local mall? As he stops in town with his new bicycle, does a police officer hassle him, asking where he got it, implying that it might be stolen? Do strangers assume he plays basketball? Each of these experiences conveys a racial message. At ten, race is not yet salient for David, because it is not yet salient for society. But it will be.

UNDERSTANDING RACIAL IDENTITY DEVELOPMENT

Psychologist William Cross, author of *Shades of Black: Diversity in African American Identity,* has offered a theory of racial identity development that I have found to be a very useful framework for understanding what is happening not only with David, but with those Black students in the cafeteria. According to Cross's model, referred to as the psychology of nigrescence, or the psychology of becoming Black, the five stages of racial identity development are *pre-encounter, encounter, immersion / emersion, internalization,* and *internalization-commitment.* For the moment, we will consider the first two stages as those are the most relevant for adolescents.

In the first stage, the Black child absorbs many of the beliefs and values of the dominant White culture, including the idea that it is better to be White. The stereotypes, omissions, and distortions that reinforce notions of White superiority are breathed in by Black children as well as White. Simply as a function of being socialized in a Eurocentric culture, some Black children may begin to value the role models, lifestyles, and images of beauty represented by the dominant group more highly than those of their own cultural group. On the other hand, if Black parents are what I call race-conscious—that is, actively seeking to encourage positive racial identity by providing their children with positive cultural images and messages about what it means to be Black—the impact of the dominant society's messages are reduced. In either case, in the pre-encounter stage, the personal and social significance of one's racial group membership has not yet been realized, and racial identity is not yet under examination. At age ten, David and other children like him would seem to be in the pre-encounter stage. When the environment cues change and the world begins to reflect his Blackness back to him more clearly, he will probably enter the encounter stage.

Transition to the encounter stage is typically precipitated by an event or series of events that force the young person to acknowledge the personal impact of racism. As the result of a new and heightened awareness of the significance of race, the individual begins to grapple with what it means to be a member of a group targeted by racism. Though Cross describes this process as one that unfolds in late adolescence and early adulthood, research suggests that an examination of one's racial or ethnic identity may begin as early as junior high school.

In a study of Black and White eighth graders from an integrated urban junior high school, Jean Phinney and Steve Tarver found clear evidence for the beginning of the search process in this dimension of identity. Among the forty-eight participants, more than a third had thought about the effects of ethnicity on their future, had discussed the issues with family and friends, and were attempting to learn more about their group. While White students in this integrated school were also beginning to think about ethnic identity, there was evidence to suggest a more active search among Black students, especially Black females. Phinney and Tarver's research is consistent with my own study of Black youth in predominantly White communities, where the environmental cues that trigger an examination of racial identity often become evident in middle school or junior high school.

Some of the environmental cues are institutionalized. Though many elementary schools have self-contained classrooms where children of varying performance levels learn together, many middle and secondary schools use "ability grouping," or tracking. Though school administrators often defend their tracking practices as fair and objective, there usually is a recognizable racial pattern to how children are assigned, which often represents the system of advantage operating in the schools. In racially mixed schools, Black children are much more likely to be in the lower track than in the honors track. Such apparent sorting along racial lines sends a message about what it means to be Black. One young honors student I interviewed described the irony of this resegregation in what was an otherwise integrated environment, and hinted at the identity issues it raised for him.

> It was really a very paradoxical existence, here I am in a school that's 35 percent Black, you know, and I'm the only Black in my classes. . . . That always struck me as odd. I guess I felt that I was different from the other Blacks because of that.

In addition to the changes taking place within school, there are changes in the social dynamics outside school. For many parents, puberty raises anxiety about interracial dating. In racially mixed communities, you begin to see what I call the birthday party effect. Young children's birthday parties in multiracial communities are often a reflection of the community's diversity. The parties of elementary school children may be segregated by gender but not by race. At puberty, when the parties become sleepovers or boy-girl events, they become less and less racially diverse.

Black girls, especially in predominantly White communities, may gradually become aware that something has changed. When their White friends start to date, they do not. The issues of emerging sexuality and the societal messages about who is sexually desirable leave young Black women in a very devalued position. One young woman from a Philadelphia suburb described herself as "pursuing White guys throughout high school" to no avail. Since there were no Black boys in her class, she had little choice. She would feel "really pissed off" that those same White boys would date her White friends. For her, "that prom thing was like out of the question."

Though Black girls living in the context of a larger Black community may have more social choices, they too have to contend with devaluing messages about who they are and who they will become, especially if they are poor or working-class. As social scientists Bonnie Ross Leadbeater and Niobe Way point out,

> The school drop-out, the teenage welfare mother, the drug addict, and the victim of domestic violence or of AIDS are among the most prevalent public images of poor and working-class urban adolescent girls. . . . Yet, despite the risks inherent in economic disadvantage, the majority of poor urban adolescent girls do not fit the stereotypes that are made about them.

Resisting the stereotypes and affirming other definitions of themselves is part of the task facing young Black women in both White and Black communities.

As was illustrated in the example of David, Black boys also face a devalued status in the wider world. The all too familiar media image of a young Black man with his hands cuffed behind his back, arrested for a violent crime, has primed many to view young Black men with suspicion and fear. In the context of predominantly White schools, however, Black boys may enjoy a degree of social success, particularly if they are athletically talented. The culture has embraced the Black athlete, and the young man who can fulfill that role is often pursued by Black girls and White girls alike. But even these young men will encounter experiences that may trigger an examination of their racial identity.

Sometimes the experience is quite dramatic. *The Autobiography of Malcolm X* is a classic tale of racial identity development, and I assign it to my psychology of racism students for just that reason. As a junior high school student, Malcolm was a star. Despite the fact that he was separated from his family and living in a foster home, he was an A student and was elected president of his class. One day he had a conversation with his English teacher, whom he liked and respected, about his future career goals. Malcolm said he wanted to be a lawyer. His teacher responded, "That's no realistic goal for a nigger," and advised him to consider carpentry instead. The message was clear: You are a Black male, your racial group membership matters, plan accordingly. Malcolm's emotional response was typical—anger, confusion, and alienation. He withdrew from his White classmates, stopped participating in class, and eventually left his predominantly white Michigan home to live with his sister in Roxbury, a Black community in Boston.

No teacher would say such a thing now, you may be thinking, but don't be so sure. It is certainly less likely that a teacher would use the word *nigger,* but consider these contemporary examples shared by high school students. A young ninth-grade student was sitting in his homeroom. A substitute teacher was in charge of the class. Because the majority of students from this school go on to college, she used the free time to ask the students about their college plans. As a substitute she had very limited information about their academic performance, but she offered some suggestions. When she turned to this young man, one of few Black males in the class, she suggested that he consider a community college. She had recommended four-year colleges to the other students. Like Malcolm, this student got the message.

In another example, a young Black woman attending a desegregated school to which she was bussed was encouraged by a teacher to attend the upcoming school dance. Most of the Black students did not live in the neighborhood and seldom attended the extracurricular activities. The young woman indicated that she wasn't planning to come. The well-intentioned teacher was persistent. Finally the teacher said, "Oh come on, I know you people love to dance." This young woman got the message, too.

COPING WITH ENCOUNTERS: DEVELOPING AN OPPOSITIONAL IDENTITY

What do these encounters have to do with the cafeteria? Do experiences with racism inevitably result in so-called self-segregation? While certainly a desire to protect oneself from further offense is understandable, it is not the only factor at work. Imagine the young eighth-grade girl who experienced the teacher's use of "you people" and the dancing stereotype as a racial affront. Upset and struggling with adolescent embarrassment, she bumps into a White friend who can see that something is wrong. She explains. Her White friend responds, in an effort to make her feel better perhaps, and says, "Oh, Mr. Smith is such a nice guy, I'm sure he didn't mean it like that. Don't be so sensitive." Perhaps the White friend is right, and Mr. Smith didn't mean it, but imagine your own response when you are upset, perhaps with a spouse or partner. He or she asks what's wrong and you explain why you are offended. Your partner brushes off your complaint, attributing it to your being oversensitive. What happens to your emotional thermostat? It escalates. When feelings, rational or irrational, are invalidated, most people disengage. They not only choose to discontinue the conversation but are more likely to turn to someone who will understand their perspective.

In much the same way, the eighth-grade girl's White friend doesn't get it. She doesn't see the significance of this racial message, but the girls at the "Black table" do. When she tells her story there, one of them is likely to say, "You know what, Mr. Smith said the same thing to me yesterday!" Not only are Black adolescents encountering racism and reflecting on their identity, but their White peers, even when they are not the perpetrators (and sometimes they are), are unprepared to respond in supportive ways. The Black students turn to each other for the much needed support they are not likely to find anywhere else.

In adolescence, as race becomes personally salient for Black youth, finding the answer to questions such as, "What does it mean to be a young Black person? How should I act? What should I do?" is particularly important. And although Black fathers, mothers, aunts, and uncles may hold the answers by offering themselves as role models, they hold little appeal for most adolescents. The last thing many fourteen-year-olds want to do is to grow up to be like their parents. It is the peer group, the kids in the cafeteria, who hold the answers to these questions. They know how to be Black. They have absorbed the stereotypical images of Black youth in the popular culture and are reflecting those images in their self-presentation.

Based on their fieldwork in U.S. high schools, Signithia Fordham and John Ogbu identified a common psychological pattern found among African American high school students at this stage of identity development. They observed that the anger and resentment that adolescents feel in response to their growing awareness of the systematic exclusion of Black people from full participation in U.S. society leads to the development of an oppositional social identity. This oppositional stance both protects one's identity from the psychological assault of racism and keeps the dominant group at a distance. Fordham and Ogbu write:

> Subordinate minorities regard certain forms of behavior and certain activities or events, symbols, and meanings as *not*

appropriate for them because those behaviors, events, symbols, and meanings are characteristic of white Americans. At the same time they emphasize other forms of behavior as more appropriate for them because these are *not* a part of white Americans' way of life. To behave in the manner defined as falling within a white cultural frame of reference is to "act white" and is negatively sanctioned.

Certain styles of speech, dress, and music, for example, may be embraced as "authentically Black" and become highly valued, while attitudes and behaviors associated with Whites are viewed with disdain. The peer groups's evaluation of what is Black and what is not can have a powerful impact on adolescent behavior.

Reflecting on her high school years, one Black woman from a White neighborhood described both the pain of being rejected by her Black classmates and her attempts to conform to her peer's definition of Blackness:

> "Oh you sound White, you think you're White," they said. And the idea of sounding White was just so absurd to me. . . . So ninth grade was sort of traumatic in that I started listening to rap music, which I really just don't like. [I said] I'm gonna be Black, and it was just that stupid. But it's more than just how one acts, you know. [The other Black women there] were not into me for the longest time. My first year there was hell."

Sometimes the emergence of an oppositional identity can be quite dramatic, as the young person tries on a new persona almost overnight. At the end of one school year, race may not have appeared to be significant, but often some encounter takes place over the summer and the young person returns to school much more aware of his or her Blackness and ready to make sure that the rest of the world is aware of it, too. There is a certain "in your face" quality that these adolescents can take on, which their teachers often experience as threatening. When a group of Black teens are sitting together in the cafeteria, collectively embodying an oppositional stance, school administrators want to know not only why they are sitting together, but what can be done to prevent it.

We need to understand that in racially mixed settings, racial grouping is a developmental process in response to an environmental stressor, racism. Joining with one's peers for support in the face of stress is a positive coping strategy. What is problematic is that the young people are operating with a very limited definition of what it means to be Black, based largely on cultural stereotypes.

OPPOSITIONAL IDENTITY DEVELOPMENT
AND ACADEMIC ACHIEVEMENT

Unfortunately for Black teenagers, those cultural stereotypes do not usually include academic achievement. Academic success is more often associated with being White. During the encounter phase of racial identity development, when the search for identity leads toward cultural stereotypes and away from anything that might be associated with Whiteness, academic performance often declines. Doing well in school becomes identified as trying to be White. Being smart becomes the opposite of being cool.

While this frame of reference is not universally found among adolescents of African descent, it is commonly observed in Black peer groups. Among the Black college students I have interviewed, many described some conflict or alienation from other African American teens because of their academic success in high school. For example, a twenty-year-old female from a Washington, D.C., suburb explained:

> It was weird, even in high school a lot of the Black students were, like, "Well, you're not really Black." Whether it was because I became president of the sixth-grade class or whatever it was, it started pretty much back then. Junior high, it got worse. I was then labeled certain things, whether it was "the Oreo" or I wasn't really Black.

Others described avoiding situations that would set them apart from their Black peers. For example, one young woman declined to participate in a gifted program in her school because she knew it would separate her from the other Black students in the school.

In a study of thirty-three eleventh-graders in a Washington, D.C., school, Fordham and Ogbu found that although some of the students had once been academically successful, few of them remained so. These students also knew that to be identified as a "brainiac" would result in peer rejection. The few students who had maintained strong academic records found ways to play down their academic success enough to maintain some level of acceptance among their Black peers.

Academically successful Black students also need a strategy to find acceptance among their White classmates. Fordham describes one such strategy as *racelessness,* wherein individuals assimilate into the dominant group by de-emphasizing characteristics that might identify them as members of the subordinate group. Jon, a young man I interviewed, offered a classic example of this strategy as he described his approach to dealing with his discomfort as being the only Black person in his advanced classes. He said, "At no point did I ever think I was White or did I ever want to be White. . . . I guess it was one of those things where I tried to de-emphasize the fact that I was Black." This strategy led him to avoid activities that were associated with Blackness. He recalled, "I didn't want to do anything that was traditionally Black, like I never played basketball. I ran cross-country. . . . I went for distance running instead of sprints." He felt he had to show his White classmates that there were "exceptions to all these stereotypes." However, this strategy was of limited usefulness. When he traveled outside his home community with his White teammates, he sometimes encountered overt racism. "I quickly realized that I'm Black, and that's the thing that they're going to see first, no matter how much I try to de-emphasize my Blackness."

A Black student can play down Black identity in order to succeed in school and mainstream institutions without rejecting his Black identity and culture. Instead of becoming raceless, an achieving Black student can become an *emissary,* someone who sees his or her own achievements as advancing the cause of the racial group. For example, social scientists Richard Zweigenhaft and G. William Domhoff describe how a successful Black student, in response to the accusation of acting White, connected his achievement to that of other Black men by saying, "Martin Luther King must not have been Black, then, since he had a doctoral degree, and Malcolm X must not have been Black since he educated himself while in prison." In addition, he demonstrated his loyalty to the Black community by taking an openly political stance against the racial discrimination he observed in his school.

It is clear that an oppositional identity can interfere with academic achievement, and it may be tempting for educators to blame the adolescents themselves for their academic decline. However, the questions that educators and other concerned adults must ask are, How did academic achievement become defined as exclusively White behavior? What is it about the curriculum and the wider culture that reinforces the notion that academic excellence is an exclusively White domain? What curricular interventions might we use to encourage the development of an empowered emissary identity?

An oppositional identity that disdains academic achievement has not always been a characteristic of Black adolescent peer groups. It seems to be a post-desegregation phenomenon. Historically, the oppositional identity found among African Americans in the segregated South included a positive attitude toward education. While Black people may have publicly deferred to Whites, they actively encouraged their children to pursue education as a ticket to greater freedom. While Black parents still see education as the key to upward mobility, in today's desegregated schools the models of success—the teachers, administrators, and curricular heroes—are almost always White.

Black Southern schools, though stigmatized by legally sanctioned segregation, were often staffed by African American educators, themselves visible models of academic achievement. These Black educators may have presented a curriculum that included references to the intellectual legacy of other African Americans. As well, in the context of a segregated school, it was a given that the high achieving students would all be Black. Academic achievement did not have to mean separation from one's Black peers. . . .

Though they may not use the language of racial identity development theory to describe it, most Black parents want their children to achieve an internalized sense of personal security, to be able to acknowledge the reality of racism and to respond effectively to it. Our educational institutions should do what they can to encourage this development rather than impede it. When I talk to educators about the need to provide adolescents with identity-affirming experiences and information about their own cultural groups, they sometimes flounder because this information has not been part of their own education. Their understanding of adolescent development has been limited to the White middle-class norms included in most textbooks, their knowledge of Black history limited to Martin Luther King, Jr., and Rosa Parks. They sometimes say with frustration that parents should provide this kind of education for their children. Unfortunately Black parents often attended the same schools the teachers did and have the same informational gaps. We need to acknowledge that an important part of interrupting the cycle of oppression is constant re-education, and sharing what we learn with the next generation.

--------------------------------- **ANALYSIS** ---------------------------------

1. Tatum notes that "the search for personal identity . . . intensifies in adolescence. . . ." What particular dimensions of adolescence does Tatum speak about here?
2. In support of her argument, Tatum cites the work of psychologist William Cross, *Shades of Black: Diversity in African American Identity* on racial identity. What, for Cross, are the stages of "racial identity development"? To what extent do you think these stages might apply regardless of racial identity?
3. What examples does Tatum use to illustrate hers and William Cross's model or framework of racialized identity?
4. How does Tatum connect the idea of personal identity with the problem of group separation as announced in her title?
5. What does Tatum mean by an "oppositional identity"?
6. What critique does Tatum offer (sympathetically, to be sure) about "Oppositional Identity Development and Academic Achievement"?

WRITING POSSIBILITIES

---

1. Earlier in the book from which this essay was taken, Tatum offers suggestions for both "dominant" and "targeted" readers:

> For those readers who are in the dominant racial category, it may sometimes be difficult to take in what is being said by and about those who are targeted by racism. When the perspective of the subordinate is shared directly, an image is reflected to members of the dominant group which is disconcerting. To the extent that one can draw on one's own experience of subordination—as a young person, as a person with a disability, as someone who grew up poor, as a woman—it may be easier to make meaning of another targeted group's experience. For those readers who are targeted by racism and are angered by the obliviousness of Whites sometimes described in these pages, it may be useful to attend to your experience of dominance where you may find it—as a heterosexual, as an able-bodied person, as a Christian, as a man—and consider what systems of privilege you may be overlooking. The task of resisting our own oppression does not relieve us of the responsibility of acknowledging our complicity in the oppression of others.

Depending on whether you believe you are among the group of readers Tatum refers to, see to what extent you can apply Tatum's theories of identity and race to your own experience. Note too, as Tatum says, that "Many of us are both dominant and subordinate. . . . There is a need to acknowledge each other's pain, even as we attend to our own."

Shelby Steele

Shelby Steele argues that discrimination's effects are not as simple as they might seem. Steele outlines a theory of "innocence," applicable to whites and blacks alike: whites, he says, want to be free of guilt over past discrimination while blacks want to believe that their situation is due entirely to discrimination. From a moral viewpoint, Steele argues, both kinds of "innocence" allow individuals to avoid responsibility for their actions, notably in ignoring the "margin of choice" to reject negative stereotypes rather than live up to their hopes and abilities.

What is especially interesting about Shelby Steele's views is that they conflict with those of his brother psychologist Claude Steele's, who argues that African Americans suffer from "stereotype vulnerability" (doing badly because you're "hexed" about supposedly bad possibilities of your own group). Yet despite differences of implication, tone, and moral framing, both Steeles offer a similar understanding of the deleterious role of stereotypes in our lives (the "our" is not an editorial "one": Claude Steele has shown that even white math students do poorly when their fears are aroused about the possibility that as a group they are the "underachievers" as, for example, compared to Asian American math students!)

I'M BLACK, YOU'RE WHITE, WHO'S INNOCENT?

RACE-HOLDING

I am a fortyish, middle-class, black American male with a teaching position at a large state university in California. I have owned my own home for more than ten years, as well as the two cars that are the minimal requirement for life in California. And I will confess to a moderate strain of yuppie hedonism. Year after year my two children are the sole representatives of their race in their classrooms, a fact they sometimes have difficulty remembering. We are the only black family in our suburban neighborhood, and even this claim to special-ness is diminished by the fact that my wife is white. I think we are called an "integrated" family, though no one has ever used the term with me. For me to be among large numbers of blacks requires con-scientiousness and a long car ride, and in truth, I have not been very conscientious lately. Though I was raised in an all-black community just south of Chicago, I only occasionally feel nostalgia for such places. Trips to the barbershop now and then usually satisfy this need, though recently, in the interest of convenience, I've taken to let-ting my wife cut my hair.

I see in people's eyes from time to time, and hear often in the media, what amounts to a judgment of people like myself: You have moved into the great amorphous middle class and lost your connec-tion to your people and your cultural roots. You have become a gen-uine invisible man. This is judgment with many obvious dimensions, many arrows of guilt. But, in essence, it charges me with selfishness and inauthenticity.

At one point I romanticized my situation, thought of myself as a marginal man. The seductive imagery of alienation supported me in this. But in America today racial marginality is hard to sell as the stuff of tragedy. The position brings with it an ugly note of self-insistence that annoys people in a society that is, at least officially, desegregated.

For better or worse, I'm not very marginal. In my middle-American world I see people like myself everywhere. We nod coolly at stoplights, our eyes connect for an awkward instant in shopping malls, we hear about one another from our white friends. "Have you met the new doctor at the hospital . . . the engineer at IBM . . . the new professor in history?" The black middle class is growing. We are often said to be sneaking or slipping or creeping unnoticed into the middle class, as though images of stealth best characterized our movement. I picture a kind of underground railroad, delivering us in the dead of night from the inner city to the suburbs.

But even if we aren't very marginal, we are very shy with one another, at least until we've had a chance to meet privately and take our readings. When we first meet, we experience a trapped feeling, as if we had walked into a cage of racial expectations that would rob us of our individuality by reducing us to an exclusively racial dimension. We are a threat, at first, to one another's uniqueness. I have seen the same well-dressed black woman in the supermarket for more than a year now. We do not speak, and we usually pretend not to see each other. But, when we turn a corner suddenly and find ourselves staring squarely into each other's eyes, her face freezes and she moves on. I believe she is insisting that both of us be more than black—that we interact only when we have a reason other than the mere fact of our race. Her chilliness enforces a priority I agree with—individuality over group identity.

But I believe I see something else in this woman that I also see in myself and in many other middle-class blacks. It is a kind of race fatigue, a deep weariness with things racial, which comes from the fact that our lives are more integrated than they have ever been before. Race does not determine our fates as powerfully as it once did, which means it is not the vital personal concern it once was. Before the sixties, race set the boundaries of black life. Now, especially for middle-class blacks, it is far less a factor, though we don't always like to admit it. Blacks still suffer from racism, so we must be concerned, but this need to be concerned with what is not so personally urgent makes for race fatigue.

I have a friend who did poorly in the insurance business for years. "People won't buy insurance from a black man," he always said. Two years ago another black man and a black woman joined his office. Almost immediately both did twice the business my friend was doing, with the same largely white client base.

Integration shock is essentially the shock of being suddenly accountable on strictly personal terms. It occurs in situations that disallow race as an excuse for personal shortcomings and it therefore exposes vulnerabilities that previously were hidden. One response to such shock is to face up to the self-confrontation it brings and then to act on the basis of what we learn about ourselves. After some struggle, my friend was able to do this. He completely revised his sales technique, asked himself some hard questions about his motivation, and resolved to work harder.

But when one lacks the courage to face oneself fully, a fear of hidden vulnerabilities triggers a fright-flight response to integration shock. Instead of admitting that racism has declined, we argue all the harder that it is still alive and more insidious than ever. We hold race up to shield us from what we do not want to see in ourselves. My friend did this at first, saying that the two blacks in this office were doing better than he was because they knew how to "kiss white ass." Here he was *race-holding,* using race to keep from looking at himself.

Recently I read an article in the local paper that explored the question of whether blacks could feel comfortable living in the largely white Silicon Valley. The article focused on a black family that had been living for more than a decade in Saratoga, a very well-to-do white community. Their neighborhood, their children's schools, their places of employment, their shopping areas and parks—their entire physical environment—were populated by affluent whites. Yet during the interview the wife said they had made two firm rules for their children: that they go to all-black colleges back east and that they do "no dating outside the race, period."

I have pushed enough black history and culture on my own children to be able to identify with the impulse behind the first of these rules. Black children in largely white situations must understand and appreciate their cultural background. But the rigidity of these rules, not to mention the rules themselves, points to more than a concern with transmitting heritage or gaining experience with other blacks. Rigidity arises from fear and self-doubt. These people, I believe, were afraid of something.

What was striking to me about their rules, especially the one prohibiting interracial dating, was their tone of rejection. The black parents seemed as determined to reject the white world as to embrace the black one. Why? I would say because of integration shock. Their integrated lives have opened up vulnerabilities they do not wish to face. But what vulnerabilities? In this case, I think, a particularly embarrassing one. On some level, I suspect, they doubt whether they are as good as the white people who live around them. You cannot be raised in a culture that was for centuries committed to the notion of your inferiority and not have some doubt in this regard—doubt that is likely to be aggravated most in integrated situations. So the rejecting tone of their rules is self-protective: *I will reject you before you have a chance to reject me.* But all of this is covered over by race. The high value of racial pride is invoked to shield them from a doubt that they are afraid to acknowledge. Unacknowledged, this doubt gains a negative power inside the personality that expresses itself in the rigidity and absolutism of their rules. Repressed fears tend always to escalate their campaign for our attention by pushing us further and further into irrationality and rigidity.

The refusal to see something unflattering in ourselves always triggers the snap from race fatigue to race-holding. And once that happens, we are caught, like this family, in a jumble of racial ironies. The parents in Saratoga, who have chosen to live integrated lives, impose a kind of segregation on their children. Rules that would be racist in the mouth of any white person are created and enforced with pride. Their unexamined self-doubt also leaves them unable to exploit fully the freedom they have attained. Race fatigue makes them run to a place like Saratoga, but integration shock makes them hold race protectively. They end up clinging to what they've run from.

Once race-holding is triggered by fear, it ensnares us in a web of self-defeating attitudes that end up circumventing the new freedom we've won over the past several decades. I have seen its corrosive effects in my own life and in the lives of virtually every black person I've known. Some are only mildly touched by it, while others seem incapacitated by it. But race-holding is as unavoidable as defensiveness itself, and I am convinced that it is one of the most debilitating, yet unrecognized, forces in black life today.

I define a *holding* as any self-description that serves to justify or camouflage a person's fears, weaknesses, and inadequacies. Holdings are the little and big exaggerations, distortions, and lies about ourselves that prop us up and let us move along the compromised paths we follow. They develop to defend against threats to our self-esteem, threats that make us feel vulnerable and that plant a seed of fear. This fear can work like wind on a brushfire, spreading self-doubt far beyond what the initial threat would warrant, so that we become even more weakened and more needy of holdings. Since holdings justify our reticence and cowardice, they are usually expressed in the form of high belief or earthy wisdom. A man whose business fails from his own indifference holds an image of himself as a man too honest to be a good businessman—a self-description that draws a veil over his weakness.

For some years I have noticed that I can walk into any of my classes on the first day of the semester, identify the black students, and be sadly confident that on the last day of the semester a disproportionate number of them will be at the bottom of the class, far behind any number of white students of equal or even lesser native ability. More to the point, they will have performed far beneath their own native ability. Self-fulfilling prophesy theory says that their schools have always expected them to do poorly, and that they have internalized this message and *done* poorly. But this deterministic theory sees blacks only as victims, without any margin of choice. It cannot fully explain the poor performances of these black students because it identifies only the forces that *pressure* them to do poorly. By overlooking the margin of choice open to them, this theory fails to recognize the degree to which they are responsible for their own poor showing. (The irony of this oversight is that it takes the power for positive change away from the students and puts it in the hands of the very institutions that failed them in the first place.)

The theory of race-holding is based on the assumption that a margin of choice is always open to blacks (even slaves had some choice). And it tries to make clear the mechanisms by which we relinquish that choice in the name of race. With the decline in racism the margin of black choice has greatly expanded, which is probably why race-holding is so much more visible today than ever before. But anything that prevents us from exploiting our new freedom to the fullest is now as serious a barrier to us as racism once was.

The self-fulfilling prophesy theory is no doubt correct that black students, like the ones I regularly see, internalize a message of inferiority that they receive from school and the larger society around them. But the relevant question in the 1990s is why they *choose* to internalize this view of themselves. Why do they voluntarily perceive themselves as inferior? We can talk about the weakened black family and countless other scars of oppression and poverty. And certainly these things have much to do with the image these students have of themselves. But they do not fully explain this self-image because none of them entirely eliminates the margin of choice that remains open. Choice lives in even the most blighted circumstances, and it certainly lives in the lives of these black college students.

I think they *choose* to believe in their inferiority, not to fulfill society's prophesy about them, but for the comforts and rationalizations their racial "inferiority" affords them. They hold their race to evade individual responsibility. Their margin of choice scares them, as it does all people. They are naturally intimidated by that eternal tussle between the freedom to act and the responsibility we must take for our actions. To some extent all of us balk in the face of this. The difference is that these students use their race to conceal the fact that they are balking. Their "inferiority" shields them from having to see that they are afraid of all-out competition with white students. And it isn't even an honest inferiority. I don't think they really believe it. It is a false inferiority, *chosen* over an honest and productive confrontation with white students and with their real fears—a strategy that allows them to stay comfortably on the sidelines in a university environment that all but showers them with opportunity.

"I'm doing okay for a black student," a student once told me. "I'm doing well considering where I came from," I have told myself. Race allows us both to hide from the real question, which is, "Am I doing what I can, considering my talents and energies?"

I see all of this as pretty much a subconscious process, fear working on a subterranean level to let us reduce our margin of choice in the name of race. Consciously, we tell ourselves that we are only identifying with our race, but fear bloats our racial identity to an unnatural size and then uses it as cover for its subversive work. The more severe the integration shock, the more fear cover is needed.

Doesn't race enhance individuality? I think it does, but only when individuality is nurtured and developed apart from race. The race-holder, inside the bubble of his separate self, feels inadequate or insecure and then seeks reassurance through race. When, instead, a sense of self arises from individual achievement and self-realization. When self-esteem is established apart from race, then racial identity can only enhance because it is no longer needed for any other purpose.

The word *individualism* began to connote selfishness and even betrayal for many blacks during the sixties. Individualism was seen as a threat to the solidarity blacks needed during those years of social confrontation. Despite the decline in racism, these connotations have lingered. Race-holding keeps them alive because they serve the race-holder's need to exaggerate the importance of race as well as to justify a fear of individual responsibility. Race-holding makes fluid the boundary between race and self, group and individual identity, so that race can swing over at a moment's notice and fill in where fears leave a vacuum.

This is a worse problem than is at first apparent because the individual is the seat of all energy, creativity, motivation, and power. We are most strongly motivated when we want something for ourselves. When our personal wants are best achieved through group action, as in the civil rights movement, we lend our energy to the group, and it becomes as strong as the sum of our energies. When the need for group action recedes, more energy is available to us as individuals. But race-holding intercedes here by affixing the race-holder too tightly to this racial identity and by causing him to see the locus of power in race rather than in himself. In this way race-holding corrupts the greatest source of power and strength available to blacks—the energy latent in our personal desires.

One of my favorite passages in Ralph Ellison's *Invisible Man* is his description of the problem of blacks as:

> not actually one of creating the uncreated conscience of [our] race, but of creating the *uncreated features of [our] face.* Our task is that of making ourselves individuals. . . . We create the race by creating ourselves and then to our great astonishment

we will have created something far more important: we will have created a culture.

These lines hold up well, more than thirty years after they were written. They seem to suggest a kind of Adam Smith vision of culture: When the individual makes himself, he makes culture. An "invisible hand" uses individual effort to define and broaden culture. In the 1990s we blacks are more than ever in a position where our common good will best be served by the determined pursuit of our most personal aspirations.

I think the means to this, and the answer to race-holding generally, is personal responsibility, a source of great power that race-holding does its best to conceal. . . .

WHITE GUILT

I don't remember hearing the phrase "white guilt" very much before the mid-sixties. Growing up black in the fifties, I never had the impression that whites were much disturbed by guilt when it came to blacks. When I would stray into the wrong restaurant in pursuit of a hamburger, it didn't occur to me that the waitress was unduly troubled by guilt when she asked me to leave. I can see now that possibly she was, but then all I saw was her irritability at having to carry out so unpleasant a task. If there was guilt, it was mine for having made an imposition of myself. Frankly, I can remember feeling a certain sympathy for such people, as if *I* was victimizing *them* by drawing them out of an innocent anonymity into the unasked-for role of racial policemen. Occasionally, they came right out and asked me to feel sorry for them. A caddy master at a country club told my brother and me that he was doing us a favor by not letting us caddy at this white club, and that we should try to understand his position, "put yourselves in my shoes." Our color had brought this man anguish and, if a part of that anguish was guilt, it was not as immediate to me as my own guilt. I smiled at the man to let him know he shouldn't feel bad and then began the long walk home. Certainly, I also judged him a coward, but in that era his cowardice was something I had to absorb. . . .

It is easy enough to say that white guilt too often has the effect of bending social policies in the wrong direction. But what exactly is this guilt, and how does it work in American life?

I think that white guilt, in its broad sense, springs from a *knowledge* of ill-gotten advantage. More precisely, it comes from the juxtaposition of this knowledge with the inevitable gratitude one feels for being white rather than black in America. Given the moral instincts of human beings, it is all but impossible to enjoy an ill-gotten advantage, much less to feel at least secretly grateful for it, without consciously or unconsciously experiencing guilt. If, as Kierkegaard says, "innocence is ignorance," then guilt must always involve knowledge. White Americans *know* that their historical advantage comes from the subjugation of an entire people. So, even for whites today for whom racism is anathema, there is no escape from the knowledge that makes for guilt. Racial guilt simply accompanies the condition of being white in America.

I do not believe that this guilt is a crushing anguish for most whites, but I do believe it constitutes an ongoing racial vulnerability, an openness to racial culpability, that is a thread in white life, sometimes felt, sometimes not, but ever present as a potential feeling. In the late sixties almost any black could charge this thread with enough current for a white to feel it. I had a friend who developed this activity into a sort of specialty. I don't think he meant to be mean, though certainly he was mean. I think he was, in that hyperbolic era, exhilarated by the discovery that his race, which had long been a liability, now gave him a certain edge—that white guilt was black power. To feel this power he would sometimes set up what he called "race experiments." Once I watched him stop a white businessman in a large hotel men's room and convince him to increase his tip to the black attendant from one to twenty dollars.

My friend's tact in this was very simple, even corny. Out of the attendant's earshot he asked the man to simply look at the attendant, a frail, elderly, and very dark man in a starched white smock that made the skin on his neck and face look as leathery as a turtle's. He sat listlessly, pathetically, on a straight-backed chair next to a small table on which sat a stack of hand towels and a silver plate for tips. Since he offered no service beyond the handing out of towels, one could only conclude the hotel management offered his lowly presence as flattery to their patrons, as an opportunity for that easy noblesse oblige that could reassure even the harried, wrung-out traveling salesman of his superior station. My friend was quick to make this point to the businessman and to say that no white man would do in this job. But when the businessman put the single back in his wallet and took out a five, my friend only sneered. Did he understand the tragedy of a life spent this way, of what it must be like to earn one's paltry living as a symbol of inferiority? And did he realize that his privilege as an affluent white businessman (ironically, he had just spent the day trying to sell a printing press to the Black Muslims for their newspaper *Muhammad Speaks*) was connected to the deprivation of this man and others like him?

But then my friend made a mistake that ended the game. In the heat of argument, which until then had only been playfully challenging, he inadvertently mentioned his father. This stopped him cold and his eyes turned inward. "What about your father?" the businessman asked. "He had a hard life, that's all." "How did he have a hard life?" Now my friend was on the defensive. I knew he did not get along with his father, a bitter man who worked nights in a factory and demanded that the house be dark and silent all day. My friend blamed his father's bitterness on racism, but I knew he had not meant to exploit his own pain in this silly "experiment." Things had gotten too close to home, but he didn't know how to get out of the situation without losing face. Now, caught in his own trap, he did what he least wanted to do. He gave forth the rage he truly felt to a white stranger in a public men's room. "My father never had a chance," he said with the kind of anger that could easily turn to tears. "He never had a fuckin' chance. Your father had all the goddamn chances, and you know he did. You sell printing presses to black people and make thousands and your father probably lives down in Fat City, Florida, somewhere, all because you're white." On and on he went in this vein, using—against all that was honorable in him—his own profound racial pain to extract a flash of guilt from a white man he didn't even know.

He got more than a flash. The businessman was touched. His eyes became mournful and finally he simply said, "You're right. Your people got a raw deal." He took a twenty-dollar bill from his wallet, then walked over and dropped it in the old man's tip plate. When he was gone my friend and I could not look at the old man, nor could we look at each other.

It is obvious that this was a rather shameful encounter for all concerned—my friend and I as his silent accomplice—trading on our racial plan, tampering with a stranger for no reason, and the stranger then buying his way out of the situation for twenty dollars, a sum that was generous by one count and cheap by another. It was not an encounter of people but of historical grudges and guilts. Yet, when I think about it now, twenty years later, I see that it had all the elements of a paradigm that I believe has been very much at the heart of racial policy-making in America since the sixties.

My friend did two things that made this businessman vulnerable to his guilt, that brought his guilt into the situation as a force. First, he put this man in touch with his own *knowledge* of his ill-gotten advantage as a white. The effect of this was to disallow the man any pretense of racial innocence, to let him know that even if he was not the sort of white who used the word *nigger* around the dinner table, he still had reason to feel racial guilt. But as disarming as this might have been, it was too abstract to do much more than crack open his vulnerability, to expose him to the logic of white guilt. This was the five-dollar intellectual sort of guilt. The twenty dollars required something more visceral. In achieving this, the second thing my friend did was something that he had not intended to do, something that ultimately brought him as much shame as he was passing out. He made a display of his own racial pain and anger. (What brought him shame was not the pain and anger but his trading on them for what turned out to be a mere twenty bucks.) The effect of this display was to reinforce the man's knowledge of ill-gotten advantage, to give credibility and solidity to it by putting a face on it. Here was human testimony, a young black beside himself at the thought of his father's racially constricted life. The pain of one man evidenced the knowledge of the other. When the businessman listened to my friend's pain, his racial guilt—normally one guilt lying dormant among others—was called out like a neglected debt he would finally have to settle. An ill-gotten advantage is not hard to bear—it can be marked up to fate—until it touches the human pain it brought into the world. This is the pain that hardens guilty knowledge.

Such knowledge is a powerful pressure when it becomes conscious. And what makes it so powerful is the element of fear that guilt always carries, fear of what the guilty knowledge says about us. Guilt makes us afraid for ourselves and so generates as much self-preoccupation as concern for others. The nature of this preoccupation is always the redemption of innocence, the reestablishment of good feeling about oneself.

In this sense, the fear for the self that is buried in all guilt is a pressure toward selfishness. It can lead us to put our own need for innocence above our concern for the problem that made us feel guilt in the first place. But this fear for the self not only inspires selfishness; it also becomes a pressure to *escape* the guilt-inducing situation. When selfishness and escapism are at work, we are no longer interested in the source of our guilt and, therefore, no longer concerned with an authentic redemption from it. Now we only want the *look* of redemption, the gesture of concern that will give us the appearance of innocence and escape from the situation. Obviously, the businessman did not put twenty dollars in the tip plate because he thought it would go to the uplift of black Americans. He did it selfishly for the appearance of concern and for the escape it afforded him.

This is not to say that guilt is never the right motive for doing good works or showing concern, only that it is a very dangerous one because of its tendency to draw us into self-preoccupation and escapism. Guilt is a civilizing emotion when the fear for the self it carries is contained—a containment that allows guilt to be more selfless and that makes genuine concern possible. I think this was the kind of guilt that, along with other forces, made the 1964 Civil Rights Act possible. But since then, I believe too many of our social policies related to race have been shaped by the fearful underside of guilt.

Black power evoked white guilt and made it a force in American institutions, just as my friend brought it to life in the businessman. Not many volunteer for guilt. Usually, it is others that make us feel it. It was the expression of black anger and pain that hardened the guilty knowledge of white ill-gotten advantage. And black power— whether from militant fringe groups, the civil rights establishment, or big city political campaigns—knew exactly the kind of white guilt it was after. It wanted to trigger the kind of white guilt in which whites fear for their own decency and innocence; it wanted the guilt of white self-preoccupation and escapism. Always at the heart of black power, in whatever form, there has been a profound anger at what was done to blacks and an equally profound feeling that there should be reparations. But a sober white guilt in which fear for the self is contained is only good for strict fairness—the 1964 Civil Rights Act that guaranteed equality under the law. It is of little value when one is after more than fairness. So black power made it its mission to have whites fear for their innocence, to feel a visceral guilt from which they would have to seek a more profound redemption. In such redemption was the possibility of black reparation. Black power upped the ante on white guilt.

With black power, all the elements of the hidden paradigm that shapes America's race-related social policy were in place. Knowledge of ill-gotten advantage could now be evidenced and deepened by black power into the sort of guilt from which institutions could redeem themselves only by offering more than fairness—by offering forms of reparation and compensation for past injustice. I believe this was the paradigm that bent our policies toward racial entitlements at the expense of racial development. In 1964, one of the assurances that Senator Hubert Humphrey and other politicians had to give Congress in order to get the landmark Civil Rights Bill passed was that the bill would not in any way require employers to use racial preferences to rectify racial imbalances. But this was before the explosion of black power in the late sixties, before the hidden paradigm was set in motion. After black power, racial preferences became the order of the day.

If this paradigm brought blacks entitlements, it also brought us the continuation of our most profound problem in American society: our invisibility as a people. The white guilt that this paradigm elicits is the kind of guilt that preoccupies whites with their own innocence and pressures them toward escapism—twenty dollars in the plate and out the door. With this guilt, as opposed to the contained guilt of genuine concern, whites tend to see only their own need for quick redemption. Blacks, then, become a means to this redemption and, as such, they must be seen as generally "less than" others. Their needs are "special," "unique," "different." They are seen exclusively along the dimension of their victimization, so they become "different" people with whom whites can negotiate entitlements, but never fully see as people like themselves. Guilt that preoccupies people with their own innocence blinds them to those who make them feel guilty. This, of course, is not racism, and yet it has the same effect as racism since it makes blacks something of a separate species for whom normal standards and values do not automatically apply.

Nowhere is this more evident today than in American universities. At some of America's most elite universities, administrators have granted concessions in response to black student demands (black power) that all but sanction racial separatism on campus—black "theme" dorms, black students unions, black yearbooks, homecoming dances, and so on. I don't believe administrators sincerely believe in these separatist concessions. Most of them are liberals who see racial separatism as wrong. But black student demands pull them into the paradigm of self-preoccupied white guilt whereby they seek a quick redemption by offering special entitlements that go beyond fairness. In this black students become invisible to them. Though blacks have the lowest grade point average of any group in American universities, administrators never sit down with them and "demand" in kind that they bring their grades up to par. The paradigm of white guilt makes the real problems of black students secondary to the need for white redemption. It also cuts these administrators off from their own values, which would most certainly discourage racial separatism and encourage higher black performance. Lastly, it makes for escapist policies; there is little difference between giving black students a separate graduation ceremony or student lounge and leaving twenty dollars in the tip plate on the way out the door. . . .

ANALYSIS

1. Steele's key argument is about *race-holding,* which he defines both by example and generalized definition. What does he mean by the term? How does he explain how race-holding contributes to the fact that black students in his classes inevitably end up at the bottom? How is this connected with "margin of choice" and "self-fulfilling prophecy"?

2. What does Steele mean by "integration shock"? How does this concept connect with his central argument?

3. How does the illustration of "white guilt" from the experience of a friend of Steele's exemplify Steele's critique of white behavior? According to Steele, what "two things" does the illustration reveal?

4. In a section of Steele's essay not reprinted here, Steele says "I think those who provoke this sort of awkwardness are operating out of a black identity that obliges them to badger white people about race almost on principle." Do you agree or disagree with this point? Explain.

5. What, finally, does Steele mean by "innocence" (for blacks or whites)?

—————————— **WRITING POSSIBILITIES** ——————————

1. As you reread Steele's essay, consider what it says about "white racism" and "victimization" of blacks in American history. Does Steele stint on this or touch on it just enough? Would there be a difference of opinion on "just enough" depending on one's race or ethnicity?

2. Steele makes a basic rhetorical move when he speaks of a TV documentary about Detroit's inner city. Though the civil rights struggle has made its achievement felt, Steele says, the disintegration of Detroit's inner city "suggests that racial victimization is not our real problem. If conditions have worsened for most of us," Steele adds, "as racism has receded, then much of the problem must be of our own making." Does Steele offer sufficient support for this analysis?

3. What is the responsibility of whites, in Steele's view ("white guilt"), for the race-holding and victimization theories of black militants today. Would you agree with him? Explain why or why not.

4. Compare Steele's essay with Beverly Tatum's. In what way are both writers saying dissimilar things? In what way might it be possible to harmonize their different viewpoints (for example that one must go through the identity-crisis aspect before one can deal responsibly with educational problems)?

5. What has been your own experience with "race-holding"? with stereotypes? with "white guilt"? Write a personal essay in which you explain autobiographically the extent to which Shelby Steele's writings either seem on target or off base.

Roger Pilon

Roger Pilon is a senior fellow and director of the Center for Constitutional Studies, Cato Institute; his essay was originally part of a forum on "Flag-Burning, Discrimination, and the Right to Do Wrong" (1990). In the context of the 1960s civil rights struggle and the Left's attack on the Vietnam War of the 1970s, Pilon's defense of both flag-burning (for which some antiwar protestors went to jail) and "private prejudice" was an act of homage to the civil rights and antiwar struggle.

Pilon admits that discrimination exists and is a "very real problem" but he has no intention of defending public *discrimination. However, with the Civil Rights Act of 1964 in mind he argues in defense of the "right to discriminate" privately and in so doing gets at the problem of institutional or structural discrimination and the difference between dealing with discrimination in terms of* intent *and* results:

> If an employer has a workforce in which blacks or women . . . are "underrepresented" with respect to the "relevant population," we presume prima facie, that he has discriminated on those proscribed grounds (race and sex) and then ask him to

prove that he has not. Thus does the burden shift—from the state to prove guilt to the defendant to prove his *innocence— not* because the statue explicitly requires it—but because practically that is the only way such a "right" can be enforced. . . . Quotas, then, are no explicit part of the 1964 act, . . . But they are there all the same. . . .

What Pilon proposes is that, instead of relying on legislation like the Civil Rights Act of 1964, we rely instead on "moral suasion and public obloquy." Whose analysis do you agree with, Pilon or Omi and Winant's "pervasive" structure of "racial formation" (148)? Why?

THE RIGHT TO DO WRONG
from The Libertarian Reader

Two questions that captured the attention of the American public in the spring of 1990 were whether we should ban the burning of the American flag and whether we should enact a new civil rights statute to broaden the rights of minorities, women, and others in the workplace. Those are distinct questions, to be sure, and have been seen as distinct by most of the public. Nevertheless, underlying them are certain common themes that go to the core of the American vision. . . .

When the Supreme Court [in 1990] found for the second time in as many years that a statute aimed at prohibiting the desecration of the American flag as a form of political protest was itself prohibited by the First Amendment to the Constitution, the Court did so by drawing upon the classic distinction between speech and its content. The statute's "restriction on expression cannot be justified without reference to the content of the regulated speech," the Court said. And "if there is a bedrock principle underlying the First Amendment, it is that the Government may not prohibit the expression of an idea simply because society finds the idea itself offensive or disagreeable."

This distinction between speech and its content is ancient, of course, finding its roots in antiquity, its modern expressions in the *philosophes* of the Enlightenment and the Founders of the American Republic. When Sir Winston Churchill observed in 1945 that "the United States is a land of free speech. Nowhere is speech freer—not even [in England] where we sedulously cultivate it even in its most repulsive forms," he was merely echoing thoughts attributed to Voltaire, that he may disapprove of what you say but would defend to the death your right to say it, and the ironic question of Benjamin Franklin: "Abuses of the freedom of speech ought to be repressed; but to whom are we to commit the power of doing it?" There is all the difference in the world between defending the right to speak and defending the speech that flows from the exercise of that right. Indeed, with perfect consistency one can condemn the burning of the flag, as most Americans do, while defending the right to burn it.

Yet for many—Americans and non-Americans alike—the distinction between speech and its content is difficult to grasp, and certainly difficult to endure. Some see the relatively explicit protections of the First Amendment as an impediment to some "right of the majority" to express its values through the democratic process. Others draw a distinction between speech and action, then claim that the First Amendment protects only the former—apparently unaware not only that speech takes many forms, many quite "active," but that all speech is action and, arguably, all action is, if not speech, at least expression. Still others point to such restrictions on speech as are found in the areas of endangerment (shouting "Fire!" in a crowded theater), defamation, and obscenity, assume those to reflect mere value or policy decisions, then ask why restrictions on flag desecration should be treated any differently.

Setting aside restrictions on obscenity as they pertain to adults, which are inexplicable anomalies in the jurisprudence of the First Amendment, the rationale for restricting speech that endangers or defames others is both persuasive and instructive. Indeed, when properly explicated, that rationale goes to the core of the American vision, as captured most generally in the Ninth Amendment, of which the First Amendment, among others, is simply a more specific manifestation. Stating that "the enumeration in the Constitution of certain rights shall not be construed to deny or disparage others retained by the people," the Ninth Amendment is fairly read as recognizing and establishing in law a general presumption in favor of liberty. Whether we call that presumption a "right to be let alone—the most comprehensive of rights and the right most valued by civilized men," as Justice Brandeis put it when exploring the idea of privacy, or a right to be free, a right to come and go as we please, to plan and live our own lives, that basic right is limited only by the equal right of others and by the express powers of government that are enumerated in the Constitution and in the constitutions of the various states. It is precisely because they implicate the rights of others, therefore, that acts that endanger or defame are not protected by the First Amendment, even when they are deemed to be "speech," whereas acts that do not implicate the rights of others are protected.

It is this fundamental principle, then, the principle of equal freedom, defined classically by our rights to life, liberty, and property, that constitutes the core of the American vision and serves as well to order systematically the countless examples of those rights—from speech to religion, contract, due process, and on and on. Far from being mere value or policy choices, when rationally related, those rights reflect a moral order that transcends our contingent values and preferences. That transcendent order—the higher or natural law, if you will—was captured most forcefully in our Declaration of Independence, of course, which states plainly that we are born free and equal, with equal moral rights to plan and live our own lives—even, by implication, when doing so offends others. Call it tolerance, call it respect: it is the mark of a free society that individuals are left free to pursue their own values, however wise or foolish, however enlightened or benighted, however pleasing or offensive to others.

But if that fundamental principle applies not simply to flag-burning, nor even simply to speech, religion, and other First Amendment issues generally, but across the board—to all questions about the relationship between the individual and his government—then we cannot shirk from that application, however unpleasant or unpopular the results may be. We turn, then, to the second of our debates and to the question whether the Civil Rights Act of 1990 is a threat to our civil rights. Plainly, underlying that question is the more basic question about just what our civil rights are. It is that more basic question to which Professor [Richard] Epstein points when he challenges not simply the proposed Civil Rights Act of 1990 but the assumptions underlying the Civil Rights Act of 1964 as well. In the Washington of 1990, neither of those challenges, but especially the latter, will earn one popular acclaim. If we are serious about getting to the heart of the matter, however, and about understanding the core of the American vision, the fundamental questions must be examined.

Now it would be one thing to respond to the basic question about what our civil rights are by answering that those rights are what the legislature says they are. That tack is all too familiar. In so responding, however, not only would we place our rights at the mercy of majorities—or, if the public choice school of thought is correct, at the mercy of special interests—but by doing so we would expose those rights to the vagaries of popular opinion, which is precisely what we have rights to protect us from. If our rights come and go according to the winds of political fashion, then we live not under the rule of law but under the rule of men. Indeed, it was precisely to secure the former that our Founders wrote a constitution in the first place, a constitution, as noted above, that was founded on the principle of equal freedom, as defined by our rights to life, liberty, and property. Subject those rights to the vagaries of public opinion and you undermine the very foundations of that moral and legal order.

Yet that is precisely what has happened over a wide area of life, including the especially wide area that is defined by our rights, or freedom, of association. As Professor Epstein observes, the civil rights acts that were enacted after the Civil War were intended simply to ensure that freed slaves would have the same civil capacities, or rights, as other free persons—rights to purchase and hold property, to make and enforce contracts, to sue and be sued, and so on. That those newly recognized rights came to be frustrated, especially in the South, by Jim Crow is appalling, of course, for the Jim Crow restraints were in direct violation of the American vision that the civil rights acts were intended to secure. And insofar as the Civil Rights Act of 1964 eliminated Jim Crow, it is to be commended. But the idea behind the early civil rights acts was to give force at last to the principle of equal freedom upon which this nation was founded, however imperfect that founding. The idea was not, most decidedly, to recognize "rights" that were inconsistent with that principle.

With the Civil Rights Act of 1964, however, that precisely is what took place. Driven by the very real problem of discrimination, but failing utterly to distinguish between the appalling institution of public discrimination, in the form of Jim Crow, and its private counterpart, the authors of the 1964 act created a "right" against private discrimination on certain grounds and in certain contexts, which has been expanded over the years. That "right," of course, is nowhere to be found in the Constitution or in its underlying principles. Indeed, its enforcement is inconsistent with that document and with those principles. For if we do have a right to be free, to plan and live our own lives as we choose, limited only by the equal right of others, then we have a right to associate, or to refuse to associate, for whatever reasons we choose, or for no reason at all. That is what freedom is all about. Others may condemn our reasons—that too is a right. But if freedom and personal sovereignty mean anything, they mean the right to make those kinds of decisions for ourselves, even when they offend others.

None of this is to defend private discrimination, of course. Rather, as in the case of flag-burning, it is to defend the *right* to discriminate. For discrimination, like flag-burning, violates no rights of others, however offensive it may otherwise be. We have no more right to associate with those who do not want to associate with us, for whatever reason, than we have to be free from the offense that flag-burning gives. Fortunately, most Americans condemn both flag-burning and discrimination. But in doing so they make value judgments, which are very different from rational judgments about the rights we have. Indeed, the whole point of rights is to enable us to pursue our ends, especially our unpopular ends. We hardly need to invoke rights to pursue popular ends.

Enter, however, this "right against discrimination" and the issues are turned on their heads. Now we may no longer choose not to associate with someone for the proscribed reasons; indeed, we have an obligation not to discriminate on those grounds. But how do we enforce such a right? After all, those who are otherwise inclined to discriminate on one or more of the proscribed grounds are not likely to announce their reasons, thereby subjecting themselves to the sanctions of the act. The answer is that, save for those rare cases in which someone openly defies the act, we have to abandon an intent test, for all practical purposes, and look instead at the effects of an individual's actions. If an employer has a workforce in which blacks or women, say, are "underrepresented" with respect to the "relevant population," we presume, prima facie, that he has discriminated on those proscribed grounds (race and sex) and then ask him to prove that he has not. Thus does the burden shift—from the state to prove guilt to the defendant to prove his *innocence*—*not* because the statute explicitly requires it—far from it—but because practically that is the only way such a "right" can be enforced. For given such a statute, and the sanctions it imposes, people simply do not go around saying they discriminated for one of the wrong reasons. By the same token, however, people who discriminate for *other* reasons, and get their numbers wrong, will be swept into the maw of this statute, from which they will extricate themselves only if they are able to convince the court that those reasons are compelling.

Quotas, then, are no explicit part of the 1964 act, nor are they of the proposed 1990 act. But they are there all the same, every bit as real as if they were written in stone. For if an employer does not get his numbers right, the burden of proving his innocence is so onerous, and the penalties for failing to do so, especially under the 1990 act, so draconian, that for all practical purposes he will operate as if quotas were explicitly in the statute. Thus those who oppose quotas, but believe in this "right against discrimination," need to rethink their position. If they are serious about enforcing such a "right," then de facto quotas are inescapable.

We return, then, to the underlying issues that join these two debates. For at a deeper level, the approach we have taken to the problem of private discrimination—admittedly, a very real problem that cries out for condemnation—is itself an affront to our founding principles. We speak, after all, of the indivisibility of freedom. And we understand that idea and its applications, for the most part, in such areas of the Constitution as the First Amendment, where our rights are relatively clear. But the principle of those First Amendment rights—that individuals are and ought to be free to express their own values and live their own lives, however much they may offend others in the process—is perfectly general. Again, most Americans find flag-burning abhorrent, just as they find discrimination abhorrent. As long, however, as those who burn flags or those who discriminate do not violate the rights of others, their right to so behave should be protected.

Indeed, we have other, more peaceful and, ultimately, more effective means of dealing with such people. In the age of communication—local, national, and global—the force of moral suasion and public obloquy in areas such as these is far more effective and far less costly than any heavy-handed resort to law, with all its unintended consequences. We need to unleash this force, not disparage it by a too hasty, and ultimately misguided, resort to legal force. And we need in particular to be careful about compromising our fundamental, founding principles, not only when our ends are noble, but especially when they are noble.

ANALYSIS

1. On what basis does Pilon argue that private discrimination is acceptable? Do you agree with him?
2. Pilon seems to *assume* that when an employer discriminates, this is a "private" matter? Would you agree with this assumption? Why or why not?
3. Is it true that public discrimination (e.g., Pilon on Jim Crow laws) really doesn't exist now? Are there differences of opinion and personal experience in this realm—i.e., if you are African American or Asian American have experienced public discriminatory practices?

WRITING POSSIBILITIES

1. Pilon defends private acts of discrimination by citing various examples. What might be other examples? Would it be acceptable for three dorm residents to say that they did not want a fourth, gay, resident among them? A black? A Mormon? Can you think of other examples to test Pilon's distinction between private and public? Discuss the pros and cons of Pilon's distinction between private and public.
2. The U.S. Commission on Civil Rights has argued in the past that "structural" discrimination is an important component of both the racial and gender scene. By "structural discrimination," the Commission refers to such seemingly neutral practices as height and weight requirements for police and firefighters—i.e., practices not targeted at any one race or group but nevertheless from the Commission's viewpoint the functional equivalent of discrimination. A similarly structural argument is to be found in William Julius Wilson's "When Work Disappears" (Chapter 5). What do you think Pilon would say about such analyses? If you accept Pilon's analysis, then the scope of "private" discrimination as he sees it is extremely limited. Review Pilon's arguments and decide if you think his analysis is better than Wilson's.

Sherman Alexie, Dennis West, and Joan M. West

The author of The Lone Ranger and Tonto Fistfight in Heaven *and the writer-director of the movie* Smoke Signals, *Alexie—a Spokane Indian—provides an adaptation of, and challenge to, pop culture images of the Indian. In other words, he says, if you want to fight movie stereotypes, make a movie of your own! (Spike Lee did the same thing, in fact.) Mockingly, Alexie asks "Does every Indian depend on Hollywood for a twentieth-century vision?" and his answer is, paradoxically, yes (in that Alexie likes much of American pop culture) and no (the stereotypes are persistent and need to be corrected). Irony and parody, as Alexie suggests, are as much counters to prejudice and discrimination as direct broadside attacks.*

SENDING CINEMATIC *SMOKE SIGNALS:*

An Interview with Sherman Alexie

Every few years or so, press kits arrive at the offices of film magazines announcing that a forthcoming film about Native Americans decisively breaks with the stereotype of the past. *Smoke Signals* is the lastest film to advertise itself so, but, unlike most of its predecessors, *Smoke Signals* delivers on its promises. A prime component of its success is that it is the first feature to have been written, directed, and coproduced by Native Americans, and also features Native Americans in all the lead roles.

The storyline is a variation of the odyssey theme. In this instance, rather than focusing on a warrior / father struggling to return to his home, the plot turns on a warrior / son struggling to physically and emotionally find an alcoholic father who fled his home and died in self-exile. Victor Joseph (Adam Beach), an abandoned son who has grown up on the Coeur d'Alene reservation in Idaho, must undertake a journey to collect the ashes of his father, Arnold Joseph (Gary Farmer), who has died in Phoenix, Arizona. Thomas Builds-the-Fire (Evan Adams) provides Victor the money he needs for the trip on condition that he is allowed to go along. Unlike Victor, Thomas has numerous positive memories of Arnold Joseph, ultimately derived from the circumstance that, when he was only an infant, Arnold had saved him from a burning building.

Their road together turns out to have a number of detours and moments of truth, all of which are interesting in and of themselves. More important than the incidents and challenges per se, however, are the effects they have on the emotional development of the two sojourners. Sherman Alexie, who wrote the script based on sections of his best-selling *The Lone Ranger and Tonto Fistfight in Heaven,* has noted that American popular culture recognizes only two major Native American profiles: the warrior and the shaman. He goes about subverting these stereotypes with various images, stories, and songs. Although some aspects of the odyssey are somber, humor often finds its way into the darkest moments. Victor and Thomas constantly jibe with one another and outsiders about what it means to be a contemporary Native American. Thomas proves to be a genuine storyteller, but his tales never dissolve into the usual hocus pocus surrounding shamans; and Victor is indeed a warrior, but he is neither stoic nor silent. Both characters are decidedly Native American, but Native Americans rooted in this time and place and not a fictionalized past.

The literary talent of Sherman Alexie, who is coproducer as well as the scriptwriter of *Smoke Signals,* is very much in evidence throughout the film. Words count for him, whether for the sheer joy of wordplay, or as a means of revealing a character. But the film is never talky in the sense of a stage play. Rather, it has the kind of intelligent and clever dialog characteristic of the best studio films of yore. In this sense, Alexie has been extremely successful in moving from writing for the printed page to writing for the screen. And his considerable success in the former bodes well for his future as a writer for the cinema. Throughout the 1990s, Alexie has garnered numerous writing awards, steadily gaining recognition as one of America's leading fiction writers. His second novel, *Indian Killer,* a current best seller, is being developed as a feature film by ShadowCatcher Entertainment, the producer of *Smoke Signals.*

In addition to his prose, Alexie is a well-known poet. His first book of poetry, *The Business of Fancydancing,* was chosen in 1992 by *The New York Times Book Review* as its Notable Book of the Year. He has since won a poetry fellowship from the National Endowment for the Arts and a Lila Wallace / Readers' Digest Writer's Award. Not coincidentally *Smoke Signals* features an original contemporary poem as its coda. The first line sounds one of the film's major themes: "How do we forgive our fathers?" The film concludes with a voice-over recitation of the poem that is a refreshing break from the dumbing-down and action-oriented approach of so many contemporary films. That the poem's author, Dick Lourie, is not a Native American also fits into the film's pattern of breaking with the expected ethnic response. Using a Native American poem for this purpose would have been far more predictable and problematic.

Smoke Signals is all the more impressive for being the debut feature of director Chris Eyre, a twenty-eight-year-old Cheyenne / Arapaho filmmaker from Oregon who has previously written and directed seven short films. He keeps the film moving at a brisk but not a hurried pace, taking time to get the most out of a scene involving frying bread, while allowing spectacular outdoor vistas to speak for themselves rather than being framed as picture postcards. Eyre gets a particularly strong performance from Evan Adams, who credibly renders Thomas as an engaging cross between a mama's boy and a traditional seer, a sometimes nerd in funny glasses who is no one's sidekick. Eyre also makes effective use of Irene Bedard, as Suzy Song, who has an understanding and affection for the deceased Arnold Joseph that his son must deal with.

No single film can be expected to undo the misinformation about Native Americans that has accumulated over many generations. Since the politically turbulent Sixties, there has been an ongoing movement by Native American film actors to combat ethnic stereotyping. In their wake have come Native American producers, directors, actors, and scriptwriters. *Smoke Signals* belongs to and advances this continuum. Hopefully, it will prove to be the first of a new wave of diverse Native American films. The ethnic group that has been featured more than any other in the history of American films is finally beginning to speak in its own voice. During the 1998 Seattle Film Festival, *Cineaste* was able to speak with Alexie about the many cultural issues embodied by and explored in his debut feature film effort, *Smoke Signals.*

Cineaste: You have called your screenplay "groundbreaking" because of its portrayal of Indians. Why?

Sherman Alexie: Well, it's a very basic story, a road trip / buddy movie about a lost father, so I'm working with two very classical, mythic structures. You can find them in everything from *The Bible* to *The Iliad* and *The Odyssey.* What is revolutionary or groundbreaking about the film is that the characters in it are Indians, and they're fully realized human beings. They're not just the sidekick, or the buddy, they're the protagonists. Simply having Indians as the protagonists in a contemporary film, and placing them within this familiar literary and cinematic structure, is groundbreaking.

Cineaste: Do you think *Powwow Highway* (1989) was one of the more worthy previous efforts?

Alexie: When it came out, I loved it, and I saw it three times at the Micro Movie House in Moscow, Idaho. But I saw it again on Bravo recently and, after working on this film, and seeing what we could do, *Powwow Highway* now seems so stereotypical. The performances are fine, but it trades in so many stereotypes, from standing in a river singing, to going up on a mountaintop to get a vision, and the generic AIM political activism. Every stereotypical touchstone of a contemporary Indian art film is there. Two scenes especially really made me cringe. When Philbert goes up on a mountain, he's supposed to leave something that means so much to him, and he leaves a Hershey bar! Then there's the scene with A Martinez, as Buddy Red Bow, where the police car's coming, and Buddy has a piece of metal or something in his hand. He jumps in the air, and there's this brief flash shot of him dressed in the full costume of an Indian warrior, throwing a tomahawk, and I just thought, "Oh God!"

Our expectations of movies about Indians were so low then that we embraced a movie like *Powwow Highway* simply because there was no other option. Looking back, *Thunderheart* is a far superior movie, just in terms of its representation. I mean, it's a generic white guy saves the day movie, but I think it's better in terms of its representation of contemporary Indians. Except for John Trudell changing into a deer *[laughs]*. I've never seen an Indian turn into a deer. I mean, I know thousands of Indians, I've been an Indian my whole life, and I've yet to see an Indian turn into an animal! And I know some very traditional Indian folks.

Cineaste: Would you comment on your fundamental approach in adapting your collection of short stories, *The Lone Ranger and Tonto Fistfight in Heaven,* for the screen?

Alexie: I've never been one of those people who compared the book and the movie of the book. That's never interested me because I've always separated them as two very distinct art forms, so I never got mad if the movie wasn't the book, or vice versa. I knew from a very young age that it was impossible to do that. I mean, you're talking about a 300-page novel versus an hour-and-a-half or two-hour movie. It's impossible to convey in a movie the entire experience of a novel, and I always knew that.

Knowing that going in, I didn't have any problems with mutating my own book. I treated my book of short stories in adapting the screenplay as though I didn't write it. Right from the get-go, I said, "OK, Sherman, you're going to do composite characters, compress time, take bits and pieces from stories you need for this screenplay, and you're not going to care." The narrative integrity of any one story was never the point, it was all about taking situations from the twenty-two short stories—it actually ended up being adapted from four short stories—taking the best you can find in this book to make the screenplay.

Cineaste: How did you think about structure?

Alexie: The cheapest kind of independent film to make is either people in a room talking. . . .

Cineaste: My Dinner with Andre?

Alexie: Yeah, or *Clerks.* It's either that or a road movie, and I didn't want to make a talking-heads movie, because that's a tough sell to begin with. It's hard to reach a large audience with a talking-heads movie and, if you put Indians in the talking heads, only four people are going to want to see it. But I knew the road movie was a very time-honored structure, and also very cheap to do. Put two guys in a car or a bus, get a camera rig, and you're fine, it's easy to film.

Cineaste: And it can be visually interesting.

Alexie: Exactly. You can let the landscape tell a lot of story. And if it's a road / buddy movie, you're going to have a lot of music, and I always knew music was going to be a part of this. There are specific music cues in the screenplay about traditional music or rock and roll music, or a combination of the two. "John Wayne's Teeth," for example, is a combination of English lyrics and Western musical rhythms along with Indian vocables and Indian traditional drums. I also wanted to use Indian artists, so as not only to make a revolutionary movie for Indians, but also to use Indian artists on the soundtrack, which fits well with the road / buddy movie structure.

There was always a template in my head for this, which was these two odd buddies, sort of Mutt and Jeff on a road trip, *Midnight Cowboy* on a bus ride. One of the original drafts of the screenplay, in fact, contained many more overt references to *Midnight Cowboy.* Joe Buck and Victor—beautiful, stoic, clueless guys—are very much alike. At the Sundance Institute, I saw a documentary about Waldo Salt, the screenwriter of *Midnight Cowboy,* that really affected me in the way I wanted to make the movie. In an interview in the documentary, Salt talked about his use of flashforwards in *Midnight Cowboy,* so that while the story is going, you learn more and more about Joe Buck and his experiences back home. It was always flashforwards, that's what he called them, that continued the story and gave you more information. Rather than stopping the movie to be expository, they kept the drama going. So in writing the screenplay, I always knew there were going to be flashforwards. *Midnight Cowboy* was really a template for me in a lot of ways, not only in its structure, but also in the screenwriting philosophies of Waldo Salt.

Cineaste: Would you comment on the screenplay's semiautobiographical elements?

Alexie: My friend and I took a trip to Phoenix, Arizona, to pick up his father's remains. At the Sundance Festival, quite a few people asked, "Were you influenced by *Powwow Highway?*," because that film's also about a trip by two Indian guys to the Southwest. "It wasn't really an influence," I said, "unless you can say that my friend's father died because of *Powwow Highway.*" The basic creative spark for *Smoke Signals* came from the trip I took with my friend. It's not my friend's story, but I placed my characters within that framework of going to pick up a father's remains. That's how the short story came about. It's more about my relationship with my father than about my friend's relationship with his father. My father is still alive, but he's had to struggle with alcoholism, as I have. It's also about the struggle within myself of being this storytelling geek like Thomas, as well as this big jock masculine guy like Victor, so it's a sort of schizophrenic multiple personality of myself that I develop within the movie.

Cineaste: Storytelling, dreams, and visions are key motifs in your book, *The Lone Ranger and Tonto,* and in *Smoke Signals.* Would you comment on their cultural and artistic significance for you?

Alexie: In the book itself, I'm rarely interested in traditional narrative. My beginnings are as a poet. My first form of writing was poetry. While there's certainly a strong narrative drive in my poetry, it was always about the image, and about the connection, often, of very disparate, contradictory images. When I began working on the screenplay, and not knowing anything about screenplays, I started reading all the typical books—you know, Syd Field and all those people—but I was not interested in their formulas for successful screenplays. In fact, after reading them and all the screenplays they admired so much, I realized that the qualities they were talking about were not what made those movies or screenplays great. It was always something that exploded outside the narrative or the structure that made the movie great, so I was always interested in going outside the narrative and traditional formats.

In my books, I've always been fascinated with dreams and stories and flashing forward and flashing back and playing with conventions of time, so in adapting the screenplay, I always knew I would use those elements. I knew there would be moments when the camera would sit still and somebody was going to talk, but I didn't want just talking heads, as I mentioned earlier. I always knew that while the person was talking, we were going to see images from the story he or she was telling. I even develop that motif, and the fact that the story of the movie is told by Thomas, so at certain points he's telling the story about himself telling the story about somebody else telling a story. So I wanted to keep those complicated layers going.

It's all based on the basic theme, for me, that storytellers are essentially liars. At one point in the movie, Suzy asks Thomas, "Do you want lies or do you want the truth?," and he says, "I want both." I think that line is what reveals most about Thomas's character and the nature of his storytelling and the nature, in my opinion, of storytelling in general, which is that fiction blurs and nobody knows what the truth is. And within the movie itself, nobody knows what the truth is.

Cineaste: Why does Thomas always close his eyes when he tells a story?

Alexie: [Laughs] That was in the book, but I don't know.

Cineaste: There is a literary tradition of blind seers, of course.

Alexie: I really don't know. The first time I wrote that story, he closed his eyes. I wrote, "Thomas closed his eyes." And it stayed.

Cineaste: For me, when I read that, it was as if he were trying to imagine it with such intensity that he had to close his eyes and move into another realm.

Alexie: It could be that! It just felt right, it just felt like something he would do.

Cineaste: We don't recall smoke signals as a motif in the book. Did you decide on the film's title?

Alexie: Yeah, I did. People keep asking me, "Why did Miramax change the title?" Well, Miramax didn't change the title, I did. In fact, I never wanted to call the movie, *This Is What It Means to Say Phoenix, Arizona.* That's the name of the short story. I love that title on the story, but it is *not* a cinematic title. There is an inverse proportional relationship between the length of movie titles and the success of the film. Very few long-titled films do well, because people forget the title.

Even though we were getting some very good Sundance coverage, people kept screwing up the movie title, and that would have killed the film. So, in looking for a title, we wanted something short and punchy, but also something that fit thematically. *Smoke Signals* fits for a number of reasons, for me. On the surface, it's a stereotypical title, you think of Indians in blankets on the plains sending smoke signals, so it brings up a stereotypical image that's vaguely humorous. But people will also instantly recognize that this is about Indians. Then, when you see the movie, you realize that, in a contemporary sense, smoke signals are about calls of distress, calls for help. That's really what this movie is about—Victor, Thomas, and everybody else calling for help. It's also about the theme of fire. The smoke that originates from the first fire in the movie is what causes these events, and the smoke from the second fire brings about the beginning of resolution. So I just thought *Smoke Signals* worked very poetically. It's something very memorable, and nobody is going to screw up that title!

Cineaste: Would you comment on the film's theme of the absent father and specifically on the ending of the film? How do you envision the future of your two young, fatherless protagonists?

Alexie: Well, I'm reminded of this quote from Gabriel Garcia Marquez that my wife has up on the refrigerator. He says something like, 'Men have been running the world for how many thousands of years, and look what we've done. It's about time we let women take over.' So that theme is in my head, the idea that in Indian cultures in particular, men have lost all their traditional roles within society. There are feminine and masculine roles within Indian society and, in many tribes, men and women played neither role, or went back and forth. But those traditional masculine roles—you know, hunter, warrior— they're all gone. I mean, driving a truck for the BIA is simply not going to fulfill your spiritual needs, like fishing for salmon or hunting for deer once did, so in some sense Indian men are much more lost and much more clueless than Indian women.

I think you'd find the same thing in every ethnic or racial community, and it's fathers who are missing. I was doing an interview yesterday, and it came to me that brown artists—African American, Chicano, Indian, and so on—write about fathers who physically leave and don't come back. White artists deal with fathers who leave emotionally, who sit in the chair in the living room but are gone. It's a theme that resonates. The actual physical presence of the father varies with ethnicity, I think, so the idea of a father leaving is nothing new for me. My father did leave to drink but he always came back. So for me it was a way of exploring that feeling of abandonment.

Cineaste: Is your vision of Indian society less dark in *Smoke Signals* than in *Long Ranger?*

Alexie: Definitely. If you chart the course of my book, or my literary work, you're going to see that pattern. I always tease literary scholars who interview me, saying, "You know, you should use the title, 'Firewater World: The Idea of Recovery in Sherman Alexie's Fiction and Poetry,' because that's really what's happened." When I first started writing I was still drinking, so *Lone Ranger and Tonto* and the first book of poems, *The Business of Fancydancing,* are really soaked in alcohol. As I've been in recovery over the years and stayed sober, you'll see the work gradually freeing itself of alcoholism and going much deeper, exploring the emotional, sociological, and psychological reasons for any kind of addiction or dysfunctions within the community. I'm looking for the causes now, rather than the effects, and I think that's what *Smoke Signals* is about. *The Lone Ranger and Tonto* is about the effects of alcoholism on its characters, and I think the adaptation, *Smoke Signals,* is more about the causes of that behavior. It's more of a whole journey, you get there and you get back.

Cineaste: There's a stunning moment in the film when Victor tells the white police chief that he doesn't drink, that he's never drunk. It seemed a declaration of a break with his father and his father's past, trying to overcome that difficult social problem.

Alexie: Exactly, that he's going to be somebody different. In my books and poems, Victor's a drinker, an alcoholic, but in the movie he's never had a drop. It's also a big break from my own work, so it's working on a couple of levels there. Not only the difference between my book Victor and my movie Victor, but, within the context of the story, it's also Victor's break away from his father, his creator, who is me.

Cineaste: Would you comment on the two young women driving their car in reverse?

Alexie: [Laughs] Well, their names are Thelma and Lucy!

Cineaste: To avoid copyright problems?

Alexie: It was an in-joke for me, playing around with the idea of a road movie. I love that movie, as an anti-road movie which deconstructs the whole macho road / buddy movie, so I wanted to put them in there as a homage to *Thelma & Louise*. It also has to do with the sense of time in the movie, then the past, present, and future are all the same, that circular sense of time which plays itself out in the seamless transitions from past to present. Within that circular sense of time, I also wanted to have this car driving in reverse. The phrase I always use is, "Sometimes to go forward you have to drive in reverse." So it's a visual metaphor for what we were doing.

It's also an Indian metaphor because our cars are always screwed up. There was a man who one summer drove his pickup all over the reservation in reverse because none of the forward gears worked. It's one of those moments that I think everybody can find amusing, but non-Indian audiences are going to say, "OK, this is funny, but what the hell's going on?," because there is no explanation for it. Indian audiences are really going to laugh, however, because they're going to completely understand it. I call those kinds of things Indian trapdoors, because an Indian will walk over them and fall in, but a non-Indian will keep on walking.

Cineaste: To get back to the music, we understand from the credits that you wrote the lyrics of five of the *Smoke Signals* songs, including "John Wayne's Teeth." Would you talk a bit about the film's use of music?

Alexie: As part of my obsessive-compulsive behavior, I guess, I had completely planned the whole movie. I knew exactly where three of the songs that I had written previously for Jim Boyd would fit in. Knowing the catalog of songs that Jim and I had written, when I was writing the screenplay I would be punching them in, knowing exactly where they would fit. I didn't want the music to be an afterthought, but an inherent and organic part of the film. Writing songs is another way of expressing ourselves. Just as I think screenplays are accessible poetry, I think songs are accessible poetry, and while I'm going to continue to write poetry that nobody reads *[laughs]*, that 2,000 people read, I also want to express myself in poetic ways that will reach a much wider audience. For me, writing songs is a way to reach a different kind of audience. Using those songs in the film, however, is also a way of telling the story, of adding more layers to the story, as you see things on screen.

"A Million Miles Away," for instance, a song that plays over one of the flashbacks, was a way of doing that, of bridging the past and the present. The lyrics of that song, sung at the beginning of the journey, are not only about the distance between Phoenix, Arizona, and the Coeur d'Alene Indian reservation, but also about the distance between people. It's a sort of battered and bruised love song. The lyrics are completely atypical of a love song, with lines like, "Some people might think you're graceful, but I think you're brittle and bent," but it's still, "Let's get a car and drive it." It's about recognizing human frailty and being in love with a person despite their frailties, so the lyrics were always an integral part of the theme of the movie.

Cineaste: What was your input as a coproducer of the film?

Alexie: Oh, everything—casting, costumes, sets, editing. I was in the editing room, and a lot of the editing ideas are mine. It was in the editing room, in fact, that I decided I wanted to direct the next one. Editing was *fun.* The whole process of editing really made me appreciate editors and realize how overlooked and underrated they are in the filmmaking process. Editors are directors and screenwriters all over again. There were many scenes that worked as we shot them, but there were also scenes that did not work, and would not have worked without the skills of our editor. It was in the editing room that I learned more than I had at any other point during the film.

In particular, it made me realize the importance of storyboards, especially in independent film, where you don't have the money to make mistakes. I started reading all these books about storyboards, catching up on the scholarship about them. Then, looking at films by directors who storyboard and those who don't, I realized how wonderfully consistent the storyboarders are and how wildly inconsistent the nonstoryboarders are. Even though the nonstoryboarders often have greater reputations, they have made some *terrible* films. Robert Altman, for example, has made classics and truly terrible films, films of such divergent qualities that it's awe-inspiring. A consistent storyboarder makes good films every time, I think.

Writing a new screenplay now, I'm very aware of editing possibilities, of transitions, so I'm really writing the screenplay as a director, whereas I didn't write *Smoke Signals* that way. I'm really conscious of scene transitions, but also about the possibilities of something not working, and trying to imagine other ways of telling this story within the editing room. So I'm editing visually, I'm doing storyboards as I'm writing, and trying to write as visually as possible.

Cineaste: In your opinion, what are the greatest challenges facing Native American societies in the U.S. today?

Alexie: The challenges to our sovereignty—artistically, politically, socially, economically. We are and always have been nations within this nation and any threats to that are dangerous. Not only in terms of the government trying to take away our sovereign rights to have casinos, to take the most crass example, but also in cultural appropriation, you know, with white people crawling into sweat lodges, and buying our religions.

Cineaste: Speaking of cultural issues, is mainstream U.S. popular culture an influence on your artistic creativity?

Alexie: I'm a thirty-one-year-old American, as well. I always tell people that the five primary influences in my life are my father, for his nontraditional Indian stories, my grandmother for her traditional Indian stories, Stephen King, John Steinbeck, and *The Brady Bunch.* That's who I am. I think a lot of Indian artists like to pretend that they're not influenced by pop culture or Western culture, but I am, and I'm happy to admit it. A lot of independent filmmakers would look down their nose at their own pop influences, or at my pop influences. It's a cultural currency. That's something that Tarantino has certainly benefited and learned from. In the best moments of his movies, he's talking about a common cultural currency, and the ways in which his characters talk about it really bring out their personalities.

Cineaste: U.S. popular culture as a lingua franca?

Alexie: Exactly, and, in the same way, I use that as a way to bridge the cultural distance between the characters in my movie and the non-Indian audience. It's a way for me, as the writer, to speak to the audience through my characters in a way that will give them something to hold onto as they're hearing and seeing something brand new.

Cineaste: There's a line in the film, and in your story, which is, "It's a good day to die." Do I recall that line from *Little Big Man?*

Alexie: Yeah, that's a *Little Big Man* reference. In every book and movie since then, it seems, the Indians always said that and I wanted to make fun of it. We used it twice in the movie, in fact. Once we said, "Sometimes it's a good day to die and sometimes it's a good day to play basketball," and another time, "Sometimes it's a good day to die and sometimes it's a good day to have breakfast." That notion has so little meaning in our lives that I wanted to make fun of it. It's never, ever, *ever,* a good day to die. There's always something better to do.

Cineaste: The film employs this sort of humor very often.

Alexie: I think humor is the most effective political tool out there, because people will listen to anything if they're laughing. The reason why someone like Rush Limbaugh is so popular is because he's damn funny. Even I—a dedicated liberal / communist / socialist kind of guy—listen to him once in a while, because you gotta know what the enemy's up to, but he makes me laugh in spite of myself. He'll be spouting this racist, homophobic, sexist, neanderthal stuff, and I'll be laughing, and thinking, "Oh God!" It's because he's funny that people respond to him. I think one thing that liberals have a decided lack of is a sense of humor. There's nothing worse than *earnest* emotion and I never want to be earnest. I always want to be on the edge of offending somebody, of challenging one notion or another, and never being comfortable not only with myself, or with my own politics or my character's politics, or their lives, but with everybody else's. Humor is really just about questioning the status quo, that's all it is.

—————— ANALYSIS ——————

1. What are the shifting attitudes Alexie reveals in regard to other movies about Native Americans?
2. Alexie says he isn't all that bothered by pop culture—at least in general. He calls it *cultural currency*. What does he mean by this term?
3. In Alexie's view, what are the crucial challenges for Native American societies today?
4. Alexie says "[N]ot only in terms of the government trying to take away our sovereign rights to have casinos . . . but also in cultural appropriation. . ." What is his *tone* in speaking of these "sovereign rights" and "casinos"? What does he mean by "cultural appropriation"?

—————— WRITING POSSIBILITIES ——————

1. Do Alexie's comments fit in with your understanding of Indian life or not? What have you learned about Native Americans in schools? From movies or books? From personal contacts or encounters?
2. What cultural themes about Indian life crop up in this interview? How would you characterize Alexie's attitudes towards such dysfunctional aspects of Reservation life as missing fathers and alcoholism?
3. At the end of the interview, Alexie says ". . . I never want to be earnest. I always want to be on the edge of offending somebody. . . ." Would you adopt such a position in order to combat stereotyping or discrimination? Who would you want to offend or challenge? How might you use humor to question the status quo?
4. Alexie raises the question of Hollywood's version of the Indian, acknowledging that he himself has been influenced both by Indian culture and popular American literature. How would this analysis work in terms of your ethnic group and its representation by the media? Are there stereotypes that you would wish to challenge (locate specific examples that you can analyze)?
5. In what way do Alexie's comments about Native Americans suggest the relevance of McLemore's summary of group identity ("Key Ideas," 2c) and group gains theories ("Key Ideas," 3b) of prejudice and discrimination (page 138)?

Elaine H. Kim

As a filmmaker and writer, Elaine Kim looks at the L.A. riots of 1992 from a personal viewpoint: here was something that affected her own Korean community even though she did not live, for much of the time, in L.A. itself. She seeks to explore "what will become of our attempts to 'become American' without dying of han—*i.e., of "frustration and rage following misfortune." She is critical of African American community leaders who regarded Korean merchants as "intruders"; she is aware of the ignorance of Koreans about the nature of "the racial hierarchy they had no part in creating"; and she is angered at the way the media have exacerbated tensions between the two communities (especially by ignoring incidents of cooperation between the two groups). Ultimately, Kim emphasizes cooperative action by both Korean and black groups to root out racism as much as possible. She argues that Korean "nationalism" must change and merge into a kind of "internationalism" and thus to see how, in Rodney King's words, "we're all stuck here for a while" and so we must try to "work it out."*

HOME IS WHERE THE *HAN* IS:
A KOREAN AMERICAN PERSPECTIVE
ON THE LOS ANGELES UPHEAVALS

About half of the estimated $850 million in material losses incurred during the Los Angeles unheavals was sustained by a community no one seems to want to talk much about. Korean Americans in Los Angeles, suddenly at the front lines when violence came to the buffer zone they had been so precariously occupying, suffered profound damage to their means of livelihood. But my concern here is the psychic damage which, unlike material damage, is impossible to quantify.

I want to explore the questions of whether or not recovery is possible for Korean Americans, and what will become of our attempts to "become American" without dying of *han*. *Han* is a Korean word that means, loosely translated, the sorrow and anger that grow from the accumulated experiences of oppression. Although the word is frequently and commonly used by Koreans, the condition it describes is taken quite seriously. When people die of *han,* it is called dying of *hwabyong,* a disease of frustration and rage following misfortune.

Situated as we are on the border between those who have and those who have not, between predominantly Anglo and mostly African American and Latino communities, from our current interstitial position in the American discourse of race, many Korean Americans have trouble calling what happened in Los Angeles an "uprising." At the same time, we cannot quite say it was a "riot." So some of us have taken to calling it *sa-i-ku,* April 29, after the manner of naming other events in Korean history—3.1 (*sam-il*) for March 1, 1919, when massive protests against Japanese colonial rule began in Korea; 6.25 (*yook-i-o*), or June 25, 1950, when the Korean War began; and 4.19 (*sa-il-ku*), or April 19, 1960, when the first student movement in the world to overthrow a government began in South Korea. The ironic similarity between 4.19 and 4.29 does not escape most Korean Americans.

Los Angeles Koreatown has been important to me, even though I visit only a dozen times a year. Before Koreatown sprang up during the last decade and a half, I used to hang around the fringes of Chinatown, although I knew that this habit was pure pretense. For me, knowing that Los Angeles Koreatown existed made a difference; one of my closest friends worked with the Black-Korean Alliance there, and I liked to think of it as a kind of "home"—however idealized and hypostatized—for the soul, an anchor, a potential refuge, a place in America where I could belong without ever being asked, "Who are you and what are you doing here? Where did you come from and when are you going back?"

Many of us watched in horror the destruction of Koreatown and the systematic targeting of Korean shops in South Central Los Angeles after the Rodney King verdict. Seeing those buildings in flames and those anguished Korean faces, I had the terrible thought that there would be no belonging and that we were, just as I had always suspected, a people destined to carry our *han* around with us wherever we went in the world. The destiny (*p'aljja*) that had spelled centuries of extreme suffering from invasion, colonization, war, and national division had smuggled itself into the U.S. with our baggage.

AFRICAN AMERICAN AND KOREAN AMERICAN CONFLICT

As someone whose social consciousness was shaped by the African American-led civil rights movement of the 1960s, I felt that I was watching our collective dreams for a just society disintegrating, cast aside as naive and irrelevant in the bitter and embattled 1990s. It was the courageous African American women and men of the 1960s who had redefined the meaning of "American," who had first suggested that a person like me could reject the false choice between being treated as a perpetual foreigner in my own birthplace, on the one hand, and relinquishing my identity for someone else's ill-fitting and impossible Anglo American one on the other. Thanks to them, I began to discern how institutional racism works and why Korea was never mentioned in my world history textbooks. I was able to see how others beside

Koreans had been swept aside by the dominant culture. My American education offered nothing about Chicanos or Latinos, and most of what I was taught about African and Native Americans was distorted to justify their oppression and vindicate their oppressors.

I could hardly believe my ears when, during the weeks immediately following *sa-i-ku,* I heard African American community leaders suggesting that Korean American merchants were foreign intruders deliberately trying to stifle African American economic development, when I knew that they had bought those liquor stores at five times gross receipts from African American owners, who had previously bought them at two times gross receipts from Jewish owners after Watts. I saw anti-Korean flyers that were being circulated by African American political candidates and read about South Central residents petitioning against the reestablishment of swap meets, groups of typically Korean immigrant-operated market stalls. I was disheartened with Latinos who related the pleasure they felt while looting Korean stores that they believed "had it coming" and who claimed that it was because of racism that more Latinos were arrested during *sa-i-ku* than Asian Americans. And I was filled with despair when I read about Chinese Americans wanting to dissociate themselves from us. According to one Chinese American reporter assigned to cover Asian American issues for a San Francisco daily, Chinese and Japanese American shopkeepers, unlike Koreans, always got along fine with African Americans in the past. "Suddenly," admitted another Chinese American, "I was scared to be Asian. More specifically, I am afraid to be mistaken for Korean." I was enraged when I overheard European Americans discussing the conflicts as if they were watching a dogfight or a boxing match. The situation reminded me of the Chinese film *Raise the Red Lantern,* in which we never see the husband's face. We only hear his mellifluous voice as he benignly admonishes his four wives not to fight among themselves. He can afford to be kind and pleasant because the structure that pits his wives against each other is so firmly in place that he need never sully his hands or even raise his voice.

BATTLEGROUND LEGACY

Korean Americans are squeezed between black and white and also between U.S. and South Korean political agendas. Opportunistic American and South Korean presidential candidates toured the burnt ruins, posing for the television cameras but delivering nothing of substance to the victims. Like their U.S. counterparts, South Korean news media seized upon *sa-i-ku,* featuring sensational stories that depicted the problem as that of savage African Americans attacking innocent

Koreans for no reason. To give the appearance of authenticity, Seoul newspapers even published articles using the names of Korean Americans who did not in fact write them.

Those of us who chafe at being asked whether we are Chinese or Japanese as the media-sought Chinese and Japanese but not Korean American views during *sa-i-ku* are sensitive to an invisibility that seems particular to us. To many Americans, Korea is but the gateway to or the bridge between China and Japan, or a crossroads of major Asian conflicts.

It can certainly be said that, although little known or cared about in the Western world, Korea has been a perennial battleground. Besides the Mongols and the Manchus, there were the *Yŏjin* (Jurched), the *Koran* (Khitan), and the *Waegu* (Wäkö) invaders. In relatively recent years, there was the war between China and Japan that ended in 1895 and the war between Japan and Russia in 1905, both of which were fought on Korean soil and resulted in extreme suffering for the Korean people. Japan's 36 years of brutal colonial rule ended with the U.S. and what was then the Soviet Union dividing the country in half at the 38th parallel. Thus, Korea was turned into a Cold War territory that ultimately became a battleground for world superpowers during the conflict of 1950–53.

BECOMING AMERICAN

One of the consequences of war, colonization, national division, and superpower economic and cultural domination has been the migration of Koreans to places like Los Angeles, where they believed their human rights would be protected by law. After all, they had received U.S.-influenced political educations. They started learning English in the seventh grade. They all knew the story of the poor boy from Illinois who became president. They all learned that the U.S. Constitution and Bill of Rights protected the common people from violence and injustice. But they who grew up in Korea watching "Gunsmoke," "Night Rider," and "McGyver" dubbed in Korean were not prepared for the black, brown, red, and yellow America they encountered when they disembarked at the Los Angeles International Airport. They hadn't heard that there is no equal justice in the U.S. They had to learn about American racial hierarchies. They did not realize that, as immigrants of color, they would never attain political voice or visibility but would instead be used to uphold the inequality and the racial hierarchy they had no part in creating.

Most of the newcomers had underestimated the communication barriers they would face. Like the Turkish workers in Germany described in John Berger and Jean Mohr's *A Seventh Man,* their toil amounted to only a pile of gestures and the English they tried to speak changed and turned against them as they spoke it. Working 14 hours a day, six or seven days a week, they rarely came into sustained contact with English-speaking Americans and almost never had time to study English. Not feeling at ease with English, they did not engage in informal conversations easily with non-Koreans and were hated for being curt and rude. They did not attend churches or do business in banks or other enterprises where English was required. Typically, the immigrant, small-business owners utilized unpaid centric American cultural practices, they knew little or nothing good about African Americans or Latinos, who in turn and for similar reasons knew little or nothing good about them. At the same time, Korean shopowners in South Central and Koreatown were affluent compared with the impoverished residents, whom they often exploited as laborers or looked down upon as fools with an aversion to hard work. Most Korean immigrants did not even know that they were among the many direct beneficiaries of the African American-led civil rights movement, which helped pave the way for the 1965 immigration reforms that made their immigration possible.

Korean-immigrant views, shaped as they were by U.S. cultural influences and official, anticommunist, South Korean education, differed radically from those of many poor people in the communities Korean immigrants served: unaware of the shameful history of oppression of nonwhite immigrants and other people of color in the U.S., they regarded themselves as having arrived in a meritocratic "land of opportunity" where a person's chances for success are limited only by individual lack of ability or diligence. Having left a homeland where they foresaw their talents and hard work going unrecognized and unrewarded, they were desperate to believe that the "American dream" of social and economic mobility through hard work was within their reach.

SA-I-KU

What they experienced on 29 and 30 April was a baptism into what it really means for a Korean to "become American" in the 1990s. In South Korea, there is no 911, and no one really expects a fire engine or police car if there is trouble. Instead, people make arrangements with friends and family for emergencies. At the same time, guns are not part of Korean daily life. No civilian in South Korea can own a gun. Guns are the exclusive accoutrement of the military and police who enforce order for those who rule the society. When the Korean Americans in South Central and Koreatown dialed 911, nothing happened. When their stores and homes were being looted and burned to the ground, they were left completely alone for three horrifying days. How betrayed they must have felt by what they had believed was a democratic system that protects its people from violence. Those who trusted the government to protect them lost everything; those who took up arms after waiting for help for two days were able to defend themselves. It was as simple as that. What they had to learn was that, as in South Korea, protection in the U.S. is by and large for the rich and powerful. If there were a choice between Westwood and Koreatown, it is clear that Koreatown would have to be sacrificed. The familiar concept of privilege for the rich and powerful would have been easy for the Korean immigrant to grasp if only those exhortations about democracy and equality had not obfuscated the picture. Perhaps they should have relied even more on whatever they brought with them here. That Koreatown became a battleground does seem like the further playing out of a tragic legacy that has followed them across oceans and continents. The difference is that this was a battle between the poor and disenfranchised and the invisible rich, who were being protected by a layer of clearly visible Korean American human shields in a battle on the buffer zone.

This difference is crucial. Perhaps the legacy is not one carried across oceans and continents but one assumed immediately upon arrival, not the curse of being Korean but the initiation into becoming American, which requires that Korean Americans take on this country's legacy of five centuries of racial violence and inequality, of divide and rule, of privilege for the rich and oppression of the poor. Within this legacy, they have been assigned a place on the front lines. Silenced by those who possess the power to characterize and represent, they are permitted to speak only to reiterate their acceptance of this role. . . .

Without a doubt, the U.S. news media played a major role in exacerbating the damage and ill will toward Korean Americans, first by spotlighting tensions between African Americans and Koreans above all efforts to work together and as opposed to many other newsworthy events in these two communities, and second by exploiting racist stereotypes of Koreans as unfathomable aliens, this time wielding guns on rooftops and allegedly firing wildly into crowds. In news programs and on talk shows, African and Korean American tensions were discussed by blacks and whites, who pointed to these tensions as the main cause of the uprising. I heard some European Americans railing against rude and exploitative Korean merchants for ruining peaceful race relations for everyone else. Thus, Korean Americans were used to deflect attention from the racism they inherited and the economic injustice and poverty that had been already well woven into the fabric of American life, as evidenced by a judicial system that could allow not only the Korean store owner who killed Latasha Harlins but also the white men who killed Vincent Chin and the white police who beat Rodney King to go free, while Leonard Peltier still languishes in prison.

As far as I know, neither the commercial nor the public news media has mentioned the many Korean and African American attempts to improve relations, Korean merchant donations to African American community and youth programs, African American volunteer teachers in classes for Korean immigrants studying for citizenship examinations, or Korean translations of African American history materials.

While Korean immigrants were preoccupied with the mantra of day-to-day survival, Korean Americans had no voice, no political presence whatsoever in American life. When they became the targets of violence in Los Angeles, their opinions and views were hardly solicited except as they could be used in the already-constructed mainstream discourse on race relations, which is a sorry combination of blaming the African American and Latino victims for their poverty and scapegoating the Korean Americans as robotic aliens who have no "real" right to be here in the first place and therefore deserve whatever happens to them.

THE *NEWSWEEK* EXPERIENCE

In this situation, I felt compelled to respond when an editor from the "My Turn" section of *Newsweek* magazine asked for a 1000-word personal essay. Hesitant because I was given only a day and a half to write the piece, not enough time in light of the vastness of American ignorance about Koreans and Korean Americans, I decided to do it because I thought I could not be made into a sound bite or a quote contextualized for someone else's agenda.

I wrote an essay accusing the news media of using Korean Americans and tensions between African and Korean Americans to divert attention from the roots of racial violence in the U.S. I asserted that these lie not in the Korean-immigrant-owned corner store situated in a community ravaged by poverty and police violence, but reach far back into the corridors of corporate and government offices in Los Angeles, Sacramento, and Washington, D.C. I suggested that Koreans and African Americans were kept ignorant about each other by educational and media institutions that erase or distort their experiences and perspectives. I tried to explain how racism had kept my parents from ever really becoming Americans, but that having been born here, I considered myself American and wanted to believe in the possibility of an American dream.

The editor of "My Turn" did everything he could to frame my words with his own viewpoint. He faxed his own introductory and concluding paragraphs that equated Korean merchants with cowboys in the Wild West and alluded to Korean / African American hatred. When I objected, he told me that my writing style was not crisp enough and that as an experienced journalist, he could help me out. My confidence wavered, but ultimately I rejected his editing. Then he accused me of being overly sensitive, confiding that I had no need to be defensive—because his wife was a Chinese American. Only after I had decided to withdraw the piece did he agree to accept it as I wrote it.

Before I could finish congratulating myself on being able to resist silencing and the kind of decontextualization I was trying to describe in the piece, I started receiving hate mail. Some of it was addressed directly to me, since I had been identified as a University of California faculty member, but most of it arrived in bundles, forwarded by *Newsweek*. Hundred of letters came from all over the country, from Florida to Washington State and from Massachusetts to Arizona. I was unprepared for the hostility expressed in most of the letters. Some people sent the article, torn from the magazine and covered with angry, red-inked obscenities scratched across my picture. "You should see a good doctor," wrote someone from Southern California, "you have severe problems in thinking, reasoning, and adjusting to your environment."

A significant proportion of the writers, especially those who identified themselves as descendants of immigrants from Eastern Europe, wrote *Newsweek* that they were outraged, sickened, disgusted, appalled, annoyed, and angry at the magazine for providing an arena for the paranoid, absurd, hypocritical, racist, and childish views of a spoiled, ungrateful, whining, bitching, un-American bogus faculty member who should be fired or die when the next California earthquake dumps all of the "so-called people of color" into the Pacific Ocean.

I was shocked by the profound ignorance of many writers' assumptions about the experiences and perspectives of American people of color in general and Korean and other Asian Americans in particular. Even though my essay revealed that I was born in the U.S. and that my parents had lived in the U.S. for more than six decades, I was viewed as a foreigner without the right to say anything except words of gratitude and praise about America. The letters also provided some evidence of the dilemma Korean Americans are placed in by those who assume that we are aliens who should "go back" and at the same time berate us for not rejecting " Korean-American identity" for "American identity." . . .

What seemed to anger some people the most was their idea that, although they worked hard, people of color were seeking handouts and privileges because of their race, and the thought of an ungrateful Asian American siding with African Americans, presumably against whites, was infuriating. How dare I "bite the hand that feeds" me by siding with the champion "whiners who cry 'racism'" because to do so is the last refuge of the "terminally incompetent"?

The racial health in this country won't improve until minorities stop erecting "me first" barriers and strive to be Americans, not African-Americans or Asian-Americans expecting privileges.

Ms. Kim wants preferential treatment that immigrants from Greece-to-Sweden have not enjoyed. . . . Even the Chinese . . . have not created any special problems for themselves or other Americans. Soon those folks are going to express their own resentments to the insatiable demands of the Blacks and other colored peoples, including the wetbacks from Mexico who sneak into this country then pilfer it for all they can.

The Afroderived citizens of Los Angeles and the Asiatic derivatives were not suffering a common imposition. . . . The Asiatics are trying to build their success. The Africans are sucking at the teats of entitlement.

Cleary I had encountered part of America's legacy, the legacy that insists on silencing certain voices and erasing certain presences, even if it means deportation, internment, and outright murder. I should not have been surprised by what happened in Koreatown or by the ignorance and hatred expressed in the letters to *Newsweek,* any more than African Americans should have been surprised by the Rodney King verdict. Perhaps the news media, which constituted *sa-i-ku* as news, as an extraordinary event in no way continuous with our everyday lives, made us forget for a moment that as people of color many of us simultaneously inhabit two Americas: the America of our dreams and the America of our experience.

Who among us does not cling stubbornly to the America of our dreams, the promise of a multicultural democracy where our cultures and our differences might be affirmed instead of distorted in an effort to destroy us?

After *sa-i-ku,* I was able to catch glimpses of this America of my dreams because I received other letters that expressed another American legacy. Some people identified themselves as Norwegian or Irish Americans interested in combating racism. Significantly, while most of the angry mail had been sent not to me but to *Newsweek,* almost all of the sympathetic mail, particularly the letters from African Americans, came directly to me. The most touching letter I received was written by a prison inmate who had served twelve years of a 35-to-70-year sentence for armed robbery during which no physical injuries occurred. He wrote:

I've been locked in these prisons going on 12 years now . . . and since being here I have studied fully the struggles of not just blacks, but all people of color. I am a true believer of helping "your" people "first," but also the helping of all people no matter where there at or the color of there skin. But I must be truthful, my struggle and assistance is truly on the side of people of color like ourselves. But just a few years ago I didn't think like this.

I thought that if you wasn't black, then you was the enemy, but . . . many years of this prison madness and much study and research changed all of this. . . . [I]t's not with each other, blacks against Koreans or Koreans against blacks. No, this is not what it's about. Our struggle(s) are truly one in the same. What happened in L.A. during the riot really hurt me, because it was no way that blacks was suppose to do the things to your people, my people (Koreans) that they did. You're my sister, our people are my people. Even though our culture may be somewhat different, and even though we may worship our God(s) different . . . white-Amerikkka [doesn't] separate us. They look at us all the same. Either you're white, or you're wrong. . . . I'm just writing you to let you know that, you're my sister, your people's struggle are my people's struggle.

This is the ground I need to claim now for Korean American resistance and recovery, so that we can become American without dying of *han*.

Although the sentiments expressed in these letters seemed to break down roughly along racial lines—that is, all writers who were identifiably people of color wrote in support—and one might become alarmed at the depth of the divisions they imply, I like to think that I have experienced the desire of many Americans, especially Americans of color, to do as Rodney King pleaded on the second day of *sa-i-ku*: "We're all stuck here for a while. . . . Let's try to work it out."

In my view, it's important for us to think about *all* of what Rodney King said and not just the words "we all can get along," which have been depoliticized and transformed into a Disneyesque catchphrase for Pat Boone songs and roadside billboards in Los Angeles. It seems to me the emphasis is on the being "stuck here for awhile" together as we await "our day in court."

Like the African American man who wrote from prison, the African American man who had been brutally beaten by white police might have felt the desire to "love everybody," but he had to amend—or rectify—that wish. He had to speak last about loving "people of color." The impulse to "love everybody" was there, but the conditions were not right. For now, the most practical and progressive agenda may be people of color trying to "work it out."

Finding Community Through National Consciousness

The place where Korean and American legacies converge for Korean Americans is the exhortation to "go home to where you belong."

Going back to Korea. The dream of going back to Korea fed the spirit of my father, who came to Chicago in 1926 and lived in the United States for 63 years, during which time he never became a U.S. citizen, at first because the law did not allow it and later because he did not want to. He kept himself going by believing that he would return to Korea in triumph one day. Instead, he died in Oakland at 88. Only his remains returned to Korea, where we buried him in accordance with his wishes.

Hasn't the dream of going back home to where you belong sustained most of America's unwanted at one time or another, giving meaning to lives of toil and making it possible to endure other people's hatred and rejection? Isn't the attempt to find community through national consciousness natural for people refused an American identity because racism does not give them that choice?

Korean national consciousness, the resolve to resist and fight back when threatened with extermination, was all that could be called upon when the Korean Americans in Los Angeles found themselves abandoned. They joined together to guard each other's means of livelihood with guns, relying on Korean-language radio and newspapers to communicate with and help each other. On the third day after the outbreak of violence, more than 30,000 Korean Americans gathered for a peace march in downtown L.A. in what was perhaps the largest and most quickly organized mass mobilization in Asian American history. Musicians in white, the color of mourning, beat traditional Korean drums in sorrow, anger, and celebration of community, a call to arms like a collective heartbeat. I believe that the mother of Edward Song Lee, the Los Angeles-born college student mistaken for a looter and shot to death in the streets, has been able to persevere in great part because of the massive outpouring of sympathy expressed by the Korean-American community that shared and understood her *han*.

I have been critical lately of cultural nationalism as detrimental to Korean Americans, especially Korean American women, because it operates on exclusions and fosters intolerance and uniformity of thought while stifling self-criticism and encouraging sacrifice, even to the point of suicide. But *sa-i-ku* makes me think again: what remains for those who are left to stand alone? If Korean Americans refuse to be victims or political pawns in the U.S. while rejecting the exhortation that we go back to Korea where we belong, what will be our weapons of choice?

In the darkest days of Japanese colonial rule, even after being stripped of land and of all economic means of survival, Koreans were threatened with total erasure when the colonizers rewrote Korean history, outlawed the Korean language, forced the subjugated people to worship the Japanese emperor, and demanded that they adopt Japanese names. One of the results of these cultural-annihilation policies was Koreans' fierce insistence on the sanctity of Korean national identity that persists to this day. In this context, it is not difficult to understand why nationalism has been the main refuge of Koreans and Korean Americans.

While recognizing the potential dangers of nationalism as a weapon, I for one am not ready to respond to the antiessentialists' call to relinquish my Korean American identity. It is easy enough for the French and Germans to call for a common European identity and an end to nationalisms, but what of the peoples suppressed and submerged while France and Germany exercised their national prerogatives? I am mindful of the argument that the resurgence of nationalism in Europe is rooted in historical and contemporary political and economic inequality among the nations of Europe. Likewise, I have noticed that many white Americans do not like to think of themselves as belonging to a race, even while thinking of people of color almost exclusively in terms of race. In the same way, many men think of themselves as "human beings" and of women as the ones having a gender. Thus crime, small businesses, and all Korean-African American interactions are seen and interpreted through the lens of race in the same dominant culture that angrily rejects the use of the racial lens for viewing yellow/white or black/white interactions and insists suddenly that we are all "American" whenever we attempt to assert our identity as people of color. It is far easier for Anglo Americans to call for an end to cultural nationalisms than for Korean Americans to give up national consciousness, which makes it possible to survive the vicious racism that would deny our existence as either Korean Americans or Americans.

Is there anything of use to us in Korean nationalism? During one thousand years of Chinese suzerainty, the Korean ruling elite developed a philosophy called *sadaejui,* or reliance of the weak on the strong. In direct opposition to this way of thought is what is called *jaju* or *juche sasang,* or self-determination. Both *sadaejui* and *juche sasang* are ways of dealing with unequal power relationships and resisting the transformation of one's homeland into a battlefield for others, but *sadaejui* has never worked any better for Koreans than it has for any minority group in America. *Juche sasang,* on the other hand, has the kind of oppositional potential needed in the struggle against silence and invisibility. From Korean national consciousness, we can recover this fierce refusal to accept subjugation, which is the first step in the effort to build community, so that we can work with others to challenge the forces that would have us annihilate each other instead of our mutual oppression.

What is clear is that we cannot "become American" without dying of *han* unless we think about community in new ways. Self-determination does not mean living alone. At least for now, that may mean mining the rich and haunted lode of Korean national consciousness while we struggle to understand how our fate is entwined with the fate of others lying prostrate before the triumphal procession of the winners of History. During the past fifteen years or so, many young Korean nationalists have been studying the legacies of colonialism and imperialism that they share with peoples in many Asian, African, and Latin American nations. At the same time that we take note of this work, we can also try to understand how nationalism and feminism can be worked together to demystify the limitations and reductiveness of each as a weapon of empowerment. If Korean national consciousness is ever to be such a weapon for us, we must use it to create a new kind of nationalism-in-internationalism to help us call forth a culture of survival and recovery, so that our *han* might be released and we might be freed to dream fiercely of different possibilities.

ANALYSIS

1. What does Kim mean by the term and concept of *han?* How does the concept function to underscore Kim's basic argument?
2. What does Kim refer to in the "battleground legacy of Korean Americans"?
3. What is Kim's view of the role American media have played in exacerbating Korean-Africa American tensions? Do you agree with her that "fascination with interethnic conflicts is rooted in the desire to excuse of [sic] minimize white racism. . . ."?
4. What does Kim mean by "Finding community through national consciousness"? But also, in what way is she ambivalent about "cultural nationalism"?
5. Kim suggests that Koreans represent "human shields" between "the poor and disenfranchised and the invisible rich"? What does she mean by this idea? If you are Korean-American, do you agree with this analysis?

WRITING POSSIBILITIES

1. Kim raises the question of whether it is possible for Korean Americans to "become American" without dying of *han.*" How might Kim's analysis of *han* apply to the experience of other groups in this country?

2. Kim explains how she reached out to African-Americans, was influenced by African-American civil rights struggles, and saw Koreans and African-Americans finding themselves in similar situations. Describe any comparable reaching out between your own and another group that you yourself are familiar with.

3. How do McLemore's categories of group identity and group gains relate to Kim's analysis of the L.A. riots?

4

AMERICAN PLURALISM: "WHAT, THEN, IS THE AMERICAN, THIS NEW MAN?"

In the following selection, the Preface to *Americans, A Collision of Histories* (pages 214–218), historian Edward Countryman explains how he views the dual subject of his book—the "colliding" and yet "shared" histories of the many groups that have made up American history. Countryman pegs his story to a chance encounter with a black airman in England:

> On a summer evening late in the 1980s [Countryman writes] a young black man stopped me to ask for directions in the English town where I used to live. That was no surprise. Asian, African, Afro-Caribbean, black British, and white people all live in the neighborhood. His speech, however, was American, and I was delighted to hear it. I speak American too, despite my long time overseas, and he was just as glad to hear me. I walked him to the pub he was seeking and we talked a while before going our ways. Neither learned the other's name.
>
> Our differences were great [Countryman continues]. He was from Texas; I still called myself a New Yorker. He was a serviceman from the nearby air base, I was a peace campaigner. He was African-American and I am white. . . . But in Royal Leamington Spa, Warwickshire, we felt what we had in common.

Throughout the Preface, the airman keeps returning in Countryman's memory as a reminder that despite differences of color, geography and occupation, he and Countryman shared a basic identity as Americans. That "Americanness," Countryman reminds us, resides in a host of things that form individuals without their realizing it (". . . I never would be one of them, however great my taste for 'real ale' and fish and chips doused in salt and vinegar. . . .") and extends backward in time and place:

If I, a white American, would understand what shaped me, if
I would not be a stranger to myself, I must understand people
who may not look like me but whose history is fundamentally, inextricably, intertwined with my own. Indeed, that history is my own . . .

For backup, Countryman appeals to Jefferson and the Declaration
of Independence, though as an historian Countryman knows full well
that a host of arguments swirl around Jefferson's significance. Was
Jefferson a racist? Was he a democrat? Was he a racist *and* a democrat? (Garry Wills has his own answer to these questions in the essay
"Storm over Jefferson.") For his part, Countryman believes that despite our new knowledge of Jefferson as a slaveholder with racist
sentiments, his matchless mantras about democratic self-government
in the Declaration have, through endless repetition and incorporation
into the fabric of our basic institutions, made this country primarily
one of "liberty" and "equality."

In this respect, Countryman's essay suggests the basic idea swirling
around such terms as *multiculturalism, diversity* and *pluralism*—the
American ideal of inclusion of all regardless of national origins, class,
or racial and ethnic backgrounds is indeed, as the historian Gordon
Wood ironically puts it, a "yearn[ing] for a world in which everyone will
love one another."

This chapter offers you different understandings of that (ostensi-
ble, actual) shared American identity postulated by Countryman.
First, there is the general set-to between historians of ethnicity Nathan
Glazer and Ronald Takaki over the very question of whether America
has been inclusivist: Glazer says this is indeed the "American ethnic
pattern" while Takaki argues that exclusion—especially racial, not
ethnic—more accurately reflects American history. Since Glazer and
Takaki also zero in on the contrary interpretations of Jefferson and
the Declaration of Independence—should Jefferson be remembered
for the idea of radical democracy or for his slaveholding and racism.
This chapter gives you a carefully nuanced assessment of Jefferson by
historian Gary Wills ("Storm over Jefferson") and allows you to decide
for yourself whether Jefferson should be preserved in the "American
pantheon" or, as the Irish diplomat Conor Cruise O'Brien once suggested, summarily kicked out.

Two essays on opposite sides of the fence—Linda Chavez's "The
Politics of Hispanic Assimilation" and Manning Marable's "We Need
New and Critical Study of Race and Ethnicity" take up changing attitudes towards race and ethnicity as a consequence of the most recent United States Census, which shows that Latinos are now poised
to become the number one minority in the country (and certainly in
the bellwether state of California): Chavez, dubbed a "multicultural

conservative" by Angela Dillard in *The Chronicle of Higher Education,* would see this new status as confirmation of her argument that Hispanics are assimilating in precisely the same way as earlier immigrants, while Marable thinks that despite demographic changes, *assimilation* is *not* the word to use and *inclusion* (or *amalgamation*) as an ideal will be just as tough for the newly enhanced *racial* minorities as it was for the older racial minorities. That's why, according to Marable, we need a "new and critical" awareness of the problems even newer groups will face in the interlinked contexts of race, class. and gender.

To tie the themes of this chapter together, a final section includes essays on the theme of "What is an American?"—a question that arises when Americans criticize—or defend—American values, move from one part of the country to another, or wonder what actually holds this quintessential country of immigrants together. Crevecoeur's classic "What, then, is the American, this new man?" sets up the basic idea of *assimilation* or the *melting pot;* Bharati Mukerjee, herself now an American citizen, defends the rights of her sister to live in America without melting into a citizen; John Miller, unhappy with precisely such noncitizens, argues that everyone who comes here should indeed be a citizen and should learn the basics of American identity (especially English); Michael Novak, concerned about Eastern and Southern European ethnic identities submerged by Americanization, contradicts the Creveceour Melting Pot idea even more directly than Mukerjee, as his title—"The Price of Being Americanized"—suggests.

To conclude the chapter, there is Langston Hughes's "Let America Be America Again," testing America's commitment to inclusion against the reality of racial exclusion in the past (and in the present).

Edward Countryman

Edward Countryman's essay tells an intriguing tale of a meeting with someone whose views are completely opposite of his own—a meeting that sparks Countryman's concern with the book on early American history that he is about to write. The story he tells is a simple one but one with important implications.

PREFACE

from Americans, A Collision of Histories

This book began with a chance encounter. On a summer evening late in the 1980s a young black man stopped me to ask for directions in the English town where I used to live. That was no surprise. Asian, African, Afro-Caribbean, black British, and white people all live in the neighborhood. His speech, however, was American, and I was delighted to hear it. I speak American too, despite my long time overseas, and he was just as glad to hear me. I walked him to the pub he was seeking and we talked a while before going our ways. Neither learned the other's name.

Our differences were great. He was from Texas; I still called myself a New Yorker. He was a serviceman from the nearby air base; I was a peace campaigner. He was African-American and I am white. In the poisoned racial atmosphere of the United States, that difference often cannot be overcome. Had we met in his native San Antonio or my native Albany or in Dallas, where I live now, we might have been polite, at best. We might have felt mutual suspicion, each representing danger to the other, especially on an open street at night. But in Royal Leamington Spa, Warwickshire, we felt what we had in common.

By then it was on my mind to attempt the theme of "being American" in historical terms. Writers have proposed many answers to that problem. There have been a distinctive "American character" and an "American political tradition." We have been "characteristically American" and a "people of plenty." One distinguished Cornell scholar when I was studying there in the late 1960s still thought he could trace an "American quest." But another was coming to see his conflicted, Janus-faced subjects as a "people of paradox."

Beginning to address these large issues, I had been wondering for some time about the significance of the American Revolution in defining our society and in releasing the nineteenth century's enormous burst of creative energy. I had been wondering as well what the price of that creativity was, and who paid it. My generation of historians had redefined the Revolution, seeing it as profoundly disruptive and transforming. Our goal had been to understand the complexities of how the United States became a separate power and Americans a separate people in the world.

The Revolution turned subjects of the British monarchy into citizens of the American Republic. It fundamentally changed relationships of power, authority, obligation, and subordination. The Revolution altered how every person and every group of the time lived their lives. All sorts of people affected the Revolution, and it affected them. The rising republic of George Washington was very different from the troubled colonies of George III. The Revolution was genuinely revolutionary.

I began wanting to see where all these changes led. Using a teacher's prerogative, I organized my courses around that problem, perhaps to my students' puzzlement. I was trying to bring together current thinking about the Revolution and the larger enterprise of American social historians who have worked on the seventeenth, eighteenth, and nineteenth centuries. Students at Warwick, Cambridge, Yale, and now Southern Methodist University all have endured my efforts. . . .

But something is missing from the current round of studies, with their stress on republicanism's American success. It is missing from accounts that would see us in terms of a single tradition or character, or in terms of a material abundance that many Americans never have enjoyed. For all my own willingness to employ Marxian ideas, it would be missing from an account framed solely in terms of social class. Ideas derived from European experience do make sense in the American context, whether we speak of the Protestant east coast heritage, Catholicism in Louisiana and New Spain or Irish immigrant Boston, the republican political tradition, or Marx's attempt to understand how capitalist society emerged and works. Nonetheless, America is not just a "neo-Europe." It cannot be understood solely in terms of its white people and their own particular heritage. My encounter with that Texas airman has helped me (I believe) to identify why that is so and what its significance is. . . .

That black airman came from Texas. In all probability his ancestors had gone there as slaves in the mid-nineteenth century, torn from places they knew and people they loved. In cotton-growing East Texas they settled on land that had been a province of Mexico not long before and that Caddo Indians regarded as their own. To borrow the astute comment of an African-American student whom I taught in Dallas, that airman *was* Texas. He *was* the South. To extend the point, he *was* America in all of the country's capacity to confuse and disrupt. So were the Lone Star State's Indians, Hispanics, and Anglos among whom he had grown up and among whom I now live.

On their way west, the ancestors of both that airman and my student probably passed through Mississippi. Counties that bear such names as Washington, Adams, Hancock, Jefferson, Lafayette,

Madison, Warren, and, for that matter, Bolivar. The white people who founded those communities came from New England as well as from Virginia and the Carolinas. They intended those history-laden names to honor the revolutionaries, whose heirs they were. They honored another history too, with county names like Issaquena, Tunica, Pontotoc, Choctaw, and Yalobusha. We need not doubt their sincerity, in either case.

But all of those counties "became southern." They turned into places of intense suffering for the people who transformed their wooded, often swampy soil into productive plantations. The Revolution, with its assertions about the equal unalienable rights of all men, may have thrown into sharp relief the contradiction between American slavery and American freedom. It may have been—it was—among the events that transformed slavery from a simple fact of life into a perceived moral abomination. It may have contributed—it did—to slavery's ultimate extinction. But the same American Revolution that set free the creative, expansive, liberating energy of the Republic's white people led to slavery's expansion and intensification for black ones. The same forces that freed my maternal ancestors to travel from overcrowded New England to the open prairies of Illinois and then back to New York State sent that airman's forebears on a very different journey.

Nor is that all. Both his ancestors and mine moved west onto soil that other people already had made their own. For the Illinois prairie to become the land of Abraham Lincoln, for the Black Belt, the Mississippi/Yazoo Delta, and East Texas to become the Cotton Kingdom, required that Indian people no longer use it their way. In 1830 it became government policy to force all Indians who lived east of the Mississippi to go west of that river, whether or not they had taken to white ways, whatever treaties had been made, whether they had fought for or against the young republic in its wars. In practice, that policy was underway well before the law was passed. Not all did go, but most were forced at gunpoint into "Indian Territory," now Oklahoma.

Among their descendants the bitterness is not forgotten. Yet today when Native American nations gather at Grand Prairie, Texas, for the National Pow Wow Championships, dancers bear a Stars and Stripes into the central arena, claiming the Republic for their own. Then Congressman and now United States Senator Ben Nighthorse Campbell made the same point in 1992, when he officiated in full Plains chief regalia as co-grand marshal of the 1992 Tournament of Roses parade in Pasadena, California.

Pasadena occupies ground that Spanish-speaking Europeans and their mixed-race progeny had claimed while English speakers were just beginning their westward push. Once it was called the Rancho San Pascual. Practically every event and process that pitted Europeans,

Africans, and Natives against one another in the East has its south-western counterpart. The great Pueblo Indian rebellion of 1680 far outstrips both the scope and the significance of eastern uprisings. British and Spanish alike encountered Indians on the same bloody, disease-ridden, alcohol-soaked terms. By the second quarter of the nineteenth century, Mexican communities and missions defined a line from Texas to Arizona and up the California coast. To the advancing Anglos, their people were semi-savages, whatever their color or language. By 1850 all those people, Indian, mestizo, and Hispanic alike, had become Americans, not by migration but by military conquest.

The expulsion of the Indian nations was at the hands of the President Andrew Jackson, who operated Tennessee and Mississippi plantations throughout his presidency. The conquest of the Far Southwest was at the hands of Jacksonians, particularly Jackson's self-proclaimed heir, the slave-owning President James K. Polk. These are the same Jackson and Polk whose version of democracy is now being offered as the American Revolution's final achievement. That interpretation of Jacksonian democracy—that it completed the Revolution's political promise—has much to commend it. Jackson himself eloquently articulated the ideology of "equal rights" that the Revolution had begun to shape, most notably in his message to Congress vetoing renewal of the Second Bank of the United States. "There are no necessary evils in government," Jackson wrote. "Its evils are only in its abuses. If it would confine itself to equal protection and, as Heaven does its rains, shower its favors alike on the high and the low, the rich and the poor, it would be an unqualified blessing." Jackson and his followers helped make the Revolution's language of equal citizenship into a powerful defense against the erosion of individual freedoms. But the link that joins romantic American democracy, slavery's expansion, the eastern Indians' stark choice to be expelled or destroyed, and the conquest of northern Mexico is not happenstance. The connection among the four is fundamental to nineteenth-century American social history.

We have our political tradition; we have a long history of people rejecting its hypocrisies; we also have a tradition of people claiming it even though it might seem to mean nothing to them. We are a people of plenty; we are also a people of want and poverty. We are a people of paradox; we also like to think we are innocent (or used to be innocent sometime in our past). I seek to explore all these matters and to offer a social history of many kinds of American people before full modernity.

Each of the founding American peoples has its own story. For the people who were here first, it is one of catastrophic defeat, near-destruction, and difficult survival. For Africans who became American, it is one of being enslaved and then painfully forging their own freedom. For English-speaking white migrants, it is a triumphant tale of colonization, independence, expansion, republicanism, and capitalist development, tempered by a tragic and bloody civil war. For Tejanos, Nuevomejicanos, and Californios, it is a story of lost possibilities. None of these stories reveals its full sense unless we see it in reference to the others. Each of these stories is different.

Nonetheless, all the stories circle around the mixture of hope and disappointment of Thomas Jefferson's proclamation that "all men are created equal." All the people in all the stories have found themselves living in a world of disruption and transformation. All of them have tried to form meaningful ties with other people in the same plight so they could establish patterns that would give their lives sense and cohesion. They have not always succeeded. Indian treaties and African-American families were broken by forces too powerful to withstand. Prairie land refused to flower, or turned out to be owned by a distant speculator. The streets of Manhattan and Lowell and San Francisco were not paved with gold. Nineteenth-century immigrants lived their lives without ever escaping the tenements to which migration first took them. Nonetheless, people kept trying to make sense of their lives, to organize the world around them, and to claim American freedom for themselves. In the sense that we all have faced those problems, we have far more in common than most of us may realize. That may be what the airman and I implicitly understood. Had he chanced to be Native American or Hispanic instead of black (or I any of those instead of white), we still might have shared the recognition.

I study American history to understand the people of whom I am a part. One result of my long stay among the British was to learn that I never would be one of them, however great my taste for "real ale" and fish and chips doused in salt and vinegar; however adept I am at driving on the left. That encounter in Leamington helped me see why. As a white American, rather than a European, I am the product of a society that many kinds of people have produced, not just the children of Europeans. Fundamentally, this book is about how we have produced categories to separate ourselves from one another but have nonetheless shared enough to call ourselves a people. The categories blur if we look at them closely, dissolving into what is shared, despite all enmity and difference.

If I, a white American, would understand what shaped me, if I would not be a stranger to myself, I must understand people who may not look like me but whose history is fundamentally, inextricably, and forever intertwined with my own. Indeed, that history is my own, just as all American history in its terrible and exciting complexity belongs to all of the American people. *Americans* offers some ideas about how that became so.

ANALYSIS
---

1. What does Countryman mean by the "colliding histories" that make up America? How does this phrase compare with Nathan Glazer's or Ronald Takaki's characterizations of American history?
2. What precisely does Countryman mean by saying that if he is to "understand" himself, he needs to know the many histories of America?

WRITING POSSIBILITIES
---

1. If you have ever traveled to another country, you may have felt what Countryman felt—that even if you liked the food and understood the driving, you would still be an "American." Explain what the circumstances of that discovery were: who you met, what you saw, felt, thought or tasted, that inspired you with that shock of recognition.
2. To what extent would you agree with Countryman that to truly understand who we are we need to become historians of America? Though much discredited, Henry Ford once said: "History is more or less bunk"; on the other hand, the American philosopher George Santyana believes that those who forget history are doomed to repeat it. What is your opinion? Use Countryman's discussion as a starting point.

Nathan Glazer

Over the years, sociologist Nathan Glazer has changed his mind several times over about the values and disvalues of affirmative action in American life. In "The American Ethnic Pattern" Glazer said no to affirmative action contending that it violates the American ethnic pattern. In a very recent essay "In Defence of Preference," he reverses himself completely and says that "preference" is absolutely necessary if we are to rest on a "moral" basis for American society. Market forces alone won't, in his new view, ensure the ideal of diversity, something he once thought possible. Knowing that Glazer is the kind of intellectual who actually changes his mind as he receives new evidence should make the reading of the his essay and of Ronald Takaki's response to it ("Reflections on Racial Patterns in America: An Historical Perspective," pages 236–253) more interesting.

THE EMERGENCE OF AN AMERICAN ETHNIC PATTERN

In the middle of the last decade, we in the United States seemed to have reached a national consensus as to how we should respond to the reality of racial and ethnic-group prejudice and racial and ethnic-group difference. Almost simultaneously, we began to move away from that consensus into new divisions and a new period of conflict and controversy. The consensus was marked by three major pieces of legislation: the Civil Rights Act of 1964, the Voting Rights Act of 1965, and the Immigration Act of 1965. Following the passage of the Civil Rights and Voting Rights acts, the Federal government intervened firmly in the South to end the one-hundred-year resistance of the white South to full political, civil, and social equality for blacks, insofar as this resistance was embodied in law and public practice. The passage of the Immigration Act of 1965 marked the disappearance from Federal law of crucial distinctions on the basis of race and national origin. The nation agreed with this act that there would be no effort to control the future ethnic and racial character of the American population and rejected the claim that some racial and ethnic groups were more suited to be Americans than others.

In the phrase reiterated again and again in the Civil Rights Act of 1964, no distinction was to be made in the right to vote, in the provision of public services, the right to public employment, the right to public education, on the ground of "race, color, religion, or national origin." Paradoxically, we then began an extensive effort to record the race, color, and (some) national origins of just about every student and employee and recipient of government benefits or services in the nation; to require public and private employers to undertake action to benefit given groups; and school systems to assign their children on the basis of their race, color, and (some) national origins. This monumental restructuring of public policy to take into account the race, color, and national origin of individuals, it is argued by Federal administrators and courts, is required to enforce the laws against discrimination on these very grounds. It is a transitional period, they say, to that condition called for in the Constitution and the laws, when no account at all is to be taken of race, color, and national origin. But others see it as a direct contradiction of the Constitution and the laws, and of the consensus that emerged after long struggle in the middle 1960s.

I will examine . . . policies in three areas: employment, school desegregation, and residential location. I will analyze the position of those who support present policies and will argue that the consensus of the middle 1960s has been broken, and that it was and remains the right policy for the United States—right for the groups that had suffered, and in some measure still suffer, from prejudice and discrimination, and right for the nation as a whole.

But the first step is to try to characterize and understand the consensus of the middle 1960s. This is not to be understood as an historically new response to the unprecedented events of those years—the vicious resistance in great parts of the South to the efforts of blacks to practice their political rights, the South's resistance to school de-segregation, the shocking assassination of a President identified with the hopes of suppressed minority groups. It is to be understood rather as the culmination of the development of a distinctive American orientation to ethnic difference and diversity with a history of almost 200 years. That orientation was shaped by three decisions. They were not taken all at once, or absolutely, or in full consciousness of their implications, but the major tendencies of American thought and political action have regularly given their assent to them.

The three decisions were:

First, the entire world would be allowed to enter the United States. The claim that some nations or races were to be favored in entry over others was, for a while, accepted, but it was eventually rejected. And once having entered into the United States—and whether that entry was by means of forced enslavement, free immigration, or conquest—all citizens would have equal rights. No group would be considered subordinate to another.

Second, no separate ethnic group was to be allowed to establish an independent polity in the United States. This was to be a union of states and a nation of free individuals, not a nation of politically defined ethnic groups.

Third, no group, however, would be required to give up its group character and distinctiveness as the price of full entry into the American society and polity.

There is of course an inevitable breathtaking arrogance in asserting that *this* has been *the* course of American history. It would be almost equally breathtaking to assert that *any* distinctive course can be discerned in the history of the shaping of the American people out of many different stocks. It is in part an act of faith to find any *one* course that the development of American society has in some way been reaching toward: It smacks of the unfashionable effort to give a "purpose," a direction, to history. Certainly this direction is not to be thought of as some unconscious immanent tendency continuing to reveal itself in American history. Direction in history is taken only in the concrete actions of men and of groups of men. Those actions in the United States have included—in direct conflict with the large direction I have described—the enslavement of the Negro, anti-immigrant and anti-Catholic movements that have arisen again and again in American life, the near extermination of the American Indian, the maintenance of blacks in a subordinated and degraded position for a hundred years after the Civil War, the lynching of Chinese, the exclusion of Oriental immigrants, the restriction of immigration from Southern and Eastern Europe, the relocation of the Japanese and the near confiscation of their property, the resistance to school desegregation, and so forth. If we are to seek a "direction" in American history that defines a distinctive approach to the relationship of the various ethnic groups that make up American society, the sequence of events just listed might well be made the central tendency of American history. Many current writers and scholars would have it so: They argue that racism defines our history—racism directed against blacks, Indians, Mexican Americans, Puerto Ricans, Filipinos, Chinese, Japanese, and some European ethnic groups. Many would have it that even the last ten years should be interpreted as a losing battle against this racism, now evident in the fact that colleges and universities resist goals and targets for minority hiring, that preferential admissions to professional schools are fought in the courts, that the attempt to desegregate the schools in the North and West has now met a resistance extremely difficult to overcome, that housing for poor and minority groups is excluded from many suburbs.

I think this is a selective misreading of American history: that the American polity has instead been defined by a steady expansion of the definition of those who may be included in it to the point where it now includes all humanity; that the United States has become the first great nation that defines itself not in terms of ethnic origin but in terms of adherence to common rules of citizenship; that no one is now excluded from the broadest access to what the society makes possible; and that this access is combined with a considerable concern for whatever is necessary to maintain group identity and loyalty. This has not been an easy course to shape or maintain, or to understand. There have been many threats to this complex and distinctive pattern for the accommodation of group difference that has developed in American society. The chief threats in the past were, on the one hand, the danger of a permanent subordination of certain racial and ethnic groups to others, of the establishment of a caste system in the United States; and on the other hand, the demand that those accepted into American society become Americanized or assimilated, and lose any distinctive group identity. The threat of the last ten years to this distinctive American pattern, however, has been of quite another sort. The new threat that followed the most decisive public actions ever taken to overcome subordination and caste status was that the nation would, under the pressure of those recently subordinated to inferior status, be permanently sectioned on the basis of group membership and identification, and that an experiment in a new way of reconciling a national polity with group distinctiveness would have to be abandoned. Many did not and do not see this latter possibility as any threat at all, but consider it only the guarantee and fulfillment of the commitment of American society to admit all peoples into full citizenship. They see the threat to a decent multigroup society rising from quite another direction: the arrogance and anger of the American people, specifically those who are descended from colonists and earlier immigrants, aroused by the effort to achieve full equality for all individuals and all groups. The prevailing understanding of the present mood is that those who have their share—and more—want to turn their backs on the process that is necessary to dismantle a caste society in which some groups are held in permanent subordination. I think this is a radical misreading of the past few years. . . .

But [my] task [here] is a rather different one: If the history of American society in relationship to many of the groups that make it up is not a history of racism, what is it? How do we define an emergent American attitude toward the problem of the creation of one nation out of many peoples? . . .

Three writers to my mind have, in recent years, given the best definition of what it meant to found a nation in this way: Seymour Martin Lipset in *The First New Nation;* Hans Kohn in his book *American Nationalism: An Interpretive Essay;* and Yehoshua Arieli in *Individualism and Nationalism in American Ideology.*

Arieli argues forcefully that the American Revolution should *not* be seen as another uprising of an oppressed nation, but as an event whose main shapers presented it as significant for the world and all its peoples:

> All the attempts made by Americans to define the meaning of their independence and their Revolution showed an awareness that these signified more than a change in the form of government and nationality. Madison spoke of the American government as one which has "no model on the face of the globe." For Washington, the United States exhibited perhaps the first example of government erected on the simple principles of nature, and its establishment he considered as an era in human history. . . . John Adams was convinced that a greater question than that of American Independence "will never be decided among men." For Jefferson, America was the proof that under a form of government in accordance "with the rights of mankind," self-government would close the circle of human felicity and open a "widespread field for the blessings of freedom and equal laws." Thomas Paine hailed the American Revolution as the beginning of the universal reformation of mankind and its society with the result "that man becomes what he ought." For Emerson, America was ". . . a last effort of the Divine Providence in behalf of the Human race."[1]

We might of course expect a second-generation sociologist, a scholar who found refuge here, and another refuge who has become

---

[1] Arieli, *op. cit.,* pp. 86–87.

a scholar in a newly founded democratic nation to respond to these claims, to reverberate to them, so to speak. We might also expect Jewish scholars to respond to these claims, for if the United States was very late in fulfilling its promise to blacks, Indians, Mexican Americans, and others—that is, those of other races—it almost from the beginning offered an open field and freedom to those who practiced another religion. Can a more searching examination, however, sustain these claims? Could it not also be said that American independence and the establishment of a new country was little more than the assertion of the arrogance of British colonists, refusing to accept a moderate overseas government more solicitous of the rights of Indians and blacks than they were, insisting on taking the land from the Indians and on the right to import and hold black men as slaves, and eventually threatening their neighbors with imperial expansion?

Our history, indeed, included all this. Even the appropriation of the name "American" for the citizens of the United States is seen by our neighbors to the north and to the south as a symbol of arrogance. Yet other interpretations of this appropriation are possible. The Americans *did* accept as the name for themselves a name with no ethnic reference, a name even with no limited geographical reference (since the Americas include all the Western Hemisphere). One side of this self-naming may be seen as a threat to the rest of the Americas and as arrogance in ignoring their existence. But another side must also be noted: the rejection by this naming of any reference to English or British or any other ethnic or racial origins, thus emphasizing in the name itself the openness of the society to all, the fact that it was not limited to one ethnic group, one language, one religion.

Lipset argues that the American nation from the beginning established and defined its national identity on the basis of its decisive break, through revolution, with England, and, by extension, with the entire old world. This weakened the ethnic identification with England. Further, two values became dominant in American society and the shaping of American character, equality and achievement, and these values can be seen sharply marked in American society from the beginning of its independent political existence.[2] One point about these two values that I would emphasize is that, by their nature, they cannot remain ethnically exclusive. And the most far-sighted of the early leaders understood this. Thus, to quote Hans Kohn:

Thomas Jefferson, who as a young man had opposed immigration, wished in 1817 to keep the doors of America open,

---

[2] Seymour Martin Lipset, *The First New Nation,* New York: Basic Books, 1963, esp. Chap. 2, "Formulating a National Identity," and Chap. 3, "A Changing American Character?"

"to consecrate a sanctuary for those whom the misrule of Europe may compel to seek happiness in other climes." . . . This proclamation of an open port for immigrants was in keeping with Jefferson's faith in America's national mission as mankind's vanguard in the fight for individual liberty, the embodiment of the rational and humanitarian ideals of eighteenth century man.

The American nation,

Hans Kohn continues, summarizing Jefferson's point of view,

was to be a universal nation—not only in the sense that the idea which it pursued was believed to be universal and valid for the whole of mankind, but also in the sense that it was a nation composed of many ethnic strains. Such a nation, held together by liberty and diversity, had to be firmly integrated around allegiance to the American idea, an idea to which everyone could be assimilated for the very reason that it was a universal idea. To facilitate the process of integration, Jefferson strongly opposed the settlement of immigrants in compact groups, and advocated their wide distribution among the older settlers for the purpose of "quicker amalgamation."[3]

Of course, to one tradition we can oppose another. If Jefferson was positive about the immigration of other groups, Benjamin Franklin was suspicious. "For many years," Arieli writes, "he strenuously argued against the wisdom of permitting the immigration of non-English settlers, who 'will never adopt our language or customs anymore than they can acquire our complexion.'[4] Undoubtedly, he was influenced by the substantial number of Germans in Pennsylvania, itself established as an open colony of refuge:

This will in a few years [Franklin wrote] become a German colony: Instead of their Learning our Language, we must learn theirs, or live as in a foreign country. Already the English begin to quit particular Neighborhoods surrounded by Dutch, being made uneasy by the Disagreeableness of dissonant Manners; and in Time, Numbers will probably quit the Province for the same Reason. Besides, the Dutch under-live, and are thereby enabled to under-work and under-sell the English; who are thereby extremely incommoded, and consequently

---

[3] Hans Kohn, *American Nationalism: An Interpretive Essay,* New York: Macmillan, 1957 (Collier Books edition, 1961, p. 144).

[4] Arieli, *op. cit.,* p. 44.

disgusted, so that there can be no cordial Affection or Unity between the two Nations.[5]

The themes are, of course, familiar ones: They were to be repeated for many groups more distant from the Anglo-American stock than the Germans, who were, after all, of related tongue and Protestant religion. And yet this was a private comment, to be set against a public one that, again to quote Kohn, "extolled Anglo-America as a place of refuge."[6]

There were two traditions from the beginning, traditions exemplified by different men and social groups, and carried in tension within the same men. Yet even to say there were two traditions makes the issue somewhat sharper than it could have been during the early history of the United States. After all, the very men who spoke about the equal rights of all men accepted slavery. If they spoke of the United States as a sanctuary for all, they clearly thought of men very like themselves who might be seeking it and were not confronted with the hard realities of men of very different culture, religion, and race taking up their offer. In addition, we must take account of the expansive rhetoric of a moment in which a nation was being founded. Yet stipulating all of these cautions, there was a development implied in the founding documents and ideas which steadily encouraged the more inclusive definitions of who was eligible to become a full participant in American life. In the Revolution and its aftermath, limitations on participation in public life by the propertyless, Catholics, and Jews were lifted. Waiting in the wings, so to speak, were other categories, implied in the founding principles. That some others waited for almost two centuries, and that their equality came not only because of founding principles but because of complex social and political developments is true; but the principles were there, exerting their steady pressure, and indeed even in 1975 much of the argument over how to define full equality for different groups revolves around a Constitution that dates to 1787.[7]

As Arieli puts it: "Whatever the impact of universal concepts on the American historical experience, the conservative and nativistic

---

[5] Kohn, *op. cit.,* pp. 143–144, quoting from Max Savelle, *Seeds of Liberty: The Genesis of the American Mind,* New York: Knopf, 1948, p. 567 f.

[6] Kohn, *op. cit.,* p. 143.

[7] On the legal position of Jews, see Oscar and Mary F. Handlin, "The Acquisition of Political and Social Rights by the Jews in the United States," *American Jewish Year Book,* Vol. 56, New York: American Jewish Committee, 1955, and Philadelphia: The Jewish Publication Society of America, 1955, pp. 43–98. There is no equally convenient summary for the legal position of Catholics, but see Anson Phelps Stokes, *Church and States in the United States,* New York: Harper and Bros., 1950, Vol. I, Chaps. V and XII.

interprets of American history, no less than their opponents, concede that American nationality has to be defined, at least to some degree, by reference to certain political and social concepts; that it is a way of life and an attitude which somehow represents ultimate social values. . . ."[8]

There is no Supreme Historian, sitting in heaven, who totes up the record and tells us which way the balance of history ran. One picks out a dominant theme, on the basis of one's experience as well as one's knowledge, and our choice is made, in part, on the basis of our hopes for the future as well as our experience. In the 1950s and 1960s men like Kohn and Arieli wanted to emphasize the inclusive tradition; in the later 1960s and in the 1970s, many historians and other scholars want to show us the exclusive tradition. . . .

In certain periods, it seems clear, one voice or another was dominant. The uprising of the white South in the Civil War marked the most determined effort to change the pattern into one in which other races and groups, labeled inferior, were to be held in permanent subjection and subordination. A new justification was to be established for this "heresy," as Arieli dubs it—and in the American context, heresy it was. Justification was to be found in religion, in pragmatic necessity, in political theory, even surprisingly enough in Auguste Comte's newfounded science of sociology, which was drawn upon to show the superiority of slave labor to Northern, immigrant, free labor, and of a society founded on slavery to one founded on free immigration.[9] . . .

In the North, exclusivism expressed itself in resistance to immigration from Eastern and Southern Europe and suspicion of immigrant settlements in the cities—of their habits, their culture, their impact on political life and on urban amenities. The Negroes were present—they always had been—but they were so few and so far down the social scale that they were scarcely seen as a threat to anything. In the South, exclusivism was directed primarily against the Negroes, though Catholics and Jews came in for their share of prejudice and, on occasion, violence. In the West, the Chinese and the Japanese were the main targets of a pervasive racism which included the Mexicans and the Indians.

The dismantling of this system of prejudice and discrimination in law and custom began in the 1930s. In the North, the ethnic groups created by the new immigration began to play a significant role in politics; and blacks, after the disenfranchisement of the 1890s, began again to appear in politics. The last mass anti-Catholic movement was the Klan's in the 1920s. It had a short life, and was in eclipse by the time Al Smith ran for President in 1928. Anti-Semitism had a longer

---

[8] Arieli, *op. cit.,* pp. 27–28.
[9] Arieli, *op. cit.,* pp. 293–305.

life, but the war against Hitler ended with the surprising discovery that anti-Semitism, so strong in the Thirties, was undergoing a rapid and unexpected deflation. And similarly with anti-Chinese and Japanese prejudice. The immigration restriction law of 1924 was modified to accept at least token numbers of people from all nations and races in 1952, and all elements of national or racial preference were expunged in 1965.

Of course, the major bastion of race discrimination was the South, and the legal subordination of the Negro there remained firm throughout the 1930s and 1940s. But twenty years of liberal domination of national politics, by a coalition in which in Northern cities blacks played an important role, finally made its effects felt in the administration of President Truman. The Armed Forces were desegregated, national demands for the enfranchisement of Southern blacks became stronger and began to receive the support of court decisions, and a major stage in the elimination of discriminatory legislation was reached with the Supreme Court decision of 1954 barring segregation in the public schools. With the Civil Rights Act of 1964 and the Voting Rights Act of 1965, the caste system of the South was dismantled. The thrust for equality now shifted from the legal position of the group to the achievement of concrete advances in economic and political strength.

Thus for the past forty years, the pattern of American political development has been to ever widen the circle of those eligible for inclusion in the American polity with full access to political rights. The circle now embraces—as premature hyperbolic statements made as long as 200 years ago suggested it would—all humanity, without tests of race, color, national origin, religion, or language. . . .

Two other elements describe the American ethnic pattern, and these are not as easily marked by the processes of political decision-making, whether by court, legislature, or war. The first additional element is that the process of inclusion set limits on the extent to which different national polities could be set up on American soil. By "polity" I refer to some degree of political identity, formally recognized by public authority. Many multiethnic societies do recognize different ethnic groups as political entities. In the Soviet Union, each is formally entitled to a separate state or autonomous region (though these distinctive units exercise their powers in a state in which all individuals and subunits are rigidly controlled by a central dictatorship). Even a group dispersed throughout the Soviet Union such as the Jews is recognized as a separate nationality; and at one time, this nationality had rights, such as separate schools, publications, publishing houses. In Eastern Europe, where successor states to the German, Russian, and Austro-Hungarian Empire were set up after World War I, once again national rights were given to groups, even to such groups as the Jews, who were dispersed throughout the national territory. In nations that have been created by migration, such as the United States, we do not have examples of something like "national rights."

But the United States is more strict than others in preventing the possibility that subnational entities will arise. Consider the case of Canada, which is also a multiethnic society. The major minority national group, the French, is a compactly settled group which was conquered in the eighteenth century: It was not created through migration into a preexisting homogeneous or multiethnic nation. There are far more extensive national rights for the French than the United States allows for any group. Bilingualism is recognized not only in the areas of French settlement, but throughout the country. It is required of civil servants. . . .

Among the possibilities for making political accommodation to groups of different ethnic character in a contemporary state, the United States falls near one end of the spectrum in denying formal recognition for any purpose to ethnic entities. In contrast to Canada, we do not ask for "ethnicity" in our census—though some government census sample surveys have recently done so—nor do we demand that each respondent select an ethnic origin.

Our pattern has been to resist the creation of formal political entities with ethnic characteristics. The pattern was set as early as the 1820s, when, as the historian of American immigration, Marcus Hansen, describes it, a number of European groups thought of establishing a New Germany or a New Ireland in the United States. . . .

No new nations would be established on American soil. We were to be, if a Federal republic, a republic of states, and even the states were not to be the carriers of an ethnic or national pattern. Most divergent from this norm, perhaps, is New Mexico, a state created out of conquered territory with a settled population, or the special rights of the Spanish-origin settlers of the Gadsden Purchase in Arizona; but even in those states, the rights of the Spanish-speaking barely lead to the creation of an ethnic state, although some militant Chicano leaders would perhaps like to see this happen.

Finally, there was a third set of decisions that defined the American ethnic pattern: Any ethnic group could maintain itself, if it so wished, on a *voluntary* basis. It would not be hampered in maintaining its distinctive religion, in publishing newspapers or books in its own language, in establishing its own schools, and, indeed, in maintaining loyalty to its old country.

This was a policy, if one will, of "salutary neglect." If immigrants could not establish new polities, they could do just about anything else. They could establish schools in their own language. They could teach their own religion, whether it was the ancient faith of Rome or the newly founded variants of Judaism and Islam developed by American blacks. When the state of Washington tried, in the early 1920s, to make public education a state monopoly, the Supreme Court said it could not.[10] Immigrants could establish their own churches and, under the doctrine of state-church separation, these would neither be more favored nor less favored than the churches of the original settlers which had once been established churches. They could establish their own hospitals, cemeteries, social service agencies to their own taste. All would be tax exempt: The state, in effect, respected whatever any group more or less wanted to consider education, or health and welfare, or religion, or charity. (Polygamy was one exception.) Indeed, the hospitals and social service agencies of these groups were even eligible for state funds, just as the institutions set up by the churches and groups of the early settlers had been. Immigrants could send money freely to their homelands, they could support the national movements of their various groups, and they could also, relatively easily, get tax exemption for their contributions to anything that smacked of religion, education, health and welfare, and charity.

There was no central public policy organized around the idea that the ethnic groups were a positive good, and therefore should be allowed whatever freedom they needed to maintain themselves. Policymakers generally never thought of the matter. It was, rather, that there was a *general* freedom, greater than in most other countries, to do what one willed. The mere fact that city planning and the controls associated with it were so much weaker than in other countries made it easy to set up churches, schools, and the like. In a society in which land could easily be bought and sold, fortunes easily made (and unmade), and mobility was high, there were, in effect, two sets of forces set loose: One force tended to break up the ethnic communities, for it was easy in American society to distance oneself from family and ethnic group, if one wanted to; but at the same time, and this is what is often forgotten, it was also easy to establish the institutions that one desired. This meant, of course, that every church divided again and

---

[10] *Pierce v. Society of Sisters,* 268 U.S. 510 (1925). Of course, as public and bureaucratic controls multiply in every part of life, this freedom is restricted, and not only for ethnic groups. It means that the establishment of church or school in a single-family house—a typical pattern—may run into zoning and planning restrictions, and often does; that the establishment of a nursery or an old-age home in less than institutional quarters fulfilling state requirements becomes almost impossible. New groups suffer probably more from these restrictions than old groups. But I note that a magnificent nineteenth-century Richard Morris Hunt-designed home for the aged in New York, maintained by an old Protestant welfare agency, is to be demolished because it cannot meet state standards of "proper" facilities for the aged. All suffer from the ever-widening reach of state controls.

again: The state was disinterested, and thus every variant of liberalism and orthodoxy could express itself freely in institutional form. It also meant there was no hindrance to the maintenance of what one wished to maintain.

One of the interesting general findings of ethnic research is that affluence and assimilation have double effects. One the one hand, many individuals become distant from their origins, throw themselves with enthusiasm into becoming full "Americans," and change name, language, and religion to forms that are more typical of earlier settlers. On the other hand, however, many use their increased wealth and competence in English to *strengthen* the ethnic group and its associations. It is hard to draw up a balance as to which tendency is stronger, because different people evaluate different effects differently. Thus undoubtedly, with longer residence in the United States, folk aspects of the culture weaken, and those attached to them feel that the original culture is lost. Yet associational and organizational forms of ethnicity are strengthened. For example, the one-room school, the *heder,* where Jewish children learned their letters, their prayers, and a bit of Bible under the tutelage of an Old World teacher, disappeared; so it become possible to say that the true old East European Jewish culture was gone. But regularly organized religious and Hebrew schools, with classrooms and teachers after the American pattern, increased greatly in number, and more Jewish children had some formal Jewish education under the organized system than under the folk system. Or, to take another example, undoubtedly, in 1975, the more folkish aspects of Ukrainian culture have weakened, both for the pre-World War II and post-World War II immigrants. This weakening is associated with assimilation and higher income. But now there are chairs for Ukrainian studies at Harvard, supported by funds raised by Ukrainian students. It is this kind of tradeoff that makes it so difficult to decide whether there is really, as Marcus Hansen suggested, a third-generation return to ethnic origins and interests. There is a return, but as is true of any return, it is to something quite different from what was there before.

In any case, whatever the character of the return, it is American freedom which makes it possible, as American freedom makes possible the maintenance and continuity and branchings out of whatever part of their ethnic heritage immigrants and their children want to pursue.

When we look now at our three sets of decisions—that all may be included in the nation, that they may not establish new nations here, and that they may, nevertheless, freely maintain whatever aspects of a national existence they are inclined to—we seem to have a classic Hegelian series of thesis, antithesis, and synthesis. The synthesis raises its own new questions, and these become steadily more sharp, to the point where many argue we must begin again with a new thesis. For the three sets of decisions create an ambiguous status for any ethnic group. The combination of first, you may become full citizens; second, you may not establish a national entity; third, you may establish most of the elements of a national entity voluntarily without hindrance, does not create an easily definable status for the ethnic group. . . .

A distinction of great importance [ethnicity] to our society is thus given no formal recognition and yet has great meaning in determining the individual's fate. In this sense, ethnicity is akin to "class" in a liberal society. Class does not denote any formal status in law and yet plays a great role in the life of the individual. Ethnicity shares with class—since neither has any formal public status—a vagueness of boundaries and limits and uncertainty as to the degree to which any person is associated with any grouping. No member of the upper, middle, or lower class—or choose what terms you wish—needs to act the way most other members of that class do; nothing but social pressure will hold him to any behavior. Similarly with persons whom we would consider "belonging" to ethnic groups: They may accept that belonging or reject it. Admittedly, there are some groups, marked by race, where belonging is just about imposed by the outside world, as against other less sharply marked groups. Nevertheless, the voluntary character of ethnicity is what makes it so distinctive in the American setting. It is voluntary not only in the sense that no one may be required to be part of a group and share its corporate concerns and activities; no one is impelled *not* to be part of a group, either. Ethnicity in the United States, then, is part of the burden of freedom of all modern men who must choose what they are to be. In the United States, one is required neither to put on ethnicity nor to take it off. Certainly this contributes to our confusion and uncertainty in talking about it.

Undoubtedly, if this nation had chosen—as others have—either one of the two conflicting ideals that have been placed before us at different times, the "melting pot" or "cultural pluralism," the ambiguities of ethnic identity in the United States and the tensions it creates would be less. Under the first circumstance, we would have chosen a full assimilation to a new identity. Many nations have attempted this: some forcefully and unsuccessfully, as did Czarist Russia in relation to certain minority groups; some with a supreme self-confidence, such as France, which took it for granted that the status of the French citizen, *tout court,* should satisfy any civilized man; some, with hardly any great self-consciousness, such as Argentina, which assimilated enormous numbers of European immigrants into a new identity, one in which they seemed quite content to give up an earlier ethnic identity, such as Spanish or Italian. If a nation does choose this path of full assimilation, a clear course is set before the immigrant and his children. Similarly, if the principle is to be that of cultural pluralism, another clear course is set. We have not set either course, neither the one of eliminating all signs of ethnic identity—through force or through the attractions of assimilation—nor the other of providing the facilities for the maintenance of ethnic identity.

But our difficulties do not arise simply because of the ambiguities of personal identity. They arise because of the concrete reality that, even in a time of political equality (or as close to political equality as formal measures can ensure), ever greater attention is paid to social and economic inequality.

If we search earlier discussions of the immigrant and of ethnic groups, we will not find any sharp attention to these inequalities. It was assumed that time alone would reduce them, or that the satisfactions of political equality would be sufficient. It was assumed, perhaps, that social and economic inequalities would be seen as *individual* deprivations, not as *group* deprivations. But there was one great group whose degree of deprivation was so severe that it was clearly to be ascribed to the group's, not the individual's, status. This was the Negro group. As we concentrated our attention in the 1960s on the gaps that separated Negroes from others, other groups of somewhat similar social and economic status began to draw attention to *their* situation. And as these new groups came onto the horizon of public attention, still others which had not been known previously for their self-consciousness or organization in raising forceful demands and drawing attention to their situation entered the process. What began as an effort to redress the inequality of the Negro turned into an effort to redress the inequality of all deprived groups.

But how is this to be done? And does not the effort to redress upset the basic American ethnic pattern? To redress inequalities means, first of all, to define them. It means the recording of ethnic identities, the setting of boundaries separating "affected" groups from "unaffected" groups, arguments among the as yet "unaffected" whether they, too, do not have claims to be considered "affected." It turned out that the effort to make the Negro equal to the *other* Americans raised the question of who *are* the other Americans? How many of them can define their own group as *also* deprived? The drawing of group definitions increased the possibilities of conflicts between groups and raised the serious question, what is legitimate redress for inequality?

In 1964, we declared that no account should be taken of race, color, national origin, or religion in the spheres of voting, jobs, and education (in 1968, we added housing). Yet no sooner had we made this national assertion than we entered into an unexampled recording of the records of the color, race, and national origin of every individual in every significant sphere of his life. Having placed into law the dissenting opinion of *Plessy* v. *Ferguson* that our Constitution is colorblind, we entered into a period of color- and group-consciousness with a vengeance.

Larger and larger areas of employment came under increasingly stringent controls so that each offer of a job, each promotion, each dismissal had to be considered in the light of its effects on group ratios in employment. Inevitably, this meant the ethnic group of each individual began to affect and, in many cases, to dominate consideration of whether that individual would be hired, promoted, or dismissed. In the public school systems, questions of student and teacher assignment became increasingly dominated by considerations of each individual's ethnic group: Children and teachers of certain races and ethnic groups could be assigned to this school but not to that one. The courts and government agencies were called upon to act with ever greater vigor to assure that, in each housing development and in each community, certain proportions of residents by race would be achieved, and a new body of law and practice began to build up which would, in this field, too, require public action on the basis of an individual's race and ethnic group. In each case, it was argued, positive public action on the basis of race and ethnicity was required to overcome a previous harmful public action on the basis of race and ethnicity.

Was it true that the only way the great national effort to overcome discrimination against groups could be carried out was by recording, fixing, and acting upon the group affiliation of every person in the country? Whether this was or was not the only way, it is the way we have taken. . . .

ANALYSIS

1. Put in your own words the essential meaning of Glazer's "American ethnic pattern." Do you agree with Glazer's formulation or not?
2. What are the specific "decisions" that Americans have made concerning the "American ethnic pattern"? What does Glazer mean by "decisions"—i.e., something hard and fast and explicit moments in our history, or looser actions over a period of time?
3. What does Glazer mean by the concept of "a selective misreading of American history"?
4. To what "voices" does Glazer refer when he says "In certain periods . . . one voice or another was dominant"?
5. According to Glazer, what does "ethnic research" reveal about the phenomena of "affluence and assimilation"? Why is this important for someone studying ethnic or racial conflict in the United States?
6. Ronald Takaki (in the following selection) criticizes Glazer for mixing the ideas of "race" and "ethnicity" which [he believes] should be kept separate and distinct. How in fact does Glazer use the concept of ethnicity? In what way and to what extent, does he talk about "race"?
7. Glazer singles out "the Negro group" (1960s usage) as *not* partaking fully of the immigrant experience of assimilation? What does he mean? What assumption does he make here?

8. What is the importance for Glazer of an "American ethnic pattern" that does not allow ethnic or religious groups to have formal status in political terms. Would Glazer, for example, reject the Canadian practice of providing monetary support to the Catholic school system? How would he analyze the situation in Northern Nigeria, where the state government wishes to impose *Sharia,* Muslim law, on the entire state?

9. In terms of argumentation, is Glazer's use of *concession* and acknowledgment of *the opposing, anti-inclusivist* position effective or not? Does Glazer deal adequately with these historical moments? Do you agree that these bad patches in American life do not confute "the central tendency of American history"? How in fact does one arrive at a "central tendency"?

10. How does Glazer use the idea of the "American ethnic pattern" to reject affirmative action? What is his reasoning here? Do you agree or disagree with it?

WRITING POSSIBILITIES

1. Pick a specific moment, event or situation in American history (e.g., pre-Civil War slavery, Jackson and the treatment of Native Americans, the exclusion of Chinese immigrants in the late nineteenth century) that both Glazer and Takaki talk about; explain how they do so, citing specific language from each of their accounts, and explain which account you think more just, appropriate and convincing, both on its own and in relation to any knowledge you may have of the situation.

2. Do you find Glazer's "American ethnic pattern" (either with or without the bad patches) appealing or not? Do you think it is relevant to social conflicts today or do you think it needs revision? Consider especially Glazer's dealings with racial and religious conflict.

3. Does Glazer do an effective job in allaying the reader's skepticism about those elements in American history which do not fit with the "central tendency" of "inclusion"?

4. Restate clearly Glazer's argument against "group" identification—i.e., the basis of affirmative action programs; explain in particular how this rejection of group identities fits in with Glazer's analysis of America's basic "ethnic pattern." (In other words, why is Glazer so wrought up about this matter?) Do you agree or disagree with Glazer's analysis and arguments? Explain.

Ronald Takaki

A Japanese-American scholar at the University of California, Berkeley, Ronald Takaki takes issue with Glazer on both the question of what American history looked like in the past and whether affirmative action is needed in the present to ensure equality. In particular, Takaki zeroes in on the confusion in Glazer's account between "ethnic" and "racial." Yes, Takaki says, if you look only at ethnic assimilation, you may see a lot of inclusion, but if you look at racial assimilation, you see very little. In effect, Takaki takes a strategy opposite to Glazer's by acknowledging some good aspects of American history but arguing that on the whole it was the bad patches that predominated (and still do).

REFLECTIONS ON RACIAL PATTERNS IN AMERICA

When Allan Bakke filed his suit against the University of California Medical School at Davis in 1974, he surely did not expect his grievance to be elevated into circles of scholarship. Yet scholarly efforts to provide a theoretical justification for Bakke's claim that affirmative action policy discriminated against whites were already well underway. Consequently, four years later, racial minorities found themselves facing a scholarly theory of "reverse discrimination" as well as the Supreme Court's *Bakke* decision itself. During this time, Nathan Glazer of Harvard University has emerged as the leading architect of this new anti-affirmative action scholarship, and his book, *Affirmative Discrimination: Ethnic Inequality and Public Policy,* spearheaded the intellectual assault on affirmative action. Published in 1975 and issued in paperback in 1978, the book has been widely read and has commanded much attention in the conference rooms of public policy makers as well as society at large.[1]

Excerpts from reviews quoted on the back cover of the paperback edition are intended to do more than announce its importance. They warn us not to ignore the book:

A tempered, factually argued, vigorous polemic against the predominant drift of public policy on racial issues over the past decade. Public issues only infrequently receive serious, sustained arguments of this high order.

—*The New York Times Book Review*

---

[1] Nathan Glazer, *Affirmative Discrimination: Ethnic Inequality and Public Policy* (New York: 1978, originally published in 1975).

Glazer writes provocatively, instead of ideologically, about a sensitive subject that needs airing.

—Business Week

His views, based on solid research, deserve the widest debate.

—The Christian Science Monitor[2]

As the excerpts suggest, the book has more than a scholarly purpose. Indeed, as Glazer himself makes clear in his 1978 Introduction, he is seeking to influence public policy makers, particularly the justices of the Supreme Court in their deliberations on affirmative action cases such as the Allan Bakke case. "In *Affirmative Discrimination*," he writes, "I attacked the justice and the wisdom of shifting from individual rights to group rights in devising policies to overcome racial and ethnic-group discrimination and its heritage." While Glazer claims that he has "no intention of 'predicting' the course of the Supreme Court," he describes the courts as the "final battleground" for the issue of affirmative action and encourages Americans who share his "vision to engage in litigation and submit amicus briefs against the new policies." In short, *Affirmative Discrimination* is Glazer's amicus brief.[3]

His book requires our attention. We could, I think, avoid his book if it were only an empirical study of employment, education and housing. But his analysis also advances a theory of an "American ethnic pattern" to interpret American history and to influence present public policy making.[4]

At the heart of Glazer's theory is a hope, a vision of a good society in which "men and women are judged on the basis of their abilities rather than their color, race, or ethnic origin." The "first principle of a liberal society," he insists, is the assertion that "the individual and the individual's interests and good and welfare are the test of a good society." Thus for Glazer, there is only one proper solution to the problem of racial inequality: the heritage of discrimination can and should be overcome by "simply attacking discrimination."[5]

A theoretician of the anti-affirmative action backlash, Glazer gives articulation to an angry popular mood, a widespread resentment against the demands of racial minorities, and a moral outrage felt by the Allan Bakkes of America. He both describes and supports the point of view of the white ethnics: "They entered a society in which they were scorned; they nevertheless worked hard, they received little

---

[2] Back cover of 1978 paperback edition.
[3] Glazer, *Affirmative Discrimination,* pp. ix, xvi, xvii.
[4] See ibid., chapters 2, 3, and 4.
[5] Ibid., pp. 220, 197, xi.

or no support from government or public agencies, their children received no special attention in school or special opportunity to attend college. . . . They contrast their situation with that of blacks and other minority groups today and see substantial differences in treatment. They consider themselves patriotic and appreciative of the United States even though they received no special benefit." While Glazer admits the comparison may be "crude and unfair," he essentially agrees with its main contention, that blacks and other racial minorities should not receive "special" opportunities, "special" treatment, and "special" benefits. Instead, they should emulate the example of the white ethnics.[6]

In his opening chapter, "The Emergence of an American Ethnic Pattern," Glazer develops the historical and theoretical underpinnings of his critique of affirmative action policies. He uses this to provide the conceptual framework for the entire book and refers to its main points throughout the study. Viewing affirmative action policies from his historical perspective, Glazer asks at the end of the book: "How have policies which so sharply reverse the consensus developed over two hundred years of American history established themselves so powerfully in a scant ten years?"[7]

But what was that "consensus" which had developed over two hundred years? According to Glazer, the mid-1960s witnessed the emergence of a "national consensus" on solutions to the problems of racial and ethnic prejudice. This consensus was reflected in three laws: the Civil Rights Act of 1964, the Voting Rights Act of 1965, and the Immigration Act of 1965. Essentially these laws prohibited discrimination based on race, color, religion, or national origin. But "paradoxically," Glazer argues, a new policy of affirmative action or "discrimination" was then instituted, and the consensus was "broken." Thus was shattered the "culmination" of the development of a "distinctive American orientation of ethnic difference and diversity with a history of almost 200 years."[8]

Glazer bases his theory of an American ethnic pattern on three historical developments or "decisions":

> First, the entire world would be allowed to enter the United States. The claim that some nations or races were to be favored in entry over others was, for a while, accepted, but it was eventually rejected. And once having entered into the United States—and whether that entry was by means of forced enslavement, free immigration, or conquest—all citizens would

---

[6] Ibid., p. 194.
[7] Ibid., p. 204.
[8] Ibid., pp. 3, 4, 5.

have equal rights. No group would be considered subordinate to another.

Second, no separate ethnic group was to be allowed to establish an independent polity in the United States. This was to be a union of states and a nation of free individuals, not a nation of politically defined ethnic groups.

Third, no group, however, would be required to give up its group character and distinctiveness as the price of full entry into the American society and polity.

All three decisions were inclusionist rather than exclusionist. Though a notion favoring the entry of particular immigrants or races was accepted "for a while," American society eventually allowed the inclusion of all racial and ethnic groups. The decisions were also egalitarian: all citizens, regardless of race, ethnicity, or religion, would have equal rights. These decisions also promoted tolerance and acceptance of cultural and ethnic diversity: a group would be allowed to maintain its cultural values and identity. Finally, all three decisions minimized, even denied, differences between the experiences of "racial" and white "ethnic" groups in American history.[9]

While Glazer describes the three decisions as integral parts of the "central" American pattern, he does acknowledge the existence of contrary "actions"—black slavery, anti-immigrant nativism, the "near extermination" of the American Indian, the lynching of Chinese, the relocation of Japanese Americans during World War II, and so forth. He even notes that, "for fifty years, between the 1890s and the 1930s, exclusivism was dominant." Nevertheless, for Glazer all of these contrary developments do not represent the "large direction," the "major tendency to a greater inclusiveness," in American history.[10]

Thus the three decisions are claimed to be major components of historical reality in America, and as a historian I had to ask whether the claim could stand the test of a rigorous and critical examination of the historical evidence. More specifically, I had to ask whether Glazer's theory of an American "ethnic" pattern could explain the history of racial minorities in America.

The first is the most important of all three decisions, for it permitted the "entire" world to enter the United States and extended "equal" rights to all citizens regardless of their means of entry. In order for us to determine whether this decision actually existed historically and whether it represented a major pattern, we need to review the history

---

[9] Ibid., p. 5.
[10] Ibid., pp. 5, 6, 7, 15, 17.

of citizenship and the right of suffrage in the United States. We also need to develop a more precise chronological measurement of how long "for a while" really was.[11]

The phrase "for a while" could refer to the early national period, when Congress made its first effort to define American citizenship in the Naturalization Law of 1790. This law specified that only free "white" immigrants would be eligible for naturalized citizenship. Clearly, this law did not allow the "entire" world to enter the United States as potential citizens or members of the body politic. Non-"white" immigrants were not permitted to be naturalized until the Walter-McCarran Act of 1952, which stated that "the right of a person to become a naturalized citizen of the United States shall not be denied or abridged because of race. . . ." What is important to note here about the first naturalization law is the fact that it remained in effect for 162 years, or for a very long time.[12]

One of the first laws to be passed by Congress, the Naturalization Law of 1790 acquired special significance in the nineteenth century due to westward expansionism and the entry of Chinese laborers into America. The two developments were closely linked. Shortly after the end of the war against Mexico, which enabled the United States to annex California, Aaron H. Palmer, a "Counsellor of the Supreme Court of the United States," submitted to Congress a plan for the extension of American markets into Asia and the importation of Chinese workers to develop American industries. "The commodious port of San Francisco," he declared, "is destined to become the great emporium of our commerce on the Pacific; and so soon as it is connected by railroad with the Atlantic States, will become the most eligible point of departure for steamers to . . . China." To build the transcontinental railroad as well as to bring the "fertile lands of California" under cultivation, Palmer recommended the immigration of Chinese. Here, in this remarkable report, was a public policy blueprint which explicitly integrated American expansion into Asia with Asiatic immigration to America.[13]

During the next three decades, tens of thousands of Chinese were recruited to work in this country. Between 1850 and 1880, the Chinese

---

[11] Ibid., p. 5.

[12] *Debates and Proceedings in the Congress of the United States,* 1789–1791, 2 vols. (Washington, D.C.: 1834), vol. 1: 998, 1284, vol. 2: 1148–56, 1162, 2264. For the Walter-McCarran Act, see Frank Chuman, *The Bamboo People: The Law and Japanese-Americans* (Del Mar, Calif.: 1976) p. 312.

[13] Aaron H. Palmer, *Memoir, geographical, political, and commercial, on the present state, productive resources, and capabilities for commerce, of Siberia, Manchuria, and the Asiatic Islands of the Northern Pacific Ocean; and on the importance of opening commercial intercourse with those countries,* March 8, 1848. U.S. Cong., Senate, 30th Cong., 1st sess., Senate misc. no. 80, pp. 1, 52, 60, 61.

population in the United States increased from 7,520 to 105,465, a fifteen-fold increase; in 1870 the Chinese constituted 8.6 percent of the total population of California and an impressive 25 percent of the wage-earning force. But the inclusion of the Chinese in the economic structure was accompanied by their political exclusion. Not "white," they were ineligible for naturalized citizenship. They were, in effect, migrant laborers, forced to be foreigners forever. Unlike white "ethnic" immigrants such as Italians, Poles, and Irish, the Chinese were a politically proscribed labor force. They were a part of America's production process but not her body politic. American businessmen expected them to be here only on a temporary basis and located them in a racially segmented labor market. Central Pacific Railroad employer Charles Crocker, for example, told a legislative committee: "I do not believe they are going to remain here long enough to become good citizens, and I would not admit them to citizenship." Crocker also explained how the presence of Chinese workers could elevate white workers in a stratified racial/occupational structure: "I believe that the effect of Chinese labor upon white labor has an elevating instead of degrading tendency. I think that every white man who is intelligent and able to work, who is more than a digger in a ditch . . . who has the capacity of being something else, can get to be something else by the presence of Chinese labor easier than he could without it. . . . There is proof of that in the fact that after we get the Chinamen to work, we took the more intelligent of the white laborers and made foremen of them." Businessmen "availed" themselves of this "unlimited" supply of "cheap" Chinese labor to build their railroads and operate their factories. After the Chinese migrant workers had completed their service, they were urged to return to their homeland, while others came to replace them. The employers of Chinese labor did not want these workers to remain in this country and become "thick" (to use Crocker's term) in American society.[14]

Enacted long before the entry of Asians into America, the Naturalization Law also had another consequence for immigrants from the east. Where white "ethnic" immigrants were legally entitled to own land in this country, Asian immigrants were subjected to a special form of discrimination. Defined as "aliens ineligible for citizenship," Chinese and other Asian immigrants were also denied, by state legislation, the right to own property in California, Washington, Arizona, Oregon, Idaho, Nebraska, Texas, Kansas, Louisiana, Montana, New Mexico, Minnesota, and Missouri. Thus Asian immigrants were excluded from the very process of land ownership, social mobility, and

---

[14] Charles Crocker, testimony, in *Report of the Joint Special Committee to Investigate Chinese Immigration,* Senate Report No. 689, 44th Cong., 2nd sess., 1876–77, pp. 667, 679, 680.

transformation of immigrants into Americans which Frederick Jackson Turner celebrated in his famous essay on the significance of the frontier in American history.[15]

Ironically, the Naturalization Law also excluded Native Americans from citizenship. Though they were born in the United States, they were regarded as members of tribes, or as domestic subjects or nationals; their status was considered analogous to children of foreign diplomats born here. As "foreigners," they could not seek naturalized citizenship, for they were not "white." Even the Fourteenth Amendment, which defined federal citizenship, did not apply to Native Americans. While Native Americans could become United States citizens through treaties with specific tribes or through allotment programs such as the Dawes Act of 1887, general citizenship for the original American was not granted until 1924.[16]

But what happened to nonwhite citizens? Did they have "equal" rights, particularly the right of suffrage? Citizenship did not necessarily carry this right, for states determined the requirements for voting. A review of this history reveals a basic political inequality between white citizens and nonwhite citizens.

The 1965 Voting Rights Act did not actually culminate a history of political inclusion for blacks. In the North, during the most important period of political inclusion—the era of Jacksonian Democracy—the establishment of universal manhood suffrage was for white men only. In reality, the inclusion of greater numbers of white men, including recent Irish immigrants, was usually accompanied by the exclusion of black citizens from the suffrage. The New York Constitution of 1821, for example, granted the vote to all free "white" male citizens who possessed a freehold, paid taxes, had served in the state militia, or had worked on the highways; it also retained the property requirement for black citizens, increasing it from $100 to $250. The Pennsylvania Constitution of 1838 went even further: it provided for universal "white" manhood suffrage and thus disenfranchised black citizens completely. In the South, except for a brief period during Reconstruction, black citizens were systematically excluded from participation in the political process. Thus the 1965 law, enacted in response to massive black pressure and protest under the leadership of Martin Luther King, was a break from a long history of denial of voting rights to racial as opposed to "ethnic" minority citizens.[17]

---

[15] Chuman, *Bamboo People,* pp. 217, 218.

[16] Felix S. Cohen, *Handbook of Federal Indian Law* (Albuquerque: 1958, originally published in 1942), pp. 153–59.

[17] See Takaki, *Iron Cages: Race and Culture in 19th-Century America* (New York: 1979), p. 111.

This difference between race and ethnicity in terms of suffrage may also be seen in the experiences of Native Americans. While the Treaty of Guadalupe-Hidalgo had offered United States citizenship to Mexicans living within the acquired territories, the 1849 Constitution of California granted the right of suffrage only to every "white" male citizen of the United States and only to every "white" male citizen of Mexico who had elected to become a United States citizen. A color line, in short, had been drawn for the granting of suffrage to American citizens in California. Native Americans were also proscribed politically in other states. The Fifteenth Amendment, which provided that the right to vote shall be denied or abridged because of race or color, did not apply to noncitizen Indians. Even after Indians were granted citizenship under the 1924 law, however, many of them were designated "Indians not taxed" or "persons under guardianship" and disenfranchised in states like Arizona, New Mexico, Idaho, and Washington.[18]

Study of the history of citizenship and suffrage disclosed a racial and exclusionist pattern. For 162 years, the Naturalization Law, while allowing various European or "white" ethnic groups to enter the United States and acquire citizenship, specifically denied citizenship to other groups on a racial basis. While suffrage was extended to white men, it was withheld from men of color. Thus what actually developed historically in American society was a pattern of citizenship and suffrage which drew a very sharp distinction between "ethnicity" and "race."

Like the first one, the second and third decisions also require our critical examination. According to Glazer, all Americans would be viewed and treated as "free individuals," not members of "politically defined ethnic groups" or "polities." Still, Americans could, if they wished, maintain an ethnic group identity on a voluntary basis. They would be allowed to have their distinctive religion, their own language, their own schools, and even to maintain their "loyalty" to their "old country."[19]

While decisions two and three may have been true for white "ethnic" groups, like the Irish and Germans, they certainly do not accurately describe the historical experiences of "racial" groups. This difference was particularly evident during World War II when Japanese Americans, unlike German Americans and Italian Americans, were forcefully interned in relocation camps. They were, in effect, defined

---

[18] Francis Newton Thorpe, ed., *The Federal and State Constitutions, Colonial Charters, and Other Organic Laws of the States, Territories, and Colonies now or heretofore forming the United States of America* (Washington: 1909), vol. 1. *Treaty of Guadalupe-Hidalgo,* p. 381, *Constitution of California,* 1849, p. 393; Cohen, *Handbook of Federal Indian Law,* pp. 155–59.

[19] Glazer, *Affirmative Discrimination,* pp. 5, 22–29.

and treated as a "polity" by the federal government. Of the 120,000 internees, 70,000 were United States citizens by right of birth. Japanese in America were not regarded as "free individuals" but as members of a polity simply because of their Japanese ancestry. In the camps, draft age Nisei men were required to fill out and sign a loyalty questionnaire entitled "Statement of United States Citizenship of Japanese Ancestry." At the end of the long list of questions, they were asked:

No. 27. Are you willing to serve in the armed forces of the United States on combat duty wherever ordered?

No. 28. Will you swear unqualified allegiance to the United States of America and faithfully defend the United States from any or all attack by foreign or domestic forces, and forswear any form of allegiance or obedience to the Japanese emperor, to any other foreign government, power or organization?

Young men of Italian or German ancestry were not subjected to such a "loyalty" test.[20]

The Native American experience also does not fit well into decisions two and three. Indians have historically been formally treated as members of polities, not as "free individuals." The Constitution of the United States recognized Indian tribes as polities: Article I, Section 2, excluded from state representation in Congress "Indians not taxed"; and Article I, Section 4, granted Congress the power to "regulate Commerce with foreign Nations . . . and with Indians Tribes." The Indian Trade and Intercourse Act of 1802 provided that no land cessions in Indian territory could be made except by "treaty" between Congress and the Indian tribe. The view of Indian tribes as polities was explicitly expressed in the 1871 case of *McKay* v. *Campbell*. Denying the Fourteenth Amendment had extended citizenship to Indians, the court ruled:

To be a citizen of the United States by reason of his birth, a person must not only be born within its territorial limits, but he must also be born subject to its jurisdiction. . . . But the Indian tribes within the limits of the United States have always been held to be distinct and independent political communities, retaining the right of self-government, though subject to the protecting power of the United States.

---

[20] "Statement of United States Citizenship of Japanese Ancestry," quoted in Michi Weglyn, *Years of Infamy: The Untold Story of America's Concentration Camps* (New York: 1976), p. 155.

The removal of Choctaws, Creeks, and Cherokees in the 1830s and the relocation of Sioux and Cheyennes on reservations in the 1870s were also based on the conception of Indian tribes as polities.[21]

This policy of defining Indians as members of tribes and as members of culturally distinct groups was used as a means to control them. The strategy can be seen in the actions of two important policy makers on Indian affairs. President Andrew Jackson, claiming Indians were culturally distinct and could not survive in white civilization, proposed their removal beyond the Mississippi River. Regarding Indian tribes as polities, Jackson was able to negotiate removal treaties with them and to transfer Indian lands into the "markett," to use the president's spelling. As Commissioner of Indian Affairs in 1872, Francis Amasa Walker saw that he could not continue Jackson's policy of removing Indians beyond the Mississippi River. By then the "markett" had already reached the Pacific Ocean, and a new future for the Indian in the West had to be defined. Walker's proposal was to "consolidate" Indian tribes onto one or two "grand reservations." According to his plan, warlike tribes would be relocated on extensive tracts in the West, and all Indian "bands" outside of the reservation would be "liable to be struck by the military at any time, without warning, and without any implied hostility to those members of the tribe" living within the reservation. For Walker, it was a policy of military convenience to treat Indian tribes as polities.[22] . . .

Federal inclusionist policies also required the Indian to give up his group character and distinctiveness as the "price" of full entry into American society and polity. Nowhere can this be seen more clearly than in the Dawes Act of 1887, also known as the Indian Allotment Act. This law, which white reformers hailed as the "Indian Emancipation Act," promised to bring to a close a "century of dishonor." What it actually did was to grant the president power, at his discretion and without the Indians' consent, to break up reservations and allot lands to individual Indians. The Dawes Act also permitted the federal government to secure tribal consent to sell "surplus" reservation lands—lands which remained after allotment had taken place—to white settlers. The effect of this policy on the Indian land base was predictable. Between 1887 and 1934, when the allotment

---

[21] Cohen, *Handbook of Federal Indian Law,* p. 155.

[22] Andrew Jackson, "First Annual Message to Congress," in James D. Richardson, ed., *A Compilation of the Messages and Papers of the Presidents, 1789–1897* (Washington: 1897), 2: 456–58; Jackson to General John Coffee, April 7, 1832, in John Spencer Bassett, ed., *Correspondence of Andrew Jackson,* 6 vols. (Washington: 1926), 4: 430; Francis Amasa Walker, *The Indian Question* (Boston: 1874), pp. 10, 62–67. *Interior for the Year 1872* (Washington: 1872), pp. 11, 63, 64, 77–79, 94, 95; *Indian Appropriation Act,* quoted in Walker, *Indian Question,* p. 5.

policy was terminated, 60 percent of the Indian land base had been transferred to whites: 60 million acres had been sold as "surplus" lands to whites by the federal government, and 27 millions acres—or two-thirds of the land allotted to individual Indians—had been transferred to whites through private transactions. This tremendous reduction of the Indian land base has had a very destructive impact on Native American cultures—their distinctive religions, languages, and ethnic group identities. The law also conferred citizenship upon the allottees and any other Indians who would abandon their tribes and adopt the "habits of civilized life." Thus the Dawes Act, offering Indians entry, exacted a "price."[23]

Still, Glazer insists that the history of American society is relation to its many groups is "not a history of racism," and he lines up three authorities to back his claim: Yehoshua Arieli, Hans Kohn, and Seymour Martin Lipset.[24]

The most revealing example of this confusion (between ethnicity and race) is Kohn's discussion of Thomas Jefferson and the founding father's conception of America as a "sanctuary" and a "Canaan." Here we have a situation where Glazer draws from Kohn to requote Jefferson and repeats Kohn's claim that Jefferson viewed America as a "universal nation," composed of "many ethnic strains." If we trace the source of the quotation, we will find that Kohn took it from Jefferson's letter to George Flower, written on September 12, 1817, and published in Volume VII of *The Writings of Thomas Jefferson,* edited by H. A. Washington. If we examine the entire letter, we will plainly see that Jefferson was actually referring to white "ethnic" immigrants—Swiss, French, and Germans. Within this context, then, America was a "sanctuary" for white immigrants fleeing from the "misrule of Europe."[25]

If we browse through Volume VII of Jefferson's *Writings,* we will come across uncontestable proof that Jefferson's inclusionism was for white ethnics only. In a letter to D. Thomas Humphreys, dated February 8, 1817, Jefferson supported a proposal for the removal of free blacks to Africa. "Perhaps the proposition now on the carpet at Washington to provide an establishment on the coast of Africa for voluntary emigrations of peoples of color," Jefferson wrote, "may be the corner stone of this future edifice." Thus, when Jefferson discussed in his letter to Flower, written only several months later, the

---

[23] For a discussion of the Dawes Act, see Takaki, *Iron Cages,* pp. 188–93.

[24] Glazer, *Affirmative Discrimination,* p. 8.

[25] Thomas Jefferson, quoted in Kohn, *American Nationalism,* requoted in Glazer, *Affirmative Discrimination,* p. 12; Jefferson to George Flower, September 12, 1817, in H. A. Washington, ed., *The Writings of Thomas Jefferson* (Washington: 1853–54), 7: 84.

"quicker amalgamation" of new settlers, he was restricting this process to white ethnic groups.[26]

Though Jefferson was the owner of 200 slaves, he advocated the abolition of slavery and the removal of blacks from America. He believed that blacks and whites could never coexist in America because of "the real distinctions" which "nature" had made between the two races. "The first difference which strikes us is that of color," Jefferson explained. "And is this difference of no importance? Is it not the foundation of a greater or less share of beauty in the two races? Are not the fine mixtures of red and white, the expressions of every passion by greater or less suffusions of color in the one, preferable to that eternal monotony, which reigns in the countenances, that immovable veil of black which covers the emotions of the other race?" To Jefferson, white was beautiful. Even blacks themselves admitted so, he thought: "Add to these, flowing hair, a more elegant symmetry of form, their own judgment in favor of whites, declared by their preference of them, as uniformly as is the preference of Oranootan for the black woman over those of his own species." Given these differences, black removal was a way to preserve white qualities. Commenting on the breeding of domestic animals, Jefferson asked: "The circumstance of superior beauty is thought worthy of attention in the propagation of our horses, dogs, and other domestic animals; why not in that of man?" In his published book, *Notes on the State of Virginia,* Jefferson described the black population as a "blot" and insisted that the black, when freed, had to be removed "beyond the reach of mixture."[27]

Jefferson even devised a plan for black removal. To remove all of them at once, he thought, was not "practicable." He estimated that such a project would take twenty-five years, during which time the slave population would have doubled. Furthermore, the value of the slaves would amount to $600 million, and the cost of transportation and provisions would add up to $300 million. Jefferson recommended instead the deportation of the future generation of blacks: black infants would be taken from their mothers and trained in industrious occupations until they reached a proper age for deportation. Since Jefferson calculated a newborn infant was worth only $22.50, the estimated loss of slave property would be reduced from $600 million to only $37.5 million. Jefferson suggested they be transported to the independent black nation of Santo Domingo. "Suppose the whole annual

[26] Jefferson to Doctor Thomas Humphreys, February 8, 1817, ibid., pp. 57–58.

[27] Thomas Jefferson, *Notes on the State of Virginia* (New York: 1964, originally published in 1785), pp. 85, 139, 133, 127; Jefferson to Dr. Edward Bancroft, January 16, 1788, in Edwin M. Betts, ed., *Thomas Jefferson's Farm Book* (Princeton: 1953), p. 10.

increase to be sixty thousand effective births," he speculated on the future of blacks in America, "fifty vessels, of four hundred tons burthen each, constantly employed in that short run, would carry off the increase of every year, and the old stock would die off in the ordinary course of nature, lessening from the commencement until its final disappearance." He was confident the effects of his plan would be "blessed." As for the taking of children from their mothers, Jefferson remarked: "The separation of infants from their mothers . . . would produce some scruples of humanity. But this would be straining at a gnat, and swallowing a camel."[28]

The third authority Glazer cites is Seymour Martin Lipset, author of *The First New Nation: The United States in Historical and Comparative Perspective*. According to Glazer, Lipset views the American Revolution as an event which weakened the ethnic identification with England and led to the emergence of equality and achievement as dominant values in American society. My own reading of Lipset suggests that he cannot be grouped with Arieli, Kohn, and Glazer himself. Where they tend to mix together ethnicity and race, Lipset makes a sharp distinction between the two: "American egalitarianism is, of course, for white men only. The treatment of the Negro makes a mockery of this value now as it has in the past."[29]

This perspective on an American "racial" pattern, while it is not developed or documented historically, leads Lipset to a very different conclusion from the one offered in Glazer's *Affirmative Discrimination*. Though both Lipset and Glazer share a similar understanding of American values, they separate on the issue of public policy and racial inequality. Where Glazer, from the perspective of the emergence of an American "ethnic" pattern, insists that all that can and should be done for blacks is to extend the legal status of equality to individuals regardless of race, Lipset contends that "perhaps the most important fact to recognize about the current situation of the American Negro is that *equality is not enough to assure his movement into the larger society*." Where Glazer asserts that all the federal government should do is to outlaw racial discrimination in employment, Lipset points out the persistence of the enormous differentiation between white and black incomes, the disproportionate rate of unemployment among blacks, and the problems of structural black unemployment—the low level of education among blacks and the elimination of unskilled labor resulting from automation. "Fair employment legislation," Lipset argues,

---

[28] Jefferson to Jared Sparks, February 4, 1824, in Paul L. Ford, ed., *The Works of Thomas Jefferson* (New York: 1892–99), 12: 334–39.

[29] Glazer, *Affirmative Discrimination,* p. 11; Seymour Martin Lipset, *The First New Nation: The United States in Historical and Comparative Perspective* (New York: 1967, originally published in 1963), pp. 379–80.

"does little good if there are no decent jobs available for which the bulk of Negroes are qualified. . . . To break this vicious cycle (of black illiteracy and unemployment), it is necessary to treat the Negro more than equally. . . ."[30]

But if Lipset is correct, how do we respond to what Glazer describes as "the remarkably rapid improvement in the black economic and occupational position in the 1960s"? If we look at certain kinds of data, we can find support for Glazer's contention that the "heritage of discrimination" can be eliminated by "simply attacking discrimination." As Glazer shows, in the North and West in 1969, the median income of black husband-wife families with family heads under thirty-five years of age was 91 percent of the median income of white families in the same category. For the nation as a whole, the median income of black husband-wife families rose from 62 percent of the median income of comparable white families in 1959 to 85 percent in 1972. During this period, blacks also made inroads into occupations of greater security and higher status. The percentage of male "Negroes and other races" (Glazer notes that this group as a whole is over 90 percent black) increased in several employment fields. Their percentages jumped from 4.9 percent in 1963 to 8.2 percent in 1973 for professional and technical workers, from 15.3 percent to 22.9 percent for white-collar workers, and from 10.7 percent to 14.9 percent for craft workers.[31]

But these advances, while important, must be analyzed within the total context of the black economic situation. While the black median income rose from 54 percent of the white median income in 1959 to 66 percent in 1969, it dropped back to 58 percent in 1972. Meanwhile, between 1959 and 1973, of all black families in poverty, those with male heads declined from 1,300,000 to 550,000, while families with female heads increased from 550,000 to 970,000. While black female-headed families constituted 23.7 percent of all black families in 1965, they increased to 34 percent in 1974, forming almost two-thirds of all black families in poverty. While blacks made important gains in several occupational fields, they remained behind whites. In 1973, only 8.2 percent of male "Negroes and other races" were professional and technical workers compared to 14.2 percent of whites, only 15.3 percent of them were white-collar workers compared to 41.7 percent of whites, and only 14.9 percent of them were craft workers compared to 21.5 percent of whites. While the unemployment rate for blacks and other races dropped from 12.6 percent (compared to 6.1 percent for whites) in 1958 to 6.7 percent (compared to 3.2 percent for whites) in 1968, it rose again to 9.9 percent (compared to 5.0 percent for whites)

[30] Lipset, *First New Nation*, pp. 381–82.
[31] Glazer, *Affirmative Discrimination*, pp. 197; 41–42.

in 1974. Furthermore, while the unemployment rate for blacks and other races sixteen to nineteen years old dropped slightly from 27.4 percent (compared to 14.4 percent for whites) in 1958 to 25 percent (compared to 11.0 percent for whites) in 1968, it soared sharply to 32.9 percent (compared to 14.0 percent for whites) in 1974. Since the publication of Glazer's book in 1975, the median income of black families has continued to remain forty or more percentage points behind the median income of white families—43 percent in 1977 and 41 percent in 1978. The number of black single-parent families headed by women has also continued to rise, from 1.4 million in 1970 to 2.3 million in 1978, and has undercut much of the gains made by black two-spouse families which Glazer highlights. For every black family that made it into the middle class, three other black families joined the bottom of American society. While black families comprised 22 percent of all low-income households in 1970, they accounted for 28 percent in 1978.[32]

The total picture suggests the black economic situation is highly complex. We must acknowledge that some black "progress" has occurred. The number of blacks in the professional, technical, white-collar, and crafts occupations has increased. But we cannot claim this improvement was wholly the result of antidiscrimination legislation. We must also take into account the general expansion of the American economy in the 1960s as well as affirmative action pressures and policies which were in operation during this time of black economic improvement. Still, while recognizing these gains, we must not overlook or diminish the importance of the overriding and persistent reality of economic inequality between blacks and whites. Blacks still lag behind whites in median incomes, still find themselves underrepresented in the higher-status and better-paying occupations, and still constitute a disproportionately large percentage of low-income and impoverished families. Moreover, underclass blacks may be facing a particularly grim future in a cybernated and service-producing economy. The high rate of black unemployment, which has been around twice the unemployment rate among whites, must be viewed within the context of a major structural shift from goods to service production; the proportion of workers in the service-producing sector of the economy has increased

---

[32] Ibid.; William J. Wilson, *The Declining Significance of Race: Blacks and Changing American Institutions* (Chicago: 1978), pp. 90, 91; *Current Population Reports,* Series P-20, Bureau of the Census, No. 340: "Household and Family Characteristics" (U.S. Government Printing Office: 1979). Table E, cited in Andrew Hacker, "Creating American Inequality," *New York Review of Books,* XXVII, No. 4:23; see also ibid for other comparisons. The most detailed study of this issue is Reynolds Farley, "Racial Progress in the Last Two Decades: What Can We Determine about Who Benefitted and Why?" paper presented at the 1979 Annual Meeting of the American Sociological Association.

from 49 percent in 1947 to 64 percent in 1968. Thus employment expansion has been located largely in clerical, professional, and administrative fields, which have higher educational and training requirements for employment.[33]

What, then, is to be done, and what would constitute responsible and informed public policies regarding the problem of racial inequality in America? How we answer this question will depend on how we perceive the problem—its nature and its history.

America, despite its racial pattern of domination and exclusion, contained a counterpointing perspective. In his resonant musings, a lonely poet—Walt Whitman—celebrated a vision of democratic tolerance and indiscriminate inclusionism. In Whitman's "America," peoples of all colors could come together, mixing in a great democracy yet respecting the rich cultural diversity of a multiracial society. Thus the poet sang:

Of every hue and caste am I, of every rank and
    religion,
A farmer, mechanic, artist, gentleman, sailor,
    quaker,
Prisoner, fancy-man, rowdy, lawyer, physician,
    priest.
I resist any thing better than my own diversity.

Whitman saluted "all the inhabitants of the earth." For the American poet, "all races and cultures" were to be "accepted, to be saluted, not to be controlled or placed in hierarchy." And in America, all were to be welcomed—"Chinese, Irish, German, pauper or not, criminal or not—all, all, without exceptions." Ours was not to be a society for "special types" but for the "great mass of people—the vast, surging, hopeful army of workers."[34]

But Whitman's was not the vision of America's public policy makers. Where the poet offered a democratic alternative, the representatives to Congress enacted the 1790 Naturalization Law and the 1882 Chinese Exclusion Act. Where the poet joyfully perceived the promise of a culturally diverse America, federal officials removed Indians and relocated Japanese Americans. Where the poet embraced an egalitarianism for all,

---

[33] Dorothy K. Newman et al., *Protest, Politics, and Prosperity: Black Americans and White Institutions, 1940 75* (New York: 1978), p. 64; Wilson, *Declining Significance of Race,* pp. 93–95.

[34] Walt Whitman, *Leaves of Grass and Selected Prose* (New York: 1958), pp. 38, 1, 25, 18, 78, 83, 89, 399–400, 340, 121, 343; Walt Whitman, in Horace Traubel, *With Walt Whitman in Canada,* 2 vols. (New York: 1915), 2: 34–35.

regardless of race, men in power like Jefferson, Rush, and Walker worked to build a homogeneous society for special types. Where the poet welcomed all immigrants into the "hopeful army of workers," corporate leaders like Crocker constructed racially divided, segmented labor markets which reflected an American racial pattern.

This pattern was discerned long ago by Herman Melville and emblematized in his description of the crew of the *Pequod* and the whaling industry's labor force. "Not one in two of the many thousand men before the mast employed in the American whale fishery, are American born, though pretty nearly all the officers are," reported Melville's Ishmael. "Herein it is the same with the American whale fishery as with the American army and military and merchant navies, and the engineering forces employed in the construction of the American Canals and Railroads. The same, I say, because in all these cases the native American liberally provides the brains, the rest of the world as generally supplying the muscles." A significant supply of the "muscles" on board the *Pequod* had been drawn from workers of color—blacks, Indians, Pacific Islanders, and Asians. The social divisions within the ship's crew represented the occupational/racial structure in American labor and society. While not all whites were officers, all officers or men on deck were white, and all workers of color were below deck.[35]

The American racial pattern which Melville depicted in 1851 still largely exists today in its basic form, and will continue long after the enactment of legislation prohibiting discrimination based on color, race, or ethnic origin, unless public policies act affirmately to overcome racial inequality. Due to racially exclusionist forces and developments in American history, racial inequality and occupational stratification have come to coexist in a mutually reinforcing and dynamic structural relationship which continues to operate more powerfully than direct forms of racial prejudice and discrimination. To diminish the significance of racial oppression in America's past and to define racial inequality as a problem of prejudice and limit the solution as the outlawing of individual acts of discrimination, as does Glazer, is effectively to leave intact the very structures of racial inequality.

--------------------------------- **ANALYSIS** ---------------------------------

1. How does Takaki summarize Nathan Glazer's "The Emergence of an American Ethnic Pattern" so as to emphasize Glazer's attack on affirmative action?

---

[35] Herman Melville, *Moby Dick, or the Whale* (Boston: 1956, originally published in 1851), p. 108.

2. In criticizing Glazer, why does Takaki attack such phrasings as the "large direction" and the "major tendency to a greater inclusiveness"?

3. What claim as "an historian" does Takaki make in examining Glazer's account of America? How does this exemplify the basic argument Takaki will make vis-à-vis Glazer's view of American history?

4. Takaki disputes the first of Glazer's three decisions by detailing the way America has not invited "the whole world" to come here and be given citizenship, or allowed all races equality of voting rights. In other words, Takaki disputes Glazer's idea of a "pattern" of inclusion; in fact, Takaki finds a pattern of exclusion. Is this an effective rebuttal to Glazer? Explain.

5. Takaki concludes his essay by reversing Glazer's optimistic assessment of America's "ethnic pattern": "The American racial pattern which Melville depicted in 1851 still largely exists today." Similarly, Takaki rejects Glazer's view that government need only ban "prejudice and individual acts of discrimination" as insufficient to deal with the "Structures of inequality such as poverty, inferior education, occupational stratification, and inner-city ghettos. . . ." For government not to "act affirmatively" on these matters, says Takaki, is "to leave intact the very structures of racial inequality." Which of these scholars offers, in your view, the best support for his argument?

Writing Possibilities

1. Sum up in your own words (in about a paragraph) what you think Glazer means by the "American ethnic pattern"; do the same for Takaki's criticism of Glazer. What, in your view, is the key difference between the two scholars? Who has the better case? Explain by citing specific examples from both Glazer and Takaki.

2. The issues between Glazer and Takaki involve both strategy—how they balance good and bad in American history—and rhetoric (how each confronts the opposing side's understanding). Assess either the strategy or the rhetoric, taking into account both evidence and language; note especially how both scholars, at key points in their arguments, make concessionary statements—i.e., those which acknowledge the good amidst the bad or vice versa.

Gary Wills

In this selection, the historian Gary Wills discusses recent attacks on the author of the Declaration of Independence, perhaps America's single-most important founding document. Mindful of the attacks on Jefferson in the present, Wills argues that we have "misconceived" Jefferson's greatness (for Wills does not doubt that Jefferson was great): we need to focus not on Jefferson's racist views, says Wills, but instead on his belief in democracy and self-government. These, argues Wills, are the crucial sources of his greatness and hence the reason not to exclude him from the pantheon of American heroes as his critics advocate.

STORM OVER JEFFERSON

Those of us who grew up in the middle of this century thought that Jefferson's star could never be dimmed, much less flicker or go out. In fact, we were surprised to learn that in the early decades of the century the star had disappeared behind clouds of hostility. Theodore Roosevelt referred to our saint as a "scholarly, timid, and shifting doctrinaire" and described any cult of him as "a discredit to my country." Roosevelt reflected the imperial mood in which America ended the nineteenth century, with naval adventurism into Cuba, the Philippines, and the Far East. The prophet of naval power at that time, Alfred Thayer Mahan (surely the only admiral who was ever the president of the American Historical Association), joined others in seeing the active government envisaged by Alexander Hamilton as the vehicle for America's rise to the status of a world power. Henry Adams, though he did not share his fellow imperialists' admiration for Hamilton, made endless fun of Jefferson for his belief that America could sustain a realistic foreign policy with the help of a few shore-hugging gunboats.

As the country moved from turn-of-the-century imperialism into the Progressive Era, reformers found that they, too, needed Hamilton's strong government for the remaking of society. The leading voice here was that of Herbert Croly, who found in Jefferson's libertarian ideals only "individual aggrandizement and collective irresponsibility." Well into the Twenties, Americans were assured that ordinary people were incapable of conducting their own affairs in a time of rapid and necessary technological innovation. Robert and Helen Lynd, famous for *Middletown* (their sociological study of Muncie, Indiana), concluded that the bewildered modern housewife could not keep up with the new tools and markets she must use, and turned her over to the advice of experts to be specially created for her guidance. Walter Lippmann, in *The Phantom Public* (1929), claimed that the average voter could not judge complex issues involved in modern public policy, and wanted boards of experts to make the real decisions, which voters would simply ratify.

It was only with the crash of the high hopes for governmental omnicompetence—it was only with the Great Depression—that a new emphasis on the plight and dignity of common people led to a resurgence of the great celebrator of the American yeoman, the plowman, the common man, the citizen. By the 1940s both political parties were invoking Jefferson—even Republicans now remembered that their own greatest president, Abraham Lincoln, called Jefferson, in his 1854 speech on the Kansas-Nebraska Act, the man "who was, is, and perhaps will continue to be, the most distinguished politician of our history." They had discovered the whole founding dream of America in Jefferson's words. The dedication of the Jefferson Memorial on April 13, 1943—the two hundredth anniversary of his birth—lodged him in that high stellar place where my contemporaries first encountered him. It seemed there would be no further wavering on the place of Jefferson at the center of America's historical commitments.

Yet Jefferson's formerly unquestioned greatness is now very thoroughly questioned. There are several confluent reasons for this, but the greatest is no doubt a deeper awareness of our national sin of slavery. When I first went to Monticello in the late 1950s, the role of slaves at that plantation complex was muted and made barely visible. The civil rights movement made such historical evasiveness impossible. The presence of slaves, their crucial labors (in a double sense), began to be marked, not only at Monticello, but at Mount Vernon, Williamsburg, and other sacred places in our history. In itself, this new clarity about our racial history should have told no more against Jefferson than against other presidents who ever owned slaves—Washington, Madison, Monroe, Jackson, Harrison, Tyler, Taylor, Andrew Johnson. But there are three things that add a special note of hypocrisy to Jefferson's purchasing and sale of human beings:

1. He was more passionate and effective in his calls for human freedom than was any other Founder.
2. He maintained an extravagant life style that kept him heavily indebted (to the very banks he called sources of corruption), and this made it impossible for him to free any but a few slaves (unlike Washington, who stayed solvent and could support the slaves he freed at his wife's death). Debt forced Jefferson to sell slaves in ways that disrupted family life, a step some other slave owners deplored and Washington was able to avoid.
3. The charge that Jefferson had a secret affair with his own slave Sally Hemings and lied about it gained new plausibility as a result of DNA testing.

A shift in the climate of any reputation leads to sharper looks at other aspects of the person's life than the one that caused that shift in the first place. So even on issues not directly related to slavery, Jefferson's credentials have come under increasing challenge. Contradictions in his policies toward Native Americans have received harsh new scrutiny, notably by Anthony Wallace in his *Jefferson and the Indians: The Tragic Fate of the First Americans*. James Morton Smith's running commentary on the Jefferson–Madison correspondence suggests that Madison was not only the deeper thinker but that he may have been a more consistent defender of liberty. A romantic picture of Jefferson the democrat who received diplomats in his slippers was dealt a blow by the great Monticello exhibit and catalog of 1993, which revealed how elitist was the life he led in France, in Virginia, and in Washington. A guest at one of his famous White House dinners wrote:

> His maitre-d'hôtel had served in some of the first families abroad, and understood his business to perfection. The excellence and the superior skill of his French cook was acknowledged by all who frequented his table, for never before had such dinners been given in the President's House, nor such a variety of the finest and most costly wines.

We can no longer forget that the fine wines, like the almost frantic collecting of art works, books, and furniture were paid for with money wrung from the bodies of Jefferson's human property. This can only make us shake our heads when Jefferson professes a creed of thrift: "Would that a missionary [might] appear who would make frugality the basis of his religious system, and go thro the land preaching it up as the only road to salvation I would join his school. . . ."

Pauline Maier's recent reappraisal of Jefferson's claim to authorship of the Declaration of Independence is evidence that Jefferson's image is under assault. She even once nominated him as "the most overrated person in American history . . . but only because of the extraordinary adulation (and, sometimes, execration) he has received and continues to receive." Conor Cruise O'Brien, in his book on Jefferson and the French Revolution adds the final insult when he calls Jefferson the son of the Parisian Terror and the father of the Oklahoma City bombing. And, as has happened in the past, a sinking of Jefferson's claims has been paired with a concomitant lifting of Hamilton's. Though Hamilton's biographer, Henry Cabot Lodge was not entirely justified in claiming that all Americans are either Jeffersonians or Hamiltonians, the two men's reputations do tend to move in contrary directions, if not quite on a historical seesaw, then as part of a sensitively poised Calder mobile.

Can we, in this climate, continue to hold that Jefferson is our "genius of liberty"? Certainly not, if that means denying some of the critical insights gained in recent years. But a reconsideration of the man may indicate that we misconceived his greatness rather than that he lacked greatness. Many people in the past thought of Jefferson as a theoretician, a French nationalist, even a metaphysician—timid, as Theodore Roosevelt thought, because so airily abstract and scholarly. Actually, of course, Jefferson despised metaphysicians. He lumped them together with the Platonists who had corrupted with their abstractions the plain moral instincts of Jesus. Jefferson was not a rigorous thinker. He was a rhetorician, an artist, an aesthete bordering on the dilettante. Henry Adams went right to the heart of this paradox when he spoke of Jefferson's "intellectual sensuousness." In discussing hypotheses, Jefferson would not sacrifice to scientific accuracy their symmetry and elegance. Even his handwriting showed his compulsion to the chaste ordering of shapes (uppercase letters were not allowed to violate the letters' formal ranks). He evened off his letters as he evened off the generations of men at a tidy nineteen years. He wanted "natural" measures of American weights and moneys, disregarding irregular intrusions of friction in his means of arriving at these all-too-neat numbers.

Not only was he an architect of talent, he was a *romantic* architect. His plantation was highly impractical because he placed it high above sublime views, where he could "ride above the storms" (and above mundane tasks), to "look down into the workhouse of nature, to see her clouds, hail, snow, rain, thunder, all fabricated at our feet!" Despite his years of obsessively collecting meteorological data, he never formulated a theory from them, as Franklin did from the experience of one storm at sea. Jefferson was the observer, who wanted to be awed by nature in its purity. When he compares his view from Monticello with other sights, they are all of untouched nature—"the Falling Spring, the Cascade of Niagara, the Passage of the Potowmac through the Blue Mountains, the Natural bridge."

In his aesthetic primitivism, Jefferson wanted to get back to a pure state of nature—pre-feudal, pre-urban, pre-monetary. The religion of Jesus was sound because non-institutional, non-theological, non-professional. It had no priests or ceremonies. Debts must be abolished periodically, to start over, to have a clean slate. America was superior to Europe, in Jefferson's eyes, because closer to nature. Europeans must be admitted into this paradise only slowly and grudgingly, if at all, lest they bring the evil fruit of their training, foreign to the ethos of our law, to "warp and bias its direction, and render it a heterogeneous, incoherent, distracted mass."

For the same reason, wrote Jefferson from France, young Americans should not be allowed to study in Europe, where, in an atmosphere of monarchs and priests, they may come to feel "the hollow, unmeaning manners of Europe to be preferable to the simplicity and sincerity of our own country." The encroachments of "civilization" must be fought off as long as possible, since "when they [Americans] get piled upon one another in large cities, as in Europe, they will become corrupt as is Europe." Since even the Bible has been corrupted by the priests, children should not be allowed to read it before they have been taught the self-evident maxims of honesty. Then they will accept from it only "the facts [that] are within the ordinary course of nature."

In Jefferson's primitivism we can discover the moral aspect of his aesthetics. For the Encyclopedists in France, for Shaftesbury in England, for Hume and Hutcheson in Scotland, the perception of moral beauty was closely allied with the aesthetic sense. That is why Jefferson thought that the sublime vistas of nature not only uplift but educate, a philosophy that he expounds in his *Notes on the State of Virginia*. Though he upheld harsh removal measures for the Native American, he thought that "his sensibility is keen" because he lives close to nature, while his natural self-control makes him "endeavour to appear superior to human events." The Indians' aesthetic sense led to "the most sublime oratory" in leaders like the Mingo chief Logan. The link between this aesthetic sensibility and moral probity was seen in the fact that "crimes are very rare among them."

Here we have to ask how Jefferson could at times be so appreciative of Native American dignity under conquest yet so blind to human worth in the oppressed African-Americans. People have thrashed about looking for a basis in intellect for this distinction, but have neglected the regnant principle with Jefferson, his sense of beauty. He found that blacks lack "the circumstance of superior beauty" that is taken into account even in animal husbandry:

> Is it [skin color] not the foundation of a greater or less share of beauty in the two races? Are not the fine mixtures of red and white, the expressions of every passion by greater or less suffusions of colour in the one, preferable to that eternal monotony, which reigns in the countenances, that immovable veil of black which covers all the emotions of the other race?

This is Jefferson's aestheticism at its worst. But he had the strengths of his weaknesses. He thought that his "beautiful people," the ordinary white yeomen, had a sense of order that was at once artistic and moral. His treatise of prosody says that all people are able to sense the order of accents that is most pleasing because of "the construction of the human ear." Why do rules jump out at us from the very nature of the English language? "The reason is that it has pleased God to make us so." Even the whole complex of grammatical constructions was grasped without rules by those who spoke Anglo-Saxon, that pre-learned language of nature that he recommended to students at his university. It was such natural beauty, existing before theories, that he thought he discerned in the poems of the Scottish bard Ossian.

This complex of aesthetic notions about natural perception gave Jefferson the assurance for one of his most famous democratic statements: "State a moral case to a ploughman & a professor. The former will decide it as well, & often better than the latter, because he has not been led astray by artificial rules." It was in the context of his letter on the sublimities of nature that Jefferson told Maria Cosway, "Morals were too essential to the happiness of man to be risked on the incertain combinations of the head. She [nature] laid their foundation therefore in sentiment, not in science." The head must make "combinations," create a chain of linked arguments, in order to reach a point that the heart leaps to directly. Jefferson even attributes the American Revolution to the direct perception of right that bypassed the head's more timid reflections:

> You [the head] began to calculate and to compare wealth and numbers: we threw up a few pulsations of our warmest blood: we supplied enthusiasm against wealth and numbers: we put our existence to the hazard, when the hazard seemed against us, and we saved our country: justifying at the same time the ways of Providence, whose precept is to do always what is right, and leave the issue to him.

His estimate of the heart's moral certitudes also made Jefferson prefer the emotional yeoman of the South to the scheming banker of the North. When he listed the attributes of the two regions, he said that Southerners were generous, candid, and "without attachment or pretensions to any religion but that of the heart," while the "chicaning" Northerners were "superstitious and hypocritical in their religion."

For Jefferson, then, the preservation of the heart's moral instinct is the true aim of education. That is why aesthetic response to a novel is a mode of moral formation:

> We are therefore wisely framed to be as warmly interested for a fictitious as for a real personage. The field of imagination is

thus laid open to our use and lessons may be formed to illustrate and carry home to the heart every moral rule of life.

Tears for another's plight, even for an imaginary character in a sentimental novel, show how the moral sense turns pain into the pleasures of benevolence: "And what more sublime delight than to mingle tears with one whom the hand of heaven hath smitten. . . ."

Jefferson the aesthete, then, is not really Jefferson the dilettante but Jefferson the moralist. *And* the democrat. He felt that human beings respond nobly to nature if their contact with it is not broken by adventitious accretions to it—by institutional religion, by systems of financial credit and debit, by cities, by theories, by governments. The defense of freedom, for him, meant not obtruding on natural man an artificial compulsion. As he wrote to Abigail Adams:

> The spirit of resistance to government is so valuable on certain occasions, that I wish it to be always kept alive. It will often be exercised when wrong, but better so than not to be exercised at all. I like a little rebellion now and then. It is like a storm in the atmosphere.

That last sentence returns us to the storms brewing in the "laboratory" below Monticello's height, and to the fundamentally artistic sense Jefferson had of politics. In his oddly mandarin way he had arrived at the basic democratic insight—that every human being is Humanity itself. It is an insight G.K. Chesterton put in many earthy ways—that we do not shout that "a Nobel Prize winner is drowning" but that "a man is drowning"; that the jury system expresses the truth that ordinary persons should be the judges of moral truth; that "democracy is like blowing your nose, you may not do it well but you ought to do it yourself." The contradictions of Jefferson had their dark side, but they also had this one dramatically benign side as well: he was the most uncommon of men, but he had a deep faith in the common man. For all his own elite life style, he was anti-elitist in principle—anti-priest, anti-banker, anti-theoretician, anti-politician. No other Founder had his deep reverence for the dignity and freedom of the individual.

Naturally, the nation has expanded on his insights—but it is to those insights it recurred when the work of expansion was to be done. The rights he found in his idealized yeoman are the model for those we try to uphold for every person in America. He voiced his faith in a rhetoric that has resonated far beyond any results he could have expected himself. His statement that "all men are created equal" is one of those formulations that ends up meaning more than it meant to mean. It became the lodestar to Lincoln, who taught us to read the

Constitution itself in the light of the Declaration of Independence. It was appealed to by Martin Luther King, Jr. The legacy of Jefferson, as passed on by Lincoln, is at the very heart of the American love of freedom. Here is the way Lincoln phrased the matter:

> The principles of Jefferson are the definitions and axioms of free society. . . . All honor to Jefferson—to the man who, in the concrete pressure of a struggle for national independence by a single people, had the coolness, forecast, and capacity to introduce into a merely revolutionary document, an abstract truth, applicable to all men and all times, and so to embalm it there, that to-day, and in all coming days, it shall be a rebuke and a stumbling-block to the very harbingers of re-appearing tyranny and oppression.

In Lincoln's own version of the American melting-pot concept, expressed in a July 10, 1858, speech in Chicago, he says that people who come from different countries, cultures, and status will be made equal in their American liberties by the Declaration. The statement that all men are equal "is the electric cord in that Declaration that links the hearts of patriotic and liberty-loving men together, that will link those patriotic hearts as long as the love of freedom exists in the minds of men throughout the world."

Jefferson's most transcendent gift may have been the gift of expression. His words continue to inspire what is deepest and best in America's struggle toward equality for all. They are applied to blacks in ways that Jefferson did not intend, and have reached others going beyond his own anticipation—women, gays, the disabled, minorities of all kinds. He intuited, with his fine sensibility, an ethos he could not always act on himself, but he conjured it up with undispellable words. That ethos was liberty, and he remains its genius. Even Henry Adams, often Jefferson's critic, had to admit that the privately visionary words of Jefferson embodied, in time, the shared public beliefs of the American citizenry.

ANALYSIS

1. According to Wills, Why has Jefferson star "dimmed"? What was his image like before it dimmed? What are the chief criticisms of Jefferson now?

2. What does Wills mean in speaking of this "new clarity about our racial history" in relationship to our attitude towards Jefferson? What in fact do we learn from the "new clarity" about Jefferson and racial history, in Wills's view?

3. Wills's defense of Jefferson involves Jefferson's attitudes towards democracy, self-government, and resistance to big government. How does Wills suggest that these concepts are intertwined?

4. From what sources, according to Wills, can we derive Jefferson's idea of "resistance to government"? (One key point: the closer man is to the state of nature, or at least to a simple state like that of ordinary yeoman—a primitivist concept—the more he is able to govern himself and thus not require government at all.)

5. After a digression on Jefferson's attitude towards Indians, Wills returns to his central theme of "Jefferson the aesthete" equals "Jefferson the moralist. *And* the democrat." How does he get, finally, to the quote from Lincoln on freedom and "Lincoln's own version of the American melting-pot concept" in the closing paragraphs of his essay?

WRITING POSSIBILITIES

1. One of the strengths of this essay is Wills's attention to rhetoric and "Jefferson's gift of expression"—as in Jefferson's extraordinary mantra that "All men are created equal." Wills's point is that the way we express something—our rhetorical presentation—is as much a source of power as the substance of what we say. How does Wills in his last paragraph apply this to the famous opening of the Declaration? What general point about language is Wills making here?

2. To what extent would you agree with Jefferson on the need to resist government? Consider on the one hand that Timothy McVeigh, the architect of the Oklahoma City bombing of a federal building in which 160 people died, claimed Jefferson as his guide, while on the other hand, a scholar like historian Gordon Wood reveres Jefferson as the apostle of democratic self-government.

Linda Chavez

In 2001, the Census Bureau reported that Latinos were about to become the nation's largest minority, having overtaken blacks in that spot, particularly in California. For Linda Chavez, however, "minority"—even if number one—mistakes the position Latinos are in. Her argument in Out of the Barrio *is precisely that the success of Latinos is not to be measured by "minority" status but rather by Latinos's assimilation into the American mainstream. The corollary here is that Hispanics do not need special treatment in order to succeed—in other words, they do not need affirmative action to prosper.*

Chavez's essay, the concluding chapter of Out of the Barrio, *raises the basic question: aren't Latinos—like blacks—often victims of group prejudice and discrimination, and in need of help by the human rights model of civic action rather than by individual action and responsibility?*

Linda Chavez is currently the president of the Center for Equal Opportunity in Washington.

TOWARD A NEW POLITICS OF HISPANIC ASSIMILATION
from Out of the Barrio

Assimilation has become a dirty word in American politics. It invokes images of people, cultures, and traditions forged into a colorless alloy in an indifferent melting pot. But, in fact, assimilation, as it has taken place in the United States, is a far more gentle process, by which people from outside the community gradually became part of the community itself. Descendants of the German, Irish, Italian, Polish, Greek, and other immigrants who came to the United States bear little resemblance to the descendants of the countrymen their forebears left behind. America changed its immigrant groups—and was changed by them. Some groups were accepted more reluctantly than others—the Chinese, for example—and some with great struggle. Blacks, whose ancestors were forced to come here, have only lately won their legal right to full participation in this society; and even then civil rights gains have not been sufficiently translated into economic gains. Until quite recently, however, there was no question but that each group desired admittance to the mainstream. No more. Now ethnic leaders demand that their groups remain separate, that their native culture and language be preserved intact, and that whatever accommodation takes place be on the part of the receiving society.

Hispanic leaders have been among the most demanding, insisting that Hispanic children be taught in Spanish; that Hispanic adults be allowed to cast ballots in their native language and that they have the right to vote in districts in which Hispanics make up the majority of voters; that their ethnicity entitle them to a certain percentage of jobs and college admissions; that immigrants from Latin America be granted many of these same benefits, even if they are in the country illegally. But while Hispanic leaders have been pressing these claims, the rank and file have been moving quietly and steadily into the American mainstream. Like the children and grandchildren of millions of ethnic immigrants before them, virtually all native-born Hispanics speak English—many speak only English. The great majority finish high school, and growing numbers attend college. Their earnings and occupational status have been rising along with their education. But evidence of the success of native-born Hispanics is drowned in the flood of new Latin immigrants—more than five million—who have come in the last two decades, hoping to climb the ladder as well. For all of these people, assimilation represents the opportunity to succeed in America. Whatever the sacrifices it entails—and there are some—most believe that the payoff is worth it. Yet the elites who create and influence public policy seem convinced that the process must be stopped or, where this has already occurred, reversed.

From 1820 to 1924 the United States successfully incorporated a population more ethnically diverse and varied than any other in the world. We could not have done so if today's politics of ethnicity had been the prevailing ethos. Once again, we are experiencing record immigration, principally from Latin America and Asia. The millions in Latin immigrants who are joining the already large native-born Hispanic population will severely strain our capacity to absorb them, unless we can revive a consensus for assimilation. But the new politics of Hispanic assimilation need not include the worst features of the Americanization era. Children should not be forced to sink or swim in classes in which they don't understand the language of instruction. The model of Anglo conformity would seem ridiculous today in a country in which 150 million persons are descended from people who did not come here from the British Isles. We should not be tempted to shut our doors because we fear the newcomers are too different from us ever to become truly "American." Nonetheless, Hispanics will be obliged to make some adjustments if they are to accomplish what other ethnic groups have.

Language and Culture

Most Hispanics accept the fact that the United States is an English-speaking country; they even embrace the idea. A *Houston Chronicle* poll in 1990 found that 87 percent of all Hispanics believed that it was their "duty to learn English" and that a majority believed English should be adopted as an official language. Similar results have been obtained in polls taken in California, Colorado, and elsewhere. But Hispanics, especially more recent arrivals, also feel it is important to preserve their own language. Nearly half the Hispanics in the *Houston Chronicle* poll thought that people coming from other countries should preserve their language and teach it to their children. There is nothing inconsistent in these findings, nor are the sentiments expressed unique to Hispanics. Every immigrant group has struggled to retain its language, customs, traditions. Some groups have been more successful than others. A majority of Greek Americans, for example, still speak Greek in their homes at least occasionally. The debate is not about whether Hispanics, or any other group, have the right to retain their native language but about whose responsibility it is to ensure that they do so.

The government should not be obliged to preserve any group's distinctive language or culture. Public schools should make sure that all children can speak, read, and write English well. When teaching children from non-English-speaking backgrounds, they should use methods that will achieve English proficiency quickly and should not allow political pressure to interfere with meeting the academic needs of students. No children in an American school are helped by being held back in their native language when they could be learning the language that will enable them to get a decent job or pursue higher education. More than twenty years of experience with native-language instruction fails to show that children in these programs learn English more quickly or perform better academically than children in programs that emphasize English acquisition.

If Hispanic parents want their children to be able to speak Spanish and know about their distinctive culture, they must take the responsibility to teach their children these things. Government simply cannot—and should not—be charged with this responsibility. Government bureaucracies given the authority to create bicultural teaching materials homogenize the myths, customs, and history of the Hispanic peoples of this hemisphere, who, after all, are not a single group but many groups. It is only in the United States that "Hispanics" exist; a Cakchiquel Indian in Guatemala would find it remarkable that anyone could consider his culture to be the same as a Spanish Argentinean's. The best way for Hispanics to learn about their native culture is in their own communities. Chinese, Jewish, Greek, and other ethnic communities have long established after-school and weekend programs to teach language and culture to children from these groups. Nothing stops Hispanic organizations from doing the same things. And, indeed, many Hispanic community groups around the country promote cultural programs. In Washington, D.C., groups from El Salvador, Guatemala, Colombia, and elsewhere sponsor soccer teams, fiestas, parades throughout the year, and a two-day celebration in a Latin neighborhood that draws crowds in the hundreds of thousands. The Washington Spanish Festival is a lively, vibrant affair that makes the federal government's effort to enforce Hispanic Heritage Month in all of its agencies and departments each September seem pathetic by comparison. The sight and sound of mariachis strolling through the cavernous halls of the Department of Labor as indifferent federal workers try to work above the din is not only ridiculous; it will not do anything to preserve Mexican culture in the United States.

Hispanics should be interested not just in maintaining their own, distinctive culture but in helping Latin immigrants adjust to their American environment and culture as well. Too few Hispanic organizations promote English or civics classes, although the number has increased dramatically since the federal government began dispensing funds for such programs under the provisions of the Immigration Reform and Control Act, which gives amnesty to illegal aliens on the condition that they take English and civics classes. But why shouldn't the Hispanic community itself take some responsibility to help new immigrants learn the language and history of their new country, even without government assistance? The settlement houses of the early century thrived without government funds. The project by the National Association of Latino Elected and Appointed Officials (NALEO) to encourage Latin immigrants to become U.S. citizens is the exception among Hispanic organizations; it should become the rule.

POLITICAL PARTICIPATION

The real barriers to Hispanic political power are apathy and alienage. Too few native-born Hispanics register and vote; too few Hispanic immigrants become citizens. The way to increase real political power is not to gerrymander districts to create safe seats for Hispanic elected officials or treat illegal aliens and other immigrants as if their status were unimportant to their political representation; yet those are precisely the tactics Hispanic organizations have urged lately. Ethnic politics is an old and honored tradition in the United States. No one should be surprised that Hispanics are playing the game now, but the rules have been changed significantly since the early century. One analyst has noted, "In the past, ethnic leaders were obliged to translate raw numbers into organizational muscle in the factories or at the polls. . . . In the affirmative-action state, Hispanic leaders do not require voters, or even protestors—only bodies." This is not healthy, for Hispanics or the country.

Politics has traditionally been a great equalizer. One person's vote was as good as another's, regardless of whether the one was rich and the other poor. But politics requires that people participate. The great civil rights struggles of the 1960s were fought in large part to guarantee the right to vote. Hispanic leaders demand representation but do not insist that individual Hispanics participate in the process. The emphasis is always on rights, never on obligations. Hispanic voter organizations devote most of their efforts toward making the process easier—election law reform, postcard registration, election materials in Spanish—to little avail; voter turnout is still lower among Hispanics than among blacks or whites. Spanish posters urge Hispanics to vote because it will mean more and better jobs and social programs, but I've never seen one that mentions good citizenship. Hispanics (and others) need to be reminded that if they want the freedom and opportunity democracy offers, the least they can do is take the time to register and vote. These are the lessons with which earlier immigrants were imbued, and they bear reviving.

Ethnic politics was for many groups a stepping-stone into the mainstream. Irish, Italian, and Jewish politicians established political machines that drew their support from ethnic neighborhoods; and the machines, in turn, provided jobs and other forms of political patronage to those who helped elect them. But eventually, candidates from these ethnic groups went beyond ethnic politics. Governor Mario Cuomo (D) and Senator Alfonse D'Amato (R) are both Italian American politicians from New York, but they represent quite different political constituencies, neither of which is primarily ethnically based. Candidates for statewide office—at least successful ones—cannot afford to be seen merely as ethnic representatives. Ethnic politics may be useful at the local level, but if Hispanic candidates wish to gain major political offices, they will have to appeal beyond their ethnic base. Those Hispanics who have already been elected as governors and U.S. senators (eight, so far) have managed to do so.

EDUCATION

Education has been chiefly responsible for the remarkable advancements most immigrant groups have made in this society. European immigrants from the early century came at a time when the education levels of the entire population were rising rapidly, and they benefited even more than the population of native stock, because they started from a much lower base. More than one-quarter of the immigrants who came during the years from 1899 to 1910 could neither read nor write. Yet the grandchildren of those immigrants today are indistinguishable from other Americans in educational attainment; about one-quarter have obtained college degrees. Second- and third-generation Hispanics, especially those who entered high school after 1960, have begun to close the education gap as well. But the proportion of those who go on to college is smaller among native-born Hispanics than among other Americans, and this percentage has remained relatively constant across generations, at about 10–13 percent for Mexican Americans. If Hispanics hope to repeat the successful experience of generations of previous immigrant groups, they must continue to increase their educational attainment, and they are not doing so fast enough. Italians, Jews, Greeks, and others took dramatic strides in this realm, with the biggest gains in college enrollment made after World War II. Despite more than two decades of affirmative action programs and federal student aid, college graduation rates among native-born Hispanics, not to mention immigrants, remain significantly below those among non-Hispanics.

The government can do only so much in promoting higher education for Hispanics or any group. It is substantially easier today for a Hispanic student to go to college than it was even twenty or thirty years ago, yet the proportion of Mexican Americans who are graduating from college today is unchanged from what it was forty years ago. When the former secretary of education Lauro Cavazos, the first Hispanic ever to serve in the Cabinet, criticized Hispanic parents for the low educational attainment of their children, he was roundly attacked for blaming the victim. But Cavazos's point was that Hispanic parents must encourage their children's educational aspirations and that, too often, they don't. Those groups that have made the most spectacular socioeconomic gains—Jews and Chinese, for example—have done so because their families placed great emphasis on education.

Hispanics cannot have it both ways. If they want to earn as much as non-Hispanic whites, they have to invest the same number of years in schooling as these do. The earnings gap will not close until the education gap does. Native-born Hispanics are already enjoying earnings comparable to those of non-Hispanic whites, once educational differences are factored in. If they want to earn more, they must become better educated. But education requires sacrifices, especially for persons from lower-income families. Poverty, which was both more pervasive and severe earlier in this century, did not prevent Jews or Chinese from helping their children get a better education. These families were willing to forgo immediate pleasures, even necessities, in order to send their children to school. Hispanics must be willing to do the same—or else be satisfied with lower socioeconomic status. The status of second- and third-generation Hispanics will probably continue to rise even without big gains in college graduation; but the rise will be slow. Only a substantial commitment to the education of their children on the part of this generation of Hispanic parents will increase the speed with which Hispanics improve their social and economic status.

ENTITLEMENTS

The idea of personal sacrifice is an anomaly in this age of entitlements. The rhetoric is all about rights. And the rights being demanded go far beyond the right to equality under the law. Hispanics have been trained in the politics of affirmative action, believing that jobs, advancement, and even political power should be apportioned on the basis of ethnicity. But the rationale for treating all Hispanics like a permanently disadvantaged group is fast disappearing. What's more, there is no ground for giving preference in jobs or promotions to persons who have endured no history of discrimination in this country— namely, recent immigrants. Even within Hispanic groups, there are great differences between the historical discrimination faced by Mexican Americans and Puerto Ricans and that faced by, say, Cubans. Most

Hispanic leaders, though, are willing to have everyone included in order to increase the population eligible for the programs and, therefore, the proportion of jobs and academic placements that can be claimed. But these alliances are beginning to fray at the edges. Recently, a group of Mexican American firemen in San Francisco challenged the right of two Spanish Americans to participate in a department affirmative action program, claiming that the latter's European roots made them unlikely to have suffered discrimination comparable to that of other Hispanics. The group recommended establishing a panel of twelve Hispanics to certify who is and who is not Hispanic. But that is hardly the answer.

Affirmative action politics treats race and ethnicity as if they were synonymous with disadvantage. The son of a Mexican American doctor or lawyer is treated as if he suffered the same disadvantage as the child of a Mexican farm worker; and both are given preference over poor, non-Hispanic whites in admission to most colleges or affirmative action employment programs. Most people think this is unfair, especially white ethnics whose own parents and grandparents also faced discrimination in this society but never became eligible for the entitlements of the civil rights era. It is inherently patronizing to assume that all Hispanics are deprived and grossly unjust to give those who aren't preference on the basis of disadvantages they don't experience. Whether stated or not, the essence of affirmative action is the belief that Hispanics—or any of the other eligible groups—are not capable of measuring up to the standards applied to whites. This is a pernicious idea.

Ultimately, entitlements based on their status as "victims" rob Hispanics of real power. The history of American ethnic groups is one of overcoming disadvantage, of competing with those who were already here and proving themselves as competent as any who came before. Their fight was always to be treated the same as other Americans, never to be treated as special, certainly not to turn the temporary disadvantages they suffered into the basis for permanent entitlement. Anyone who thinks this fight was easier in the early part of this century when it was waged by other ethnic groups does not know history. Hispanics have not always had an easy time of it in the United States. Even though discrimination against Mexican Americans and Puerto Ricans was not as severe as it was against blacks, acceptance has come only with struggle, and some prejudices still exist. Discrimination against Hispanics, or any other group, should be fought, and there are laws and a massive administrative apparatus to do so. But the way to eliminate such discrimination is not to classify all Hispanics as victims and treat them as if they could not succeed by their own efforts. Hispanics can and will prosper in the United States by following the example of the millions before them.

─────────────────────── **ANALYSIS** ───────────────────────

1. In Chavez's view, why has assimilation become a "dirty word"? How does Chavez refute this rejection of assimilation?
2. Why does Chavez distinguish between "Hispanic leaders" and "the rank and file"?
3. How does Chavez criticize reliance on the Census Bureau report that "23 percent of Hispanics live in poverty compared with only 7.7 percent of non-Hispanic whites"?
4. Discussing the low rate of Hispanic political participation, Chavez rejects solutions to the problem through making the political process easier ("election law reform, postcard registration, election materials in Spanish") or by resorting to traditional "ethnic politics." How does she support this argument?
5. Education, says Chavez, has been the most important agency of immigrant success; why, in her view, has this not turned out to be the case for Hispanics? What does she mean by saying that "Hispanics cannot have it both ways."
6. According to Chavez, how has America changed in the past century so that immigrants now have an easier time of it than before?

─────────────── **WRITING POSSIBILITIES** ───────────────

1. Chavez rejects "affirmative action politics" as a solution to the problems Hispanics face. How does she support this position? Do you agree with her argument here?
2. According to Angela D. Dillard in *Multicultural Conservatism,* the problem with minority conservatives like Chavez is their refusal to recognize structural impediments to success in the economic or political world. One version of such structural impediments—i.e., globalization of the economy, downsizing of factories to improve the bottom line— can be found in William Julius Wilson's "When Work Disappears" (Chapter 5, pages 348–356); how would Chavez answer Wilson's argument? How would you?
3. Chavez argues against bilingual education, even as a means of bringing non-English Hispanics into English-language proficiency. A ballot proposition in 1998, supported by a majority of Latinos, agreed with Chavez but others—including bilingual teacher-professionals, disagreed. Look up discussions of bilingual education on the Web and decide for yourself who has the best case. Explain why you agree or disagree with Chavez.

Manning Marable

An influential scholar of race and ethnicity, Manning Marable, in the following essay, proposes a "new and critical" approach to the study of race and ethnicity. What he means can be gleaned immediately by turning to his last paragraphs, where he suggests that while traditional "white racism" is on the decline:

> its place is being taken by a qualitatively new color line of spiraling class inequality and extreme income stratification, mediated or filtered through old discourses and cultural patterns more closely coded by physical appearance, legal and racial classification, and language.

Ultimately, Marable says, a new ethnic studies must have both a "broad perspective" and at the same time insist on vital "distinctions." Where, in the recent past, it has been a mark of progress to deal generally with "Asian American" identities, in particular Japanese and Chinese immigrants, increased immigration from other countries means that particular approach no longer can be maintained exclusively:

> as Indians, Pakistanis, Indonesians, Vietnamese, Arabs, Cambodians, and other increasingly enter the discussion regarding the definition of what the Asian-American category should mean, the conversation will become even more complicated.

Marable does a superb job of summarizing theories of race and ethnicity; the question, finally, is how we might want to respond to his ultimate point—i.e., that while racism is declining, new forms of economic, racial, and ethnic conflicts are now on the upswing. Is Marable right, for example, in saying that a "new color line" of economic—not racial—inequality has dawned or that while the older black-white conflicts have subsided, new inter-ethnic issues (blacks and Chicanos in L.A. differing about the role of immigration) will have to be dealt with by coming generations? There is much to ponder in Marable's packed paragraphs.

WE NEED NEW AND CRITICAL STUDY OF RACE AND ETHNICITY

When Nelson Mandela was elected president of a newly democratic South Africa in 1994, an entire period of racial history came dramatically to an end. Since the 1960's, the United States has witnessed the rise of an affluent African-American middle class and the dismantling of the last vestiges of legal segregation. In Europe, growing numbers of ethnic and racial minorities have had an impact on governments and political parties on both the left and the right. Such recent historical events illustrate how the meaning of race and the way it is expressed through political power are being rapidly transformed across the world. But while a great deal of scholarly attention has gone into studying both race and ethnicity, too often the discussion has been mired in old debates and definitions. To understand the changes around us, we need a new and critical study of the increasingly complicated relationship between race and ethnicity.

Part of today's confusion stems from the fact that the concepts of race and ethnicity have evolved very differently. Race is a dynamic social construct that has its roots in the transatlantic slave trade, the establishment of plantation economies based on enslaved labor, and the ideological justification for the vast extermination of millions of indigenous Americans. White Americans have thought of themselves in terms of racial categories for several centuries.

By contrast, ethnicity is a relatively recent concept. There are no references to ethnicity per se in the social-science literature of the 19th and early 20th centuries. Ethnicity surfaced as an important category of analysis in the writings of sociologists during the Great Depression, as a means to describe the diverse immigrant populations that came largely from Southern and Eastern Europe. Later, ethnicity was used to describe the development of modern European nationalism and the conflicts developing among various communities defined by their cultural and social traditions.

Because of the hegemony of race and racism in the social development of the United States, European immigrants who arrived here quickly learned that the key to their advancement and power was to claim the status of being white. In other words, during the 19th century race was much more powerful than what we might today call ethnicity in determining the lives of most new immigrants.

The Irish experienced severe discrimination upon their arrival. But within several generations, they had become "white." They had assimilated the values of privilege and the language and behavior of white domination that permitted them to claim status within the social hierarchy. Conversely, immigrants from Latin America and Asia were frequently "racialized" by both legislative means and de facto segregation. After the U.S.–Mexican War of 1846–48, the United States incorporated roughly half of Mexico's entire territory into its own legal boundaries. Slavery, which had previously been abolished by the Mexican government, was reestablished. Only Mexicans who were defined as Spanish or white could claim U.S. citizenship: American Indians, peasants, and mestizos were treated as inferior groups.

Small wonder that there are currently major academic disagreements over the meanings and materiality of both race and ethnicity. For example, should race be subsumed under ethnicity as a subcategory? Or is race an exceptional social category in its own right, because of its peculiar historical development, discourses, relations with culture, etc., which set it apart from ethnicity? To what extent, if at all, should race be measured by biological, genetic, or cultural differences among groups? Can ethnic minority groups who are at least partly defined by their legal racial categories, such as African-Americans, be guilty of "racism" themselves? And what of the complex relationships among racialized ethnicities—Asian-Americans, American Indians, Latinos, and African-Americans?

Many different theoretical approaches have been proposed to address such questions. At one end of the ideological spectrum stand the racial-ethnic theorists, the multiculturalists, who insist that racialized ethnic groups should be studied together. The historian Ronald Takaki is a prominent example. In several influential studies, Takaki has, in essence, said that racialized minorities are fundamentally different from other ethnic groups because they share a common history of oppression. African-Americans came to this country involuntarily, in chains. American Indians were subjected to a deliberate policy of genocidal extermination. A common history of residential segregation, economic subordination, and political disenfranchisement has created the basis for a comprehensive approach to the study of such ethnic minority groups. Similarly, Johnnella E. Butler, a professor of English and ethnic studies, has defined "people of color" as a social category that includes "those who have not and do not assimilate."

Social scientists such as Robert Allen and Robert Blauner provide a variant of that argument, using political economy to understand race. Both scholars have proposed that racialized minorities share not only uniquely different social histories from white people, but also that their existence is strikingly similar to that of a colonized nation.

In *Black Awakening in Capitalist America,* Allen has suggested that black America is an oppressed colony inside the United States. The capitalist economic system uses racism as a means to exploit black and brown labor, and to keep white workers from joining with them. Blauner's *Racial Oppression in America* has argued that white ethnic groups may have experienced intolerance and exploitation, but that they were never "colonized," never confined to a subordinate status the way African-Americans and other racialized minorities were. The process of racial and class underdevelopment was therefore not accidental, but absolutely essential to the consolidation of white power.

At the opposite end of the spectrum are the cultural universalists, who, for divergent reasons, attack or dismiss all kinds of ethnic studies that factor in race. In *Beyond the Melting Pot* (1963), the social scientists Nathan Glazer and Daniel Patrick Moynihan laid out his argument, saying that ethnic identity is not biologically based, but rather a product of social forces and voluntary choices. As for African-Americans, Glazer and Moynihan took white ethnic groups as the standard, urging black people to strive to acquire the lifestyles, family patterns, and work habits of whites to diminish racial tensions.

More recently, a new school of universalists implies that any recognition of a unique status for racialized ethnic groups veers dangerously toward racial essentialism and separatism. Two leading intellectuals in this school of thought are Werner Sollors and Sean Wilentz.

In a series of provocative works, Sollors has vilified those who emphasize the discontinuities and conflicts among various racial and ethnic groups. For Sollors, "ethnicity" is an "invention," nothing more; all Americans, regardless of their respective racial or ethnic identities, share far more with each other—culturally, socially, and politically—than they don't share. In an essay in *The Chronicle,* Wilentz accused many ethnic-studies scholars of depicting "the United States chiefly in terms of ethnic (or racial) identities and antagonisms and, in some cases, . . . proclaim[ing] that ethnic groups should defend their cultures from assimilation into a hegemonic mainstream 'American' civilization." The American-studies program he directs at Princeton University, however, he noted, has taken a different approach, emphasizing fundamental cultural commonalities rather than differences.

Finally, there are the social theorists of race and ethnicity, who frankly do put forward essentialist and identity-bound models of cultural difference. The most influential school of thought, presently expressed in many black-studies programs, is Afrocentricity. It is a concept initially developed by Molefi Asante, former chair of black studies at Temple University, and bases itself on an oppositional stance toward Eurocentrism, the cultural ideology and supremacist practices of the white West, and on a belief in the enduring meaning of race and ethnicity.

Therefore, it is not surprising that a national conversation around issues of race and social diversity, such as the 1997–98 President's Race Initiative, is so difficult to carry out. The discourse about race continues to be politically charged, both in public policy and on our campuses, and people generally talk past each other—precisely because there is no consensus, in abstract theory or in the real world, on what is meant by race and ethnicity.

As a field of scholarship, the study of race and ethnicity is the intellectual product of vast historical and social changes within U.S. society. The field is still in the process of evolving, but its essential character was forged in the demographic, political, and cultural transformations of 20th-century American society that occurred in response to protests about white indifference.

At the dawn of the 20th century, American universities rarely focused on racial groups except to explore them as communities with "problems"—as in "the Negro problem." Black higher education was confined to about 100 academic institutions that had been constructed in the decades after the Civil War, and it was at those underfinanced but proud colleges that the black intellectual tradition of scholarship was first nurtured.

Then, as Northern industrial and manufacturing jobs became available to black people around the turn of the century, millions trekked out of the South in the Great Migration. Later, in the 1940's and 1950's, several million people from Mexico crossed the border to work in the Southwest. By the 1960's, every major city in the United States had substantial numbers of people from ethnic minority groups whose identity was defined, at least in part, by their race. As those people arrived on white campuses, they demanded changes in the curriculum that reflected their own experiences and intellectual traditions. African-American studies came first, to be followed by Chicano studies and Asian-American studies.

The development of Native American studies was different. For years, the study of American Indian cultures and societies had been dominated by white, frequently ethnocentric and even racist, anthropologists. American Indians, who usually thought of themselves in terms of their tribal identities, did not begin to develop a part-Indian cultural identity until the 1950's, when the federal government began to expel more than 100 tribes from lands promised them by historic treaties. The militancy that such policies provoked finally came together in the 1980's in a demand for Native American studies.

As a result, that field today has two very different types of institutional structures: many traditional programs initiated and led by white scholars at predominantly white universities, which focus on anthropological, linguistic, historical, and folkloric themes, and the more radical Indian-studies programs, frequently connected with the network of tribal colleges. (The second group often defines its research outside the boundaries of ethnic studies, saying that Indian Americans are the only "indigenous" people in the United States.)

For the most part, African-American studies, as a field, was at first only marginally affected by the emergence of those newer programs. The racialized discourse and framing of inquiry along the boundaries of the black experience limited the development of comparative studies. Similarly, the male-dominated hierarchies and paradigms in African-American studies on many campuses limited interaction with the emerging interdisciplinary programs in women's, gender, and queer studies.

Ethnic-studies programs that explicitly examined the interactions, comparisons, and contacts among racialized minorities came later. The first of the major ethnic-studies departments to develop was, not surprisingly, in ethnically diverse California. The department of ethnic studies at the University of California at Berkeley was founded in 1969, at the height of the antiwar and Black Power movements, and was originally conceived of as an umbrella-like structure, with four interdependent programs operating within one department. Four separate majors and curricula were established, in Native American studies, Chicano studies, Asian-American studies, and Afro-American studies.

Within several years, serious problems had developed in the program. Because each major focused on a single racial ethnicity, students and faculty members alike tended to function only in their narrow area of scholarly interest. Few undertook comparative research. Moreover, there was internal competition for resources, and cooperation among the divisions sometimes broke down completely. Nevertheless, for nearly 20 years Berkeley's model prevailed in the dozens of ethnic-studies programs that developed. Then, as significant numbers of Asian-American students enrolled in elite universities throughout the country, their presence on campuses helped to promote a new approach to teaching ethnic studies, with a broader comparative and global focus.

The department of ethnic studies at the University of California at San Diego, founded in 1991, was representative of the new directions in the field. Courses previously taught under separate academic menus of Asian-American, Chicano, American Indian, and African-American studies were integrated in one rigorous, comparative core curriculum. Faculty members were recruited largely on their academic interest in comparative ethnic research. The department has also recently begun the process of creating graduate programs.

As of 1996, there were nearly 100 ethnic-studies programs throughout the United States, and approximately 30 of them were full departments. The most successful share several characteristics. First, and perhaps foremost, they offer courses that fulfill undergraduate core-curriculum or general-distribution requirements. Second, and related, they avoid racialization and ghettoization, refusing to limit the study of race and ethnicity to Latino, Asian-American, American Indian, and African-American students and scholars. Successful programs nearly always also have the authority to initiate appointments and recruit and retain their own faculty members, who are well-grounded in a traditional academic discipline and who define their primary field of research in broadly interdisciplinary and comparative terms.

To be sure, that can create tensions. At a number of programs, by the mid-1980's some older faculty members—hired in the initial wave of institutionalization, often without scholarly credentials—had ceased to function as intellectuals beyond their normal responsibilities as classroom instructors. At times, they developed a siege mentality, admonishing junior faculty members never to work with traditional departments or other interdisciplinary programs like women's studies. But much of the most innovative and creative scholarship is produced at the borders, the intellectual spaces between old disciplines. At its best, ethnic studies expands inquiry and provides innovative ways of thinking about traditional ideas.

Nevertheless, the central recurring dilemmas of scholarship in ethnic studies continue to be the twin problems of cultural amalgamation and racial essentialism. I say "twin problems" because those two different tendencies nevertheless have a subterranean unity.

First, look at cultural amalgamationists. As I've noted above, many people who study race and ethnicity tend to homogenize groups into a broad political construct: "people of color." That concept has tremendous utility in highlighting the commonalities of oppression and resistance that racialized ethnic groups have experienced; our voices and visions cannot properly be understood or interpreted in isolation from one another. But to argue that all people of color are therefore equally oppressed and share a common politics is dubious at best.

The opposite tendency—essentialism ("identitarianism," in the literary critic and activist Gayatri Spivak's term) encapsulates our respective racialized groups within the narrow terrain of our own experiences. In our own separate languages, from the vantage point of our respective grievances, we trust only in ourselves, cursing the possibility that others unlike ourselves might share a similar destiny.

Most scholars of ethnic studies today don't fall into either trap. We recognize both the profound divergences *and* the parallels in the social construction of ethnicity. Different ethnic groups retain their own unique stories, insights and reflections, triumphs and tragedies from their sojourns through American life. None of that can take away from the deep structural parallels, especially in the processes of racial oppression, in struggles for survival and resistance, and in efforts to maintain cultural and social integrity and identity. Those create the dynamic social framework that brings us together.

But let us take seriously the dynamic, dialectical characteristics of social change that define the framework of American race and ethnicity. Most scholars agree that racialization is a social and historical process—that "races" are not fixed categories. They are permeated by the changing contours of class, gender, nationality, and sexual orientation. If that is true, then we must also recognize that an "oppressed race" in one historical epoch, such as the Irish or the Ashkenazi Jews, can be incorporated into the privileged strata of whiteness. Racial designations of identical cultural groups may differ from country to country and in diverse places and times.

The general tendency of most people in the United States is to think about race and racism parochially solely within a North American context and within our current moment in history. A much richer perspective about race can be obtained from a comparative approach. In South Africa, for example, a racialized society very different from that in the United States developed, with a "coloured" group forming something of a buffer between black and white groups. Under the former regime of apartheid, certain Asian nationalities such as the Japanese, could be classified as white, while others, like the Chinese, were relegated to the lower status of coloureds. Even today, African-American traveling to South Africa are usually racially "coded by their appearance as coloured, but generally have political orientation and cultural consciousness that is defined as black in local terms. South Africa, thus highlights how fluid racial categories can be.

In colonial Brazil, the importation of more than four million enslaved Africans was the foundation for the construction of a distinctive racialized society. Color and phenotype were important criteria for placing an individual within the racial hierarchy. But social class, education, family background, and other elements were also extremely important in interpreting racial distinctions. For more than a century, Brazilians have used the expression "Money lightens the skin," which suggests how a minority of Brazilian blacks have been able to scale the hierarchy of whiteness through the acquisition of material wealth and cultural capital. Until recently, that was rarely the case in the United States. But the situation is changing.

Moreover, the state always has a vested interest in the management of diversity. The U.S. government's decision in 1971 to create a new "ethnic, but not racial" category of "Hispanic" on its census form is the best recent example of state manipulation of the politics of difference. The designation "Hispanic" was imposed on more than fifteen million citizens and resident aliens who had very different nationalities, racial-ethnic identities, cultures, social organizations, and political histories.

The Puerto Rican people had been in every respect a "nation" incorporated into the political system of the United States, in much the same way that Mexicans in the Southwest had been brought into the country. Both groups were racialized national minorities within the hierarchy of American race relations. By contrast, most Cuban-Americans who had fled to the United States following the Cuban revolution of 1959 were immediately granted the status of whiteness. To this day, their legal status and access to material resources from the U.S. government is strikingly different from that of black Hispanics from the Dominican Republic or Panama.

The Hispanic category on the census encompasses both Puerto Rican-Americans and Cuban-Americans, as well as such extraordinarily different groups as: upper middle-class immigrants from Argentina, Uruguay, and Chile, who are phenotypically white and culturally European; black working-class Panamanians and Dominicans; the anti-Castro

Cuban exiles of 1959–61 who now form much of Florida's ruling political elite and professional class; and Mexican-American farm workers in California's agricultural districts. Which of those distinct nationalities and cultural groups will largely set the standards for what the Hispanic legal and social construct may become?

The central driving force today behind the configuration of the U.S. racial formation is immigration, and it is creating a host of new problems for our understanding of race and ethnicity. Nationwide, about a third of the total growth rate of the U.S. labor force comes from legal and illegal immigration. According to an Urban Institute study, more than 90 percent of the new immigrant population settles in urban areas where there are high concentrations of black Americans. That means that native-born black workers increasingly find themselves in sharp competition with foreign-born non-whites.

In some cities, black workers complain that they have been fired or have lost low-wage jobs because they are not fluent in Spanish. Increasingly, some Latino and Asian-American groups are using laws against discrimination achieved by the civil-rights movement to attack what many African-Americans see as hard-won gains. For instance, in late 1994 Tirso del Junco, the only Latino on the Board of Governors of the U.S. Postal Service, charged that African-Americans were "over-represented" within the Postal Service work force.

In the area of education, the gains achieved by African-Americans during the 1960's and 1970's are also being reversed. The percentage of graduating black seniors who went on to college leveled off in the 1980's and started to descend. By contrast, 51 percent of all 1980 Asian-American high-school seniors had enrolled in four-year colleges by February 1982, compared with 37 percent of all white seniors, 33 percent of African-American seniors, and 20 percent of Hispanic seniors. In terms of business development, the Census Bureau estimated in 1987 that about 6 percent of all Asian-Americans owned businesses, compared with 6.5 percent of all white people, 2 percent of Hispanics, 1.5 percent of African-Americans, and 1 percent of American Indians.

Those and other striking differences in opportunities and upward mobility of racialized ethnics set the context for increasing social and legal conflicts, from the black and Latino violence in 1992 in Los Angeles, which was aimed squarely against Korean establishments, to the debate two years later in California over Proposition 187, which denied undocumented immigrants access to education and health-care services. Asian-Americans voted overwhelmingly for the initiative; most black voters rejected it, but by a narrow margin of 53 percent opposed and 47 percent in favor. With the initiative's passing, black-Latino conflicts intensified in poor urban communities such as Compton, where underfinanced schools, public-health facilities, and social services had already reached a crisis.

Conflicts among America's racialized ethnic groups are also exacerbated by the significant differences—based on social class, nationality, language, and religion—that subdivide each grouping. The Asian-American category includes Japanese-Americans, who have higher median family incomes than whites, and the Hmong of southeast Asia, who are one of the poorest U.S. population groups. There is significant class stratification and polarization within the Chinese community, with a growing professional and corporate group facing tens of thousands of working poor people. Moreover, the attempt to construct a pan-ethnic Asian-American identity and cultural/political consciousness is historically a very recent phenomenon and remains extremely contested.

All of that means that ethnic studies must both have a broad perspective—and at the same time be careful to make distinctions. Much of the focus in Asian-American studies, for example, has concentrated largely on the experiences of Japanese and Chinese immigrants. But as Indians, Pakistanis, Indonesians, Vietnamese, Arabs, Cambodians, and others increasingly enter the discussion regarding the definition of what the Asian-American category should mean, the conversation will become even more complicated.

Ethnic studies will also have to contend with the continuing attempt to differentiate some "model" minority groups from other minority groups. In today's period of globalization, corporate capital requires a multicultural, multinational management and labor force. Racialized ethnic consumer markets in the United States represent hundreds of billions of dollars; African-Americans alone spend more than $350-billion annually. To better exploit those vast consumer markets, capital has developed a strategy of manipulating cultural diversity to maximize profit.

In terms of the governmental, financial, and corporate interests, certain ethnic minorities are seen as being connected with powerful geopolitical countries such as China and Japan. At a symbolic level, the prestige or power of a nation-state's economy in the global marketplace is inevitably translated in the United States and Western industrialized countries into public policies, which in turn impact the representation and treatment of different groups. Ideologically and culturally, the so-called backward peoples who have been historically identified with Africa, the Caribbean, and much of Latin America and southern Asia are at a distinct disadvantage in racist Western societies.

A century ago, W.E.B. Du Bois predicted that the problem of the 20th century would be "the problem of the color-line." Although many Americans still think about race in largely biological and socially static terms, in a paradigm of black versus white, that historical color line is now being transformed. A new racial formation is evolving rapidly in the United States, with a new configuration of racialized ethnicity, class, and gender stratification and divisions. Increasingly the pheno-typical, color-based categories of difference that only a generation ago appeared rigid and fixed are being restructured and reconfigured against the background of globalized capitalism and neoliberal govern-ment policies worldwide.

In a curious way, William Julius Wilson was both right and wrong when he predicted the "declining significance of race" nearly two decades ago. Traditional white racism is certainly declining. But its place is being taken by a qualitatively new color line of spiraling class inequality and extreme income stratifications, mediated or filtered through old discourses and cultural patterns more closely coded by physical appearance, legal and racial classification, and language.

What the critical study of racialized ethnicities can bring into focus is how and why such domestic and global processes are cur-rently unfolding, and what can be done to challenge them.

ANALYSIS

1. Look again at the quotation from Marable at the end of the previous selection that begins "its place is being taken . . .". This is an extraor-dinarily compressed discussion. Marable packs in a lot of ideas and concerns, so it really requires careful unpacking to see exactly what connections Marable is making between class, inequality, older "racial" classifications, and new racial immigration. Reread the passage and see if you are absolutely clear about what Marable is claiming. Do you agree or disagree with Marable? Why?

2. In Marable's view, what are the basic conflicts over understanding the terms *race* and *ethnicity?* Omi and Winant (Chapter 3), for example, argue that the two terms have been confused since the 1920s; Takaki maintains that we should not mix the two together, substituting "eth-nicity" for "race." How does Marable deal with this issue?

3. What does Marable mean by saying that the "central recurring dilemma . . . in ethnic studies," is "the twin problems of cultural amal-gamation and racial essentialism"?

4. By "amalgamationists," Marable means those who want to deal with different groups by in effect homogenizing them, putting them all to-gether under a common construct, e.g., "people of color." The opposite tendency, "essentialism" or "identitarianism" keeps racialized groups within their own separate categories. Most scholars, though, Marable argues, don't fall into this either-or trap. They believe that there are both "divergences *and* parallels" in the experience of different ethnic and racial groups. How does this apply to Takaki? To Glazer?

5. Marable also looks at social change in time and place; for example a group pilloried in one era or one place, he notes, may be saluted in others. Can you find examples of this phenomenom in your own expe-rience or from what you yourself have seen, especially in contrasting

countries or cultures? How might such changes illustrate Marable's contention about "how fluid racial categories can be."

WRITING POSSIBILITIES

1. At the conclusion of his essay, Marable turns to the present moment and the problems that immigration creates for racial and ethnic communities—e.g., where "native-born black workers increasingly find themselves in sharp competition with foreign-born non-whites." This has led to increasing problems in education, to social and legal conflicts, to the exacerbation of conflict by "significant differences—based on social class, nationality, language, and religion—that subdivide each grouping." From your own experience, illustrate some aspect of these conflicts. Note that Marable says class, nationality, language and religion may "subdivide each grouping"; can you find examples of this internal division from your own group?

2. How would you compare and contrast Marable's views on "amalgamation" and Linda Chavez' views (pages 262–269) on "assimilation"? Which view strikes you as currently applicable? What are your reasons?

Hector St. John Crevecoeur

Born in France, Crevecoeur lived for many years in this country and liked what he saw (or imagined he saw). Crevecoeur's question, "What is an American?" is often cited as the first definition of American identity as the melting pot: *immigrants come to this country, abandon their old prejudices, religious enmities, political fears and anxieties, and take on a new and common identity, that of "American." And they live, as Crevecoeur maintains he had seen them live, in peace and harmony, no matter where they came from or what their religious faith originally was. Crevecoeur's rhetorical question offers a powerful argument for the makeover-idea of total assimilation: get rid of the past, accept the new, and rejoice.*

WHAT IS AN AMERICAN?

What, then, is the American, this new man? He is neither an European nor the descendant of an European; hence that strange mixture of blood, which you will find in no other country. I could point out to you a family whose grandfather was an Englishman, whose wife was Dutch, whose son married a French woman, and whose present four sons have now four wives of different nations. *He* is an American, who, leaving behind him all his ancient prejudices and manners, receives new ones from the new mode of life he has embraced, the new government he obeys, and the new rank he holds. He becomes an American by being received in the broad lap of our great Alma Mater. Here individuals of all nations are melted into a new race of men, whose labours and posterity will one day cause great changes in the world. Americans are the western pilgrims who are carrying along with them that great mass of arts, sciences, vigour, and industry which began long since in the East; they will finish the great circle. The Americans were once scattered all over Europe; here they are incorporated into one of the finest systems of population which has ever appeared, and which will hereafter become distinct by the power of the different climates they inhabit. The American ought therefore to love this country much better than that wherein either he or his forefathers were born. Here the rewards of his industry follow with equal steps the progress of his labour; his labour is founded on the basis of nature, self-interest; can it want a stronger allurement? Wives and children, who before in vain demanded of him a morsel of bread, now, fat and frolicsome, gladly help their father to clear those fields whence exuberant crops are to arise to feed and to clothe them all, without any part being claimed, either by a despotic prince, a rich abbot, or a mighty lord. Here religion demands but little of him: a small voluntary salary to the minister and gratitude to God; can he refuse these? The American is a new man, who acts upon new principles; he must therefore entertain new ideas and form new opinions. From involuntary idleness, servile dependence, penury, and useless labour, he has passed to toils of a very different nature, rewarded by ample subsistence. This is an American.

ANALYSIS

1. What does Crevecoeur mean by saying that the American "acts upon new principles"?

2. There may be some problems with Crevecoeur's depiction of the melting pot idea of assimilation in America. Ben Franklin for example (cited in Glazer, page 225–226), suspected that German immigrants in colonial America would never assimilate. Could this be explained as a difference in "strategy"—Crevecoeur's utopian attitude, Franklin's pessimistic one—or a difference in actual perceptions and understandings? To what extent does Crevecoeur tone and way of talking suggest some possibilities of answering such questions?

3. Do you think Crevecoeur's account of the new American applied to blacks as well as whites? Does it invalidate the melting pot idea if it doesn't? (Read Crevecoeur's Letter IX, "Description of Charles Town; Thoughts on Slavery; On Physical Evil; A Melancholy Scene" from *Letters From an American Farmer* to help form your answer to this question [not reprinted here].)

WRITING POSSIBILITIES

1. Is it necessarily the case that immigrants want to leave behind "all," e.g., their "ancient prejudices"? Also consider whether present immigrant or ethnic groups wish to melt so completely as Creveceour says they do; read (pages 288–289) Michael Novak's "The Price of Being Americanized" to see what might be said on behalf of *not* melting.

Bharati Mukerjee

Born in India, transplanted briefly to Canada (which she disliked, despite its multiculturalism), Bharati Mukerjee is a novelist and now an American citizen. Her sister, who has lived and worked in this country for thirty years, is not a citizen; she is a legal immigrant who, as Mukerjee says, "clings to her Indian citizenship and hopes to go home to India when she retires." Though Mukerjee says she and her sister have "polite arguments over the ethics of retaining an overseas citizenship," neither one will budge from their respective positions. Here then is a test case for the idea of being "American." Is someone who is not a citizen nevertheless an "American" in some sense? Or no sense? Mukerjee defends her sister—in fact she wonders if she, not her sister, is the freak. But probably most readers of the New York Times *would be skeptical about her sister's decision. The rhetorical question is: How does Mukerjee present her sister's choice in such a way as to overcome our likely objections and persuade us that there is a case for the American identity of a legal immigrant?*

TWO WAYS TO BELONG IN AMERICA

THE "ALIEN" ISSUE DIVIDES SISTERS

This is a tale of two sisters from Calcutta, Mira and Bharati, who have lived in the United States for some 35 years, but who find themselves on different sides in the current debate over the status of immigrants. I am an American citizen and she is not. I am moved that thousands of long-term residents are finally taking the oath of citizenship. She is not.

Mira arrived in Detroit in 1960 to study child psychology and preschool education. I followed her a year later to study creative writing at the University of Iowa. When we left India, we were almost identical in appearance and attitude. We dressed alike, in saris; we expressed identical views on politics, social issues, love and marriage in the same Calcutta convent-school accent. We would endure our two years in America, secure our degrees, then return to India to marry the grooms of our father's choosing.

Instead, Mira married an Indian student in 1962 who was getting his business administration degree at Wayne State University. They soon acquired the labor certifications necessary for the green card of hassle-free residence and employment.

Mira still lives in Detroit, works in the Southfield, Mich., school system, and has become nationally recognized for her contributions in the fields of pre-school education and parent-teacher relationships. After 36 years as a legal immigrant in this country, she clings passionately to her Indian citizenship and hopes to go home to India when she retires.

In Iowa City in 1963, I married a fellow student, an American of Canadian parentage. Because of the accident of his North Dakota birth, I bypassed labor-certification requirements and the race-related "quota" system that favored the applicant's country of origin over his or her merit. I was prepared for (and even welcomed) the emotional strain that came with marrying outside my ethnic community. In 33 years of marriage, we have lived in every part of North America. By choosing a husband who was not my father's selection, I was opting for fluidity, self-invention, blue jeans and T-shirts, and renouncing 3,000 years (at least) of caste-observant, "pure culture" marriage in the Mukherjee family. My books have often been read as unapologetic (and in some quarters overenthusiastic) texts for cultural and psychological "mongrelization." It's a word I celebrate.

Mira and I have stayed sisterly close by phone. In our regular Sunday morning conversations, we are unguardedly affectionate. I am her only blood relative on this continent. We expect to see each other through the looming crises of aging and ill health without being asked. Long before Vice President Gore's "Citizenship U.S.A." drive, we'd had our polite arguments over the ethics of retaining an overseas citizenship while expecting the permanent protection and economic benefits that come with living and working in America.

Like well-raised sisters, we never said what was really on our minds, but we probably pitied one another. She, for the lack of structure in my life, the erasure of Indianness, the absence of an unvarying daily core. I, for the narrowness of her perspective, her uninvolvement with the mythic depths or the superficial pop culture of this society. But, now, with the scapegoating of "aliens" (documented or illegal) on the increase, and the targeting of long-term legal immigrants like Mira for new scrutiny and new self-consciousness, she and I find ourselves unable to maintain the same polite discretion. We were always unacknowledged adversaries, and we are now, more than ever, sisters.

"I feel used," Mira raged on the phone the other night. "I feel manipulated and discarded. This is such an unfair way to treat a person who was invited to stay and work here because of her talent. My employer went to the I.N.S. and petitioned for the labor certification. For over 30 years, I've invested my creativity and professional skills into the improvement of *this* country's pre-school system. I've obeyed all the rules, I've paid my taxes, I love my work, I love my students, I love the friends I've made. How dare America now change its rules in midstream? If America wants to make new rules curtailing benefits of legal immigrants, they should apply only to immigrants who arrive after those rules are already in place."

To my ears, it sounded like the description of a long-enduring, comfortable yet loveless marriage, without risk or recklessness. Have we the right to demand, and to expect, that we be loved? (That, to me, is the subtext of the arguments by immigration advocates.) My sister is an expatriate, professionally generous and creative, socially courteous and gracious, and that's as far as her Americanization can go. She is here to maintain an identity, not to transform it.

I asked her if she would follow the example of others who have decided to become citizens because of the anti-immigration bills in Congress. And here, she surprised me. "If America wants to play the manipulative game, I'll play it too," she snapped. "I'll become a U.S. citizen for now, then change back to Indian when I'm ready to go home. I feel some kind of irrational attachment to India that I don't to America. Until all this hysteria against legal immigrants, I was totally happy. Having my green card meant I could visit any place in the world I wanted to and then come back to a job that's satisfying and that I do very well."

In one family, from two sisters alike as peas in a pod, there could not be a wider divergence of immigrant experience. America spoke to me—I married it—I embraced the demotion from expatriate aristocrat to immigrant nobody, surrendering those thousands of years of "pure culture," the saris, the delightfully accented English. She retained them all. Which of us is the freak?

Mira's voice, I realize, is the voice not just of the immigrant South Asian community but of an immigrant community of the millions who have stayed rooted in one job, one city, one house, one ancestral culture, one cuisine, for the entirety of their productive years. She speaks for greater numbers than I possibly can. Only the fluency of her English and the anger, rather than fear, born of confidence from her education, differentiate her from the seamstresses, the domestics, the technicians, the shop owners, the millions of hard-working but effectively silenced documented immigrants as well as their less fortunate "illegal" brothers and sisters.

Nearly 20 years ago, when I was living in my husband's ancestral homeland of Canada, I was always well-employed but never allowed to feel part of the local Quebec or larger Canadian society. Then, through a Green Paper that invited a national referendum on the unwanted side effects of "nontraditional" immigration, the Government officially turned against its immigrant communities, particularly those from South Asia.

I felt then the same sense of betrayal that Mira feels now. I will never forget the pain of that sudden turning, and the casual racist outbursts the Green Paper elicited. That sense of betrayal had its desired effect and drove me, and thousands like me, from the country.

Mira and I differ, however, in the ways in which we hope to interact with the country that we have chosen to live in. She is happier to live in America as expatriate Indian than as an immigrant American. I need to feel like a part of the community I have adopted (as I tried to feel in Canada as well). I need to put roots down, to vote and make the difference that I can. The price that the immigrant willingly pays, and that the exile avoids, is the trauma of self-transformation.

ANALYSIS

1. Mukerjee contrasts the "polite conversations" she has had with her sister with "what was really on our minds." What was on Mukerjee's mind? For example, how does she criticize her sister's decision? On the other hand, why does she now feel that she must defend her sister's decision and become less an adversary, more a sister?

2. We do need to make an important distinction here. Mira was asked to come to this country by her employer, who petitioned the I.N.S. (the Immigration and Naturalization Service) for the labor certification. According to Mukerjee, the I.N.S. is now targeting long-term legal immigrants for closer inspection, and at this Mukerjee's sister explodes. How, Mira says, can they change the rules? Do you sympathize with Mira here or still feel she ought to become a citizen?

3. Mukerjee says her sister's description of life in America is like that of "a long-enduring, comfortable yet loveless marriage, without risk or recklessness. Have we the right to demand, and to expect, that we be loved?" What is her point here? Do you agree with it?

WRITING POSSIBILITIES

1. Does Mukerjee persuade you that her sister's "Americanization" is an acceptable or valid choice? Why or why not? What methods of persuasion does she use? Are they effective?

2. The hard issue is the matter of being a permanent legal immigrant. What, according to Mukerjee, are the values of someone in such a position?

3. For John H. Miller (pages 290–292), citizenship is probably top priority for an immigrants' becoming an American. Given his arguments, how would you assess Mukerjee's sister's decision to *not* opt for citizenship?

Michael Novak

Scholar and theologian, Novak has had a varied career. In this short excerpt from his path-breaking book of 1971, Novak offers a cri de coeur *about the failure of majority "Anglo" (or WASP) culture to understand Eastern-European/Southeastern-European ethnicity Novak's own background—i.e., Slovak, Polish, Italian, and Greek. The question is whether Novak's critique of the rejection of these varied ethnicities still holds.*

THE PRICE OF BEING AMERICANIZED
from The Rise of the Unmeltable Ethnics

My grandparents, I am sure, never guessed what it would cost them and their children to become "Americanized."

In their eyes, no doubt, almost everything was gain. From the oppression experienced by Slovaks at the hands of the Austro-Hungarian empire, the gain was liberty; from relative poverty, opportunity; from an old world, new hope. (There is a town in Pennsylvania, two hundred miles from where they now lie buried, called "New Hope.")

They were injured, to be sure, by nativist American prejudices against foreigners, by a white Anglo-Saxon Protestant culture, and even by an Irish church. (Any Catholic church not otherwise specified by nationality they experienced and described as "the Irish church.")

What price is exacted by America when into its maw it sucks other cultures of the world and processes them? What do people have to lose before they can qualify as true Americans?

For one thing, a lot of blue stars—and silver and gold ones—must hang in the window. You proved you loved America by dying for it in its wars. The Poles, Italians, Greeks, and Slavs whose acronym Msgr. Geno Baroni has made to stand for all the non-English-speaking ethnic groups—pride themselves on "fighting for America." When my father saw my youngest brother in officer's uniform, it was one of the proudest days of his life . . . even though it (sickeningly) meant Vietnam.

I don't have other figures at hand. But when the Poles were only four percent of the population (in 1917–19) they accounted for twelve percent of the nation's casualties in World War I. "The Fighting Irish" won their epithet by dying in droves in the Civil War.

There is, then, a blood test. "Die for us and we'll give you a chance."

One is also expected to give up one's native language. My parents decided never to teach us Slovak. They hoped that thereby we would gain a generation in the process of becoming full Americans.

They kept up a few traditions: Christmas Eve holy bread, candle-light, mushroom soup, fish, and poppyseed. My mother baked *ko-lacky. Pirohi,* however, more or less died with my grandmother, who used to work all day making huge, steaming pots of potato dumplings and prune dumplings for her grandchildren. No other foods shall ever taste so sweet.

My parents, so far as I know, were the first Slovaks in our town to move outside the neighborhoods traditional for our kind of people and move into the "American" suburbs. There were not, I recall, very many other Catholics in the rather large, and good, public school I attended from grades two until six. I remember Mrs. S., the fifth-grade teacher, spelling "Pope Pius" with an "o" in the middle, and myself with gently firm righteousness (even then) correcting her.

What has happened to my people since they came to this land nearly a century ago? Where are they now, that long-awaited fully Americanized third generation? Are we living the dream our grand-parents dreamed when on creaking decks they stood silent, afraid, hopeful at the sight of the Statue of Liberty? Will we ever find that se-cret relief, that door, that hidden entrance? Did our grandparents choose for us, and our posterity, what they should have chosen?

Now the dice lie cold in our own uncertain hands.

ANALYSIS

1. Novak says that for his grandparents, "everything was gain" in coming to America. What does he mean by this?
2. What does Novak mean by being "Americanized"?
3. On the other hand, Novak suggests that there was, and is, a price for being Americanized? Novak wrote this about conditions around 1971; do you think immigrants and refugees today still pay a price for being Americanized?

WRITING POSSIBILITIES

1. In *Ethnic Options,* sociologist Mary Waters critiques Novak's view of ethnicity because it does not differentiate between ethnicity and race. Ethnicity, Waters maintains, is a construction, and one best denomi-nated by the term *symbolic ethnicity.* According to this view, being Irish or Italian is a voluntary matter, a pleasurable experience only (community, tradition, family ties), and with only the "good" parts chosen. Race, on the other hand, is not voluntary and often involves unpleasurable experiences. (Takaki makes a similar point in "Reflec-tions on Racial Patterns in America," pages 236–252). Would you agree with Waters here? Why or why not? What has been your own experi-ence in describing and/or defining your own ethnic heritage?

John J. Miller

Miller argues that assimilation is in trouble because intellectuals on both the Left and the Right no longer believe in it as an ideal. Those on the Right, says Miller, think that assimilation never really happened—that the Ellis Island immigrants never really did become American. On the other side leftist intellectuals, according to Miller, insist on multiculturalism only and see Americanization as a kind of "ethnic cleansing." Miller proposes a middle ground that would support immigration but also insist on assimilation. Immigrants, says Miller, need to become part of American society and not mere "sojourners" in it. They must learn English, live by this country's laws, and become citizens.

Nativists too, says Miller, must keep their end of the bargain. They must do what assimilationists and Americanization spokesmen in the 1920s and earlier did—pass on the "ideals that bind us together." This would mean rejecting bilingual education (which rarely teaches children to speak, read, and write in English), rejecting "government racial-preference policies" (which treat people "as members of groups rather than as individuals"), and keeping, not eliminating, mandatory tests for immigrants in American history and citizenship.

BECOMING AN AMERICAN

WASHINGTON

At a soccer game against Mexico in February, the American national team listened in frustration as a chorus of boos erupted during "The Star-Spangled Banner." Thousands of fans threw cups and bottles at the United States players, often striking them. They also attacked someone in the stands who tried to unfurl an American flag.

The match didn't take place in Mexico City but in Los Angeles. Most of the fans were Mexican or Mexican-American. The extreme reactions to their behavior were disheartening but predictable. On one side, the columnist Pat Buchanan declared that "the Melting Pot is freezing over." On the other, a *Los Angeles Times* editorialist said that critics of the fans were "xenophobic, nativist, protectionist and isolationist."

The United States is in the midst of as assimilation crisis—one inspired not by immigrants but by an American intelligentsia that has abandoned the struggle to help newcomers assimilate. Neither Left nor Right knows how to respond to a troubling incident like the Los Angeles soccer match.

On the Right, nativists argue that immigrants are not capable of becoming American: "Immigration is a failure because assimilation, contrary to national myth, never really occurred," Chilton Williamson wrote recently in the magazine *Chronicles*. Mr. Williamson, an editor and writer for the conservative monthly, claims that the Ellis Island generation of immigrants never actually became American.

On the Left, multiculturalists say that immigrants should not have to become American. As Juan Perea, a law professor at the University of Florida, says, "Americanization must either be completely reworked or abandoned as a premise of American identity." For many in the academic world, assimilation is nothing but a gentrified form of ethnic cleansing.

Both sides have unfortunately ceded a sensible middle ground that supports some level of immigration but also insists on assimiliation. As a result, many native-born Americans are confused about what, if anything, they should ask of immigrants.

The Americanization movement of the early 20th century provides an effective blueprint for how the United States should greet today's immigrants. The original Americanizers believed that newcomers and natives would have to reach an accord. Immigrants needed to become part of American society, rather than mere sojourners in it. They had responsibilities to their new home, like learning English, living by its laws and earning citizenship. Ultimately, they were to dedicate themselves to the principles embodied in the Declaration of Independence and the Constitution that define American nationhood.

Natives had to keep their end of the bargain. "From the moment [the immigrant] arrives in America, he needs the creative, aggressive attention of American institutions," wrote Frances Kellor, a leading Americanizer, in 1916. She and others set up classes and lectures and wrote publications on the English language, American history and naturalization. They used various private and public institutions, including corporations, schools and government offices, as engines of assimilation. They gave speeches and held parades.

Many immigrants encountered severe discrimination, and in the 1920's nativist groups like the Ku Klux Klan helped pass restrictive legislation that slowed immigration to a trickle. For two decades before that, however, the original Americanizers strove for the immigrant's full acceptance in and of American society.

Today, Americans no longer know how to pass on the ideals that bind us together. A mishmash of public policies actively inhibit the Americanization of immigrants. Public schools engage in the charade of bilingual education, which rarely teaches children to speak, read and write in English as well as they could. Often it leaves them illiterate in two languages and fluent in none. That failure is the reason that so many Hispanic and Asian parents in California support Proposition 227, a state initiative that would get rid of bilingual education and replace it with English-language immersion classes.

Government racial-preference policies treat people as members of groups rather than as individuals, classifying them by the color of their skin. The overburdened Immigration and Naturalization Service flirts with the idea of eliminating the mandatory test on American history and government for new citizens—a change that threatens to lower the standards of naturalization so far that the only requirement for full citizenship could consist of filling out an application form, as if becoming an American were on a par with getting a driver's license. The State Department looks the other way as more countries encourage dual loyalties by enacting dual-citizenship laws that extend political privileges, including the vote, to select American citizens.

In a remarkably short period, the United States has forgotten what to ask of its newcomers. We must rediscover the lost idea of Americanization. Whether we welcome few immigrants or many, we should give every stranger a chance and a reason to become a patriotic American.

ANALYSIS

1. What is the force of Miller's opening anecdote about the soccer game in relation to his overall argument?
2. For Miller, what exactly is the "immigration crisis"?
3. What are the arguments Miller cites about immigration and assimilation from the "Right"? from the "Left"? Whose arguments strike you as more persuasive?
4. As against Right and Left, what are Miller's own views and arguments?
5. Miller assumes that bilingual education is a way of not learning English, but those who support it say it's a way of easing the transition from native language-use to English. How would supporters of bilingual education counter Miller's assumptions?

WRITING POSSIBILITIES

1. Is your own experience as either a member of a group or as an individual such that you could supply evidence for or against Miller's basic thesis or subissues?
2. Which accords more with your views, Mukherjee's essay or Miller's? Why?
3. There are at least three models of "assimilation" relevant to Miller's argument (1) the "melting pot" (as in Crevecoeur), (2) Separatism (Black Power or Sherman Alexie on Indian "sovereignty"), and (3) Pluralism or multiculturalism (akin to Glazer's "ethnic pattern" where individual groups retain their *cultural* identity, not their political, and don't subsume that cultural identity under the idea of an

undifferentiated "American"). Where is Miller on this issue? Which model gets your vote and why?

4. Miller's essay touches on many subissues that require further investigation: learning English-only (versus bilingual education); earning citizenship (no resident aliens, like Bharati Mukherjee's sister in "Two Ways to Belong in America"); no affirmative action policies (because they treat people as members of groups, not as individuals); and testing for understanding of American history and principles of citizenship. For each of these subissues, do you agree or disagree? Why?

Langston Hughes

Hughes' poem is widely reprinted and needs no analysis. But in a collected edition of Hughes's poetry read his later and angrier poetry— e.g., "Harlem," with its famous line "What happens to a dream deferred?". To what extent can "Let America Be America Again" be reconciled with the more pessimistic later poems?

LET AMERICA BE AMERICA AGAIN

Let America be America again.
Let it be the dream it used to be.
Let it be the pioneer on the plain
Seeking a home where he himself is free.

(America never was America to me.)

Let America be the dream the dreamers dreamed—
Let it be that great strong land of love
Where never kings connive nor tyrants scheme
That any man be crushed by one above.

(It never was America to me.)

O, let my land be a land where Liberty
Is crowned with no false patriotic wreath.

The free?
Who said the free? Not me?
Surely not me? The millions on relief today?
The millions who have nothing for our pay
For all the dreams we've dreamed
And all the songs we've sung
And all the hopes we've held
And all the flags we've hung,
The millions who have nothing for our pay—
Except the dream we keep alive today.

O, let America be America again—
The land that never has been yet—
And yet must be—the land where *every* man is free.
The land that's mine—the poor man's, Indian's, Negro's, Me!
But opportunity is real, and life is free,
Equality is in the air we breathe.

(There's never been equality for me,
Nor freedom in this "homeland of the free.")

Say who are you that mumbles in the dark?
And who are you that draws your veil across the stars?

I am the poor white, fooled and pushed apart,
I am the red man driven from the land.
I am the refugee clutching the hope I seek—
But finding only the same old stupid plan
Of dog eat dog, of mighty crush the weak.
I am the Negro, "problem" to you all.
I am the people, humble, hungry, mean—
Hungry yet today despite the dream.
Beaten yet today—O, Pioneers!
I am the man who never got ahead,
The poorest worker bartered through the years.
Yet I'm the one who dreamt our basic dream
In that Old World while still a serf of kings,
Who dreamt a dream so strong, so brave, so true,
That even yet its mighty daring sings
In every brick and stone, in every furrow turned
That's made America the land it has become.
O, I'm the man who sailed those early seas
In search of what I meant to be my home—
For I'm the one who left dark Ireland's shore,
And Poland's plain, and England's grassy lea,
And torn from Black Africa's strand I came
To build a "homeland of the free."

Who made America,
Whose sweat and blood, whose faith and pain,
Whose hand at the foundry, whose plow in the rain,
Must bring back our mighty dream again.
    O, yes,
    I say it plain,
    America never was America to me,
    And yet I swear this oath—
    America will be!

5

THE AMERICAN DREAM: CLASS IN AMERICA

In "When Money Is Everything, Except Hers," *New York Times* reporter Dirk Johnson tells of a working-class high school girl who has to fend off nasty comments from the upper-class kids she goes to school with; she almost doesn't make it. She is even ready to drop out of the honors class that might be her ticket to a scholarship and a move up the ladder of mobility.

Wendy Williams's story may lead to all sorts of insidious questions—questions that may already be surfacing in your own mind. Was Wendy in all that bad a shape? Shouldn't she just have been a little tougher, endured the taunts, and gone into that honors class intent on improving her lot through that most powerful of American enterprises, education?

Or conversely, think of the contingencies here: the powerful undertow of sibling and parental difficulties, the psychology of withdrawal in the face of stigmatizing taunts, the hopelessness and perhaps even despair that can overcome young people caught in problematic situations. Indeed, what if this were a poorer school district with no school psychologist to take Wendy firmly in hand (or a psychologist forced to deal abstractly with hundreds of basket cases in huge schools of 2,000 or 3,000 students)?

What do we think of Wendy's life-chances from here on out? An optimistic scenario? A pessimistic one? A mixed and muddled one? Who knows how the Wendy Williameses of the world will turn out?

Finally, one might question the journalist's own slant on Wendy's story. Look at that headline for example (perhaps not the journalist's fault but significant nevertheless)—"Money Is Everything, Except Hers." From a liberal point of view, that headline gets at the irony of the American culture of material success for the few, while from a conservative point of view it may be a needless and cynical tarnishing of a basic American value—not "money" (don't be a fool!) but the enterprise and energy that goes into bettering one's lot.

Liberal commentators (Mantsios and Wilson, in this chapter and Mike Rose in Chapter 1) would argue that the Wendy Williameses of

America áre the victims of a class structure and an ambiguous American Dream which enlarges opportunities primarily for the wealthy and diminishes those for the working poor, the middle class, minorities, and women. In this view, individuals are not likely to emerge from psychological and sociological despair. Such commentators will also point to the theme of "the rich getting richer, the poor are getting poorer" theme (percurrent in the media and even in so conservative a source as the *Wall Street Journal Almanac*). The crucial matter, in this view, would be to change the nature of opportunity, enlarging and equalizing it so as to provide better chances for the Wendy Williameses of this world.

On the other hand, conservative commentators (Alm and Cox in this chapter) would argue that the crucial thing is not present constraints but future *mobility* and the American Dream of hopefulness: through education (especially in this technological and information era), hard work, and perseverance: individuals who assume responsibility for their own lives can overcome the limitations surrounding them and truly succeed. Such critics also point to the "culture" of victimization and the collapse of family values (Clarence Thomas in this chapter) as crucial in creating a climate of hopelessness and despair. As to "the rich getting richer theme," Cox and Alm mount a powerful case that argues that if you inspect the numbers carefully, no one ever remain permanently at the bottom of the pool, that as the decades roll by, individuals and families both keep moving up the ladder of mobility. The crucial matter is individual effort and willpower, not alteration of the social structure in any major way. We should stop whining and got on with our lives.

Somewhere in between the liberals and the conservatives is Eric Liu's viewpoint in "A Chinaman's Chance: Reflections on the American Dream" pages 319–327). Liu is aware of the "reactionary" aspects of the American Dream ideology (so he's a liberal) but also a believer in the role of "opportunity" and generation-binding that the Dream represents (he's a conservative). Here then is the particular place where the battle over class and the American Dream is joined.

Dirk Johnson

Wendy Williams's story, told so carefully by Dirk Johnson, might make readers wonder how typical Wendy's story is. The reader wonders if her discouragement in the face of taunts about the affluent gear she can't afford is common to large numbers of young Americans. The problem is if it's not common, then Wendy is simply an exception to the rule and not worth worrying about. Evidently Johnson, and the editors of the New York Times, felt Wendy's story does say something about American culture at large. The question is, do you as a reader think so? Does it resonate with your experience or not?

In addition, if we turn to the essay by economist and journalist Alm and Cox (in this chapter) which argues that no one ever stays poor for very long in America, then Wendy's plight might take on a different coloration. We might as readers be skeptical about her difficulties in coping and think that probably millions of others who face such difficulties will manage to survive without much trouble, and perhaps even (as Alm and Cox would have it) actually prosper. The argument here would rest on Alm and Cox's statistics—on the reports from studies of income as to how many people from what different socioeconomic classes actually do or don't move up the ladder of opportunity and mobility that American society (arguably) affords.

WHEN MONEY IS EVERYTHING, EXCEPT HERS

DIXON, Ill.—Watching classmates strut past in designer clothes, Wendy Williams sat silently on the yellow school bus, wearing a cheap belt and rummage-sale slacks.

One boy stopped and yanked his thumb, demanding her seat.

"Move it, trailer girl," he sneered.

It has never been easy to live on the wrong side of the tracks. But in the economically robust 1990's, with sprawling new houses and three-car garages sprouting like cornstalks on the Midwestern prairie, the sting that comes with scarcity gets rubbed with an extra bit of salt.

Seen through the eyes of a 13-year-old girl growing up at Chateau Estates, a fancy name for a tin-plain trailer park, the rosy talk about the nation's prosperity carries a certain mocking echo.

The everyday discussion in the halls of Reagan Middle School in this city about 100 miles west of Chicago touches on computer toys that can cost $1,000, family vacations to Six Flags or Disney World and stylish clothes that bear a Nike emblem or Tommy Hilfiger's coveted label.

Unlike young people a generation ago, those today must typically pay fees to play for the school sports teams or band. It costs $45 to play in the youth summer soccer league. It takes money to go skating on weekends at the White Pines roller rink, to play laser tag or rock-climb at the Plum Hollow Recreation Center, to mount a steed at the Horseback Riding Club, to gaze at Leonardo DiCaprio and Kate Winslet at the Plaza Cinemas, to go shopping for clothes at Cherry-vale Mall.

To be without money, in so many ways, is to be left out.

"I told this girl: 'That's a really awesome shirt. Where did you get it?'" said Wendy, explaining that she knew it was out of her price range, but that she wanted to join the small talk. "And she looked at me and laughed and said, 'Why would you want to know?'"

A lanky, soft-spoken girl with large brown eyes, Wendy pursed her lips to hide a slight overbite that got her the nickname Rabbit, a humiliation she once begged her mother and father to avoid by sending her to an orthodontist.

For struggling parents, keenly aware that adolescents agonize over the social pecking order, the styles of the moment and the face in the mirror, there is a no small sense of failure in telling a child that she cannot have what her classmates take for granted.

"Do you know what it's like?" asked Wendy's mother, Veronica Williams, "to have your daughter come home and say, 'Mom, the kids say my clothes are tacky,' and then walk off with her head hanging low."

This is not the desperate poverty of Chicago housing projects, where the plight of empty pockets is worsened by the threat of gangs and gunfire. Wendy lives in relative safety in a home with both parents. Her father, Wendell Provow, earns $9 an hour as a welder. Her mother works part-time as a cook for Head Start, a Federal education program.

Unlike students in some urban pockets, isolated from affluence, Wendy receives the same education as a girl from a $300,000 house in the Idle Oaks subdivision. The flip side of that coin is the public spectacle of economic struggle. This is a place small enough where people know the personal stories, or, at least, repeat them as if they did.

Even in this down-to-earth town, where a poor boy nicknamed Dutch grew up to become President, young people seem increasingly enchanted with buying, having, spending and status.

R. Woodrow (Woody) Wasson, the principal at Reagan Middle School, makes it a point to sit down with every child and ask them about their hopes and dreams.

"They want to be doctors, lawyers, veterinarians and, of course, professional athletes," said Mr. Wasson, whose family roots here go back to the 19th century. "I don't remember the last time I heard somebody say they wanted to be a police officer or a firefighter. They want to do something that will make a lot of money and have a lot of prestige."

He said a teacher in a nearby town has been trying to recruit high school students for vocational studies to become tool-and-die artisans, a trade that can pay $70,000 a year.

"The teacher can't fill the slots," Mr. Wasson said. "Nobody's interested in that kind of work."

It is not surprising that children grow up believing that money is so important, given the relentless way they are targeted by marketers.

"In the past, you just put an ad in the magazine," said Michael Wood, the director of research for Teen-Age Research Unlimited, a marketing consultant in suburban Chicago. "Now savvy marketers know you must hit them at all angles—Web sites, cable TV shows, school functions, sporting events."

He noted the growth of cross-promotions, like the deal in which actors on the television show "Dawson's Creek," which is popular among adolescents, wear clothes by J. Crew and appear in its catalogue.

But young people get cues in their everyday lives. Some spending habits that would once have been seen as ostentatious—extravagant parties for small children, new cars for teenagers—have become familiar trappings of middle-class comfort.

The stock market, although it is sputtering now, has made millionaires of many people in Main Street towns. Building developers here recently won approval to build a gated community, which will be called Timber Edge.

"Wendy goes to school around these rich kids," her mother said, "and wonders why she can't have things like they do."

A bright girl with a flair for art, writing and numbers, Wendy stays up late most nights, reading books. *The Miracle Worker* was a recent favorite.

But when a teacher asked her to join an elevated class for algebra, she politely declined. "I get picked on for my clothes and living in the trailer park," said Wendy, who never brings anyone home from school. "I don't want to get picked on for being a nerd, too."

Her mother, who watched three other daughters drop out of school and have babies as teen-agers, has told Wendy time and again: "Don't lose your self-esteem."

One time a boy at school was teasing Wendy about her clothes— "They don't even match," he laughed—and her humble house in the trailer park.

She listened for a while. He kept insulting her. So she lifted a leg— clothed as it was in discount jeans from the Farm & Fleet store—and kicked him in the shins.

He told the authorities. She got the detention.

It became clear to Wendy that the insults were not going to stop. It also became clear that shin-kicking, however deserved, was not going to be the solution.

She went to a guidance counselor, Cynthia Kowa Basler, a dynamic woman who keeps close tabs on the children, especially girls who fret about their weight and suddenly stop eating lunch.

"I am large," she tells the girls, "and I have self-esteem."

Wendy, who knew that Mrs. Basler held sessions with students to increase their self-confidence, went to the counselor. "I feel a little down," Wendy told her. The counselor gathered eight students, including other girls like Wendy, who felt embarrassed about their economic station.

In this school named for Ronald Reagan, the students were told to study the words of Eleanor Roosevelt.

One of her famous quotes was posted above the counselor's desk: "No one can make you feel inferior without your consent."

As a group, the students looked up the definition of inferior and consent.

And then they read the words out loud.

"Again," the counselor instructed.

"Louder," the counselor insisted.

Again and again, they read the inspirational words.

In role-playing exercises, the children practiced responses to taunts, which sometimes called for nothing more than a shrug.

"Mrs. Basler told us to live up to our goals—show those kids," Wendy said. "She told us that things can be a lot different when you're grown up. Maybe things will be the other way around then."

Wendy smiled at the notion.

Life still has plenty of bumps. When Wendy gets off the school bus—the trailer park is the first stop, so everyone can see where she lives—she still looks at her shoes.

She still pulls her shirt out to hide a belt that does not quite make the grade. And she still purses her lips to hide an overbite. But her mother has noticed her smiling more these days. And Wendy has even said she might consider taking an advanced course in math, her favorite subject.

"I want to go to college," Wendy said the other day. "I want to become a teacher."

One recent day, she popped in to the counselor's office, just to say hello, then walked back down the halls, her arms folded around her schoolbooks.

Mrs. Basler stood at the doorway and watched her skip away, a student with so much promise, and so many obstacles.

For the girl from Chateau Estates, it is a long way from the seventh grade to college.

"She's going to make it," the counselor said, with a clenched fist and a voice full of hope.

ANALYSIS

1. What is the implication of the student who asks Wendy "What would you want to know for?" What is its effect on Wendy? How would you respond to such a question?
2. What are the indicators of economic class in Wendy's situation (hers and her family's both)? What particulars of class does Johnson make us aware of as he tells Wendy's story? (Consider class as both income and lifestyle.)
3. How does Dirk Johnson illuminate the social significance of Wendy's story—i.e., through what combination of narrative anecdote, quotation, and summary of situations?
4. How does the counselor get Wendy to see the possibilities of an alternative response to the feelings of inadequacy and rejection?
5. What is Johnson's "summary view" at the end of the article? Does he imply a sense of hopefulness about Wendy or not?

WRITING POSSIBILITIES

1. Have you ever been in a situation similar to Wendy's? Describe it as even-handedly as possible, using anecdote and quotation as appropriate, and then indicate your present assessment of that situation.
2. Johnson's story is about economic class (low-income working-class parents, lifestyle contrasts in the vein of the Tommy Hilfiger sweater). But given the presence of Wendy's overweight counselor who admits to having difficulties in coping herself, how could Johnson's story be extended to cover other aspects of rejection, prejudice, and discrimination? Pick an area you know something about and construct a rejective situation different from the socioeconomic scene that Wendy Williams inhabits.
3. Johnson's story is implicitly an indictment of gross class differentials in American society, but could it be reframed, turned inside out in a way, so as to be a story about an *individual* who doesn't have the cultural and psychological understanding to cope with something most people have to cope with most of the time—rejection? Try your hand at rewriting Johnson's story to imply a different perspective on Wendy Williams's plight.

Gregory Mantsios

Mantsios's "Class in America" is a powerful essay, developing a striking collection of data on inequality in America in terms of both money and lifestyles. Reprinted many times, the essay repays careful study because it makes a persuasive argument that if we really believe in equality as the essence of the American Dream, we will have to do much more for those at the bottom of the social scale. Mantsios summarizes his argument this way:

> When we look at society and try to determine what it is that keeps most people down—what holds them back form realizing their potential as healthy, creative, productive individuals— we find institutionally oppressive forces that are largely beyond individual control. Class domination is one of these forces.

There is however one antidote to the position Mantsios adopts. What if, despite your initial "class standing," you were able to improve your class position? What if, in other words, mobility *in terms of income meant that although you might start poor, you won't end up poor, i.e., you might be in the lower-middle class initially (like your parents) but after a generation or two, you have moved up—maybe one class, maybe two, who knows? Mantsios, as noted, doesn't address this question (and he'd probably reject it as another specious notion of the Dream ideology), yet it would seem to be crucial to his argument. This is the basic issue from various viewpoints that Mantsios, Eric Liu, and Cox and Alm explore in this chapter.*

CLASS IN AMERICA:
MYTHS AND REALITIES (2000)

People in the United States don't like to talk about class. Or so it would seem. We don't speak about class privileges, or class oppression, or the class nature of society. These terms are not part of our everyday vocabulary, and in most circles they are associated with the language of the rhetorical fringe. Unlike people in most other parts of the world, we shrink from using words that classify along economic lines or that point to class distinctions: phrases like "working class," "upper class," and "ruling class" are rarely uttered by Americans.

For the most part, avoidance of class-laden vocabulary crosses class boundaries. There are few among the poor who speak of themselves as lower class; instead, they refer to their race, ethnic group, or geographic location. Workers are more likely to identify with their employer, industry, or occupational group than with other workers, or with the working class.[1]

Neither are those at the other end of the economic spectrum likely to use the word "class." In her study of thirty-eight wealthy and socially prominent women, Susan Ostrander asked participants if they considered themselves members of the upper class. One participant responded, "I hate to use the word 'class.' We are responsible, fortunate people, old families, the people who have something." Another said, "I hate [the term] upper class. It is so non-upper class to use it. I just call it 'all of us,' those who are wellborn."[2]

It is not that Americans, rich or poor, aren't keenly aware of class differences—those quoted above obviously are; it is that class is not in the domain of public discourse. Class is not discussed or debated in public because class identity has been stripped from popular culture. The institutions that shape mass culture and define the parameters of public debate have avoided class issues. In politics, in primary and secondary education, and in the mass media, formulating issues in terms of class is unacceptable, perhaps even un-American.

There are, however, two notable exceptions to this phenomenon. First, it is acceptable in the United States to talk about "the middle class." Interestingly enough, such references appear to be acceptable precisely because they mute class differences. References to the middle class by politicians, for example, are designed to encompass and attract the broadest possible constituency. Not only do references to the middle class gloss over differences, but these references also avoid any suggestion of conflict or exploitation.

This leads us to the second exception to the class-avoidance phenomenon. We are, on occasion, presented with glimpses of the upper class and the lower class (the language used is "the wealthy"

---

[1] See Jay MacLead, *Ain't No Makin' It: Aspirations and Attainment in a Lower-Income Neighborhood* (Boulder, Colo.: Westview Press, 1995); Benjamin DeMott, *The Imperial Middle* (New York: Morrow, 1990); Ira Katznelson, *City Trenches: Urban Politics and Patterning of Class in the United States* (New York: Pantheon Books, 1981); Charles W. Tucker, "A Comparative Analysis of Subjective Social Class: 1945–1963," *Social Forces,* no. 46, June 1968, pp. 508–514; Robert Nisbet, "The Decline and Fall of Social Class," *Pacific Sociological Review,* vol. 2, Spring 1959, pp. 11–17; and Oscar Glantz, "Class Consciousness and Political Solidarity," *American Sociological Review,* vol. 23, August 1958, pp. 375–382.

[2] Susan Ostander, "Upper-Class Women: Class Consciousness as Conduct and Meaning," in G. William Domhoff, *Power Structure Research,* Beverly Hills, CA, Sage Productions, 1980, pp. 78–79. Also see, Stephen Birmingham, *America's Secret Aristocracy,* Boston, Little Brown, 1987.

and "the poor"). In the media, these presentations are designed to satisfy some real or imagined voyeuristic need of "the ordinary person." As curiosities, the ground-level view of street life and the inside look at the rich and the famous serve as unique models, one to avoid and one to aspire to. In either case, the two models are presented without causal relation to each other: one is not rich because the other is poor. Similarly, when social commentators or liberal politicians draw attention to the plight of the poor, they do so in a manner that obscures the class structure and denies class exploitation. Wealth and poverty are viewed as one of several natural and inevitable states of being: differences are only differences. One may even say differences are the American way, a reflection of American social diversity.

We are left with one of two possibilities: either talking about class and recognizing class distinctions are not relevant to U.S. society, or we mistakenly hold a set of beliefs that obscure the reality of class differences and their impact on people's lives.

Let us look at four common, albeit contradictory, beliefs about the United States.

Myth 1: The United States is fundamentally a classless society. Class distinctions are largely irrelevant today, and whatever differences do exist in economic standing are, for the most part, insignificant. Rich or poor, we are all equal in the eyes of the law, and such basic needs as health care and education are provided to all regardless of economic standing.

Myth 2: We are, essentially, a middle-class nation. Despite some variations in economic status, most Americans have achieved relative affluence in what is widely recognized as a consumer society.

Myth 3: We are all getting richer. The American public as a whole is steadily moving up the economic ladder, and each generation propels itself to greater economic well-being. Despite some fluctuations, the U.S. position in the global economy has brought previously unknown prosperity to most, if not all, North Americans.

Myth 4: Everyone has an equal chance to succeed. Success in the United States requires no more than hard work, sacrifice, and perseverance: "In America, anyone can become a millionaire; it's just a matter of being in the right place at the right time."

In trying to assess the legitimacy of these beliefs, we want to ask several important questions. Are there significant class differences among Americans? If these differences do exist, are they getting bigger or smaller, and do these differences have a significant impact on the way we live? Finally, does everyone in the United States really have an equal opportunity to succeed?

THE ECONOMIC SPECTRUM

We will begin by looking at differences. An examination of available data reveals that variations in economic well-being are in fact immense. Consider the following:

- The wealthiest 20 percent of the American population holds 85 percent of the total household wealth in the country. That is, they own nearly seven-eighths of all the consumer durables (such as houses, cars, and stereos) and financial assets (such as stocks, bonds, property, and savings accounts).[3]
- Approximately 144,000 Americans, or 0.1 percent of the adult working population, earn more than $1 million annually, with many of these individuals earning over $10 million and some earning over $100 million annually. It would take the average American, earning $34,000 per year, more than 65 lifetimes to earn $100 million.[4]

Affluence and prosperity are clearly alive and well in certain segments of the United States population. However, this abundance is in contrast to the poverty and despair that is also prevalent in the United States. At the other end of the spectrum:

- A total of 13 percent of the American population—that is, one of every eight[5]—live below the government's official poverty line (calculated in 1999 at $8,500 for an individual and $17,028 for a family of four).[6] These poor include a significant number of homeless people—approximately two million Americans.
- Approximately one out of every five children in the United States under the age of eighteen lives in poverty.[7]

The contrast between rich and poor is sharp, and with nearly one-third of the American population living at one extreme or the other, it

---

[3] Jared Bernstein, Lawrence Hishel, and John Schmitt, *The State of Working America: 1998–99,* ILR Press, Cornell University Press, 1998, p. 262.

[4] The number of individuals filing tax returns showing a gross adjusted income of $1 million or more in 1997 was 144,459 (Internal Revenue Service, *Statistics of Income Bulletin, Summer 1999,* Washington, DC, 1999, p. 268). The total civilian employment in 1997 was 129,588,000 (U.S. Bureau of Labor Statistics, 1997).

[5] Joseph Dalaker, U.S. Bureau of the Census, "Current Population Reports," series pp. 60–207, *Poverty in the United States: 1998.* Washington, DC, U.S. Government Printing Office, 1999, p. v.

[6] "Preliminary Estimates of Weighted Average Poverty Thresholds in 1999," Department of Commerce, Bureau of Census, 2000.

[7] Ibid, p. v.

is difficult to argue that we live in a classless society. The income gap between rich and poor in the United States (measured as the percentage of total income held by the wealthiest 20 percent of the population versus the poorest 20 percent) is approximately 11 to 1, one of the highest ratios in the industrialized world. The ratio in Japan and Germany, by contrast, is 4 to 1.[8]

Reality 1: There are enormous differences in the economic status of American citizens. A sizable proportion of the U.S. population occupies opposite ends of the economic spectrum.

In the middle range of the economic spectrum:

- Sixty percent of the American population hold less than 4 percent of the nation's wealth.[9]
- While the real income of the top 1 percent of U.S. families skyrocketed by 89 percent during the economic growth period from 1977 to 1995, the income of the middle fifth of the population actually declined by 13 percent during that same period.[10] This led one prominent economist to describe economic growth as a "spectator sport for the majority of American families."[11]

The level of inequality is sometimes difficult to comprehend fully with dollar figures and percentages. To help his students visualize the distribution of income, the well-known economist Paul Samuelson asked them to picture an income pyramid made of children's blocks, with each layer of blocks representing $1,000. If we were to construct Samuelson's pyramid today, the peak of the pyramid would be much higher than the Eiffel Tower, yet almost all of us would be within six feet of the ground.[12] In other words, the distribution of income is heavily skewed; a small minority of families take the lion's share of national income, and the remaining income is distributed among the vast majority of middle-income and low-income families. Keep in mind that Samuelson's pyramid represents

---

[8] See The Center on Budget and Policy Priorities, Economic Policy Institute, "Pulling Apart: State-by-State Analysis of Income Trends," January 2000, fact sheet; U.S. Department of Commerce, "Current Population Reports: Consumer Income," Washington, DC, 1993; The World Bank, "World Development Report: 1992," Washington, DC, International Bank for Reconstruction and Development, 1992; The World Bank "World Development Report 1999/2000," pp. 238–239.

[9] Jared Bernstein et al., op. cit., p. 262.

[10] Derived from Ibid, p. 95.

[11] Alan Blinder, quoted by Paul Krugman, in "Disparity and Despair," *U.S. News and World Report,* March 23, 1992, p. 54.

[12] Paul Samuelson, *Economics,* 10th ed., New York, McGraw-Hill, 1976, p. 84.

the distribution of income, not wealth. The distribution of wealth is skewed even further.

Reality 2: The middle class in the United States holds a very small share of the nation's wealth, and its income—in constant dollars—is declining.

Lottery millionaires and celebrity salaries notwithstanding, evidence suggests that the level of inequality in the United States is getting higher. Census data show the gap between the rich and the poor to be the widest since the government began collecting information in 1947. Furthermore, the percentage of households earning between $25,000 and $75,000 has been falling steadily since 1969, while the percentage of households earning less than $25,000 has actually increased between 1989 and 1997.[13] And economic polarization is expected to increase over the next several decades.[14]

Reality 3: The middle class is shrinking in size, and the gap between rich and poor is bigger than it has ever been.

AMERICAN LIFESTYLES

At last count, nearly 35 million Americans across the nation lived in unrelenting poverty.[15] Yet, as political scientist Michael Harrington once commented, "America has the best dressed poverty the world has ever known."[16] Clothing disguises much of the poverty in the United States, and this may explain, in part, its middle-class image. With increased mass marketing of "designer" clothing and with shifts in the nation's economy from blue-collar (and often better-paying) manufacturing jobs to white-collar and pink-collar jobs in the service sector, it is becoming increasingly difficult to distinguish class differences based on appearance.[17]

Beneath the surface, there is another reality. Let us look at some "typical" and not-so-typical lifestyles.

---

[13] "Money Income of Households, Families, and Persons in the United States: 1992," U.S. Department of Commerce, "Current Population Reports: Consumer Income" series P60–184, Washington, DC, 1993, p. B6. Also, Jared Bernstein et al., op. cit., p. 61.

[14] Paul Blumberg, *Inequality in an Age of Decline,* New York, Oxford University Press, 1980.

[15] U.S. Census Bureau, 1999, op. cit., p. v.

[16] Michael Harrington, *The Other America,* New York, Macmillan, 1962, p. 12–13.

[17] Stuart Ewen and Elizabeth Ewen, *Channels of Desire: Mass Images and the Shaping of American Consciousness,* New York, McGraw-Hill, 1982.

American Profile No. 1

Name: Harold S. Browning

Father: manufacturer, industrialist

Mother: prominent social figure in the community

Principal child-rearer: governess

Primary education: an exclusive private school on Manhattan's Upper East Side

Note: a small well-respected primary school where teachers and administrators have a reputation for nurturing student creativity and for providing the finest educational preparation

Ambition: "to become President"

Supplemental tutoring: tutors in French and mathematics

Summer camp: sleep-away camp in northern Connecticut

Note: camp provides instruction in the creative arts, athletics, and the natural sciences

Secondary education: a prestigious preparatory school in Westchester County

Note: classmates included the sons of ambassadors, doctors, attorneys, television personalities, and well-known business leaders

After-school activities: private riding lessons

Ambition: "to take over my father's business"

High-school graduation gift: BMW

Family activities: theater, recitals, museums, summer vacations in Europe, occasional winter trips to the Caribbean

Note: as members of and donors to the local art museum, the Brownings and their children attend private receptions and exhibit openings at the invitation of the museum director

Higher education: an Ivy League liberal arts college in Massachusetts

Major: economics and political science

After-class activities: debating club, college newspaper, swim team

Ambition: "to become a leader in business"

First full-time job (age 23): assistant manager of operations, Browning Tool and Die, Inc. (family enterprise)

Subsequent employment: *3 years*—executive assistant to the president, Browning Tool and Die
Responsibilities included: purchasing (materials and equipment), personnel, and distribution networks
4 years—advertising manager, Lackheed Manufacturing (home appliances)
3 years—director of marketing and sales, Comerex, Inc. (business machines)

Present employment (age 38): executive vice president, SmithBond and Co. (digital instruments)
Typical daily activities: review financial reports and computer printouts, dictate memoranda, lunch with clients, initiate conference calls, meet with assistants, plan business trips, meet with associates
Transportation to and from work: chauffeured company limousine
Annual salary: $315,000
Ambition: "to become chief executive officer of the firm, or one like it, within the next five to ten years"

Present residence: eighteenth-floor condominium on Manhattan's Upper West Side, eleven rooms, including five spacious bedrooms and terrace overlooking river
Interior: professionally designed and accented with elegant furnishings, valuable antiques, and expensive artwork
Note: building management provides doorman and elevator attendant; family employs au pair for children and maid for other domestic chores

Second residence: farm in northwestern Connecticut, used for weekend retreats and for horse breeding (investment/hobby)
Note: to maintain the farm and cater to their needs when they are there, the Brownings employ a part-time maid, groundskeeper, and horse breeder

Harold Browning was born into a world of nurses, maids, and governesses. His world today is one of airplanes and limousines, five-star restaurants, and luxurious living accommodations. The life and lifestyle of Harold Browning is in sharp contrast to that of Bob Farrell.

American Profile No. 2

Name: Bob Farrell

Father: machinist

Mother: retail clerk

Principal child-rearer: mother and sitter

Primary education: a medium-size public school in Queens, New York, characterized by large class size, outmoded physical facilities, and an educational philosophy emphasizing basic skills and student discipline

Ambition: "to become President"

Supplemental tutoring: none

Summer camp: YMCA day camp

Note: emphasis on team sports, arts and crafts

Secondary education: large regional high school in Queens

Note: classmates included the sons and daughters of carpenters, postal clerks, teachers, nurses, shopkeepers, mechanics, bus drivers, police officers, salespersons

After-school activities: basketball and handball in school park

Ambition: "to make it through college"

High-school graduation gift: $500 savings bond

Family activities: family gatherings around television set, bowling, an occasional trip to the movie theater, summer Sundays at the public beach

Higher education: a two-year community college with a technical orientation

Major: electrical technology

After-school activities: employed as a part-time bagger in local supermarket

Ambition: "to become an electrical engineer"

First full-time job (age 19): service-station attendant
Note: continued to take college classes in the evening
Subsequent employment: mail clerk at large insurance firm, manager trainee, large retail chain
Present employment (age 38): assistant sales manager, building supply firm
Typical daily activities: demonstrate products, write up product orders, handle customer complaints, check inventory
Transportation to and from work: city subway
Annual salary: $39,261
Ambition: "to open up my own business"
Additional income: $6,100 in commissions from evening and weekend work as salesman in local men's clothing store
Present residence: the Farrells own their own home in a working-class neighborhood in Queens

Bob Farrell and Harold Browning live very differently: the lifestyle of one is privileged; that of the other is not so privileged. The differences are class differences, and these differences have a profound impact on the way they live. They are differences between playing a game of handball in the park and taking riding lessons at a private stable; watching a movie on television and going to the theater; and taking the subway to work and being driven in a limousine. More important, the difference in class determines where they live, who their friends are, how well they are educated, what they do for a living, and what they come to expect from life.

Yet, as dissimilar as their lifestyles are, Harold Browning and Bob Farrell have some things in common. They live in the same city, they work long hours, and they are highly motivated. More important, they are both white males.

Let us look at someone else who works long and hard and is highly motivated. This person, however, is black and female.

American Profile No. 3

Name: Cheryl Mitchell
Father: janitor
Mother: waitress
Principal child-rearer: grandmother
Primary education: large public school in Ocean Hill-Brownsville, Brooklyn, New York
Note: rote teaching of basic skills and emphasis on conveying the importance of good attendance, good manners, and good work habits; school patrolled by security guards
Ambition: "to be a teacher"
Supplemental tutoring: none
Summer camp: none
Secondary education: large public school in Ocean Hill-Brownsville
Note: classmates included sons and daughters of hairdressers, grounds-keepers, painters, dressmakers, dish-washers, domestics
After-school activities: domestic chores, part-time employment as babysitter and housekeeper
Ambition: "to be a social worker"
High-school graduation gift: corsage
Family activities: church-sponsored socials
Higher education: one semester of local community college
Note: dropped out of school for financial reasons
First fill-time job (age 17): counter clerk, local bakery
Subsequent employment: file clerk with temporary service agency, supermarket checker
Present employment (age 38): nurse's aide at a municipal hospital
Typical daily activities: make up hospital beds, clean out bedpans, weigh patients and assist them to the bathroom, take temperature readings, pass out and collect food trays, feed patients who need help, bathe patients, and change dressings
Annual salary: $14,024
Ambition: "to get out of the ghetto"
Present residence: three-room apartment in the South Bronx, needs painting, has poor ventilation, is in a high-crime area
Note: Cheryl Mitchell lives with her four-year-old son and her elderly mother

When we look at the lives of Cheryl Mitchell, Bob Farrell, and Harold Browning, we see lifestyles that are very different. We are not looking, however, at economic extremes. Cheryl Mitchell's income as a nurse's aide puts her above the government's official poverty line.[18] Below her on the income pyramid are 35 million poverty-stricken Americans. Far from being poor, Bob Farrell has an annual income as an assistant sales manager that puts him in the fifty-first percentile of the income distribution.[19] More than 50 percent of the U.S. population earns less money than Bob Farrell. And while Harold Browning's income puts him in a high-income bracket, he stands only a fraction of the way up Samuelson's income pyramid. Well above him are the 144,000 individuals whose annual salary exceeds $1 million. Yet Harold Browning spends more money on his horses than Cheryl Mitchell earns in a year.

Reality 4: Even ignoring the extreme poles of the economic spectrum, we find enormous class differences in the lifestyles among the haves, the have-nots, and the have-littles.

Class affects more than lifestyle and material well-being. It has a significant impact on our physical and mental well-being as well.

Researchers have found an inverse relationship between social class and health. Lower-class standing is correlated to higher rates of infant mortality, eye and ear disease, arthritis, physical disability, diabetes, nutritional deficiency, respiratory disease, mental illness, and heart disease.[20] In all areas of health, poor people do not share the same life chances as those in the social class above them. Furthermore, lower-class standing is correlated with a lower quality of treatment for illness and disease. The results of poor health and poor treatment are borne out in the life expectancy rates within each class. Researchers have found that the higher your class standing, the higher your life expectancy. Conversely, they have also found that within each age group, the lower one's class standing,

---

[18] This is based on the 1999 poverty threshold of $13,290 for a family of three.

[19] Based on a median income in 1998 of $38,885.

[20] E. Pamuk, D. Makuc, K. Heck, C. Reuben, and K. Lochner, *Socioeconomic Status and Health Chartbook, Health, United States, 1998,* Hyattsville, MD, National Center for Health Statistics, 1998, pp. 145–159; Vincente Navarro "Class, Race, and Health Care in the United States," in Bersh Berberoglu, *Critical Pespectives in Sociology,* 2nd ed., Dubuque, IA, Kendall/Hunt, 1993, pp. 148–156; Melvin Krasner, *Poverty and Health in New York City,* United Hospital Fund of New York, 1989. See also U.S. Dept. of Health and Human Services, *Health Status of Minorities and Low Income Groups,* 1985; and Dan Hughes, Kay Johnson, Sara Rosenbaum, Elizabeth Butler, and Janet Simons, *The Health of America's Children,* The Children's Defense Fund, 1988.

the higher the death rate; in some age groups, the figures are as much as two and three times as high.[21]

Reality 5: From cradle to grave, class standing has a significant impact on our chances for survival.

The lower one's class standing, the more difficult it is to secure appropriate housing, the more time is spent on the routine tasks of everyday life, the greater is the percentage of income that goes to pay for food and other basic necessities, and the greater is the likelihood of crime victimization.[22] Class can predict chances for both survival and success.

CLASS AND EDUCATIONAL ATTAINMENT

School performance (grades and test scores) and educational attainment (level of schooling completed) also correlate strongly with economic class. Furthermore, despite some efforts to make testing fairer and schooling more accessible, current data suggest that the level of inequity is staying the same or getting worse.

In his study for the Carnegie Council on Children 15 years ago, Richard De Lone examined the test scores of over half a million students who took the College Board exams (SATs). His findings were consistent with earlier studies that showed a relationship between class and scores on standardized tests; his conclusion: "the higher the student's social status, the higher the probability that he or she will get higher grades."[23] Fifteen years after the release of the Carnegie report, College Board surveys reveal data that are no different; test scores still correlate strongly with family income.

---

[21] E. Pamuk et al., op. cit.; Kenneth Neubeck and Davita Glassberg, *Sociology: A Critical Approach,* New York, McGraw-Hill, 1996, pp. 436–438; Aaron Antonovsky, "Social Class, Life Expectancy, and Overall Mortality," in *The Impact of Social Class,* New York, Thomas Crowell, 1972, pp. 467–491. See also Harriet Duleep, "Measuring the Effect of Income on Adult Mortality Using Longitudinal Administrative Record Data," *Journal of Human Resources,* vol. 21, no. 2, Spring 1986.

[22] E. Pamuk et al., op. cit., fig. 20; Dennis W. Roncek, "Dangerous Places: Crime and Residential Environment," *Social Forces,* vol. 60, no. 1, September 1981, pp. 74–96.

[23] Richard De Lone, *Small Futures,* New York, Harcourt Brace Jovanovich, 1978, pp. 14–19.

Average Combined Scores by Income
(400 to 1600 scale)[24]

Family Income	Median Score
More than $100,000	1130
$80,000 to $100,000	1082
$70,000 to $80,000	1058
$60,000 to $70,000	1043
$50,000 to $60,000	1030
$40,000 to $50,000	1011
$30,000 to $40,000	986
$20,000 to $30,000	954
$10,000 to $20,000	907
less than $10,000	871

These figures are based on the test results of 1,302,903 SAT takers in 1999.

A little more than 20 years ago, researcher William Sewell showed a positive correlation between class and overall educational achievement. In comparing the top quartile (25%) of his sample to the bottom quartile, he found that students from upper-class families were twice as likely to obtain training beyond high school and four times as likely to attain a postgraduate degree. Sewell concluded: "Socioeconomic background . . . operates independently of academic ability at every stage in the process of educational attainment."[25]

Today, the pattern persists. There are, however, two significant changes. On the one hand, the odds of getting into college have improved for the bottom quartile of the population, although they still remain relatively low compared to the top. On the other hand, the chances of completing a college degree have deteriorated markedly for the bottom quartile. Researchers estimate the chances of completing a four-year college degree (by age 24) to be 19 times as great for the top 25 percent of the population as it is for the bottom 25 percent. "Those from the bottom quartile of family income . . . are faring worse than they have at any time in the 23 years of published Current Population Survey data."[26]

---

[24] Derived from The College Entrance Examination Board, "1999, A Profile of College Bound Seniors: SAT Test Takers," *www.collegeboard.org/sat/cbsenior/yr1999/NAT/natbk499.html#income*

[25] William H. Sewell, "Inequality of Opportunity for Higher Education," *American Sociological Review,* vol. 36, no. 5, 1971, pp. 793–809.

[26] The Mortenson Report on Public Policy Analysis of Opportunity for Postsecondary Education, "Postsecondary Education Opportunity," Iowa City, IA, September 1993, no. 16.

Reality 6: Class standing has a significant impact on chances for educational attainment.

Class standing, and consequently life chances, are largely determined at birth. Although examples of individuals who have gone from rags to riches abound in the mass media, statistics on class mobility show these leaps to be extremely rare. In fact, dramatic advances in class standing are relatively few. One study showed that fewer than one in five men surpass the economic status of their fathers.[27] For those whose annual income is in six figures, economic success is due in large part to the wealth and privileges bestowed on them at birth. Over 66 percent of the consumer units with incomes of $100,000 or more have some inherited assets. Of these units, over 86 percent reported that inheritances constituted a substantial portion of their total assets.[28]

Economist Harold Wachtel likens inheritance to a series of Monopoly games in which the winner of the first game refuses to relinquish his or her cash and commercial property for the second game. "After all," argues the winner, "I accumulated my wealth and income by my own wits." With such an arrangement, it is not difficult to predict the outcome of subsequent games.[29]

Reality 7: All Americans do not have an equal opportunity to succeed. Inheritance laws ensure a greater likelihood of success for the offspring of the wealthy.

SPHERES OF POWER AND OPPRESSION

When we look at society and try to determine what it is that keeps most people down—what holds them back from realizing their potential as healthy, creative, productive individuals—we find institutionally oppressive forces that are largely beyond their individual control. Class domination is one of these forces. People do not choose to be poor or working class; instead, they are limited and confined by the opportunities afforded or denied them by a social and economic system. The class structure in the United States is a function of its economic system—capitalism, a system that is based

---

[27] De Lone, op. cit., pp. 14–19.

[28] Howard Tuchman, *Economics of the Rich,* New York, Random House, 1973, p. 15.

[29] Howard Wachtel, *Labor and the Economy,* Orlando, FL, Academic Press, 1984, pp. 161–162.

on private rather than public ownership and control of commercial enterprises, and on the class division between those who own and control and those who do not. Under capitalism, these enterprises are governed by the need to produce a profit for the owners, rather than to fulfill collective needs.

Racial and gender domination are other such forces that hold people down. Although there are significant differences in the way capitalism, racism, and sexism affect our lives, there are also a multitude of parallels. And although race, class, and gender act independently of each other, they are at the same time very much interrelated.

On the one hand, issues of race and gender oppression cut across class lines. Women experience the effects of sexism whether they are well-paid professionals or poorly paid clerks. As women, they face discrimination and male domination, as well as catcalls and stereotyping. Similarly, a black man faces racial oppression, is subjected to racial slurs, and is denied opportunities because of his color. Regardless of their class standing, women and members of minority races are confronted with oppressive forces precisely because of their gender, color, or both.

On the other hand, class oppression permeates other spheres of power and oppression, so that the oppression experienced by women and minorities is also differentiated along class lines. Although women and minorities find themselves in subordinate positions vis-à-vis white men, the particular issues they confront may be quite different, depending on their position in the class structure. Inequalities in the class structure distinguish social functions and individual power, and these distinctions carry over to race and gender categories.

Power is incremental, and class privileges can accrue to individual women and to individual members of a racial minority. At the same time, class-oppressed men, whether they are white or black, have privileges afforded them as men in a sexist society. Similarly, class-oppressed whites, whether they are men or women, have privileges afforded them as whites in a racist society. Spheres of power and oppression divide us deeply in our society, and the schisms between us are often difficult to bridge.

Whereas power is incremental, oppression is cumulative, and those who are poor, black, and female have all of the forces of classism, racism, and sexism bearing down on them. This cumulative oppression is what is meant by the double and triple jeopardy of women and minorities.

Furthermore, oppression in one sphere is related to the likelihood of oppression in another. If you are black and female, for example, you are much more likely to be poor or working class than you would be as a white male. Census figures show that the incidence of poverty varies greatly by race and gender.

Chances of Being Poor in America[30]

White male/ female	White female head*	Hispanic male/ female	Hispanic female head*	Black male/ female	Black female head*
1 in 10	1 in 4	1 in 4	1 in 2	1 in 4	1 in 2

* Persons in families with female householder, no husband present.

In other words, being female and being nonwhite are attributes in our society that increase the chances of poverty and of lower-class standing.

Reality 8: Racism and sexism compound the effects of classism in society

---

ANALYSIS

1. Mantsios begins by characterizing the basic themes of the American Dream credo; what for him are the four essential elements of this credo or ideology?

2. What key questions does Mantsios think we need to ask in order to assess the "legitimacy" of this Dream credo?

3. What, for Mantsios, constitutes the idea of social class? How does income enter the picture? Lifestyles? Do you agree with Mantsios that Americans avoid the use of the term *class?*

4. Mantsios asserts that "Class affects more than lifestyle and material well-being. . . ." How does it affect lifestyle and well-being? What is the "more" part, according to Mantsios?

5. The most shocking bit of evidence in Mantsios's essay is perhaps his assertion that "Test scores still correlate strongly with family income." Does it shock you? Or is this a chicken-egg phenomenon, i.e., which came first? Do high intelligence people (assuming the SAT's measure that in some way) gravitate toward situations of success and prosperity? Or is it that the money comes first and then "buys" a good education, and hence good test scores?

6. "Class standing, and consequently life chances, are largely determined at birth. Although examples of individuals who have gone from rags to riches abound in the mass media, statistics on class mobility show these leaps to be extremely rare . . . dramatic advances in class standing are relatively few." What does Mantsios mean by "determined at birth"? What evidence does Mantsios offer in support of this contention?

7. How generally would you assess Mantsios's case? What evidence does he offer to support his general thesis that "institutionally oppressive forces . . . beyond individual control" such as "class domination" are the real forces that keep "most people down"?

---

[30] Derived from Census, 1999, op. cit., p. vi.

WRITING POSSIBILITIES

1. Mantsios acknowledges that the chances of getting into college have improved for the bottom quartile but notes that the chances for that quartile actually *completing* a college degree have "deteriorated markedly." Is this the result of affirmative action? Of open admissions (e.g., at City College of New York, before the program was closed down)? Could one argue that poorly prepared students in either case are obviously the ones not to complete a degree? How do you think Wendy Williams ("Money Is Everything, Except Hers") would fair in this respect?

2. ". . . statistics on class mobility show these leaps [from rags to riches] to be extremely rare . . . dramatic advances in class standing are relatively few." Interview your parents and if possible your grandparents: How do *they* see their progress or lack of it in terms of class standing? In terms of "dramatic" advances (or simply advances)?

3. Some critics of Mantsios's class-inequality argument suggest that another way to look at the matter is to see that what had once been only the rich man's preserve (cars, good clothing, air conditioners, VCRs) is now the privilege of even the poorest citizens. America, Michael Harrington once said, "has the best dressed poverty the world has ever known." In other words, while technically most people might stay wherever they or their families started on the socioeconomic ladder, their position has enormously improved for the better. Read the selection by Cox and Alm to see if you agree with theirs or Mantsios's positions.

Eric Liu

The American idea of success—the American Dream—can be succinctly illustrated by this statement of President Clinton's, quoted in Jennifer Hochschild's Facing Up to the American Dream: *"The American dream that we were all raised on is a simple but powerful one—if you work hard and play by the rules you should be given a chance to go as far as your God-given ability will take you."*

Eric Liu's understanding of the Dream ideology is considerably more nuanced than Clinton's, but it is like Clinton's and unlike Gregory Mantsios's (pages 302–318) in finally offering a ringing endorsement of the American Dream. Consider how, in fact, Liu negotiates between liberal criticism of the Dream and conservative enthusiasm for it.

A CHINAMAN'S CHANCE:
REFLECTIONS ON THE AMERICAN DREAM

A lot of people my age seem to think that the American Dream is dead. I think they're dead wrong.

Or at least only partly right. It is true that for those of us in our twenties and early thirties, job opportunities are scarce. There looms a real threat that we will be the first American generation to have a lower standard of living than our parents.

But what is it that we mean when we invoke the American Dream?

In the past, the American Dream was something that held people of all races, religions, and identities together. As James Comer has written, it represented a shared aspiration among all Americans—black, white, or any other color—"to provide well for themselves and their families as valued members of a democratic society." Now, all too often, it seems the American Dream means merely some guarantee of affluence, a birthright of wealth.

At a basic level, of course, the American Dream is about prosperity and the pursuit of material happiness. But to me, its meaning extends beyond such concerns. To me, the dream is not just about buying a bigger house than the one I grew up in or having shinier stuff now than I had as a kid. It also represents a sense of opportunity that binds generations together in commitment, so that the young inherit not only property but also perseverance, not only money but also a mission to make good on the strivings of their parents and grandparents.

The poet Robert Browning once wrote that "a man's reach must exceed his grasp—else what's a heaven for?" So it is in America. Every generation will strive, and often fail. Every generation will reach for success, and often miss the mark. But Americans rely as much on the next generation as on the next life to prove that such struggles and frustrations are not in vain. There may be temporary setbacks, cutbacks, recessions, depressions. But this is a nation of second chances. So long as there are young Americans who do not take what they have—or what they can do—for granted, progress is always possible.

My conception of the American Dream does not take progress for granted. But it does demand the *opportunity* to achieve progress—and values the opportunity as much as the achievement. I come at this question as the son of immigrants. I see just as clearly as anyone else the cracks in the idealist vision of fulfillment for all. But because my parents came here with virtually nothing, because they did build something, I see the enormous potential inherent in the ideal.

I happen still to believe in our national creed: freedom and opportunity, and our common responsibility to uphold them. This creed is what makes America unique. More than any demographic statistic or economic indicator, it animates the American Dream. It infuses our mundane struggles—to plan a career, do good work, get ahead—with purpose and possibility. It makes America the only country that could produce heroes like Colin Powell—heroes who rise from nothing, who overcome the odds.

I think of the sacrifices made by my own parents. I appreciate the hardship of the long road traveled by my father—one of whose first jobs in America was painting the yellow line down a South Dakota interstate—and by my mother—whose first job here was filing pay stubs for a New York restaurant. From such beginnings, they were able to build a comfortable life and provide me with a breadth of resources—through arts, travel, and an Ivy League education. It was an unspoken obligation for them to do so.

I think of my boss in my first job after college, on Capitol Hill. George is a smart, feisty, cigar-chomping, take-no-shit Greek-American. He is about fifteen years older than I, has different interests, a very different personality. But like me, he is the son of immigrants, and he would joke with me that the Greek-Chinese mafia was going to take over one day. He was only half joking. We'd worked harder, our parents doubly harder, than almost anyone else we knew. To people like George, talk of the withering of the American Dream seems foreign.

It's undeniable that principles like freedom and opportunity, no matter how dearly held, are not enough. They can inspire a multiracial March on Washington, but they can not bring black salaries in alignment with white salaries. They can draw wave after wave of immigrants here, but they can not provide them the means to get out of our ghettos and barrios and Chinatowns. They are not sufficient for fulfillment of the American Dream.

But they are necessary. They are vital. And not just to the children of immigrants. These ideals form the durable thread that weaves us all in union. Put another way, they are one of the few things that keep America from disintegrating into a loose confederation of zip codes and walled-in communities.

What alarms me is how many people my age look at our nation's ideals with a rising sense of irony. What good is such a creed if your are working for hourly wages in a deadend job? What value do such platitudes have if you live in an urban war zone? When the only apparent link between homeboys and housepainters and bike messengers and investment bankers is pop culture—MTV, the NBA, movies, dance music—then the social fabric is flimsy indeed.

My generation has come of age at a time when the country is fighting off bouts of defeatism and self-doubt, at a time when racism and social inequities seem not only persistent but intractable. At a time like this, the retreat of one's own kind is seen by more and more of my peers as an advance. And that retreat has given rise again to the notion that there are essential and irreconcilable differences among the races—a notion that was supposed to have disappeared from American discourse by the time my peers and I were born in the sixties.

Not long ago, for instance, my sister called me a "banana."

I was needling her about her passion for rap and hip-hop music. Every time I saw her, it seemed, she was jumping and twisting to

Arrested Development or Chubb Rock or some other funky group. She joked that despite being the daughter of Chinese immigrants, she was indeed "black at heart." And then she added, lightheartedly, "You, on the other hand—well, you're basically a banana." Yellow on the outside, but white inside.

I protested, denied her charge vehemently. But it was too late. She was back to dancing. And I stood accused.

Ever since then, I have wondered what it means to be black, or white, or Asian "at heart"—particularly for my generation. Growing up, when other kids would ask whether I was Chinese or Korean or Japanese, I would reply, a little petulantly, "American." Assimilation can still be a sensitive subject. I recall reading about a Korean-born Congressman who had gone out of his way to say that Asian-Americans should expect nothing special from him. He added that he was taking speech lessons "to get rid of this accent." I winced at his palpable self-hate. But then it hit me: Is this how my sister sees me?

There is no doubt that minorities like me can draw strength from our communities. But in today's environment, anything other than ostentatious tribal fealty is taken in some communities as a sign of moral weakness, a disappointing dilution of character. In times that demand ever-clearer thinking, it has become too easy for people to shut off their brains: "It's a black/Asian/Latino/white thing," says the variable T-shirt. "You wouldn't understand." Increasingly, we don't.

The civil-rights triumphs of the sixties and the cultural revolutions that followed made it possible for minorities to celebrate our diverse heritages. I can appreciate that. But I know, too, that the sixties—or at least, my generation's grimy, hazy vision of the decade—also bequeathed to young Americans a legacy of near-pathological race consciousness.

Today's culture of entitlement—and of race entitlement in particular—tells us plenty about what we get if we are black or white or female or male or old or young.

It is silent, though, on some other important issues. For instance: What do we "get" for being American? And just as importantly, What do we owe? These are questions around which young people like myself must tread carefully, since talk of common interests, civic culture, responsibility, and integration sounds a little too "white" for some people. To the new segregationists, the "American Dream" is like the old myth of the "Melting Pot": an oppressive fiction, an opiate for the unhappy colored masses.

How have we allowed our thinking about race to become so twisted? The formal obstacles and the hateful opposition to civil rights have long faded into memory. By most external measures, life for minorities is better than it was a quarter century ago. It would seem that the opportunities for tolerance and cooperation are commonplace.

Why, then, are so many of my peers so cynical about our ability to get along with one another?

The reasons are frustratingly ambiguous. I got a glimpse of this when I was in college. It was late in my junior year, and as the editor of a campus magazine, I was sitting on a panel to discuss "The White Press at Yale: What Is to Be Done?" The assembly hall was packed, a diverse and noisy crowd. The air was heavy, nervously electric.

Why weren't there more stories about "minority issues" in the Yale *Daily News?* Why weren't there more stories on Africa in my magazine, the foreign affairs journal? How many "editors of color" served on the boards of each of the major publications? The questions were volleyed like artillery, one round after another, punctuated only by the applause of an audience spoiling for a fight. The questions were not at all unfair. But it seemed that no one—not even those of us on the panel who *were* people of color—could provide, in this context, satisfactory answers.

Toward the end of the discussion, I made a brief appeal for reason and moderation. And afterward, as students milled around restlessly, I was attacked: for my narrow-mindedness—*How dare you suggest that Yale is not a fundamentally prejudiced place!*—for my simplemindedness—*Have you, too, been co-opted?*

And for my betrayal—*Are you just white inside?*

My eyes were opened that uncomfortably warm early summer evening. Not only to the cynical posturing and the combustible opportunism of campus racial politics. But more importantly, to the larger question of identity—my identity—in America. Never mind that the aim of many of the loudest critics was to generate headlines in the very publications they denounced. In spite of themselves—against, it would seem, their true intentions—they got me to think about who I am.

In our society today, and especially among people of my generation, we are congealing into clots of narrow commonality. We stick with racial and religious comrades. This tribal consciousness-raising can be empowering for some. But while America was conceived in liberty—the liberty, for instance, to associate with whomever we like—it was never designed to be a mere collection of subcultures. We forget that there is in fact such a thing as a unique American identity that transcends our sundry tribes, sets, gangs, and cliques.

I have grappled, wittingly or not, with these questions of identity and allegiance all my life. When I was in my early teens, I would invite my buddies overnight to watch movies, play video games, and beat one another up. Before too long, my dad would come downstairs and start hamming it up—telling stories, asking gently nosy questions, making corny jokes, all with his distinct Chinese accent. I would stand back, quietly gauging everyone's reaction. Of course, the guys loved it. But I would feel uneasy.

What was then cause for discomfort is now a source of strength. Looking back on such episodes, I take pride in my father's accented English; I feel awe at his courage to laugh loudly in a language not really his own.

It was around the same time that I decided that continued attendance at the community Chinese school on Sundays was uncool. There was no fanfare; I simply stopped going. As a child, I'd been too blissfully unaware to think of Chinese school as anything more than a weekly chore, with an annual festival (dumplings and spring rolls, games and prizes). But by the time I was a peer-pressured adolescent, Chinese school seemed like a badge of the woefully unassimilated. I turned my back on it.

Even as I write these words now, it feels as though I am revealing a long-held secret. I am proud that my ancestors—scholars, soldiers, farmers—came from one of the world's great civilizations. I am proud that my grandfather served in the Chinese Air Force. I am proud to speak even my clumsy brand of Mandarin, and I feel blessed to be able to think idiomatically in Chinese, a language so much richer in nuance and subtle poetry than English.

Belatedly, I appreciate the good fortune I've had to be the son of immigrants. As a kid, I could play Thomas Jefferson in the bicentennial school play one week and the next week play the poet Li Bai at the Chinese school festival. I could come home from an afternoon of teen slang at the mall and sit down to dinner for a rollicking conversation in our family's hybrid of Chinese and English. I understood, when I went over to visit friends, that my life was different. At the time, I just never fully appreciated how rich it was.

Yet I know that this pride in my heritage does not cross into prejudice against others. What it reflects is pride in what my country represents. That became clear to me when I went through Marine Corps Officer Candidates' School. During the summers after my sophomore and junior years of college, I volunteered for OCS, a grueling boot camp for potential officers in the swamps and foothills of Quantico, Virginia.

And once I arrived—standing 5'4", 135 pounds, bespectacled, a Chinese Ivy League Democrat—I was a target straight out of central casting. The wiry, raspy-voiced drill sergeant, though he was perhaps only an inch or two taller than I, called me "Little One" with as much venom as can be squeezed into such a moniker. He heaped verbal abuse on me, he laughed when I stumbled, he screamed when I hesitated. But he also never failed to remind me that just because I was a little shit didn't mean I shouldn't run farther, climb higher, think faster, hit harder than anyone else.

That was the funny thing about the Marine Crops, it is, ostensibly, one of the most conservative institutions in the United States. And yet, for those twelve weeks, it represented the kind of color-blind equality of opportunity that the rest of society struggles to match. I did not feel uncomfortable at OCS to be of Chinese descent. Indeed, I drew strength from it. My platoon was a veritable cross section of America: forty young men of all backgrounds, all regions, all races, all levels of intelligence and ability, displaced from our lives (if only for a few weeks) with nowhere else to go.

Going down the list of names—Courtemanche, Dougherty, Grella, Hunt, Liu, Reeves, Schwarzman, and so on—brought to mind a line from a World War II documentary I once saw, which went something like this: The reason why it seemed during the war that America was as good as the rest of the world put together was that America *was* the rest of the world put together.

Ultimately, I decided that the Marines was not what I wanted to do for four years and I did not accept the second lieutenant's commission. But I will never forget the day of the graduation parade: bright sunshine, brisk winds, the band playing Sousa as my company passed in review. As my mom and dad watched and photographed the parade from the rafters, I thought to myself: this is the American Dream in all its cheesy earnestness. I felt the thrill of truly being part of something larger and greater than myself.

I do know that American life is not all Sousa marches and flag-waving. I know that those with reactionary agendas often find it convenient to cloak their motives in the language of Americanism. The "American Party" was the name of a major nativist organization in the nineteenth century. "America First" is the siren song of the isolationists who would withdraw this country from the world and expel the world from this country. I know that our national immigration laws were once designed explicitly to cut off the influx from Asia.

I also know that discrimination is real. I am reminded of a gentle old man who, after Pearl Harbor, was stripped of his possessions without warning, taken from his home, and thrown into a Japanese internment camp. He survived, and by many measures has thrived, serving as a community leader and political activist. But I am reluctant to share with him my wide-eyed patriotism.

I know the bittersweet irony that my own father—a strong and optimistic man—would sometimes feel when he was alive. When he came across a comically lost cause—if the Yankees were behind 14–0 in the ninth, or if Dukakis was down ten points in the polls with a week left—he would often joke that the doomed party had "a Chinaman's chance" of success. It was one of those insensitive idioms of a generation ago, and it must have lodged in his impressionable young mind when he first came to America. It spoke of a perceived stacked deck.

I know, too, that for many other immigrants, the dream simply does not work out. Fae Myenne Ng, the author of *Bone,* writes about how her father ventured here from China under a false identity and arrived at Angel Island, the detention center outside the "Gold Mountain" of San Francisco. He got out, he labored, he struggled, and he suffered "a bitter no-luck life" in America. There was no glory. For him, Ng suggests, the journey was not worth it.

But it is precisely because I know these things that I want to prove that in the long run, over generations and across ethnicities, it *is* worth it. For the second-generation American, opportunity is obligation. I have seen and faced racism. I understand the dull pain of dreams deferred or unmet. But I believe still that there is so little stopping me from building the life that I want. I was given, through my parents' labors, the chance to bridge that gap between ideals and reality. Who am I to throw away that chance?

Plainly, I am subject to the criticism that I speak too much from my own experience. Not everyone can relate to the second-generation American story. When I have spoken like this with some friends, the issue has been my perspective. *What you say is fine for you. But unless you grew up where I did, unless you've had people avoid you because of the color of your skin, don't talk to me about common dreams.*

But are we then to be paralyzed? Is respect for different experiences supposed to obviate the possibility of shared aspirations? Does the diversity of life in America doom us to a fractured understanding of one another? The question is basic: Should the failure of this nation thus far to fulfill its stated ideals incapacitate its young people, or motivate us?

Our country was built on, and remains glued by, the idea that everybody deserves a fair shot and that we must work together to guarantee that opportunity—the original American Dream. It was this idea, in some inchoate form, that drew every immigrant here. It was this idea, however sullied by slavery and racism, that motivated the civil-rights movement. To write this idea off—even when its execution is spotty—to let American life descend into squabbles among separatist tribes would not just be sad. It would be a total mishandling of a legacy, the squandering of a great historical inheritance.

Mine must not be the first generation of Americans to lose America. Just as so many of our parents journeyed here to find their version of the American Dream, so must young Americans today journey across boundaries of race and class to rediscover one another. We are the first American generation to be born into an integrated society, and we are accustomed to more race mixing than any generation before us. We started open-minded, and it's not too late for us to stay that way.

Time is of the essence. For in our national political culture today, the watchwords seem to be *decline* and *end*. Apocalyptic visions and dark millennial predictions abound. The end of history. The end of progress. The end of equality. Even something as ostensibly positive as the end of the Cold War has a bittersweet tinge, because for the life of us, no one in America can get a handle on the big question, "What Next?"

For my generation, this fixation on endings is particularly enervating. One's twenties are supposed to be a time of widening horizons, of bright possibilities. Instead, America seems to have entered an era of limits. Whether it is the difficulty of finding jobs from some place other than a temp agency, or the mountains of debt that darken our future, the message to my peers is often that this nation's time has come and gone; let's bow out with grace and dignity.

A friend once observed that while the Chinese seek to adapt to nature and yield to circumstance, Americans seek to conquer both. She meant that as a criticism of America. But I interpreted her remark differently. I *do* believe that America is exceptional. And I believe it is up to my generation to revive that spirit, that sense that we do in fact have control over our own destiny—as individuals and as a nation.

If we are to reclaim a common destiny, we must also reach out to other generations for help. It was Franklin Roosevelt who said that while America can't always build the future for its youth, it can—and must—build its youth for the future. That commitment across generations is as central to the American Dream as any I have enunciated. We are linked, black and white, old and young, one and inseparable.

I know how my words sound. I am old enough to perceive my own naïveté but young enough still to cherish it. I realize that I am coming of age just as the American Dream is showing its age. Yet I still have faith in this country's unique destiny—to create generation after generation of hyphenates like me, to channel this new blood, this resilience and energy into an ever more vibrant future for *all* Americans.

And I want to prove—for my sake, for my father's sake, and for my country's sake—that a Chinaman's chance is as good as anyone else's.

ANALYSIS

1. What does Liu mean by distinguishing between the "basic level" of the Dream—"prosperity and the pursuit of material happiness"—and "a sense of opportunity that binds generations together in commitment"?

2. Unlike Mantsios, Liu makes no mention of "class" but you might infer something of where class enters his essay by his remarks on his parents and upbringing: "I think of the sacrifices made by my own parents . . . they were able to build a comfortable life and provide me with a breadth of resources . . . and an Ivy League education. . . ." Where would you place Liu's parents and family in the charts of class differences in Mantsios's essay?

3. Liu speaks of the present era's "near-pathological race consciousness"; what does he mean by this? How does he develop it in the essay? To

what extent would you agree or disagree with Liu that race presents a crucial problem of the American Dream?

4. Liu offers a crucial autobiographical example—his experience in the Marine Officer Candidates School—to insist on the idea that race is finally irrelevant as one pursues one's goals in America today. Do you think his one example is persuasive or not? Explain.

5. Do you agree with Mantsios that we have in America a class system supported by myths? Or do you concur with Liu in believing the possibilities of the American Dream? Explain why you agree or disagree with the terminology of either "class" or the "American Dream," cite both writers.

WRITING POSSIBILITIES

1. To what extent would you agree with Liu's belief that race does not matter as much as the critics of the Dream have argued? Would you agree that an earlier era has bequeathed to young Americans a legacy of "near-pathological race consciousness"?

2. Liu speaks for the value of "assimilation," though he recognizes that it "can still be a sensitive subject." Do you agree with Liu that success (material and otherwise) depends on assimilation?

Richard Alm and Michael Cox

*In Alm and Cox's essay, you will find an analytic piece that deals with the statistical argument over inequality. Don't glaze over! All the arguing of pessimists like Michael Mantsios (*Class in America: Myths and Realities, *pages 302–318) or optimists like Liu (previous selection) and Alm and Cox ultimately comes down to numbers: how many are better off, how many are poorer? Whether writers say so or not, they all—no matter what their ideological persuasion—make certain assumptions about statistical facts. And until we get some kind of statistical sense about the facts, we're arguing in the dark. In the following selection, you can get a rough idea of what the statistical arguments are about. It's not conclusive by any means, but at least you will have a sense of what kinds of particular issues crop up when anyone says either that "the rich are getting richer" or that "the poor are getting poorer."*

Cox is an economist with the Federal Reserve Bank in Atlanta; Alm is a journalist. Together, they have written a lively book which argues that, contrary to those of Gregory Mantsios (pages 302–318), the poor are not getting poorer and the rich, if getting richer, are simply doing what all of us—poor, middle class, and upper class are doing, i.e., benefiting from the American Dream. Mobility is indeed the name of the game for Alm and Cox, and the Dream is myth for them. No, say Cox and Alm, the real myth is the myth of rich and poor itself. They offer two basic arguments: (1) The standard of living has increased so dramatically over the years that what might have been a rich man's prerogative 30 years ago is now available even to the poor. (They might have been watching Rorie Kennedy's film about Appalachia, where VCR's were easily available.) and (2) Treasury Department tax returns, which track individuals *and families over the years, show that few people stay in the same spot they originally were—in fact, over the years, they move up two or three big leaps (quintiles) and get themselves out of poverty into the middle class or out of the middle class into even the upper classes.*

As you can see, such an argument contradicts Gregory Mantsios's and William Julius Wilson's and lends solid statistical support to a writer like Justice Clarence Thomas below.

Cox and Alm's piece—an excerpt from their book—is easy reading and you should have little trouble following their arguments. To help you deal with the conflict between Cox and Alm and such a pessimist as Gregory Mantsios, consult a critical review of Myths of Rich and Poor *by Michael M. Weinstein.*

BY OUR OWN BOOTSTRAPS
from Myths of Rich and Poor

"Land of opportunity." Anywhere in the world, those three words bring to mind just one place: the United States of America.

Opportunity defines our heritage. The American saga entails waves of immigrant farmers, shopkeepers, laborers, and entrepreneurs, all coming to the United States for the promise of a better life. Some amassed enormous fortunes—the Rockefellers, the Carnegies, the DuPonts, the Fords, the Vanderbilts, to name just a few. Even today, America's opportunity is always on display. Bill Gates in computer software, Ross Perot in data processing, Bill Cosby and Oprah Winfrey in entertainment, Warren Buffett in investing, Sam Walton in retailing, Michael Jordan in sports, and Mary Kay Ash in cosmetics could head a list of the many thousands who catapulted from society's lower or middle ranks to the top. Many millions more, descendants of those who arrived with little more than the clothes on their backs and a few bucks in their pockets, took advantage of an open economic system to improve their lot in life through talent and hard work.

Even pessimists acknowledge that the Gateses, Perots, Cosbys, Winfreys, Buffetts, Waltons, Jordans, and Ashes are getting filthy rich, along with Wall Street's wheeler-dealers, Hollywood moguls, and big-league ballplayers. At the nation's 350 largest companies, top executives' median total compensation in 1996 was $3.1 million, or 90 times what a typical factory hand earns. We often hear that ordinary Americans aren't keeping up, that success isn't as easy, or at least not as democratic, as it once was. At the close of the twentieth century, one disturbing vision portrays the United States as a society pulling apart at the seams, divided into separate and unequal camps, an enclave of fat cats gorging themselves on the fruits of others' labor surrounded by a working class left with ever more meager opportunities.

The most-cited evidence of ebbing opportunity is the *distribution of income*—the slicing up of the American pie. Examining the data, analysts seize on two points. First, there's a marked inequality in earnings between society's haves and have-nots. Second, and perhaps more ominous, the gap between the richest and poorest households has widened over the past two decades. The Census Bureau provides the statistical ballast for these claims. In 1997, the top 20 percent of American households received almost half of the nation's income. Average earnings among this group are $122,764 a year. The distribution of income to the four other groups of 20 percent was as follows: The second fifth had 23.2 percent, with average earnings of $57,582; the third fifth had 15.0 percent, with average earnings of $37,177; the fourth fifth had 8.9 percent, with average earnings of $22,098. The bottom 20 percent earned 3.6 percent of the economic pie, or an average of $8,872 a year (see Figure 1).

The case for the existence of a growing rift between rich and poor rests on longer-term trends in the same Census Bureau data. Since 1975, only the top 20 percent of Americans managed to expand their allotment of the nation's income—from 43.2 percent to 49.4 percent.

FIGURE 1   Slicing Up the American Pie

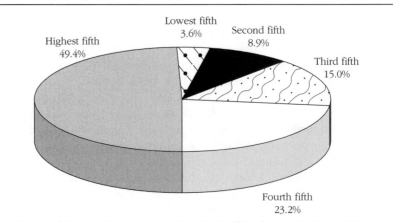

Shares of National Income Earned by Each Fifth of Households in 1997.

Over the same period, the distribution to the middle three groups slipped slightly. The share going to the lowest 20 percent of income earners fell from 4.4 percent to 3.6 percent. The shift of income toward the upper end of the distribution becomes even more striking when it's put in dollars. After adjusting for inflation, the income of households in the bottom 20 percent increased by only $207 from 1975 to 1997. The top tier, meanwhile, jumped by $37,633 (see Figure 2).

Once again, the pessimists have it wrong. The income distribution only reveals how one group is doing relative to others at a particular moment. That kind of you-vs.-me score keeping has little to do with whether any American can get ahead. By its very nature, opportunity is individual rather than collective. Even for an individual, the concept can't be divorced from its time element, an assessment of how well someone is doing today relative to yesterday, or how he can expect to do tomorrow compared to today. How many of us worked our way up? How quickly did we move from one rung to the next? How many of us fell? Studies of income inequality cannot say whether individuals are doing better or worse. They lump together Americans who differ in age, educational level, work effort, family and marital status, gender

FIGURE 2   A Caste Society?

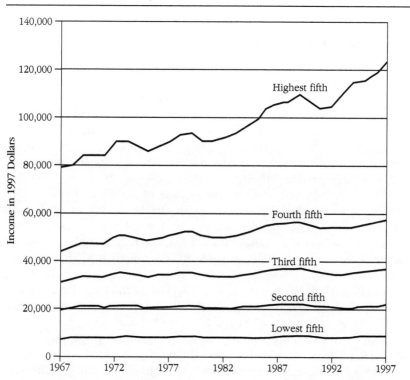

and race. The sample never stays the same from one year to another, and researchers haven't a clue about what happened to any individual in the income distribution.

Annual snapshots of the income distribution might deserve attention if we lived in a caste society, with rigid class lines determining who gets what share of the national income—but we don't live in a caste society. It takes a heroic leap to look at the disparity between rich and poor and conclude that any one individual's chances of getting ahead aren't what they used to be. Even the most sophisticated income-distribution statistics fail to tell us what we really want to know: Are the majority of Americans losing their birthright—a chance at upward mobility? Static portraits, moreover, don't tell us whether low-income households tend to remain at the bottom year after year. By definition, a fifth of society will always inhabit the lowest 20 percent of the income distribution. We don't know, however, whether individuals and families stay there over long periods. It's no great tragedy if the bottom rung is where many Americans start to climb the ladder of success. To argue that upward mobility is being lost, we would have to show that the poorest remain stuck where they are, with little hope of making themselves better off. Nothing could be further from the truth.

Making It from Bottom to Top

How can we gauge *opportunity*—the prospects for getting ahead? The best way involves identifying individuals and tracking them year by year, capturing the highs and lows of income over a lifetime. When combined with such personal data as age, education, and marital status, individual earnings profiles pinpoint income changes that occur along life's journey. It's no easy task to keep tabs on specific income earners in a mobile, fast-changing society. The statistical mills of government and private industry produce few numbers on long-term earnings—year-by-year data on the income of particular persons. One source of such information does exist: the University of Michigan's Panel Survey on Income Dynamics, the longest tracking study ever done on Americans' earnings. Since 1968, the university has collected detailed information on more than 50,000 Americans. This mass of data, carefully designed to provide a statistically valid picture of the nation as a whole, has over the years served as the basis for hundreds of studies. A sample from this database allows us to follow the ebbs and flows in income for 17 years. It's a period long enough to capture the real stories of our economic lives—the hirings, firings, raises, promotions, retirements, windfalls, and financial setbacks.

Tracking individuals' income over time gives a startlingly different view of income distribution than the Census Bureau's static analysis.

TABLE 1   Moving On Up

Income Quintile, 1975	Percent in Each Quintile, 1991				
	1st	2nd	3rd	4th	5th
1st (Lowest)	5.1	14.6	21.0	30.3	29.0
2nd	4.2	23.5	20.3	25.2	26.8
3rd (Middle)	3.3	19.3	28.3	30.1	19.0
4th	1.9	9.3	18.8	32.6	37.4
5th (Highest)	0.9	2.8	10.2	23.6	62.5

Let's begin where others find the most disappointing trends: with the Americans in the bottom 20 percent of income earners in 1975. The inference typically drawn from the Census Bureau data is that these Americans should be worse off in the 1990s. The University of Michigan sample says it just isn't so. Only 5 percent of those in the bottom fifth in 1975 were still there in 1991. Where did they end up? A majority made it to the top three fifths of the income distribution—middle class or better. Most amazing of all, almost 3 out of 10 of the low-income earners from 1975 had risen to the uppermost 20 percent by 1991. More than three-quarters found their way into the two highest tiers of income earners for at least one year by 1991 (see Table 1).

In fact, the poor make the most dramatic gains when one looks at income distribution. Those who started in the bottom 20 percent in 1975 had an inflation-adjusted gain of $27,745 in average income by 1991. Among workers who began in the top fifth, the increase was just $4,354. The rich may have gotten a little richer, but the poor have gotten much richer (see Table 2).

The University of Michigan data suggest that low income is largely a transitory experience for those willing to work, a place Americans may visit but rarely stay. Nearly a quarter of those in the bottom tier in 1975 moved up the next year and never again returned. By contrast, long-term hardship turned out to be rare: Less than 1 percent of the

TABLE 2   The Poor Are Getting Richer Faster

Income Quintile, 1975	Average Income, 1975	Average Income, 1991	Absolute Gain
1st (Lowest)	$1,263	$29,008	$27,745
2nd	$6,893	$31,088	$24,195
3rd (Middle)	$14,277	$24,438	$10,161
4th	$24,568	$34,286	$9,718
5th (Highest)	$50,077	$54,431	$4,354

Figures are in 1997 dollars.

sample remained in the bottom fifth every year from 1975 to 1991. Labor Department data confirm that long-term poverty afflicts only a relatively small number of Americans. In the early 1990s, the median duration of a poverty spell was 4.2 months. Only a third of the nation's 36 million classified as poor by the Census Bureau had been below the poverty line for 24 or more months. With those figures in mind, the long-term poverty rate shrinks to 4 percent, compared to the overall official rate of 13.3 percent in 1997.

Other tiers of income earners in the University of Michigan sample show the same pattern of upward mobility seen in the bottom fifth. Among the second-poorest 20 percent in 1975, more than 70 percent had moved to a higher bracket by 1991, a quarter reaching the top echelon. From the middle group, almost half of the income earners managed to make themselves better off. Even a third of the people from the next-to-highest 20 percent could be found among the top fifth of income earners after 17 years. All through the University of Michigan data, there's a consistent, powerful upward thrust toward the top of the income distribution.

The sample shows, too, that the rise in income can be swift, especially for those with education and skills. More than half of those in the lowest 20 percent in 1975 had reached one of the top three tiers within four years. Two-thirds of these people made that leap within six years, and three-fourths did it in nine years. Not surprisingly, it's the young who move up most quickly. Among respondents 20 to 24 years old in 1975, workers who finished college saw their inflation-adjusted income increase fivefold, to $44,159, in 1991. A typical college graduate with work experience rose from the next-to-lowest bracket to the top one in about a decade. High-school graduates who were in their early twenties in 1975 doubled their average incomes to $30,271 in 17 years. They moved quickly up to the next-to-highest echelon of income earners with a few years of experience, but tended to stay there through 1991. Even high-school dropouts weren't completely shut off from opportunity. Their earnings also rose, although much more slowly than those of any other group, going from $12,741 in 1975 to $20,918 in 1991. They were without question better off, even if they lost ground to their better-educated contemporaries (see Figure 3).

The University of Michigan sample also tells us what happened to those who were in the top tier in 1975. Nearly 66 percent of them could still be found in the top tier in 1991, and 23 percent slipped just one bracket, leaving them in the second fifth of income earners. Less than 1 percent of the richest fifth in 1975 plummeted all the way to the bottom of the income distribution in 17 years. The fate of the well-to-do offers a comforting conclusion: Once households move up the income ladder, they rarely get pushed back down again. Those in the middle groups showed a similar tendency to avoid downward mobility.

FIGURE 3   Income Mobility by Education: Even Dropouts Earn More

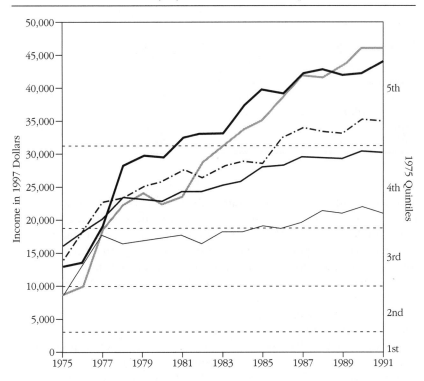

Tracking individuals gives a truer verdict on upward mobility, but it still doesn't provide a perfect measure of changes in living standards. Some progress is still overlooked. In cataloguing how much Americans consume, the argument was that income doesn't march in lock-step with living standards. It's just as true here. From 1975 to 1991, overall income in the United States rose, shifting each fifth of the University of Michigan sample upward in absolute terms. As a result, individuals will be better off even if they fail to make any relative gains. A worker at the midpoint of the bottom 20 percent of income earners today, for example, lives better than someone in a similar spot did almost two decades later.

Using a constant yardstick—living standards prevailing in 1975—we can see that absolute gains are larger than the relative ones (see Table 3).

By 1991, two-thirds of the workers in the bottom fifth were better off than those in the middle tier of 1975. Almost three-fifths of them made it to the top tier for at least one year between 1976 and 1991. Every other income group experienced the same strong upward push, suggesting that the vast majority of those in the sample

TABLE 3   Living Standards on the Rise

Income Quintile 1975	Percent in Each 1975 Quintile, 1991					In 5th 1975 Quintile Sometime in 1976–91
	1st	*2nd*	*3rd*	*4th*	*5th*	
1st (Lowest)	2.3	14.0	17.6	26.9	39.2	57.0
2nd	2.1	19.9	19.9	25.2	32.9	52.6
3rd (Middle)	2.2	15.6	24.1	32.0	26.1	48.2
4th	1.0	6.6	16.0	30.0	46.4	78.6
5th (Highest)	0.3	2.5	7.7	20.1	69.4	98.4

attained comfortable living standards in the 17-year period. Even those who failed to finish high school had achieved a living standard comparable to that of the upper middle in 1975. For all the anguish about downward mobility and long-term poverty, the University of Michigan sample shows it's a reality for only a tiny fraction of Americans. A mere 2 percent of the bottom fifth failed to attain higher living standards by the early 1990s.

The Treasury Department, using a similar income-tracking analysis, affirms that most Americans still have a good shot at upward mobility. In a 1992 analysis covering nine years, researchers found that 86 percent of those in the lowest 20 percent of income earners in 1979 had moved to a higher grouping by 1988. Moreover, 66 percent reached the middle tier or above, with almost 15 percent making it all the way to the top fifth of income earners. Among Americans who started out above the bottom fifth in 1979, the Treasury found the same movement up the income ladder. Nearly 50 percent of those in the middle tier, for example, rose into the top two groupings, overwhelming whatever downward mobility that took place (see Figure 4).

The Treasury study used a database of income-tax returns from 14,351 households. The sample is entirely different from the University of Michigan's, so there's no chance the Treasury is merely rehashing the same statistics. The study using the University of Michigan data shows more upward mobility, probably because it examines a period twice as long.

In addition to confirming that most Americans are still getting ahead in life, the Treasury study verifies that the quickest rise occurs among the young, an antidote to the prevailing ennui among the so-called Generation X. It also found that wage and salary income was primarily responsible for pushing people upward in the distribution, indicating that work, not luck, is the widest path to opportunity. Ours is not a "Wheel of Fortune" economy, where a few

FIGURE 4   A Second Opinion from the Treasury

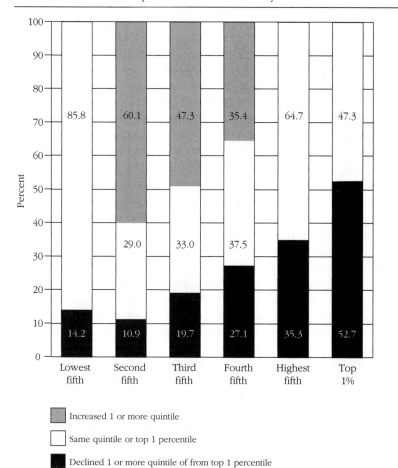

Increased 1 or more quintile

Same quintile or top 1 percentile

Declined 1 or more quintile of from top 1 percentile

lucky individuals win big, leaving paltry gains to the great mass of people. Most of us get ahead because we strive to make ourselves and our families better off.

By carefully tracking individuals' incomes over many years, both the University of Michigan data and the Treasury study show that our economic system is biased toward success. These results should go a long way toward quelling fears of an America polarized between privileged rich and permanently poor. The rich may indeed be getting richer. We ought to have little problem with that. The poor are also getting richer. We ought to celebrate that. Indeed, what's so encouraging is the ability of those who start out in the lowest income brackets to jump into the middle and upper echelons. There's evidence that most Americans are making their way up the income distribution through education, experience, and hard work.

That's what the American Dream, a dream of opportunity, is all about.

Minorities, Women Doing Better

It's a dream that's open to all segments of society. Even if society as a whole isn't going downhill, there's still worry about whether one group or another has missed the prosperity of the mainstream. We've already seen that the poor, while still very much with us, are better off than they used to be, and that bottom-rung households typically consume more in the 1990s than the middle class did a quarter century ago. The remaining concerns center on minorities and women: Are they sharing in the country's upward thrust of living standards and incomes? That's not the same as asking whether they've attained full economic equality. Without a doubt, most minorities and women aren't doing as well as the white-male norm, partly because of such socioeconomic factors as education and job tenure, partly because of discrimination. We can, however, assert that an otherwise healthy economy is working if most minorities and women are making consistent progress toward equality.

The answer, once again, isn't in rhetoric or anecdote but in facts and figures. African-Americans clearly made strides over the past generation. On average, they still earn less than whites, but the gap is shrinking. Among black male, full-time workers with year-round jobs, the average income rose to 72 percent of whites' average income in 1996, compared with 65 percent in 1973. Black women's average income moved from 46 percent of white men's in 1973 to 59 percent in 1996. The disparity in average income between black and white women went from 15.4 percent to 13 percent. After adjusting for inflation, the proportion of African-American families earning more than $75,000 has tripled since 1970, to 9 percent. In 1998 the poverty rate for African-Americans fell to 26.5 percent, the lowest since the government began collecting data on blacks' poverty in 1959.

Minority businesses often face greater hurdles in raising capital, finding skilled labor, and developing markets, but African-American entrepreneurial activity is still flourishing. The census of U.S. businesses, taken every five years, found that the number of black-owned businesses stood at 620,912 in 1992, up 46.4 percent from the previous reading and a whopping 281 percent since 1967. From 1987 to 1992, total sales increased 63 percent to an inflation-adjusted $36 billion. In 1976, they were just $4.5 billion. Most minority enterprises are small, but at least 17 African-American-owned companies have revenues of

$100 million or more, topped by TLC Beatrice International Holding's $2.2 billion.

Blacks' college enrollment rose from 1.1 million in 1975 to 1.8 million in 1995. As a result, African-Americans raised their representation between 1983 to 1996 in many high-paying professions, such as financial managers, personnel executives, accountants and auditors, psychologists, and editors and reporters. What's more, minorities are no longer bearing the brunt of hard times. In 1982, the layoff rate was 45 percent greater for blacks than for whites. By 1993, the rate for blacks was the same as that for whites. Minorities actually gained jobs during the 1990–91 recession, whereas in the recessions between 1950 and 1975, minorities suffered job loss at a rate nearly double that of whites.

For Hispanics, economic fortunes have been somewhat mixed. On the positive side, the number of Hispanic-owned businesses rose from 100,000 in 1967 to 422,373 in 1987 and 862,605 in 1992. Sales soared 150 percent, to $86 billion, eclipsing the gains made by African-Americans. The gain since 1967 was a staggering 506 percent. College enrollment among Hispanics jumped from 411,000 in 1975 to 1.2 million in 1995, allowing Hispanics to take a larger share of the good jobs in white-collar occupations. Hispanics' incomes show signs of slipping back, however. Although many families are making their way up the income ladder, the group's overall income hasn't kept pace with that of whites and African-Americans. Hispanics' median weekly earnings fell from 75 percent of whites' in 1986 to 67 percent in 1996. One possible reason: Continuing immigration brings in new waves of low-skilled, low-paid workers, overwhelming the statistical gains of longer-term resident Hispanics who are improving their education and skills.

For women, the past quarter century has brought progress by almost any measure. For starters, women are a growing presence in the business world. They are starting their own companies at twice the rate of men. In the 1990s, women owned 7.7 million businesses in the United States, up from fewer than 402,000 in the early 1970s. The portion of all U.S. companies owned by women rose from 4.6 percent in 1972 to 33.2 percent in 1992. At major corporations, women now hold 10 percent of the top management positions—a figure that represents steady gains but still disappoints women's groups. In the future, more women will no doubt get prestigious titles because the pipeline is filling with candidates: The number of female vice presidents doubled in the past decade and the number of senior vice presidents rose 75 percent. About 40 percent of business travelers are women, up from 1 percent in 1970, another indication that women are taking on more responsibilities in the workplace. Women aren't just taking on the burdens of executive life. They're also reaping the material rewards of success: One-third of today's Porsche buyers are women, up from just 3 percent just a few years ago.

Women are moving into higher-paying, traditionally male jobs. They've had their strongest employment gains among the ranks of managers and professionals. Overall, women make up about 46 percent of the labor force, but hold half of the jobs as managers and professionals. Among financial managers, 50 percent are women, up from 24 percent in 1975. Women fill 45 percent of the ranks of professors, an increase from 31 percent in 1975. Women computer analysts rose from 15 percent to 30 percent of the profession in two decades. A quarter of America's lawyers are women, compared with just 7 percent in 1975. The percentage of police officers and detectives who are women increased from 3 percent in 1975 to 14 percent today.

Education has played a key role in women's economic gains. In 1970, 55 percent of college freshmen were men and 45 percent were women. Today, the ratio is just the opposite. In 1970, only 13 percent of Ph.D.s went to women. Now, the figure is up to 40 percent. In the past quarter century, women's representation among law school graduates jumped from 5 percent to 45 percent. Degrees in dentistry climbed from 2 percent to 40 percent. Medical degrees increased from 8 percent to 38 percent. What's more, women are quickly adopting cutting-edge technologies that enhance employment prospects. They accounted for only 20 percent of Americans on-line in as recently as 1994. By 1998, two out of five Web surfers were women.

With their success in business, the workplace, and academia, women are shrinking the earnings gap between themselves and men. Among full-time wage and salary workers, women on average now earn 75 percent of what men do, up from 62 percent in 1970. The pay gap gets smaller for more recent entrants into the labor force, suggesting it will continue to narrow. Among women aged 20 to 24, pay is almost 92 percent of men's. It's 86 percent for women aged 25 to 29. By contrast, working women over age 50 earn less than 70 percent of what men do. Each year, more women move past their mates in earning power. Among married couples, 28 percent of working wives brought home a bigger paycheck than their husbands in 1995, up from 24 percent just eight years ago.

One piece of data suggests how much more even the economy is becoming: Among workers between the ages of 27 and 33 who have never had children, the wage gap between the sexes all but disappears, with women earning 98 percent of men's wages. As women march out of colleges, graduate schools, and professional programs with newly minted diplomas, it only seems right that, other things being equal, they earn just about what men do.

Variations in pay involve a hodgepodge of variables, not just gender but occupation, age, work experience, education, lifestyle choices, union membership, and motivation. Even expectations vary: A mid-1990s survey by the consulting firm Korn/Ferry found that 14 percent of women aspired to be their company's chief executive officer, compared with 46 percent of men. The differences help explain why minorities and women still earn less. Black and Hispanic workers, for example, have fewer years of schooling, a crucial factor in pay. Many women take time away from work for childbearing and family responsibilities, so they average fewer years in the labor force. For women who leave the workforce, the median amount of time before returning is 4.5 years. As a result, a typical 40-year-old woman may find herself five years behind her male contemporaries in seniority. Motherhood even influences what jobs women take. Some women, knowing that they might interrupt their careers, choose occupations where hours are flexible and skills deteriorate at a slower rate. These jobs are often lower-paying. Women are more likely to work at home, an option that usually doesn't enhance career advancement. Four-fifths of work-at-home women are married and three-fourths have children. According to the Department of Labor, these women put in fewer hours and earn approximately 25 percent less than their on-site counterparts. The choice of working at home apparently involves a significant financial sacrifice, but the flexibility it affords makes it worthwhile for many families.

Differences in social and family situations can lead to economic disparities. Over the years, dozens of statistical studies have attempted to account for inequality in wages and income, looking at such factors as education, experience, and occupation. Wage gaps for minorities and women shrink, but they don't completely disappear. Adjusting for differences in education, for example, brings African-Americans to within 80 percent or 90 percent of whites' incomes. The unexplained 10 percent to 20 percent isn't necessarily a result of discrimination. There might be additional factors that researchers haven't taken into account. By the same token, equal wages wouldn't rule out the presence of discrimination: A group might be considered underpaid if its members get a substandard return on years of schooling or work experience. Wage differences don't equate with racial or sexual discrimination.

Will minorities and women ever catch up to white men? Not as long as work experience, occupational choice, and other factors contributing to earnings gaps remain. The elusiveness of full equality shouldn't blind us to the fact that the U.S. economic system has opened itself to minorities and women in the past quarter century, allowing them to make significant improvements in their status. Overall, minorities and women may continue to lag behind white men because of education, experience, and other socioeconomic reasons. Even so, it doesn't mean minorities and women don't have opportunity for upward mobility. In the age of equal-employment laws, affirmative action, and general disapproval of racist and sexist attitudes, job discrimination based on sex or ethnicity isn't the barrier it once was. For minorities and women, the path to success will lie in the virtues a thriving economy rewards on a consistent basis—education, experience, work effort. . . .

In the United States, getting ahead isn't a great mystery. The economy provides opportunity—more, in fact, than ever before—but it's up to each of us to grab it. Success isn't random. Luck and Daddy's money aren't the way most Americans get to the top. More often than not, the rewards go to education, experience, talent, ambition, vision, risk taking, readiness to change, and just plain hard work. Young people aren't guaranteed success any more than their parents were. Their chances will improve, though, if they make the right choices in life. Opportunity lies in the advice given by generations of parents and teachers: Study, work hard, and save. In short, the best advice for economic success is this: Listen to your elders. . . .

INEQUALITY IS NOT INEQUITY

Judging from the public debate, at least some Americans would prefer a more equal distribution of income to a less equal one, perhaps on moral grounds, perhaps as a part of an ideal of civic virtue. There's no *economic* reason, however, to prefer one pattern of income distribution over another. In fact, the income statistics do little but confirm what's obvious: America isn't an egalitarian society. It wasn't designed to be. Socialism, a failed and receding system, sought to impose an artificial equality. Capitalism, a successful and expanding system, doesn't fight a fundamental fact of human nature—we vary greatly in capabilities, motivation, interests, and preferences. Some of us are driven to get ahead. Some of us are just plain lazy. Some of us are willing to work hard so we can afford a lifestyle rich in material goods. Some of us work just hard enough to provide a roof overhead, food, clothes, and a few amenities. It shouldn't come as a surprise that our incomes vary greatly.

Income inequality isn't an aberration. Quite the opposite, it's perfectly consistent with the laws that govern a free-enterprise system. In the early 1970s, three groups of unemployed Canadians, all in their twenties, all with at least 12 years of schooling, volunteered to participate in a stylized economy where the only employment was making woolen belts on small hand looms. They could work as much or as little as they liked, earning $2.50 for each belt. After 98 days, the results were anything but equal: 37.2 percent of the economy's income went to the 20 percent with the highest earnings. The bottom 20 percent received only 6.6 percent. This economic microcosm tells us one thing: Even among similar people with identical work options, some workers will earn more than others.

In a modern economy, incomes vary for plenty of reasons having little to do with fairness or equity. Education and experience, for example, usually yield higher pay. As industry becomes more sophisticated, the rewards to skilled labor tend to rise, adding to the number of high-income earners. Location matters. New Yorkers earn more than Mississippians. Lifestyle choices play a part, too. Simply by having an additional paycheck, two-income families make more money than those with a single breadwinner. Longer retirements, however, will add to the number of households with low income, even if many senior citizens live well from their savings. Demographic changes can twist the distribution of income. As the Baby Boom enters its peak earning years, the number of high-income households ought to rise. Economic forces create ripples in what we earn. The ebb and flow of industries can shift workers to both ends of the income distribution. Layoffs put some Americans into low-income groups, at least temporarily. Companies with new products and new technologies create jobs and, in most cases, share the bounty by offering workers higher pay. In technology industries, bonuses and stock options are becoming more common. Higher rates of return on investments—with, for example, a stock-market boom—will create a windfall for households with money riding on financial markets.

In and of itself, moreover, income distribution doesn't say much about the performance of an economy or the opportunities it offers. A widening gap isn't necessarily a sign of failure, nor does a narrowing one guarantee that an economy is functioning well. As a matter of fact, it's quite common to find a widening of income distribution in boom times, when almost everyone's earnings are rising rapidly. All it takes is for one segment of the workforce to become better off faster than others. However, the distribution can narrow in hard times, as companies facing declining demand cut back on jobs, hours, raises, and bonuses. In fact, we often see a compression of incomes in areas where people are sinking into poverty.

There's no denying that our system allows some Americans to become much richer than others. We must accept that, even celebrate it. Opportunity, not equality of income, is what made the U.S. economy grow and prosper. It's most important to provide equality of opportunity, not equality of results. There's ample evidence to refute any suggestion that the economy is no longer capable of providing opportunity for the vast majority of Americans. At the end of the twentieth century, upward mobility is alive and well. Even the lower-income households are sharing in the country's progress. What's more, data suggest that the populist view of America as a society torn between haves and have-nots, with rigid class lines, is just plain wrong. We are by no means a caste society.

ANALYSIS
---

1. How do Alm and Cox summarize their opponents' arguments? How does providing this summary help convince the reader of Alm and Cox's fairness?

2. Why, according to Alm and Cox, do "the pessimists have it wrong" about wealth and poverty? What does it mean to be a pessimist in this sense?

3. "Opportunity," Alm and Cox argue, "is individual rather than collective." What do they mean by this? As an *assumption,* could you offer the contrary view: that opportunity is collective rather than individual (as in Hillary Clinton's much-debated suggestion that "it takes a village to raise a child")?

4. Why do Alm and Cox reject Census Bureau figures for income? Why do they prefer the Michigan Panel Studies in Income Dynamics (PSID)? What in fact do the PSID figures reveal about low-income experience?

5. How do Alm and Cox use Treasury Department figures about individual tax returns to further support their claims?

6. What evidence do Alm and Cox offer to support the view that minorities and women are also moving up?

WRITING POSSIBILITIES
---

1. Quite apart from their economic arguments, Alm and Cox adopt an informal and ingratiating tone that enables even economic illiterates to get something out of their analyses. How, for example, do the opening paragraphs establish this free and easy approach to potentially difficult issues? Does the tone here, for that matter, make it easy for you to understand what they're saying or do you still find yourself puzzled? Explain your understanding by pointing to particulars in the essay that either please or trouble you.

2. Any one economic argument—like any technical discussion in any field—is hard for laypeople to evaluate; but one way that even laymen can tackle such a problem is by simple comparison and contrast with other, opposed, viewpoints. Thus if you compare and contrast Alm and Cox's basic assertion that America is indeed a land of opportunity (measured eventually by increasing income levels in almost all classes) with the contrary assertions of Gregory Mantsios or William Julius Wilson, you might, even as a layperson, be able to decide some of the pros and cons about that basic assertion. So look at either the Mantsios or Wilson essay, both of which argue that opportunity (through education, especially) is limited either by income, to begin with (Mantsios), and/or by economic forces beyond the control of the individual (Wilson). Summarize in your own words the analyses of Alm and Cox, on the one hand, and of either Mantsios or Wilson on the other, and then explain why you think one or the other writer(s) offer the better case for their position.

Michael M. Weinstein

Perhaps the most important criticism of Alm and Cox (previous selection) lies in Weinstein's op-ed piece. He says, for example, that the idea that the formerly poor rising up several notches doesn't make much sense if those "poor" are the children of rich parents working initially at part-time jobs but then in adulthood going on to at least five-figure incomes. Cox and Alm defend themselves on this point by arguing as follows: "Yes, a lot of the poor are students but they get counted as poor just like everyone else." This would be a useful issue in considering the pros and cons of the rich-poor argument and its statistical backup.

AMERICA'S RAGS-TO-RICHES MYTH

Income Mobility Fails to Soften the Blow of Growing Inequality

Americans cling to the conceit that they have unrivaled opportunity to move up and, alas, down the income ladder. This notion, that families that occupy the bottom rungs of the income ladder readily exchange places with those that occupy higher rungs, breeds indifference to the most glaring economic fact of the past quarter-century: widening inequality. The gap in earnings, for example, between college and high school graduates more than doubled.

Yet in a recent Op-Ed piece in *The New York Times,* W. Michael Cox and Richard Alm acknowledge that the wealth of poor families has been falling at the same time that the wealth of rich families has been rising, and ask, "So what?"

Mr. Cox and Mr. Alm suggest that mobility along the income ladder is serving as an antidote to inequality. But exactly how much mobility is there? According to them, quite a lot. "America isn't a caste society," they say, citing a study by the Federal Reserve that shows that only 5 percent of the poorest 20 percent of people stayed in that lowest income group over a 17-year period. Everyone else moved higher.

But this stunning statistic is stunningly misleading. Prof. Peter Gottschalk of Boston College points out that the Fed study counts teenagers and young adults from upper-income families who work part time while in school as moving upward when they find higher-paying jobs after graduation. This upward mobility of students hardly answers the enduring question: How many grown-ups are trapped in low-paying jobs?

The answer is, a lot. America's conceit is just that—a conceit.

Mr. Gottschalk and Prof. Sheldon Danziger of the University of Michigan have looked at the plight of children during the 1970's and 80's. They separate children into five groups according to their family's income. About 6 in 10 of the children in the lowest group—the poorest 20 percent—in the early 1970's were still in the bottom income group 10 years later. Almost 9 in 10 children in the bottom group remained in the bottom two income groups 10 years later. Neither of these figures budged in the 1980's, providing solid evidence that mobility did not rise over the 20-year period. About 70 percent of poor black children in the early 1970's were still poor a decade later.

The upshot is that few families occupying the low rungs of America's income ladder get rich.

Economists provide no rule for figuring out how much mobility a society needs to counter the impact of any given amount of inequality. But there is indirect evidence that mobility is not high enough in this country to provide an adequate safety valve for those on the bottom rungs. Even if mobility was high enough 30 years ago to justify a so-what attitude toward inequality, it seems improbable that it could be high enough today, given that mobility has remained constant but inequality has reached extreme levels. Another sobering indicator: mobility is no higher in the United States than in Western Europe, where living standards are comparable and there is only a fraction as much inequality.

Some inequality is essential for capitalism. High incomes are the reward for studying long hours, working hard and investing in risky businesses. But high incomes can result for reasons that have little to do with merit, reflecting rich parents, luck or manipulation of the political process. Inequality driven by such factors can breed social division, anger and a politics of resentment. It also belies the notion that America gives everyone a fair chance.

Economists are in general reluctant to tamper with market-driven incomes. The risk of squashing incentives and innovation can be great. But there is a compelling case for eradicating one virulent form of inequality: poverty. The richest country in the history of the universe tolerates a poverty rate of about 20 percent among its children, and about 35 percent among its black children. No conceit about mobility, real or imagined, can excuse that unconscionable fact.

ANALYSIS

1. What is the essential criticism that Weinstein makes of Alm and Cox's thesis about everyone in America rising above their initial social class?

———— WRITING POSSIBILITIES ————

1. In *Insight on the News* (March 8, 1999), available via the Web on *Infotrac,* Eli Lehrer praises Cox and Alm's thesis but does offer brief critical comments from other writers: "Yes, it is true that the poor people probably have more today than they did in 1970," says Thomas Geoghegan, "But it was easier to be poor in the past . . . you had vastly . . . more poor people in 1938 but they lived in places where you could walk anywhere and there were support networks for them that just don't exist today." "Sure people have more things and sure per-capita incomes have gone up for the rich but, on balance, people have more things because you need to have more things. You can't get to a job without a car and you probably can't get a job if you don't have a telephone. . . ."

2. Mark Weisbrot, the director of research at the left-leaning Preamble Center in Washington, makes an even harsher assessment. "Sure we have things like CD players and microwaves that we didn't have 20 or 30 years ago, but that doesn't mask the fact that living standards have declined for the great majority of the American workforce. Thirty years ago, a family could survive on the median income, today they can't."

3. Look up the whole review on the Web, use Weinstein's critique of Alm and Cox, and/or use the pro and con quotations immediately above to fashion your own observations about whether (as Lehrer puts it) the "good times are rolling" for everyone or only for selected groups. The chief issues to consider are the standard of living argument (today's poor live like yesterday's kings; no, it takes more goods to be poor now than it did in the past), the college student argument (the so-called poor who are moving up the income ladder are just college students—not ordinary poor people; no they get counted as poor like everyone else), the needs argument (you need more to survive now than in the past; no, you don't really need much beyond food, clothing, and shelter); and the income mobility argument (everyone is moving up; not only college students are moving up).

4. At your library find Mishel and Bernstein's *State of Working America 1998–1999.* Using the same criterion of tracking individuals as Alm and Cox, but with different results, Mishel and Bernstein don't see movement up the mobility ladder: "large transitions" in income over a period of time "are uncommon," they say: "41.0 percent of persons in the bottom fifth in 1969 were also in the bottom fifth in 1994" they note as well. The percent of people staying in the same fifth in each pair of years (1968–1969 and 1990–1991) is pretty constant, hovering between the low of almost 63 percent to a high of about 66 percent (the lower percentage = greater income mobility, and vice versa). Is there much room for hope here? Examine Mishel and Bernstein's argument carefully and explain whose statistics and arguments most persuade you of the case for or against the Alm and Cox thesis that most people are indeed fulfilling the American Dream by moving up on the mobility ladder.

William Julius Wilson

For a black sociologist (now Malcolm Wiener Professor of Social Policy at Harvard University), Wilson may be seen as taking an unusual tack in this article. He says there is crime and violence in the urban ghetto and there's no use putting one's head in the sand about it. But in contrast to conservative writers (e.g., Clarence Thomas, pages 358–367) who would argue that such effects stem from such causes as lack of individual responsibility or family values, Wilson insists that we've got to look at such beyond-the-individual factors as technological change, global competition (for example the disappearance of the thousands of jobs in the once formidable U.S. steel industry), and the flight of the black middle class to the suburbs (ironically as a result of the civil rights struggle). Ultimately, Wilson says, any solution to the plight of the disadvantaged will require some form of government aid and intervention.

Wilson's views have been criticized by Joe Klein (The New Republic, October 26, 1996) for ignoring the role of values in inner-city decay: "His own empirical work," Klein writes, "shows that these poor people are different, sadly, from you and me. They are isolated from us; they have different values. And it seems very clear that their problems were neither entirely caused by the loss of work, nor will they be entirely solved by government action."

WHEN WORK DISAPPEARS

The disappearance of work in the ghetto cannot be ignored, isolated or played down. Employment in America is up. The economy has churned out tens of millions of new jobs in the last two decades. In that same period, joblessness among inner-city blacks has reached catastrophic proportions. Yet in this Presidential election year, the disappearance of work in the ghetto is not on either the Democratic or the Republican agenda. There is harsh talk about work instead of welfare but no talk of where to find it.

The current employment woes in the inner city continue to be narrowly defined in terms of race or lack of individual initiative. It is argued that jobs are widely available, that the extent of inner-city poverty is exaggerated. Optimistic policy analysts—and many African-Americans—would prefer that more attention to devoted to the successes and struggles of the black working class and the expanding black middle class. This is understandable. These two groups, many of whom have recently escaped from the ghetto, represent a majority of the African-American population. But ghetto joblessness still afflicts a substantial—and increasing—minority: it's a problem that won't go away on its own. If it is not addressed, it will have lasting and harmful consequences for the quality of life in the cities and, eventually, for the lives of all Americans. Solutions will have to be found—and those solutions are at hand.

For the first time in the 20th century, a significant majority of adults in many inner-city neighborhoods are not working in a typical week. Inner cities have always featured high levels of poverty, but the current levels of joblessness in some neighborhoods are unprecedented, for example, in the famous black-belt neighborhood of Washington Park on Chicago's South Side, a majority of adults had jobs in 1950; by 1990, only 1 in 3 worked in a typical week. High neighborhood joblessness has a far more devastating effect than high neighborhood poverty. A neighborhood in which people are poor but employed is different from a neighborhood in which people are poor and jobless. Many of today's problems in the inner-city neighborhoods—crime, family dissolution, welfare—are fundamentally a consequence of the disappearance of work.

What causes the disappearance of work? There are several factors, including changes in the distribution and location of jobs, and in the level of training and education required to obtain employment. Nor should we overlook the legacy of historic racial segregation. However, the public debate around this question is not productive because it seeks to assign blame rather than recognizing and dealing with the complex realities that have led to economic distress for many Americans. Explanations and proposed solutions to the problem are often ideologically driven.

Conservatives tend to stress the importance of values, attitudes, habits and styles. In this view, group differences are reflected in the culture. The truth is, cultural factors do play a role; but other, more important variables also have to be taken into account. Although race is clearly a significant variable in the social outcomes of inner-city blacks, it's not the *only* factor. The emphasis on racial differences has obscured the fact that African-Americans, whites and other ethnic groups have many common values, aspirations and hopes.

An elderly woman who has lived in one inner-city neighborhood on the South Side of Chicago for more than 40 years reflects: "I've been here since March 11, 1953. When I moved in, the neighborhood was intact. It was intact with homes, beautiful homes, mini-mansions, with stores, Laundromats, with Chinese cleaners. We had drugstores. We had hotels. We had doctors over on 39th Street. We had doctors' offices in the neighborhood. We had the middle class and upper middle class. It has gone from affluent to where it is today. And I would like to see it come back, that we can have some of the things we had. Since I came in young, and I'm a senior citizen now, I would like to see some of the things come back so I can enjoy them like we did when we first came in."

In the neighborhood of Woodlawn, on the South Side of Chicago, there were more than 800 commercial and industrial establishments in 1950. Today, it is estimated that only about 100 are left. In the words of Loïc Wacquant, a member of one of the research teams that worked with me over the last eight years: "The once-lively streets—residents remember a time, not so long ago, when crowds were so dense at rush hour that one had to elbow one's way to the train station—now have the appearance of an empty, bombed-out war zone. The commercial strip has been reduced to a long tunnel of charred stores, vacant lots littered with broken glass and garbage, and dilapidated buildings left to rot in the shadow of the elevated train line. At the corner of 63d Street and Cottage Grove Avenue, the handful of remaining establishments that struggle to survive are huddled behind wrought-iron bars. . . . The only enterprises that seem to be thriving are liquor stores and currency exchanges, those 'banks of the poor' where one can cash checks, pay bills and buy money orders for a fee."

The state of the inner-city public schools was another major concern expressed by our urban-poverty study respondents. The complaints ranged from overcrowded conditions to unqualified and uncaring teachers. Sharply voicing her views on these subjects, a 25-year-old married mother of two children from a South Side census tract that just recently became poor stated: "My daughter ain't going to school here. She was going to a nursery school where I paid and of course they took the time and spent it with her, because they was getting the money. But the pubic schools, no! They are overcrowded and the teachers don't care."

A resident of Woodlawn who had left the neighborhood as a child described how she felt upon her return about the changes that had occurred: "I was really appalled. When I walked down 63d Street when I was younger, everything you wanted was there. But now, coming back as an adult with my child, those resources are just gone, completely. . . . And housing, everybody has moved, there are vacant lots everywhere."

Neighborhoods plagued by high levels of joblessness are more likely to experience low levels of social organization: the two go hand in hand. High rates of joblessness trigger other neighborhood problems that undermine social organization, ranging from crime, gang violence and drug trafficking to family breakups. And as these controls weaken, the social processes that regulate behavior change.

Industrial restructuring has further accelerated the deterioration of many inner-city neighborhoods. Consider the fate of the West Side black community of North Lawndale in Chicago: since 1960, nearly half of its housing stock has disappeared; the remaining units are mostly run-down or dilapidated. Two large factories anchored the economy of this neighborhood in its good days—the Hawthorne plant of Western Electric, which employed more than 43,000 workers, and an International Harvester plant with 14,000 workers. But conditions rapidly changed. Harvester closed its doors in the late 1960's. Sears moved most of its offices to the Loop in downtown Chicago in 1973. The Hawthorne plant gradually phased out its operations and finally shut down in 1984.

"Jobs were plentiful in the past," attested a 29-year-old unemployed black man who lives in one of the poorest neighborhoods on the South Side. "You could walk out of the house and get a job. Maybe not what you want, but you could get a job. Now, you can't find anything. A lot of people in this neighborhood, they want to work but they can't get work. A few, but a very few, they just don't want to work."

The more rapid the neighborhood deterioration, the greater the institutional disinvestment. In the 1960's and 1970's, neighborhoods plagued by heavy abandonment were frequently redlined (identified as areas that should not receive or be recommended for mortgage loans or insurance); this paralyzed the housing market, lowered property values and encouraged landlord abandonment.

As the neighborhood disintegrates, those who are able to leave depart in increasing numbers; among these are many working- and middle-class families. The lower population density in turn creates additional problems. Abandoned buildings increase and often serve as havens for crack use and other illegal enterprises that give criminals—mostly young blacks who are unemployed—footholds in the community. Precipitous declines in density also make it even more difficult to sustain or develop a sense of community. The feeling of safety in numbers is completely lacking in such neighborhoods.

Problems in the new poverty or high-jobless neighborhoods have also created racial antagonism among some of the high-income groups in the city. The high joblessness in ghetto neighborhoods has sapped the vitality of local businesses and other institutions and has led to fewer and shabbier movie theaters, bowling alleys, restaurants, public parks and playgrounds and other recreational facilities. When residents of inner-city neighborhoods venture out to other areas of the city in search of entertainment, they come into brief contact with citizens of markedly different racial or class backgrounds. Sharp differences in cultural style often lead to clashes.

Some behavior on the part of residents from socially isolated ghetto neighborhoods—for instance, the tendency to enjoy a movie in a communal spirit by carrying on a running conversation with friends and relatives or reacting in an unrestrained manner to what they see on the screen—is considered offensive by other groups, particularly black and white members of the middle class. Expressions of disapproval, either overt or with subtle hostile glances, tend to trigger belligerent responses from the ghetto residents, who then purposely intensify the behavior that is the source of irritation. The white and even the black middle-class moviegoers then exercise their option and exit, expressing resentment and experiencing intensified feelings of racial or class antagonism as they depart.

The areas surrendered in such a manner become the domain of the inner-city residents. Upscale businesses are replaced by fast-food chains and other local businesses that cater to the new clientele. White and black middle-class citizens complain bitterly about how certain areas of the central city have changed—and thus become "off-limits"— following the influx of ghetto residents.

The negative consequences are clear: where jobs are scarce, many people eventually lose their feeling of connectedness to work in the formal economy; they no longer expect work to be a regular, and regulating, force in their lives. In the case of young people, they may grow up in an environment that lacks the idea of work as a central experience of adult life—they have little or no labor-force attachment. These circumstances also increase the likelihood that the residents will rely on illegitimate sources of income, thereby further weakening their attachment to the legitimate labor market.

A 25-year-old West Side father of two who works two jobs to make ends meet condemned the attitude toward work of some inner-city black males:

"They try to find easier routes and had been conditioned over a period of time to just be lazy, so to speak. Motivation nonexistent, you know, and the society that they're affiliated with really don't advocate hard work and struggle to meet your goals such as education and stuff like that. And they see who's around them and they follow that same pattern, you know. . . . They don't see nobody getting up early in the morning, going to work or going to school all the time. The guys they be with don't do that . . . because that's the crowd that you choose— well, that's been presented to you by your neighborhood."

Work is not simply a way to make a living and support one's family. It also constitutes a framework for daily behavior because it imposes discipline. Regular employment determines where you are going to be and when you are going to be there. In the absence of regular employment, life, including family life, becomes less coherent. Persistent unemployment and irregular employment hinder rational planning in daily life, the necessary condition of adaptation to an industrial economy.

It's a myth that people who don't work don't want to work. One mother in a new poverty neighborhood on the South Side explained her decision to remain on welfare even though she would like to get a job: "I was working and then I had two kids. And I'm struggling. I was making, like, close to $7 an hour. . . . I had to pay a baby-sitter. Then I had to deal with my kids when I got home. And I couldn't even afford medical insurance. . . . I was so scared, when my kids were sick or something, because I have been turned away from a hospital because I did not have a medical card. I don't like being on public aid and stuff right now. But what do I do with my kids when the kids get sick?"

Working mothers with comparable incomes face, in many cases, even greater difficulty. Why? Simply because many low-wage jobs do not provide health-care benefits, and most working mothers have to pay for transportation and spend more for child care. Working mothers also have to spend more for housing because it is more difficult for them to qualify for housing subsidies. It is not surprising, therefore, that many welfare-reliant mothers choose not to enter the formal labor market. It would not be in their best economic interest to do so. Given the economic realities, it is also not surprising that many who are working in these low-wage jobs decide to rely on or return to welfare, even though it's not a desirable alternative for many of the black single mothers. As one 27-year-old welfare mother of three children from an impoverished West Side neighborhood put it: "I want to work. I do not work but I want to work. I don't want to just be on public aid."

As the disappearance of work has become a characteristic feature of the inner-city ghetto, so too has the disappearance of the traditional married-couple family. Only one-quarter of the black families whose children live with them in inner-city neighborhoods in Chicago are husband-wife families today, compared with three-quarters of the inner-city Mexican families, more than one-half of the white families and nearly one-half of the Puerto Rican families. And in census tracts with poverty rates of at least 40 percent, only 16.5 percent of the black families with children in the household are husband-wife families.

There are many factors involved in the precipitous decline in marriage rates and the sharp rise in single-parent families. The explanation most often heard in the public debate associates the increase of out-of-wedlock births and single-parent families with welfare. Indeed, it is widely assumed among the general public and reflected in the recent welfare reform that a direct connection exists between the level of welfare benefits and the likelihood that a young woman will bear a child outside marriage.

However, there is little evidence to support the claim that Aid to Families With Dependent Children plays a significant role in promoting out-of-wedlock births. Research examining the association between the generosity of welfare benefits and out-of-wedlock childbearing and teen-age pregnancy indicates that benefit levels have no significant effect on the likelihood that African-American girls and women will have children outside marriage. Likewise, welfare rates have either no significant effect or only a small effect on the odds that whites will have children outside marriage. The rate of out-of-wedlock teen-age child-bearing has nearly doubled since 1975—during years when the value of A.F.D.C., food stamps and Medicaid fell, after adjusting for inflation. And the smallest increases in the number of out-of-wedlock births have not occurred in states that have had the largest declines in the inflation-adjusted value of A.F.D.C. benefits. Indeed, while the real value of cash welfare benefits has plummeted over the past 20 years, out-of-wedlock childbearing has increased, and postpartum marriages (marriages following the birth of a couple's child) have decreased as well.

It's instructive to consider the social differences between inner-city blacks and other groups, especially Mexicans. Mexicans come to the United States with a clear conception of a traditional family unit that features men as breadwinners. Although extramarital affairs by men are tolerated, unmarried pregnant women are "a source of opprobrium, anguish or great concern," as Richard P. Taub, a member of one of our research teams, put it. Pressure is applied by the kin of both parents to enter into marriage.

The family norms and behavior in inner-city black neighborhoods stand in sharp contrast. The relationships between inner-city black men and women, whether in a marital or nonmarital situation, are often fractious and antagonistic. Inner-city black women routinely say that black men are hopeless as either husbands or fathers and that more of their time is spent on the streets than at home.

The men in the inner city generally feel that it is much better for all parties to remain in a nonmarital relationship until the relationship dissolves rather than to get married and then have to get a divorce. A 25-year-old unmarried West Side resident, the father of one child, expressed this view:

"Well, most black men feel now, why get married when you got six to seven women to one guy, really. You know, because there's more women out here mostly than men. Because most dudes around here are killing each other like fools over drugs or all this other stuff."

The fact that blacks reside in neighborhoods and are engaged in social networks and households that are less conducive to employment than those of other ethnic and racial groups in the inner city clearly has a negative effect on their search for work. In the eyes of employers in metropolitan Chicago, these differences render inner-city blacks less desirable as workers, and therefore many are reluctant to hire them. The white chairman of a car transport company, when asked if there were differences in the work ethic of whites, blacks and Hispanics, responded with great certainty:

"Definitely! I don't think, I know: I've seen it over a period of 30 years. Basically, the Oriental is much more aggressive and intelligent and studious than the Hispanics. The Hispanics, except Cubans of course, they have the work ethic [sic]. The Hispanics are *mañana, mañana, mañana*—tomorrow, tomorrow, tomorrow." As for native-born blacks, they were deemed "the laziest of the bunch."

If some employers view the work ethic of inner-city poor blacks as problematic, many also express concerns about their honesty, cultural attitudes and dependability—traits that are frequently associated with the neighborhoods in which they live. A white suburban retail drug-store manager expressed his reluctance to hire someone from a poor inner-city neighborhood. "You'd be afraid they're going to steal from you," he stated. "They grow up that way. They grow up dishonest and I guess you'd feel like, geez, how are they going to be honest here?"

In addition to qualms about the work ethic, character, family in-fluences, cultural predispositions and the neighborhood milieu of ghetto residents, the employers frequently mentioned concerns about applicants' language skills and educational training. They "just don't have the language skills," stated a suburban employer. The president of an inner-city advertising agency highlighted the problem of spelling:

"I needed a temporary a couple months ago, and they sent me a black man. And I dictated a letter to him. He took shorthand, which was good. Something like 'Dear Mr. So-and-So, I am writing to ask about how your business is doing.' And then he typed the letter, and I read the letter, and it's 'I am writing to ax about your business.' Now you hear about them speaking a different language and all that, and they say 'ax' for 'ask.' Well, I don't care about that, but I didn't say 'ax,' I said 'ask.'"

Many inner-city residents have a strong sense of the negative attitudes that employers tend to have toward them. A 33-year-old employed janitor from a poor South Side neighborhood had this ob-servation: "I went to a couple jobs where a couple of the recep-tionists told me in confidence: 'You know what they do with these applications from blacks as soon as the day is over?' They say, 'We rip them and throw them in the garbage.'" In addition to concerns about being rejected because of race, the fears that some inner-city residents have of being denied employment simply because of their inner-city address or neighborhood are not unfounded. A welfare mother who lives in a large public housing project put it this way:

"Honestly, I believe they look at the address and the—your atti-tudes, your address, your surround—you know, your environment has a lot to do with your employment status. The people with the best addresses have the best chances. I feel so, I feel so." . . .

What can be done? I believe that steps must be taken to galvanize Americans from all walks of life who are concerned about human suffering and the public policy direction in which we are now moving. We need to generate a public-private partnership to fight social inequality. The following policy frameworks provide a basis for further discussion and debate. Given the current political climate, these proposals might be dismissed as unrealistic. Nor am I suggesting that we can or should simply import the social policies of the Japanese, the Germans or other Western Europeans. The question is how we Americans can address the problems of social inequality, including record levels of joblessness in the inner city, that threaten the very fabric of our society. . . . [In the sections following, deleted here, Wilson recommends that local, state and federal governments "Create Standards for Schools," "Improve Child Care," "Establish City-Suburban Partnerships," and "Reintroduce the W.P.A.—" the large public-works program initiated in 1935 by President Franklin D. Roosevelt."]

The long-term solutions that I have advanced would reduce the likelihood that a new generation of jobless workers will be produced from the youngsters now in school and preschool. We must break the cycle of joblessness and improve the youngsters' preparation for the new labor market in the global economy.

My framework for long-term and immediate solutions is based on the notion that the problems of jobless ghettos cannot be separated from those of the rest of the nation. Although these solutions have wide-ranging application and would alleviate the economic distress of many Americans, their impact on jobless ghettos would be profound. Their most important contribution would be their effect on the children of the ghetto, who would be able to anticipate a future of economic mobility and harbor the hopes and aspirations that for so many of their fellow citizens help define the American way of life.

--------------- **ANALYSIS** ---------------

1. Wilson's essay exemplifies two interconnected ways of argumentation—problem solution analysis and cause-effect analysis. The problem (and the effect) is high joblessness in the inner city; the cause, for Wilson, are a trio of economic and social factors—company downsizing, global economics, the civil rights revolution. Towards the end of his essay, Wilson tentatively and briefly offers some solutions to the problem he poses, although his primary interest in this essay is to lay out the problem and its causes.

2. What does Wilson mean when he refers to the inner city? What kinds of people is he talking about—e.g., poor people who are actually working (the "working poor")? People on welfare?

3. What evidence does Wilson offer for high joblessness in the inner city?

4. To what extent does Wilson suggest that "cultural" factors might be a cause of such joblessness? What does he mean by culture in this sense? Why does he tend to dismiss the role of culture?

5. To what extent does Wilson believe that race is a factor in joblessness? How does Wilson deal with the conservative analysis of the disappearance of work?

6. How does Wilson connect industrial restructuring to such matters as schooling, neighborhood problems, and racial antagonism? How does Wilson use details of the Woodlawn area in Chicago to illustrate his argument?

7. Why does Wilson maintain that "it's a myth that people who don't work don't want to work"? What support does he bring to his contention?

8. How does Wilson view the "disappearance of the traditional married-couple family" in comparison to Clarence Thomas (following selection)? How does he refute the argument that welfare dependency is the cause of out-of-wedlock births?

9. Wilson quotes Pete Hamill on the "underclass" and "cycles of welfare dependency." The sociologist Herbert Gans has argued that the term "underclass" stereotypes people and makes it seem that they can't be helped. Wilson disagrees with this analysis, although, like Hamill, he has offered the comparable idea of "cycles of poverty." What do Hamill and Wilson himself mean by this idea of "cycles" of poverty?

WRITING POSSIBILITIES

1. What is the connection Wilson makes between inner-city neighborhoods and the job qualifications employers are looking for? Do you think the employers Wilson quotes are seen by Wilson as prejudiced or not? Develop two versions of an employer's statement to a work-training agency, one in which you lay it on the line and explain that you can't afford to hire employees with poor work habits, the other in which you say that out of a hopeful spirit you will accept some workers who may or may not have proper work habits and that you will train them yourself to ensure their future success. What difficulties did you face in writing both statements?

Clarence Thomas

At the opposite end of the spectrum from William Julius Wilson is Supreme Court Justice Clarence Thomas. Thomas argues that racial discrimination is no excuse for shirking the individual responsibility that actually determines success or failure. In an eloquent speech to the Federalist Society, Thomas argues that we have become addicted to getting help from the "benevolent state" rather than taking on the responsibility for our own actions and our fate. Even if you're a die-hard proponent of affirmative action and welfare as we once knew it, you can't help but be affected by Thomas's personal life-stories, his tone and language, and his ethical insistence on "responsibility." (Thomas' position, in a much less inflammatory way, has been echoed recently by such "multicultural conservatives" as John H. McWhorter in Losing the Race: Self-Sabotage in Black America *(New York, 2000) and Debra J. Dickerson in* An American Dream, *(New York, 2001).)*

VICTIMS AND HEROES IN THE "BENEVOLENT STATE"

I would like to thank my friends here at the Federalist Society for once again inviting me to be a part of an important and timely conference. And I would like to begin by returning to a topic I touched upon in my last speech at a conference cosponsored by this organization: personal responsibility. It says something about the current state of affairs in our society that a conference on victims—that is, a conference on the rise of the practice of blaming circumstances for one's situation rather than taking responsibility for changing things for the better—is even necessary. As many of you have heard me say before, the very notion of submitting to one's circumstances was unthinkable in the household in which I was raised. The mere suggestion that difficult circumstances could prevail over individual effort would evoke a response that my brother and I could lip-sync on cue: "Old man can't is dead; I helped bury him." Or, another favorite response: "Where there is a will, there is a way." Under this philosophy—the essential truth of which we all recognize in our hearts—victims have no refuge.

It may have seemed harsh at the time to be told that failure was one's own fault. Indeed, there may have been many circumstances beyond our control. But there was much that my family and my community did to reinforce this message of self-determination and self-worth, thereby inoculating us against the victim plague that was highly contagious in the hot, humid climate of segregation. What has become clear to me over the years, as I have witnessed the transformation of our society into one based upon victims rather than heroes, is that there is a more positive message to be gained from adversity: success (as well as failure) is the result of one's own talents, morals, decisions, and actions. Accepting personal responsibility for victory as well as for defeat is as liberating and empowering as it is unpopular today. Overcoming adversity not only gives us our measure as individuals, but it also reinforces those basic principles and rules without a society based upon freedom and liberty cannot function.

In those years of my youth, there was a deep appreciation of heroes and heroic virtue. Art, literature, and even popular culture (unlike today) often focused on people who demonstrated heroic virtues—courage, persistence, discipline, hard work, humility, triumph in the face of adversity, just to mention a few. These building blocks of self-reliance were replicated and reinforced at home, school, and church. The "rags to riches" Horatio Alger stories were powerful messages of hope and inspiration to those struggling for a better life. And, many of us used to read and dream about heroes—not to mention our favorite television heroes, something perhaps unbelievable these days. I am certain that many of you who attended grammar school in the 1950s or earlier probably remember reading a favorite account of the integrity and work ethic of George Washington, or of Abraham Lincoln, or of George Washington Carver, or even of some baseball or football legend. It seemed that we all had heroes (not role models, a term of far more recent vintage). Indeed, it would have been odd for a child of several decades ago not to have had a hero.

But today, our culture is far less likely to raise up heroes than it is to exalt victims—individuals who are overcome by the sting of oppression, injustice, adversity, neglect, or misfortune. Today, victims of discrimination, racism, poverty, sickness, and societal neglect abound in the popular press. Today, there are few (if any) heroes. Often, it seems that those who have succumbed to their circumstances are more likely to be singled out than those who have overcome them.

What caused this cultural shift—from an emphasis on heroes to a preoccupation with victims? Why are there more victims and virtually no heroes recognized today? Why in years past was there much less of an emphasis on victimage?

I think two things contributed to this change in the state of affairs. The first is that our political and legal systems now actively encourage people to claim victim status and to make demands on society for reparations and recompense. The second is that our culture actually seeks to denigrate or deconstruct heroes. Why would a civilized society travel down two such destructive paths? Why has it become no more admirable to rise valiantly above one's circumstances than it is to submit to them—all the while aggressively transferring responsibility for one's condition to others?

Let's begin with our political and legal systems—how have they contributed to this state of affairs? The classical conception was that government and the law were meant to ensure freedom and equality of opportunity by giving people the most room possible for self-provision and self-determination. James Madison made this point in *The Federalist Papers* when he observed that the "protection" of the "diversity of faculties in men" was the "first object" of government. And, in more recent times, the great political economist Friedrich von Hayek—who witnessed totalitarianism first hand—made a similar point when he observed that "the chief aim of freedom is to provide both the opportunity and the inducement to insure the maximum use of the knowledge that an individual can acquire."

Between the New Deal and the 1960s, a far different view began to hold sway—namely, that the role of the state was to eliminate want, suffering and adversity. Freedom was no longer simply a right to self-provision and self-determination, but was instead a right to make demands on government and society for one's well-being and happiness. That is the import of Franklin Roosevelt's "Citizen Bill of Rights," which spoke of freedom from want—rights to minimum income, housing, and other "adequate protections from economic fears." And, I think it is axiomatic that the call for such new rights (if not claims) became ever more prevalent in the 1950s and 1960s.

No doubt, this gradual transformation in ideas took root and flourished (at least in part) because of the aggregate growth in wealth and resources we were witnessing in this country during the course of the 20th century. Against the background of this prosperity, poverty stood out in bold relief and in uncomfortably stark contrast—even as the number of people suffering from it shrank. It is not surprising that people began to think that, in a world of seemingly unlimited resources, adversity could be eliminated, or, at the very least, remedied. The ideal of the "benevolent state" took hold. In our "enlightened" society, neglect, misfortune, and injustice did not have to be accepted as inevitable facts of life. Good government and laws could step in when necessary, as many believed they had successfully done during two World Wars, the Great Depression, and the Civil Rights Movement.

If one assumes that suffering and adversity can be eliminated, but sees a number of people continuing to suffer from adversity or misfortune, then there must be some forces in society that relegate the "have nots" to this fate. Or, at the very least, the less fortunate are being ignored. Those facing adversity, hence, are victims of a society that is not doing as much as it could (if it so desired), and these victims can (and should) stake a legitimate claim against the political and legal systems for recompense. On this view, neglect or selfishness on the part of society and government is responsible for the sting of oppression, injustice, and misfortune that the unfortunate and "have nots" feel today.

In light of this modern ideology, is it any surprise that people identify themselves as victims and make demands on the political systems for special status and entitlements? Our culture expects (and, indeed, encourages) people to do exactly that. Consider, for example, the creation and continued expansion of the welfare state and other social programs in this country. How often have we heard proponents of these programs lull the poor into thinking that they are hopeless victims, incapable of triumphing over adversity without "benevolent intervention" by the state? How often have we heard these proponents encouraging the less fortunate in our society to become indignant about their situation in life and more demanding on the political system to find solutions to their problems?

It is not only in the political system, though, that we see our society and its leaders succumbing to the modern ideology of victimhood. As with the political system, people today also are strongly encouraged to make demands on the legal system by claiming victim status. Indeed, the legal system has, in many ways, become a significant driving force behind the modern ideology of victimhood. Courts are viewed as an effective means of forcing (or at least pressuring) political institutions into meeting demands for protected status and new rights or entitlements. Pointing to perceived "victimization" by "the system" or by others in society, our legal culture has often told the least fortunate in our society that their last hope is to claim special legal rights and benefits, or to seek exoneration for the harmful, criminal consequences of their acts. The least fortunate are encouraged to turn to legal arguments that admit defeat and that challenge the moral authority of society. In these ways, courts are called upon to solve social problems—by creating special rules, and by crafting remedies that will satisfy the claims and demands of victim groups but that do not apply to all of us.

Appealing to the legal system, though, was not as easy a task as making demands on the political system. Our legal system has traditionally required that redress for grievances only be granted after very exacting standards have been met. There had to be, for example, very distinct, individualized harm. And, the definition of harm was circumscribed by a traditional understanding of adjudication under the common law, where narrow disputes regarding traditional property rights were resolved among private parties who could not settle matters on their own. Very generalized claims of misfortune or oppression or neglect—the kinds of assertions made in the political system—would not easily fit into this common mold of court activity. It would not be enough for people to be indignant, angry, and demanding about their situation in life. There would have to be an assertion of a legal wrong and a persuasive argument that a legal remedy was available.

The pressure of victimology "revolutionized"—and that word does not always have positive connotations—the courts and the law. For those in our culture seeking to use the courts as agents of social change, poverty, unemployment, social deviancy, and criminal behavior were not just unfair conditions in our society that could be eliminated if only people or politicians cared. Instead, these abstract problems were personified as the direct actions of local schools, churches, businesses, and other social institutions so that they could be sued for causing individualized harm to the victims. Based on this new kind of harm—a kind of legalistic understanding of "victimage"—the courts were said to be obligated to recognize special rights and protected status under the law.

Take, for example, welfare rights and due process. Beginning with *Goldberg v. Kelly,* our cases underscored the importance of welfare as a means of preventing social malaise, promoting the general welfare, and securing the blessings of liberty for all Americans. The rights to life, liberty, and property were, in effect, transformed from freedom from government interference into a right to welfare payments. There are countless other examples in legal literature and judicial opinions—some have argued that inner city minorities and the poor should not be held responsible for the consequences of their criminal acts because of oppression and misfortune; and, of course, there is the debate now raging about preferences based on sex, race, and ethnicity.

This change in our political and legal systems has been accompanied by the rise of the "victim group." These groups are quite useful to public officials for building coalitions for future political support and legitimacy as well. And, for the courts, "victim groups" provide useful justification or cover for energizing the legislative process, changing the legislative agenda, forcing reconsideration of spending priorities, and transforming public debate.

But the rise of victimhood, and its perpetuation by government and the law, is only part of the modern tragedy. There is also the dearth of heroes in our culture. Significantly, as the number of these "victim groups" has escalated, there has been a corresponding decline in the amount of attention that our culture has paid to heroes or, even worse, a conscious attempt to cheapen their achievement. Today, success or a commitment to fighting for noble ideas is attributed to self-interest, revenge, self-aggrandizement, insecurity, or some psychological idiosyncrasy. Just thumb through recently published biographies in the library or bookstore—in many of them, it is not a conscious effort to be virtuous or to do good, but instead a series of unforeseeable and external forces, that lead to greatness or success. And, in many of these biographies, we are introduced to the uncut, "never before seen" foibles, mistakes, and transgressions of people our culture idealized for centuries. The message—that these so-called heroes are really just regular people capable of folly and vice who happened to have a few good breaks. In *Democracy in America,* Alexis de Tocqueville anticipated this state of affairs when he said: "historians who live in democratic times do not only refuse to admit that some citizens may influence the destiny of a people, but also take away from the people themselves the faculty of modifying their own lot and make them depend on an inflexible providence or a kind of blind fatality."

Now, the problem these days is not that there are no people who should be singled out as heroes. Rather, as Daniel Boorstin suggests in his book, *The Image,* society is preoccupied with celebrities. And heroism and celebrity status are two very different things. The word hero refers to people of great strength, integrity, or courage who are recognized and admired for their accomplishments and achievements. The word celebrity, on the other hand, refers to a condition—the condition of being much talked about. It is a state of notoriety or famousness. As Boorstin says, "a celebrity is a person who is known for his well-known-ness." Thus, while a hero is distinguished by his achievement, celebrities are created by the media and are simply a trademark. Celebrities are, in short, neither good nor bad—they are just a big name. Publicity is the defining feature of a celebrity's existence, and, unlike a hero who will become greater as time passes, time destroys celebrities. Over time the glare of publicity, as Boorstin notes, melts away the celebrity by shedding light and heat on his vices and commonplaceness.

This pattern of ignoring and deconstructing heroes—and focusing instead on the ephemeral celebrity who is known for his well-knownness rather than character or individual worth—stems from the rise of radical egalitarianism. In the 1960's, many of the cultural elite saw a need to ensure absolute equality. On this view, differences in ability and level of achievement are random or uncontrolled; and to permit these characteristics to dictate human happiness and well-being would therefore be unfair. Celebrity status, in contrast, is not a problem for egalitarians, for as Boorstin notes, "anyone can become a celebrity, if only he can get into the news and stay there." Certainly, real achievement is not necessarily required.

It should surprise no one that our culture now has far less difficulty recognizing celebrities that it does those who achieve success as a result of personal effort and character traits that we traditionally would consider heroic. Denigrating heroic virtue—in other words, chalking heroism up to circumstance—its quite well with the notion that we must all be the same and that there can be no significant differences in our achievement, social standing, or wealth.

Anyone can see what these intellectual currents have done to the ideals of human dignity, personal responsibility, and self-determination. Preoccupation with victim status has caused people to focus covetously on what they do not have in comparison to others, or on what has happened to them in the past. Many fail to see the freedom they do have and the talents and resources that are at their disposal.

Our culture today discourages, and even at times stifles, heroic virtues—fortitude, character, courage, a sense of self-worth. For so many, the will, the spirit, and a firm sense of self-respect and self-worth have been suffocated. Many in today's society do not expect the less fortunate to accept responsibility for (and overcome) their present circumstances. Because they are given no chance to overcome their circumstances, they will not have the chance to savor the triumph over adversity. They are instead given the right to fret and complain, and are encouraged to avoid responsibility and self-help. This is a poor substitute for the empowering rewards of true victory over adversity. One of my favorite memories of my grandfather is how he would walk slowly by the corn field, admiring the fruits of his labor. I have often thought that just the sight of a tall stand of corn must have been more nourishing to his spirit than the corn itself was to his body.

But the culture of victimology—with its emphasis on the so-called "benevolent state"—delivers an additional (and perhaps worse) blow to dignity and self-worth. When the less fortunate do accomplish something, they are often denied the sense of achievement which is so very important for strengthening and empowering the human spirit. They owe all their achievements to the "anointed" in society who supposedly changed the circumstances—not to their own efforts. Long hours, hard work, discipline, and sacrifice are all irrelevant. In a world where the less fortunate are given special treatment and benefits—and, significantly, where they are told that whatever gains or successes they have realized would not be possible without protected status and special benefits—the so-called beneficiaries of state-sponsored benevolence are denied the opportunity to derive any sense of satisfaction from their hard work and self-help. There is not a one among us who views what others do for us the same way we view what we do for ourselves. No matter how much we appreciate the help, it is still just that—help, not achievement.

It also bears noting that our culture's preoccupation with grouping victims has balkanized society. The "We/They" mentality of calling oneself a victim of society breeds social conflict and calls into question the moral authority of society. The idea that whole groups or classes are victims robs individuals of an independent spirit—they are just moving along with the "herd" of other victims. Such individuals also lack any incentive to be independent, because they know that as part of an oppressed group they will neither be singled out for the life choices they make nor capable of distinguishing themselves by their own efforts.

As victim ideology flourishes, and people are demoralized by its grip, more and more people begin to think that they must claim victim status to get anywhere in this world. Indeed, is it any surprise that anyone and everyone can claim to be a victim of something these days? In his book *The Abuse Excuse,* Alan Dershowitz criticizes countless examples of conditions that "victimize" people and thereby release them from responsibility for their actions. Here are just a few examples:

- the "black rage defense," which asserts that blacks who are constantly subjected to oppression and racial injustice will become uncontrollably violent;
- "urban survival syndrome," which claims that violent living conditions justify acts of aggression in the community;
- "self-victimization syndrome," which maintains that people become less productive and creative, and become severely depressed, as a result of societal neglect and discrimination.

Most significantly, there is the backlash against affirmative action by "angry white males." I do not question a person's belief that affirmative action is unjust because it judges people based on their sex or the color of their skin. But something far more insidious is afoot. For some white men, preoccupation with oppression has become the defining feature of their existence. They have fallen prey to the very aspects of the modern ideology of victimology that they deplore.

Some critics of affirmative action, for example, fault today's civil rights movement for demanding equality yet supporting policies that discriminate based on race. These critics expect the intended beneficiaries of the civil rights regime to break away from the ideology of victimhood: to cherish freedom, to accept responsibility, and, where necessary, to demonstrate fortitude in the face of unfairness. I do not quarrel with this. But these critics should hold themselves to the same standards, resisting the temptation to allow resentment over what they consider reverse discrimination to take hold of their lives and to get the best of them. They must remember that if we are to play the victim game the very people they decry have the better claim to victim status.

Of course, de-emphasizing heroism exacerbates all these problems. Human beings have always faced the temptation to permit adversity or hate to dominate and destroy their lives. To counter this tendency, society had heroes—people capable of overcoming the very adversity or injustice that currently affects today's victims. They rose above their circumstances and inherent inperfections. Heroes cherished freedom, and tried to accomplish much with what little they had. Heroes demonstrated perseverance in the face of adversity and used hardship as a means to strive for greater virtue. And heroes accepted responsibility—they did what they did despite fear and temptation, and tried to do the right thing when presented with a choice between good and evil. It is awfully hard for society to inculcate these values without some useful models from the past and present.

I may not have realized it as a child, but my grandfather was a hero who had a tremendous impact on my life. He certainly would not be a celebrity by today's standards. Though barely able to read and saddled with the burdens of segregation, he worked hard to provide for his family. He was a deeply religious man who lived by the Christian virtues. He was a man who believed in responsibility and self-help. And though this could not bring him freedom in a segregated society, it at least gave him independence from its daily demeaning clutches.

In all the years I spent in my grandparents' house, I never heard them complain that they were victims. Now, they did not like segregation or think that it was right. In fact, there was no question that it was immoral and that anyone who promoted it was morally reprehensible. But there was work to be done. I assure you that I did not enjoy the demands he placed on us. I saw no value in rising with the chicken, and, unlike him, I was not obsessed with what I will call the "reverse dracula syndrome": that is, fear that the rising sun would catch me in bed. It would not be until I was exposed to the most fortunate and best educated in our society that I would be informed that all this time I had been a victim. I am sure you can imagine what it was like when I returned home to Savannah, and informed my grandparents that with the education I had received because of their tremendous foresight and sacrifice, I had discovered our oppressed and victimized status in society. Needless to say relations were quite strained, and our vacation visits were somewhat difficult. My grandfather was no victim and he didn't send me to school to become one.

There are many people like my grandfather alive today. The cultural elite does not honor them as the heroes they are, but instead views them as people who are sadly ignorant of their victim status or who have forgotten where they came from. Our social institutions do not train today's young to view such people as heroes and do not urge them to emulate their virtues.

In idealizing heroic virtue and criticizing the victim ideology of our day, I am not saying that society is free from intractable and very saddening injustice and harm. That would not be true. But, the idea that government can be the primary instrument for the elimination of misfortune is a fundamental misunderstanding of the human condition. There has always been bad and suffering in the world, and we must admit that wrongs have been and will continue to be committed. People will always be treated unfairly—we can never eliminate oppression or adversity completely, though we can and should fight injustice as best we can.

But keep in mind that all of us are easily tempted to think of ourselves as victims and thereby permit adversity to be the defining feature of our lives. In so doing, we deny the very attributes that are at the core of human dignity—freedom of will, the capacity to choose between good and bad, and the ability to endure adversity and to use it for gain. Victimhood destroys the human spirit.

I also am not saying that we should expect everyone to be a hero all of the time. We humans are weak by our very nature; all of us at times will permit hardship to get the very best of us. But having a set of norms to guide us and to push us along—the stuff of heroes—can be a source of great strength. If we do not have a society that honors people who make the right choices in the face of adversity—and reject the bad choices—far fewer people will make the right choices. Ultimately, without a celebration of heroic virtue, we throw ourselves into the current state of affairs, where man is a passive victim incapable of triumphing over adversity and where aggression, resentment, envy and other vice thwart progress and true happiness.

What I am saying is that it requires the leadership of heroes and the best efforts of all to advance civilization and to ensure that its people follow the path of virtue. And, because of the role law has played in perpetuating victim ideology, and because of the influence law can have in teaching people about right and wrong, lawyers have a special obligation here. We should seek to pare back the victimology that pervades our law, and thereby encourage a new generation of heroes to flourish.

I am reminded of what Saint Thomas a Kempis wrote more than 500 years ago about the human spirit. His standard is a useful one for thinking about the instruction that our law should be offering: "take care to ensure that in every place, action, and outward occupation you remain inwardly free and your own master. Control circumstances, and do not allow them to control you. Only so can you be a master and ruler of your actions, not their servant or slave; a free man. . . ."

ANALYSIS

1. Thomas's key term, and the one audiences respond to, is *responsibility*. What does Thomas mean by this protean term? In what varied ways does Thomas illustrate and define the meaning of the term responsibility for him?

2. Jennifer Hochschild, in criticizing the "American Dream," argues that one must distinguish between "necessary" and "sufficient" conditions for success. How might this apply to Thomas's arguments?

3. What point does Thomas actually make about welfare? At first he seems to say it's necessary for the general welfare (preventing social malaise) but then argues that the rights to life, liberty, and so forth were improperly "transformed . . . into a right to welfare payments."

4. Generally, Thomas rejects the idea of affirmative action; how then do you explain those paragraphs in which he criticizes some attacks on it?

WRITING POSSIBILITIES

1. Does Thomas offer evidence for the way media emphasize victims rather than heroes? To what extent do you think this occurs? What examples might you cite on behalf of Thomas's argument? (Check out popular biographies in the tabloids or in bookstores as possibilities.)

2. Do you agree with Thomas's assumption that art and popular culture should portray the heroic rather than the nonheroic?

3. In almost all his speeches (as well as this one), Thomas makes use of his own and his family's personal history to support his contentions. How effective is his use of the stories about his grandfather's success in life? Are his stories open to the possibility that other autobiographical stories (by his listeners, by us) could be cited in direct contrast to his own? What stories are present in your family's history that might illustrate or contravene Thomas's stories?

4. Wilson says that many people "do not expect the less fortune to accept responsibility for their present circumstances." To what extent would these statements apply to Wendy Williams's story ("Money Is Everything, Except Hers")? How does Thomas's emotive *language* work in such statements as these to persuade us of the merit of his assertions?

5. Thomas argues that we over-emphasize social causes and pay little attention to the way individuals fight adverse conditions. William Julius Wilson argues the reverse: that the individual is powerless in the face of globalized, technological changes. How does each writer advance his argument? Where is the weakest spot in each? Who, in your view, does the best job of analyzing present-day situations and proposing ways to improve them?

6. Take a sample of output from the mass medium of your choice (TV, newspapers, cable news, etc.) and test Thomas's assertions about how popular culture plays up victims and plays down heroes. Consider this especially in the case of human interest economic or social stories (e.g., about the homeless, the working poor, racial discrimination, etc.) Do you think the media over-emphasizes such victim-stories or (perhaps) doesn't emphasize them enough? Explain. (One quick-access suggestion: on the Web, try the key words "Welfare Reform" to see what comes up, as Clinton-era welfare changes are now coming to a five-year terminus.)

6

GENDER IN AMERICAN LIFE

In the excerpt from her autobiography (pages 371–377), former NOW President Patricia Ireland explains why she became a feminist: small indignities (stewardesses had to wear a cute little pillbox hat like Jackie Kennedy's), lack of respect (the sexualized "stew" syndrome) and above all economics: her husband required immediate surgery for an impacted tooth but Ireland discovered to her shock that Pan Am's medical insurance didn't extend to her husband. Why? Because *she* was not the "spouse"; only men could be spouses.

Though enormous changes in attitude and practice have taken place over the last 30 years, the issue of what is properly a male or female role is still with us. And likewise, the arguments continue to swirl around the biological-cultural divide. In the opening section of "What Women Really Want" (pages 379–390), Michael Segell brings up fresh supplies on the biological front to argue that men and women are distinct biological forms, born of Darwinian evolutionary struggles: the "bitchfesters" and "dickfesters" both, he says pungently, better get with the program. On the other hand, Susan Lorber in "The Social Construction of Gender" (pages 391–400) expresses today's dominant consensus that with some exceptions it's not biology but culture that makes men and women who they are.

In the face of the abstract arguments by Segell and Lorber, it's a relief to turn to several practical issues. On the wage-equity front, Diana Furchgott-Roth and Christine Stolba and Ellen Bravo all argue over whether, and why, women still earn only 74 cents to the male dollar, while on the issue of Title IX mandates, Donna LoPiano and Stephen Erber square off as to whether Title IX means a disaster for men's sports or a boon to women's. (401–415; 417–424)

Male violence is always in the news, tied especially to male athletes. Don Sabo, a former All-American football player, argues in "Pigskin, Patriarchy and Pain" (pages 425–428) that athleticism, male violence and patriarchy are all built on the ideology that men must dominate others by learning to accept pain—even when it hurts; Sabo wants to overthrow the patriarchal idea because of its damage to individuals *and* to society as a whole. On the other hand, Michael Segell in "What Women Really Want" would disagree with Sabo, finding in intense athletic competition something that enhances the lives of both men and women.

On the other side of the male-female ledger, some would argue that men are in greater difficulty now than women. Again, Michael Segell's opening salvo on behalf of evolutionary biology has an edge to it. As a journalist, Segell talked to young men who simply didn't know how to deal with women now that feminism has made its impact felt so deeply. Segell wants men to be more aggressive and competitive (that's their real nature, he says) and thus make them more confident in front of women. And this in turn will make women want them—women, he says, want strong men. (After all, he might point out, don't female robins pick the males with the best territory?) Warren Farrell, an ex-vice president of NOW is on the other side of the fence but would agree with Segell, arguing that men have always been an endangered species because they are "success objects," with all the anxieties and stresses that a need to succeed implies.

bell hooks (she insists on lower case) closes off the debate by striking a note at once severely polemical (patriarchy is the charge, though here from a black woman's perspective) and yet ultimately conciliatory and helpful: men and women she argues are indeed "comrades"—or ought to be.

Patricia Ireland

The crucial point in Ireland's story is made by her remark towards the end: "I found it incredible," she writes, "that none of the women employed by Pan Am had challenged the insurance discrimination before me." It pays to read or reread Ireland's account to see why she was the only one to do this.

Consider Ireland's strategy here in her retrospective account of how she became a feminist. She tells her story pretty much as a personal account, but along the way hints at those aspects of the social scene that made her a candidate for activism: her eventual husband ("James hated the way stewardesses were treated. . . ."), the antiwar movement of the late 1960s, time spent in the artists and hippie community of Miami's Coconut Grove, her readings in de Beauvoir and other feminists. These and other forces in the social milieu made her, as she says, into a "budding feminist." Eventually (and here we move back towards the earlier sections of the essay), she tells a pilot to cook a steak for himself (but, she says to us, "I refrained from telling him where he could stick it.") In other words, Ireland is quite artful in presenting her gradual transition from acceptance to rejection of the stewardess's stereotypical role. When she is told by Pan Am that her husband is not covered by her health insurance, she is certainly primed to seek out NOW's assistance and to go on the offensive.

WHAT WOMEN WANT
from What Women Want

Hey, Patricia. Fix me a steak while we wait this one out." The captain emerged from the cockpit, adjusting his hat to a jaunty angle, and turned into the jetway. "Make it medium rare."

In training school I'd been taught that the captain was, if not God Himself, at least a minor deity. I moved into the galley and fired up the grill.

Pan Am had received another bomb threat that day, and our flight from Miami International to Piarco Airport in Trinidad had been temporarily grounded. This wasn't anything out of the ordinary at the time; bomb scares and skyjackings—especially from Miami—had become relatively routine. Armed U.S. sky marshals were a common sight on our flights; we stewardesses could always spot them by the pained looks on their faces (their concealed guns and holsters made it difficult for them to sit comfortably in the cramped-economy seats). This time, after herding a lot of unhappy passengers back to the safety of the terminal, I returned to gather my own belongings. That's when the captain emerged, ordering dinner.

So a future president of the National Organization for Women found herself alone in the galley of an evacuated 727 that might blow up at any moment, cooking this guy a filet. Medium rare.

As blasé as I'd become about bomb threats, it suddenly occurred to me that this one might just be the real thing. I had resigned myself to the other hazards of a lowly flight attendant's role: the long hours, low pay, leering passengers, groping copilots. But in that moment I realized that I had no real obligation to lay my own life on the line for our captain's dinner. If he didn't feel obliged to risk going down with the ship, why should I? I turned off the grill. I left the plane.

He was sitting comfortably in the crew lounge, reading a newspaper. I approached, smiling.

"Captain?"

"Hmmm?"

"Cook your own steak."

Ever the cordial flight attendant, I refrained from telling him where he could stick it.

In retrospect, that incident was a turning point. A small thing, really, just a moment of rebellion. It didn't feel important at the time; after all, I told myself, I was just expressing aggravation. It didn't immediately change my career, my relationships, or anyone's attitude about me. But it was a first step toward taking some real control over my own life. No matter where we are in life, it's important to seize these moments of opportunity and take the next step—whatever that may be—to gain more control. It doesn't matter if the step seems small. No change is insignificant. It *does* make a difference.

Individuals don't act in a vacuum. We're part of history—of the world events happening around us, all the time. We reflect and mirror and react to them daily.

While I was wandering up and down aisles serving coffee, tea, and a tightly packaged version of my stewardess persona to passengers on either side, the 1960s were happening, too, and it was much more than sex, drugs, and rock 'n' roll. The civil rights movement, the antiwar movement, the gay rights movement, and a newly revived feminist movement all were gaining strength and visibility. There was the sense, shared by many people of many different backgrounds, that the limits of anyone's role could be expanded—exploded—and that this was the right thing to do.

Even those stewardesses who didn't identify with the burgeoning feminist movement, or with *any* of the other political movements of the sixties, were affected by the atmosphere. Oh, some still clung to the fantasy of meeting her knight in shining armor: an oil baron, perhaps (sitting in first class), who would sweep that lucky stewardess off her feet and into a Bel Air mansion. Personally, I never witnessed such an event. But most of us, like so many other women in our country, were starting to look at ourselves in a different light, to value ourselves more, to demand more respect from others.

Despite all the loud turmoil, social experimentation, and exploration and expression of individual freedom going on in our country in the late 1960s, the airline industry remained rooted in the past. The industry still presented fifties-style advertising schemes to the public, like Continental's "We Really Move Our Tails For You!" and National's "I'm Cheryl—Fly Me!" Painfully oblivious to the social upheaval of the day, all the major airlines gleefully perpetuated the notion that flight attendants were pretty bimbos, there to service men.

Because it was difficult at best to develop a sense of self-worth working as stewardesses, many of us looked elsewhere. I worked with flight attendants who were Girl Scout troop leaders, church choir directors, and volunteers at rape crisis centers and county courthouses in their spare time. Many flight attendants had a second job, not just for the money but to ensure their primary identity would be based on more than running up and down airplane aisles. Of course, whether we did it for pay or not, women's work continued to be service work, caretaking work. The doors leading into the halls of real political and economic power and influence were still shut tight against us.

Working as a stewardess continued to be a never-ending struggle to maintain some kind of identity apart from the caretaker/seductress persona that the airline insisted we constantly wear: In defending its women-only hiring policy regarding flight attendants (*Pan Am* v. *Diaz,* 1967), the company hypocritically argued that passengers preferred women attendants, because our "maternal" presence had a calming influence on them. But if the airline considered you overweight, all respect for the "maternal" image went out the window—you were gone. In fact, motherhood was grounds for dismissal.

This extraordinary double message that we were given about motherhood is still prevalent in our culture today. Motherhood is good, beautiful, necessary, and important, we are told; but it is treated as unattractive, irresponsible, and worthless. Mothers deserve to be put on a pedestal, begifted and adored; but mothers are second-class citizens, undeserving of society's practical support.

Though I never suffered the indignity of choosing between a child and a job, slowly but surely I began to feel the need for a lot more respect—in the air and on the ground. Here I was: a highly skilled employee who could rattle off emergency instructions in three languages, deliver a baby at thirty thousand feet, and evacuate a 747 in ninety seconds upside down, underwater, in the dark—and I was being sold for my smile! It was getting harder and harder to stay in character as the EverPleasant Flight Attendant. How could I respect myself if I couldn't respect the way I acted in uniform twenty days or more each month? . . .

At first my growing dissatisfaction manifested itself in rather unproductive activity. I still had one thing in common with many of my coworkers: the will and the way to get knee-walking drunk. I don't even remember how many layovers were spent partying and drinking in hotel rooms, taking the party—complete with glasses and rapidly emptying bottles—out into lobbies, skinny-dipping in pools, laughing at the irate complaints of the hotel managers. I used the booze to keep from having to deal with my life. That way I didn't have to face the question, What's wrong and what would I rather be doing?

But just because we were drinking buddies didn't mean that I wasn't starting to alienate some of my coworkers. I had been reading Simone de Beauvoir's *The Second Sex* and articles by feminists in this country, and these writings spoke to me. Inevitably, I tried out my new ideas on the people closest at hand: Some were more receptive than others. In a swelteringly hot crew van on the way from the airport to the hotel in Buenos Aires, exhausted at the end of a sixteen-hour shift, I was engaged in an interesting discussion with the copilot about how women's work—especially housework—was undervalued and underpaid, when the captain turned around and interjected, "I think my wife's got a good deal, a damned good deal. We have a maid for the housework, so she really doesn't do anything all day. But *I* come home after a long flight, and she's got this list of demands . . ."

All conversation in the van stopped dead, and everyone looked at me to see if I'd explode. I obliged them.

"Isn't that the ultimate sign of wealth!" I snapped. "To be able to afford a slave who doesn't *do* anything?"

I was a little shocked at myself after saying this. I hadn't been aware of thinking anything like that. But it came from somewhere inside me, somewhere real.

After a few moments of stunned silence, he started to laugh. "Boy, Patricia. You really *have* gone off the deep end!"

End of conversation. True, by letting my anger and sarcasm get the best of me, I'd blown my chance to have a persuasive conversation; then again, I thought I'd made a pretty snappy comeback, and I felt pretty good about it. Years of experience with political leadership would later teach me that I can make my arguments passionately and still be persuasive—if I don't let indignant rage get in the way; but I wasn't quite there yet!

My anger (and all my futile attempts to bury it) was symptomatic of something that was happening inside me. I was at another real turning point in my life: Willing, and *almost* ready, for change, I didn't yet possess the tools to make that change on my own. This is the most frustrating phase in the process of change: The beginnings of consciousness, awareness of self, painful dissatisfaction with self and world, and the desire for great change in both are the first unsettling glimmerings that tell us a turning point has been reached—when you *know,* but don't have the slightest idea yet what to *do* about it all.

As a budding feminist, I hadn't left my armchair (or jumpseat, as the case may be). Mouthing off in crew buses hardly made me a political activist. When getting drunk or belligerent became too exhausting, I went out exploring on layovers. Once, I got lost hiking in El Salvador. I wandered through a poverty-stricken village in the countryside, flies swarming over me under a baking sun. Women and children stared. I felt ugly, odd: a tall, pale woman from some other world who did not belong here at all. I felt I had absolutely nothing of use to give or to share. Somehow, I imagined, they knew that. An old farmer, speaking an Indian dialect that I could not understand, finally pointed me toward a road with a bus stop. Saved from further introspection and terror—about myself, my future, the world—for another day. . . .

My first tepid foray into activism was the Pillbox Hat Incident.

Although it had already fallen out of fashion by the late 1960s, this annoying bit of once high-fashion headgear, popularized by Jacqueline Kennedy, was required wearing for stewardesses whenever we were on the ground in uniform. The utterly useless hats invariably mashed our hair into a rat's nest of tangles. As soon as we were airborne we'd tear them off, then run to the tiny bathrooms and try desperately to comb ourselves back into some semblance of presentability. It wasn't just vanity: Our coiffure had been legally mandated to look perfect; nobody wanted any bad-hair reports to get back to the grooming supervisor.

The compulsory wearing of pillbox hats may not seem like a burning human rights issue, but it was a source of real stress and a general waste of energy. We might land and take off several times a day, traveling up and down Central America or the Caribbean on flights that lasted little more than half an hour. With 125 passengers on board waiting for magazines and Bloody Marys, we really didn't have time to be beauticians on each leg of the trip.

Finally, ten of us sent a letter to our base manager, John Lorenz, complaining that the pillbox hat requirement constituted discrimination against female flight attendants. After all, none of Pan Am's male pursers had to deal with this moronic bit of millinery.

Lorenz's response dripped sarcasm. Men and women at Pan Am had always worn different uniforms, he wrote, and always would. Would we be satisfied, he asked, if the company required men to wear brassieres and skirts? (We might have been, but we knew he'd say no if we decided to take him up on it.) The message was clear: Decisions about how we dressed, like everything else about us, would continue to be made by men in a corporate boardroom; if we didn't like it, tough.

Such humbling experiences tended to kill any enthusiasm for activism among the stewardess ranks, but for some reason, Lorenz's discouraging response had a different effect on me. It made me mad to be treated that way. It made me feel small and foolish and helpless. But it also made me determined to start fighting back against some of the systematically demeaning elements of my job. Although our letter had brought us nothing but sarcasm, it was a first step of sorts. I'd had a tiny taste of activism. And regardless of the outcome, I liked it! In some small but essential way, I was inspired.

If I was going to stand up for my rights again, though, I needed a better issue—a more clear-cut incident of discrimination, one in which we stewardesses had much more of a direct *economic* stake. The opportunity soon came in the form of James's impacted wisdom teeth.

We had no large appliances left to pawn off for quick cash when his teeth began to really hurt him, so I breathed a sigh of relief at the thought of Pan Am's medical coverage. His benefits as the spouse of an airline employee would be a lifesaver. Dutifully, I headed down to the company insurance offices to fill out paperwork. I was probably a bit naive—this being my first experience with major medical costs of any sort—but I certainly didn't expect problems. Imagine my surprise upon being told that Pan Am's insurance didn't cover my husband, even though it covered my fellow employees' wives. This was like a splash of ice water right in my face. If I'd been a man, my family would have been protected. Because I was a woman, my family was not.

I shouldn't have been so shocked. The airline and its competitors were much more interested in their bottom lines than in anything as esoteric as equal rights. Short-shrifting stewardesses was easy, relatively risk-free, and a sure way to show higher profits. Up until 1966, stewardesses faced mandatory retirement at age thirty-two or upon marriage—whichever came first. And, even after that policy fell, it would be another decade before flight attendants could become pregnant without getting fired.

What a great deal for the airlines! The entire operation was geared to ensure that we female flight attendants didn't take too big a chunk out of profits. (Stewardesses are still paid so little that, in many cases, new hires qualify for food stamps.) The industry could get away with it, even after the collapse of the mandatory retirement policy, because stewardesses generally didn't stay on the job long, and very few of us were active in the union or held union posts. If the airlines could keep moving us out at a relatively young age, they didn't have to worry about providing pensions or long-term health care benefits, not to mention maternity leave or child care. Ultimately, they were assured of a cheap and exploitable labor force through the constant turnover of young, female employees.

I didn't think about any of this at the time. Instead, I assumed there had been some kind of mistake. So I went to my supervisor and told him what had happened. "That's just the way it is," he said. And finally, something inside me snapped.

My anger—and a newfound sense of confidence—was fed by the certainty that this double standard was blatantly unfair; there was no way Pan Am could get away with it. The role of ditsy stewardess who could be counted on to keep her mouth shut was no longer one I was willing to play. Anyway, I had no choice. Neither James nor I had the money to cover his oral surgery. I decided to fight.

Had I tried to take on insurance practices in the airline industry ten years earlier, I would have been in trouble. But after the explosion of civil rights activities in the sixties, I knew that a lot of groundwork had already been laid for this case. I had never in my life been to a political meeting or demonstration organized by the revitalized feminist movement. But I identified with the movement from a distance, and instinctively felt that, in some way, I was a part of it. Help was out there; I just had to figure out who to call.

I looked up the local chapter of the National Organization for Women in a phone book and left a message on their answering machine.

ANALYSIS

1. Ireland describes the 1960s view of the stewardess as involving a "caretaker/seductress persona." What is a "persona"? Why is a stewardess both "caretaker" and "seductress"?
2. What "tools" might Ireland have lacked in the first real "turning point" of her life?
3. How does Ireland make clear to the present-day reader what the pillbox hat symbolized for her generation? Can you think of contemporary clothing accessories whose symbolic meaning might have to be explained to a future generation?
4. Why did Ireland eventually believe that the "impacted wisdom tooth" issue was a more powerful one than the pillbox hat issue?
5. Ireland explains that it was "affirmative action" that got her a victory over Pan Am. How does Ireland's build up to this point through telling the story of injustice (the treatment of her husband's medical bills) make you sympathize with affirmative action requirements, regardless of whether in principle you approve or disapprove of the concept itself? Or *did* it make you sympathize? If not, why not?

WRITING POSSIBILITIES

1. Ireland's story is a good model of how someone changes over a period of time; there are key turning points that she mentions (either explicitly or implicitly) and many significant contexts (social climate, reading,

personal relationships) that helped her change. Have you experienced a similar development? What did it involve? Are you (or were you) surprised at the outcome?

2. On the basis of this chapter from her book, what would you say that "women want"? Is this what you want?

3. Have you ever relied on governmental aid or a pressure group's assistance (e.g., NOW) to get what you thought you deserved? Justice itself? What were the circumstances?

4. Does Ireland's account of her early feminism apply in today's world? Explain to what extent it still applies and to what extent it has changed.

Michael Segell

Like the movie of the same name, Michael Segell in "What Women Really Want" may not win votes from women by telling them "what women want." In his view, women want aggressive, highly competitive men who will make the best mates and fathers of future babies and provide both wife and children with the best support possible. "Men are naturally aggressive," [Segell writes], "obsessed with dominating each other . . . because over the eons during which the male brain was laying down its circuitry, the benefits conferred by these traits helped us get the girl. The dickfesters . . . need to get with this simply evolutionary plan."

As a journalist, Segell has interviewed a number of young men, who, he says, were confused and bewildered about what it means to be a man—this because feminism has chased the old manly idea of the aggressive male out of sight and replaced it with nothing more than a politically correct wussy ideal of a man. In particular, Segell contends that men are reluctant to get married now (a key device for civilizing male aggressiveness) because they're so confused about what women really want. Seemingly women don't want hairy-chested and aggressive males, but that's what nature—according to Segell—dictates men are; hence massive confusion, retreat, and chagrin. Segell himself doesn't want to go back to that old hairy-chested ideal but, on the other hand, he's not happy with what he sees in the present. His solution, therefore, is "the stand-up guy," the fellow who is assertive, competitive, sexually charged but also responsible, thoughtful, and generative (in later years).

Segell's basic pitch is what is known as evolutionary biology (or psychology), i.e., where Darwinian evolutionary ideas about male and female nature provide scientific underpinning for the social roles of men and women. In fact, for Segell and the evolutionary psychologists he follows, it's actually women who determine what men are like, because it's their preferences (presumably uncontaminated by feminist political correctness) that shape what men are like. Women want to marry aggressive men because they know they're the kind who will take care of them and "the nippers" (as Segell puts it so colorfully).

In contrast to Segell, Susan Lorber (in the essay immediately following Segell's) adopts today's dominant model of social construction: culture, not biology, is basically what makes men and women. Yes, she says, biology has some small impact on sex and gender, but, in reality, the primary thing is the way any one culture—its stereotypes, media transmissions, family practices—shapes that biological heritage.

The importance of the debate cannot be underestimated. Go for the biological only, like Segell, and you seem to endorse male aggressiveness in the extreme, plus a kind of biological determinism that few want to accept. Go with Lorber, on the other hand, and perhaps you're going to be guilty of what the philosopher Susan Koertge calls "biodenial," i.e., a flouting of what (arguably) are indeed biological limits on what women or men can do or achieve.

What Women Really Want
from Standup Guy

It's eight A.M. on a Monday morning and, buzzing with antiinflammatories to minimize the soft-tissue paralysis I'm guaranteed to be suffering by noon, I lace up my hockey skates and adjust the fifteen pounds of protective equipment I've strapped, taped, and velcroed onto my creaking body, which is already howling in protest. I'm surrounded in a malodorous locker room at Chelsea Piers, a magnificent sports complex in lower Manhattan, by my frisky, youthful teammates, all but a few of whom are New York City firemen, about as noble and manly a group of guys as you could hope to assemble in one room. Some of them have just come off a graveyard shift and chatter noisily about the pasta sauces, ragouts, and vats of stew they've prepared for the coming week at the firehouse, meaning they had a quiet, alarm-free night. Others will be heading to various stations around the city after our game. Some will probably get paged during the contest and have to leave to rescue trapped infants from four-alarm infernos or bridge painters dangling by their safety harnesses from collapsed rigging high above the East River. We all knock helmets in the Police and Fire Hockey League, which includes teams from the police department, FBI, and Drug Enforcement Agency. Hockey is popular among the firefighters, and they signed up too many guys for one team, but not enough for two. So I and a couple of other ringers were recruited to round out the second team.

As they do for a lot of men, sports to me present allegories of real substance. The minidramas that unfold over forty-eight or sixty stop-time minutes on a court or rink, over nine innings on a field of dreams, or during a deranging five-set tennis match in hundred-degree heat reveal much about their dramatis personae. Courage and composure, guile and grace, strength and skill—many of the same talents essential to prevailing in nonsporting milieus—are on display to be disparaged, admired, or rewarded. Being a member of the cast, as opposed to just watching the drama, is the fun part: every new game situation presents a different test, and I love being tested, even if, just as it was in childhood, it's only pretend.

It's no secret that the most successful men are intensely competitive—although simply being competitive, as I'm willing to testify, doesn't necessarily guarantee success. Today, however, a man who loves to compete—or, in anthropological terms, sees other men as "hostile forces of nature"—is not always admired. Although men are still allowed to ritualize their urge to bang up against each other on the playing fields, manly aggression is routinely knocked in many real-life venues, particularly those inhabited by the arbiters of the new politically correct behavioral codes. Among the ways men have been asked to change by gender rhetoricians, this one has flummoxed them more than any other, causing many young men, in particular, to shrink from manhood's larger contests. If the alleged contemporary female preference for sensitive men were true—if Kate and her girlfriends really did crave the metaphysical-poet type, as they claim—this new bias would have to rank as one of nature's great reversals, for women have always encouraged tough and forceful engagement with the world. Evidence of their complicity still abounds, and sometimes this plain truth is drilled into you even on the hockey rink.

This morning we play the FBI, the nastiest and most viciously competitive team in the league, although the drug cops are not exactly known for their gentility on the ice, either. Clearly, there's some kind of hierarchical thing going on here, a federal versus local rivalry at work. The FBI goons have gleaming, perfectly matched uniforms in the colors of the flag, naturally, with the stars and stripes emblazoned across the front of their jerseys; all new equipment; a row of expensive new sticks stacked behind their bench; even a team manager, who proffers high-carb sports drinks to the players after a shift. Our federal tax dollars at work. The rest of us wear twenty-year-old pads and skates salvaged from our high school or college teams and pull on shirts-and-skins-style sleeveless pullovers to distinguish us from our opponents. Someone tried to take up a collection to buy matching jerseys imprinted with our team nickname, the Hosers, but no one was interested in coughing up the twenty bucks apiece.

Many of the feds were recruited from Ivy League or Big Ten schools that had terrific hockey teams, so in addition to being talented players, many of them are gifted in the IQ department—and with all their supercop psychotraining, they aren't above messing with the heads of their opponents. Their second-line center, a short, quick man with disturbing cobalt eyes, disgorges a stream of trash talk before each face-off. "I know where your sister lives," he'll say with a smirk, his implication totally mystifying. Or, "Still keep up with your old Yippie pals?" (I'm the only one old enough in the league to even remember the Yippies.) But every once in a while, he'll astound me with a bit of personal knowledge, indicating he's done some real snooping. "So, how are the twins?" he'll ask just before the puck is dropped, then win the face-off easily. I wonder how he even knows my name, much less the fact that my youngest kids are twins.

This morning, our third game this season against the feds, I'm whipped. I've been staring at a computer screen all weekend trying to honor various deadlines, and I haven't gotten much sleep. But on my first shift, parked in front of the net, I score by tipping in a shot from the point, having eluded for a split second my chatty nemesis, whose job was to cover me. On my second shift, I thread the puck through the opposing defensemen to my left wing, who scores, and suddenly we're up by a pair over the feisty feds, who dominated us in the first two games. Feeling a little cocky, I decide to engage my noisy opponent before the ensuing face-off. "I hear your wife is going to have a baby," I tell him, having overheard him gush about his incipient parenthood in the next locker room. "Who's the father?" Shifting into robocop mode, he effectively tunes me out and controls the face-off.

This is supposedly a no-checking league, although plenty of hitting goes on. My opponent is a master at staging an apparently inadvertent collision, and on my third shift he's looking for me, although I don't know it at the time. I don't have his training in mind reading and constantly watching my back. As I circle at center ice about to receive a pass—a screw-your-buddy pass, it turns out—he lunges for the puck, and for me, burying his shoulder in my solar plexus. He may not be big, but like a lot of hockey players he has a low center of gravity, with meaty thighs and a powerful butt, and he levels me, sprawling backward as he pretends the hit was just one of those unavoidably random atomic events in a high-speed game. The referee looks at the two of us laid out on the ice, apparently decides no malice was intended, and lets play go on. The feisty fed springs to his feet and rejoins the play.

I lie gasping on the blue line, hoping my neck bones will remember where they're supposed to be and reconfigure themselves in something that resembles a natural alignment, my retinal rods quivering and sprinkling little points of light across my visual field. As I drag myself back to the bench, calling out for a replacement, I laugh at the silly thought bobbing on the surface of my foamy brainpan: This is all women's fault.

The idea isn't that silly, actually. Evolutionary biologists think of men as a vast breeding experiment run by women, because everything we do in relation to them, and often with and to each other, provides clues to our desirability as mates. In this view, we evolved in response to women's preferences. Men are naturally aggressive, obsessed with dominating each other, and inclined to take risks, because over the eons during which the male brain was laying down its circuitry, the benefits conferred by these traits helped us get the girl. The dickfesters and other men who feel overlooked by desirable women need to get with this simple evolutionary plan. Join a hockey club and practice your dominance technique. Fight for the big job. Stay competitive. Because women are watching, and comparing notes.

Of course, "dominance" is a loaded word in today's touchy social climate. Men's healthy desire to leapfrog over rivals, along with our affinity for pissing contests, wars, and the Super Bowl, is often maligned, in male bashspeak, as "testosterone poisoning." But if that's the case—to take the breeding-experiment metaphor a step further—the estrogen-afflicted are helping to skew the data. Some of the wiser feminists know this and are willing to admit it. "Male oppression is not just attributable to men," says Felicia Pratto, a psychologist and feminist scholar at Stanford, "but to a cooperative relationship between men and women."

Is this feminist heresy? How do women participate in their own oppression? Like everything else, it starts with sex, says Pratto. As do most other female animals, women expend more effort (and thus risk more) than men in launching their kids—and are therefore pickier about choosing an ambitious and prosperous mate who will keep the nippers well fed, clothed, and tutored at the finest academies. According to evolutionary theory, men have responded to this selective pressure by learning to monopolize the material wealth their partners would want or need—thus making themselves attractive—and by keeping those goods out of the clutches of other men.

So over time, this adaptation to female choosiness helped mold a male noodle specially equipped with the desire to keep lower-ranking men in their place, accumulate disproportionate wealth, and back political causes that keep a lid on women's power. Men who were particularly apt at hip-checking rival suitors into the tarpits while bearing food, furs, and the deed to a capacious and well-appointed condo fathered and raised more children, who inherited a special talent for beating down others.

The gender differences in what Pratto calls "social dominance orientation" explain why men favor ideologies that squash social groups unlike their own—wage and income controls are a favorite hobbyhorse—while women wave the flag for social equality. Men are far more supportive of defense spending, the use of troops in foreign countries, and the death penalty, while women tend to back funding for welfare, education, health, and programs for the poor. A man's obsession with status also predicts the career he chooses. Men overwhelmingly hold jobs that enhance their hierarchical positions—three quarters of all lawyers and judges and more than 90 percent of police (and 100 percent of hockey-playing FBI agents) are men—whereas three quarters of all social service providers are women. Along with their political views, this makes men, in Pratto's view, "rankers" (*My salary/house/dick is bigger than yours*) and women "linkers" (*Peoples of the world: Unite*).

As disloyal as it may be to say it, Pratto knows that women continue to be actively involved in tweaking our obsession with status and rank. By preferring and selecting trophy husbands (the bitch-festers' résumé man), they encourage male competition, which in turn reinforces social stratification and the sexist cultural practices that enable it. Surveys of accomplished women, including those who call themselves feminists, indicate that they seek even higher-status men for themselves and their daughters. And, though the practices are supported by men, it is upper-class women in India, China, and much of Africa who impose veiling, footbinding, and infibulation on young women to make them "marriageable" to a man with a fat wallet. The obvious benefits that accrue to both mother and bride go a long way toward easing the guilt they may feel for having to cooperate in their sisters' oppression.

It's an old story, succinctly articulated by the very modern slacker/cartoonist Holden in the movie *Chasing Amy:* "Life is about money and chicks." History is filled with colorful examples of how cultural success (money) translates into reproductive success (chicks). Moulay Ismail the Bloodthirsty, the emperor of Morocco from 1672 to 1727, had 888 acknowledged offspring, produced by a harem of five hundred women that was managed by a senior wife. In the royal courts of China and the Middle East, the harems were even larger. The Arabian caliph al-Mutawakkil, who ruled his kingdom from 847 to 851, reportedly had four thousand concubines. The Egyptian Abdur Rahman III topped out at 6,300. As Holden might say, the more money, the more chicks.

Dominant men don't have to enslave women to mate with them, though, as Pratto knows. From Thomas Jefferson to Bill Clinton, Louis B. Mayer to Jack Nicholson, Babe Ruth to Magic Johnson, Nabokov to Picasso, overachievers have been magnets to women. Social dominance theory is writ large in a man like Sir James Goldsmith—a corporate raider and one of the richest men in the world. Among his several palaces, the tycoon has built a huge compound in Mexico, where he's surrounded by ex-wives and current and former mistresses, one of whom he has married (others have borne him children). Once, on vacation in Sardinia, his wife and children were lodged in a sea-side villa, his mistress across the water. Goldsmith went back and forth by speedboat, keeping everybody happy.

"When you marry you mistress," Goldsmith has said in the tradi-tion of Moulay Ismail, "you create a vacancy." . . .

Another Monday morning, another scrum with the goons from the FBI. Two weeks ago, after we played this team, I made the mistake of telling my wife about my feud with the scrappy federal agent. She ex-amined my scraped and swollen lip, which interfered with my oppo-nent's elbow during a corner tussle, and threw me a look—that look—which she used to back up with the following admonition: "Don't be stupid. You know how you can get. I really don't want to have to raise our kids by myself." Now, of course, she only has to give me the look, and I say the words for her.

Last year, after a twenty-five-year layoff, I started playing hockey again. I was asked to coach my son Tom's mite team, and gradually got drawn back into playing. As I slowly rediscovered some of my skills, I remembered why I was so attracted to the sport as a young boy and up until my last game in college: it's played at an exhilarating pace and requires split-second reactions and decisions. Its constantly shifting geometry focuses my mind in a way that no other activity—save, say, sex—does. It's got speeding missiles and moving targets. Its greatest appeal, though, is that it satisfies my desire to experience, however artificially, danger. To my middle-aged mind and body, that danger is relative but real—and to my usually underaroused metabo-lism, absolutely necessary to feeling alive.

When I was twelve, my father, then a trial attorney, knew this about me and decided in his wisdom to send me to a boys' school with a good hockey team. Dad figured that the key to reforming my youthful talents, which demonstrated special aptitudes for hopping trains, stealing cars, and busting my nose on the rink, was good old martial discipline—and a lot of exercise. "I'm doing this for your own good," I remember him saying, reciting the popular parental mantra, which was also invoked while delivering corporal punishment. "If I don't, you'll end up dead or in jail."

Dad believed my waywardness was due at least in part to the company I kept—my pals were all tough, working-class, Irish Catholic kids, whose penchant for mischief certainly equaled my own—never suspecting my affinity for trouble and risky adventures might have been innate. Today, he could get a pretty good sense of how attracted I am to activities with a higher-than-average probability of making me a paraplegic or my wife a widow simply by measuring my resting pulse rate. Seventy beats per minute is normal; sixty is common among well-trained athletes, mountaineers, and other Xtreme sports fanatics; fifty is typical of test pilots and serial killers. Recently, during a routine physical, I clocked a forty-eight.

A reptilian nervous system is the physiological hallmark of what psychologists call the Type T (for thrill-seeking) personality. Type T's chase risk, uncertainty, intensity, and novelty just to arouse themselves to the level everyone else is at when they get out of bed in the morning. As my father intuited, low-idlers may live fast but often die young. One in five fighter pilots, for instance, will have to eject from a doomed plane, and one in twelve will die on the job.

Among this group of thrill-chasers—in America, about 20 to 30 percent of the population—men far outnumber women. Psychological tests reveal that we score twice as high as they do on measurements of aggression and impulsivity—a combination researchers uncharitably refer to as "psychoticism." Like astronaut Buzz Aldrin, who dozed while waiting for hundreds of thousands of gallons of hydrogen fuel to ignite beneath him and hurtle him toward the moon, they are almost unmoved, both psychologically and physiologically, by potentially fatal risk.

This particular trait is key to understanding the connection between the sangfroid of the *Top Gun* joyrider and the cool, impassive hostility of the Boston Strangler. The only thing that separates them, as my father intuited, is socialization. Personality researcher David Lykken, a psychologist at the University of Minnesota, says, "The hero and the psychopath are two twigs on the same genetic branch."

Type T's inhabit extreme characterological outposts, but many other men are also blessed with an inherent desire to take risks that far exceeds most women's. On psychological tests, this trait is measured as "harm avoidance." "Psychoticism," or this wicked cocktail of aggression, impulsivity, and risk-taking behavior, nudges us toward the achievement contests, the endpoints of which, of course, are the female prize.

Male risk-taking may have evolved to facilitate a baser instinct, but it's a trait that continues to serve the commonweal. The loftiest expressions of this innate urge are documented daily. Every year, the Carnegie Hero Fund Commission reviews eight hundred to a thousand incidents of selfless bravery in America and awards the 10 percent of the rescuers they deem truly heroic a medal and a stipend. Since the awards were established in 1904, more than 90 percent of these citations have gone to men. Many of the players in the Police and Fire Hockey League—even some of the rabid FBI agents—would be candidates for citation were it not for the fact that part of their job description is to save lives.

Women often complain that men are insensitive, but like most hardwired traits, emotional restraint has real advantages, particularly as a subtle courtship device (just ask any woman how she feels about a firefighter in rescue gear). In the more overtly competitive eras of our dark evolutionary history, the ability to suppress fear had obvious adaptive utility. Today, the ability to stay cool under attack—one of the largest gender differences to emerge in research done by personality researchers—still serves men well: in cutthroat boardrooms, a negotiator who reveals his emotions wages a losing battle. And when facing life-or-death situations, a tendency to act first and feel later is an almost godly gift. After seeing a man and his four-year-old son sucked into deep, cold water after slipping down a cliff on the Oregon coast, Christopher Hockert, a thirty-five-year-old glazier from Grant's Pass and a recent Carnegie Hero, shed his boots and jacket and dived in. "I didn't really think about it," he said. "I just figured if I didn't succeed, at least I could save myself, and I could always say I tried my best."

In sync with the grand design of the breeding experiment, the ancestral female was really helping herself by selecting those among us who could best keep their cool. . . .

No big deal. An elbow to the jaw is an honest, direct form of communication, easy to read and easy to respond to. At least I know it's coming. There's no subterfuge, no hidden intent, none of the lingering toxicity of passive aggression—the leadership and courtship styles du jour. It's easy to forgive, too. He's just being aggressive, as he should be.

A dirty word, "aggressive," but again, a reliable measure of a man's social dominance—and thus how attractive he is to women. In the past few years, curbing male aggression (and encouraging it in females) has become kind of a clarion call among feminists and New Age men. In nearly all studies of aggression, the subject of more research than just about any other human behavior, boys and men demonstrate far more confrontational behavior and rough-and-tumble play than girls and women, and are responsible for almost all violent crime. According to a well-known feminist jeremiad, our inherent pathology—our "psychoticism"—taints even our most artful creations: the rhythms of Beethoven's Ninth Symphony, as we've all heard, are really the tympanic expressions of male rage and the universal urge to rape.

Although men are overwhelmingly responsible for all murders, muggings, gang violence, rape, and spousal abuse, violence is an aberrational by-product of aggression. "We wouldn't have so much of the behavior if it didn't work not only for the individual—as a means of maintaining one's autonomy and the integrity of one's life—but for the species," says Robert Cairns, a psychologist at Duke University who has studied aggression for three decades. "It's not just a virus that's been inserted into our behavior."

An early-life example: Boys, rankers manqués, learn the efficacy of an aggressive problem-solving style—confrontation—almost the moment their first toy is snatched from them. The up-front approach, which initially shocks everyone in the play group, including first-time moms, resolves conflict quickly. The strategy serves him well throughout his life: when a dispute has been settled, boys and men are much more likely to make up afterward, as opposed to girls, whose grudges can last indefinitely.

In fact, according to Cairns, girls may actually be meaner—agents of a different, and sometimes more destructive, aggression. Around age ten, they develop a powerful, sophisticated social weaponry that, although not physically assertive, uses alienation, rumormongering, and ostracization to vanquish a rival. This style of passive aggression can emotionally devastate the victim, who often has no idea why, or even by whom, she's being attacked. The junior linkers' strategy of organizing informal social networks as a way of ganging up on a peer not only prolongs conflict but kindles larger in-group discord. As girls enter adulthood, they become even more skilled at using gossip, aspersions, and social ostracization to assault their adversaries. Margaret Mead once remarked that women should stay off the battlefield because they'd be too brutal. Unable to handle direct confrontation, they'd end up blowing everyone away when more modest strategies might suffice.

All linkers, large and small, seem to know this about themselves and go to great lengths—a classic female weakness—to avoid conflict. In a famous study of kids' games, researchers found that girls played less competitively in smaller groups and their games were shorter, partly because they were unskilled at resolving disputes. When a quarrel began, the game typically broke up because no one made an effort to resolve the problem. Boys, on the other hand, quarreled all the time, but not once was a game terminated because of a dispute, and no game was interrupted for more than seven minutes.

Despite its bad press, aggression, skillfully and maturely deployed, sets the stage for manly cooperation. Whether on the ballfield or in the boardroom, in the Marines or in the mailroom, boys and men quickly run up against each other to establish a hierarchy and create an ordered environment in which they can work together best. To the female sensibility, this jockeying for position and rank is just another pissing contest (although they quietly pay close attention to the results). But to rankers, who learned from women a long time ago that all men are not equal, a hierarchy is a tool of cooperation and social integration. Even picking a fight, many psychologists say, is a common way for men to relate to each other, check each other out, and sometimes—mystifyingly to women—take a first step toward friendship.

Of course, the key to making this work is having women hover around the edges of the competition—the breeding experiment—implicitly offering themselves as the prize. Without them, the consequences of male hierarchical jostling can be dire, not just for the men involved but for society as a whole. Lost in the debates about the root causes of violence in America is the simple fact that most acts of aggression are committed by single men. Marriage has long had a civilizing influence on the energies of young rankers: disproportionate gender ratios and the absence or presence of family life have more to do with historical rates of nasty aggression in America than "testosterone poisoning." In the nation's early days, when the number of men far exceeded the number of women, homicidal fights were common in towns like Sutter's Mill, where the ratio of men to women was twenty to one. Within six months after their arrival, a fifth of the men were dead. Other frontier towns, like Leadville, Colorado, had homicide rates eighteen times that of Boston, which had more even gender ratios. In the Western towns that were settled by families, however, there was little violence and premature death. These correlations have persisted throughout the nation's history. By 1950, the percentage of unmarried men was about the same everywhere, and the rate of violent death fell to very low levels. With the decline of the family, the rise in illegitimacy rates, and competition for scarce jobs, the inner cities have become modern frontier towns, and rates of aggression have again soared.

Sometimes the results of women's breeding experiments don't turn out as planned. . . .

Ah, but again I imagine that chorus of protest, this time perhaps from the bitchfesters. Yes, Kate would acknowledge, up until the very recent past the surest way women could acquire power was to marry it, but we are now in the midst of a cultural sea change. As they continue to shrug off the cloak of male oppression and increase their access to power and wealth on their own, women are acting more like men, both in the boardroom and the bedroom. Furthermore, Sarah would argue, as their independence grows they'll be less interested in judging a man by his ability to rise above other men—and women—and they'll acquire for themselves the pelf that historically has attracted them. When you're making big bucks of your own, a cute surfer with a nice bod and good sense of humor will do.

Surely, part of what Kate would argue is true. Women have discovered the expediency—if not always the gratification—of acting sexually aggressive, even if they often resort to such behavior, as the bitchfest participants admitted, only out of necessity and even then reluctantly. But her vision of lady doctors and lawyers marrying beach bums and potters is unlikely to be realized anytime soon, and probably not ever. Current surveys show high-powered women want superpowerful men: recently, when asked what traits they sought in a husband, fifteen women's leaders, all of them veterans of feminism's earliest skirmishes, routinely used high-status words like "very rich," "brilliant," and "genius." Even Kate and Sarah's mate test—their lucky candidate had to have read John Donne, cultivated a sophisticated international palate, and studied classical music—was a poorly disguised status check. Broader surveys of the world's industrialized nations show that today's financially successful women continue to demonstrate the universality of this fundamental mate preference: they want men who are more successful than they are. Even in Sweden, the most gender-equal society in the world, these partialities hold true. That's not to say the issue isn't fraught; as one highly accomplished woman told me at a dinner party, "Ideally, I want my husband to make one dollar more than me."

However modern, that's a formula for marital happiness that leaves only a small margin for error and a lot of room for conflict. Of course, from the long view of evolutionary biology, conflict between the sexes is as natural and inevitable as their essential differences— between the male need to seek status and rank and the female need to link. Together, men's and women's pursuits of their respective agendas act as an engine of evolutionary change, as each party struggles to outmanipulate the other. When one party introduces a new strategy, it sets off what biologists call a coevolutionary arms race. To stay in the game, the other sex is required to work out a new defense.

But it's precisely because men have yet to work out an adequate response to feminism—and devise a formula for marital happiness that's also acceptable to modern women—that the gender war continues to slog along. Certainly women over the past thirty years have adopted a new strategy—they've refashioned themselves, redefined the nature of mutual dependence and partnership, and changed their expectations of their long breeding experiment. Many men's "new defense" has been to let their wives and children fend for themselves or to withdraw from the mating pool altogether. Even those of us who are attracted to and marry accomplished women still often confuse them with rivals, other "hostile forces of nature," and aren't entirely comfortable when they make one dollar more than us.

So what would the standup guy, wherever he is, recommend as an appropriate and strategic "defense," however overdue it may be? For men who have retreated from the mating contests, the best defense is a good offense: they need to reaffirm the value of their natural aggression and desire to take risks, and reenter the competitions that determine who gets the girl. As the former astronaut Walt Cunningham told me recently, "When in doubt, act." The rest of us need to adopt a new code of behavior that enables us to indulge our innate ranking proclivities without alienating the linkers we're aiming to attract.

We need sexual manners.

ANALYSIS

1. What is the best evidence Segell brings to his assertions about men's real nature? Are there any kinds of evidence he cites that you would question or challenge?
2. A good part of the fun of Segell's essay is its jocularity and pungent rhetoric—"bitchfesters" and "dickfesters" indeed. The question is, how seriously should we take this jocularity and jock-talk? Is Segell simply out to get a rise from his readers? Is he emulating the shock-jock king Howard Stern? Is there a serious and less-than-nasty side to Segell's outrageousness?
3. "Men are naturally . . ." (says Segell), and right there we have fighting words for almost anyone. How do you tell what is nature and what is culture? Who gets to decide? On what basis?
4. Segell says that men "far outnumber women" in the "thrill-chaser" department; thrill-chasers as a group (men and women both) amount to "about 20 to 30 percent of the population." But wouldn't that also mean that 70 to 80 percent of both men and women are *not* thrill-chasers, are not highly aggressive and competitive? Is Segell's argument limited by this admission?

WRITING POSSIBILITIES

1. Segell argues that through marriage women have been the tamers of overly-aggressive males. Is he right? How does this view of marriage compare and contrast with your own view?
2. Segell says that about 20 to 30 percent of the population are thrill chasers (and mostly men). How does this assertion intersect with Susan Lorber's assertion (following selection) that there is great *variability* among men and women, and that variability is what is really at stake when we talk about male and female differences?
3. Segell agrees that men, being naturally aggressive, are responsible for most of the violence in the world, especially if they are not married. Why then does he oppose the feminists' "clarion call" to reduce male aggression and violence? Is there a contradiction in his views?

Judith Lorber

At considerable distance from Michael Segell's point of view, Judith Lorber lays out a careful statement of the social construction viewpoint about sexuality: namely, that biological sex is different from social gender. Lorber is no dummy, nor an ideologue—"Neither sex nor gender are pure categories," she notes early in her essay—but she does insist that much of what passes for the biological (compare to Segell) is really a set of male and female roles created by social means and enforced by social authority. If it weren't for that fact, she would insist, we wouldn't have the many changes over the centuries in what is proper for a man and woman to do, as in fact we do have. (Victorian women, as it now emerges, were thought to be especially good copyists because they were the sex that could "reproduce"!) Read Lorber's essay keeping in mind Segell's and locate the crucial differences about sex and gender they both exhibit.

THE SOCIAL CONSTRUCTION OF GENDER

Until the eighteenth century, Western philosophers and scientists thought that there was one sex and that women's internal genitalia were the inverse of men's external genitalia: the womb and vagina were the penis and scrotum turned inside out (Laqueur 1990). Current Western thinking sees women and men as so different physically as to sometimes seem two species. The bodies, which have been mapped inside and out for hundreds of years, have not changed. What has changed are the justifications for gender inequality. When the social position of all human beings was believed to be set by natural law or was considered God-given, biology was irrelevant; women and men of different classes all had their assigned places. When scientists began to question the divine basis of social order and replaced faith with empirical knowledge, what they saw was that women were very different from men in that they had wombs and menstruated. Such anatomical differences destined them for an entirely different social life from men.

In actuality, the basic bodily material is the same for females and males, and except for procreative hormones and organs, female and male human beings have similar bodies (Naftolin and Butz 1981). Furthermore, as has been known since the middle of the nineteenth century, male and female genitalia develop from the same fetal tissue, and so infants can be born with ambiguous genitalia (Money and Ehrhardt 1972). When they are, biology is used quite arbitrarily in sex assignment. Suzanne Kessler (1990) interviewed six medical specialists in pediatric intersexuality and found that whether an infant with XY chromosomes and anomalous genitalia was categorized as a boy or a girl depended on the size of the penis—if a penis was very small, the child was categorized as a girl, and sex-change surgery was used to make an artificial vagina. In the late nineteenth century, the presence or absence of ovaries was the determining criterion of gender assignment for hermaphrodites because a woman who could not procreate was not a complete woman (Kessler 1990, 20).

Yet in Western societies, we see two discrete sexes and two distinguishable genders because our society is built on two classes of people, "women" and "men." Once the gender category is given, the attributes of the person are also gendered: Whatever a "woman" is has to be "female"; whatever a "man" is has to be "male." Analyzing the social processes that construct the categories we call "female and male," "women and men," and "homosexual and heterosexual" uncovers the ideology and power differentials congealed in these categories (Foucault 1978). This article will use a familiar area of social life—sports—to show how myriad physiological differences are transformed into similar-appearing, gendered social bodies. My perspective goes beyond accepted feminist views that gender is a cultural overlay that modifies physiological sex differences. That perspective assumes either that there are two fairly similar sexes distorted by social practices into two genders with purposefully different characteristics or that there are two sexes whose essential differences are rendered unequal by social practices. I am arguing that bodies differ in many ways physiologically, but they are completely transformed by social practices to fit into the salient categories of a society, the most pervasive of which are "female" and "male" and "women" and "men."

Neither sex nor gender are pure categories. Combinations of incongruous genes, genitalia, and hormonal input are ignored in sex categorization, just as combinations of incongruous physiology, identity, sexuality, appearance, and behavior are ignored in the social construction of gender statuses. Menstruation, lactation, and gestation do not demarcate women from men. Only some women are pregnant and then only some of the time; some women do not have a uterus or ovaries. Some women have stopped menstruating temporarily, others have reached menopause, and some have had hysterectomies. Some women breastfeed some of the time, but some men lactate (Jaggar 1983; 165fn). Menstruation, lactation, and gestation are individual experiences of womanhood (Levesque-Lopman 1988), but not determinants of the social category "woman," or even "female." Similarly, "men are not always sperm-producers, and in fact, not all sperm producers are men. A male-to-female transsexual, prior to surgery, can be socially a woman, though still potentially (or actually) capable of spermatogenesis" (Kessler and McKenna [1978] 1985, 2).

When gender assignment is contested in sports, where the categories of competitors are rigidly divided into women and men,

chromosomes are now used to determine in which category the athlete is to compete. However, an anomaly common enough to be found
in several women at every major international sports competition are
XY chromosomes that have not produced male anatomy or physiology
because of a genetic defect. Because these women are women in
every way significant for sports competition, the prestigious International Amateur Athletic Federation has urged that sex be determined
by simple genital inspection (Kolata 1992). Transsexuals would pass
this test, but it took a lawsuit for Renée Richards, a male-to-female
transsexual, to be able to play tournament tennis as a woman, despite
his male sex chromosomes (Richards 1983). Oddly, neither basis for
gender categorization—chromosomes nor genitalia—has anything to
do with sports prowess (Birrell and Cole 1990).

In the Olympics, in cases of chromosomal ambiguity, women
must undergo "a battery of gynecological and physical exams to see if
she is 'female enough' to compete. Men are not tested" (Carlson 1991,
26). The purpose is not to categorize women and men accurately, but
to make sure men don't enter women's competitions, where, it is felt,
they will have the advantage of size and strength. This practice
sounds fair only because it is assumed that all men are similar in size
and strength and different from all women. Yet in Olympics boxing
and wrestling matches, men are matched within weight classes. Some
women might similarly successfully compete with some men in many
sports. Women did not run in marathons until about twenty years
ago. In twenty years of marathon competition, women have reduced
their finish times by more than one-and-one-half hours; they are expected to run as fast as men in that race by 1998 and might catch up
with men's running times in races of other lengths within the next
fifty years because they are increasing their fastest speeds more rapidly than are men (Fausto-Sterling 1985, 213–18).

The reliance on only two sex and gender categories in the biological and social sciences is as epistemologically spurious as the reliance
on chromosomal or genital tests to group athletes. Most research designs do not investigate whether physical skills or physical abilities are
really more or less common in women and men (Epstein 1988). They
start out with two social categories ("women," "men"), assume they
are biologically different ("female," "male"), look for similarities
within them and differences between them, and attribute what they
have found for the social categories to sex differences (Gelman, Coll-
man, and Maccoby 1986). These designs rarely question the categorization of their subjects into two and only two groups, even though
they often find more significant within-group differences than be-
tween-group differences (Hyde 1990). The social construction perspective on sex and gender suggests that instead of starting with the
two presumed dichotomies in each category—female, male; woman,
man—it might be more useful in gender studies to group patterns of

behavior and only then look for identifying markers of the people likely to enact such behaviors.

WHAT SPORTS ILLUSTRATE

Competitive sports have become, for boys and men, as players and as spectators, a way of constructing a masculine identity, a legitimated outlet for violence and aggression, and an avenue for upward mobility (Dunning 1986; Kemper 1990, 167–206; Messner 1992). For men in Western societies, physical competence is an important marker of masculinity (Fine 1987; Glassner 1992; Majors 1990). In professional and collegiate sports, physiological differences are invoked to justify women's secondary status, despite the clear evidence that gender status overrides physiological capabilities. Assumptions about women's physiology have influenced rules of competition; subsequent sports performances then validate how women and men are treated in sports competitions.

Gymnastic equipment is geared to slim, wiry, prepubescent girls and not to mature women; conversely, men's gymnastic equipment is tailored for muscular, mature men, not slim, wiry prepubescent boys. Boys could compete with girls, but are not allowed to; women gymnasts are left out entirely. Girl gymnasts are just that—little girls who will be disqualified as soon as they grow up (Vecsey 1990). Men gymnasts have men's status. In women's basketball, the size of the ball and rules for handling the ball change the style of play to "a slower, less intense, and less exciting modification of the 'regular' or men's game" (Watson 1987, 441). In the 1992 Winter Olympics, men figure skaters were required to complete three triple jumps in their required program; women figure skaters were forbidden to do more than *one*. These rules penalized artistic men skaters and athletic women skaters (Janofsky 1992). For the most part, Western sports are built on physically trained men's bodies:

> Speed, size, and strength seem to be the essence of sports. Women *are* naturally inferior at "sports" so conceived.
>
> But if women had been the historically dominant sex, our concept of sport would no doubt have evolved differently. Competitions emphasizing flexibility, balance, strength, timing, and small size might dominate Sunday afternoon television and offer salaries in six figures. (English 1982, 266, emphasis in original)

Organized sports are big businesses and, thus, who has access and at what level is a distributive or equity issue. The overall status of women and men athletes is an economic, political, and ideological issue that has less to do with individual physiological capabilities than with their cultural and social meaning and who defines and profits from them (Messner and Sabo 1990; Slatton and Birrell 1984). Twenty years after the passage of Title IX of the U.S. Civil Rights Act, which forbade gender inequality in any school receiving federal funds, the *goal* for collegiate sports in the next five years is 60 percent men, 40 percent women in sports participation, scholarships, and funding (Moran 1992).

How access and distribution of rewards (prestigious and financial) are justified is an ideological, even moral, issue (Birrell 1988, 473–76; Hargreaves 1982). One way is that men athletes are glorified and women athletes ignored in the mass media. Messner and his colleagues found that in 1989, in TV sports news in the United States, men's sports got 92 percent of the coverage and women's sports 5 percent, with the rest mixed or gender-neutral (Messner, Duncan, and Jensen 1993). In 1990, in four of the top-selling newspapers in the United States, stories on men's sports outnumbered those on women's sports 23 to 1. Messner and his colleagues also found an implicit hierarchy in naming, with women athletes most likely to be called by first names, followed by black men athletes, and only white men athletes routinely referred to by their last names. Similarly, women's collegiate sports teams are named or marked in ways that symbolically feminize and trivialize them—the men's team is called Tigers, the women's Kittens (Eitzen and Baca Zinn 1989).

Assumptions about men's and women's bodies and their capacities are crafted in ways that make unequal access and distribution of rewards acceptable (Hudson 1978; Messner 1988). Media images of modern men athletes glorify their strength and power, even their violence (Hargreaves 1986). Media images of modern women athletes tend to focus on feminine beauty and grace (so they are not really athletes) or on their thin, small, wiry androgynous bodies (so they are not really women). In coverage of the Olympics,

> loving and detailed attention is paid to pixie-like gymnasts; special and extended coverage is given to graceful and dazzling figure skaters; the camera painstakingly records the fluid movements of swimmers and divers. And then, in a blinding flash of fragmented images, viewers see a few minutes of volleyball, basketball, speed skating, track and field, and alpine skiing, as television gives its nod to the mere existence of these events. (Boutilier and SanGiovanni 1983, 190)

Extraordinary feats by women athletes who were presented as mature adults might force sports organizers and audiences to rethink their stereotypes of women's capabilities, the way elves, mermaids, and ice queens do not. Sports, therefore, construct men's bodies to be powerful; women's bodies to be sexual. As Connell says,

> The meanings of the bodily sense of masculinity concern, above all else, the superiority of men to women, and the exaltation of hegemonic masculinity over other groups of men which is essential for the domination of women. (1987, 85)

In the late 1970s, as women entered more and more athletic competitions, supposedly good scientific studies showed that women who exercised intensely would cease menstruating because they would not have enough body fat to sustain ovulation (Brozan 1978). When one set of researchers did a yearlong study that compared 66 women—21 who were training for a marathon, 22 who ran more than an hour a week, and 23 who did less than an hour of aerobic exercise a week—they discovered that only 20 percent of the women in any of these groups had "normal" menstrual cycles every month (Prior et al. 1990). The dangers of intensive training for women's fertility therefore were exaggerated as women began to compete successfully in arenas formerly closed to them.

Given the association of sports with masculinity in the United States, women athletes have to manage a contradictory status. One study of women college basketball players found that although they "did athlete" on the court—"pushing, shoving, fouling, hard running, fast breaks, defense, obscenities, and sweat" (Watson 1987, 441), they "did woman" off the court, using the locker room as their staging area:

> While it typically took fifteen minutes to prepare for the game, it took approximately fifteen minutes after the game to shower and remove the sweat of an athlete, *and* it took another thirty minutes to dress, apply make-up and style hair. It did not seem to matter whether the players were going out into the public or getting on a van for a long ride home. Average dressing time and rituals did not change. (Watson 1987, 443)

Another way women manage these status dilemmas is to redefine the activity or its result as feminine or womanly (Mangan and Park 1987). Thus women bodybuilders claim that "flex appeal is sex appeal" (Duff and Hong 1984, 378).

Such a redefinition of women's physicality affirms the ideological subtext of sports that physical strength is men's prerogative and justifies men's physical and sexual domination of women (Hargreaves 1986; Messner 1992, 164–72; Olson 1990; Theberge 1987;

Willis 1982). When women demonstrate physical strength, they are labeled unfeminine:

> It's threatening to one's takeability, one's rapeability, one's femininity, to be strong and physically self-possessed. To be able to resist rape, not to communicate rapeability with one's body, to hold one's body for uses and meanings other than that can transform what *being a woman means.* (MacKinnon 1987, 122, emphasis in original)

Resistance to that transformation, ironically, was evident in the policies of American women physical education professionals throughout most of the twentieth century. They minimized exertion, maximized a feminine appearance and manner, and left organized sports competition to men (Birrell 1988, 461–62; Mangan and Park 1987).

SOCIAL BODIES AND THE BATHROOM PROBLEM

People of the same racial ethnic group and social class are roughly the same size and shape—but there are many varieties of bodies. People have different genitalia, different secondary sex characteristics, different contributions to procreation, different orgasmic experiences, different patterns of illness and aging. Each of us experiences our bodies differently, and these experiences change as we grow, age, sicken, and die. The bodies of pregnant and nonpregnant women, short and tall people, those with intact and functioning limbs and those whose bodies are physically challenged are all different. But the salient categories of a society group these attributes in ways that ride roughshod over individual experiences and more meaningful clusters of people.

I am not saying that physical differences between male and female bodies don't exist, but that these differences are socially meaningless until social practices transform them into social facts. West Point Military Academy's curriculum is designed to produce leaders, and physical competence is used as a significant measure of leadership ability (Yoder 1989). When women were accepted as West Point cadets, it became clear that the tests of physical competence, such as rapidly scaling an eight-foot wall, had been constructed for male physiques—pulling oneself up and over using upper-body strength. Rather than devise tests of physical competence for women, West Point provided boosters that mostly women used—but that lost them test points—in the case of the wall, a platform. Finally, the women themselves figured out how to use their bodies successfully. Janice Yoder describes this situation:

> I was observing this obstacle one day, when a woman approached the wall in the old prescribed way, got her fingertips grip, and did an unusual thing: she walked her dangling legs up the wall until she was in a position where both her hands and feet were atop the wall. She then simply pulled up her sagging bottom and went over. She solved the problem by capitalizing on one of women's physical assets: lower-body strength. (1989, 530)

In short, if West Point is going to measure leadership capability by physical strength, women's pelvises will do just as well as men's shoulders.

The social transformation of female and male physiology into a condition of inequality is well illustrated by the bathroom problem. Most buildings that have gender-segregated bathrooms have an equal number for women and for men. Where there are crowds, there are always long lines in front of women's bathrooms but rarely in front of men's bathrooms. The cultural, physiological, and demographic combinations of clothing, frequency of urination, menstruation, and child care add up to generally greater bathroom use by women than men. Thus, although an equal number of bathrooms seems fair, equity would mean more women's bathrooms or allowing women to use men's bathrooms for a certain amount of time (Molotch 1988).

The bathroom problem is the outcome of the way gendered bodies are differentially evaluated in Western cultures: Men's social bodies are the measure of what is "human." Gray's *Anatomy,* in use for 100 years, well into the twentieth century, presented the human body as male. The female body was shown only where it differed from the male (Laqueur 1990, 166–67). Denise Riley says that if we envisage women's bodies, men's bodies, and human bodies "as a triangle of identifications, then it is rarely an equilateral triangle in which both sexes are pitched at matching distances from the apex of the human" (1988, 197). Catharine MacKinnon also contends that in Western society, universal "humanness" is male because

> virtually every quality that distinguishes men from women is already affirmatively compensated in this society. Men's physiology defines most sports, their needs define auto and health insurance coverage, their socially defined biographies define workplace expectations and successful career patterns, their perspectives and concerns define quality in scholarship, their experiences and obsessions define merit, their objectification of life defines art, their military service defines citizenship, their presence defines family, their inability to get along with each other—their wars and rulerships—

define history, their image defines god, and their genitals define sex. For each of their differences from women, what amounts to an affirmative action plan is in effect, otherwise known as the structure and values of American society. (1987, 36)

THE PARADOX OF HUMAN NATURE

Gendered people do not emerge from physiology or hormones but from the exigencies of the social order, mostly, from the need for a reliable division of the work of food production and the social (not physical) reproduction of new members. The moral imperatives of religion and cultural representations reinforce the boundary lines among genders and ensure that what is demanded, what is permitted, and what is tabooed for the people in each gender is well known and followed by most. Political power, control of scarce resources, and, if necessary, violence uphold the gendered social order in the face of resistance and rebellion. Most people, however, voluntarily go along with their society's prescriptions for those of their gender status because the norms and expectations get built into their sense of worth and identity as a certain kind of human being and because they believe their society's way is the natural way. These beliefs emerge from the imagery that pervades the way we think, the way we see and hear and speak, the way we fantasize, and the way we feel. There is no core or bedrock human nature below these endlessly looping processes of the social production of sex and gender, self and other, identity and psyche, each of which is a "complex cultural construction" (Butler 1990, 36). The paradox of "human nature" is that it is *always* a manifestation of cultural meanings, social relationships, and power politics—"not biology, but culture, becomes destiny" (Butler 1990, 8).

Feminist inquiry has long questioned the conventional categories of social science, but much of the current work in feminist sociology has not gone beyond adding the universal category "women" to the universal category "men." Our current debates over the global assumptions of only two categories and the insistence that they must be nuanced to include race and class are steps in the direction I would like to see feminist research go, but race and class are *also* global categories (Collins 1990; Spelman 1988). Deconstructing sex, sexuality, and gender reveals many possible categories embedded in the social experiences and social practices of what Dorothy Smith calls the "everyday/everynight world" (1990, 31–57). These emergent categories group some people together for comparison with other people without prior assumptions about who is like whom. Categories can be broken up and people regrouped differently into new categories for comparison. This process of discovering categories from similarities and differences in people's behavior or responses can be more meaningful for feminist research than discovering similarities and differences between "females" and "males" or "women" and "men" because the social construction of the conventional sex and gender categories already assumes differences between them and similarities among them. When we rely only on the conventional categories of sex and gender, we end up finding what we looked for—we see what we believe, whether it is that "females" and "males" are essentially different or that "women" and "men" are essentially the same.

ANALYSIS

1. In general, Lorber argues that discrimination against women exists because discussions of men's and women's behavior depends on the assumption that biology—not "social roles" or the "social construction" of sex and gender—rules. How does Lorber go about building her case for this argument? Do you agree with her analysis? Where do you think she provides the strongest arguments? The weakest?
2. Specifically, what is the difference between *sex* and *gender* as Lorber uses the terms? Is this distinction a familiar one to you or not? Why or why not?
3. What does Lorber mean by suggesting that "neither sex nor gender are pure categories"?
4. Throughout the essay, Lorber refers in various ways to the "social construction" of sexuality and gender or to the "social roles" that both sex and gender involve. What does she mean by these terms?
5. According to Lorber, how does discrimination between men and women occur in sports?
6. What does Lorber mean in saying that "access and distribution of rewards (prestigious and financial) . . . is an ideological, even moral, issue. . . . "?
7. A key argumentative point for Lorber is the idea that research in sex and gender is off-base unless it groups "patterns of behavior" together regardless of sex or gender; what is her point here?
8. How does Lorber use the "bathroom problem" to suggest ultimate sources of sexual inequality? Do you find her argument strange or puzzling? Why?

WRITING POSSIBILITIES

1. In the concluding paragraphs of her essay, Lorber argues that "There is no core or bedrock human nature. . . . The paradox of 'human nature' is that it is *always* a manifestation of cultural meanings, social relationships, and power politics. . . ." Based on your assessment of the use of evidence and theoretical overviews, how would you adjudicate

between Lorber, who insists on the "social construction" of gender, and Segell, who sees biology only at work in sex and gender?

2. Rather than continue with traditional research into "male" and "female" categories, Lorber proposes the study of "emergent categories." What does she mean by this? How is it reflected in this essay? Would you agree that conventional research into male/female behavior is no longer relevant? (Look up recent discussions, e.g., of health problems relating to men versus women, as an added piece of support or contradiction to Lorber's position.)

3. In "Social Bodies and the Bathroom Problem," Lorber criticizes mere equality in the number of women's and men's bathrooms. Explain why she does this and whether or not you agree with her argument.

Diana Furchtgott-Roth and Christine Stolba, and Ellen Bravo

The nationally syndicated columnist Molly Ivins says that pay equity is the key issue feminism presents ("Equal pay is the essence of feminism"): men make more than women—have in the past, do so in the present, will keep doing so in the future. (One survey, for example, suggests that women make 82 cents to the male $1.00.) Diana Furchtgott-Roth and Christine Stolba however dispute this argument and show that "among people ages twenty-seven to thirty-three who have never had a child, women's earnings are close to 98 percent of men's."

But enter now a critical review of the American Enterprise study itself, in Ms. *magazine. Here, Ellen Bravo criticizes the assumptions of that study. Why, she asks, are women only the ones to take care of children and raise families, thus forcing them off the career ladders that cut down their lifetime earnings?*

Here is where the rubber meets the road. Consider the careful analyses of the American Enterprise report and the criticisms of it by Bravo and decide for yourself to what extent discrimination and/or rational choice inhabits the world of men and women's earning power.

WOMEN'S FIGURES: THE ECONOMIC PROGRESS OF WOMEN IN AMERICA

INTRODUCTION

This monograph analyzes women's condition in American society and challenges some enduring assumptions about women's social and economic progress. The study makes no effort or claim to be exhaustive in the topics it covers or the information presented for each topic; instead, it presents data that illustrate the difficulty in constructing plausible—much less conclusive—evidence from market outcomes to support claims that American women are second-class citizens.

The study also gives a statistical rendering of the often-neglected historical record of women's progress. An examination of historical patterns in voting, marriage, education, employment, and other areas reveals the momentous though gradual changes that have taken place in American society. The authors have tried to provide figures from 1920 up to the present. They believe the year 1920 is an excellent starting point for mapping women's progress, for it was in that year, with the passage of the Nineteenth Amendment to the Constitution, that women achieved the right to vote. Since then, American women have achieved a great deal more.

One hundred years ago, American women were an unequal class in American society, complete with unequal laws, unequal schools, unequal access to political institutions, and unequal access to many markets.[1] Women not only were excluded from some labor markets, but also were not allowed to own some forms of property. To find the causes of the inequality of women was simple: one needed to look no further than to federal, state, and local statutes, which in turn engendered unequal attitudes and expectations. Despite those statutes, however, many women ran farms on the frontier and participated actively in nineteenth-century life.

The twentieth century has witnessed many changes in the legal, social, and economic status of women. The inequality of institutions that characterized the early years of the century have largely vanished. Legal barriers to women's entering and participating fully in markets have been removed. In their stead, equality of opportunity reigns. Employers in the United States may not engage in sex discrimination involving unequal pay for equal work or in discriminatory hiring or promotion practices.[2] Numerous court cases have upheld the statutes. In *Price Waterhouse* v. *Hopkins,* the Supreme Court ruled that Ann Hopkins, who had been denied a partnership at a major accounting firm, had been the subject of unfair discrimination. While some wage discrimination may persist, it does not appear to be pervasive in the American economy. The equality of opportunity that now exists is the result only partly of government intervention to remove legal barriers; it is also the result of nongovernmental forces such as changes in social attitudes that have come with time, changes in technology, and markets' reacting to those changes.

Markets are at their most efficient with equality of opportunity. Without equality of opportunity for market participants, market

---

[1] A market provides the opportunity for willing buyers and sellers to exchange products.

[2] Equal Pay Act of 1963 and Title VII of the Civil Rights Act of 1964.

outcomes are not truly competitive. Competition has led generations of Americans to strive for greater achievements not because outcomes were guaranteed to be the same, but because competition rewards effort, ingenuity, and capability regardless of the demographic characteristics of the participants. Competitive markets yield the greatest innovations and the most benefits for both consumers and producers. Competitive markets, however, will lead to equality of outcome for market participants only if they are truly identical in all respects. Identical outcomes are impossible in competitive markets to the extent that people differ.

Thus, equality of opportunity in America has not necessarily translated into identical market outcomes for women and men. Some market-oriented observers of the status of women in America find nothing unnatural, unsettling, or unexpected in a wide range of disparate outcomes resulting from equal opportunity in free and competitive markets. Those observers do not see unequal outcomes as the necessary consequence of discrimination. Instead, they point to an array of market and other explanations ranging from a transition from former discriminatory practices to differences in experience, education, and skills, as well as to differences in preferences, motivations, and expectations as reasons to expect nonidentical outcomes.

According to those market advocates, *equal opportunity* should be the primary policy objective of government, since federal, state, and local governments currently provide American women with sufficient equal opportunity protections through a complex web of statutes and regulations. While isolated instances of sex discrimination occur, available statutes can remedy any harm. To those observers, American women—and, indeed, all Americans—benefit most from equal economic opportunity to participate in free and open competitive markets without further intrusion from the government.

But other observers of the status of women in America see differences in outcomes as the failure rather than the efficiency of markets. They do not believe that market outcomes should necessarily be the product of free exchange between buyers and sellers, and they see the nonidentical outcomes of men and women in the U.S. markets as the result of a sinister system that is inherently unfair to women and in need of further government market intervention. Some claim that the failure to reach *equality of outcome* is evidence that opportunities are, in fact, not yet equal, that current legal remedies are inadequate, and that further government intervention is necessary.[3] Such

---

[3] This is clearly the position adopted by the National Association of Women Business Owners, despite the obvious gains made by women in business. In an open letter released last year to Governor Pete Wilson of California, the NAWBO argued that women still lacked the opportunities available to men; see "Let's Stop

observations have led to the claim that equality of outcome, rather than equality of opportunity, should be the goal for public policy and consequently further government intervention is needed.

Still other observers claim that the failure to reach equality of outcome reflects the fact that women are victims of their social condition.[4] According to those claims, women do not fully benefit from equal opportunity because many women accept social stereotypes that determine their preferences, motivations, and expectations. Thus, American women are denied the same rights, privileges, and opportunities as men as a consequence of American socialization. The suggested remedy is considerable government intervention on behalf of women.

Finally, there are those who claim that a failure to reach equality of outcomes for men and women in America is simply an artifact of market failure. Specifically, the market does not reward women with their rightful wage. Those market skeptics fail to recognize the legitimacy of simple market differences; instead, their common theme is that currently available legal remedies are inadequate and that further government intervention is necessary.[5]

A sampling of recent statements from some organizations gives the impression that American women are locked in a losing battle with men in almost all areas of society.[6] According to those groups, women suffer from lower wages, compulsory occupational segregation, and the burden of a "glass ceiling," to name just a few. But the story of the evolution of American markets shows that women are closing the gap. That we discuss in the following section. After showing how poverty disproportionately affects women in the third section, we describe standards of evidence for sex discrimination and show why those standards ought to be higher for the indirect evidence

---

the Affirmative Action Misinformation Campaign," open letter to Pete Wilson, June 8, 1995, *PR Newswire*. Feminist leader Gloria Steinem, as recently as February 1996, claimed that expanded affirmative action policies are necessary to "rescue women who have fallen into a river of discrimination." See Karen De Witt, "Feminists Gather to Affirm the Relevancy of Their Movement," *New York Times,* Saturday, February 3, 1996.

[4] For a good analysis of this issue, as well as the debate between "gender feminism" and "equity feminism," see Christina Hoff Sommers, *Who Stole Feminism?* (New York: Simon and Schuster, 1994); also see Gertrude Himmelfarb's review of Sommers, "A Sentimental Priesthood," *Times Literary Supplement,* November 11, 1994; and Irving Kristol, "Sex Trumps Gender," *Wall Street Journal,* Wednesday, March 6, 1996.

[5] A market skeptic holds the view that women's outcomes are the result of discrimination rather than economic supply and demand characteristics.

[6] See, for example, Eleanor Smeal, as quoted in Kevin Merida, "Feminist Expo '96 Billed as Rebirth of the Women's Movement," *Washington Post,* February 4, 1996, p. A22.

proffered by the current advocates of women as victims. The final section provides the conclusion.

WOMEN ARE CLOSING THE GAP

Most recent data indicate that women are closing the formerly wide gulfs that separated them from men in terms of economic, social, and educational status. This section examines the narrowing of gaps between the sexes in wages, educational achievement, labor force participation, occupational choices, and election to public office.

Wages

Women are closing the gap with men in wages and income levels. In the 1960s, protesters wore "59¢" buttons to publicize the fact that women allegedly earned only fifty-nine cents for every dollar earned by a male. Today, some groups such as the National Organization for Women (NOW) claim that women are still punished with lower wages, earning somewhere between sixty to eighty-nine cents for every dollar earned by a male. Those claims fail to recognize the multiple factors that affect income levels.

Employment compensation is perhaps the bloodiest battleground in the wars between the sexes. It is also the area in which the most blatant distortion of statistics has occurred. In particular, two rhetorical devices loom large over nearly every report on the subject of employment compensation: the "wage gap" and the "glass ceiling." Cited constantly by those skeptical of market outcomes, those popular mantras have been used to argue that income inequality between the sexes is the direct result of discrimination on the part of employers and that government intervention is the only way to rectify that injustice. The statistics and arguments deployed as evidence for the existence of both the "wage gap" and the "glass ceiling" do not, however, withstand close examination. Frequently cited as evidence of sex discrimination in employment compensation is the "wage gap." In *Facts on Working Women,* the U.S. Department of Labor reports that the ratio of women's median weekly earnings to men's is 76.4 percent.[7] Even in traditionally female occupations, where women outnumber men, women still earn less than men. This is a disturbing figure, but how was it calculated? What does it really tell us about income differences?

---

[7] U.S. Department of Labor, *Facts on Working Women,* no. 95–1 (Washington, D.C.: Government Printing Office, May 1995).

Economist June O'Neill has argued that such numbers, removed from their context, tell us little about the existence of discrimination, for they do not take into consideration important determinants of income, such as lifetime education and work experience. A U.S. Department of Labor study concludes that the existence and effect of discrimination "on the earnings gap [are] hard to measure,"[8] and data demonstrate that between 1920 and 1980 women's wages grew at a rate 20 percent faster than men's wages.[9]

Even though discrimination is frequently blamed for income differentials, a host of choices made by men and women—personal choices made *outside* the work environment—have important implications for men's and women's earnings. Those choices often have a negative effect on pensions, promotions, and total wages.

Recent economic literature on choices made by women in the working world emphasizes that multiple forces in the market play an important part in determining compensation. Occupation, seniority, absenteeism, and intermittent work-force participation are all critical variables in accounting for pay disparities. In other words, those who assume that discrimination is solely to blame for wage differences are drawing unsubstantiated conclusions. The issue is far more complex.

Decisions that affect seniority and absenteeism are particularly important to understand. For example, a higher percentage of women's work years are spent away from work, owing to childbearing and family responsibilities.[10] Hence, women's opportunities for promotion may not be so great as those of their male colleagues. That in itself is not evidence of discrimination, but of personal decisions made by women. Sally Pipes, an economist and president of the Pacific Research Institute for Public Policy, has suggested that many women do not want to reach parity at the highest levels of the corporate world. She cited a recent study by Korn/Ferry that found only 14 percent of women surveyed aspiring to reach the position of CEO, compared with 46 percent of the men surveyed.[11] A 1992 management study cited by the *Economist* reached a similar conclusion. It suggested not only that men "work more hours than women and spend more years in the workforce," but that "women were one-third as likely (14 percent to 44 percent) as men to aspire to be top dog."[12]

It is likely that women, who are most frequently children's primary caregivers, take the responsibilities of motherhood into consideration

---

[8] Ibid.

[9] U.S. Department of Labor, *1993, Handbook on Women Workers* (Washington, D.C.: Government Printing Office, 1993), p. 27.

[10] U.S. Bureau of the Census, *Current Population Reports,* Series P-70, no. 10 (Washington, D.C.: Government Printing Office, 1987).

[11] Sally Pipes, "Glass Ceiling? So What?" *Chief Executive,* April 1996.

[12] Sally Pipes, "Through a Glass, Darkly," *Economist,* August 10, 1996.

FIGURE 1   Estimated Earnings of Women Ages 16–29 as a Percentage of Men's Earnings, Controlling for Demographic and Job Characteristics 1974–1993

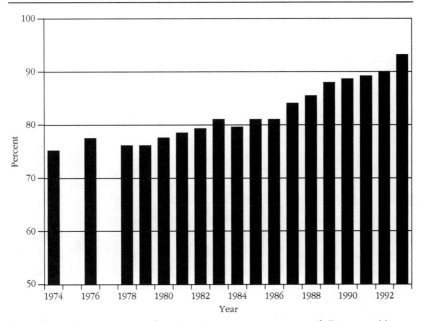

Note: This estimate accounts for education, race, age, part- or full-time, public- or private-sector status, production or non-production occupation, and union status. Data for 1975 and 1977 are not available. *Source:* David A. Macpherson and Barry T. Hirsch, "Wages and Gender Composition: Why Do Women's Jobs Pay Less?' *Journal of Labor Economics,* vol. 13 (July 1995): p. 466, table A1.

when making employment decisions. Thus, as we noted earlier, many women, planning to interrupt their careers at some point in the future to have children, choose fields where job flexibility is high, salaries are lower, and job skills deteriorate at a slower rate than others. Furthermore, men and women choose different fields of study, which result in different income levels after graduation. Since that is the case, comparing incomes by the highest degree earned does not measure discrimination and produces numbers that are politically useful but meaningless in practice.[13] Given those educational and career choices, comparing the *average* wages of men and women is not a comparison of like units. It is another misleading comparison.

Figures 1, 2, and 3 show estimates of the ratio of women's to men's earnings in three different age groups from a data series constructed

---

[13] Katherine Post and Michael Lynch, "Free Markets, Free Choices: Women in the Workforce," Pacific Research Institute, December 11, 1995.

FIGURE 2   Estimated Earnings of Women Ages 30–40 as a Percentage of Men's Earnings, Controlling for Demographic and Job Characteristics 1974–1993

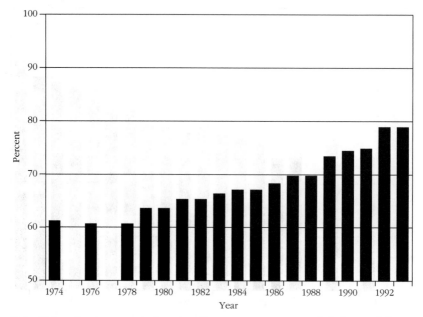

Note: This estimate accounts for education, race, age, part- or full-time, public- or private-sector status, production or non-production occupation, and union status. Data for 1975 and 1977 are not available. *Source:* David A. Macpherson and Barry T. Hirsch, "Wages and Gender Composition: Why Do Women's Jobs Pay Less?" *Journal of Labor Economics,* vol. 13 (July 1995): p. 466, table A1.

by David Macpherson and Barry Hirsch.[14] They control for education, age, race, part- or full-time status, private- and public-sector status, production and nonproduction occupational status, and union status. We can see that women's wages have been steadily rising relative to men's wages in all age groups over the period 1974 to 1993. The greatest gains for women have been in the youngest age group, age sixteen to twenty-nine, for whom wages rose from 74 percent to 92 percent over that period, as shown in figure 1. It is significant that the younger the age group, the higher the wage relative to men's. The *National Longitudinal Survey of Youth* found an even smaller gap between men's and women's earnings: among people ages twenty-seven to thirty-three who have never had a child, women's earnings are

---

[14] David A. Macpherson and Barry T. Hirsch, "Wages and Gender Composition: Why Do Women's Jobs Pay Less?" *Journal of Labor Economics,* vol. 13, July 1995, pp. 426–71.

FIGURE 3   Estimated Earnings of Women Ages 45 and Older as a Percentage of Men's Earnings, Controlling for Demographic and Job Characteristics 1974–1993

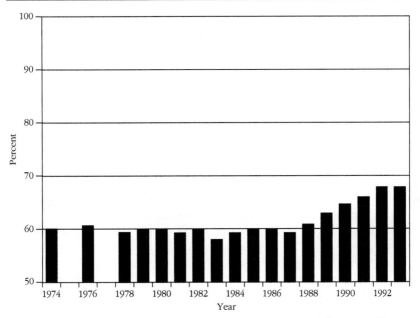

Note: This estimate accounts for education, race, age, part- or full-time, public- or private-sector status, production or non-production occupation, and union status. Data for 1975 and 1977 are not available. *Source:* David A. Macpherson and Barry T. Hirsch, "Wages and Gender Composition: Why Do Women's Jobs Pay Less?" *Journal of Labor Economics,* vol. 13 (July 1995): p. 466, table A1.

close to 98 percent of men's.[15] As June O'Neill notes, "When earnings comparisons are restricted to men and women more similar in their experience and life situations, the measured earnings differentials are typically quite small."[16]

Yet some continue to promote discrimination as the primary cause of earnings differences between men and women. In January 1996 the *New York Times* reported on an American Bar Association study that purported to show setbacks for women lawyers. The study showed that despite the visible inroads women have made into the profession, they continue to face lower rates of promotion and lower wages than their male counterparts, and concluded that discrimination was still rampant in law offices nationwide.

---

[15] June O'Neill, "The Shrinking Pay Gap," *Wall Street Journal,* October 7, 1994.
[16] Ibid.

Included in the study, however, were some quotations from women lawyers that bear closer scrutiny. The study noted that those women lawyers "say that they are less willing to make extreme personal sacrifices" and that they "expect employers to accommodate their life needs," including having children.[17] What this shows, then, is that some women lawyers have made choices regarding priorities that might ultimately have a negative effect on their professional success. If a lawyer is expected to work a consistent sixty-hour week to become a partner, then a woman or man who requests scaled-back hours cannot expect to be promoted at the same rate. What appears to be happening (and what is ignored by those who cite discrimination) is that women in many professions are making decisions about work and family priorities that can result in fewer women's reaching the top of their fields.

That trend is rarely recognized by those who measure success solely by women's performance in the professional world. Nonwork factors frequently assume equal importance: a Department of Labor study found that "63 percent of mothers with children age five and under gave high priority to getting paid leave to care for children."[18] Those women recognized that caring for their children meant higher rates of absenteeism and thus fewer opportunities for promotions—a trade-off they were willing to make.

Many mothers, including unmarried mothers, often work to help support their families. It may be unfair that the bulk of childcare responsibilities continues to fall to mothers rather than to fathers, but it is not clear that most women see motherhood as a burden. According to Elizabeth Fox-Genovese, "Even highly successful women frequently want to spend much more time with their young children than the sixty-hour weeks required by the corporate fast tracks will permit."[19] The quandary many women face when they combine work and motherhood is a painful one, but it is a matter of choices made by individuals. Women are not the only ones making such choices: an increasing number of men are changing the schedules of their professional lives to have more time with their families. Although the consequences of those individual choices are sometimes negative for women's professional lives, that is not in itself evidence of discrimination.

---

[17] Nina Bernstein, "Equal Opportunity Recedes for Most Female Lawyers," *New York Times,* January 8, 1996.

[18] U.S. Department of Labor, "Executive Summary," *Working Women Count: A Report to the Nation* (Washington, D.C.: Government Printing Office, 1994).

[19] Elizabeth Fox-Genovese, *Feminism Is Not the Story of My Life* (New York: Doubleday, 1996).

Ellen Bravo

GO FIGURE

Oh, the thorny problem of the wage gap—what's the right wing to do? They used to say that women didn't deserve as much money as men. But hey, it's the dawn of the twenty-first century; you can't stand by that outdated notion anymore. So in the name of progress, the right has decided to prove that the gap simply doesn't exist. Select a few statistics here, throw in some rosy predictions there, pin any disparity on the choices women themselves have made, and voilá!—the wage gap disappears.

The arguments against the gap are all set out in *Women's Figures: An Illustrated Guide to the Economic Progress of Women in America,* by Diane Furchtgott-Roth and Christine Stolba, published by the conservative American Enterprise Institute. The authors maintain that young women without children make almost the same amount as men in their fields. Therefore, wherever women earn less than men, factors other than discrimination are at play. Women "choose" lower-paying jobs because these positions offer "much-needed flexibility." Women earn less because they work fewer hours and take more breaks from work to spend time with their children. And women just haven't been in the workforce long enough to gain the experience necessary to rise to the top. Given the growing array of flexible options at work, the greater number of women in jobs previously dominated by men, and the simple passage of time, those women who want to reach the top will be able to do so. Or so say the wage-gap vaporizers.

First off, let's admit it: there's a tiny bit of truth in their argument. Young women who don't have any children and who are just entering the workforce do earn roughly the same salaries as men in their fields. *Women's Figures* would have you believe that those equal paychecks will last. If only it were so. Wait five or ten years. Even if she doesn't take time off to have a family, and puts in the same amount of "face time," the woman who started out on a par with the guy next to her will have gotten fewer raises, smaller bonuses, and less frequent promotions. It's certainly not because she's less competent. This truth was brought home to professors and administrators at the Massachusetts Institute of Technology recently. The university conducted a pay-equity study that confirmed women professors' gut feeling that they weren't faring as well as their male colleagues. It wasn't that the university offered unequal pay—at least not at first. But over the years, men were offered research grants more often than women, given better teaching assignments, nominated for awards more often. And all of that led to higher salaries. MIT is doing something about the problem,

thanks to the establishment of a committee on women faculty. Yet
Furchtgott-Roth and Stolba want us to think there's no problem, so
why remedy the situation?

And what about jobs that aren't quite equal, although the work is
at least comparable by anyone's standards? Why do maintenance
workers make more than cleaning women? The authors of *Women's
Figures* don't have an answer to that, since it's a fact that in *any* job
or profession where women concentrate, the salaries are lower than
in those where men predominate—even when they're doing virtually
the same work.

Despite the figures in *Women's Figures,* it's hard to find jobs in
which women make what men do.

- The Web is one of the newest industries around. But female Internet technology professionals pull in only 88 percent of what
  men in the field make. Same job, equal seniority, but the paychecks don't match.
- Women in executive, administrative, and managerial positions
  earn 68 percent of what their male counterparts bring home.
- Female general surgeons take home 77 percent of the average
  male general surgeon's salary.
- Overall, women still earn only 76 cents for every dollar a man
  earns. Part of the reason is the poverty wages many women
  earn. Twelve percent of women in year-round, full-time jobs
  earned less than $12,500 in 1998. The figures for women of color
  are even worse—16 percent of African-American women and 24

percent of Latinas had such low earnings. Nevertheless, the wage gap between men and women in the U.S. has decreased—it was 59 cents to a dollar in 1961, when the Census Bureau first began looking at pay equity. But the improvement isn't just because women's wages have gone up; it's also because of a drop in men's earnings. Downsizing and the closing of manufacturing plants have forced men to take lower-paying jobs. Men of color have been particularly hard hit by declining pay.

What about Furchtgott-Roth and Stolba's other arguments?

- Women choose lower-paying jobs because they offer more flexibility. That's really playing fast and loose with statistics and with logic. Women may cheerfully choose to be child care workers, but they hardly choose to live in poverty as a result. And forget about flexibility. Most women can't get time off to care for their families. Half of the workforce—mostly the low-paid half—isn't covered by the Family and Medical Leave Act. And many of those who are covered can't afford time off because it's unpaid. Meanwhile, 80 percent of working-poor mothers have less than one week of sick leave, which they have to use to care for family members as well as themselves.
- Women work fewer hours and take more time off than men. Furchtgott-Roth and Stolba are right about women making sacrifices to care for their families. The question is, should there be a penalty for that? And if so, how long should it last? One study of professional women showed that years after they had taken an average of only 8.8 months of family leave, they still earned 17 percent less than women who had not taken leave. For lower-wage women, taking time off can have even worse repercussions. It may mean losing a job altogether.
- Women haven't been in the workforce long enough to earn what men do. Forget it. We've already seen that women make less compared to men as time goes on, not more.

There are other ways *Women's Figures* flouts both statistics and logic. It argues that the reason women are so underrepresented in many occupations is that those jobs require physical strength and involve great hazards. Yet this hardly explains why women make up a scant 3.4 percent of airline pilots or navigators, 10 percent of engineers, and 27 percent of physicians. Nor does it explain the discrepancy between the wage and the inherent worth of work traditionally done by women. Whey do accountants make more than kindergarten teachers when both jobs require equal levels of training?

Job	Women's Median Weekly Earnings	Men's Median Weekly Earnings	Women's Salaries as a Percentage of Men's
Accountants and Auditors	$618	$821	75.3%
Bookkeepers, Accounting, and Auditing Clerks	$426	$455	93.6%
Cashiers	$259	$302	85.8%
College and University Professors	$769	$998	77.1%
Computer Programmers	$715	$884	80.9%
Computer Systems Analysts and Scientists	$890	$996	89.4%
Construction Workers	$408	$545	74.9%
Editors and Reporters	$616	$812	75.9%
Elementary School Teachers	$677	$749	90.4%
Engineers	$831	$1,011	82.2%
Executive and Administrative Positions	$626	$915	68.4%
Farmworkers	$262	$285	91.9%
Financial Managers	$703	$1,017	69.1%
Food Preparation Service Workers	$271	$303	89.4%
Health Technologists and Technicians	$486	$588	82.7%
Lawyers	$951	$1,350	70.4%
Legal Assistants	$581	$561	103.6%
Pharmacists	$985	$1,146	86%
Physicians	$966	$1,255	77%
Psychologists	$621	$740	83.9%
Real Estate Sales Agents	$575	$763	75.4%
Registered Nurses	$734	$774	94.8%
Secretaries, Stenographers, and Typists	$436	$484	90.1%
Social Workers	$568	$609	93.3%
Textile, Apparel, and Furnishing Machine Operators	$285	$318	89.6%
Truck Drivers	$371	$520	71.3%
Waiters	$282	$343	82.2%

Source: U.S. Department of Labor, Women's Bureau, 1998

The truth is, women's earnings are still much lower than men's—and so low period—for complex reasons, most of which come down to the persistence of sex segregation and the legacy of discrimination.

- Sex Segregation: While there has been growing opportunity in jobs formerly closed to women, most women do the same jobs they've always done, and those jobs pay less than comparable jobs done by men. Even within certain occupations, such as sales, women are clustered in the lower-paying jobs. For instance, women constitute 82 percent of employees in gift and novelty shops but only 19 percent of those in higher-paying car dealerships. Women of color are concentrated in the lowest-paying jobs, including domestic workers, nurse's aides, and sewing machine operators.
- Discrimination: The continuation of discrimination holds women back—whether it is the traditional "We don't want a woman doing that job" or something more subtle, such as when women are left out of informal gatherings where people pass on skills, connections, and workplace savvy. Because of the expense and often the humiliation involved, women who experience this type of discrimination tend to leave jobs in higher numbers than those who don't. This affects their earnings as well as their opportunities for advancement.

We know how to end both the wage gap and poverty wages. We need to lobby for comparable pay standards that guarantee that the jobs done by women are valued as much as those done by men. We need to continue to push for women to enter traditionally male fields, like construction and engineering. We need to expand equal-pay protection to part-time workers. And certainly not least, we need to organize—to join unions and to become activists.

By masking the wage gap, the right hopes to eliminate the fight for these solutions: you don't need better pay, honey, you just need to embrace the choices you've made, or make different ones.

Why do they think women will buy this lie? Go figure.

ANALYSIS

1. Furchgott-Roth and Stolba says that "among people . . . who have never had a child, women's earnings approach 98 percent of men's earnings." Bravo attacks this very point. Why, she argues, should women make "sacrifices to care for their families" and then indeed pay a "penalty" for such sacrifices (and for some time too, not just in the immediate moment). What assumptions do Furchgott-Roth and Stolba

and Ellen Bravo, respectively, make about women and child-care? Can either or both of their assumptions be questioned? Explain.

2. Furchtgott-Roth and Stolba say that women in engineering (and some other fields) make "as much as" a man. Bravo cites figures to dispute this. What do you think?

―――――――――― **Writing Possibilities** ――――――――――

1. Regardless of whether you follow the statistics and arguments here, what is your sense of the tone and style of these presentations—their rhetorical power directed at you as an audience? In other words, which piece is more persuasive? Explain your preference by citing specific language from both Furchtgott-Roth and Stolba, and Ellen Bravo.

2. A key issue here "personal choice": Furchtgott-Roth and Stolba argue that women choose low-paying or part-time jobs; Bravo disagrees, implying that women choose those jobs because men don't take on the responsibilities of family and child-rearing. Explain which presentation, in your view, is better.

3. Have you experienced differential earnings, wages, or salaries? Explain how your experience intersects with either of the arguments presented here.

Donna Lopiano, and Stephen P. Erber

Before *you read Lopiano and Erber's conflicting arguments about Title IX, look at the "Compliance Checklist" from the* New York Times *and see which items you yourself would be unhappy about (all the items show favoritism to boys).*

In his essay, Erber details the way in which a number of college athletic programs have suffered cuts in athletics for men and the "freezing" of opportunities for women, resulting—says Erber—in a situation where "neither gender comes out a winner." Erber's argument is a pragmatic one: despite any ideal aims, "proportionality" as a principle ruins athletic opportunities for both men and women. Decisions made by various athletic programs, Erber maintains, simply apply a mechanical quota system to bring their programs into line with the proportionality requirement, despite destroying significant possibilities for athletic performances for both sexes.

Donna Lopiano addresses the pragmatic issue that Erber raises by saying that indeed, colleges can keep opportunities for men's programs intact while at the same time "increasing opportunities for women . . . but only by avoiding easy choices. . . ." After listing those choices, (see paragraphs beginning "Before any college . . .", and "We also need to start at the opposite end . . ."), Lopiano adds her own pragmatic note: by adhering to court rulings, colleges will avoid costly lawsuits. Finally, Lopiano brings up her heavy gun—the ethical issue of "equal treatment."

10 For Title IX: A Compliance Checklist
from the New York Times, *June 23, 1997*

Vivian Acosta and Linda Carpenter, professors at Brooklyn College, have been in the forefront in the movement for Title IX Compliance. Here, they have provided 10 places to look to see if your daughter's athletic experience is equitable. A "yes" to any of the following indicates that Title IX violations may exist.

- The boys' basketball team plays at the prime time of 7 P.M. and the girls' team plays at 5 P.M. as the warm-up game.
- My daughter's team uses the larger locker room of the entire student body; some of the boys' teams have separate locker room facilities.
- Transportation to the games is provided by vans driven by the coaches for the girls' teams; buses with drivers are used for the boys' teams.
- Our booster club buys shoes for our football team but our female athletes buy their own shoes.
- The coach of our baseball team is full time; the coach for our softball team is part time. We have 10 teams for boys and 10 for girls; we have 10 head coaches for the girls, and 10 head coaches plus 6 assistant coaches for the boys.
- When budget constraints require our school to downsize its program, it cut an equal number of boys' and girls' teams.
- The cheerleaders and pep band attend the boys' games but not the girls' games.
- Letters and trophies are presented to male athletes at a traditional banquet; certificates are given to female athletes at the last game.
- We have lights and a dugout on our baseball field; our softball field has neither.
- The boys practice in the new gym and the girls practice in the old gym.

TITLE IX: IT'S TIME TO LIVE
UP TO THE LETTER OF THE LAW

Donna Lopiano

The U.S. Court of Appeals for the First Circuit has upheld a district-court decision finding Brown University and its athletic program in violation of Title IX of the Education Amendments of 1972.

Brown argued that it should be permitted to offer fewer athletic opportunities for women because men are more interested in sports than women are. A lawsuit was filed soon after Brown eliminated varsity-level teams for women in gymnastics and volleyball.

To comply with Title IX, Brown has threatened to drop men's "minor" sports (such as wrestling or gymnastics) and to blame it all on Title IX and women's sports. Sour grapes? Sure sounds like it. Let's not forget that the Brown lawsuit began after Brown had spent $250,000 to buy out the football coach's contract and then dropped two men's and two women's sports to balance the budget. Worse yet, Brown then spent well over half-a-million dollars litigating the Title IX case, a sum that could have brought the university's sports program into compliance with the statute. What is going on here? This just doesn't make any sense.

The Brown decision is consistent with other court decisions. In other cases in which institutions have dropped a women's sports program—despite the fact that women on campus were clearly under-represented in athletics—the courts have sided with the female plaintiffs. Colleges and universities need to recognize that women will continue going to court to enforce the law. So isn't it time that institutions stop wasting money in legal fees and get on with the job of expanding opportunities for women athletes?

June 23, 1997, will mark the 25th anniversary of the passage of Title IX, the federal law prohibiting sex discrimination by educational institutions receiving federal money. Yet most colleges and universities still do not comply with the law. Has progress been made? Definitely. The glass is not as empty as it was in 1972, when women were receiving less than 1 per cent of all athletic-scholarship dollars and still buying their own uniforms and equipment. But the glass is only half full. At the college level, across all divisions of the National Collegiate Athletic Association, twice as many men as women participate in sports. (The proportions are the same at the high-school level.) Women are still receiving $179-million less than men in college athletic scholarships each year. (Men receive $356-million annually.) And women's-sports budgets are far short of the budgets for men's sports.

Let us remember that sports are not just fun and games. At the college level, athletic scholarships and admissions preferences for athletes translate into access to education. At the junior-high and high-school levels, participation in sports makes a huge impact on girls' lives: It is associated with pluses such as better grades and graduation rates, increased confidence and self-esteem, and reduced risk of breast cancer, osteoporosis, and heart disease later in life. It is no accident that 80 per cent of the executive women in Fortune 500 companies identify themselves as having been "tomboys" and say that they played sports when they were young.

So why are so many high schools, colleges, and universities still fighting the law? In 1972, almost 100 per cent of the money in college athletics went to support athletic programs for men. The money wasn't there, and still isn't there, to give women equal athletic opportunities unless male athletes and coaches are willing to accept a smaller piece of the financial pie, and unless all athletes take a cut in traditional levels of support. Therein lies the problem. On every campus, one or two men's sports—usually football and basketball—traditionally have received a disproportionate share of the athletics budget (30 to 60 per cent) and are powerful enough to reject an effort to reduce their "standard of living." College presidents (and high-school principals) take the easy way out by cutting men's "minor" sports and blaming it on the women—pitting victims against victims.

Some supporters of men's teams say they are concerned that decisions like that in the Brown case will lead institutions to cut athletics opportunities for men. This issue is beside the point. The real point is that institutions need to stop hiding behind the threat of cutting men's teams and start increasing opportunities for women. Historically, institutions made progress in the 1970s in opening up athletics opportunities for women. But then they slowed down their efforts, and they got caught. When you commit a traffic violation, you can try to make excuses, but that rarely works. Or you can change your driving habits.

Can an institution keep sports opportunities for men intact while increasing opportunities for women? Yes, but only by avoiding easy choices and taking some less-than-popular steps.

Cutting the level of men's participation needs to be a last choice. Before any college or university does that, every one of its sports should cut back on excessive expenditures. Doing so may mean eliminating a spring-break trip or one or two regular-season games. Maybe uniforms should be bought every other year or every three years. The point is that all sports—including the powerhouses like football and basketball—need to find ways to tighten their belts without cutting back on student participation.

We also need to start at the opposite end of the continuum by asking if we can generate more revenues. Colleges and universities need to put more effort into raising money for women's sports; they need to promote those sports, so that women's teams generate bigger gate receipts. They put the time and effort into raising money for men's sports; now put the same time and effort into women's sports.

Colleges and universities also should remember that expanding opportunities for women is not only right; over the long term, it is in their best financial interest to do so. Quite simply, colleges and universities risk further costly lawsuits if they don't "do the right thing." Even if institutions manage to avoid lawsuits, they may not be able to avoid negative publicity. As of October 1, 1996, institutions of higher education are required to publish annually their expenditures on men's and women's sports under a new federal law, the Gender Equity in Athletics Disclosure Act. Public embarrassment can be a strong force that creates change.

Remember, the 20-year-olds of the 1970s are the first generation of mothers and fathers who grew up fully believing that their daughters were going to have equal opportunities in sports. These 40-year-olds of the 1990s are now being asked to support their institutions of higher learning in a big way. How will they feel if their daughters are not receiving the same opportunities as their sons? Moms and dads of female athletes are paying taxes and tuition. They want equal treatment for their children.

The smart colleges and universities will quickly take the high ground. Institutions need to promise to achieve rates of male and female participation in athletics that are in proportion to the enrollment of male and female students. If they develop a plan that will achieve such results within five years, no one is likely to sue.

The bottom line is the need for strong ethical leadership by college and university presidents. They need to admit that sports are as important to our daughters as to our sons. They need to ask their alumni and alumnae to step up to the donation plate to help keep athletic opportunities for men while, at the same time, adding opportunities for women. They need to require Title IX self-evaluation studies that would show them just what their athletics directors are— or are not—doing to increase opportunities for women. They need to require their athletics directors to submit written plans with reasonable timetables to insure compliance with Title IX. Finally, they need to monitor those plans to see that progress is being made. Otherwise, they—like Brown—may end up in court.

While the Brown University decision can be viewed as a victory for women's sports, that victory will be hollow if other college presidents and educational institutions fail to do the right thing for our daughters who play sports.

"PROPORTIONALITY" WILL KEEP BOTH MALE AND FEMALE ATHLETES OUT OF THE GAME

Stephen P. Erber

Once again, a court has ruled that "proportionality" is an accurate measure of an institution's compliance with Title IX of the Education Amendments of 1972 and an accurate test of whether or not the institution discriminates against women. And, once again, proportionality becomes the death knell of men's intercollegiate athletics and Olympic sports.

Proportionality refers to whether a college or university provides intercollegiate athletic opportunities for male and female students in numbers substantially proportional to their enrollment.

In a case closely watched by colleges and universities around the nation, the U.S. Court of Appeals for the First Circuit ruled 2 to 1 that Brown University had failed to pass any of the three tests that the U.S. Education Department uses to determine compliance with Title IX, the 1972 federal law that prohibits sex discrimination at colleges and universities receiving federal money. The decision upheld a similar ruling of March 29, 1995, by a U.S. District Court.

Why was this case so closely watched? Because it was perceived as a benchmark for how athletics administrators can keep their programs in compliance with Title IX. If they do not comply with the statute, they risk an investigation by the U.S. Department of Education's Office for Civil Rights (the government agency charged with enforcing Title IX) and a possible loss of their federal support. To my knowledge, no college or university has suffered such a loss as a result of non-compliance with Title IX, but some of those subjected to an O.C.R. investigation may ultimately have preferred to have done so.

The Johns Hopkins University was subjected to just such an investigation for more than two and a half years, from 1992 to 1995. University officials told me that the process, initiated by a complaint and labeled by the university as a "fishing expedition," included an O.C.R. investigator who asked the men's tennis coach if the university provided presses for racquets. The investigator apparently was unaware that presses are for wooden racquets, which has been supplanted by metal, fiberglass, and graphite racquets at least 15 years earlier. Understandably, officials at Johns Hopkins called the investigation a "flagrant misuse of federal agency money and manpower."

Title IX is an excellent statute and deserves much of the credit for the meteoric growth in both the number of women's athletics programs and the number of girls and women participating in varsity athletics in high school and college. However, one unintended consequence of Title IX has been that many colleges and universities have dropped men's programs simply to meet an artificial quota, which the test of proportionality imposes.

Ironically, following the passage of Title IX, Brown University became a pioneer in expanding athletic opportunities for women. From 1972 to 1978, it added women's teams in basketball, crew, cross country, field hockey, gymnastics, lacrosse, soccer, softball, squash, swimming, track and field, and volleyball. Brown is considered a leader in women's athletics, offering 17 varsity sports for women, placing it far ahead of most colleges and universities. Brown women participate in varsity sports at a rate nearly three times the average for women at American colleges and universities.

So why is Brown in trouble? Because, when the university elected to drop two men's and two women's teams in 1991 to balance its budget (no bowl revenue for the football team at Brown) nine women sued the institution for violating Title IX. Brown's crimes were—and, apparently, still are—threefold. First, the district court that heard the Brown case ruled that the university had not recently expanded its women's athletic program. (However, it had built one of the best women's programs in the nation in the approximately six year following the passage of Title IX. In hindsight, the university would have been better served if it had spread that expansion over a 20-year period.)

Second, the judge said that Brown was not meeting the athletic abilities and interests of its female students. Yet the institution had followed o.c.r. guidelines and conducted a survey of its students that indicated that only 35 to 45 per cent of the women were interested in varsity athletics. Finally, the judge ruled that the proportion of women athletes at Brown (about 40 per cent after Brown cut the women's gymnastics and volleyball teams) was not equal to the proportion of women who were undergraduates (slightly more than 50 per cent).

In the original ruling, Judge Raymond Pettine advised that the easiest way for Brown to comply with Title IX would be to arrange the numbers so that women would constitute 51 per cent of the students participating in athletics, thereby "mirroring" the undergraduate enrollment. Judge Pettine said that Brown could do that by reducing athletic opportunities for men or eliminating the athletics programs altogether.

The recent court ruling reaffirmed that position. Although no college or university has elected to eliminate athletics entirely, many administrators are, unfortunately, focusing their attention on proportionality (taking their lead from the courts) as the simplest and least-expensive way to come into compliance with Title IX. In doing so, institutions are choosing to eliminate or reduce opportunities for men to participate in athletics.

As a result of recent court rulings, including those involving Brown, men's sports such as gymnastics, swimming, and wrestling are on the verge of extinction. Because these sports do not generate large revenues, universities consider them expendable when looking for something to cut. Since 1982, 99 colleges have eliminated wrestling and 64 have eliminated men's swimming. Men's gymnastics has shrunk from 133 teams in 1975 to 32 today and is literally fighting for its life. Yet the quality of our Olympic teams in these sports depends on the athletes coming up through college programs.

Following are examples of how proportionality is affecting two campuses.

The wrestling team at California State University at Bakersfield finished third in the National Collegiate Athletic Association's Division 1 championship in 1996. This was a remarkable feat for a small school competing against major universities, all of which had budgets much larger than Bakersfield's. The head coach at Bakersfield was selected as national coach of the year, and its assistant coach received a similar honor. But wrestling at Bakersfield may be eliminated, because athletic departments at all California State universities have been ordered by the courts to insure (by 1998–99) that the proportion of their women athletes is within 5 per cent of the total number of women enrolled.

That requirement is particularly onerous for Bakersfield, because approximately 60 per cent of its student body are women. An especially high proportion of those women are "non-traditional" students, that is, women older than 22, who have gone back to college, perhaps after raising a family.

Bakersfield supports six men's sports and six women's sports, and women make up about 40 per cent of the school's athletes. With a relatively small pool of women who can or want to be varsity athletes, how can Bakersfield meet the court-ordered requirements? Simple: Eliminate men's swimming and wrestling, which is exactly what is has proposed to do. And how does this nonsensical decision eradicate discrimination against women or increase athletics opportunities for women? It doesn't. It merely satisfies an artificially imposed quota.

Pennsylvania State University, with one of the most prominent, successful, and broad athletic programs in the nation (29 varsity sports), recently decided to "cap" the size of its men's team rosters, a practice that has become known as "roster management." The purpose is to move Penn State closer to proportionality. In reality, the practice means telling seven or eight students who pay tuition (known as walk-ons: remember the film *Rudy?*) and are willing to commit themselves to the training, discipline, and regimentation required to be a varsity wrestler that they can no longer participate— even though their participation costs the university relatively little.

At the same time, the decision allows the coaches of women's varsity teams to limit their rosters. If they are not required to expand their teams, some of these coaches may well prefer not to take on extra work and students; they may take the easy way out and refuse to accept female walk-ons. So much for accommodating the interests and abilities of the underrepresented gender.

In another sex-discrimination case, *Pederson* v. *LSU,* last January Judge Rebecca Doherty stated that the "proportionality test" is inappropriate in determining Title IX compliance, because the test assumes that men and women on all campuses are equally interested and able to participate in athletics. The language of the Title IX statute explicitly says that it should not be interpreted as requiring any educational institution to grant "preferential or disparate treatment" to members of one sex to bring male and female participation rates into proportion with enrollments. But many courts seem to be requiring institutions to do exactly that.

The real shame in all of this is that by allowing colleges and universities to come into compliance with Title IX by eliminating opportunities for men, o.c.r. and the courts actually are freezing opportunities for women, and neither gender comes out a winner. If Brown University currently has 500 men but only 300 women participating in varsity athletics (close to the actual numbers), the institution can comply with Title IX by reducing the number of male athletes to 300. Then 200 Brown University women who might want to participate in the future miss out forever on the opportunity, and so do 200 Brown University men. Where are the winners?

ANALYSIS

1. What is the principle of "proportionality" that is at the heart of this dispute?
2. What does Lopiano mean by "ethical leadership"?
3. Whose arguments (Lopiano's or Erber's) do you find most persuasive and why? How would you counter the arguments of the opposition?

WRITING POSSIBILITIES

1. What has been the experience of your own school in complying with Title IX? Does it bear out either Lopiano or Erber's analyses?

Don Sabo

The women's movement has awakened men to the possibility that they are exploited as much as women by what Sabo refers to as "patriarchy." Men may also suffer disadvantages in personal and family life from following the dictates of the male model.

Don Sabo was an All-American football player at SUNY at Buffalo, he now teaches courses in Sports and Society at Buffalo and at Daemen College in Buffalo. He has written extensively on issues involving sports and masculinity. Sabo's most recent book, Prison Masculinities, *is about male prison life.*

PIGSKIN, PATRIARCHY, AND PAIN

I am sitting down to write as I've done thousands of time over the last decade. But today there's something very different. I'm not in pain.

A half-year ago I underwent back surgery. My physician removed two disks from the lumbar region of my spine and fused three vertebrae using bone scrapings from my right hip. The surgery is called a "spinal fusion." For seventy-two hours I was completely immobilized. On the fifth day, I took a few faltering first steps with one of those aluminum walkers that are usually associated with the elderly in nursing homes. I progressed rapidly and left the hospital after nine days completely free of pain for the first time in years.

How did I, a well-intending and reasonably gentle boy from western Pennsylvania, ever get into so much pain? At a simple level, I ended up in pain because I played a sport that brutalizes men's (and now sometimes women's) bodies. *Why* I played football and bit the bullet of pain, however, is more complicated. Like a young child who learns to dance or sing for a piece of candy, I played for rewards and payoffs. Winning at sport meant winning friends and carving a place for myself within the male pecking order. Success at the "game" would make me less like myself and more like the older boys and my hero, Dick Butkus. Pictures of his hulking and snarling form filled my head and hung over my bed, beckoning me forward like a mythic Siren.[1] If I could be like Butkus, I told myself, people would adore me as much as I adored him. I might even adore myself. As an adolescent I hoped sport would get me attention from the girls. Later, I became more practical-minded and I worried more about my future. What kind of work would I do for a living? Football became my ticket to a college scholarship which, in western

---

[1] A monster in Greek mythology whose singing lured sailors to their deaths.— Eds.

Pennsylvania during the early sixties, meant a career instead of getting stuck in the steelmills.

My bout with pain and spinal "pathology" began with a decision I made in 1955 when I was 8 years old. I "went out" for football. At the time, I felt uncomfortable inside my body—too fat, too short, too weak. Freckles and glasses, too! I wanted to change my image, and I felt that changing my body was one place to begin. My parents bought me a set of weights, and one of the older boys in the neighborhood was solicited to demonstrate their use. I can still remember the ease with which he lifted the barbell, the veins popping through his bulging biceps in the summer sun, and the sated look of strength and accomplishment on his face. This was to be the image of my future.

That fall I made a dinner-table announcement that I was going out for football. What followed was a rather inauspicious beginning. First, the initiation rites. Pricking the flesh with thorns until blood was drawn and having hot peppers rubbed in my eyes. Getting punched in the gut again and again. Being forced to wear a jock-strap around my nose and not knowing what was funny. Then came what was to be an endless series of proving myself: calisthenics until my arms ached; hitting hard and fast and knocking the other guy down; getting hit in the groin and not crying. I learned that pain and injury are "part of the game."

I "played" through grade school, co-captained my high school team, and went on to become an inside linebacker and defensive captain at the NCAA Division I level. I learned to be an animal. Coaches took notice of animals. Animals made first team. Being an animal meant being fanatically aggressive and ruthlessly competitive. If I saw an arm in front of me, I trampled it. Whenever blood was spilled, I nodded approval. Broken bones (not mine of course) were secretly seen as little victories within the bigger struggle. The coaches taught me to "punish the other man," but little did I suspect that I was devastating my own body at the same time. There were broken noses, ribs, fingers, toes and teeth, torn muscles and ligaments, bruises, bad knees, and busted lips, and the gradual pulverizing of my spinal column that, by the time my jock career was long over at age 30, had resulted in seven years of near-constant pain. It was a long road to the surgeon's office.

Now surgically freed from its grip, my understanding of pain has changed. Pain had gnawed away at my insides. Pain turned my awareness inward. I blamed myself for my predicament; I thought that I was solely responsible for every twinge and sleepless night. But this view was an illusion. My pain, each individual's pain, is really an expression of a linkage to an outer world of people, events, and forces. The origins of our pain are rooted *outside,* not inside, our skins.

The Pain Principle

Sport is just one of the many areas in our culture where pain is more important than pleasure. Boys are taught that to endure pain is courageous, to survive pain is manly. The principle that pain is "good" and pleasure is "bad" is crudely evident in the "no pain, no gain" philosophy of so many coaches and athletes. The "pain principle" weaves its way into the lives and psyches of male athletes in two fundamental ways. It stifles men's awareness of their bodies and limits our emotional expression. We learn to ignore personal hurts and injuries because they interfere with the "efficiency" and "goals" of the "team." We become adept at taking the feelings that boil up inside us—feelings of insecurity and stress from striving so hard for success—and channeling them in a bundle of rage which is directed at opponents and enemies. This posture toward oneself and the world is not limited to "jocks." It is evident in the lives of many nonathletic men who, as tough guys, deny their authentic physical or emotional needs and develop health problems as a result.

Today, I no longer perceive myself as an *individual* ripped off by athletic injury. Rather, I see myself as just *one more man among many men* who got swallowed up by a social system predicated on male domination. Patriarchy has two structural aspects. First, it is an hierarchical system in which men dominate women in crude and debased, slick and subtle ways. Feminists have made great progress exposing and analyzing this dimension of the edifice of sexism. But it is also a system of *intermale dominance,* in which a minority of men dominates the masses of men. This intermale dominance hierarchy exploits the majority of those it beckons to climb its heights. Patriarchy's mythos of heroism and its morality of power-worship implant visions of ecstasy and masculine excellence in the minds of the boys who ultimately will defend its inequities and ridicule its victims. It is inside this institutional framework that I have begun to explore the essence and scope of "the pain principle."

Taking It

Patriarchy is a form of social hierarchy. Hierarchy breeds inequity and inequity breeds pain. To remain stable, the hierarchy must either justify the pain or explain it away. In a patriarchy, women and the masses of men are fed the cultural message that pain is inevitable and that pain enhances one's character and moral worth. This principle is expressed in Judeo-Christian beliefs. The Judeo-Christian god inflicts or permits pain, yet "the Father" is still revered and loved. Likewise, a chief disciplinarian in the patriarchal family, the father has the right to inflict pain. The "pain principle" also echoes throughout traditional western sexual morality; it is better to experience the pain of *not* having sexual pleasure than it is to have sexual pleasure.

Most men learn to heed these cultural messages and take their "cues for survival" from the patriarchy. The Willie Lomans[2] of the economy pander to the profit and the American Dream. Soldiers, young and old, salute their neo-Hun[3] generals. Right-wing Christians genuflect before the idols of righteousness, affluence, and conformity. And male athletes adopt the visions and values that coaches are offering: to take orders, to take pain, to "take out" opponents, to take the game seriously, to take women, and to take their place on the team. And if they can't "take it," then the rewards of athletic camaraderie, prestige, scholarship, pro contracts, and community recognition are not forthcoming.

Becoming a football player fosters conformity to male-chauvinistic values and self-abusing lifestyles. It contributes to the legitimacy of a social structure based on patriarchal power. Male competition for prestige and status in sport and elsewhere leads to identification with the relatively few males who control resources and are able to bestow rewards and inflict punishment. Male supremacists are not born, they are made, and traditional athletic socialization and fundamental contribution to this complex social-psychological and political process. Through sport, many males, indeed, learn to "take it"—that is, to internalize patriarchal values which, in turn, become part of their gender identity and conception of women and society.

My high school coach once evoked the pain principle during a pre-game peptalk. For what seemed an eternity, he paced frenetically and silently before us with fists clenched and head bowed. He suddenly stopped and faced us with a smile. It was as though he had approached a podium to begin a long-awaited lecture. "Boys," he began, "people who say that football is a 'contact sport' are dead wrong. Dancing is a contact sport. Football is a game of pain and violence! Now get the hell out of here and kick some ass." We practically ran through the wall of the locker room, surging in unison to fight the coach's war. I see now that the coach was right but for all the wrong reasons. I should have taken him at his word and never played the game!

---

[2] The main character in *Death of a Salesman,* Arthur Miller's play about the tragedy of the common man.—Eds.

[3] Contemporary version of one who is indiscriminately destructive.—Eds.

---------------------------------- **ANALYSIS** ----------------------------------

1. How does Sabo connect "the pain principle" and the idea of hierarchy? What does Sabo mean by emphasizing the role of "intermale dominance"?
2. Sabo speaks of the "initiation rites" that he endured as a fledgling football player; what were these rites? What did Sabo learn from them?
3. In what way is "pain" for Sabo "rooted *outside*" rather than inside?
4. Sabo links "neo-Hun generals" (a joke of course), "Right-wing Christians," and "male athletes," all of whom "take orders . . . take pain . . . take women. . . ." Why are "Right-wing Christians" attacked here? Do you agree with the attack on any or all of these targets? Why or why not?

---------------------------- **WRITING POSSIBILITIES** ----------------------------

1. Towards the end of his essay, Sabo argues that "becoming a football player . . . contributes to the legitimacy of a social structure based on patriarchal power. Male competition for prestige and status in sport . . . leads to identification with the relatively few males who control resources and are able to bestow rewards and inflict punishment." Sabo builds up to these high-level abstractions from the base of his own experience, feminist theory, and extrapolations from feminist theory. Given the high level of abstraction here, one can question whether Sabo provides support for his argument, but assume that we provisionally accept his hypothesis (that in fact is the meaning of *hypothesis*—something eventually to be confirmed, denied, or revised) and test out its possibilities. Consider your own experience with participation in sports and/or with being a spectator of sports. Consider also the stereotypes, images, language, and implications of media coverage of sports. With that in mind, to what extent would you (or would you not) assent to Sabo's broad argument?

Warren Farrell

Originally a vice president of NOW (the National Organization of Women), Warren Farrell has turned away from some aspects of feminism, particularly as they involve seeing men as the aggressive, violent, harassing dominators of women. Moreover says Farrell, men's lives are in danger because, despite feminism, men are deemed to be the sex that must take on the major burdens of life and marriage. Hence, as he argues at length in The Myth of Male Power, *men experience greater stresses in their lives than women, evince psychological difficulties in reconciling the need to succeed with the need to be human, and ultimately show greater suicide rates as a testimony to the damages they endure. As Farrell says in this essay, "few understand the sexism directed against men." Farrell is the author of* Why Men Are the Way They Are *(1986) and* The Myth of Male Power *(1993); the essay here originally appeared in* Family Therapy Network *(November/December 1988).*

MEN AS SUCCESS OBJECTS

For thousands of years, marriages were about economic security and survival. Let's call this Stage I in our culture's conception of marriage. Beginning in the 1950s, marriages became focused on personal fulfillment and we entered into the era of the Stage II relationship. In Stage II, love was redefined to include listening to each other, joint parenting, sexual fulfillment, and shared decision-making. As a result, many traditional marriages consummated in Stage I failed under the new Stage II expectations. Thus we had the great surge of divorces beginning in the '60s.

The increasing incidence of divorce altered the fundamental relationship between women, men, and the workplace. Before divorce became common, most women's income came from men, so discrimination in favor of a woman's husband benefited her. But, as the divorce rate mushroomed, the same discrimination often hurt her. Before divorce became a common expectation, we had two types of inequality— women's experience of unequal rights in the workplace and men's experience of unequal responsibility for succeeding in the workplace. To find a woman to love him, a man had to "make his mark" in the world. As women increasingly had to provide for themselves economically, we confined our examination of inequality between the sexes to inequality in the workplace. What was ignored was the effect of inequality in the homeplace. Also ignored was a man's feeling that no woman would love him if he volunteered to be a full-time househusband instead of a full-time provider. As a result, we falsely assumed that the experience of inequality was confined to women.

Because divorces led to a change in the pressures on women (should she *become* a doctor, marry a doctor, or have a career and marry a doctor?), that change became "news" and her new juggling act got attention in the media. Because the underlying pressures on men did not change (women still married men who earned more than they did), the pressure on men to succeed did not change, and, therefore, received no attention. With all the focus on discrimination against women, few understood the sexism directed against men.

The feminist perspective on relationships has become like fluoride in water—we drink it without being aware of its presence. The complaints about men, the idea the "men are jerks," have become so integrated into our unconscious that even advertisers have caught on.

After analyzing 1,000 commercials in 1987, researcher Fred Hayward found that when an ad called for a negative portrayal in a male-female interaction, an astonishing 100 percent of the time the "bad guy" was the man.

This anti-male bias isn't confined to TV commercials. A sampling of the cards in the "Love and Friendship" section of a greeting card store revealed these gems:

> If they can send one man to the moon, why can't they send them all?

> When you unzip a man's pants . . . his brains fall out.

> If we can make penicillin out of moldy cheese . . . maybe we can make men out of the low-lifes in this town.

A visit to the bookstore turns up titles like *No Good Men.* Imagine *No Good Women* or *No Good Jews.* And what do the following titles have in common? *Men Who Can't Love; Men Who Hate Women and the Women Who Love Them; Smart Women/Foolish Choices; Successful Women, Angry Men; Peter Pan Syndrome.*

Feminism-as-fluoride has left us acknowledging the working mother ("Superwoman") without even being aware of the working father. It is by now well recognized that, even among men who do more housework or more childcare than their wives, almost never does the man truly share the 24-hour-a-day psychological responsibility of ministering to everyone's needs, egos, and schedules.

But it is not so widely recognized that, despite the impact feminism has had on the contemporary family, almost every father still remains 24-hour-a-day psychological responsibility for the family's financial well-being. Even women who earn more than their husbands tell me that they know their husbands would support their decision to earn as much or as little as they wish. If a woman marries a successful man, then she knows she will have an option to work or not, but not an obligation. Almost all men see bringing home a healthy salary as an obligation, not an option.

A woman today has three options.

Option 1: Full-time career.
Option 2: Full-time family.
Option 3: Some combination of career and family.

A man sees himself as having three "slightly different" options:

Option 1: Work full time.
Option 2: Work full time.
Option 3: Work full time.

The U.S. Bureau of the Census explains that full-time working males work an average of eight hours more per week on their jobs than full-time working females.

Since many women now earn substantial incomes, doesn't this relieve the pressure on men to be a wallet? No. Why? Because successful women do exactly what less-successful women do—"marry up," that is, marry a man whose income is greater than her own. According to statistics, if a woman cannot marry up or marry someone with a high wage-earning potential, she does not marry at all. Therefore, a man often reflexively backs away from a woman he's attracted to when he discovers she's more successful than he is because he senses he's only setting himself up for rejection. Ultimately, she'll dump him for a more successful man. She may sleep with him, or live with him, but not marry him unless she spots "potential." Thus, of top female executives, 85 percent don't get married; the remaining 15 percent almost all marry up. Even successful women have not relaxed the pressure on men to succeed.

Ask a girl in junior high or high school about the boy whom she would "absolutely love" to ask her out to the prom and chances are almost 100 percent that she would tell you her fantasy boy is *both* good-looking *and* successful (a jock or student leader, or someone who "has potential"). Ask a boy whom he would absolutely love to ask out to the prom and chances are almost 100 percent his fantasy girl is good-looking. Only about 25 percent will also be interested in a girl's "strong career potential" (or her being a top female jock). His invisible curriculum, then, taught him that being good-looking is not enough to attract a good-looking girl—he must be successful *in addition* to being good-looking. This was his experience of inequality: "Good-looking boy does not equal good-looking girl." Why are boys willing to consider themselves unequal to girls' attention until they hit their heads against 21 other boys on a football field?

In part, the answer is because boys are addicted. In all cultures, boys are addicted to the images of beautiful women. And in American culture this is enormously magnified. Boys are exposed to the images of beautiful women about 10 million times per year via television, billboards, magazines, etc. In the process, the naturally beautiful girl becomes a *genetic celebrity*. Boys become addicted to the image of the quasi-anorexic female. To be the equal of this genetic celebrity, the adolescent boy must become an *earned celebrity* (by performing, paying on dates, etc.). Until he is an earned celebrity, he feels like a groupie trying to get a celebrity's attention.

Is there an invisible curriculum for girls and boys growing up? Yes. For girls, "If you want to have your choice among boys, you had better be beautiful." For boys, it's "You had better be handsome *and* successful." If a boy wants a romantic relationship with a girl he must not only be successful and perform, he must pay and pursue—risk sexual rejection. Girls think of the three Ps—performing, paying and pursuing—as male power. Boys see the three Ps as what they must do to earn their way to female love and sexuality. They see these not as power, but as compensations for powerlessness. This is the adolescent male's experience of inequality.

ANALYSIS

1. According to Farrell, in what ways do men and women look at each other differently? What is the consequence of this difference? Do you think Farrell is right?
2. According to Farrell's analysis, why are men's options limited?
3. What is the antimale bias that Farrell finds in contemporary culture? Do you agree that it's there?

WRITING POSSIBILITIES

1. How does Farrell's view of men's lives differ from that of Michael Segall? Which version most accords with your own experience?
2. Farrell wrote this piece in 1988; does its premise still hold true? Pick a generalization and test it against your own experience, against what you find true in media and/or in relation to other writing you are familiar with.

bell hooks

Where white feminists sometimes see only a basic conflict between men and women, bell hooks sees both conflict and, most importantly, comradeship. For black women and men, hooks argues, the shared experience of racism makes for a closer relationship between the sexes than in the case of white men and women. hooks does not spare black men from criticism about chauvinist behavior but she does see that a common struggle against discrimination must be undertaken by both men and women. hooks' positive position on gender matters is contained in the dual statements that, on the one hand, "Men do oppress women," and on the other, "People are hurt by rigid sex role patterns." hooks also makes an emphatic point about the importance of class matters in dealing with both race and gender; for her, in many instances, gender discrimination is dwarfed by what she sees as capitalism's nasty exploitation of everyone in a marginalized position regardless of race or gender.

hooks teaches at the CUNY (City University of New York) Graduate Center and has written extensively on issues of race, class and gender, in Ain't I a Woman, Feminist Theory, *and* Talking Back. *In a notable dialogic exchange with Cornel West, she has examined the problem of the black intellectual in contemporary culture.*

MEN: COMRADES IN STRUGGLE

Feminism defined as a movement to end sexist oppression enables women and men, girls and boys, to participate equally in revolutionary struggle. So far, contemporary feminist movement has been primarily generated by the efforts of women—men have rarely participated. This lack of participation is not solely a consequence of anti-feminism. By making women's liberation synonymous with women gaining social equality with men, liberal feminists effectively created a situation in which they, not men, designated feminist movement "women's work." Even as they were attacking sex role divisions of labor, the institutionalized sexism which assigns unpaid, devalued, "dirty" work to women, they were assigning to women yet another sex role task: making feminist revolution. Women's liberationists called upon all women to join feminist movement but they did not continually stress that men should assume responsibility for actively struggling to end sexist oppression. Men, they argued, were all-powerful, misogynist oppressor—the enemy. Women were the oppressed—the victims. Such rhetoric reinforced sexist ideology by positing in an inverted form the notion of a basic conflict between the sexes, the implication being that the empowerment of women would necessarily be at the expense of men.

As with other issues, the insistence on a "woman only" feminist movement and a virulent anti-male stance reflected the race and class background of participants. Bourgeois white women, especially radical feminists, were envious and angry at privileged white men for denying them an equal share in class privilege. In part, feminism provided them with a public forum for the expression of their anger as well as a political platform they could use to call attention to issues of social equality, demand change, and promote specific reforms. They were not eager to call attention to the fact that men do not share a common social status; that patriarchy does not negate the existence of class and race privilege or exploitation; that all men do not benefit equally from sexism. They did not want to acknowledge that bourgeois white women, though often victimized by sexism, have more power and privilege, are less likely to be exploited or oppressed, than poor, uneducated, nonwhite males. At the time, many white women's liberationists did not care about the fate of oppressed groups of men. In keeping with the exercise of race and/or class privilege, they deemed the life experiences of these men unworthy of their attention, dismissed them, and simultaneously deflected attention away from their support of continued exploitation and oppression. Assertions like "all men are the enemy," "all men hate women" lumped all groups of men in one category, thereby suggesting that they share equally in all forms of male privilege. One of the first written statements which endeavored to make an anti-male stance a central-feminist position was "The Redstocking Manifesto." Clause III of the manifesto reads:

> We identify the agents of our oppression as men. Male supremacy is the oldest, most basic form of domination. All other forms of exploitation and oppression (racism, capitalism, imperialism, etc.) are extensions of male supremacy: men dominate women, a few men dominate the rest. All power situations throughout history have been male-dominated and male-oriented. Men have controlled all political, economic, and cultural institutions and backed up this control with physical force. They have used their power to keep women in an inferior position. All men receive economic, sexual, and psychological benefits from male supremacy. All men have oppressed women. (1970, p. 109)

Anti-male sentiments alienated many poor and working class women, particularly non-white women, from feminist movement. Their life experiences had shown them that they have more in common with men of their race and/or class group than bourgeois white women. They know the sufferings and hardships women face in their communities; they also know the sufferings and hardships men face and they have compassion for them. They have had the experience of struggling with them for a better life. This has been especially true for black women. Throughout our history in the United States, black women have shared equal responsibility in all struggles to resist racist oppression. Despite sexism, black women have continually contributed equally to anti-racist struggle, and frequently, before contemporary black liberation effort, black men recognized this contribution. There is a special tie binding people together who struggle collectively for liberation. Black women and men have been united by such ties. They have known the experience of political solidarity. It is the experience of shared resistance struggle that led black women to reject the anti-male stance of some feminist activists. This does not mean that black women were not willing to acknowledge the reality of black male sexism. It does mean that many of us do not believe we will combat sexism or woman-hating by attacking black men or responding to them in kind.

Bourgeois white women cannot conceptualize the bonds that develop between women and men in liberation struggle and have not had as many positive experiences working with men politically. Patriarchal white male rule has usually devalued female political input. Despite the prevalence of sexism in black communities, the role black women play in social institutions, whether primary or secondary, is recognized by everyone as significant and valuable. In an interview with Claudia Tate (1983), black woman writer Maya Angelou explains her sense of the different role black and white women play in their communities:

> Black women and white women are in strange positions in our separate communities. In the social gatherings of black people, black women have always been predominant. That is to say, in the church it's always Sister Hudson, Sister Thomas, and Sister Wetheringay who keep the church alive. In lay gatherings it's always Lottie who cooks, and Mary who's going to Bonita's where there is a good party going on. Also, black women are the nurturers of children in our community. White women are in a different position in their social institutions. White men, who are in effect their fathers, husbands, brothers, their sons, nephews, and uncles say to white women or imply in any case: "I don't really need you to run my institutions. I need you in certain places and in those places you must be kept—in the bedroom, in the kitchen, in the nursery, and on the pedestal." Black women have never been told this. . . .

Without the material input of black women, as participants and leaders, many male-dominated institutions in black communities would cease to exist; this is not the case in all white communities.

Many black women refused participation in feminist movement because they felt an anti-male stance was not a sound basis for action. They were convinced that virulent expressions of these sentiments intensify sexism by adding to the antagonism which already exists between women and men. For years black women (and some black men) had been struggling to overcome the tensions and antagonisms between black females and males that is generated by internalized racism (i.e., when the white patriarchy suggests one group has caused the oppression of the other). Black women were saying to black men, "we are not one another's enemy," "we must resist the socialization that teaches us to hate ourselves and one another." This affirmation of bonding between black women and men was part of anti-racist struggle. It could have been a part of feminist struggle had white women's liberationists stressed the need for women and men to resist the sexist socialization that teaches us to hate and fear one another. They chose instead to emphasize hate, especially male woman-hating, suggesting that it could not be changed. Therefore no viable political solidarity could exist between women and men. Women of color, from various ethnic backgrounds, as well as women who were active in the gay movement, not only experienced the development of solidarity between women and men in resistance struggle, but recognized its value. They were not willing to devalue this bonding by allying themselves with anti-male bourgeois white women. Encouraging political bonding between women and men to radically resist sexist oppression would have called attention to the transformative potential of feminism. The anti-male stance was a reactionary perspective that made feminism appear to be a movement that would enable white women to usurp white male power, replacing white male supremacist rule with white female supremacist rule.

Within feminist organizations, the issue of female separatism was initially separated from the anti-male stance; it was only as the movement progressed that the two perspectives merged. Many all-female sex-segregated groups were formed because women recognized that separatist organizing could hasten female consciousness-raising, lay the groundwork for the development of solidarity between women, and generally advance the movement. It was believed that mixed groups would get bogged down by male power trips. Separatist groups were seen as a necessary strategy, not as a way to attack men. Ultimately, the purpose of such groups was integration with equality. The positive implications of separatist organizing were diminished when radical feminists, like Ti Grace Atkinson, proposed sexual separatism as an ultimate goal of feminist movement. Reactionary separatism is rooted in the conviction that male supremacy is an absolute aspect of our culture, that women have only two alternatives: accepting it or withdrawing from it to create subcultures. This position eliminates any need for revolutionary struggle and it is in no way a threat to the status quo. In the essay "Separate to Integrate," Barbara Leon (1975) stresses that male supremacists would rather feminist movement remain "separate and unequal." She gives the example of orchestra conductor Antonia Brico's efforts to shift from an all-women orchestra to a mixed orchestra, only to find she could not get support for the latter:

> Antonia Brico's efforts were acceptable as long as she confined herself to proving that women were qualified musicians. She had no trouble finding 100 women who could play in an orchestra or getting financial backing for them to do so. But finding the backing for men and women to play together

in a truly integrated orchestra proved to be impossible. Fighting for integration proved to be more a threat to male supremacy and, therefore, harder to achieve.

The women's movement is at the same point now. We can take the easier way of accepting segregation, but that would mean losing the very goals for which the movement was formed. Reactionary separatism has been a way of halting the push of feminism. . . .

During the course of contemporary feminist movement, reactionary separatism has led many women to abandon feminist struggle, yet it remains an accepted pattern for feminist organizing, e.g. autonomous women's groups within the peace movement. As a policy, it has helped to marginalize feminist struggle, to make it seem more a personal solution to individual problems, especially problems with men, than a political movement which aims to transform society as a whole. To return to an emphasis on feminism as revolutionary struggle, women can no longer allow feminism to be another arena for the continued expression of antagonism between the sexes. The time has come for women active in feminist movement to develop new strategies for including men in the struggle against sexism.

All men support and perpetuate sexism and sexist oppression in one form or another. It is crucial that feminist activists not get bogged down in intensifying our awareness of this fact to the extent that we do not stress the more unemphasized point which is that men can lead life affirming, meaningful lives without exploiting and oppressing women. Like women, men have been socialized to passively accept sexist ideology. While they need not blame themselves for accepting sexism, they must assume responsibility for eliminating it. It angers women activists who push separatism as a goal of feminist movement to hear emphasis placed on men being victimized by sexism; they cling to the "all men are the enemy" version of reality. Men are not exploited or oppressed by sexism, but there are ways in which they suffer as a result of it. This suffering should not be ignored. While it in no way diminishes the seriousness of male abuse and oppression of women, or negates male responsibility for exploitative actions, the pain men experience can serve as a catalyst calling attention to the need for change. Recognition of the painful consequences of sexism in their lives led some men to establish consciousness-raising groups to examine this. Paul Hornacek (1977) explains the purpose of these gatherings in his essay "Anti-Sexist Consciousness-Raising Groups for Men":

Men have reported a variety of different reasons for deciding to seek a C-R group, all of which have an underlying link to the feminist movement. Most are experiencing emotional pain as a result of their male sex role and are dissatisfied with it. Some have had confrontations with radical feminists in public or private encounters and have been repeatedly criticized for being sexist. Some come as a result of their commitment to social change and their recognition that sexism and patriarchy are elements of an intolerable social system that needs to be altered . . .

Men in the consciousness-raising groups Hornacek describes acknowledge that they benefit from patriarchy and yet are also hurt by it. Men's groups, like women's support groups, run the risk of overemphasizing personal change at the expense of political analysis and struggle.

Separatist ideology encourages women to ignore the negative impact of sexism on male personhood. It stresses polarization between the sexes. According to Joy Justice, separatists believe that there are "two basic perspectives" on the issue of naming the victims of sexism: "There is the perspective that men oppress women. And there is the perspective that people are people, and we are all hurt by rigid sex roles." Many separatists feel that the latter perspective is a sign of co-optation, representing women's refusal to confront the fact that men are the enemy—they insist on the primacy of the first perspective. Both perspectives accurately describe our predicament. Men *do* oppress women. People *are* hurt by rigid sex role patterns. These two realities co-exist. Male oppression of women cannot be excused by the recognition that there are ways men are hurt by rigid sex roles. Feminist activists should acknowledge that hurt—it exists. It does not erase or lessen male responsibility for supporting and perpetuating their power under patriarchy to exploit and oppress women in a manner far more grievous than the psychological stress or emotional pain caused by male conformity to rigid sex role patterns.

Women active in feminist movement have not wanted to focus in any way on male pain so as not to deflect attention away from the focus on male privilege. Separatist feminist rhetoric suggested that all men shared equally in male privilege, that all men reap positive benefits from sexism. Yet the poor or working class man has been socialized via sexist ideology to believe that there are privileges and powers he should possess solely because he is male often finds that few if any of these benefits are automatically bestowed him in life. More than any other male group in the United States, he is constantly concerned about the contradiction between the notion of masculinity he was taught and his inability to live up to that notion. He is usually "hurt," emotionally scarred because he does not have the privilege or power society has taught him "real men" should possess. Alienated, frustrated, pissed off, he may attack, abuse, and oppress an individual woman or women, but he is not reaping positive benefits from his support and perpetuation of sexist ideology. When he beats or rapes women, he is not exercising privilege or reaping positive rewards; he may feel satisfied in exercising the only form of domination allowed him. The ruling class male power structure that promotes his sexist abuse of women reaps the real material benefits and privileges from his actions. As long as he is attacking women and not sexism or capitalism, he helps to maintain a system that allows him few, if any, benefits or privileges. He is an oppressor. He is an enemy to women. He is also an enemy to himself. He is also oppressed. His abuse of women is not justifiable. Even though he has been socialized to act as he does, there are existing social movements that would enable him to struggle for self-recovery and liberation. By ignoring these movements, he chooses to remain both oppressor and oppressed. If feminist movement ignores his predicament, dismisses his hurt, or writes him off as just another male enemy, then we are passively condoning his actions.

The process by which men act as oppressors and are oppressed is particularly visible in black communities, where men are working class and poor. In her essay "Notes For Yet Another Paper on Black Feminism, or Will The Real Enemy Please Stand Up?," (1979) black feminist activist Barbara Smith suggests that black women are unwilling to confront the problem of sexist oppression in black communities:

> By naming sexist oppression as a problem it would appear that we would have to identify as threatening a group we have heretofore assumed to be our allies—Black men. This seems to be one of the major stumbling blocks to beginning to analyze the sexual relationships/sexual politics of our lives. The phrase "men are not the enemy" dismisses feminism and the reality of patriarchy in one breath and also overlooks some major realities. If we cannot entertain the idea that some men are the enemy, especially white men and in a different sense Black men too, then we will never be able to figure out all the reasons why, for example, we are beaten up every day, why we are sterilized against our wills, why we are being raped by our neighbors, why we are pregnant at age twelve, and why we are at home on welfare with more children than we can support or care for. Acknowledging the sexism of Black men does not mean that we become "man-haters" or necessarily eliminate them from our lives. What it does mean is that we must struggle for a different basis of interaction with them.

Women in black communities have been reluctant to publicly discuss sexist oppression, but they have always known it exists. We too have been socialized to accept sexist ideology and many black women feel that black male abuse of women is a reflection of frustrated masculinity—such thoughts lead them to see that abuse is understandable, even justified. The vast majority of black women think that just publicly stating that these men are the enemy or identifying them as oppressors would do little to change the situation; they fear it could simply lead to greater victimization. Naming oppressive realities, in and of itself, has not brought about the kinds of changes for oppressed groups that it can for more privileged groups, who command a different quality of attention. The public naming of sexism has generally not resulted in the institutionalized violence that characterized, for example, the response to black civil rights struggles. (Private naming, however, is often met with violent oppression.) Black women have not joined the feminist movement not because they cannot face the reality of sexist oppression; they face it daily. They do not join feminist movement because they do not see in feminist theory and practice, especially those writings made available to masses of people, potential solutions.

So far, feminist rhetoric identifying men as the enemy has had few positive implications. Had feminist activists called attention to the relationship between ruling class men and the vast majority of men, who are socialized to perpetuate and maintain sexism and sexist oppression even as they reap no life-affirming benefits, these men might have been motivated to examine the impact of sexism in their lives. Often feminist activists talk about male abuse of women as if it is an exercise of privilege rather than an expression of moral bankruptcy, insanity, and dehumanization. For example, in Barbara Smith's essay, she identifies white males as "the primary oppressor group in American society" and discusses the nature of their domination of others. At the end of the passage in which this statement is made she comments: "It is not just rich and powerful capitalists who inhibit and destroy life. Rapists, murderers, lynchers, and ordinary bigots do too and exercise very real and violent power because of this white male privilege." Implicit in this statement is the assumption that the act of committing violent crimes against women in either a gesture or an affirmation of privilege. Sexist ideology brainwashes men to believe that their violent abuse of women is beneficial when it is not. Yet feminist activists affirm this logic when we should be constantly naming these acts as expressions of perverted power relations, general lack of control over one's actions, emotional powerlessness, extreme irrationality, and in many cases, outright insanity. Passive male absorption of sexist ideology enables them to interpret this disturbed behavior positively.

As long as men are brainwashed to equate violent abuse of women with privilege, they will have no understanding of the damage done to themselves, or the damage they do to others, and no motivation to change.

Individuals committed to feminist revolution must address ways that men can unlearn sexism. Women were never encouraged in contemporary feminist movement to point out to men their responsibility. Some feminist rhetoric "put down" women who related to men at all. Most women's liberationists were saying "women have nurtured, helped, and supported others for too long—now we must fend for ourselves." Having helped and supported men for centuries by acting in complicity with sexism, women were suddenly encouraged to withdraw their support when it came to the issue of "liberation." The insistence on a concentrated focus on individualism, on the primacy of self, deemed "liberatory" by women's liberationists, was not a visionary, radical concept of freedom. It did provide individual solutions for women, however. It was the same idea of independence perpetuated by the imperial patriarchal state which equates independence with narcissim and lack of concern with triumph over others. In this way, women active in feminist movement were simply inverting the dominant ideology of the culture—they were not attacking it. They were not presenting practical alternatives to the status quo. In fact, even the statement "men are the enemy" was basically an inversion of the male supremacist doctrine that "women are the enemy"—the old Adam and Eve version of reality.

In retrospect, it is evident that the emphasis on "man as enemy" deflected attention away from focus on improving relationships between women and men, ways for men and women to work together to unlearn sexism. Bourgeois women active in feminist movement exploited the notion of a natural polarization between the sexes to draw attention to equal rights effort. They had an enormous investment in depicting the male as enemy and the female as victim. They were the group of women who could dismiss their ties with men once they had an equal share in class privilege. They were ultimately more concerned with obtaining an equal share in class privilege than with the struggle to eliminate sexism and sexist oppression. Their insistence on separating from men heightened the sense that they, as women without men, needed equality of opportunity. Most women do not have the freedom to separate from men because of economic inter-dependence. The separatist notion that women could resist sexism by withdrawing from contact with men reflected a bourgeois class perspective. In Cathy McCandless' essay "Some Thoughts About Racism, Classism, and Separatism," she makes the point that separatism is in many ways a false issue because "in this capitalist economy, none of us are truly separate" (1979). However, she adds:

Socially, it's another matter entirely. The richer you are, the less you generally have to acknowledge those you depend upon. Money can buy you a great deal of distance. Given enough of it, it is even possible never to lay eyes upon a man. It's a wonderful luxury, having control over who you lay eyes on, but let's face it: most women's daily survival still involves face-to-face contact with men whether they like it or not. It seems to me that for this reason alone, criticizing women who associate with men not only tends to be counterproductive; it borders on blaming the victim. Particularly if the women taking it upon themselves to set the standards are white and upper or middle class (as has often been the case in my experience) and those to whom they apply these rules are not.

Devaluing the real necessities of life that compel many women to remain in contact with men, as well as not respecting the desire of women to keep contact with men, created an unnecessary conflict of interest for those women who might have been very interested in feminism but felt they could not live up to the politically correct standards.

Feminist writings did not say enough about ways women could directly engage in feminist struggle in subtle, day-to-day contacts with men, although they have addressed crises. Feminism is politically relevant to the masses of women who daily interact with men both publicly and privately, if it addresses ways that interaction, which usually has negative components because sexism is so all-pervasive, can be changed. Women who have daily contact with men need useful strategies that will enable them to integrate feminist movement into their daily life. By inadequately addressing or failing to address the difficult issues, contemporary feminist movement located itself on the periphery of society rather than at the center. Many women and men think feminism is happening, or happened, "out there." Television tells them the "liberated" woman is an exception, that she is primarily a careerist. Commercials like the one that shows a white career women shifting from work attire to flimsy clothing exposing flesh, singing all the while "I can bring home the bacon, fry it up in the pan, and never let you forget you're a man" reaffirm that her careerism will not prevent her from assuming the stereotyped sex object role assigned women in male supremacist society.

Often men who claim to support women's liberation do so because they believe they will benefit by no longer having to assume specific, rigid sex roles they find negative or restrictive. The role they are most willing and eager to change is that of economic provider. Commercials like the one described above assure men that women can be breadwinners or even "the" breadwinner, but still allow men to dominate them. Carol Hanisch's essay "Men's Liberation" (1975) explores the attempt by these men to exploit women's issues to their own advantage, particularly those issues related to work:

> Another major issue is the attempt by men to drop out of the work force and put their women to work supporting them. Men don't like their jobs, don't like the rat race, and don't like having a boss. That's what all the whining about being a "success symbol" or "success object" is really all about. Well, women don't like those things either, especially since they get paid 40% less than men for working, generally have more boring jobs, and rarely are even allowed to be "successful." But for women working is usually the only way to achieve some equality and power in the family, in their relationship with men, some independence. A man can quit work and pretty much still remain the master of the household, gaining for himself a lot of free time since the work he does doesn't come close to what his wife or lover does. In most cases, she's still doing more than her share of the housework in addition to wife work and her job. Instead of fighting to make his job better, to end the rat race, and to get rid of bosses, he sends his woman to work—not much different from the old practice of buying a substitute for the draft, or even pimping. And all in the name of breaking down "role stereotypes" or some such nonsense.

Such a "men's liberation movement" could only be formed in reaction to women's liberation in an attempt to make feminist movement serve the opportunistic interests of individual men. These men identified themselves as victims of sexism, working to liberate men. They identified rigid sex roles as the primary source of their victimization and though they wanted to change the notion of masculinity, they were not particularly concerned with their sexist exploitation and oppression of women. Narcissism and general self-pity characterized men's liberation groups. Hanisch concludes her essay with the statement:

> Women don't want to pretend to be weak and passive. And we don't want phony, weak, passive acting men any more than we want phony supermen full of bravado and little else. What women want is for men to be honest. Women want men to be bold—boldly honest, aggressive in their human pursuits. Boldly passionate, sexual and sensual. And women want this for themselves. It's time men became boldly radical. Daring to go to the root of the own exploitation and seeing

that it is not women or "sex roles" or "society" causing their unhappiness, but capitalists and capitalism. It's time men dare to name and fight these, their real exploiters.

Men who have dared to be honest about sexism and sexist oppression, who have chosen to assume responsibility for opposing and resisting it, often find themselves isolated. Their politics are disdained by antifeminist men and women, and are often ignored by women active in feminist movement. Writing about his efforts to publicly support feminism in a local newspaper in Santa Cruz, Morris Conerly explains:

> Talking with a group of men, the subject of Women's Liberation inevitably comes up. A few laughs, snickers, angry mutterings, and denunciations follow. There is a group consensus that men are in an embattled position and must close ranks against the assaults of misguided females. Without fail, someone will solicit me for my view, which is that I am 100% for Women's Liberation. That throws them for a loop and they start staring at me as if my eyebrows were crawling with lice.
>
> They're thinking, "What kind of man is he?" I am a black man who understands that women are not my enemy. If I were a white man with a position of power; one could understand the reason for defending the status quo. Even then, the defense of a morally bankrupt doctrine that exploits and oppresses others would be inexcusable.

Conerly stresses that it was not easy for him to publicly support feminist movement, that it took time:

> . . . Why did it take me some time? Because I was scared of the negative reaction I knew would come my way by supporting Women's Liberation. In my mind I could hear it from the brothers and sisters. "What kind of man are you?" "Who's wearing the pants?" "Why are you in that white shit?" And on and on. Sure enough the attacks came as I had foreseen but by that time my belief was firm enough to withstand public scorn.
>
> With growth there is pain . . . and that truism certainly applied in my case.

Men who actively struggle against sexism have a place in feminist movement. They are our comrades. Feminists have recognized and supported the work of men who take responsibility for sexist oppression—men's work with batterers, for example. Those women's liberationists who see no value in this participation must re-think and re-examine the process by which revolutionary struggle is advanced. Individual men tend to become involved in feminist movement because of the pain generated in relationships with women. Usually a woman friend or companion has called attention to their support of male supremacy. Jon Snodgrass introduces the book he edited, *For Men Against Sexism: A Book of Readings* (1977), by telling readers:

> While there were aspects of women's liberation which appealed to men, on the whole my reaction was typical of men. I was threatened by the movement and responded with anger and ridicule. I believed that men and women were oppressed by capitalism, but not that women were oppressed by men. I argued that "men are oppressed too" and that it's workers who need liberation! I was unable to recognize a hierarchy of inequality between men and women (in the working class) not to attribute it to male domination. My blindness to patriarchy, I now think, was a function of my male privilege. As a member of the male gender case, I either ignored or suppressed women's liberation.
>
> My full introduction to the women's movement came through a personal relationship. . . . As our relationship developed, I began to receive repeated criticism for being sexist. At first I responded, as part of the male backlash, with anger and denial. In time, however, I began to recognize the validity of the accusation, and eventually even to acknowledge the sexism in my denial of the accusations.

Snodgrass participated in the men's consciousness-raising groups and edited the book of readings in 1977. Towards the end of the 1970s, interest in male anti-sexist groups declined. Even though more men than ever before support the idea of social equality for women, like women they do not see this support as synonymous with efforts to end sexist oppression, with feminist movement that would radically transform society. Men who advocate feminism as a movement to end sexist oppression must become more vocal and public in their opposition to sexism and sexist oppression. Until men share equal responsibility for struggling to end sexism, feminist movement will reflect the very sexist contradictions we wish to eradicate.

Separatist ideology encourages us to believe that women alone can make feminist revolution—we cannot. Since men are the primary agents maintaining and supporting sexism and sexist oppression, they can only be successfully eradicated if men are compelled to assume responsibility for transforming their consciousness and the consciousness of society as a whole. After hundreds of years of anti-racist struggle, more than ever before non-white people are currently calling attention to the primary role white people must play in anti-racist struggle. The same is true of the struggle to eradicate sexism—men have a primary role to play. This does not mean that they are better equipped to lead feminist movement; it does mean that they should share equally in resistance struggle. In particular, men have a tremendous contribution to make to feminist struggle in the area of exposing, confronting, opposing, and transforming the sexism of their male peers. When men show a willingness to assume equal responsibility in feminist struggle, performing whatever tasks are necessary, women should affirm their revolutionary work by acknowledging them as comrades in struggle.

ANALYSIS

1. How does hooks analyze the differences between the experience of black women and white women? On what basis does she argue that black women and black men have a special understanding of liberation struggles?
2. Why, according to hooks, have many black women rejected feminism? I.e., what does she say about the antimale attitude of feminism? Do you judge this to be true of feminism today?
3. hooks asserts that "All men support and perpetuate sexism and sexist oppression in one form or another." Does she offer support for this assertion? What might be said in support of it? Against it? In the section dealing with "sexist oppression in black communities," what is hooks' criticism of women in such communities?
4. What, on the other hand, does hooks see as the importance of "the pain men experience" to the struggle for equality between men and women?
5. ". . . the emphasis on 'man as enemy'," hooks writes, "deflected attention away from . . . improving relationships between women and men, ways for men and women to work together to unlearn sexism." hooks also speaks here of "[B]ourgeois women. . . ." What does she mean by criticizing such women's attitudes toward men (442)?

WRITING POSSIBILITIES

1. At the close of her essay, hooks asserts that men must be "compelled to assume responsibility for transforming their consciousness and the consciousness of society as a whole." In what respects does she want this kind of transformation to occur?
2. How does hooks's analysis invoke race and class as ways to understand more deeply the nature of gender in contemporary society? Where do you particularly agree or disagree with hooks's analysis?

7

RELIGION IN
MULTICULTURAL AMERICA

The story of Mildred Rosario's tangles with the doctrine of church-state separation ("[Prayer] Gets Teacher Axed," pages 450–451) is but one of many, distinguished only by the wonderfully flamboyant front-page coverage of the *New York Post:* who could beat the "Bible Belted" headline or the double-page spread inside about Rosario being done in by the educational bureaucracy? (Though to be fair, the *Post* also ran an Op-Ed piece in defense of the Board of Education's firing of Rosario.) And indeed, many such incidents can be found almost every day around the country: a judge wants to post the Ten Commandments in his courtroom (and the ACLU objects); a Board of Education makes a move against the teaching of evolution as nothing but "theory," to be taught alongside Creationism (biology teachers object); a Catholic priest is turned down (initially) for the post of Chaplain to Congress—and Catholics wonder if anti-Catholic prejudice is operating (atheists wonder how come there is even a chaplain in Congress to begin with). And during the 2000 presidential campaign, Senator Lieberman's enthusiastic references to God and religion invited many different opinions as to whether these represented a new opening towards the values of religion or, contrariwise, a problematic intrusion of religion into the public sphere.

In more formal terms, such incidents raise the question of the Establishment Clause of the First Amendment to the Constitution which dictates that Congress shall "make no law respecting an establishment of religion, or prohibiting the free exercise thereof. . . ." This is the "wall of separation" between church and state which Mildred Rosario ostensibly breached, and strict constitutionalists would argue that Ms. Rosario's little prayer represented (even as a symbolic act) an "establishment of religion" (the Jehovah's Witness parent who sued the school board thought so). Many on the other side have argued either that Rosario's prayers did not constitute an "establishment of religion" or at the most that they represented a minor matter and were a decent and humane act.

The two readings by Jefferson on this issue—the "Letter to the Danbury Baptists" and the "Act for Establishing Religious Freedom" provide some historical background for the possible intentions of Jefferson, the Enlightenment figure most directly associated with the idea of church-state separation. The contrastive readings by Michael Novak and Lee Albert take the wall of separation story into issues raised by the 2000 presidential campaign, Novak arguing that the "wall" as a metaphor no longer has any authority, Albert's arguing that bringing religion into politics is, for one group or another, to reject the American principle of respect for "diversity."

The student essay on a debate about teaching Creationism and evolutionary theory in Kansas illustrates how church-state issues touch—and surprisingly, to the student—even what appears to be simple scientific truth: a cry from the back of the class at the end of the debate deeply unsettled the writer—"Don't you believe in miracles?"

Finally, the chapter concludes with two essays about the personal dimensions of religious faith: Stephen Dubner's "Choosing My Religion" and Geraldine Brooks's "Faith is a Compromise: What Does the Koran Say About Nasreen's Nose Ring?" These are not matters for the Supreme Court, but rather for every individual and family: religious faith changes within the context of the society in which it is situated, and most certainly in American society, where experimentation and the value of heterogeneity operate often in conflict with the ideal of religious unity and communal faith.

New York Post, June 16, 1998 by Angela Mosconi and Susan Edelman

The New York Post *story on the Mildred Rosario incident should be read along with the accompanying Op-Ed commentary from the* Post *and a day's worth of letters on the case from the* New York Times. *A public school teacher, Rosario was summarily fired for leading her elementary students in prayer on the death of one of their classmates: the problem came to the attention of the New York City School Board because the parent of one member of the class, a Jehovah's Witness, complained about the intrusion of religious matters in a secular environment.*

Bible Belted: School Prayer Gets Teacher Axed

A Bronx junior-high-school teacher has been fired for talking about God and leading her sixth-graders in prayer.

Mildred Rosario, a self-described born-again Christian, told students at IS 74 in Hunts Point that a drowned classmate was "in heaven" and that "Jesus, our Savior," came "to save all the human race."

She then prayed with the 11- and 12-year-old kids by going from one to the other and placing her hands over their heads.

Board of Education officials said Rosario, who was fired Friday, violated laws requiring the separation of church and state.

"We do follow the Constitution and state laws regarding the teaching of religion," said spokesman David Galarza.

Rosario—who showed up at the school yesterday to clear out her desk—waved the Bible, hugged teary-eyed students and said her firing was unfair.

"A lot of programs are brought into our schools where they talk about condoms, drugs and everything else, but we cannot talk about God," she told the *Post.*

"This is an injustice. Without Him, nothing is possible."

Rosario, 43, a member of the Pentecostal church and mother of two, was booted on Friday from her job at IS 74—one of a dozen low-performing schools under the direct supervision of Schools Chancellor Rudy Crew. She has taught at the school since September.

Her firing followed a complaint from the guardian of one of the students in the class, an 11-year-old girl who is a Jehovah's Witness.

"It shouldn't have happened in school," said the woman who blew the whistle, the child's sister-in-law.

Rosario said the subject came up June 8 after a student in her homeroom class questioned her about the recent death of fellow sixth-grader Christopher Lee.

Lee, 11, was stepping over rocks in the Bronx Kill a week earlier when he was pulled under by a rising tide and drowned.

"Mrs. Rosario, did Christopher Lee go to heaven?" an 11-year-old girl asked.

"Of course, he went to heaven," the teacher replied.

Rosario said she then told the students if they wanted to sit and talk about God it was their "free will" and right to do so.

"I told them whoever doesn't want to participate in this conversation should go use the computer or read some books," said Rosario, who teaches mostly bilingual sixth-, seventh- and eighth-graders at the Bryant Avenue school.

Rosario said all 29 students remained for the discussion.

Rosario said she told students about heaven and said that Chris is "at peace . . . I told them about the great love of God, that he sent Jesus, our Savior, to die for us, and that he came to save all the human race."

She then led the prayer.

"I told the principal our public school system is messed up because we're taking Jesus, prayers, and God out of school," she said. "Why do we have to hide something so special and beautiful that the students want to know?"

Civil libertarians were aghast at Rosario's "poor judgment" and "inappropriate behavior."

"She was teaching Christian doctrine, and there might have been children of other faiths in that room for whom Christ was not the messiah," said Sheldon Friedberg, executive director of the Greater New York Region of the National Conference for Community and Justice, a group founded by Christians and Jews.

When you teach a single point of view without letting the students know—particularly at that impressionable age—that there are other viewpoints as well, then you're treating them unfairly. You may be planting ideas in their heads that their parents don't want put there."

While a prohibition against prayer in public schools has sparked protests and court fights in Alabama and several other states, the issue has rarely arisen in New York City with its rainbow of religions.

"I've never heard of anything like this," said Norman Siegel, executive director of the New York Civil Liberties Union.

"This is the first time I've heard of such an explicit a recognition of Jesus Christ and God in a public school."

BOARD WAS RIGHT TO STRIKE
LIKE LIGHTNING

Andrea Peyser

It isn't often the sluggish Board of Education acts with lightning swiftness to correct a wrong committed in the distant Bronx.

But the board acted quickly, decisively—and properly—when it gave the boot to one Mildred Rosario, a teacher who imposed her born-again Christian beliefs on the most captive of audiences: a sixth-grade class.

Now, as might be expected, some parents in the often-troubled Bronx, where Godlessness might account for a portion of the ills, are unhappy about Rosario's ouster.

Rosario doesn't dispute the basic facts:

One day, she sat down a class of pubic-school students—a group representing a variety of religious denominations—and informed the little sinners that God sent Jesus our Savior, to die for us.

"And he came to save all the human race."

Then she led the kids, one by one, in Christian prayer.

As you can imagine, Rosario has put the gentlest spin on her outrageous effort to convert the school group into junior members of her Pentecostal faith. She insists she merely offered to talk about God with the children, who were grieving for a fellow student who drowned accidentally.

"I told them whoever doesn't want to participate in this conversation should go and use the computer or read some books," Rosario told the *Post's* Angela Mosconi.

What do you know? "They all wanted to say and listen," Rosario said.

The view of Rosario's actions was a bit different inside IS 74, in Hunts Point.

As one observer sees it, to a bunch of 11-year-olds, Rosario's queries, "Do you accept Jesus as your savior?" and "Do you want me to pray for you?" sounded less like optional offers of religious guidance than a teacher's orders.

"They didn't really have any choice," a source at the school told me.

How could they? When you were in sixth grade and a teacher said words to the effect—"Today, class, would you like to discuss your multiplication tables?"—I don't think any among us would have felt comfortable replying, "Sorry, I'd rather stare into space."

Before Rosario is made into some kind of martyr, two other factors—things that may have contributed to her being exiled so quickly—should be taken into consideration.

Apparently, she is not the brightest light at IS 74. Although she has been teaching three years, Rosario has only been at this particular school for one year; sources say she did not receive a satisfactory rating at her previous assignment.

Also, despite clear and uncompromising federal law separating church and state, and the fact that New York City kids represent a veritable religious Tower of Babel, Rosario sees absolutely nothing amiss in witnessing for her religious sect in the public schools.

After the school forwarded a parent's complaint about Rosario's unorthodox—not to mention illegal—religious instruction to the Board of Ed, the board called her in for a meeting.

"She basically said all that and more to the kids," a source said. "And then she put what she did in writing."

In short, Mildred Rosario, fueled by the belief that she understands the will of God, believes she is in the right. And everyone who disagrees is wrong.

Lack of judgment, a quality this teacher possesses in abundance, is not even the greatest of her sins. It is her lack of humility.

There is a good reason this country does not allow religious indoctrination in its public schools. We are a society that cherishes each individual's right to religious freedom. At the same time, sixth-grade students, by law, do not have any choice whether to sit in a classroom: they simply must.

So when you ram your particular faith down the throats of public school kids, you are, by definition, denying their right to religious freedom.

There is a place for religion in the lives of students. It is in the home, church, synagogue or mosque of their families' choice.

Bronx parents worried about their children's religious training must know that their borough contains many houses of worship. Each one, no doubt, is more than willing to accept kids of any age.

PARENTS CALL FIRING "A DAMN SHAME"

Angela Mosconi and Neil Graves

Parents at IS 74 yesterday were virtually unanimous in their support for teacher Mildred Rosario, fired for talking about Christ and praying in class.

"Because you mentioned God? Come on!" shouted one of several parents in a mob of kids who greeted Rosario with cheers and hugs when she showed up at the Bronx school waving a bible.

"It's a damn shame," said Lee Murray, 54, whose grandson, Jason Stewart, was one of Rosario's pupils.

"Even if it was prayer, that's what's missing from the schools today. There would be better kids in this world today if prayer was in school," added Murray, who said her grandson has improved "so much" since taking Rosario's bilingual class.

Flor Guzman, who's 12-year-old son, Steven, prayed with Rosario, said Rosario was like a second mother to her child, who suffers from asthma.

"She always took care of him," Guzman said. "I wish every teacher could mention God at least once in the school."

Angry parents said Principal Leroy Johnson promised that a Board of Education representative would meet with them today to explain why Rosario was fired.

Rosario, who is several credits short of obtaining her permanent teacher's license, said she was told by officials she will probably never work in the city system again.

When she pulled up at the school in a van with her husband and son, more than 15 pupils ran down the street to greet her.

Some of the kids, who affectionately call Rosario "Mami," cried.

"It's a real dumb reason they got rid of her," said Juan Ruiz, 13. "We talk about guns and condoms—and they give us condoms to have safe sex on the streets. But then we can't talk about the one who made us.

"I really want my teacher back," Juan said, adding that Rosario even came to his house to drop off books and check on him after he broke an arm.

"She helped me when I was failing. She was the only one who cared about me."

Rosario hinted she may sue the board.

"I'll take this to the Supreme Court if I have to," she said.

When asked if she had a lawyer, she replied, "Right now, my lawyer is God."

LETTERS ON ROSARIO CASE

PROSELYTIZING TEACHER VIOLATED STUDENTS' RIGHTS

To the Editor:

It is interesting that Tom DeLay, the House majority whip, the Rutherford Institute and other conservative political and religious groups have come out to defend the right of Mildred Rosario, a New York City public school teacher, to proselytize in the classroom (news article, June 26).

You say she asked students "if anyone would like to accept Jesus as their personal Saviour" and then laid her hand on their foreheads and invoked Jesus to protect them and their families. Mr. DeLay and others seem to view her dismissal as a violation of religious freedom, but the real violation came when she used her position as a teacher to proselytize her students.

The religious right claims to be concerned with religious freedom in the public school classroom, but this incident shows that its real interest is in converting children to Christianity.

REBECCA LESSES
New York, June 26, 1998

To the Editor:

As a faculty member at the City University of New York, I was astonished to read (news article, June 26) that a staunch enforcer of academic standards like Mayor Rudolph W. Giuliani would give a second chance to a public school teacher dismissed for asking sixth-graders "to accept Jesus as their personal Saviour." If precious class time is devoted to the laying on of hands, how will Mildred Rosario's students acquire the basic skills they will later need to avoid remediation in college?

At CUNY, they won't have a prayer.

ELISABETH GITTER
New York, June 26, 1998

*The writer is a professor of English,
John Jay College of Criminal Justice, CUNY.*

To the Editor:

Your July 3 editorial "Prayer in a Bronx School" points out how Mildred Rosario's action "has humanized" the issue. The school principal calls for a moment of silence for a fifth grader who has drowned. Faced with questions from students related to the mysteries of life and death, Mrs. Rosario seems to have clearly crossed a line in providing answers from her religious faith that amounted to impermissible proselytizing in a public school. However, that school cannot provide answers that can only come out of religious traditions.

Those parents who supported Mrs. Rosario should have the freedom to choose the kind of schools that can provide the answers they wish for their children. The affluent can afford private-school tuition; moderate-income families can afford parochial-school tuition. But poor parents need a means-tested school choice voucher system like that approved by the Wisconsin Supreme Court.

(Msgr.) HARRY J. BYRNE
New York, July 4, 1998

ANALYSIS

1. What is the buried allusion (and pun) in the *Post's* "Bible Belted"? (Check the dictionary.)
2. Read the "Bible Belted" news story, the Op-Ed pieces from the *Post,* and the letters on the story from the *New York Times* and decide for yourself, on the merits of the particular case, whether you would have fired Ms. Rosario. (455–456)
3. After reading the selection of letters to the editor which appeared in the *New York Times* following Ms. Rosario's suspension, act as a surveyor (*not an arguer*): what range of opinions do you find among these letter writers? What reasons, for and against, do they provide in the case of Ms. Rosario?

WRITING POSSIBILITIES

1. Compose your own letter to the editor about Ms. Rosario's decision to lead prayers for a classmate who died: explain whether you think she was right or wrong and the reasoning behind your decision. Also indicate what kind of newspaper you're writing to—the tabloid *Post* or the august *Times.*

Article 1, Bill of Rights
(The Establishment Clause)

Mildred Rosario's decision to lead her young students in prayers in a public school brings up the perennial question of what America's founding fathers had to say about church-state relationships. There are two key sources here. One is simply the First Amendment to the Constitution (i.e., the very first article of the Bill of Rights) and the key phrase that Congress shall make "no law respecting an establishment of religion"—the "Establishment" clause as it is known. Another is a set of two statements by Thomas Jefferson on the "wall" of separation between church and state. It was Jefferson who coined the metaphor of the "wall," although commentators often argue that the "wall" wasn't meant even by Jefferson to be as high as often interpreted.

ARTICLE I[1]

Congress shall make no law respecting an establishment of religion, or prohibiting the free exercise thereof; or abridging the freedom of speech, or of the press; or the right of the people peaceably to assemble, and to petition the Government for a redress of grievances.

Thomas Jefferson

AN ACT FOR ESTABLISHING RELIGIOUS FREEDOM

Although the Assembly received this bill in 1779, it was not enacted until 1786 in reaction against proposed assessments for the establishment which had been in part stimulated and focused by Madison's Memorial. As passed by the Assembly a clause of the Virginia Declaration of Rights was substituted in the text as here reproduced. It is widely noted that Jefferson ranked this act as one of his most significant achievements.

SECTION I. Well aware that the opinions and belief of men depend not on their own will, but follow involuntarily the evidence proposed to their minds; that Almighty God hath created the mind free, and manifested his supreme will that free it shall remain by making it altogether insusceptible of restraint; that all attempts to influence it by

---

[1] The first ten amendments were adopted in 1791.

temporal punishments, or burthens, or by civil incapacitations, tend only to beget habits of hypocrisy and meanness, and are a departure from the plan of the holy author of our religion, who being lord both of body and mind, yet choose not to propagate it by coercions on either, as was in his Almighty power to do, but to exalt it by its influence on reason alone; that the impious presumption of legislature and ruler, civil as well as ecclesiastical, who, being themselves but fallible and uninspired men, have assumed dominion over the faith of others, setting up their own opinions and modes of thinking as the only true and infallible, and as such endeavoring to impose them on others, hath established and maintained false religions over the greatest part of the world and through all time: That to compel a man to furnish contributions of money for the propagation of opinions which he disbelieves and abhors, is sinful and tyrannical; that even the forcing him to support this or that teacher of his own religious persuasion, is depriving him of the comfortable liberty of giving his contributions to the particular pastor whose morals he would make his pattern, and whose powers he feels most persuasive to righteousness; and is withdrawing from the ministry those temporary rewards, which proceeding from an approbation of their personal conduct, are an additional incitement to earnest and unremitting labours for the instruction of mankind; that our civil-rights have no dependance on our religious opinions, any more than our opinions in physics or geometry; and therefore the proscribing any citizen as unworthy the public confidence by laying upon him an incapacity of being called to offices of trust or emolument, unless he profess or renounce this or that religious opinion, is depriving him injudiciously of those privileges and advantages to which, in common with his fellow-citizens, he has a natural right; that it tends also to corrupt the principles of that very religion it is meant to encourage, by bribing with a monopoly of worldly honours and emoluments, those who will externally profess and conform to it; that though indeed these are criminals who do not withstand such temptation, yet neither are those innocent who lay the bait in their way; that the opinions of men are not the object of civil government, nor under its jurisdiction; that to suffer the civil magistrate to intrude his powers into the field of opinion and to restrain the profession or propagation of principles on supposition of their ill tendency is a dangerous falacy, which at once destroys all religious liberty, because he being of course judge of that tendency will make his opinions the rule of judgment, and approve or condemn the sentiments of others only as they shall square with or differ from his own; that it is time enough for the rightful purposes of civil government for its officers to interfere when principles break out into overt acts against peace and good order; and finally, that truth is great and will prevail if left to herself; that she is the proper and sufficient antagonist to error, and has nothing to fear from the conflict unless by human interposition disarmed of her natural weapons, free argument and debate; errors ceasing to be dangerous when it is permitted freely to contradict them.

Section II. We the General Assembly of Virginia do enact that no man shall be compelled to frequent or support any religious worship, place, or ministry whatsoever, nor shall be enforced, restrained, molested, or burthened in his body or goods, or shall otherwise suffer, on account of his religious opinions or belief; but that all men shall be free to profess, and by argument to maintain, their opinions in matters of religion, and that the same shall in no wise diminish, enlarge, or affect their civil capacities.

Section III. And though we well know that this assembly, elected by the people for their ordinary purposes of legislation only, have no power to restrain the acts of succeeding Assemblies, constituted with powers equal to our own, and that therefore to declare this act to be irrevocable would be of no effect in law; yet we are free to declare, and do declare, that the rights hereby asserted are of the natural rights of mankind, and that if any act shall be hereafter passed to repeal the present or to narrow its operations, such act will be an infringement of natural right.

Thomas Jefferson

[Jefferson's] Letter to the Danbury Baptists

To some extent informal letters written during the later years of Jefferson's and Madison's lives are at least as important in understanding their attitudes toward the question of "Church and State" as the formal documents they drafted or the constitutional arrangements they contrived. The following represent rather than exhaust this kind of source.

Readers will note how the letter is a wholly conventional response, and might question whether it provides a likely foundation for the "wall of separation" it allegedly supports.

Messrs. Nehemiah Dodge, Ephraim Robbins, and Stephen S. Nelson, a Committee of the Danbury Baptist Association, in the State of Connecticut.

January 1, 1802.

Gentlemen—The affectionate sentiments esteem and approbation which you are so good as to express towards me, on behalf of the Danbury Baptist Association, give me the highest satisfaction. My duties dictate a faithful and zealous pursuit of the interests of my constituents, and in proportion as they are persuaded of my fidelity to those duties, the discharge of them becomes more and more pleasing.

Believing with you that religion is a matter which lies solely between man and his God, that he owes account to none other for his faith or his worship, that the legislative powers of government reach actions only, and not opinions, I contemplate with sovereign reverence that act of the whole American people which declared that their legislature should "make no law respecting an establishment of religion, or prohibiting the free exercise thereof," thus building a wall of separation between church and State. Adhering to this expression of the supreme will of the nation in behalf of the rights of conscience, I shall see with sincere satisfaction the progress of those sentiments which tend to restore to man all his natural rights, convinced he has no natural right in opposition to his social duties.

I reciprocate your kind prayers for the protection and blessing of the common Father and Creator of man, and tender you for yourselves and your religious association, assurances of my high respect and esteem.

JEFFERSON ON THE QUESTION OF FAST DAYS

To the Rev. Mr. Millar

Washington, January 23, 1808.

Sir,—I have duly received your favor of the 18th, and am thankful to you for having written it, because it is more agreeable to prevent than to refuse what I do not think myself authorized to comply with. I consider the government of the United States as interdicted by the Constitution from intermeddling with religious institutions, their doctrines, discipline, or exercises. This results not only from the provision that no law shall be made respecting the establishment or free exercise of religion, but from that also which reserves to the States the powers not delegated to the United States. Certainly, no power to prescribe any religious exercise, or to assume authority in religious discipline, has been delegated to the General Government. It must then rest with the States, as far as it can be in any human authority. But it is only proposed that I should *recommend*, not prescribe a day of fasting and prayer. That is, that I should *indirectly* assume to the United States an authority over religious exercises, which the Constitution has directly precluded them from. It must be meant, too, that this recommendation is to carry some authority, and to be sanctioned by some penalty on those who disregard it; not indeed of fine and imprisonment, but of some degree of proscription, perhaps in public opinion. And does the change in the nature of the penalty make the recommendation less a *law* of conduct for those to whom it is directed? I do not believe it is for the interest of religion to invite the civil magistrate to direct its exercises, its discipline, or its doctrines; nor of the religious societies; that the General Government should be invested with the power of effecting any uniformity of time or matter among them. Fasting and prayer are religious exercises; the enjoining them an act of discipline. Every religious society has a right to determine for itself the times for these exercises, and the objects proper for them, according to their own particular tenets; and this right can never be safer than in their own hands, where the Constitution has deposited it.

I am aware that the practice of my predecessors may be quoted. But I have ever believed, that the example of State executives led to the assumption of that authority by the General Government, without due examination, which would have discovered that what might be a right in a State government, was a violation of that right when assumed by another. Be this as it may, every one must act according to the dictates of his own reason, and mine tells me that civil powers alone have been given to the President of the United States, and no authority to direct the religious exercises of his constituents.

I again express my satisfaction that you have been so good as to give me an opportunity of explaining myself in a private letter, in which I could give my reasons more in detail than might have been done in a public answer; and I pray you to accept the assurances of my high esteem and respect.

ANALYSIS

1. Look again at Ms. Rosario's case in the light of the First Amendment's rejection of an "established" church; does the prayer Ms. Rosario led her students in seem to you to involve (perhaps symbolically) such establishing of a "state church"?

WRITING POSSIBILITIES

1. Jefferson's statement to the Danbury Baptists has occasioned controversy. In this letter it would seem Jefferson says point-blank that church and state must be kept separate (the "wall of separation"). That would

mean, in the case of Ms. Rosario, that anything even remotely like the prayer she led her students in would be a violation of the First Amendment and its "establishment" clause. But some readers of Jefferson's Letter to the Baptists say this is hardly a full statement—it's a casual, knock-off letter in response to another letter, not a considered and elaborated statement of Jefferson's principles. And this being the case, we shouldn't (so these analysts would say) press zealously on the establishment idea and worry that every infraction is a violation of church and state separation. Look at Jefferson's letter again, examine its tone and language, and see if you think his letter can be taken with utmost seriousness or (rather) with a grain of salt.

Lee Albert

A professor of law, Albert advances a view of the role of religion in public affairs that contrasts with that of Michael Novak (pages 462–470). Albert argues that while religion offers many benefits to understanding public policy debates, its role should be constrained through habits of prudence and compromise (not by the courts or laws, a surprising point by a law professor). Paradoxically in fact, Albert argues, Americans crave the rigid distinctions afforded by legal decisions in the touchy areas of church-state relations, but Albert remains skeptical that law is the best approach to any area involving pluralistic respect for different religious faiths.

GOD IN THE PUBLIC SQUARE

We are a Christian nation, the U.S. Supreme Court declared more than a century ago. That was gratuitous and inappropriate, not because it was not true, but because it was (and is). Happily, such declarations have disappeared from Supreme Court opinions. But that expression of religiosity seems tepid compared with the robust resurgence of faith and prayer in the 2000 presidential campaign.

In the beginning, candidate George W. Bush spoke about how Jesus had changed his life and about the need for a religious revival in America. Not to be outdone, Al Gore asserted that Jesus provides him with learning on hard political questions.

In a surprise choice that reclaimed a share of faith and piety for his party, Gore selected an observant Jew, Joe Lieberman, as his running mate. Lieberman readily accepted campaign responsibility for religion on the bustings and vigorously demonstrated that prayer and spirituality do not belong exclusively to the Moral Majority or Republican Right. Lieberman observed "a new spiritual awakening to be welcomed" because there is "a constitutional place for religion in our public life." He also identified an intimate link between moral principles and religion.

Although God talk and piety are customary quadrennial features of American political life, recent public expressions of piety go well beyond the usual bland assertions of faith in a generic deity that most believers (and some non-believers) can embrace. It is, after all, a singular event when a Jewish organization, the Anti-Defamation League of B'nai B'rith, rebukes a Jewish candidate for excessive talk of God and professions of faith in the public square.

The high visibility of religion in the 2000 presidential campaign demonstrates the expressive, important and contentious role that faith continues to play in American life. Is this good for society, politics and religion? What hazards are presented by a high religious profile and a powerful secular reaction of disapproval and an occasional display of hostility toward religion?

The short answer is that religion is too important a source of views and learning to be an alien and unwelcome intruder in the political arena. But the uses and misuses of religion are sufficiently grave to warrant a great deal of care in mixing politics and religion.

Political campaigns occur in the public square, those many places in which we explore the issues raised in a political campaign. The same First Amendment of our Constitution that mandates separation of church and state also guarantees in sweeping terms freedom of expression. That free speech guarantee has maximal force and minimal qualification when addressing political speech in the public square.

The compromises and accommodations that are endemic to most constitutional freedoms are least applicable to political speech, for among the varied goals of free expression, making democracy work is the clearest and most widely accepted. The public square is sacrosanct free speech terrain because it is the stage for the play of democracy. The Constitution does not interdict or qualify God talk in the public square.

This ample space for religion in the public square is as it should be. Religion has provided the foundation for some of the most important social movements in the nation's history. To take some familiar examples, religion has played a critical role in public discourse about abolition of slavery, extensions of the right to vote, civil rights, capital punishment and abortion.

Like it or not, there are many believers among us, and they see and feel a connection between their faith and public issues. To bar or restrict religion from the public square would be to banish widely shared fundamental belief systems from our political discourse.

Religion is not only a source for defining issues and for formulating a position on them for many believers. Religion also provides such people an informing calculus for assessing the character of candidates and for judging the intensity with which they hold their announced positions. God talk in the public square gets high marks for relevancy. That it does not provide illumination for others is not of moment. Beliefs need not garner unanimity to be an essential part of political discourse.

Nor does God talk fail a test of civic virtue, civility or good citizenship. It is neither unusual nor wrong for people to seek to have their beliefs accepted or at least recognized as reasonable and valid. People generally are more willing to accept defeat in public life after their views have been given a respectful airing and consideration. On the other hand, people are far less willing to acquiesce in democratic decisions when their views have been dismissed as irrelevant or alien to our public life.

To be sure, there are occasions in which religious persons seek to impose their beliefs on others, including non-believers. But surely believers are not alone in this behavior. To take a volatile example, supporters and opponents of choice for abortions equally seek to impose their views on society. Guido Calabresi, a law professor, now a federal judge, has persuasively argued that the Supreme Court's cavalier dismissal of a deeply and widely held conviction on when life begins as irrelevant to the Constitution in Roe vs. Wade greatly contributed to the impassioned and bitter polarization that followed the decision (and the failure of the decision to generate consent after nearly three decades).

Telling people that their views do not count is very different from saying that they do not prevail on this occasion. The latter is the give and take of politics that is familiar and acceptable; the former rejects a part of our identity and most people do not quietly accept that.

Hence there are few legal constaints on religion in political campaigns. But there are and should be powerful restraints, based on prudence, not constitutional principle. That in itself is a problem. As a nation, we govern less well with self-restraint based on the dictates of prudence and civility than with the unequivocal commands of seemingly clear rules of law.

But just as there are powerful reasons for having religion in the public square, there are monumental reasons for care in its uses. Indeed, the virtual absence of legal limits is one of them.

We are a nation of great diversity among both believers and non-believers. There are an uncountable number of sects and faiths in the nation and a comparable number of ways of not believing in a traditional deity. Without great care, expressions of faith in public arenas have a high potential to divide and marginalize people, again both believers and non-believers.

Marginalizing segments of the nation's population, branding them as outsiders, is the reason it was inappropriate for the Supreme Court to declare us a Christian nation and for Joe Lieberman to declare that religion was the foundation of morality. Lieberman's statement insults the many non-believers in traditional faiths who have high moral standards and ignores the many believers who do not (as the Anti-Defamation League reminded him).

Much that purports to be religion in political campaigns constitutes pandering, hawking of faith and marketing of God in a manner that insults, demeans and trivializes both religion and political discourse. God talk seems to be highly susceptible to such debasement, though it is not alone in this regard. Much other talk in the public square is tasteless, vacuous and devoid of content.

To avoid sectarianism and divisiveness, the public square often witnesses a kind of homogenized civil religion comprised of faintly Christian platitudes that affirm religious beliefs while avoiding anything of theological or social significance. This pabulum, of course, does not do justice to the rich variety and depth of religious faiths in the nation.

Then there is religious jingoism, the portrayal of America as the special object of God's blessing and the special recipient of God's mission. To take one fairly recent and egregious example, it was said that we won the Cold War by God's grace. These may be alluring incantations of faith, but they do not grace God or politics. Instead, they reinforce wariness and disquiet over religion in politics.

Even when authentic, the elaboration of religious justifications for political positions may not advance dialogue. Rightly or wrongly, many people of little or no faith find religious justifications for controversial policy positions to signal the end rather than the beginning of conversation. We are familiar with occasions when religious discourse polarizes positions and makes the search for common ground and intermediate premises more difficult.

Finally, Joe Lieberman's recent invocation of the Fifth Commandment to honor thy father and mother as a justification for Medicare coverage of prescription drugs reminds us that neither the Bible nor other ancient religious texts speak closely or directly to contemporary social and economic issues. In sum, a lack of effectiveness or cogency in religious argument is an excellent reason for forbearance.

Religion in the public square also may blur the line between the state and religion, a line based on constitutional principle, not prudence. It is easy to confound religion with politics when candidates put on a mantle of spirituality. Such posturing, for example, encourages the mischievous but widespread perception of the president as the moral leader of the United States. It is enough that the president is the political head of a vast and powerful nation. Morality may be left to those who are better trained and situated to carry out that difficult role in a diverse nation of many faiths.

Religion in the public square is not all talk, for the talk may encourage believers to seek a greater role for religion in society. Hence, accompanying God talk today are heady support for prayer before high school football games (for what do they pray?) and at school-yard flagpoles; for the posting of the Ten Commandments in public sites, including schools and courtrooms; for the transference of publicly funded social welfare programs to religious institutions, and for school vouchers that facilitate attendance at parochial schools.

These measures seem to follow in the wake of the resurgence of religion in the presidential campaign. But they differ from pure political speech in that the Constitution that creates a barrier between church and state has a great deal to say about the legality of these measures. Indeed, the Supreme Court has addressed some of them. The breeding of measures that may violate the separation of church and state is yet another reason for circumspection in the play of religion and politics.

Religion on the campaign trail is an untidy and unruly force. Because it also is a source of illumination and understanding for believers, religion is an inescapable part of our quadrennial democratic exercise.

ANALYSIS

1. In what way does Albert praise the *value* of religious entry into the political arena?
2. When Albert comes to his major argumentative point—that some limits should be placed on religious statements in the public sphere—how does he specify what those limits are and how they should be placed? Would you agree with his formulation here?

WRITING POSSIBILITIES

1. Do you agree with Albert's sense of the values that religious statement offers for public debate? Explain why, using examples of issues expressed by statements in this chapter or any that have come to the fore in your own experience. Be sure to indicate the *principles* on which you base your argument.
2. How do you assess Albert's main point that religious talk needs to be constrained in certain ways? Explain how you see Albert's arguments unfolding, the principles behind them, and your agreement or disagreement with both arguments and principles.
3. Albert's position is diametrically opposed to that of Michael Novak's, (pages 467–470). Read his analysis of both the past history of the Jeffersonian arguments for separation of church and state and his discussion of the present-day values of moving away from separation. To what extent do you think Novak and Lee Albert would agree or disagree on these issues?

Michael Novak

A theologian with the American Enterprise Institute, Michael Novak argues here that (1) Jefferson's seeming insistence on strict church-state separation ignores the historical realities (Jefferson in the "Letter to the Danbury Baptists," Novak argues, was simply making an expedient political move to garner needed votes) and (2) that the present-day realities of life in the public square require the moral leavening of religious values in politics. Novak's position contrasts in most respects with that of Lee Albert, in the previous selection.

FAITH IN SEARCH OF VOTES

WASHINGTON.
On the two-thousandth anniversary of His birth, it was bound to happen. George W. Bush, asked to name the philosopher most influential in his life, replied, "Jesus Christ, because He changed my heart." Not to be outdone, Al Gore confessed on television that he himself had been "born again," that is, had consciously accepted Jesus Christ as his personal Savior. And John McCain's campaign ran TV ads in South Carolina praising him for the moving sermons he had preached for Christmas in a North Vietnamese prison.

Not since the first days of American independence have we seen such public expressions of faith. Many will question whether this injection of religion is good for American politics; others may wonder if it is good for religion. But conventional wisdom about the separation of church and state notwithstanding, this is a hopeful phenomenon, and not one that would have offended our founders.

Consider that the first act of the First Continental Congress in 1774 was to call for public prayer so that war might be averted. During the early days of the republic, the largest Sunday service in the United States was held in the Capitol—the second-largest was in the Supreme Court.

Nor was God absent from political campaigns. Jefferson's famous letter about the wall of "separation" between church and state was itself a campaign ploy to hold the votes of the Baptists of New England in the run-up to a hot campaign. Under the aegis of church establishments, Baptists, Methodists and others had been horse-whipped, jailed—even tarred and feathered—for preaching without a license, which they refused to request, from states. Their license, they said, came from the Word of God. For this reason, the single most active force insisting on this "wall of separation" were the dissident evangelical churches, the lineal ancestors of today's so-called religious right.

Jefferson, one of the least orthodox of the founders, for the most part kept his personal religious beliefs private. But during his term in the White House, he composed a "Philosophy of Jesus Christ," and he later enlarged it into "The Jefferson Bible," a compendium (in four languages) of the moral teachings of Jesus, which he called "the most sublime and benevolent code of morals which has ever been offered to man."

Almost to a man, the signers of the Declaration of Independence held that Christian moral teaching (which they understood as aligned with Jewish moral teaching) was necessary to republican government. Tocqueville noted 50 years later how universal this belief still was: "I do not know if all Americans have faith in their religion—for who can read the secrets of hearts?—but I am sure that they think it is necessary to the maintenance of republican institutions."

Why did the founders believe this? Christianity had learned one reason from Judaism and one on its own. First, as every story in the Bible is about individual decisions of will—yes or no to the Lord—human history is the history of liberty, and liberty is history's golden thread. Second, humans should "give to Caesar what is Caesar's, and to God what is God's"—in other words, religion and state do not compete in a zero-sum game; each is important to the other, but they operate on different planes.

The early Americans grasped a logic now forgotten. The practice of liberty is constituted by sober reflection and deliberate choice—a willingness to be relied upon and held accountable. In short, liberty requires moral virtues like sobriety, prudence, courage, dispassion and coolness under fire. While without religion a few people may be able to practice such virtues, at least some of the time, experience shows that the many cannot do so over long periods of time.

George Washington, in his Farewell Address, said it best:

"Of all the dispositions and habits which lead to political prosperity, Religion and morality are indispensable supports. . . . Let us with caution indulge the supposition, that morality can be maintained without religion. Whatever may be conceded to the influence of refined education on minds of peculiar structure, reason and experience both forbid us to expect that National morality can prevail in exclusion of religious principle." (Some scholars think "minds of peculiar structure" was an allusion to Jefferson.)

In our system, church and state need fences, but religion and politics go together like air and lungs. As a result, in no other republic (not in Europe nor Asia) is religion so lively as here, nor civil society and grassroots political action so vigorous.

Freedom of conscience means that not all citizens make the same religious commitments, and pluralism means that each of us sometimes feels "left out" when others articulate their beliefs. That's how we learn from one another. That's how we glimpse regions of the soul unknown to us. That, too, is one of the glories of America.

From a very early period, however, that glory has been dimmed by a curious reluctance to discuss religion, a deliberate inarticulateness. Jefferson excused it thus: "It is in our lives and not our words that our religion must be read."

So also George W. Bush recently pleaded that his faith defied being put in to words for others: "Well, if they don't know, it's going to be hard to explain."

Tocqueville called this "a religion believed in without discussion," and the problem with it is that people inarticulate about their beliefs cannot defend them intellectually. Their behavior may be warmed by faith, but their intellect remains untouched and cold. A faith cast in shallow soil shrivels in the day's heat.

Religion cannot be reduced to good behavior, to solipsism or to matters merely of the heart and the emotions. A scriptural name given to Jesus is "Word" (in Greek, "Logos"), hardly a call for inarticulateness on our part. Not for nothing did America's early religious leaders create Harvard, Yale, Princeton and other universities. Our current intellectual weakness is not due to Jewish or Christian faith, but to ourselves.

When John F. Kennedy was elected president, this could still be thought of as a Protestant "mainline" country. No more.

The power and influence of the nonbelieving segment of America has grown considerably during the past 40 years. Non-Christian sex education has been forced on the schools, traditional expressions of Christian belief in public life have been forbidden, and fixed truths ("We hold these truths to be self-evident") have been relativized.

More than ever before, religious persons of all faiths judge both that the nation's public life has become hostile to them and that its public culture is no longer worthy of moral respect.

The loyalty of such people to this experiment in republican self-government should not be lost. Neither should it be trifled with. Presidential candidates, having made their point, should tread lightly. Political figures need to be forthright about their core beliefs, but they should remember that their role is not that of clergymen.

We should be glad that the old pluralism of give-no-offense, lowest-common-denominator mumble is giving way to a new and more mature pluralism: frank public discussion of the diverse convictions that move us. In the next century, religion is likely no longer to be "believed in without discussion." Arguments in public will be many and hot. We are becoming confident enough of each

other's bona fides to say who we are, each of us; to listen respect-
fully to those who differ; and to argue with one another civilly. In a
shining city on the hill, that's how it should be.

ANALYSIS

1. By what means does Novak support his position that religion must be
   a vital part of political life?
2. What does Novak mean by "religion"?

WRITING POSSIBILITIES

1. Novak argues that we have misunderstood Jefferson's writings on separation of church and state, as in the interpretation of Jefferson's "Letter to the Danbury Baptists." Look up a discussion of this letter, for
   example in Leonard W. Levy's *The Establishment Clause,* and explain
   in an essay whether you agree or disagree with Novak's reading of the
   historical evidence.
2. Novak insists that morality requires religion and hence that "religion
   and politics go together like air and lungs." Would you agree or disagree with Novak's argument? With his assumption that politics is a
   matter exclusively of morality?
3. Novak and Lee Albert both refer to the role of "prudence" in political
   and religious affairs—but they do so in divergent ways. Reread both essays and explain in an essay of your own whether you agree with Novak
   that religion and politics do go together as "air and lungs" or with Albert that politics, unlike religion, requires "prudence and compromise."

Michael Jacobs

Michael Jacobs wrote this paper, reproduced exactly as he handed it in for a section of "American Pluralism," a required course at SUNY Buffalo. After a few paragraphs of introduction, it gets down to the nitty-gritty—the debate on evolution versus Creationism sparked by the Kansas State Board of Education's decision [since rescinded] to require teachers to teach Darwinian evolution as only a theory and to present Creationism as a legitimate alternative to Darwinian theory. Jacobs tells the story of the debate and its surprising climax with appropriate subtlety and, finally, drama. He also supplied two papers from the Internet (not reproduced here) on both sides of the question. To my mind, this is in miniature an almost perfect paper. Although I carped at the relative brevity of the presentation of creation science, I am satisfied, rereading it, that Michael has done a good job. In any case, you are welcome to comment on it in your own way.

A Place in the Classroom

Since Darwin's return from the Galapagos Islands, man has stood in bitter debate with his fellow man over the origin of his specie. In the years following the publication of *The Origin of Species by Means of Natural Selection* (Darwin: 1859), the world has witnessed this conflict take drastic turns in either direction. Perhaps one of the most famous incidents where the two ideologies of creationism and evolution have faced off was the "Scopes Monkey Trial" of 1925. In this affair, a biology teacher in Dayton, Tenn., was accused of illegally teaching human evolution in his classroom. The trial, which saw two of the country's most prestigious attorneys in opposition, fundamentalist William Jennings Bryan and progressive Clarence Darrow, quickly became a media extravaganza. Scopes, the teacher accused, was eventually found guilty: A verdict that fortified religion's unspoken authority over America's educational system of the day.

Despite the verdict of the Scopes trial, Darwin's theory of evolution grew to be the western world's most accepted scientific explanation of mankind's origin. Ultimately, all educational institutions in the U.S. came to embrace its teachings. That is, until now. Recently, the Kansas State Board of Education passed legislation permitting the teaching of religious creationism in the science classroom. Along with this decision came the eradication of questions on biological evolution in all standardized tests. While the publicized motive of this decree is to offer students a variety of viewpoints on the subject of human origin, most oppositionists believe its merely an attempt to reintroduce religion into the classroom of skirting secular legislation.

The conflict between Darwin and Genesis will never be settled, at least not in this lifetime. Regardless, the question remains: Does creationism have a place in the science classroom?

Perhaps the biggest argument in favor of creationism is the notion that, like evolution, it is a viable theory behind the derivation of human beings. As such, they contest, it holds just as much legitimacy in a classroom setting. According to traveling creationist, Steve Grohman, the Kansas State Board of Education's decision "is not a case of substituting creationism for evolution. Rather it is the attempt to make evolution seem speculative, unscientific, and just a belief."[1] Accompanying this widely accepted idea of pro-creationists is a series of proposals that attempt to debunk the credibility of biological evolution.

One proposal, in particular, suggests that many foundations of evolutionary theory were spawned from either hoaxes or mere short sightedness. One example is cited on the web page of a fundamentalist group called A.L.P.H.A. It is titled, *50 Reasons to Leave Your Faith (evolution)*. In reference to the "Piltdown Man," fossils discovered early in the twentieth century, the article reads:

> Discovered in 1912 by Charles Dawson, a medical doctor and amateur paleontologist who discovered a mandible and a small piece of a skull in a gravel pit near Piltdown, England. The jawbone was ape-like but the teeth had human characteristics. The skull piece was very human-like. These 2 specimens were combined to form dawn man, which was supposedly 500,000 years old. However, the whole thing turned out to be an elaborate hoax. The skull was indeed human (about 500 years old) but the jaw was that of a modern ape whose teeth had been filed to look like human wear. The success of this hoax for 50 years, despite the scrutiny of the best authorities in the world, led Solly Zuckerman to say, "It is doubtful if there is any science at all in the search for mans fossil ancestry."

Ultimately, examples such as these are meant to illustrate a necessity for an alternate approach to explaining the origin of man. The reason being that evolution thrives in the wake of a multitude of hoaxes and mistakes. How, inquire creationists, can educators rely on a theory (evolution) that has so many holes in it? Those in favor of biological evolution have a simple reply: It's the best one we've got. Essentially, evolutionists argue that their theory of the origin of mankind is simply that: A theory. Unlike creationism, they continue, it's a *scientific* theory. They claim that evolution was never taught as a fact. "It was never intended to be a history of biology. It is a system

---

[1] Knappick, p. 1.

through which people can explain observations made within human grasp."[2] Yes, evolution is only a theory. However, so is gravity. Yet, no one denies its existence because it cannot be seen or touched. Science, by definition, is a theory in itself. To dismiss evolution on the grounds that it can not be proven is to dismiss science altogether.

Many opposed to the inclusion of creationism in the science classroom often avoid arguments on which belief is correct. Instead, they simply declare that creation, regardless of its plausibility, is not, by definition, a science. For a theory or fact to be considered a viable scientific explanation of one's environment, it must develop from a strict procedure of observations, hypotheses, testing, and conclusions. This is known as the scientific method. According to such scientists and others opposed to the Kansas legislature, a belief in god and his creation of the universe developed not from the scientific method, but from faith. How can you test the existence of god? What observations can be made to propose that the earth was created in six days and on the seventh, god rested? These are questions asked by skeptics of creationism. For many, creationism is not science. It's theology.

Before I devulge my extensive opinion on the subject, I would like to tell a story. Recently, I was asked to participate in a classroom debate for a course titled, American Pluralism. The topic: Is Kansas's decision to allow creationism in the science classroom justified? Being a man of little religious faith, I chose the platform against the legislation. My preparation for the in-class discussion was minimal. I simply read a few articles, wrote down a few quotes, and developed a basis for my argument. The rest, I decided, would be improvised. I had no intention of questioning anyone's faith. Nor was I out to disprove the existence of a higher power. I was going to merely attempt to give reasons as to why creationism had no place in a science curriculum.

When the day of the debate came, four students, myself included, were called up to the front of the class. It was a fairly small classroom, considering the amount of students taking the course, and I was a tad uneasy having a mob of kids right on top of me—The reason being that I was about to touch on a very sensitive topic.

"We're all mature adults here," I quickly convinced myself. "There's nothing to worry about."

After a brief lecture by a fellow student in favor of the legislation, it was my turn to speak. I hastily approached the microphone and set down a piece of paper with a few notes scribbled on it. I hardly remember what I said; something about scientific method versus theology. I can't recall exactly. I soon ran out of ideas, summarized my argument, and took my seat. I remember being very glad that I was

---

[2] Knappick, p. 2.

not the only one arguing the side I had chosen. Two other students on my particular platform were left to speak. After they made their cases, the professor opened the floor up to questions. This, I recall, was when rationale left the room.

Despite being one of three panelists opposed to creationism, I was targeted by the religious faction of the class and bombarded with a barrage of loud and sarcastic questions. At first I welcomed the onslaught.

"I must have really made a good case," I told myself confidently. Soon, however, I realized that I'd done more than that; I had pissed a lot of people off. It was as though I was the only speaker in the room. Every question, and there were many, was directed towards me. I attempted to answer each inquiry as objectively as possible. However, it was no use. No matter how I structured my retort, the mob grew angrier. Even the girl on the panel that argued in favor of creationism got in on it. I was a marked man.

Nervous and anxious to leave, I looked at another student's watch. It was five minutes until the class would be dismissed. Almost out of the woods, I said the words that might have gotten me lynched.

"You're right," I yelled to a girl in the rear of the classroom, "you can't deny the legitimacy of a theory if you can't disprove it. But every time someone attempts to question an impractical element of the Bible, you people say it can't be comprehended by mortal man." I continued in a sarcastic tone, "It's a miracle." The class grew silent. What the hell did I just say?

"O.K.," interrupted my professor, "we'll end it here."

Then, from an astonished voice buried somewhere in the room I heard, "You don't believe in miracles?"

I left the classroom and ventured to my car, all the while in disbelief of the drama that had just unfolded. What did I say? What did I do wrong? I asked myself these questions the entire ride home. I walked rather slowly from my car to my apartment. I began to grow angry about the entire incident.

"Disconnected Bible beaters," I said out loud. "What the hell did I do?"

Suddenly, it hit me. I stood at the entrance to my building, key in the door, in the realization of how things got so out of hand. I didn't call anyone a derogatory name, nor did I insult anyone's opinion. I was simply on the wrong side of an inevitable argument: RELIGION. It made perfect sense. The class dismissed the notion that I was arguing for a side, not necessarily myself. Thus, I was attacked. Why? Not because they're unintelligent. They were blinded by religion. Since the dawn of man, whenever that was, religion has been the cause for more abandonment of good judgment and rationale than any other entity on earth. Its been the catalyst for wars and riots, greed and hysteria. There's something about a belief in a higher power that makes human beings avoid reality. It's the reason why so many bars, in an effort to dissuade brawls, never used to allow the discussion of two particular topics: politics and religion.

I realized that the class was not angry at me or anything I had said. They were merely incensed that someone dared to question their religion; and much more, its undeniable authority in all aspects of life— especially the classroom. I was targeted merely because I was stupid enough to take the first question. In this , they had helped argue my point. Forget scientific method and dismiss the notion of miracles. Creationism has no place in a science classroom for no other reason than the fact that it insights blind and intense emotion. The Philadelphia Native American Riots of 1844 were a testament to this notion.[3]

Ultimately, the science class is a place where theories and facts, developed from impartial testing, are taught and explained. The subject material must exist on an impartial platform because it is always subject to change. Scientific approaches to explaining the aesthetics of the universe are not made to favor a particular ideology. They are made to discover the truth. Such is the very foundation of science. Religion, on the other hand, is anything but impartial. Furthermore, it can not change. To compromise the teachings of Christianity is to oppose its true essence. Lastly, how does one choose which story of creation to teach; Christian, Jewish, Islamic. Why not Ancient Greco or Roman? Introducing theology creates the new dilemma of deciding whose religion is more significant.

Bibliography

Web articles

American Atheists, *Kansas Evolution Debate Flares Again; Change Ordered in Teaching Standards.*
About Biotech, *The Scientific Method—Elegant Experiments.*
Knappick, Jacquieline, *Creationism is Gaining Popularity.*

Books

Binder, Frederick M./Reimers, *The Way We Lived: Essays and Documents in American Social History—Volume I: 1607–1877;* 1988. D.C. Heath and Company: Lexington Mass.
Harten, Lucile B., *Evolution: Trials and Tribulations;* 1982. Idaho Museum of Natural History.

---

[3] A bloody conflict between Catholic immigrant and native-born Protestant inhabitants of the city over whose version of the Bible could be used in the classroom.

ANALYSIS
---

1. How does Jacobs present himself as a narrator and speaker in this essay?

WRITING POSSIBILITIES
---

1. Have you ever been in a classroom debate in which a surprising development like that which Jacobs describes suddenly erupts? Tell the story.

Stephen J. Dubner

Stephen Dubner, raised as a Catholic in childhood and now a Jew by choice, explains what religious faith meant to him in the past and what it means now as a conscious and deliberate matter: ". . . for my parents— and now, for me—there is a pointed difference. We have chosen our religion. . . . This is a particularly American opportunity. . . ."

As his last sentence indicates, Dubner is concerned with the social dimension of American religious values—that dimension which permits, perhaps even encourages, individuals to choose their faith and not simply submit to the national faith. The question here might be simply, what are the disvalues—as well as the values—of such individual choice? Does it fragment more than it unites? Does it leave too many people isolated from viable religious communities, pursuing their own bent regardless of the social consequences? Or, contrariwise, does it simply indicate the health of a society which, as Jack Miles (the author of God: A Biography*) is quoted as saying, "we are bound to be more tolerant and experimental" in a country which "has absorbed . . . many different religious traditions . . ."?*

CHOOSING MY RELIGION

Can you know who you are if you don't know who your god is? To reject your parents' faith for another is wrenching and liberating, and more Americans are doing it than ever before.

Not long ago, I was having Shabbos dinner with three friends. I am still new to all this. As the candles were lighted and a song was sung, I stumbled along. We washed our hands, then said the blessing as we dried them. I did know that you weren't supposed to speak until the bread had been blessed, so I went back to the table.

As I sat there, another silent ritual came to mind. I was raised in upstate New York and was the last of eight children. When it was your birthday, you had to eat your entire piece of cake without saying a word. If you broke your silence, a penalty awaited: molasses would be poured over your bare feet, then chicken feed sprinkled on, and you'd have to walk through the chicken coop and let the hens peck away.

Although the penalty was carried out a few times (never on me), what I remember best is the struggle to keep the silence, no matter how much everyone baited you. The whole thing was nonsense, and I had never thought about where it came from—until that Shabbos dinner a few weeks ago, when I suddenly wondered if one silence weren't somehow related to the other.

I did not grow up Jewish, but my parents did. Florence Greenglass and Solomon Dubner, both born in Brooklyn, were the children of Russian and Polish immigrants. On Christmas Eve of 1942, when Florence was a 21-year-old ballet dancer, she was baptized as a Roman Catholic. Two years later, she met Sol, a 28-year-old soldier home on furlough. The son of Orthodox Jews, he, too, was about to become a Catholic.

Unlike St. Augustine or Thomas Merton, my parents did not embrace Catholicism to atone for a wanton past. Unlike Saul of Tarsus, who became St. Paul, they saw no visions, heard no voices. Theirs were sober conversions of faith, brought about by no force or crises, or at least none visible from the surface.

The fallout was dramatic; no one in their families went to their wedding, and Sol's father never spoke to him again. They built new lives from top to bottom. They even changed their names. My mother chose Veronica as her baptismal name and has used it ever since; Sol, not surprisingly, became Paul.

They began having children, moved to a rural sprawl outside Albany and continued having children. After Joseph, the first son, and Mary, the first daughter, the rest of us had to settle for Joseph or Mary as our middle names. My namesake was St. Stephen, the first Christian martyr who I remember early on, was stoned to death by Jews.

We took our Catholicism very seriously. We never missed Mass; our father was a lector, and both our parents taught catechism. At 3 in the afternoon on Good Friday, we gathered in the living room for 10 minutes of silence in front of a painting of the Crucifixion. On top of a battered bookcase, our mother kept a simple shrine: a large wooden crucifix, a statue of a beatific Virgin Mary and several devotional candles, all nestled on a thick piece of red felt. Once a year, when our grandmother was due to visit, the shrine was packed away in a cardboard box. This wasn't a sin, our mother assured us, and was absolutely necessary, to keep our grandmother "from getting hysterical."

It did seem strange that our Jewish aunts and uncles and cousins almost never visited—not that I had the slightest idea of what a Jew or Judaism was. Our neighbors were farmers and auto mechanics named O'Donnell and Vandemeer. Only when our father died, when he was 57 and I was 10, did a handful of Jewish relatives make the trip upstate. Because our grandmother was dead by then, the shrine stayed put.

The matter of our having been Jewish was half footnote, half secret. A jar of gefilte fish sometimes found its way into the refrigerator, and our parents occasionally resorted to Yiddish for private conversations. But their ardent Catholicism allowed for scant inquiry into a different religious past. My brother Dave remembers asking our mother, when he was 7, why they had become Catholic. "Because we were young and we were searching for the truth, and we found it," she told him.

If I had known then what I know now, I might have recognized the remnants of my parents' past—for a religious conversion, I have come to learn, is imperfect. At best, the convert is a palimpsest. The old writing will always bleed through. The gefilte fish, the birthday cake routine, the way our father would burst into "My Yiddishe Mama"—it all reminds me of the Marranos, the Jews who were forced during the Spanish Inquisition to convert to Catholicism and wound up practicing their Judaism, in secret. Hundreds of years later, some fully assimilated Marrano families still clung to old Jewish rituals with no idea where they had come from.

But for my parents—and now, for me, as I am becoming a Jew—there is a pointed difference. We have *chosen* our religion, rejecting what we inherited for what we felt we needed. This is a particularly American opportunity and one that is being exploited in ever-increasing numbers. To be convinced, you only need to stick your head into an overflowing Catholic conversion workshop, a mosque filled with American-born blacks, a 5,000-member "megachurch" that caters to forward-looking Protestants or a tiny Pentecostal church packed with Hispanic immigrants who came here as Catholics. "Religious switching is more common now than it has ever been in American history," says Dean Hoge, a sociology professor at Catholic University in Washington, D.C., who has conducted many religious surveys.

Statistics on religious affiliation are notoriously slippery: the Government isn't allowed to gather such data, and the membership claims of religious organizations aren't entirely reliable. But, according to "One Nation Under God" (1993), by Barry A. Kosmin and Seymour P. Lachman, perhaps the most ambitious study to date of Americans and their religions, about 30 percent of Americans now switch denominations in their lifetimes. Kosmin and Lachman, who used a survey of 113,000 people, conclude that the most common reason for a switch is, predictably, intermarriage, followed by a shift in religious conviction and a geographical change.

To be sure, the majority of shifts are not particularly dramatic, tending to be from one Protestant denomination to another. (In a study of 500 people from 33 to 42 years old who had been confirmed as Presbyterians, Hoge found that 33 percent had already made a move, usually to another mainline Protestant denomination.) Still, Kosmin says, "There are more spiritual searches now than ever before, mainly because people are freer than ever before to search."

There is also the common phenomenon of intensely renewing your religion of birth as an adult—an especially strong movement among American Jews and middle-class blacks. Such journeys often fall under what is known as Hansen's Law, or the third-generation syndrome, noted by the sociologist Marcus Lee Hansen in the 1930's. According to Hansen's Law, a person looks beyond his parents' religion, which was watered down by assimilation, to the religion of his grandparents, splicing traditional rituals and beliefs into his modern life.

Americans born after World War II, simultaneously facing their parents' deaths and watching their children grow up with a flimsy religious identity, are particularly susceptible to Hansen's Law. The recent surge in American spirituality has sent even the most secular adults into what has become a religion bazaar, where the boundaries are far more fluid and the rules less rigid than when they were children. As late as 1960, even a Protestant-Catholic marriage might have kept at least one set of in-laws out of the church; since then, the charge toward ecumenism has been relentless.

Jack Miles, a former Jesuit and the author of the recent "God: A Biography," told me why he thought this is so: because America has long been that rare country where a religious identity, as opposed to a political identity, is optional. As citizens of a country that has absorbed, with a fair amount of grace, so many different religious traditions, we are bound to be more tolerant and experimental. Miles himself is proof: after leaving the seminary in 1970, he considered converting to Judaism, then flirted with Buddhism and is now a practicing Episcopalian.

By now, choosing a religion is no longer a novel idea. And sometimes all the switching can seem comically casual. At the first meeting of a Judaism class I've been taking, we all announced why we had come. "I grew up Catholic in New Zealand—Catholic school, the whole bit," said one earnest young man, who was there with his Jewish girlfriend. "I had more than my share of whacks on the behind. And, well, as I learned more about Judaism, I thought it was a cracking good religion, so I'm here to see more about it."

The movement toward choosing religion, rampant as it is, shouldn't be surprising. Ours is an era marked by the desire to define—or redefine—ourselves. We have been steadily remaking ourselves along ethnic, political, sexual, linguistic and cultural lines, carefully sewing new stripes into our personal flags and waving them with vigor. Now, more than ever, we are working on the religious stripe.

That, of course, is a tricky proposition, since religion comprises practically every strand of identity we possess, and since so many religious rituals are also our most important family rituals. Disengaging yourself from your family's religion often means disengaging yourself, to some extent, from your family.

Lately, I have fallen in with and sought out a variety of converts— or seekers or returnees or born-agains, as they variously call themselves. Judith Anderson, 34, is a practicing Buddhist who was raised, she said, in a "devoutly atheistic" Jewish family in Teaneck, N.J. Like many Jews who practice Buddhism, she hasn't renounced her Jewishness; still, her parents are distressed with the spiritual layer she has added to her life, and she is torn between satisfying herself and appeasing them.

"My heart really hurts right now," she told me. "If they knew half of what goes on in the Buddhist center I belong to, or half of what I say in the morning when I do chants, it would absolutely freak them out. So I will probably always edit what I say and what I expose them to." She keeps a small Buddhist shrine in her Manhattan apartment; when her parents visit, she takes most of it down.

Three of my four sisters are still practicing Catholics; none of my brothers are. Most of them are curious about my God-wrestling, as we sometimes call it, but they don't seem to want or need it for themselves. My mother, meanwhile, remains the most devoted Catholic I have ever known. Two summers ago, I was sitting with her on a screened-in porch in the Adirondacks. Everyone else was off swimming or fishing. To that point, I hadn't asked her how she felt about my push toward Judaism, since I was pretty sure I knew. Now, though, I decided to go ahead with the question.

She tilted her face toward me and almost smiled. "How can I tell you what to believe?" she said. "You have to be true to your own conscience, and you have to do what you think is right." Her answer surprised me and pleased me.

"But," she went on, "I see this as the loss of a great opportunity for you." She respected Judaism, she explained, but only as the foundation for Catholicism.

Her tone of voice encouraged no argument. A door slammed, and my niece ran in, dripping wet, wanting to tell Grandma about her swim. I was relieved to be interrupted. For the first time, I had felt the sting of rebuke that, a half-century ago, my parents must have felt tenfold.

It may be that the transcendent mystery of a religious conversion, like the transcendence of sex, is incommunicable. A conversion is a tangle of loneliness, ambition, fear and, of course, hope. It is never tidy. The memoirs written by converts are generally one of two kinds: the breathless account of an irreversible epiphany (I tend to be skeptical of these) and the story wherein a convert pokes around his soul and his mind, yet arrives at no more concrete an explanation than a pressing desire to change the course of his life.

The current boom in choosing religion exists precisely because such inquiry is allowed today—as opposed to when my parents converted. There has never been a more liberal time and place than pre-millennial America to explore a given religion, both intellectually and spiritually. Fifty years ago, challenging a religious text or arguing with doctrine bordered on the heretical; now it is fashionable. Most denominations have become adept as packaging themselves, at disseminating their doctrines and rewards. "It's supply-side religion," Barry Kosmin says. "It's a free-market situation, and anything you can do to survive in that market, you'll do."

What the trends don't reveal, of course, is the fiercely personal nature of any religious search. Daniel Dunn, 26, a database programmer is Boca Raton, Fla., who grew up in the United Church of Christ, became a Catholic after a serious water-skiing accident left him wondering why he hadn't died. "I would go every Sunday and sit in the back pew, just watching and listening to the weekly Scriptures," Dunn says. "I was able to relate to each one in some way, which I hadn't been able to do as a young person."

Everyone who chooses a religion is running toward—and away from—his own mountain of questions. As adults, at least people know how to ask those questions and, just as important, how to argue—with their religions, their consciences, their families. They experience the intoxicating jolt of learning a religion with the intellect of an adult rather than the rote acceptance of a child.

I recently met a 22-year-old woman named Fatima Shama, whose mother is a devout Catholic from Brazil and whose father, a Palestinian Muslim, isn't very religious, Shama said. Shama grew up Catholic in the Bronx; she saw Islam, as practiced by her aunts, as exceedingly anti-female. At college, though, she discovered literary interpretations of the Koran, many written by women.

"I realized that everything I'd been taught as a child was wrong," she told me. "I began to separate out the Islamic religion from the Arabic culture, to learn what was really what." She now practices

Islam, albeit a more liberal form than her aunts do, and insists that she will marry an Arab-American Muslim. "All my brothers and sisters, they think I'm whacked," Shama said. "They always say to me, 'Where did you come from?'"

I have been asked the same question, now that I am becoming a Jew—or, as some would argue, as I am learning to be the Jew that I have always been. I was, after all, born of a Jewish mother; curious as my religious provenance may be, my bloodline would provide entry into either the state of Israel or a concentration camp.

Four years ago, I first sat down with my mother and a tape recorder. I had to know at least a little bit about my Jewish family, and how Florence Greenglass became Veronica Dubner. And I had to understand what made me so badly want to be Jewish when both my mother and father wanted so badly not to be.

What could be called the first existential thought of Florence Greenglass's life occurred in 1931, when she was 10. In bed with a cold, she heard her friends playing stickball outside and realized that, with or without her, life would go rambling on. From that day, she pondered the ephemerality of her existence, and her fate.

Her father, Harry, was an agnostic, a quietly affable man who ran a candy store on Lincoln Place in Brooklyn. Florence had an older sister and a mother, Esther, who disapproved of most things that Florence was interested in. Harry and Esther, born poor in Russia, were now inching toward the middle class. They were the only Jews in their neighborhood, which was mostly Catholic. Florence's grandmother was Orthodox and devout, but the rest of the family observed only Passover and a few other holidays.

Florence considered her Jewishness largely inconsequential. "Except I do remember one time, this girl standing up in class, in sixth grade," she told me. "This very, very blond girl, her name was Ann Ross. And she said, 'My father thinks that Hitler has the right idea about the Jews.' That was kind of a blow, to hear somebody comes out and say that."

When Florence was 13, she began studying ballet in Manhattan. Her teacher, Asta Souvorina, was about 60, a former Russian ballerina and actress who had fled Moscow in 1917. Madame Souvorina, as her students always called her, had converted to Catholicism from Russian Orthodoxy. She was domineering, charming, melodramatic, an intellectual, a storyteller—a mentor in every sense. Florence became her star dancer, performing in her small company and later in nightclub acts.

Florence and some of the other girls virtually lived at the studio, where Mme. Souvorina held forth on many subjects. When she mentioned the Epistles of St. Paul, Florence was curious: she had no idea that a living, breathing person, a Jew no less, had left behind such a dramatic record of his newfound faith, and such a compelling explanation of everlasting life. She read Paul's letters and felt they had the ring of truth.

"Well, if you really believe, you ought to do something about it," Mme. Souvorina told her. "You ought to get baptized, because that's what Jesus said you should do."

But Florence had much to reconcile—the Virgin Birth, for instance, seemed highly implausible. Her search was long and gradual. She devoured literature and asked endless questions of priests and her Catholic friends. One day, she went to Mass at the Church of the Blessed Sacrament, on West 71st Street in Manhattan, just down Broadway from Mme. Souvorina's studio. She was 21.

Even now, after more than 50 years, my mother's eyes brighten at the memory, and her voice shoots up an octave. "The priest was saying, 'God said, This is my beloved son in whom I am well pleased. Hear Him.' Those words were the key to my conversion, actually— '*hear* Him, listen to Jesus and do what He said. And all of a sudden, everything made sense."

About two years ago, I asked my mother how she ultimately came to accept the Virgin Birth and the Resurrection on a literal level. "First of all, it's told in Scripture," she said. But how had she come to believe Scripture? "Because you feel that Scripture was divinely inspired, for one thing—it's not a fairy tale that's made up." But how was she convinced that the Gospels canonized in the New Testament were divinely inspired, as opposed to all the conflicting gospels that didn't make it in?

A long, jagged pause. "It's the gift of faith," she said, "and faith is a gift."

It's the gift of faith, and faith is a gift. Where could I go with that? I recalled how our parents used to parry any questions about Catholicism: faith, they told us, is a treasure that can neither be questioned nor fully explained.

Florence was baptized at Blessed Sacrament, and her new faith immediately became the most valuable thing in her life. Esther, her mother, was heartsick and furious—what kind of daughter would betray the family, betray the Jews? Esther tried to plead, bully, threaten her daughter out of it. Veronica, as she now called herself, put up a font of holy water in her bedroom; when she came home, it was missing. "My mother told me I was to blame for her arthritis," she remembers. "And when my father died, she said he died because of me."

She had anticipated her mother's anger. "But you see, this was calculated—you know what you're going to have to give up," she says. "And to me, it was worth it. It's like the story in the Scripture, where you sell everything you have to buy this pearl of great value.

That's what you do when you find that pearl—you pay the price. And I could not have lived with myself if I hadn't done it."

A confession: much of the time my mother is telling me about her conversion, I am thinking about my father. When she mentions a book that influenced her, I ask if he read it, too. I prod her to remember more of his life, to think of more people I can interview about what he was like as a Jew and why he converted.

ANALYSIS

1. How does Dubner explain his family's commitment to Catholicism? His and his siblings varying responses in later life to that religious choice? What would you infer as to Dubner's idea of religious life and religious commitment—what does it involve?

2. Dubner says of himself that, "Going off to college, I had a sharply defined religious identity that I was eager to shed." Why was he so eager?

3. What leads Dubner to Judaism? How does he chronicle this passage from one faith to another?

4. How does Dubner characterize the responses of his mother and siblings to his new choice? What tone does he adopt in dealing with such a delicate situation?

WRITING POSSIBILITIES

1. If you have ever thought of changing your religious faith, or if you have indeed changed, how does your experience compare or contrast with that of Stephen Dubner? Using Dubner's essay as a model, explain how and why you chose to change.

2. In the same special issue of the *New York Times Magazine* from which Dubner's essay is taken, there is Marshall Sella's essay on atheism and agnosticism; find the essay—"Faith is a Fraud, Godless and Proud of It," *New York Times Magazine,* December 7, 1997—and discuss how you react to Sella's descriptions of those who reject religious faith itself.

Geraldine Brooks

Concern with religion is hardly to be confined to the politics of church and state separation. In fact, as Diane Winston makes clear in "Campuses Are a Bellwether for Society's Religious Revival" in The Chronicle of Higher Education *(January 16, 1998), university campuses are the sites of intense concern over the personal nature of religious faith and spiritual awareness. Whether on campuses or off, experimentation and mixing and matching of traditions now takes place within particular religious communities, as Geraldine Brooks's article here suggests and as the intriguing title emphasizes.*

FAITH IS A COMPROMISE

What Does the Koran Say about Nasreen's Nose Ring?

The American Muslim population is growing fast. There's the terrorist stigma to worry about, mosques to be built—and daughters who love Jim Morrison.

On a Saturday night in suburban Virginia, Sharifa Alkhateeb is putting on a purple head scarf before rushing out for a potluck dinner at the local mosque. Meanwhile, her 16-year-old daughter, nose pierced, baggy jeans dangling from her hips, hangs out with her non-Muslim girlfriends. Returning home after 10, Sharifa finds a note pinned to the living-room door.

"Mom, can I stay over at Jessie's, please? Use the pager—that's what it's for."

Sharifa tugs off her head scarf and sighs. "Sometimes I wonder if I'll survive her teens." Even more than most parents, she worries about her daughter staying out at night. Like many Muslims, she believes unmarried women shouldn't socialize with men outside the family, even the fathers and brothers of close friends. Still, she trusts her daughter. Despite her appearance, Nasreen is a committed Muslim who doesn't date.

When Americans think of Islam, their image is often of fundamentalists in faraway lands, not the Muslims at the local mall. But numbering about six million, Muslims are almost as numerous in the United States as Jews, with roughly half of American Muslims born here. A Muslim in the United States now is twice as likely to be African-American as Arab. Meanwhile, Muslims raised in repressive countries are opening up in the noisy forum of American free speech. They are protesting anti-Islamic stereotypes, asking for halal meat in

school cafeterias and developing a faith-based feminism that may ultimately prove to be American Muslims' biggest contribution to Islam.

The Alkhateeb family's blond brick colonial sits amid manicured
boxwoods in Great Falls, Va., an affluent community where signs
touting "estate" lots for sale sprout among horse barns about 15
miles northwest of Washington. But a calendar by the fridge reminds the Alkhateebs that they also live in the Ummah—the community of Islam—where the year is 1418. Sharifa Alkhateeb, born in
the United States, is an academic adviser to foreign graduate students and a part-time intercultural trainer for teachers in the Fairfax
County school system. Her husband, Mejdi, is an Iraqi immigrant
and computer scientist who runs his own company.

Their closest mosque, the All-Dulles Area Muslim Society, occupies an unmarked floor of a bland office building in Herndon, amid a
typical Northern Virginia sprawl of tract homes and strip malls. At the
mosque's Saturday potluck, Sharifa places a pan of cinnamon-spiced
kebabs beside Malaysian glass noodles, Egyptian braised lamb, Pakistani chicken biriani and chocolate brownies baked by an African-
American. Mejdi heads to one side of the room, to sit with the men,
while Sharifa joins a women's table where the dress is as diverse as
the food. Most wear some kind of head cover.

In 1990, Sharifa compiled a directory of mosques in the greater
Washington area. There were nine. When she updated the booklet in
1994, there were 39, and at least 6 more have appeared since. While a
few serve a single ethnic group and hold firmly to national traditions,
the majority welcome all comers. And that usually means preaching
an Islam all kinds of Muslims—Middle Easterners, Asians, Africans and
American-born—can agree on. Harsh customs like obligatory face
veils or female genital mutilation, which have crept into the religion
in various Islamic lands, are virtually nonexistent.

At Sharifa's table, the talk is mostly about children: whether a
teen-age son should be allowed to watch "Executive Decision," a film
that portrays Muslims as terrorists; how to get permission for a child
to miss class on a Muslim holiday; whether a daughter can transfer
out of a school with gangs and drugs. "Don't say you want to change
schools because of gangs," counsels Sharifa, who has worked in education for 30 years. "The authorities can't admit they have a rotten
school. Find some positives about the school you want to move her
to—it's got a better music program, more language classes."

As vice president of the North American Council for Muslim
Women, Sharifa often dispenses this sort of advice. This can involve
anything from writing memos to the imams at local mosques urging
them to preach against domestic violence, to exhorting a conference
of Muslim women in Turkey to pass a resolution condemning Taliban

repression in Afghanistan, to helping develop guidelines for Federal employees that allow them to read the Koran or cover their hair at work. She even advises brides-to-be on formulating Islamic wedding contracts (1,300-year-old precursors of modern prenuptial agreements) that protect their rights. "Muslim women are quite capable of speaking up for ourselves," Sharifa says. "We're not waiting for Western women to pour their loveliness into our heads."

While she fights for women's rights inside the mosque, she struggles for a greater Muslim role in the wider political debate. She thinks part of the problem is that Muslim immigrants often come from countries where saying the wrong thing could get them killed. They have to be introduced to the American notion that activism is expected rather than suspect.

At a recent meeting at the Herndon mosque, Sharifa urges a roomful of parents to get involved in their children's education. She encourages them to volunteer any skills they may have—driving, editing, cooking, computer programming—to become more familiar with the school and gain more influence over what happens there. One mother tells how volunteering as a classroom aide allowed her to steer her daughter's end-of-year celebration from a dance, which she considered un-Islamic, to a sports carnival. From the back of the hall, a father raises his hand. Muslims, he says, have skills passed to them through the Koran; namely, God's rules on how to live. Why not offer to give a course on that? "I think the public school would think that's a theological way of looking at the world and wouldn't be interested in promoting that idea," replies Sharifa diplomatically. "When we volunteer in schools, we shouldn't wear our religion on our shoulder. We should be willing to be part of the whole spectrum of American society."

Sharifa Alkhateeb got to know part of the spectrum of American society during an unsettled childhood in Philadelphia. Every year, a delegation of nuns would come to see her Czech-born mother, who converted to Islam before she married a Yemeni. "They would beg her to leave us," she recalls. Instead, it was the children who left, in flight from the strictness of their father. Of five children, "everyone ran away except me," Sharifa says. She stayed, plunging deeper into Islam than any of her siblings.

At the Community College of Philadelphia and the University of Pennsylvania in the late 1960's and early 1970's, fellow students who were initially puzzled by her covered hair eventually came to call her "the guru." "They came to me for advice, I guess because I was the only one who wasn't on something." She was 22 years old when an Iraqi-born computer-science student heard her speak at Muslim student's convention. He wrote to her and they met—chaperoned by an Egyptian couple. "I sat on the sofa next to the wife; Mejdi sat on the other side, next to the husband. And that was how we talked, for 10 days. On the 11th, we got married at Niagra Falls." They've been to-gether 27 years.

They moved to Great Falls about 10 years ago, into an all-American subdivision with Neighborhood Watch and July 4th fireworks on a nearby farm. The Irish-American neighbors are friendly, but Sharifa politely declines invitations to their St. Patrick's Day parties. "It's a hol-iday that's mostly about drinking, so what would we do there?" she says. The neighbors also have sons, and she doesn't want her daughters to become too closely acquainted with them.

Sharifa worries about her daughters. She worries that the eldest, a fashion-design student in New York, may want to marry a Saudi. "I'm not sure that most men raised in that culture would allow a woman enough room to grow," she says. She worries about her middle daugh-ter, trying to balance a job as a diversity trainer with marriage and a toddler. But most of all, she worries about Nasreen, her youngest.

A picture on the kitchen wall shows Nasreen at 9, reading the Koran, her hair tucked away in a scarf. She was in Iraq with her daughter, visiting relatives, when the Persian Gulf war erupted. While her father contrived their exit, she posed as a mute for almost a month to conceal her nationality. But when she finally got home, her head scarf branded her an enemy to her schoolmates. "It was, 'Every Muslim is a terrorist, every Muslim is Arab,'" she says. "The kids in my school knew nothing about the world. I felt harassed, beaten up mentally." On the school bus, pupils taunted her as "scarf head" and tried to snatch the cloth from her hair. Nasreen abandoned the scarf when she began middle school. She says she'll put it back "sometime in the future," but she's not sure when. "I love my religion; I'm very proud of it," she says. "I just wish people in this country were more accepting of other cultures."

On a Friday evening, before heading out to a girlfriend's house, she sits with her mother and her eldest sister, who comes home most weekends, in a living room decorated with oriental carpets and Ara-bic calligraphy. Upstairs, her own room features Jim Morrison posters and pictures of fashion models. Nasreen loves art and would like to work in theatrical makeup. She demonstrates how easily she can change her own appearance, twisting her nose ring so that it sits out of sight and tucking strands of wavy hair over the ornaments stud-ding her ears. "My conservative look," she declares.

Sharifa gives a rueful smile. "I raised my daughters to question everything—to weigh all opinions, including mine." Sometimes, she says, she wishes she hadn't taught them quite so well. "But I know that there's less chance of someone walking all over them, whether it's a male in his male-chauvinist way or a woman as they try to rise in their professions. You can't be a quiet person in this country and make it."

She is mad at Nasreen for piercing her body and disappointed that she doesn't wear a scarf. But she also wants the world to understand that a Muslim woman with a nose ring is just as Muslim as a woman in a veil. "The Koran says, 'Let there be no compulsion in religion,' and while covering is important, it's not the most important thing. The most important thing is that you feel connected to God."

Sharifa renews her own connection to god in the five daily prayers that mark the passing of each Muslim's day. But on Fridays, the Muslim holy day, she makes the connection public by attending communal prayers. The closest Friday prayers are just across the road at the Embassy of Saudi Arabia. But she can't get there soon enough to avoid walking past some men, which the Saudis forbid. So she must drive to George Washington University, where an auditorium is packed with students, professors and office workers, standing shoulder to shoulder in stocking feet. Sharifa takes her place with the women, behind a lattice at the rear of the auditorium. Sometimes, the lattice is covered by a sheet, to further segregate male from female worshipers. "It's an overzealous young Spanish convert who puts it up," Sharifa says. "I always take it down."

Afterward, in the corridor, Sharifa greets a young friend, Huma Abedin, office manager for Hillary Rodham Clinton. Downstairs, in the street, she looks around for a place to grab a quick lunch. The closest restaurant is a T.G.I.F.—Thank God It's Friday. Sharifa laughs. "Who says it's impossible to be American and Muslim?" Inside, she orders a virgin daiquiri and a club sandwich: "Hold the ham. And the bacon."

ANALYSIS

1. What conflicts does Nasreen face as she tries to negotiate between her parents's values and those of the secular society around here?

2. What context, religious or not, does Brooks analysis of Nasreen's problems offer?

WRITING POSSIBILITIES

1. If you have experienced the kind of (gentle) conflict between yourself and your family over religious or communal traditions, try to explain to a general audience what that conflict involved and the extent to which it was resolved. Provide key anecdotes to help your reader understand the nature of the conflict and its resolution.

8

CHANGE IN AMERICA

The idea of changing one's mind, institutions, or government is about as American as apple pie: Jefferson thought that a revolution every ten years would be a fine thing for the body politic; Franklin is famous for his (erotic) "errata"—the printer's symbol for corrections—and Whitman said it wonderfully, "Do I contradict myself? Very well then, I contradict myself, (I am large, I contain multitudes)." And let us not forget either Horatio Alger and the American Dream of success or the Dream's evil twin, as in *The American Tragedy* of Theodore Dreiser.

Studs Terkel's oral history of C. P. Ellis's conversion from Ku Klux Klan racist to human rights activist (pages 492–500) exemplifies a version of change that goes back to the Puritans and Ben Franklin— the individual who sees the error of his ways, resolves on a new course of behavior, and makes a public declaration of his repentance. Ellis was a leader of the Ku Klux Klan in Raleigh, South Carolina, but eventually came to renounce the hatred and violence which the Klan stood for. What led to this change of heart? As in all cause-effect reasoning, Ellis' motives for changing his attitude are more complex than he himself perhaps realized, but it is possible to see the influence of both internal sources (conscience) and external (social pressure, governmental programs). In one way or another, this combination of the internal and external figures is in all the essays in this chapter.

On the internal (conscience) side, there is Doug Bandow's libertarian essay whose title says it all—"Private Prejudice, Private Remedy"; Tom Watson's account of fighting discrimination with a personal act (he resigned) in "The American Way of Golf"; and Studs Terkel's revealing interview with a Klansman turned civil rights activist.

On the external side, demonstrating or urging a changed role for government and statute law, there is Jay Walljasper's account of "social engineering" in Montgomery County, Maryland, and Kenny Fries's argument on behalf of better Social Security payments so that the disabled can more easily earn a living.

The essay by Suzanne Pharr, "A Match Made in Heaven, Lesbian Leftie Chats with a Promise Keeper" illustrates a different aspect of the possibilities for change, namely how dialogue can make us reconsider previously frozen attitudes and stereotypes. In a different direction, essays by Wendy Shalit ("Among the Gender Benders") and Nat Hentoff ("Speech Codes") attack already implemented modes of change and argue that they are worse than the problems they sought to cure. Ellis Cose in "Affirmative Action and the Dilemma of the 'Qualified'" takes up the arguments for overturning of affirmative action mandates, in particular that affirmative action is a haven for the unqualified.

Finally, and almost as if questioning a whole legacy of argument about multiculturalism, pluralism, and even human rights talk, Richard Rorty's pugnacious "What's Wrong With Rights Talk" argues that instead of debating endlessly over "rights" (the rightness or wrongness of affirmative action in the abstract, for example) we would do better to act in the American pragmatic spirit and focus on specific problems and specific solutions, abandoning ideology, dogmatism, and perhaps "rights" themselves!

Studs Terkel and C. P. Ellis

C. P. Ellis's account makes for riveting reading. We learn how and why he became a member of the Ku Klux Klan (one of the most vicious racist organizations in the past, now masquerading under a guise of openness) and how he got out of the Klan to become a spokesman for integration and civil rights. Studs Terkel comments on Ellis's narrative.

OCCURRENCE IN DURHAM

from Stud Terkel's Race, How Black and Whites Think and Feel About the American Obsession

The year is 1978.

We're in his office in Durham, North Carolina. He is business manager of the International Union of Operating Engineers. On the wall is a plaque: "Certificate of Service, in recognition to C. P. Ellis for your faithful service to the city in having served as a member of the Human Relations Council, February, 1977."

At one time, he had been Exalted Cyclops of the Durham chapter of the Ku Klux Klan.

He is fifty-three years old.

My father worked in a textile mill in Durham. He died at forty-eight years old. It was probably from cotton dust. Back then, we never heard of brown lung. I was seventeen years old and had a mother and sister depending on somebody to make a livin'. It was just barely enough insurance to cover his burial. I had to quit school and go to work. I was about eighth grade when I quit.

> He recounts his daily humiliations at school because of his raggedy clothes; his sense of shame; his love for his father, who took him to ballgames and "fishin'," who deprived himself of the barest of amenities for his boy's sake, who "got plastered on weekends because he worked so hard and he'd done the best he could the entire week and there seemed to be no hope."
>
> He remembers his early workdays, pumping gas, running a bread route, raising four children, one blind and retarded, "I hug his neck, tell him I love him, I don't know whether he knows me or not, but I know he's well taken care of."

I worked my butt off and never seemed to break even. They say to abide by the law, do right and live for the Lord, and everything'll work out. It just kept getting worse and worse.

I will never forget: outside our house—rent, forty-eight dollars a month, way more than half my weekly wages—there was a 265-gallon oil drum. What I would do every night, I would run up to the store and buy five gallons of oil and climb up the ladder and pour it in that 265-gallon drum. I could hear that five gallons when it hit the bottom of that oil drum, splatters, and it sounds like it's nothin' in there. But it would keep the house warm for the night. Next day you'd have to do the same thing.

I began to say there's somethin' wrong with this country. I really began to get bitter. I tried to find somebody. I began to blame it on black people. I had to hate somebody. Hatin' America is hard to do because you can't see it to hate it. You gotta have somethin' to look at to hate. [*Laughs.*] The natural person for me to hate would be black people, because my father before me was a member of the Klan. As far as he was concerned, it was the savior of the white people. It was the only organization that would take care of the white people. So I began to admire the Klan.

The first night I went with the fellas, they knocked on the door and gave the signal. They sent some robed Klansmen to talk to me and give me some instructions. I was led into a large meeting room and this was the time of my life! It was thrilling. Here's a guy who's worked hard all his life and struggled all his life to be something, and here's the moment to be something. I will never forget it. Four robed Klansmen led me into the hall. The light were dim and all you could see was an illuminated cross. I knelt before the cross. I had to make certain vows and promises. We promised to uphold the purity of the white race, fight communism, and protect white womanhood.

After I had taken my oath, there was loud applause goin' through the buildin', musta been at least four hundred people. It was a thrilling moment for C. P. Ellis.

The majority of 'em are low-income whites, people who don't really have a part in something. They have been shut out as well as the blacks. Some are not very well-educated either. Just like myself. We had a lot of support from doctors and lawyers and police officers.

I can understand why people join extreme right-wing or left-wing groups. They're in the same boat I was in. Shut out. Deep down inside, we want to be part of this great society. Nobody listens, so we join these groups.

He tells of recruiting young people, "teachin' the principles of the Klan. When they came in the door, we had 'Dixie' playin' and they were just thrilled to death.

"I had a call one night from one of our kids. He was about twelve. He said, 'I just been robbed downtown by two niggers.' I'd had a couple of drinks and that really teed me off. I go downtown and I saw two young black people. I said, 'Nigger, you seen a little white boy up here? I just got a call from him and was told some niggers robbed him of fifteen cents.' I pulled my .32 out and put it right at his head. I said, 'I always wanted to kill a nigger and I think I will make you the first one.' I nearly scared the kid to death and he struck off."

This was the time when the civil-rights movement was really beginnin' to peak. The blacks were beginnin' to demonstrate and picket downtown stores. I will never forget some black lady I hated with a purple passion. Ann Atwater. Every time I'd go downtown, she'd be leading a boycott. How I hated—pardon the expression, I don't use it now—how I just hated that black nigger. Big, fat heavy woman. She'd pull about eight demonstrations, and first thing you know they had two, three blacks at the checkout counter. Her and I had some pretty close confrontations.

We'd go to the city-council meetings, and the blacks would be there and we'd be there. It was a confrontation every time. I didn't hold back anything. The councilmen and county commissioners began to call us at night on the telephone. "C. P., glad you came to that meeting last night." We visited the city leaders in their homes and talked to 'em privately. It wasn't long before they would call me up. "The blacks are comin' up tonight and makin' outrageous demands. How about some of you people showin' up?"

We'd load up our cars and we'd fill up half the council chambers, and the blacks the other half. During these times, I carried weapons, outside my belt. We would wind up just hollerin' and fussin' at each other. As a result of our fightin' one another, the city council still had their way. They didn't want to give up control to the blacks *nor* the Klan. They were usin' us.

I began to realize this later down the road. One day I was walkin' downtown and a certain city-council member saw me comin'. I expected him to shake my hand, because he was talking to me at night on the telephone. I had been in his home and visited him. He crossed the street. Oh shit, I began to think, somethin's wrong here. Most of 'em are merchants, maybe an attorney, an insurance agent, people like that. As long as they kept low-income whites and low-income blacks fightin', they're gonna maintain control.

I began to get that feeling after I was ignored in public. I thought: Bullshit, you're not gonna use me anymore. That's when I began to do some really serious thinkin'.

I spent a lot of sleepless nights. I still didn't like blacks. I didn't want to associate with 'em. I didn't, until I met a black person and talked to him eyeball to eyeball. Or a Jewish person. I found out they're people just like me. They cried, they cussed, they prayed, they had desires. Just like myself. Thank God, I got to the point where I can look past labels. But at that time, my mind was closed.

I remember one Monday-night Klan meeting. I said something was wrong. Our city fathers were using us. And I didn't like to be used. The reactions of the others were not too pleasant: "Let's just keep fightin' them niggers."

I'd go home at night and I'd have to wrestle with myself. I'd look at a black person walkin' down the street, and the guy'd have ragged shoes or his clothes would be worn. That began to do somethin' to me inside. I went through this for about six months. I felt I just had to get out of the Klan. But I wouldn't get out.

> He recounts a turning-point: an HEW grant of $78,000 to the state AFL-CIO, to help solve racial problems in the schools. A meeting was called of blacks, whites, liberals, conservatives, Klansmen, NAACP people. "I said, 'No way am I comin' with all those niggers.' A White Citizens Council guy says, 'Let's go, it's tax money bein' spent.' I walk in the door and I knew most of 'em by face, 'cause I seen 'em demonstratin' around town. Ann Atwater was there. [Laughs.] I just forced myself to go in and sit down."

The meeting was moderated by a great big black guy, but he was very nice. He said, "I want you all to feel free to say anything you want to say." Some of the blacks stand up and say it's white racism. I took all I could take. I asked for the floor and cut loose. I said, "No, sir, it's black racism. If we didn't have niggers in the schools, we wouldn't have the problems we got today."

I will never forget. Howard Clement, a black guy, stood up. He said, "I'm certainly glad C. P. Ellis come, because he's the most honest man here tonight." I thought, "What's that nigger tryin' to do?" [*Laughs.*] At the end of that meeting, some blacks tried to come up and shake my hand, but I wouldn't do it. I walked off.

> He continues: On the second night, it was easier; things were off his chest. On the third night, he is astonished that a black man suggests Ellis and Ann Atwater as cochairs of the key committee. "I thought to myself, 'Hey, there ain't no way I can work with that gal.' Finally, I agreed to accept it, 'cause at this point I was tired of fightin'."

How could I work with Ann Atwater? It was impossible. But it was in our hands. We had to make it a success. This gave me another sense of belongin', a sense of pride. Here's a chance for a low-income white man to be somethin'. Her and I began to reluctantly work together. [*Laughs.*] She had as many problems workin' with me as I had workin' with her.

One night I called her: "Ann, you and I should have a lot of differences and we got 'em now. But there's somethin' laid out here before us, and if it's gonna be a success, you and I are gonna have to make it one. Can we lay aside some of these feelin's?" She said, "I'm willing if you are." I said, "Let's do it."

My old friends would call me at night: "C. P., what the hell is wrong with you? You're sellin' out the white race." This began to make me have guilty feelin's. Here I am all of a sudden makin' an about-face and tryin' to deal with my feelin's, my heart. My mind was beginnin' to open up. I was beginnin' to see what was right and what was wrong. I don't want the kids to fight forever.

> During this time, he had been doing maintenance work at Duke University. The president, Terry Sanford, gave him ten days off with pay, recognizing the importance of this venture. There were days and nights of knocking on doors, with little positive response. He was rebuffed by whites; she, by blacks. This odd coupling was too much for most others to take.

One day, Ann and I just sat down and began to reflect. Ann said, "My daughter came home cryin' every day. She said her teacher was makin' fun of her in front of the other kids." I said, "Boy, same thing happened to my kid. White liberal teacher was makin' fun of Tim Ellis's father, the Klansman, in front of other peoples. He came home cryin'." At this point—[*He pauses, swallows hard, stifles a sob.*]—I begin to see, here we are, two people from the far ends of the fence, havin' identical problems, except her bein' black and me bein' white. From that moment on, I tell ya, that gal and I worked together good. I begin to love the girl, really. [*He weeps.*]

The amazing thing about it, her and I, up to that point, had cussed each other, bawled at each other, hated each other. Up to that point, we didn't know each other. We didn't know we had things in common.

We worked at it with the people who came to these meetings. They talked about racism, sex education, about teachers not bein' qualified. After seven, eight nights of real intense discussion, these people who had never talked to each other before, all of a sudden came up with resolutions. It was really somethin', you had to be there to get the tone and feelin' of it.

I still didn't like integration, but the law says you gotta do this and I've gotta do what the law says, okay? The most disheartening thing was the school system refused to implement our resolutions. So I decided to run for school board.

I spent eighty-five dollars on the campaign. The guy runnin' against me spent several thousand. I really had nobody on my side. The Klan turned against me. The low-income whites turned against me. The liberals didn't particularly like me. The blacks were suspicious to me. The blacks wanted to support me, but they couldn't muster up enough to support a Klansman on the school board. [*Laughs.*] But I made up my mind that what I was doin' was right, and I was gonna do it regardless what anybody said.

I was invited to the Democratic women's social hour as a candidate. Didn't have but one suit to my name. Had it six, seven, eight years. I had it cleaned, put on the best shirt I had and a tie. Here were all these high-class wealthy candidates shakin' hands. I walked up to the mayor and stuck out my hand. He gave me that handshake with that rag type of hand. He said, "C. P., I'm glad to see you." But I could tell by his handshake he was lyin' to me. This was botherin' me. I know I'm a low-income person. I know they were sayin', "What's this little dude runnin' for the school board?" Yet they had to smile and make like they were glad to see me. I begin to spot some black people in that room. I automatically went to 'em and that was a firm handshake. They said, "I'm glad to see you, C. P." I knew they meant it—you can tell about a handshake.

I got 4,640 votes. The guy beat me by 2,000. Not bad for eighty-five bucks and no constituency.

The whole world was openin' up. I was learnin' new truths that I had never learned before. I was beginnin' to look at a black person, shake hands with him, and see him as a human bein'. I hadn't got rid of all this stuff. I've still got a little bit of it. But somethin' was happin' to me. It was almost like bein' born again. It was a new life. I didn't have these sleepless nights I used to have when I was active in the Klan and slippin' around at night. I could sleep at night and feel good about it. I'd rather live now than at any time in history. It's a challenge.

He worked mornings at Duke and attended high school in the afternoon. "I was the only white in class and the oldest by far." He studied biology, "took the books home at night, and sure enough I graduated. I got the diploma at home."

A union was being organized at work. "I wasn't pro-union. My daddy was antilabor, too. But we were workin' seven days in a row, starvin' to death." In recruiting for the union, he discovered "I knew how to organize, how to stir people up." [Laughs.] The result was an overwhelming union victory. He was elected chief steward and appointed business agent.

When I began to organize, I began to see far deeper. I began to see people again bein' used. Blacks against whites. I say this without hesitancy: management is vicious. There's two things they want to keep: all the money and all the say-so. They don't want these poor workin' folks to have any of that. I begin to see management fightin' me with everything they had. Hire anti-union law firms, bad-mouth unions. I worked as business rep for five years and was seein' all this.

Last year I ran for business manager of the union. He's elected by the workers. The guy who ran against me was black and the membership was seventy percent black. I thought: Claiborne, there's no way you can beat that black guy. People know your background. Even though you've made tremendous strides, those black people are not gonna vote for you.

The company used my past against me. They put out pictures with a robe and a cap: Would you vote for a Klansman? They wouldn't deal with the issues. I immediately called for a mass meeting. I said, "Okay, this is Claiborne Ellis. This is where I come from. I want you to know, you black ladies here. I was at one time a member of the Klan. I want you to know because they'll tell you about it."

I invited some of my old black friends. Howard Clement kidded me a little bit. "I don't know what I'm doin' here, supporting an ex-Klansman." [*Laughs.*] He said, "I know where C. P. Ellis come from. I knew as he grew and growed with him. I'm tellin' you now, Follow, follow this Klansman." [*He pauses, swallows hard.*] "Any questions?" "No," the black ladies said. "Let's get on with the meeting, we need Ellis." [*He laughs and weeps.*] Boy, black people sayin' that about me. I won, 134 to 41. Four to one.

It makes you feel good to go into a plant and butt heads with professional union-busters. You see black people and white people join hands to defeat the racist issues they use against people. Can you imagine a guy who's got an adult-high-school diploma runnin' into professional college graduates who are union-busters? I work seven days a week, nights and on Saturday and Sunday. The salary's not great, but I can't quit. I got a taste of it. [*Laughs.*]

I tell people there's a tremendous possibility to stop wars, the battles, the struggles, the fights between people. People say, "That's an impossible dream. You sound like Martin Luther King." An ex-Klansman who sounds like Martin Luther King! [*Laughs.*] I don't think it's an impossible dream. It's happened in my life. It's happened in other people's lives in America.

When the news came over the radio that Martin Luther King was assassinated, I got on the telephone and began to call other Klansmen. We just had a real party at the service station. Really rejoicin' 'cause that sonofabitch was dead. Our troubles are over with. They say the older you get, the harder it is for you to change. That's not necessarily true. Since I changed, I've set down and listened to tapes of Martin Luther King. I listen to it and tears come to my eyes, 'cause I know what he's sayin' now. I know what's happenin'.

> The phone rings. A conversation. "This was a black guy who's director of Operation Breakthrough in Durham. I had called his office. I'm interested in employin' some young black person, who's interested in learnin' the labor movement. I want someone who's never had an opportunity, like myself. Just so he can read and write, that's all."

1989

What worries me is that racism is getting worse. In the last ten years, the White House has been promoting it. It has become more open. There was a time when it was getting better, but these last two administrations have set it back. With Reagan and Bush, it's like a nod to say okay, try it again. And it's being tried.

I don't think anybody is born full of hate, born a racist. At the Democratic Convention, the cameras zoomed in on one Klansman. He was saying, "I hope Jesse Jackson gets AIDS and dies." I felt sympathy for him. That's the way my old friends used to think. Me, too. And my father.

After I left the Klan, I felt guilt, isolation, rejection. I wound up getting counseling. I was getting calls from former Klan friends, "You betrayed us." I began to question myself. But now at sixty-three, with this new light, I feel good about myself.

Sometimes I see my old Klan friends. Sometimes they speak to me, sometimes they don't. I don't worry about it. I wish them well; they're human beings, I think some of them changed a little bit.

But they're not willing to come out with it. They're afraid to change their own life because they're afraid of life. It would have been easier for me if I had gone on being a member of the Klan. It's been a struggle. Any change is.

My children have all changed along with me. They were with me when I was in the Klan and they painfully left with me. Now they feel the way I do. We used to say the word "nigger." Not anymore. When my oldest son came home with a black girl, I was shocked at first. It wasn't serious; he married somebody else. But when I met her, I felt like I was a great liberal. I don't like the word "liberal." I like the word "progressive."

Most of my friends in Durham are progressive, but there's an economic barrier. Their station is higher than mine. I don't feel comfortable in their homes. Sometimes I find myself standing in the corner in a social gathering and that ought not to be. But the black people in my union are progressive, too. I feel comfortable with them.

Companies fighting our union still bring up my Klan past. It thrills me when they do it, because it backfires on 'em every time. Cargill Grain tried it recently. My picture was put up on the company bulletin board: C. P. Ellis is not the kind of man you want as a leader. The workers just tore the picture off the wall and went back to work.

Our union, seventy-percent black and thirty-percent white, have negotiated one of the best contracts we ever had. One of the greatest satisfactions in my life was to see forty low-income black women negotiate and win. It's the first contract in Durham that had Martin Luther King's birthday as a paid holiday. The company at first said no, but we insisted. At the very last moment, they said okay. I wish you could have seen the faces of the black people light up. Some of the whites said, "We're not going to take Martin Luther King's birthday off." We said, "Okay, idiots, work." Of course, they didn't work. Of course, they took the day off with pay.

Some of my old friends are cautious around me and say "black" instead of the other word. They almost say it, but catch themselves and stop. I respect it and I'm glad they respect me that much. Maybe I expect something that's impossible. Maybe it'll never get settled, unless we sit down and listen to each other as individuals. Skinheads and blacks will find they have much in common. Jews and Arabs, too.

I have the same fundamental beliefs I've had for a long time. But it's hard to find a church out here that preaches the social gospel. I'm visiting churches now trying to find one. I believed Christ cared about poor people. That's something I learned after I left the Klan. I do a lot of riding, and I do most of my thinking on the road, when I'm on to my next meeting.

I think Christ was a god in the flesh. He cares about individuals, he cares about how we're treated. It's got to bother Him to see people hungry, to see people under the bridges, homeless, starving. I think if He came back today, he'd be extremely disappointed.

─────────────────── **ANALYSIS** ───────────────────

1. To what extent do you think Ellis' entry into the Klan was foreordained by virtue of his father's membership? Other early circumstances of his life?

2. How does Ellis, looking back, use the scapegoat idea of prejudice to explain his earlier attitudes?

3. For Ellis, what begins the process of moving away from the Klan? I.e., what is the effect of him when a city-council member turns away from him?

4. A turning point, says Terkel, is the HEW (Department of Health, Education and Welfare) grant of $78,000 to help solve racial problems in the schools. What might be the pros and cons of such governmental intervention in local affairs?

5. Ellis notes that his Klan friends would call him up and ask him why he was "selling out the white race"? Why doesn't he buy into this bit of peer pressure?

6. How does Ellis analyze the root causes of racial antagonism, as he now looks back on them (and presumably as a result of attending high school now)?

WRITING POSSIBILITIES

1. What is the interplay between racial and economic forces in Ellis' account? Does it simply involve "low-income whites, people who don't really have a part in something" or is there more to it—habits and traditions, white self-definitions, family traditions? How seriously should we take Ellis' comment on his "progressive" friends in Durham whose "station is higher than mine"?

2. Some critics wonder if Ellis is sincere or not in his conversion story. What might be said on one side or the other as you reread his account and look for evidences of sincerity?

3. Have you ever held attitudes in the past which you rejected later? Using either an essay or self-interview format (you can be Studs Terkel to yourself), explain what you thought or felt and how you changed.

Doug Bandow

Bandow's essay represents a libertarian challenge to many of the essays in this text. Bandow argues that prejudice is private behavior and hence should be met with private responses—not with governmental legislation, as for example William Julius Wilson urges at the end of "When Work Disappears" (pages 348–356). To illustrate his point, Bandow argues that the discriminatory behavior of a particular Eddie Bauer store should have been met by a boycott and a letter to the CEO, not by more antidiscrimination legislation. For some, such individual action represents the way all great reform movements have begun— abolition, women's suffrage—but for others, individual action at some point will need to be replaced by institutional and governmental change. Bandow, a senior fellow at the conservative Cato Institute, is the author of The Politics of Plunder *(1990).*

PRIVATE PREJUDICE, PRIVATE REMEDY

There may be no more politically contentious issue than race. The federal government has created a vast racial spoils system that often helps those who least need assistance. To be well-educated and well-connected—that is, successful—is to gain the most from a system supposedly intended to help the victims of discrimination.

But the perversion of such programs is not the most important reason to dismantle racial norming, quotas, preferences, and other forms of discrimination against the "majority." Justice should be based on individual, not group, treatment. To favor someone simply because he or she is black (or Hispanic, or whatever) is morally wrong. Doing so is also, in the long run, socially destructive, causing everyone to look at almost everything through a racial lens. The most elemental decisions about education and employment become political; even private relationships increasingly polarize as everyone squabbles over their supposed "entitlement" by color. . . .

Race also underlies most of the other critical issues facing our society: crime, economic opportunity, education, poverty, welfare. Too many political debates quickly descend into vicious squabbles over race, even though the solutions are usually simple to discern. African-Americans are almost invariably the victims of perverse government policies, which, though racially neutral on their face, have a highly disparate impact. The minimum wage disproportionately bars urban youth from the job market; welfare disproportionately disrupts inner-city families and communities. And so on. Here, too, less state control and more individual freedom and community responsibility are the answer.

Yet to criticize government intervention on race, especially the tendency of people to turn every private dispute, no matter how small, into a public crisis—via a formal lawsuit, government prosecution, or federal program—carries with it a responsibility to criticize acts of private discrimination and intolerance. That is, if we really believe that public law should not reach every obnoxious private act, then people who are moral as well as free should practice the alternative: applying social sanctions.

The need for private action is probably greater than realized by most middle-class whites. Imagine stopping by the mall and buying a shirt that you liked. Imagine returning to the shop the next day wearing the shirt. Imagine being accosted by two security guards, demanding to see the receipt for your shirt—which, not surprisingly, you didn't think to bring with you. Imagine being ordered to strip off the shirt and, even though a cashier remembered selling you one, told to bring in the receipt to retrieve your shirt.

Seem improbable? If you're a middle-aged white, it's inconceivable. Any employee going up to such a customer and saying, "Excuse me, sir—that shirt looks like the type we stock. Where's your receipt?" would earn a quick trip to the unemployment line.

But an Eddie Bauer clothing store in a Washington, D.C., suburb forced Alonzo Jackson, a 16-year-old black male, to literally give the shirt off of his back to store security personnel. He went home in his t-shirt. He did find the receipt, though not without some effort. The store's management wasn't entirely satisfied: explained spokeswoman, Cheryl Engstrom, "The amount on the receipt matched the purchase, although the stub didn't specifically indicate whether or not it was the same shirt." However, Engstrom added, the store "gave him the benefit of the doubt and let him keep it anyway." Mr. Jackson was lucky the store guards weren't checking underwear as well as shirts.

The treatment of Alonzo Jackson dramatically demonstrates why race remains such a painful and divisive issue. Store personnel implicitly accused Jackson of being a criminal and took his property—because he was black. It took a torrent of angry letters and phone calls from whites and blacks alike before the company formally apologized.

That young black males are treated badly because they are young black males is not new. Cab drivers are less likely to pick up and jewelers less likely to buzz into locked shops African-American males. Stores are, as Jackson certainly knows, more likely to suspect young black males of shoplifting.

The fear of African-American men is shared by many African-Americans—black cab drivers also pass by black pedestrians. It was Jesse Jackson, of all people, who once observed that "There is nothing more painful to me at this stage in my life than to walk down the street and hear footsteps and start thinking about robbery—then look around and see someone white and feel relieved."

Yet this understandable fear of a small number of predators who commit a disproportionate share of crimes penalizes the vast majority of African-Americans who are not only decent, law-abiding people, but also the primary victims of crime. Explains the Justice Department, "Black households, Hispanic households, and urban households were the most likely to experience crime." In fact, blacks are 50 percent more likely than others to be victimized by a violent crime. People like Alonzo Jackson are paying twice—they are more likely to suffer from crime and be suspected of being criminals.

And that has a larger social impact. Such treatment can only fan anger, frustration, and resentment. Victimology has become big business, with most everyone wanting to be called, and recompensed for allegedly being a victim. But there are real victims, like Jackson.

What can we do? Some of the answers, as noted earlier, are better policy. Crime must be detected, punished, and deterred, especially in poor neighborhoods, where residents are so vulnerable. The government's educational monopoly must be broken, giving disadvantaged students a chance to receive a real education. The economy needs to be deregulated and opened to help everyone, rather than controlled to enrich special interests, such as labor unions, which back laws like the Davis-Bacon Act, which restrict the hiring of minorities.

Racism is harder to address, especially through government. Some race-based decisions, like those of cab drivers who pass by blacks, reflect reasons other than prejudice. Are we really prepared to penalize people who, even if wrongly, believe their lives might be in danger—especially when today's antidiscrimination laws have misfired, creating a quota mentality and encouraging disappointed jobseekers to routinely scream racism?

We especially need to steer clear of the quota temptation that has so entranced politicians in Washington and across the nation. When the high school in Piscataway Township, New Jersey, facing the need to lay off one of ten business education teachers, fired Sharon Taxman because she was white, it compounded rather than alleviated injustice. Cases like this also ensure that anger, frustration, and resentment will rise among whites as well as blacks.

At the same time, the kind of racist behavior exhibited by Eddie Bauer should be criticized and treated as socially unacceptable. As it was when consumers of all races demanded that Eddie Bauer apologize to Alonzo Jackson, else they would take their business elsewhere.

And this is how it should be. As individuals, we need to insist that racism is wrong. That means speaking out and taking action when necessary. The burden for doing so falls especially heavily on those of us who don't believe that every instance of offensive behavior should be a crime. If political society is to do less, as it should, then civil society must do more. It becomes the duty of every one of us to help shape society's moral code.

Analysis

1. What kind of support does Bandow offer for his argument? Consider what he says about quotas and the root causes of the Eddie Bauer case. Do you agree with Bandow that, insofar as quotas are concerned, the governmental cure is worse than the original problem? Why or why not?
2. How do you assess Bandow's discussion of black crime and his rootcause solution to it? Does Bandow offer sufficient evidence in support of his contention that the real issue is how to cut down on black male crime in the first place?

WRITING POSSIBILITIES
---

1. Bandow's essay contrasts starkly with that of William Julius Wilson (pages 348–356) in arguing for the personal cause and personal solution to prejudice and discrimination. But what if prejudice and discrimination are the product of broad social forces (as in Wilson's example of globalization and technological change)? Summarize both Bandow's and Wilson's argument and then explain why you favor one or the other.

2. Have you ever engaged in a boycott, as Bandow recommends? If so, why? What was the upshot?

3. If you faced ethnic or racial or religious slurs or joking from a group of friends and were offended by such slurs or joking, would you speak out or defer to group comraderie? Have you ever been in such a situation (e.g., where no one realized you had a Jewish grandfather or were yourself gay or feminist or conservative or radical, and so forth)? How did you feel? What did you do?

Suzanne Pharr

In her essay, Susanne Pharr reveals how she changed her mind about the Promise Keepers, a religious organization dedicated to male "headship." She implies that perhaps her liberal audience ought to think twice about the possibilities of such cross-group dialogues as she herself had. The encounter Pharr says made her realize what it takes to talk to people "different from ourselves" yet still live with them "in harmony."

A MATCH MADE IN HEAVEN
Lesbian Leftie Chats with a Promise Keeper

In February, as I boarded a plane to Portland, Oregon, I overheard a man say to a woman, "We're almost all Promise Keepers on this flight. We are returning from an Atlanta meeting of 43,000 pastors."

"Forty-three thousand pastors," I thought. "That's like 43,000 organizers because they have influence over their congregations." I entered the plane thinking, "We're sunk."

For the last couple of years I have been watching the growth of the Promise Keepers with fascination and fear. As a Southern lesbian-feminist and anti-racist worker, I am keenly interested in any group of white men organizing around issues related to women and people of color.

As a long-time community organizer, I have to admire the brilliance of the Promise Keepers' organizing strategy. How smart it is to recognize not only the anger and confusion that men have about this changing society, but also their desire for connection and purpose. How smart to bring them into sports stadiums around the country to sing, touch, do the wave, and bond through physical and emotional contact they rarely allow themselves.

I believe the Promise Keepers are the ground troops in an authoritarian movement that seeks to merge church and state. It does not matter that a rightwing agenda is not overt in the formative stages of this movement; when the leaders are ready to move their men in response to their agenda, they will have thousands disciplined to obey and command.

The plane was full of men dressed in casual clothes, many sporting new Promise Keepers shirts. During the flight, they stood in the aisles, talking excitedly. The scene reminded me of the 1987 March on Washington, which I attended along with thousands of lesbians and gay men. For the first time in our lives, we were the majority in airplanes, subways, buses, restaurants, and the streets. The experience was exhilarating. The Promise Keepers on the plane seemed to be having a similar experience, as though they had found each other for the first time.

After trying to escape through reading, I finally gave up and began chatting with the man next to me, dressed in a blue work shirt and jeans and reading a Tom Clancy novel. He reminded me very much of my brothers from rural Georgia. I asked if he was returning from Atlanta. "Yes," he replied. "I've just been to the Promise Keepers meeting, and I'm returning to my small town in Oregon."

I told him that I was a feminist, a civil-rights worker, and a lesbian, that I have very mixed feelings about the Promise Keepers, and that I wanted him to tell me about them.

He told me that he was pastor at a Baptist church, married, father of a teenage son, and that he would enjoy talking about his experience with the Promise Keepers. "You are the second homosexual I've ever met," he said, adding with a grin, "I think." With that introduction, we launched into an hour-and-a-half-long conversation.

The pastor told me that the first thing the Promise Keepers make clear is that men are responsible for all that's wrong with the family; they are not victims.

I told him that was going a little too far for this feminist—I think women might have some responsibility for the negative side of the ledger, too.

He said the Promise Keepers were not to dominate their wives but to lead them. When I asked what this meant, he said, "Man's role is laid out in the Bible—'As God is to man, man is to the family'— and it is to take charge of his family. This means listening to their needs and wishes, then deciding what is best for them."

I said, "As a feminist, I am deeply concerned about shared decision-making, about equality."

"We share the conversations, but I make the decisions," he said. "My job is to lead."

This talk about leadership made me feel that I was in a time warp in which the women's movement had never occurred. I thought about the current status of women struggling with families, jobs, and intimate relationships. I thought about stories I have read that mention how pleased some Promise Keepers' wives are to have their husbands taking a dominant role in the family. With some sadness I considered how damning this is of many male-female relationships: that men are often so absent emotionally that women would be willing to give up autonomy in order to gain their husbands' presence.

I suggested the Promise Keepers could make an enormous contribution to women if they added an additional promise to their credo: that they would not lift their hand against women, and that they would stop other men from committing violence against women and children.

The Promise Keepers are against harming women, he said. They want to protect them. But adding an eighth promise would have to be up to the leadership.

Of everything that happened to this pastor at the meeting, the most life-changing, he said, was racial reconciliation. He said he had never thought about himself as someone prejudiced or discriminatory, and he came to recognize it in himself: "I'm not an emotional man, but I cried along with the audience when the men of color were called to the stage and they could not get there because they were intercepted by white pastors hugging them, shaking their hands, pounding them on the back."

The pastors were sent home, he said, to work to bring about racial reconciliation in their churches.

Since my conversation with the pastor on the airplane, Ralph Reed has been calling for racial reconciliation in the wake of the recent rash of black church burnings in the South. At a meeting with black pastors, Reed admitted that the Christian Coalition has a history of being on the "wrong side" when it comes to race. Now it wants to be on the right side, he says. But why? Calls from the Christian Coalition and the Promise Keepers for racial reconciliation do not include any effort to end institutional racism, or to stop coded attacks on "welfare mothers" or immigrants or affirmative action. Rather, moving into black churches gives the religious right a foothold in the black community. In this way, the call for racial reconciliation is one of the most insidious aspects of the Promise Keepers and their allies on the Christian right. Just as the right is hungry for people of color who are willing to denounce affirmative action and the civil-rights struggles that have traditionally benefited their communities, the Promise Keepers' recruitment of black church leaders looks like a way to persuade the black community to act against its own best interests.

I asked the pastor about the Promise Keepers' attitudes toward lesbians and gays.

The pastor said it was not for a Promise Keeper to judge homosexuals ("That is God's job") but that they believe homosexuality is immoral because the Bible says it is.

"This is not judging?" I thought.

He said that he was sure there were many of us who were fine people but that we suffered from being identified with our "fringe" people who marched in those San Francisco parades.

I asked him if Jesus today would not be thought of as gay—an unmarried thirty-three-year-old who spent almost all of his time with twelve close male friends, one of whom in particular was "beloved."

He said, "No doubt if Jesus returned today, he might not be accepted in many churches."

We then talked about how few were the references in the Bible to same-sex relationships and how many were the references to sharing wealth, caring for those who have less, and opening one's home and heart to others. Why, then, did fundamentalists not have a strong economic agenda for the redistribution of wealth?

It's true, he said. This is a contradiction.

In the end, I thought we had communicated honestly with each other and that on some points, we had moved toward one another in understanding. It seemed to me that a great difference between us was his belief in the literal truth of the Bible, and my belief that it is a historical document with great spiritual content. I told him I thought that almost all of Christendom falls somewhere between those two positions. He agreed.

I wondered, can people who have very different beliefs and cultural practices live in peace with one another?

My final question to him was: Can you and I live in homes side by side, borrow sugar from one another, and encourage our children to play together? He said yes.

This conversation led me to think more deeply about the difference between the right's leaders (those engaged in an organizing strategy that threatens democracy) and its followers (those searching for solutions to social and economic instability, whose heartfelt beliefs make them easy targets for manipulation). Many progressives write off the latter, discarding them as ignorant or mean.

Our conversation stayed on my mind for weeks afterwards, and I thought of this one Promise Keeper with respect and continued interest. Then one day he phoned me long distance from his small town, saying he was just calling to keep in touch and to say what a profound effect our conversation had had on him.

"It eliminated whole areas of ignorance for me," he said.

"Me too," I replied.

My conversations with this Promise Keeper made me understand that progressive people must rethink their relation to the American right.

How do we point out the differences between the generals of this army and their recruits?

How do we talk to people who are different from ourselves?

How do we hold different beliefs and still live in harmony?

Is there any hope for preventing the merger of church and state if we do not hold authentic conversations with those who believe fervently in the inerrancy of the Bible?

How do we get closer to people's real needs and their values in our organizing for change?

Finally, how do we carry on this conversation and organize as progressives committed to equal rights for everyone—nothing more, nothing less?

ANALYSIS

1. Where do Pharr and the pastor disagree about the roles of husbands and wives?

2. What is the difference in tone and language about racial tolerance between what Pharr says on the plane to the Promise Keeper friend and what she later talks about to the audience of *The Progressive?* Does Pharr present evidence for her suspicion that the Promise Keepers represent attempts "to persuade the black community to act against its own best interests"?

3. Do you agree with Pharr's implication that there's a big difference between leaders and followers in organizations like the Promise Keepers? Explain.

WRITING POSSIBILITIES

1. Have you ever had a conversation of opposites like this, one in which modest understanding was achieved? Ignorance dispelled on both sides? Explain what is was like and model your essay on Pharr's (i.e., on the dual *purposes* of presenting your original *speaker-self* and your present *writer-speaker* self.)

2. To what extent does Pharr's *rhetorical strategy* provide for *identification* between herself and her auditor? As you read Pharr's essay, to what extent do you (or don't you) find such identification between yourself and some, none, or all of Pharr's understandings and beliefs?

Tom Watson

Tom Watson's story illustrates almost perfectly Doug Bandow's idea of individual moral action as the best solution to prejudice. Watson sees discrimination within his own golfing world and resolves to attack it as best he can, both by resigning from the Kansas City Golf Club he has played in since childhood and by writing this op-ed piece to demonstrate his commitments to a national audience.

THE AMERICAN WAY OF GOLF

Golf has changed slowly through the decades, yet it is growing phenomenally, nationally and internationally. There are more players from more segments of society, more new courses, more women, and more and better opportunities for young and old to learn the game. That's all good; golf is healthy (and healthful), wealthy and still wise.

Yet this has been a troubled and historic year. For the past century, golf in America has been largely the sport of the privileged, a game for white Protestant men to learn and master at private country clubs. Most such clubs have had restrictive and highly secret membership policies. Jews, Hispanics, blacks, single women and others who sought the comforts of a private club with its pool, dining room and lush golf course, not to mention elevated social standing and potential business contacts, were left out or left to fend for themselves.

Golf didn't care. The game produced its great champions: Bobby Jones, Hagen and Nelson, Hogan, Palmer and Nicklaus. Each was white, none was Jewish, and each was accepted by the public and the privileged. The game flourished.

Then last August, at our P.G.A. championship at the Shoal Creek Country Club in Birmingham, Ala., the inevitable happened. The club's founder was quoted, or misquoted, as saying after an interview that blacks were not allowed to play at Shoal Creek because "that just isn't done down here."

Suddenly, the closet door flew open. Why should a major golf championship, in this day and age of social advances, be played at a site where such discrimination toward fellow Americans prevails? The unspeakable had been spoken and the reaction was swift and sure.

The furor took the story from the sports pages to the front page; corporate sponsors of the tournament telecast withdrew their $2 million in advertising. In rapid order, Shoal Creek agreed to open its membership, and the PGA Tour stated that its tournaments would be played only at clubs that agreed to membership policies that did not discriminate on the basis of race, gender or religion.

(Because of the new P.G.A. policy, a few golf courses are no longer available for tournament play; the members chose not to abdicate control over their policies.)

Then, late last year, I resigned from the Kansas City Country Club, where I had played golf since I was 6 years old. I had heard that my club had denied membership to a popular and distinguished business leader, Henry Bloch, who happened to be Jewish, the only possible reason for rejection. My decision to resign was a matter of personal conscience, brought to the forefront all the more because my wife and children are Jewish, though I am not.

At least two conflicting forces are involved in this snarling issue of privacy and openness. First, Americans cherish their freedom of choice, assembly and their individual rights to say, do and think anything they want within the law. On the other hand, and equally fundamental, we presuppose the merit of the Golden Rule and equal rights for every citizen. We abhor bigots and bigotry, hypocrisy and repression.

Truly American, I am in conflict with myself. The Bloch family certainly belongs, and indeed now does officially belong, among the members at my former club. It was painful for my family and me when I resigned to protest the Blochs' initial rejection, the secrecy of that decision and the lack of explanation for it.

Still, I fervently support the right of any group of people to band together in private association, just so long as they *choose to admit* their own discriminatory practices. There are significant differences among us. I see nothing wrong with private clubs, be they for men, women, Jews, blacks, Catholics, Hispanics, Asians, whomever. Just let them own up to it, not hide it.

There is no doubt in my mind that public posture and private practice are replete with hypocrisy. How many executives defiantly withdraw their advertising dollars in support of a civil rights protest only to leave the office and relax at a discriminatory private club? Should any club recruit one black member just to "integrate" the membership, obey P.G.A. policies and retain its televised tournament?

Perhaps someday Capitol Hill will establish quotas: religious quotas for my old club, gender quotas at the all-male Butler National Golf Club near Chicago and racial quotas at Shoal Creek. To aid the economically disenfranchised, we have found that legislation is vital to equality. But let's not wait for government or the P.G.A. or a corporate sponsor to dictate what they think we ought to do.

Let's discriminate right now, each one of us, privately, between what is right and what is wrong. At work, at the country club, at home with the children (especially at home with the children), let's make our own personal choices that help, rather than hurt. And let's start soon.

Analysis

1. Midway through the essay, Watson reveals a possible conflict of interest in the case under discussion: his wife and children are Jewish, he is not. The Kansas City Golf Club, in Watson's view, had rejected for membership a businessman who would seem to have met all the criteria for acceptance except that he was Jewish. Watson says that his decision to resign from the Club was not motivated by any personal interest—it was rather, he says, "a matter of personal conscience." How does Watson convince you that this is the case? How, in other words, does he support the argument that *conscience* is his guide throughout the op-ed piece?

Writing Possibilities

1. Watson takes up the crucial issue of choice—the "right of any people to band together in private association, just so long as they *choose to admit* their own discriminatory practices." Do you agree with this argument? Why or why not? How does Watson support it? How might it apply to other groups and situations—e.g., the right of gay leaders in the Boy Scouts?
2. Choose a case of presumed discrimination that you have experienced, write an op-ed piece like Watson's that details the circumstances of the case and your own view as to whether private moral action (like Bandow's) or public laws (like the Civil Rights Commission's) ought to be the alternative.

Jay Walljasper

According to Walljasper, the editor of the Utne Reader, *residential segregation results from the piling up of expensive homes in one or another area, and then such a piling up in turn becomes the bane of integrated schooling. How can there be amicable relationships among different races if the economic classes are shunted off one by one into separate ghettos and gated communities? Furthermore, if communities offer only high-priced homes, thus excluding low-income and most minority group members, the schools will also remain one-class, one-race entities. As Walljasper tells the story, Maryland's Montgomery County broke the logjam and set up the possibility for greater integration (class and race) of its neighborhoods by use of building codes and tax incentives. Walljasper's enthusiastic article does however raise a question for some of its readers: what if we don't like such "social engineering"? What if we don't want to risk a home purchase in the name of social experimentation?*

A FAIR SHARE IN SUBURBIA

Devonshire East, in many people's minds, embodies the American Dream in full glory. A subdivision of new homes set among a stand of trees, Devonshire's winding streets and $275,000 property values seem to guarantee a haven of comfort and satisfaction. Even critics of soulless suburban architecture might find something to like in these brick town houses, whose handsome design recalls classic neighborhoods in nearby Washington, DC. Located in Montgomery County, Maryland, which is the sixth-wealthiest county in the nation and is full of blossoming high-tech businesses and federal agencies like the National Institutes of Health, Devonshire East is home to the managerial and professional class that has benefited so enormously from the nineties economic boom.

It's also home to Michelle Dove, a 37-year-old-African-American single mother, and her three kids—two of whom are now attending college. How she affords to live in Devonshire East, on top of college costs, with the modest salary of an elementary school teacher is no miracle of financial planning. It's the result—a small miracle itself—of Montgomery County's housing policy. Every subdivision of more than fifty units built here over the past twenty-two years has been required to include a share of affordable housing (between 12.5 and 15 percent). Even more surprising, a third of these affordable units have been set aside for purchase by the county's public housing authority or nonprofit groups that rent to lower-income families.

Dove rents her three-bedroom apartment for $991, well below the market rate in this county (where the median price for a new town house is $189,000 and the average new single-family house exceeds $300,000), from Interfaith Housing Coalition, a group of congregations involved in social issues. Devonshire East's affordable units maintain the same look and architectural standards as the market-rate town houses across the street, but costs are kept down by tucking a second apartment atop each ground-floor unit.

"I like living here," Dove says. "It's nice and quiet. I'm just a nine-minute drive from work and my daughter goes to a very nice middle school." She says she's felt no tension from her more upscale neighbors since moving here four years ago and notes, "There's a good sense of community among the people living right here on the street."

Dove's hope is someday to buy her own house in Montgomery County, the place where she grew up and now teaches in the local schools. This would be an impossible dream in many wealthy suburban enclaves, where sky-high home prices and restrictive zoning codes bar many folks—including young people who grew up in these towns as well as teachers, firefighters, nurses, office workers and other middle-income employees who play a vital role in the life of the community. Even current residents facing economic setbacks due to divorce, lay-offs, death in the family or medical bills find themselves unable to continue living in their own hometown. But Montgomery County's "Fair Share" housing legislation, called the Moderately Priced Housing law and enacted in 1974, requires that all new developments include housing affordable for people making approximately 65 percent or less of the county's median income. The MPH law has fostered the creation of 10,000 moderately priced units in the past two decades. At least two-thirds of these homes are available for sale, offering people like Michelle Dove a chance they otherwise would not have.

Montgomery County's record in opening up suburban neighborhoods to people of lesser means is gaining national attention now that affordable housing is being recognized as not simply an inner-city problem. A recent report from the Department of Housing and Urban Development notes that one-third of families with "worst case" housing needs now live in the suburbs—almost 2 million households. This crisis has led to the adoption of Fair Share housing legislation (sometimes called "inclusionary zoning") in many places—other affluent counties ringing Washington, DC, as well as the states of Connecticut and New Jersey, plus Tallahassee, Florida; Burlington, Vermont; and several dozen communities in California. Although inspired by Montgomery County's efforts, none of these programs go so far as Montgomery County in reserving some of the units for public housing families. Also, in most places the Fair Share laws rely on voluntary incentives rather than mandatory requirements.

The success of Montgomery County's housing policies is also being touted by a growing number of policy-makers and activists who identify the concentration of poverty as one of America's most damaging social problems. Fair Share housing has become a central element of innovative regional strategies aimed at reducing social inequities and insuring the vitality of America's metropolitan areas. David Rusk, a former mayor of Albuquerque who has become a prominent spokesperson for regional solutions to urban problems, says, "As a society we are now slowly lowering the barriers defined by race but raising the ones defined by income. Among American communities

Montgomery County stands out for its integrated neighborhoods—integrated by both racial and ethnic group and, most uncommonly, by income class."

In researching his book on regional strategies for urban revitalization—*Inside Game/Outside Game: Winning Strategies for Saving Urban America,* forthcoming in March—Rusk compared Montgomery County to Oakland County, Michigan, near Detroit. In 1970 both counties were wealthy white enclaves bordering troubled central cities. On an index of economic segregation, with 100 representing absolute segregation by income, they each measured 27. By 1990, class segregation in Montgomery County had remained at a low and stable level, inching up six-tenths of a point on this scale, while Oakland County shot upward eleven points—a direct result of Montgomery County's Fair Share housing ordinance, according to Rusk.

Rusk points out that Montgomery County's housing policies are local rather than regional, covering just part of an area with 4.5 million people that includes two states as well as the District of Columbia. He admits that the county's Fair Share housing law has had limited impact in boosting the fortunes of poor people in inner-city Washington, but it has prevented the county from becoming a fortress for the privileged. Montgomery County's population is ethnically diverse (13.4 percent African-American, 7.6 percent Hispanic, 9.6 percent Asian-American), with 5 percent of residents living below the poverty level. Moreover, poor households are found throughout the county, not just in the hand-me-down older housing near the District of Columbia line: Two-thirds of the affordable units created in compliance with the Fair Share ordinance have been built in the newer, more affluent western portion of the county.

Oakland County, on the other hand, replicates the same pattern of clear-cut economic and racial segregation that devastated Detroit. Its poor and minority residents are clustered in certain portions of the county, notably the hard-hit city of Pontiac. The per capita income ratio between the wealthiest and poorest census tracts in Oakland County is 15 to 1, compared with 6 to 1 in Montgomery County.

One of Rusk's allies in this emerging regional movement is Myron Orfield, a Minnesota state legislator who describes how fast-growing areas such as the rich suburbs of Oakland County are able to capture most of the benefits of economic growth in a region while passing the social costs to poorer central cities and working-class suburbs. Affluent communities are able to do this, Orfield explains, through exclusionary zoning; ordinances that prohibit smaller houses, establish minimum lot sizes, require two-car garages or restrict multifamily dwellings. The overall effect is to outlaw affordable housing, forcing low- and many middle-income people to live elsewhere in the metropolitan region in spite of the fact that they contribute directly to the well-being of these upper-income suburbs. "These are the people who take care of wealthy surbur-banites' kids, take care of their parents at the rest home, serve them coffee, answer the phone in their offices, yet they can't live in these communities," says Russ Adams, who works closely with Orfield as director of the Alliance for Metropolitan Stability, an activist group in the Minneapolis–St. Paul area.

Exclusionary zoning forces poor people—especially minorities—to cluster in certain neighborhoods, creating new stresses for social ser-vices and the social fabric in those communities. Even as the tax base shrinks, taxes often rise to meet low-income people's increased need for local government services, and problems more prevalent in poor communities intensify: crime, underachieving public schools and a culture of hopelessness. All of this, along with America's ongoing anxiety about race, fuels middle-class and business flight from these communities, usually in the direction of the newer suburbs that prac-tice exclusionary zoning.

In a nutshell, this is the story of American cities since World War II. But it is not the way things must turn out. "If you want different outcomes," Rusk notes, "you need to change the rules. Fair Share housing is one of the key rules you need." The Portland, Oregon, met-ropolitan area recently incorporated Fair Share housing principles into its long-range regional plan, which will be implemented by local gov-ernments. "It's a huge victory," says local affordable-housing activist Tasha Harmon, who notes that a recent study shows a deficit of 35,000 low-income housing units in the region. "But there's a lot of work to do to see that it actually happens."

The Portland measure drew support not just from social justice activists, who believe that low- and middle-income people will be better able to fill the new jobs being created in upscale suburbs if they can live in the vicinity, but also from environmentalists, who see it as a chance to reduce auto traffic by allowing people who work in these booming communities to live closer to their jobs. Homebuilders, worried about how Fair Share housing would affect new-home sales, lobbied against the measure, and so did some sub-urban mayors who feared that their communities would be stuck with a disproportionate share of low-income housing. But because Portland's Fair Share principles are merely guidelines in a regional planning document, not concrete proposals being debated by a city council, there have been few objections from the public at large.

Measures designed to mix low-income housing into affluent sub-urbs usually spark substantial criticism wherever they are proposed. "Fair Share housing goes right to the heart of people's fear about race and class," Rusk notes. The fiercest opponents are people who think they've insulated themselves from the problems of modern urban life by settling in a suburb that practices exclusionary zoning. They often mount intense campaigns against Fair Share ordinances, framing their opposition as resistance to social engineering schemes rather than as unwillingness to live near poor or minority people.

Yet exclusionary zoning is social engineering in its purest form, Rusk points out. "You can see the social engineering right on the signs that say 'New Houses from $149,000.'" He adds that critics of Fair Share housing overlook the fact that mixing of incomes (although not races) was an ordinary feature of American life until the suburban boom of midcentury, when subdivisions began to be developed along strict economic lines and zoning codes became more exclusionary. Even silk-stocking neighborhoods in the years before World War II were sprinkled with inexpensive apartments above stores and the occasional boardinghouse.

Now, Myron Orfield explains, "people are afraid of affordable housing [because] they fear they will be the only ones to do it and they will get piled up on." In this sort of climate, how did Montgomery County enact such a far-reaching Fair Share housing policy? One answer is its form of government, in which the county board, rather than municipal government, is invested with most of the decision-making authority. This has made the Fair Share ordinance more effective and politically palatable: It covers the entire county with the exception of two older municipalities and six villages, so there is less fear about one community absorbing the social costs associated with low-income housing while others do not. Montgomery County's system represents a step toward the kind of regional government advocated by Rusk, Orfield and others proposing regional strategies for urban revitalization.

Another part of the answer is the particulars of the place. Montgomery County (population: 819,000)—probably better known to most people as the place where Bethesda, Silver Spring, Chevy Chase and Takoma Park are located—stood out in the sixties and seventies as a peculiar political anomaly: liberal suburbia. Many of the folks who came to Washington to work on New Frontier and Great Society social programs built houses in the suburban stretches of Maryland, bringing along their beliefs in can-do government. In 1965 it became one of the first places below the Mason-Dixon line to pass a fair housing law banning racial discrimination. By 1970, however, it became clear that racial integration would stall in this prosperous county if economic segregation was not addressed. The League of Women Voters and local civil rights groups began pressing the county council for legislation to insure a supply of affordable housing in all neighborhoods. The result, after years of organizing and debate, was the Moderately Priced Housing law.

Developers immediately objected, claiming the ordinance violated their rights under the "takings" clause of the U.S. Constitution, which has been interpreted to mean that citizens must be compensated when government action diminishes the value of their property. But the MPH law had been drafted with this objection in mind, and the county council decided that it did not violate the takings clause since developers were granted a density bonus: the opportunity to develop more units than zoning ordinances permitted in exchange for building the required affordable units. As they began constructing the affordable units (known as Moderately Priced Dwelling Units, or MPDUs) developers realized that the ordinance increased their profits, and they've been supportive of it ever since. Tom Doerr, a local developer, notes a distinct advantage of the program from the point of view of homebuilders: During periods when the housing market is slow they can continue constructing MPDUs, which are assured of immediate sales.

The MPDU program still encounters occasional resistance from local residents—especially as Montgomery County loses its distinction as a liberal bastion—who worry that lower-income households in their midst will drag down property values and spawn ghetto-style social problems. But a recently released study by the Innovative Housing Institute analyzed real estate transactions from 1992 to 1996 in eight Montgomery County subdivisions and found that the change in property values of homes located directly next to MPDUs was no different than that of other homes in the same subdivision or in the same ZIP code.

Deep-seated fears about poor and minority people are not easy to allay with statistics, but a twenty-year track record has convinced the vast majority of county residents that low-income people will not harm their neighborhoods. In researching his book, David Rusk door-knocked the streets of an upscale Montgomery County subdivision adjacent to MPDUs, asking people how they liked the neighborhood. In more than twenty interviews only two of the upscale homeowners even mentioned the MPDUs: a white retired Army colonel and an Asian-American realtor. The colonel, who was an officer of the homeowners association, admitted he was "a little apprehensive when I first moved into the neighborhood, but it's turned out OK." The realtor pointed out that although the units look the same at first glance, a closer look shows they were not constructed with the same overall quality, but added, "The county's housing laws are the best laws we have. . . . Montgomery County is a very good place."

This is the program's greatest achievement: proving that people can get along. "In 99 percent of the cases it works out fine," says Lillian Durham, assistant director of resident services for the Housing

Opportunities Commission (HOC), Montgomery County's public housing authority. "People figure out how to get along. But when there are problems it's often about lifestyle. If there's a big family with a lot of people coming and going, the neighbors may think it's drug traffic."

Durham runs HOC's counseling services, which aim to head off cultural clashes between public housing families, 70 percent of whom are African-American, and others in a county that is 74 percent white. A counselor visits every public housing family soon after they move in, offering help with specific problems and general advice—such as, don't park cars on the lawn, don't go outside in pajamas or a bathrobe, don't yell at your kids out the window. To a large extent, poor and minority families are expected to conform to suburban middle-class standards, but in most cases they're willing to do it in exchange for what they see as the advantages of living in a well-off neighborhood.

"We don't want our units to stick out," notes Roy Appletree, assistant executive director of HOC, as he gets down on his knees to rearrange the position of a concrete drain basin so that it will better catch the flow of rainwater from a gutter spout. "And it's very important for our residents, too."

Appletree is giving me a tour of subdivisions with HOC properties, and to his satisfaction I can rarely guess the ones rented to public housing families. "The whole idea of this," Appletree says, "is that when you disperse low-income folks, institutions are better able to absorb problems—schools, recreation programs, hospitals. I hate correlating social needs with income, but there is a tipping point where a concentration of poor people overwhelms the local institutions. Like the hospital in a low-income neighborhood that gets all the hard emergency-room cases."

"Schools are the classic example," he adds, as we drive into another subdivision with a sign announcing "homes from the mid-$300,000s." We pass a school bus, with high school kids of all races and ethnicities jumping off and walking toward home in groups of twos and threes. "In these subdivisions you've got the rich, the middle class and the poor all going to school together. The kids socialize with each other. If there are kids with less support at home, at least here they are not so concentrated."

"Moving poor children and their families from an inner-city ghetto to a prosperous suburb is likely to increase their chances to do well in school," notes Rusk. "Even if the home environment is nurturing, a kid in an inner city is surrounded by poverty. He's surrounded by few examples of kids who have succeeded and done well in the world. There are no after-school jobs. Teachers and counselors at schools have lowered expectations. That's why I say housing policy is education policy."

Montgomery County's HOC rents about 1,000 MPDUs to low- and moderate-income families (out of a total of some 5,300 units of public housing in the county), while nonprofit housing groups like the Interfaith Housing Coalition own a number of additional low-cost units. Even though the program is limited to people living or working in Montgomery County, it's still very competitive. Cutbacks in Department of Housing and Urban Development funding since the Republicans gained control of Congress in 1994 make matters worse because the housing authority now has very little money to purchase new MPDUs as they come up for sale.

The majority of Montgomery County's MPDUs are not rented to public housing families but sold to middle-income families as part of a program open to anyone living or working in Montgomery County who makes 65 percent or less of the county's $63,000 median household income. Again, it's a very competitive process. Eric Larsen, the county's MPDU coordinator, notes that 1,800 buyers are now on the waiting list for homes that are being built at the rate of 250 a year. However, because this program operates as an automatic part of the housing market—whenever new developments are built, new MPDUs are sold—it's not dependent on government funding beyond a few administrative costs.

Buyers of MPD homes in Montgomery County are 26 percent white, 46 percent Asian-American, 23 percent African-American and 5 percent Hispanic, with an average household income of $26,500. For people like Bonnie and Dave Ellsbury, a white couple who earn $10 an hour as a data entry worker and $12 an hour as an office furniture installer, it means they and their four children can afford to live in the county where they both grew up and now work. If they had not been able to buy their four-bedroom MPD house last year for $112,000 in a subdivision where most houses go for $200,000, they would have had to move out of the county to a cheaper area much farther from their jobs. Bonnie, 34, who lived in public housing for a number of years as a single mother, attended homebuying classes offered by HOC, one of many career and financial planning programs offered by the housing authority.

"I love owning a house," she says. "The yard, it's not huge, but it's ours. The kids go to school with all the other kids in the neighborhood, and there's no problem. No one looks down on us."

"We have an awful lot of people who would not be living in this county if it were not for this program," notes Richard Ferrara, executive director of HOC. The Fair Share housing ordinance has made Montgomery County different from most suburban areas across the country, both in the idealistic goal of mixing households of different incomes and the perhaps more self-serving purpose of heading off urban decline in its own midst.

The complex set of economic, social and racial forces that have overwhelmed America's urban neighborhoods don't suddenly disappear at the city limits. Many suburbs, especially those adjacent to central cities, are now experiencing the same spiral of poverty, crime and decay as inner cities. They are losing middle-class residents and established businesses to newer developments springing up on the edges of metropolitan regions. These suburbs sometimes find themselves in worse shape than central cities. In metropolitan Los Angeles, for instance, eighty-six suburbs now have a lower tax base per household than the city.

The Fair Share housing ordinance protects Montgomery County from these trends by making sure that lower-income people are not concentrated in struggling communities. By limiting the scope of exclusionary zoning, Montgomery County has been able to stabilize its less wealthy communities and stem middle-class flight. The benefits of this are enjoyed not just by lower-income families who have access to a wider choice of places to live but by a large number of county residents who can be more secure that they won't one day feel forced to sell their homes out of fear of an encroaching ghetto.

"These policies represent a win-win solution all the way around," David Rusk explains. "You integrate lower-income families into middle-class communities and middle-class schools. And you don't add to the concentration of poverty in the older, more humble middle-class neighborhoods."

ANALYSIS

1. How does Walljasper use the story of Michelle Dove to illustrate his point?
2. What is the argument over "exclusionary zoning"?
3. Homeowners fear loss of property values when poor and minority people move into their neighborhood; how does Walljasper say Montgomery County officials dealt with these fears?
4. What is the significance of "takings"?

WRITING POSSIBILITIES

1. How do you think your parents would react to Montgomery County's solution to the creating of a broad base of housing?
2. Walljasper's article refers to the issue of "social engineering." Assume you are either a new homeowner, told about mowing your lawn properly or not having loud parties or not parking your car outside the garage, *or*

a new a homebuilder anxious to make a decent profit on a new home in an area like Montgomery County. In either instance, how would you react to the infringements on your freedom by virtue of the Fair Share housing law or its corollary social controls?

Kenny Fries

In contrast to his painfully remembered autobiography Body, Remember, *Fries writes in an analytic and persuasive mode to argue that the Social Security system "provides harsh disincentives for people with disabilities who want to enter the work force."*

In debaters' terms, Fries' essay illustrates a classic mode—"the need for a change." After detailing his own initial success in working on his own and receiving the crucial Social Security benefits that enabled him to do so, Fries goes on to explain how he loses medical care and supplemental income if he makes so much as a dollar over the meager yearly maximum of $2,000. And in addition, he points out, Social Security guidelines allow for only a $700 a month benefit for housing—hardly enough to cover most rents in major cities these days.

Having established in his own instance a need *for a change, Fries then supports his case by offering* examples *of other individuals' problems and by an* attack *on assumptions—the "medical model" of disability and the Social Security Administration's unrealistic benefit levels.*

Finally, Fries offers a (brief) generalized plan of change ("make the benefits correspond to our needs") and (again briefly) the desirable benefits of change: "If we were able to work as much as we could . . . without risking our disability status . . . not only would we be better off, but so would the rest of society." (last paragraph)

GETTING TO WORK

It's been ten years since the passage of the Americans with Disabilities Act (ADA). When signed by President George Bush, it was called "the most far-reaching civil rights legislation since the Civil Rights Act of 1964." Many of us who live with disabilities thought the ADA would create an array of employment opportunities since it requires employers to make "reasonable accommodations" to allow those with disabilities to work. Considering the economic boom that has left many businesses without the workers they need, people with disabilities should be joining the work force in record numbers.

But this has not proved to be the case. While the unemployment rate for the entire population hovers around 4 percent, 70 percent of working-age adults with disabilities are still unemployed, a figure that basically has not changed since the ADA's passage.

One reason is that Social Security provides some harsh disincentives for people with disabilities who want to enter the work force.

Twelve years ago, due to issues related to my congenital disability (I am missing bones in both legs), I was no longer able to perform routine daily tasks I used to take for granted. I couldn't do my own grocery shopping, take out the garbage, or do the dishes. Still can't. And since I couldn't make my living as an arts administrator anymore, I applied for Social Security.

Initially, Social Security provided me just enough money to pay rent and utility bills while I adapted to a new way of life. After a year on Social Security Disability Income (SSDI), I became eligible for Medicare. Since I also qualified for Supplemental Security Income (SSI), a means-tested program whose benefits vary from state to state, I also was eligible for Medicaid. The two health insurance programs paid all of my medical bills, and Medicaid reimbursed me for travel to doctors' appointments. I was able to get food stamps, which helped keep me fed. And eventually I qualified for five hours per week of state-supported "homemaking" assistance for the daily tasks I could no longer do on my own.

During the past five years, I have tried other ways to support myself. In 1996, I received a two-book contract for a prose memoir and an anthology of work by writers with disabilities. I began teaching in a low-residency graduate writing program, and I was able to instruct my students mostly through the mail. I could work at home and keep my own schedule, which I need to do because of my disability. But this work—writing and teaching part time—comes with neither health insurance nor retirement benefits.

When I signed my book contract, I designed, with the help of a disability advocate, a Plan to Achieve Self-Support (PASS), one of the work incentives that allows a person with a disability on SSI to train for or begin work without diminishing your SSI check. I could not be where I now am if not for this program and the help of my SSI caseworker and a few other employees of the Social Security Administration.

However, because I eventually made more money than I was allowed to under the eligibility rules for SSDI, I lost my Medicare coverage last year. Luckily, I've still got Medicaid, and the Massachusetts Medicaid program is one with good benefits. But the doctor who has seen me since I was an infant works in New York City, and therefore I have to pay him out of pocket, and I have to shell out for any X-rays or other tests I need when I visit him.

Soon, I will have to make a decision about whether I can afford to keep working. Once I earn a certain amount, I will no longer qualify for Medicaid. I will also become ineligible for the state-supported "homemaking" help I need.

Although it is clear that my disability-related expenses will increase as I age, I cannot go over the $2,000 resource limit. This is the uppermost amount the statutes allow a person to own in cash and other liquid resources (usually excluding ownership of a home and a car) and still be eligible for SSI and its auxiliary benefits, which include Medicaid.

So now I'm faced with a choice: Do I cut back on my work so I can still get SSI, or do I risk working without these benefits?

I am not the only disabled person who is in such a quandary. I know of many others. One husband and his wife annulled their marriage so she could get the assistance she needs after multiple sclerosis left her unable to care for herself.

Another woman had to apply for a waiver from the Secretary of Health in order to marry her partner. Otherwise, she would have lost the benefits that pay for her respirator, which just happens to keep her alive.

A woman with spina bifida inherited $35,000 from her grandparents, which she invested. But because her bank account is over the $2,000 resource limit, she has lost her Medicaid benefits, which paid her $2,000 disability-related monthly drug bill. This woman wants to work part-time to help pay her medical expenses, but if she does she will lose her disability status, forcing her to go see doctors who may not understand her particular medical history or current physical situation.

According to SSI regulations, this woman could decide to "spend down" her inheritance to again be eligible for SSI and Medicaid. That is, instead of investing the money that can help her care for herself as she ages, she would have to spend $33,000 on items that would not be considered "resources." Although I can think of many enjoyable ways to spend more than $33,000 in less than a month's time, none of them makes sense considering the extra money it takes to live as a person with a disability.

Benefits for the disabled are terribly outdated. According to Social Security rules, "sustained gainful employment" is $700 per month. Once you earn more than that for nine months (called a "trial work period"), you are ineligible, which is why I lost my SSDI back in 1996. But who considers earning $700 per month "sustained gainful employment"? In many cities, $700 a month will not even cover rent.

Or consider the regulations SSI uses to calculate monthly "income exclusions"—income you are allowed to keep before it reduces the amount of your SSI check. There is only a $20 general income exclusion, and the earned income exclusion is $65, plus one-half of any additional income earned each month. And these regulations are nothing in comparison to the more byzantine rules it would take more than the space of this article to describe.

These regulations put enormous hurdles in our way. Many disabled persons want to work and are fully capable of doing so. But it's gotten to the point where we just can't afford it. We can't go without our insurance benefits, and we can't afford to pay for them ourselves.

Last December, President Clinton signed the Work Incentives Improvement Act, which was designed to address just this problem. But the government is still, in effect, telling us that we have to stay poor and unemployed if we want the security of the health insurance and other assistance we need. The new law leaves it to each state to set its own varying thresholds for deciding how much income you can make and still keep Medicaid. And the new regulations do not modify the outdated resource limits. My choice—to work, or to keep receiving the assistance I need—remains essentially the same.

There are other reasons why persons with disabilities have not entered the work force in higher numbers.

One is in the way the ADA is written, using the intentionally ambiguous term "reasonable accommodations." This can mean many things to many employers. And enforcement of the law has been spotty, at best.

Another part of the answer lies surely in the stereotypes and fears about disabled people that still pervade our society. Can you think of a movie that addresses the day-to-day life of a paraplegic once rehabilitation is over? Those who live with disabilities are not part of public discourse. That's because people with disabilities are not thought of as having day-to-day lives. Once a person is disabled, what else is there to know other than that they are still disabled or that they've "recovered"?

A debilitating medical model underlies our society's view of the disabled. That model focuses on the physical impairment, which needs to be overcome or cured. Instead of seeing the forces outside the body, outside the impairment, outside the self as essential to a disabled person's successful negotiation with an often hostile society (whether the barriers be financial, physical, or discriminatory), this view of disability—where cure and eradication of difference are paramount goals—puts the blame squarely on the individual when a physical impairment cannot be overcome.

Historian Paul K. Longmore points out that the medical model creates a class of persons with disabilities who are "confined within a segregated economic and social system and to a socioeconomic condition of childlike dependency."

Thanks to disability rights advocates and artists with disabilities, this model is under assault. And the ADA has created a legal framework to begin viewing disability in a way that shifts the focus from the impairment to how, as social scientist Victor Finkelstein says, "the nature of society . . . disables physically impaired people."

The assumptions behind Social Security for the disabled remain mired in the past, just as the benefits do. It's time to take a closer look at these assumptions, and it's time to make the benefits correspond to our needs. Otherwise, they will continue, in practice, to undermine the goals of the ADA and to sabotage the attempts of those of us with disabilities who want to include work as part of our lives.

If we were able to work as much as we could when we could, to save and invest the money we earn without risking our disability status, health insurance, and other benefits, not only would we be better off, but so would the rest of society.

ANALYSIS

1. Does Fries convince you of his basic argument that the Social Security system needs to change?
2. Does Fries answer objections that might be put by proponents of the present system? Why would the "rest of society" benefit?
3. Does Fries seem guilty of special pleading or does he offer a valid, general argument?

WRITING POSSIBILITIES

1. Fries attacks the "medical model" of disability, for its inadequate assumptions about disability and the place of the disabled in contemporary society. Explain what you think he means here and whether you would agree with this criticism.
2. Have you had a disastrous experience with an official body like Social Security? Explain what your situation involved and what you can recommend that might have changed the situation.
3. Try a contrarian possibility here: assume you are an official spokesperson for the Social Security Administration. What defense of the system could you make? What kind of criticism could you level at Fries?

Nat Hentoff

Renowned as a free-speech advocate, jazz critic, and pro-life spokesman, Hentoff criticizes speech codes on college and university campuses—i.e., those official collections of rules about what kind of language cannot be used, generally on the grounds that it stigmatizes a particular group. On the pro side, such codes may inhibit the kind of linguistic nastiness that becomes a way of dehumanizing a particular group and thus a way, eventually, of physically attacking them; on the con side, there is the potent argument in favor of meeting hate speech not with rules and regulations but with more free speech—energizing those who are revulsed at the hate speech types.

SPEECH CODES

During three years of reporting on anti-free-speech tendencies in higher education, I've been at more than twenty colleges and universities—from Washington and Lee and Columbia to Mesa State in Colorado and Stanford.

On this voyage of initially reverse expectations—with liberals fiercely advocating censorship of "offensive" speech and conservatives merrily taking the moral high ground as champions of free expression—the most dismaying moment of revelation took place at Stanford.

In the course of a two-year debate on whether Stanford, like many other universities, should have a speech code punishing language that might wound minorities, women, and gays, a letter appeared in the *Stanford Daily*. Signed by the African-American Law Students Association, the Asian-American Law Students Association, and the Jewish Law Students Association, the letter called for a harsh code. It reflected the letter and the spirit of an earlier declaration of Canetta Ivy, a black leader of student government at Stanford during the period of the grand debate. "We don't put as many restrictions on freedom of speech," she said, "as we should."

Reading the letter by this rare ecumenical body of law students (so pressing was the situation that even Jews were allowed in), I thought of twenty, thirty years from now. From so bright a cadre of graduates, from so prestigious a law school would come some of the law professors, civic leaders, college presidents, and even maybe a Supreme Court justice of the future. And many of them would have learned—like so many other university students in the land—that censorship is okay provided your motives are okay.

The debate at Stanford ended when the president, Donald Kennedy, following the prevailing winds, surrendered his previous position that once you start telling people what they can't say, you will end up telling them what they can't think. Stanford now has a speech code.

This is not to say that these gags on speech—every one of them so overboard and vague that a student can violate a code without knowing he or she has done so—are invariably imposed by student demand. At most colleges, it is the administration that sets up the code. Because there have been racist or sexist or homophobic taunts, anonymous notes or graffiti, the administration feels it must *do something*. The cheapest, quickest way to demonstrate that it cares is to appear to suppress racist, sexist, homophobic speech.

Usually, the leading opposition among the faculty consists of conservatives—when there is opposition. An exception at Stanford was law professor Gerald Gunther, arguably the nation's leading authority on constitutional law. But Gunther did not have much support among other faculty members, conservative or liberal.

At the University of Buffalo Law School, which has a code restricting speech, I could find just one faculty member who was against it. A liberal, he spoke only on condition that I not use his name. He did not want to be categorized as a racist.

On another campus, a political science professor for whom I had great respect after meeting and talking with him years ago, has been silent—students told me—on what Justice William Brennan once called "the pall of orthodoxy" that has fallen on his campus.

When I talked to him, the professor said, "It doesn't happen in my class. There's no 'politically correct' orthodoxy here. It may happen in other places at this university, but I don't know about that." He said no more.

One of the myths about the rise of PC (politically correct) is that, coming from the left, it is primarily intimidating conservatives on campus. Quite the contrary. At almost every college I've been, conservative students have their own newspaper, usually quite lively and fired by a muckraking glee at exposing "politically correct" follies on campus.

By and large, those most intimidated—not so much by the speech codes themselves but by the Madame Defarge–like spirit behind them—are liberal students and those who can be called politically moderate.

I've talked to many of them, and they no longer get involved in class discussions where their views would go against the grain of PC righteousness. Many, for instance, have questions about certain kinds of affirmative action. They are not partisans of Jesse Helms or David Duke, but they wonder whether progeny of middle-class black families should get scholarship preference. Others have a question about abortion. Most are not prolife, but they believe that fathers should have a say in whether the fetus should be sent off into eternity.

Jeff Shesol, a recent graduate of Brown and now a Rhodes scholar at Oxford, became nationally known while at Brown because of his comic strip, "Thatch," which, not too kindly, parodied PC students. At a forum on free speech at Brown before he left, Shesol said he wished he could tell the new students at Brown to have no fear of speaking freely. But he couldn't tell them that, he said, advising the new students to stay clear of talking critically about affirmative action or abortion, among other things, in public.

At that forum, Shesol told me, he said that those members of the left who regard dissent from their views as racist and sexist should realize that they are discrediting their goals. "They're honorable goals," said Shesol, "and I agree with them. I'm against racism and sexism. But these people's tactics are obscuring the goals. And they've resulted in Brown no longer being an open-minded place." There were hisses from the audience.

Students at New York University Law School have also told me that they censor themselves in class. The kind of chilling atmosphere they describe was exemplified last year as a case assigned for a moot court competition became subject to denunciation when a sizable number of law students said it was too "offensive" and would hurt the feelings of gay and lesbian students. The case concerned a divorced father's attempt to gain custody of his children on the grounds that their mother had become a lesbian. It was against PC to represent the father.

Although some of the faculty responded by insisting that you learn to be a lawyer by dealing with all kinds of cases, including those you personally find offensive, other faculty members supported the rebellious students, praising them for their sensitivity. There was little public opposition from the other students to the attempt to suppress the case. A leading dissenter was a member of the conservative Federalist Society.

What is PC to white students is not necessarily PC to black students. Most of the latter did not get involved in the N.Y.U. protest, but throughout the country many black students do support speech codes. A vigorous exception was a black Harvard law school student during a debate on whether the law school should start punishing speech. A white student got up and said that the codes are necessary because without them, black students would be driven away from colleges and thereby deprived of the equal opportunity to get an education.

A black student rose and said that the white student had a hell of a nerve to assume that he—in the face of racist speech—would pack up his books and go home. He's been familiar with that kind of speech all his life, and he had never felt the need to run away from it. He'd handled it before and he could again.

The black student then looked at his white colleague and said that it was condescending to say that blacks have to be "protected" from racist speech. "It is more racist and insulting," he emphasized, "to say that to me than to call me a nigger."

But that would appear to be a minority view among black students. Most are convinced they do need to be protected from wounding language. On the other hand, a good many black student organizations on campus do not feel that Jews have to be protected from wounding language.

Though it's not much written about in reports on the language wars on campuses, there is a strong strain of anti-Semitism among some—not all, by any means—black students. They invite such speakers as Louis Farrakhan, the former Stokely Carmichael (now Kwame Touré), and such lesser but still burning bushes as Steve Cokely, the Chicago commentator who has declared that Jewish doctors inject the AIDS virus into black babies. That distinguished leader was invited to speak at the University of Michigan.

The black student organization at Columbia University brought to the campus Dr. Khallid Abdul Muhammad. He began his address by saying: "My leader, my teacher, my guide is the honorable Louis Farrakhan. I thought that should be said at Columbia Jewniversity."

Many Jewish students have not censored themselves in reacting to this form of political correctness among some blacks. A Columbia student, Rachel Stoll, wrote a letter to the *Columbia Spectator:* "I have an idea. As a white Jewish American, I'll just stand in the middle of a circle comprising . . . Khallid Abdul Muhammad and assorted members of the Black Students Organization and let them all hurl large stones at me. From recent events and statements made on this campus, I gather this will be a good cheap method of making these people feel good."

At UCLA, a black student magazine printed an article indicating there is considerable truth to the *Protocols of Elders of Zion.*[1] For months, the black faculty, when asked their reactions, preferred not to comment. One of them did say that the black students already considered the black faculty to be insufficiently militant, and the professors didn't want to make the gap any wider. Like white liberal faculty members on other campuses, they want to be liked—or at least not too disliked.

Along with quiet white liberal faculty members, most black professors have not opposed the speech codes. But unlike the white liberals,

---

[1] *Protocols of the Elders of Zion* Documents forged by anti-Semites and introduced in the late nineteenth century as "proof" of an international Jewish conspiracy.—EDS.

many honestly do believe that minority students have to be insulated from barbed language. They do not believe—as I have found out in a number of conversations—that an essential part of an education is to learn to demystify language, to strip it of its ability to demonize and stigmatize you. They do not believe that the way to deal with bigoted language is to answer it with more and better language of your own. This seems very elementary to me, but not to the defenders, black and white, of the speech codes.

Consider University of California president David Gardner. He has imposed a speech code on all the campuses in his university system. Students are to be punished—and this is characteristic of the other codes around the country—if they use "fighting words"—derogatory references to "race, sex, sexual orientation, or disability."

The term "fighting words" comes from a 1942 Supreme Court decision, *Chaplinsky* v. *New Hampshire,* which ruled that "fighting words" are not protected by the First Amendment. That decision, however, has been in disuse at the high court for many years. But it is thriving on college campuses.

In the California code, a word becomes "fighting" if it is directly addressed to "any ordinary person" (presumably, extraordinary people are above all this). These are the kinds of words that are "inherently likely to provoke a violent reaction, *whether or not they actually do."* (Emphasis added.)

Moreover, he or she who fires a fighting word at any ordinary person can be reprimanded or dismissed from the university because the perpetrator should "reasonably know" that what he or she has said will interfere with the "victim's ability to pursue effectively his or her education or otherwise participate fully in university programs and activities."

Asked Gary Murikami, chairman of the Gay and Lesbian Association at the University of California, Berkeley: "What does it mean?"

Among those—faculty, law professors, college administrators—who insist such codes are essential to the university's purpose of making *all* students feel at home and thereby able to concentrate on their work, there has been a celebratory resort to the Fourteenth Amendment.

That amendment guarantees "equal protection of the laws" to all, and that means to all students on campus. Accordingly, when the First Amendment rights of those engaging in offensive speech clash with the equality rights of their targets under the Fourteenth Amendment, the First Amendment must give way.

This is the thesis, by the way, of John Powell, legal director of the American Civil Liberties Union, even though that organization has now formally opposed all college speech codes—after a considerable civil war among and within its affiliates.

The battle of the amendments continues, and when harsher codes are called for at some campuses, you can expect the Fourteenth Amendment—which was not intended to censor *speech*—will rise again.

A precedent has been set at, of all places, colleges and universities, that the principle of free speech is merely situational. As college administrators change, so will the extent of free speech on campus. And invariably, permissible speech will become more and more narrowly defined. Once speech can be limited in such subjective ways, more and more expression will be included in what is forbidden.

One of the exceedingly few college presidents who speaks out on the consequences of the anti-free-speech movement is Yale University's Benno Schmidt:

> Freedom of thought must be Yale's central commitment. It is not easy to embrace. It is, indeed, the effort of a lifetime. . . . Much expression that is free may deserve our contempt. We may well be moved to exercise our own freedom to counter it or to ignore it. But universities cannot censor or suppress speech, no matter how obnoxious in content, without violating their justification for existence. . . .
>
> On some other campuses in this country, values of civility and community have been offered by some as paramount values of the university, even to the extent of superseding freedom of expression.
>
> Such a view is wrong in principle and, if extended, is disastrous to freedom of thought. . . . The chilling effects on speech of the vagueness and open-ended nature of many universities' prohibitions . . . are compounded by the fact that these codes are typically enforced by faculty and students who commonly assert that vague notions of community are more important to the academy than freedom of thought and expression. . . .
>
> This is a flabby and uncertain time for freedom in the United States.

On the Public Broadcasting System in June, I was part of a Fred Friendly panel at Stanford University in a debate on speech codes versus freedom of expression. The three black panelists strongly supported the codes. So did the one Asian-American on the panel. But then so did Stanford law professor, Thomas Grey, who wrote the Stanford code, and Stanford president Donald Kennedy, who first opposed and then embraced the code. We have a new ecumenicism of those who would control speech for the greater good. It is hardly a new idea, but the mix of advocates is rather new.

But there are other voices. In the national board debate at the ACLU on college speech codes, the first speaker—and I think she had a lot to do with making the final vote against codes unanimous—was Gwen Thomas.

A black community college administrator from Colorado, she is a fiercely persistent exposer of racial discrimination.

She started by saying, "I have always felt as a minority person that we have to protect the rights of all because if we infringe on the rights of any persons, we'll be next.

"As for providing a nonintimidating educational environment, our young people have to learn to grow up on college campuses. We have to teach them how to deal with adversarial situations. They have to learn how to survive offensive speech they find wounding and hurtful."

Gwen Thomas is an educator—an endangered species in higher education.

ANALYSIS

1. In criticizing "political correctness," Hentoff argues that "an essential part of an education is to learn to demystify language, to strip it of its ability to demonize and stigmatize you. They [proponents of speech codes] do not believe [as Hentoff does] that the way to deal with bigoted language is to answer it with more and better language." What does Hentoff mean by "demystify"? Do you think Hentoff's position is too idealistic or absolutely necessary?

WRITING POSSIBILITIES

1. Hentoff notes that "what is PC to white students is not necessarily PC to black students." What point does Hentoff make here? Explain whether you agree or disagree with Hentoff on this matter?
2. Hentoff writes, "Students at New York University Law School have . . . told me that they censor themselves in class." The example offered was a case in a moot court competition that, as Hentoff summarized things, might have "hurt the feelings of gay and lesbian students. The case concerned a divorced father's attempt to gain custody of his children on the grounds that their mother had become a lesbian. It was against PC to represent the father." How would you have reacted to the issue here?
3. Have you ever censored yourself in a class discussion? Hentoff notes that the most common issues involve affirmative action and abortion, but there may be other matters as well. Explain what the situation was, what you did or did not say, and why you chose to do what you did.
4. Hentoff argues "that the way to deal with bigoted language is to answer it with more and better language of your own." What might "more and

better language of your own" involve? Can you think of an example? Explain whether you would agree or not with Hentoff's "elementary" solution, using the arguments—pro and con—touched on in his essay.

5. Have you ever been the subject of hate talk and/or a hate crime? How does your experience compute in relation to Hentoff's absolute-free-speech arguments? To what extent would you, on the basis of your own experience, agree or disagree with Hentoff's analysis?

Wendy Shalit

In this tart review-essay, Wendy Shalit in the conservative journal Commentary *reviews two recent challenges to the conventional gender system, focusing primarily on a memoir by Sandra Lipsitz Bem,* An Unconventional Family. *Bem's volume explains how she and her husband brought up their children as "truly egalitarian" and treated them like "gender pioneers," liberating them from the conventional "sex-and-gender system." Shalit's review is a sardonic one: she suggests that for all the gender-bending here, the children of the Bems have pretty much come out as "surprisingly normal," that is, as one of them admits, "I can't really say I've transcended gender." Indeed, Jeremy Bem says to his mother, "I would advise you to make it clearer to me that it's okay to have conventional desires as well as unconventional ones."*

AMONG THE GENDER BENDERS

After almost three decades of boil and bubble, the academic field of women's studies has not only cooked down but has been served up and thoroughly ingested. In 700 or so undergraduate and graduate institutions around the country, women's-studies programs boast their own tenured faculty and produce their own voluminous literature. This literature is readily divisible into two principal genres: the theoretical tract, and the first-person-singular sexual narrative.

For the most part, works in the former category are devoted to proving that all differences between men and women are "socially constructed" and, even more energetically, to disproving the opposite belief, labeled "biological determinism" or "essentialism"—the belief, that is, that biological differences exist or, worse still, matter. In the anti-essentialist world view, little boys and girls are not male and female; rather, they can be arranged along a continuum displaying, in the words of one professor of women's studies, their relative "commitment to hegemonic femininity and masculinity." The good news is that, if caught early enough, one's hegemonic commitment to a sex—especially the male sex—can be reversed.

As for the second genre, sometimes called the "herstory" tradition, this sets itself in counterpoise to *his*tory, which records such things as wars, political successions, and similarly unedifying matters. The object of "herstory" is "the removal of male self-glorification from history." This it accomplishes by offering "accounts of the human past and human activity that consider women as being at the center of society, not at the margins." Such accounts can range across the totality of human experience, but in practice they often consist of the author's "celebrating" her own sexuality by writing about what she did and with whom. (Naming names is particularly revered as a "transgressive" act.)

Of the two types, the personal sexual narrative has become the more popular, lapping out of the academy and into better bookstores everywhere. And little wonder. It is not just that anti-essentialist theorizing is utterly false to reality, though it is certainly that. No lesser a problem is the prose in which anti-essentialist arguments are invariably couched. Here, for instance, is Judith Butler, a professor of humanities at Johns Hopkins and a veritable goddess in the anti-essentialist world for her 1990 work, *Gender Trouble: Feminism and the Subversion of Identity,* urging her readers to

> consider not only that the ambiguities and incoherences with and among heterosexual, homosexual, and bisexual practices are suppressed and redescribed within the reified framework of the disjunctive and asymmetrical binary of masculine/feminine, but that these cultural configurations of gender confusion operate as sites for intervention, exposure, and displacement of these reifications.

It does not help matters that Professor Butler has steadfastly bristled at attempts to make her explain what she means—or, rather, to "linguistify [her] positionality." And so one can hardly blame readers for preferring the likes of Naomi Wolf, Kathryn Harrison, or Joyce Maynard. Each of them has been only too ready to linguistify her positionality, horizontal and otherwise.

Yet, truth to say, the tell-all genre has its limitations as well, having mainly accomplished a task one might once have thought impossible—rendering the obscene boring, and the salacious banal. Still, not to despair: as if to rescue a terminally devolving situation, we have lately been graced with what may seem like a new feminist genre but is really a hybrid, melding the best of antiessentialism with the best of "herstory." Enter two new books, one by a novelist, the other by a professor.

The novelist is Catherine Texier, and her offering is *Breakup: The End of a Love Story,** written after her husband of eighteen years left her for another woman. . . .

Unfortunately, . . . her book is rather shorter on analysis than one might wish (not that one would wish it longer). But in any case, a more substantial treat awaits in *An Unconventional Family* by Sandra Lipsitz Bem,† a professor of psychology and women's studies at Cornell. Bem often writes about her children, her husband, and herself, and since the early 70's has held herself up as an expert practitioner of nonsexist child-rearing. "Like many feminist scholars," she explains in *An Unconventional Family,* "I live my life with little separation between the personal, the professional, and the political. My theory and my practice are thus inextricably intertwined."

The contents of *An Unconventional Family* certainly confirm this claim. Part One, "Coming Together," tells the story of how Sandra met her husband Daryl ("Courtship"), followed by an analysis of their dating career ("Why Daryl?"). In Part Two, "Writing Our Own Script," Bem gives us a tour of her anti-essentialist ideology, deconstructing each "phase" of its implementation in her own family; thus, we have a chapter on "Egalitarian Partnering," another on "Feminist Child-Rearing," and, as an extra added attraction, a blow-by-blow account of her personal battles in academia ("My Unorthodox Career"). Finally, in Part Three, "Evaluating Our Experiment," Bem interviews her two grown children, Jeremy and Emily, prodding them to assess "what the consequences were for [them] of our so consciously trying to raise them in a gender-liberated, anti-homophobic, and sex-positive way."

All parents have hopes for their children, but Sandra Bem had specific ones. She is, after all, the author of *The Lenses of Gender* (1993), a book which argues "that in order to interrupt the social reproduction of male power, we need to dismantle not only androcentrism and biological essentialism but also gender polarization and compulsory heterosexuality." So it is not surprising to learn in *An Unconventional Family* that when young Sandra met young Daryl—she was then a senior psychology major at Carnegie Institute of Technology in Pittsburgh—that she "loved" most was this: "The fact that he was male and I was female had not seemed to be part of our chemistry."

Soon after their wedding in 1965—in the great tradition of untraditional marriages, the pair performed the ceremony themselves—Sandra and Daryl Bem vowed to "function as truly egalitarian partners." Not only did Sandra know "there was no way I would be

---

* Doubleday, 159 pp., $19.95.
† Yale University Press, 209 pp., $20.00.

willing to do what I presumed a good wife was supposed to do for her husband: namely, wash his floor, darn his socks, cook his meals, raise his children." She even took pride in quashing Daryl's job offers, and taught him to take pride in it as well: "This loss of total independence gave Daryl a moment's pause . . . , but he quickly recovered, and we excitedly moved on to framing an egalitarian philosophy." Before long, the two lovebirds were featured in *Ms.* magazine, where a confident Sandra declared that "I believe we are unlikely to get divorced."

As for the children, those little "gender pioneers," Sandra alternated with Daryl as the parent "on-duty." A sign in the kitchen signified to little Jeremy and Emily whose turn it was to be responsible for them, with two pointy breast marks on a figure signifying "mommy's turn," a figure with one pointy crotch mark signifying "daddy's turn." To liberate them from the tyranny of "the culture's sex-and-gender system," Bem writes, "we never allowed there to be a time . . . when they didn't know that some people had partners of their own sex and other people had partners of the other sex." Sandra and Daryl "censored" (her word) certain books and television programs with inappropriate "gender" messages, and, when all else failed, used white correcting fluid to change pronouns in books from male to female.

At the Bems', everyone often traipsed around in the buff. Sandra made a point of "putting tampons in and taking them out" in front of the children to demonstrate that women's blood was not "yucky," and the children were encouraged to "experiment sexually" in the privacy of their third-floor bedrooms. Experimenting intellectually, however, was another matter. When little Jeremy demanded that the pages of a book he was being read from be flipped over rapidly so that he could yell out the numbers, his mother became alarmed. Jeremy's "mathematical giftedness," as she puts it, had all the earmarks of a "nightmare. After all, mathematics is a field in which few American women have yet entered the highest levels, and that gender disparity could have easily made Jeremy even more disrespectful of women's intelligence." Luckily, by the time his parents were through with him, little Jeremy was so gender-liberated he had come to think the word "heorshe" was an English pronoun.

Given their parents' ideological weirdness, it is a relief to report that the Bem children, both now in their early twenties, have ended up surprisingly normal. True, they have tried to fulfill their parents' expectations: Emily does not shave her body hair, and Jeremy still dons a skirt on occasion—just as he once wore barrettes to nursery school. But, as we learn in the final chapter, Emily mostly dates boys, wears makeup, and keeps a doll collection, while Jeremy admits that "I can't really say I've transcended gender" (though it still "bothers" him that he is interested in "conventionally gendered" topics like "math and computer programming and physics").

Jeremy, in fact, rebukes his mother for her child-rearing practices. "If you were doing it all over again," she dutifully records him as saying, "I would advise you to make it clearer to me that it's okay to have conventional desires as well as unconventional ones." Emily, for her part, complains that her mother made her feel "unnatural to be a girl." Does this give Sandra pause? Does it make her think there might be something to this "nature" business after all? Not for the merest moment. She and her husband, she (manfully?) concludes, must have been "much more gendered as parents than [we] had intended."

Nor, it turns out, is this the only unexpected development to have tested the resilience of the Bem doctrine. Reader, it seems that Daryl and Sandra are no longer married. Nowhere near enough is made of this startling disclosure, which is mentioned only in passing; but perhaps the base facts are enough. "We did split up about four years ago," Bem writes, "and both of us became involved in relationships with people of our own sex."

A failure for the couple who once voted themselves most "unlikely to divorce"? Far from it: a crowning achievement. True, the Bems "are no longer close-coupled"—*close-coupled?*—but "Till death do us part is not the only—or even the best—criterion of whether and how we met our goals." After all, they intended from the beginning to "provide at least one concrete example of an alternative to the traditional heterosexual family." By running off with members of their own sex, they have carried their program to its triumphant conclusion.

Yes, anti-essentialism is a wonderful thing, as the doyennes of women's studies have long maintained. Just ask Jeremy and Emily.

ANALYSIS

1. Shalit is basically hostile to the books she reviews here. Does she, or does she not, in your view, keep that hostility in bounds, so that we get a fair presentation of the material in the books?

WRITING POSSIBILITIES

1. At the end, Shalit mockingly suggests that the book's "anti-essentialism" is not born out by the gender trajectories of the Bems' children. "Anti-essentialism" refers to the social construction argument (see Judith Lorber's essay, pages 391–400) that gender is basically a matter of social creation, not of "essential" or innate biological forces. Conversely, to what extent does Shalit assert or imply that there are certain biological

constraints on sexuality that no amount of gender-bending can really alter? Does she prove her point? Would you agree or disagree with it? Why? (You will probably wish to reread Lorber's essay.)

Ellis Cose

In a period when affirmative action programs are under increased attack or have actually been dismantled—e.g., by a ballot measure in California, by the Hopwood decision at the University of Texas Law School—it is appropriate to look back to Ellis Cose's "ambivalent" defense of such programs and his thoughtful answer to the question about the seeming acceptance of the less than "qualified" under affirmative action regimens.

A contributing editor for Newsweek, *Ellis Cose is an African American journalist and the author of* A Nation of Strangers, *a history of immigration, and most recently* A Man's World, How Real is Male Privilege—and How High is Its Price?

AFFIRMATIVE ACTION AND THE DILEMMA OF THE "QUALIFIED"
from The Rage of a Privileged Class

When the talk turns to affirmative action, I often recall a conversation from years ago. A young white man, a Harvard student and the brother of a close friend, happened to be in Washington when the Supreme Court ruled on an affirmative action question. I have long since forgotten the question and the Court's decision, but I remember the young man's reaction.

He was not only troubled but choleric at the very notion that "unqualified minorities" would dare to demand preferential treatment. Why, he wanted to know, couldn't they compete like everyone else? Why should hardworking whites like himself be pushed aside for second-rate affirmative action hires? Why should he be discriminated against in order to accommodate *them?* His tirade went on for quite a while, and he became more indignant by the second as he conjured up one injustice after another.

When the young man paused to catch his breath, I took the occasion to observe that it seemed more than a bit hypocritical of him to rage on about preferential treatment. A person of modest intellect, he had gotten into Harvard largely on the basis of family connections. His first summer internship, with the White House, had been arranged by a family member. His second, with the World Bank, had been similarly arranged. Thanks to his nice internships and Harvard degree, he had been promised a coveted slot in a major company's executive training program. In short, he was already well on his way to a distinguished career—a career made possible by preferential treatment.

My words seemed not to register, and that did not surprise me. Clearly he had never thought of himself as a beneficiary of special treatment, and no doubt never will. Nor is it likely that either his colleagues or his superiors would be inclined to look down on him as an undeserving incompetent who got ahead on the basis of unfair advantage and was keeping better-qualified people out of work. Yet that assumption is routinely made about black beneficiaries of "affirmative action."

In February 1993, for instance, *Forbes* magazine published an article purporting to demonstrate "how affirmative action slows the economy." The authors referred approvingly to a 1984 poll that "found one in ten white males reporting they had lost a promotion because of quotas." They went on to argue that the poll "was quite possibly accurate. Indeed, it could be an underestimate."

It's impossible from the article to be certain just what poll *Forbes* is citing, but it appears to be a never-published telephone survey by Gordon S. Black Corporation for *USA Today* in which one-tenth of white males answered yes to a much broader question: "Have you yourself ever lost a job *opportunity* or educational *opportunity* at least *partially* as a result of policies and programs aimed at promoting equal opportunity for minorities?" (Emphasis mine.) That, of course, is a very different question from the one *Forbes* reported.

In 1993, *Newsweek* magazine commissioned a national poll that framed the question more narrowly. That poll, interestingly, found even more white males claiming to have been victimized by affirmative action. When asked, "Have you ever been a victim of discrimination or reverse discrimination in getting a promotion?" 15 percent of white males said that they had—the same percentage reporting such discrimination in "getting a job."

Let's assume for the sake of discussion that the *Forbes* figure is correct, and that ten percent of white males do indeed believe that some quota-driven minority person has snatched a position that would otherwise have gone to them. Let's further assume that the ratio holds across occupational categories, so that one out of ten white men in managerial and professional jobs (which, after all, is the group *Forbes* caters to) believes he was unfairly held back by a black or Hispanic colleague's promotion.

Blacks and Hispanics make up 10 percent of the total employees in such jobs, and white males make up 46 percent. So if one out of every ten white males has been held back by a black or Hispanic, that would mean that nearly half of those blacks and Hispanics received promotions they didn't deserve at the expense of white men. (If the *Newsweek* numbers are right, and if we assume that racial and ethnic minorities were the beneficiaries of the "reverse discrimination" suffered by whites, the percentage of minorities who have been unfairly promoted is even higher.) Yet if so many minorities are being promoted ahead of whites, why do black and Hispanic professionals, on average, earn less and hold lower positions than whites? It could be that despite their unfair advantage, minority professionals are so incompetent that whites still manage to get ahead of them on merit. Or it could be that white males who think minorities are zooming ahead of them are way off the mark. *Forbes,* for whatever reason, chose not to consider that possibility. Just as it chose not to consider that the alternative to a system based on "quotas" is not necessarily one based on merit. Or that affirmative action might conceivably result in some competent people getting jobs. Instead, the *Forbes* writers simply assumed such problematic possibilities away. Indeed, like many arguments against affirmative action, their article was not a reasoned analysis at all, but an example of pandering to the anger and anxieties of white males who believe they and their kind are being wronged. And the editors of *Forbes* have plenty of company.

In April 1991, for example, a white Georgetown University law student, Timothy Maguire, set off a tempest in Washington's scholarly and legal communities by questioning the academic quality of blacks admitted to the law school. In an article entitled "Admissions Apartheid," written for a student-controlled paper, Maguire charged that the black law students were in general not as qualified as the whites. The blacks, he said, had lower average scores on the Law School Admissions Tests and lower grade point averages—an allegation based on documents he perused, apparently surreptitiously, while working as a file clerk in the student records office.

The article polarized the campus. On one side were those who demanded that Maguire be expelled for unethical behavior in reading and publishing confidential information. They also raised questions about his mastery of statistics, pointing out that the "random sample" on which he based his conclusions was nothing of the sort, since the files he rifled were only a small selection and included the scores of many applicants who had not been admitted. On the other side were those who saw Maguire as a champion of free speech, a courageous young man who—at risk of public censure—had undertaken to disseminate information that deserved to be debated in a public arena. Maguire apparently saw himself as a victim of leftist ideologues, declaring at one point, according to the *Washington Post,* "It's painful not being politically correct."

In the midst of the ruckus, and after a leak focused attention on Maguire's own academic background, he admitted that his own LSAT scores were below the median for Georgetown students. Interestingly, in light of his charges, coverage of the controversy did not highlight the fact that Maguire got into Georgetown through a special screening program for "low testers," people who would not have been admitted on the basis of their scores but were in effect given extra credit for showing other evidence of promise, dedication, or commitment. In Maguire's case, the fact that he had been a Peace Corps volunteer in Africa weighed heavily in his favor. In short, he was every bit as much a beneficiary of special preference as the black students he scorned.

Shortly after it began, the uproar died down. And despite the protests of the black student organization and others, Maguire was permitted to graduate with his class. Though he was formally reprimanded for violating confidentiality, an agreement worked out by attorneys specifically barred the reprimand from becoming part of his official transcript. Maguire, in short, was allowed to resume a normal life and to put both the controversy and his need for special preference behind him.

Unlike the black students he assailed, who will find their careers haunted by the specter of affirmative action, and who will often be greeted by doubts about their competence whatever their real abilities, Maguire is not likely to suffer because he got into law school on grounds other than academic performance. In other words, he will never be seen as an affirmative action man but simply as a lawyer— entitled to all the recognition conferred by his prestigious degree and all the privileges granted to those presumed to be professionally "qualified."

Why should the presumption of competence differ for black and white graduates of the same school? One answer may be that blacks should be scrutinized more carefully because they are more likely to have met lower admission standards. While that is true in many cases, it is far from true that every black student admitted to a selective school is academically inferior (in any sense of the word) to every white student admitted. Nor is it true, as Maguire's case illustrates, that whites do not receive special treatment in academia. Just as Maguire benefited from a program for "low testers," others benefit from "diversity" policies in East Coast schools that favor residents of Wyoming over those of Connecticut, or from policies that favor relatives of alumni (or children of faculty members, donors, and other influential figures) over those with no family connections. Sometimes universities wish to attract mature students or veterans, or to nurture relationships with certain high schools by admitting their graduates.

One reason for such policies, as virtually any admissions officer will attest, is that prior academic performance is a far from perfect predictor of who will succeed in any specific school, much less who will succeed in life. And that rationale is apparently accepted even by many fervent opponents of affirmative action, since nonracial preferences never seem to elicit anything like the animosity provoked by so-called racial quotas. And even if we grant that many blacks who gain admission with the help of affirmative action are not objectively "qualified," precisely the same can be said about certain children of alumni or about the student who caught the admissions committee's eye because he spent a year on a mission of mercy in Malaysia.

Moreover, determining what it means to be "qualified" is not as easy as it is often made to seem. Ted Miller, who was associate dean of admissions at Georgetown Law at the time of the Maguire imbroglio, points out that many older white professors there—"if they were being honest"—would admit that they could not have met the standards exceeded by the school's typical black student today. As the number of applicants escalated during the 1940s, notes Miller, law schools turned to the LSAT as "an artificial means" to help them sift through applications. And as the numbers continued to increase, the minimum score needed to get into the more exclusive schools (the "qualified threshold") rose. Yet many of those who met the lower standards of the past nonetheless turned out to be distinguished lawyers. Obviously, they were not "unqualified," even if their test results would not win them admission to a prestigious law school today. By the same token, reasons Miller, as long as black students are capable of doing the work, who is to say they are "unqualified"?

Whatever one thinks of Miller's argument, it is unlikely that hostility to affirmative action programs would suddenly vanish if it could be established that "quota" recruits are in fact "qualified." If that were the only issue, programs favoring the children of alumni, say, would provoke the same animus directed at affirmative action. So the primary cause of the hostility must lie elsewhere. And the most logical place to look for it is in American attitudes about race.

In a country largely stuck in a state of denial, any such inquiry is fraught with peril. For one thing, and for any number of reasons, Americans have a devil of a time being honest (even with ourselves) when it comes to race. And because determining what our basic attitudes are is so difficult, agreeing on what those attitudes mean may well be impossible.

Not to put too fine a point on it, some people lie—almost reflexively under certain circumstances—about their attitudes regarding race, as public opinion experts have long known. Moreover, the phrasing of the question and the race of the interviewer can make a huge difference in what people say.

In 1989, for instance, pollsters for ABC News and the *Washington Post* asked a random sample of whites, "Do you happen to have a close friend who is black?" When the question was asked by a black, 67 percent of respondents answered yes. When a white asked, the percentage dropped to 57. Conversely, 67 percent of blacks told a black caller they had a close friend who was white, while 79 percent gave the same answer to a white interviewer.

On the question of whether the problems faced by blacks were "brought on by blacks themselves," the variation in responses was even greater. When interviewed by whites, 62 percent of whites said yes. When the same question was asked by blacks, the number dropped to 46 percent. Similarly, when whites were asked by blacks whether it was "very important" for children to attend racially mixed schools, 39 percent said yes, compared to 29 percent who thought so when asked by whites. In all, ABC/*Washington Post* pollsters found that answers varied significantly on more than half of the thirty-three race-related questions in the survey, depending on the race of the interviewer. The disparity might well have been greater if the interviewees could have been absolutely certain of the race of the person on the other end of the telephone line.

Even when the race of the interviewer is not an issue, when people know (or assume) they are talking to someone of their own racial stock, honesty is hardly assured—certainly not in morally charged areas, and especially not when people sense that what they feel is "politically correct." Hence, any poll on race must be taken with more than a few grains of salt. When pollsters ask, in one way or another, "Are you a racist?" people know what they are supposed to say. As a consequence, polling has proven to be problematic in political campaigns that pit black and white candidates against each other, because a gap exists between those who say they will vote for a candidate of another race and those who actually will in the privacy of the voting booth. There is no real reason to believe that polls measuring racial attitudes in general are any more accurate. The presumption, instead, should be that they understate the dimensions of racial bias and disharmony. If that presumption is true, the statistics reported below are all the more stunning for what they reveal about the pervasiveness and perdurability of racial stereotypes.

In 1990, 62 percent of whites across America told pollsters for the University of Chicago's National Opinion Research Center (NORC) that they believed blacks were lazier than whites. Fifty-one percent thought blacks likely to be less patriotic. Fifty-three percent said blacks were less intelligent. On every relevant measure of merit or virtue, blacks were judged inferior to whites. What the survey means, in short—despite a widespread belief to the contrary—is that

America remains a color-struck society; and there is an abundance of data corroborating that finding.

Two less ambitious polls patterned in part on the National Opinion Research Center's study—in Wisconsin and Los Angeles—yielded results that were strikingly similar. New Yorkers polled in 1992 for the American Jewish Committee rated blacks less intelligent and lazier than the Irish and Italians. Another survey, of 185 employers in the Chicago area, found that those responsible for hiring tended to associate blacks—at least blacks in the central city—with crime, illiteracy, drug use, and a poor work ethic. Many employers had developed strategies (such as recruiting in suburbs and predominantly white schools and advertising in neighborhood and ethnic publications) that allowed them to avoid large numbers of black job applicants. The study, conducted by University of Chicago sociologists Kathryn Neckerman and Joleen Kirschenman, did not focus specifically on firms hiring for professional or executive positions, so its relevance to highly educated blacks is a matter of conjecture; but other research by the same scholars has found that many employers generalize stereotypes of the black underclass to all black applicants.

Not surprisingly, people who see blacks as lazier than whites tend to be among those most strongly opposed to affirmative action. To Tom Smith, director of NORC's general social survey, the reason is obvious: "Negative images lead people to conclude these groups don't deserve this special help." Indeed, it's fairly easy to understand why anyone might have a hard time with the idea that lazy, unintelligent, violence-prone people (whom Americans believe to be disproportionately black and Hispanic) deserve any special consideration at all. . . .

Stephen Carter, author of *Reflections of an Affirmative Action Baby,* argues that people of color might be much better served by the free market than by any explicit scheme of racial preferences. "Left to itself, the market isn't racist at all," he writes, "and if highly qualified minority scholars or lawyers or doctors are a more valuable commodity than white ones, a free market will naturally bid up their price. That is what markets do (at least in the absence of regulation) when valuable commodities are in short supply; outstanding professionals who are members of desirable minority groups are expensive for the same reason that gold or diamonds are expensive. And that is evidently the result that the market currently produces, at least at the top end."

How is one to square Carter's view with Haynes's lament that the top ranks of Fortune 500 companies remain all but closed to African Americans, and that even large companies not on the Fortune 500 list have locked the CEO's office to blacks (except a conspicuous few, such as the late Reginald Lewis, who bought TLC Beatrice International Holdings in 1987, and Richard Parsons, who was named chief executive officer of Dime Savings Bank in 1990). "Certainly, given the fact that the first wave of minority group executives entered Fortune 500 companies in the late 1960s, certainly by now one would have made it, at least to be one of the top three executives in a Fortune 500 company," says Haynes. "I can't think of anyone who's made it to the top. By the law of averages, one of us, even if we didn't stay there, should have gotten to be chief financial officer."

One reason Haynes and Carter disagree is that they are looking at different markets. The market for law partners or university faculty members is considerably larger than the market for Fortune 500 CEOs. To put it another way, a law firm with one hundred partners or a university with two hundred faculty slots might easily see how they could profit by naming blacks to a few of those posts. A firm with only one CEO, however, is likely to view things differently. In my profession, there is considerable evidence of Carter's market theory in action. It is generally accepted among newspaper executives that a big-city daily needs at least some minority journalists in order to do an adequate job. As a result, the bidding for black, Hispanic, and Asian reporters considered top-notch can sometimes get furious. A few years ago, Ben Bradlee, then editor of the *Washington Post,* became so annoyed that the *New York Times* was trying to recruit his best black reporters that he wrote a note to the *Times* editor volunteering to send him a list of them. Despite the intense competition for black reporters, however, the top tier of newspaper management remains overwhelmingly white. None of the nation's biggest and most prestigious papers (or the three major news magazines) has installed an African American as its principal editor.

There are reasons for the scarcity of blacks at the top, some having to do with race and some not, but anyone who sees newspapers and other large organizations as nothing more than economic units in a gigantic market is bound to miss many of them. Newspapers in the real world are not elegant abstractions full of people with perfect knowledge and perfect access, driven purely by a desire to maximize profit. They are much more (for lack of a better word) *human* than that.

Even economists these days don't hew to the view that the "market" always knows what is best. Economist Herbert Stein, for instance, tells the story of two men, one an economist and one not, who were out for a stroll when the noneconomist stopped dead in his tracks and exclaimed, "Look, there's a $20 bill lying on the sidewalk!" The economist responded, "No, there can't be. If there had been, it would already have been picked up."

People don't always know where the money lies in life, and as a result they don't always make decisions that maximize their wealth, even if that is their intention. And often that is *not* their intention. Human beings, after all, are not bloodless calculators. They often act in romantic, altruistic, or merely mysterious ways. The same sort of emotional attachment that can lead a father to try to fulfill his dreams through his son, or a mother to sacrifice everything, including life itself, for the welfare of her family, operate—though generally in much milder ways—in the work environment, which is as much a social organization as an economic one. So decisions get made, and people get accepted (and rapidly promoted), for reasons that have nothing to do in a direct way with profit maximization. Perhaps a corporate officer sees a younger version of himself in the appearance and style of a certain young man. Or maybe a subordinate shares a passion for an exotic sport, or for a particular kind of after-hours entertainment. And even for competent people, especially blacks, such social binding can present a problem. As Edward Jones observes: "The kinds of social relationships, the kinds of acceptance by others [needed to advance], or not within your control. You can't make somebody love you or root for you."

Moreover, however much corporate mandarins like to think of themselves as risk-seeking entrepreneurs, most senior executives of established firms avoid risk whenever they can—not only looking out for their own economic welfare by negotiating compensation packages that never go down, regardless of their performance, but by rejecting any personnel move that seems a radical departure from the norm. And in many conservative corporate cultures, moving a black person into a sensitive job would be seen as an unacceptable risk, irrespective of that person's abilities. As the *New York Times* executive insinuated in explaining his hesitation to promote a certain black man, the very fact that a black had never previously held the post constituted part of the argument as to why one should not. Only after the "first black" managed to succeed would that particular barrier be removed.

The hesitation to move blacks along may have nothing to do with personal prejudice, but with a perception that putting a black person in a visible slot might have economic consequences—a perception that makes sense if one assumes (whatever the reality) that some segments of the market or some players who influence the market might be disturbed to see a black person in a job where only whites are normally seen. In assessing the comfort level of whites with very visible blacks, most executives have only assumptions to guide them, and those assumptions tend to be conservative, often to the point of rigidity. Until very recently, for instance, one big-city paper had an explicit policy against running more than one minority op-ed columnist a day, regardless of the columns' subject matter, perspectives, or quality. The assumption apparently was that while whites were comfortable with one nonwhite pictured in the commentary section of the newspaper, they would not be comfortable with more. So the editor had taken it upon himself to protect his readers from encountering too many minority writers.

Even if there were no explicit racial criteria at work, the market model would have obvious limits. Assuming that a market existed for "good people" and that it was to the economic advantage of the firm to make sure that such people were allowed, relative to others in the organization, to go as far as their abilities could take them, how would the organization recognize the best talent? To many, the answer seems obvious. That is exactly what they assume corporations are already doing. Isn't it self-evident that simply out of economic self-interest, a firm would do everything within its power to ensure that the best people were in the most appropriate jobs? . . . [M]any people (perhaps most) end up in jobs for reasons that seem to have little to do with merit. Edward Irons and Gilbert Moore, in their research on black bankers, were surprised to find that "virtually 100 percent of the interviewees indicated that the most important criterion for promotions was 'who you know,' or 'being plugged into the political system.'" Technical competence, in their eyes, counted for little.

Perhaps we can dismiss the bankers interviewed by Irons and Moore as extremists of some sort, but it's much more difficult to dismiss the mountain as academic studies, personal narratives, and anecdotal evidence that reveals the workplace as a social institution run largely on the basis of favoritism, stereotypes, and unexamined (often incorrect) suppositions. While affirmative action may have aggravated the problem, for all we know it has not. It may just be that *that is the way the workplace works*—or at least the way it has worked so far.

Hence, one is not quite sure what to make of Stephen Carter's declaration of war on racial preferences, or of the fact that he apparently expects an army of black professionals to join his crusade. The time will come, he speculates, when "we, the professionals who are people of color, decide to say that we have had enough—enough of stereotyping, enough of different standards, enough of the best-black syndrome." But Carter's stirring rhetoric obscures an important question. If in fact affirmative action does not account for all the problems he so eloquently pinpoints, then what, upon reflection, should be the response? If stereotyping, double standards, and professional ceilings exist quite independently of formal racial preference programs, how eager should we be to join the movement to abolish affirmative action? And if we assume that people in general, and employers in particular, tend to be marginally competent in assessing merit and potential irrespective of race, what are we to think of Carter's desire "to show the world that we who are black are not so marked by our history of racist oppression that we are incapable of intellectual achievement on the same terms as anybody else."

The problem he addresses is a real one. Yet the presumption of lesser competence is a cross borne not only by blacks who were "affirmative action hires," but at one time or another by many blacks who were not; by most blacks, in fact, who have ever found themselves working for a major American institution. That presumption is difficult, if not impossible, to overcome, which raises the obvious question of exactly what proof it would take to "show the world" that blacks are capable of real intellectual achievement.

I suspect that those inclined to believe in the possibility of genuine black achievement will accept that proposition even in the absence of absolute proof; or will note that blacks throughout history have already accomplished so much that yet another demonstration is unnecessary; or will point out that blacks, as Americans, deserve to be treated as individuals and equals without having to prove their worth first. On the other hand, those not inclined to believe that blacks are capable of any real intellectual achievement will reject "proof" of it with one of several responses. They may praise the black person who finally "shows" them as an "exception," and therefore not really black. Or they may claim that whatever feat of genius a black person performs, it is a simple intellectual parlor trick that demonstrates nothing at all. Or they may accept the proffered proof but then demand that blacks pass yet another test, that black professionals, for instance, make the black crime rate equal the white crime rate before they presume the right to be treated as equals. Common sense, in short, dictates that there is no such thing as proving such a proposition to a world unwilling to believe it, and no need to prove it to a world disposed to accept it.

To expect that abolishing affirmative action would make black intellectual capability easier to prove strikes me as more than a little naive. Just as to argue, as Carter does, that "affirmative action has done nothing at all for the true victims of racism" strikes me as myopic. Putting aside the question of whether affirmative action has truly benefited most members of any class, who exactly are these "true victims of racism"? Presumably, in Carter's mind, they are the poor souls who populate the underclass. Yet if you believe the volumes of evidence that show racial problems and racial stereotypes percolating through every level of American society, you could argue that just about every American, whatever his or her race, is a true victim of racism.

For all my problems with Carter's analysis, I believe he has a compelling point: that affirmative action or racial preference programs will never bring blacks into parity with whites. And I'm sure that others who might disagree with much of what he says would not disagree with him on that. Roosevelt Thomas, founder of the

American Institute for Managing Diversity, comes to a similar conclusion about affirmative action from a different set of premises. "Sooner or later, affirmative action will die a natural death. Its achievements have been stupendous, but if we look at the premises that underlie it, we find assumptions and priorities that look increasingly shopworn," he wrote in 1990 in the *Harvard Business Review.*

I will return to Thomas later. Suffice it to say here that like many black professionals, I find myself profoundly ambivalent on the question of affirmative action. I don't believe that it works very well, nor that it can be made to satisfy much of anyone. Moreover, I believe that programs based on racial preferences are inherently riddled with the taint and the reality of unfairness. I don't, however, believe that such programs belong on any list of the most odious things to have befallen America. And I certainly don't believe—despite the anguished cries of untold numbers of white men—that such programs have had much to do with the inability of any but a handful of whites to get hired or promoted. I believe, rather, that affirmative action has been made the scapegoat for a host of problems that many Americans simply don't wish to face up to; and that while a huge and largely phony public debate has raged over whether affirmative action is good or bad, the reality is much more nuanced and complex. In recent days, that debate has sometimes pitted so-called black conservatives against so-called black liberals. Yet I doubt that if pressed to the wall, the two sides would find themselves in much disagreement—at least over the essential bankruptcy of affirmative action as a policy to foster workplace equality. Where their more fundamental disagreement lies is in their assessment of the virtues of whites. Would whites treat everyone more equally if affirmative action wasn't gumming up the works? Without the millstone of affirmative action, would corporations and other large organizations be more capable of judging people on performance, potential, and merit rather than on preconceptions and office politics? Would acceptance as full members of the American family come easier if the prod were taken away? One side, in effect, says yes, and the other says no.

These are not questions of fact, for the future, by definition, is unknown. They are essentially questions of faith—of whether one believes in the ability and willingness of those whites who still control the majority of important institutions in America to do what they have not done thus far: ensure that no group is systematically penalized as a consequence of color.

In March 1961, when John F. Kennedy signed Executive Order 10925, which created the President's Committee on Equal Employment Opportunity and brought the phrase affirmative action into common usage, he apparently had little more than that in mind: "The contractor will not discriminate against any employee or applicant for employment because of race, creed, color or national origin . . . [and] will take affirmative action to ensure that applicants are employed, and that employees are treated during employment, without regard to their race, creed, color, or national origin." The difficulty companies had in carrying out that simple injunction is a story much too tangled and complicated even to begin to detail here; but the fact that they in large measure did not carry it out explains both why we are still debating affirmative action more than three decades later and why so many blacks are reluctant to take a leap of faith.

Imagine a brown, unpopular child who wants more than anything to be a runner. His classmates refuse to let him run with them, or even to practice on *their* track. When he dares to go near it, they taunt him, and then they push him away. A kindly official, noticing the harassment, decides to give the boy a break. He declares that even if the other children will not let the brown kid practice with them, they must let him run in every scheduled public race. Moreover, since the boy is at a disadvantage because he has not been allowed to practice with them, the official orders all the other boys to give him a five-yard head start.

At the first race approaches, the boy is both apprehensive and elated. He is unsure of his own abilities but delighted that he will finally have a chance to show all the other kids what he can do, and he is comforted by the thought that once he does they will finally accept him as a peer. On the day of the race, however, an unexpected thing happens. Even before he starts to run, the crowd pelts him with garbage and stones. When the race begins, he stumbles and the other kids catch up with him. Some pass him with looks of concern and sympathy, others pass with looks of scorn, and a few even elbow him or kick him as they scamper on their way.

The experience repeats itself race after race; and as the child struggles to understand why he is being treated so, he learns that the people in the crowd suffer from a strange affliction, that though they can see him well enough to abuse him, no one up there can really see what he is going through. Those in the stands can see, at most, a fraction of the objects that fly his way; and those who are hurling them can't understand their force. He learns that many of the onlookers pity him, that some refuse to throw stones and even whisper words of encouragement, but that most deeply resent the fact that the other kids had to let him into the race, and that they resent his five-yard head start even more.

Though the official has given a very public and heartfelt explanation for the special treatment, loudmouths in the bleachers focus increasingly on the unfairness of the brown kid's head start. Why is it necessary? If he must run, why can't he start with the other kids?

Could he be genetically inferior? If so, why is he running at all? And why in the blazes can't he ever win even with a head start? Could he have a psychological problem? Is he lazy? Is he stupid? Is something in his culture keeping him from keeping up?

Soon the questions have reached such a pitch that the mere sight of the kid on the track is enough to whip the crowd into a frenzy. The child, as he comes to understand the anger of the mob, realizes that even with a five-yard head start, he will never win. And he doesn't know whether he should ask for a bigger lead, give up the one he has, or simply abandon the race.

ANALYSIS

1. How does Cose analyze the *Forbes* and *Newsweek* polls showing that whites believe they have been discriminated against by affirmative action policies? Does his analysis convince you?
2. According to Cose, what criteria other than academic performance do college admissions officers use? Why don't such criteria arouse debate?
3. Cose makes an important point about polling by noting the discrepancy between answers dependent on the race of the poll-taker; does he convince you?
4. How, according to Cose, do stereotypes of blacks affect judgment of particular black applicants?

WRITING POSSIBILITIES

1. Towards the end of his essay, Cose says he is "profoundly ambivalent on the question of affirmative action" but goes on to ask whether, without such policies, corporations and organizations would be "more capable of judging people on performance, potential, and merit rather than on preconceptions and office politics"? Cose admits that the question can't be answered easily—they are, he says, "essentially questions of faith." What does Cose mean by this phrase? How would you answer such a question of faith and persuade your audience, through examples and reasons, that the answer might be either positive or negative?
2. Defenders of affirmative action often rely on the effect of such policies on women; in California for example, a ballot initiative to drop affirmative action policies by the state was opposed on the grounds that small-business opportunities for women had been increased immeasurably by affirmative action loan programs. Assuming this record of loans to women's businesses was factually true, how would you deal with the ethical issue of equality: why should one sex be given special privileges over another?

3. George Will has argued that while affirmative action programs were originally begun to improve diversity in business organizations, they have spread inappropriately to educational institutions. Does Wills rely on an arguable assumption that educational and business opportunities are and ought to be entirely separate matters? Would you agree or disagree with Will's assumption? Why or why not?

4. In an unusual intellectual move, sociologist Nathan Glazer has reversed himself on the question of affirmative action. Glazer's essay in Chapter 4 ("The American Ethnic Pattern") was part of a book-length study urging rejection of the then-new affirmative action programs on the grounds that they violated the "American Ethnic Pattern" (no special political aid to particular groups). But recently Glazer has said that the dismal record over the years of admission of African Americans to colleges and universities now requires acceptance of "preference" ("In Defence of Preference," *The New Republic,* April 6, 1998) and of the "moral" criterion of "diversity"—for example by adding a "Striver's Score" to the SAT admission factor ("Yes, the SAT Should Account for Race," *The New Republic,* September 27, 1999). In this last article Glazer was opposed by the sociologist Angela Thernstrom; both Glazer's argument and Thernstrom's are easily accessible on *The New Republic's* own website or via such common search engines as Yahoo: just punch in "Glazer, Nathan," go to the "Next Searches" and run down the list until you come to the running title for the symposium of which Glazer and Thernstrom were a part—"The End of Meritocracy." Read (or reread) Glazer's "American Ethnic Pattern" (Chapter 4) and the later articles from *The New Republic,* together with Thernstrom's reply to Glazer's SAT essay in the same *New Republic* website and explain to what extent you agree or disagree with Glazer's new defence of the "moral" merit of "preference" and "diversity" in college or university admissions.

5. A conservative attack on the new criterion of "diversity" can be found in Jason L. Riley's "The Diversity Defense" (*Commentary,* April 2001). Riley argues that the University of Michigan's policy of attaching new importance to "diversity" as a criterion of admission conflicts dramatically with a university's need to accept only the most "qualified" students, regardless of skin color, sex, national origin, and so forth. Riley refutes recent arguments by William G. Bowen and Derek Bok in *The Shape of the River* (1998) that affirmative action in Ivy League schools did not result in hordes of unqualified students—quite the contrary, according to Bowen and Bok, graduation rates showed these affirmative action admissions as fully competitive with others. But Riley says that (among other criticisms) Bowen and Bok in claiming high graduation rates simply ignored "the alarmingly high *drop-out* rates of students admitted under preferential quotas. . . . " Read Riley's essay, find other reviews of Bowen and Bok's study, and in an essay discuss the two key issues here—the ethical one (diversity is a good thing, regardless of performance) and the intellectual one (universities exist only for intellectual goals).

Richard Rorty

A philosopher of American pragmatism ('what's right is what works' would be a crude definition), Richard Rorty takes on the contemporary assumption that "rights" are the crucial engine of social progress. Rorty argues that the minute you mention rights you're in the realm of the "nonnegotiable." Who can argue for or against them—rights are simply there and that's it. As Rorty says here, rights talk "makes political morality not a result of political discourse—of reflection, compromise, and choice of the lesser evil—but rather an unconditional moral imperative. . . . " Some would say, That's exactly the point: abortion is not something that can be a "lesser evil," human rights under Pol Pot or in genocidal Rwanda are not subject to "compromise," and so forth. Rorty raises a tough point. He is criticizing his own group—the Left to which he belongs—but he is saying that there are some cases in which "rights talk" is so counterproductive as to be, in effect, wrong.

WHAT'S WRONG WITH "RIGHTS"

If one accepts the premise that the basic responsibility of the American left is to protect the poor against the rapacity of the rich, it's difficult to argue that the postwar years have been particularly successful ones. As Karl Marx pointed out, the history of the modern age is the history of class warfare, and in America today, it is a war in which the rich are winning, the poor are losing, and the left, for the most part, is standing by.

Early American leftists, from William James to Walt Whitman to Eleanor Roosevelt, seeking to improve the standing of the country's poorest citizens, found their voice in a rhetoric of fraternity, arguing that Americans had a responsibility for the well-being of their fellow man. This argument has been replaced in current leftist discourse by the rhetoric of "rights." The shift has its roots in the fact that the left's one significant postwar triumph was the success of the civil-rights movement. The language of "rights" is the language of the documents that have sparked the most successful attempts to relieve human suffering in postwar America—the series of Supreme Court decisions that began with *Brown* v. *Board of Education* and continued through *Roe* v. *Wade*. The *Brown* decision launched the most successful appeal to the consciences of Americans since the Progressive Era.

Yet the trouble with rights talk, as the philosopher Mary Ann Glendon has suggested, is that it makes political morality not a result of political discourse—of reflection, compromise, and choice of the lesser evil—but rather an unconditional moral imperative: a matter of corresponding to something antecedently given, in the way that the will of God or the law of nature is purportedly given. Instead of saying, for example, that the absence of various legal protections make the lives of homosexuals unbearably difficult, that it creates unnecessary human suffering for our fellow Americans, we have come to say that these protections must be instituted in order to protect homosexuals' rights.

The difference between an appeal to end suffering and an appeal to rights is the difference between an appeal to fraternity, to fellow-feeling, to sympathetic concern, and an appeal to something that exists quite independently from anybody's feelings about anything—something that issues unconditional commands. Debate about the existence of such commands, and discussion of which rights exist and which do not, seems to me a philosophical blind alley, a pointless importation of legal discourse into politics, and a distraction from what is really needed in this case: an attempt by the straights to put themselves in the shoes of the gays.

Consider Colin Powell's indignant reaction to the suggestion that the exclusion of gays from the military is analogous to the pre-1950s exclusion of African Americans from the military. Powell angrily insists that there is no analogy here—that gays simply do not have the rights claimed by blacks. As soon as the issue is phrased in rights talk, those who agree with Powell and oppose what they like to call "special rights for homosexuals" start citing the Supreme Court's decision in *Bowers* v. *Hardwick*. The Court looked into the matter and solemnly found that there is no constitutional protection for sodomy. So people arguing against Powell have to contend that *Bowers* was wrongly decided. This leads to an argumentative impasse, one that suggests that rights talk is the wrong approach.

The *Brown* v. *Board of Education* decision was not a discovery of a hitherto unnoticed constitutional right, or of the hitherto unnoticed intentions of the authors of constitutional amendments. Rather, it was the result of our society's long-delayed willingness to admit that the behavior of white Americans toward the descendants of black slaves was, and continued to be, incredibly cruel—that it was intolerable that American citizens should be subjected to the humiliation of segregation. If *Bowers* v. *Hardwick* is reversed, it will not be because a hitherto invisible right to sodomy has become manifest to the justices. It will be because the heterosexual majority has become more willing to concede that it has been tormenting homosexuals for no better reason than to give itself the sadistic pleasure of humiliating a group designated as inferior—designated as such for no better reason than to give another group a sense of superiority.

I may seem to be stretching the term "sadistic," but I do not think I am. It seems reasonable to define "sadism" as the use of persons weaker than ourselves as outlets for our resentments and frustrations, and especially for the infliction of humiliation on such people in order to bolster our own sense of self-worth. All of us have been guilty, at some time in our lives, of this sort of casual, socially accepted sadism. But the most conspicuous instances of sadism, and the only ones relevant to politics, involve groups rather than individuals. Thus Cossacks and the Nazi storm troopers used Jews, and the white races have traditionally used the colored races, in order to bolster their group self-esteem. Men have traditionally humiliated women and beaten up gays in order to exalt their own sense of masculine privilege. The central dynamic behind this kind of sadism is the simple fact that it keeps up the spirits of a lot of desperate, beaten-down people to be able to say to themselves, "At least I'm not a nigger!" or "At least I'm not a faggot!"

Sadism, however, is not the only cause of cruelty and needless suffering. There is also selfishness. Selfishness differs from sadism in being more realistic and more thoughtful. It is less a matter of a sense of one's own worth and more a matter of rational calculation. If I own a business and pay my workers more than the minimum necessary to keep them at work, there will less for me. My paying them less is not sadistic, but it may well be selfish. If I prevent my slaves, or the descendants of my ancestors' slaves, from getting an education, there will be less chance for them to compete with me and my descendants for the good jobs. If suburbanites cast their votes in favor of financing public education through locally administered property taxes, there will be less chance for the children in the cities to be properly educated, and so to compete with suburban children for membership in a shrinking middle class. All these calculated actions are cruel and selfish, but it would be odd to call them sadistic.

Our knowledge of sadism is relatively new—it is something we have only begun to get a grip on with the help of Freud, and philosophers like Sartre and Derrida, who have capitalized on Freud's work. But it is as if the thrill of discovering something new has led us to forget other human impulses; on constant guard against sadism, we have allowed selfishness free reign.

Just as rights talk is the wrong approach to issues where appeals to human sympathy are needed, sadism is the wrong target when what is at hand is selfishness. But this is the way American leftists have learned to talk—and think—about the world.

You would not guess from listening to the cultural politicians of the academic left that the power of the rich over the poor remains the most obvious, and potentially explosive, example of injustice in contemporary America. For these academics offer ten brilliant unmaskings of unconscious sadism for every unmasking of the selfishness intrinsic to American political and economic institutions. Enormous ingenuity and learning are deployed in demonstrating the complicity of this or that institution, or of some rival cultural politician, with patriarchy or heterosexism or racism. But little gets said about how we might persuade Americans who make more than $50,000 a year to take more notice of the desperate situation of their fellow citizens who make less than $20,000.

Instead, we hear talk of "the dominant white patriarchal heterosexist culture." This idea isolates the most sadistic patterns of behavior from American history, weaves them together, and baptizes their cause "the dominant culture." It is as if I listed all the shameful things I have done in my life and then attributed them to the dark power of "my true, dominant self." This would be a good way to alienate myself from myself, and to induce schizophrenia, but it would not be a good way to improve my behavior. For it does not add anything to the nasty facts about my past to blame them on a specter. Nor does it add anything to the facts about the suffering endured by African Americans and other groups to invent a bogeyman called "the dominant culture."

The more we on the American left think that study of psychoanalytic or sociological or philosophical theory will give us a better grip on what is going on in our country, the less likely we are to speak a political language that will help bring about change in our society. The more we can speak a robust, concrete, and practical language— one that can be picked up and used by legislators and judges—the more use we will be.

ANALYSIS

1. What might Rorty mean by speaking of political morality as involving "political discourse— . . . reflection, compromise, and choice of the lesser evil" as against an "unconditional moral imperative." Might this apply to the pro-choice, pro-life debate? In what way, on your view?

2. To test whether you agree with Rorty or not, consider his discussion of gays in the military. Rorty examines Colin Powell's view that one cannot analogize the exclusion of gays in the military with the former discrimination against blacks in the military because (as Powell argued) gays do not have the rights that blacks do. Rorty attacks this rights-argument. On what basis? Does he convince you that "rights talk" here is "the wrong approach"?

3. Does Rorty's argument amounts to nothing more than what he says at the end—avoid the left's infatuation with high-powered talk ("heterosexism," "racism") and use "a robust, concrete, and practical language"? Would you be willing to give up such terms as "racism" or "sexism"? Why or why not?

——————— Writing Possibilities ———————

1. Consider again Rorty's words:

   . . . the trouble with rights talk . . . is that it makes political morality not a result of political discourse—of reflection, compromise,
   and choice of the lesser evil—but rather an unconditional moral
   imperative: a matter of corresponding to something antecedently
   given, in the way that the while of God or the law of nature is
   purportedly given.

   Have you seen examples of such "unconditional" talk in any of the essays in this text? For any such essay, cite specific examples of such talk
   and then develop an essay in which you either agree or disagree with
   Rorty view that such "unconditional" talk is a problem. Or: find a recent editorial or op-ed column in the newspaper or from a news-
   magazine and explain to what extent you think it could be Rorty-ized;
   cite specific examples, especially, of talk that is "not a result of political discourse. . . ."

2. Have you ever experienced a situation which might be Rorty-ized? A
   controversy on campus (or even within your family) where "rights
   talk" got in the way more than it helped? Explain the situation and
   offer sufficient detail and example to make the reader understand, and
   perhaps agree with, the position you have adopted. Contrariwise, find
   a situation which resists the Rorty strategy and explain it for an on-
   the-fence reader.

3. The popular campus speaker Paul Rogat Loeb, author of *Soul of a Citizen, Living With Conviction in a Cynical Time,* cites Rorty's ideas as
   justification for the view that we ought to be telling stories about "specific lives and situations" if we are to really affect others and feel
   deeply about a problem ourselves:

   Concrete, particularized stories [Loeb writes] help us feel the emotional weight of the world's troubles without so burdening us that
   we despair of ever being able to change things. As the philosopher
   Richard Rorty reminds us, the best way to promote compassion
   and solidarity is not by appealing to some general notion of goodness, but by encouraging people to respond to specific human
   lives. Responsibility in this view is not an abstract principle but a
   way of being. It exists only in the doing.

   Can you find in your own experience an example of a "particularized
   story" that meets Loeb's specifications? Would you agree with Loeb
   that it is better to respond to an individual life (and tell the story of
   that life) rather than talk about abstract and general ethical principles?

CREDITS

Abu-Jaber, Diana, "On Reading Differences" by Diana Abu-Jaber, originally appeared in *Ploughshares* vol 16, no. 223.

Albert, Lee, "God in the Public Square," *The Buffalo News* 10/15/00. Used with permission.

Alcaraz, Lala, "L.A. Cucaracha Urban Sketch Journal" from *Urban Latino Cultures (La Vida Latina en L.A.)* pp. 83–84, 89. Copyright © 1999 Corwin Press. Reprinted by permission of Crown Press, Inc.

Anonthasy, Monk Phen, from *Voices from Southeast Asia: The Refugee Experience in the United States,* by John Tenhula (New York: Holmes & Meier, 1991). Copyright © 1991 by Holmes & Meier Publishers, Inc. Reproduced by permission of the publisher.

Anzaldua, Gloria, from *Borderlands/La Frontera: The New Mestiza* © 1987, 1999 by Gloria Anzaldua. Reprinted by permission of Aunt Lute Books.

Bandow, Doug, used with permission from *The Freeman,* now known as *Ideas on Liberty.*

Blew, Mary Clearman, from *Bone Deep in Landscaping: Writing, Reading, and Place* by Mary Clearman Blew. Copyright © 1999 by the University of Oaklahoma Press. Reprinted with Permission.

Bravo, Ellen, reprinted by permission of *Ms.* Magazine, © 1999/2000.

Brooks, Geraldine, used with permission of Geraldine Brooks.

Chang-Rae Lee, "Mute in an English-Only World" from *The New York Times* 4/18/96. Used with permission.

Chavez, Linda, from Out of the Barrio, by Linda Chavez. Copyright © 1991 by BasicBooks, a division of HarperCollins Publishers, Inc. Reprinted by permission of Basic Books, a member of Perseus Books, L.L.C.

Cose, Ellis, page 111–133 from *The Rage of The Privileged Class* by Ellis Cose. Copyright © 1993 by Ellis Cose. Reprinted by permission of Harper-Collins Publishers, Inc.

Countryman, Edward, "Preface" from *Americans: A Collision of Histories* by Edward Countryman. Copyright © 1996 by Edward Countryman. Reprinted by permission of Hill and Wang, a division of Farrar, Straus and Giroux, L.L.C.

Cox, Michael and Richard Alm, copyright © 1999 by W. Michael Cox and Richard Alm. Reprinted by permission of Basic Books, a member of Perseus Books, L.L.C.

De Marco Torgovnick, Marianne, "On Being White, Female, and Born in Bensonhurst" from *Crossing Ocean Parkway.* Published by The University of Chicago Press. Used with permission.

Ellis, C.P., and **Studs Terkel,** copyright © 1992. *Race: How Blacks and Whites Feel About the American Obsession* by Studs Terkel. Reprinted by permission of The New Press. (800) 233-4830.

Erber, Stephen P., used with permission of Stephen P. Erber, Muhlenberg College.

Farrell, Warren, "Men as Success Objects," from *The Myth of Male Power* (Penguin © 1993, ISBN: 0425181448). Essay first appeared in *Family Therapy Network* (Nov/Dec 1988). Used with permission.

Finnegan, William, reprinted by permission of International Creative Management, Inc. Copyright © 1997 William Finnegan.

Fries, Kenny, "Getting to Work: For the Disabled, Opportunity Out of Reach," originally appeared in *The Progressive.* Copyright © 2000 by Kenny Fries. Reprinted by permission of the author.

Furchgott-Roch, Diane and Christine Stolba, reprinted with the permission of *The American Enterprise Institute for Public Policy Research,* Washington, DC.

Glazer, Nathan, from *Affirmative Discrimination: Ethnic Inequality and Public Policy* by Nathan Glazer. Copyright © 1975 by Nathan Glazer. Reprinted with permissions of Basic Books, a member of Perseus Books, L.L.C.

Hentoff, Nat, used with permission of the author.

Hooks, Bell, from "Men: Comrades in Struggle" from *Feminist Theory: From Margin to Center by Bell Hooks.* Published by South End Publishing, Cambridge, MA. Used with permission.

Hughes, Langston, from *The Collected Poems of Langston Hughes* by Langston Hughes, Copyright © 1994 by The Estate of Langston Hughes. Used by permission of Alfred A. Knopf, a division of Random House, Inc.

Ireland, Patricia, from *What Women Want* by Patricia Ireland. Copyright © 1996 by Patricia Ireland. Used by permission of Dutton, a division of Penguin Putnam, Inc.

Jacobs, Michael, "A Place in the Classroom," used with permission.

Johnson, Dirk, from *The New York Times,* 10/14/98, pp. 1. Used with permission.

Kim, Elaine, copyright © 1993 from *Reading Rodney King: Urban Uprising* by Elaine H. Kim. Reproduced by permission of Routledge, Inc., part of the Taylor & Francis Group.

Lerner, Gerda, from *Why History Matters* by Gerda Lerner, copyright © 1997 by Gerda Lerner. Used by permission of Oxford University Press.

Lippard, Lucy, copyright © 1997 *The Lure of The Local: A Sense of Place in a Multicentered Society* by Lucy R. Lippard. Reprinted by permission of The New Press. (800) 233-4830.

Liu, Eric, author of "The Accidental Asian: Notes of a Native Speaker," and editor of the anthology, *Next: Young American Writers on the New Generation.* Used with permission.

LoPiano, Donna, used with permission of the author.

Lorber, Judith, "The Social Construction of Gender" from *The 1992 Cheryl Miller Lecture,* pp. 47–55, copyright © 1992 by Sage Publications. Reprinted by Permission of Sage Publications, Inc.

Loury, Glenn C., "Free at Last? A Personal Perspective on Race and Identity in America," from *Commentary,* October 1992, by permission; all rights reserved.

Malcolm X, used with permission of Chelsea House Publishers.

Mantsios, Gregory, from *Race, Class, & Gender in the United States: An Integrated Study, 5th ed.* Paula Rothenberg, editor. (New York, NY: Worth Publishing, 2001). Reprinted by permission of the author.

Marable, Manning, from *Dispatches from The Ebony Tower: Intellectuals Confront The African-American Experience* edited by Manning Marable © 2000 Columbia University Press. Reprinted with the permission of the publisher.

McBride, James, "School" from *The Color of Water* by James McBride, copyright © 1996 by James McBride. Used by permission of Riverhead Books, a division of Penguin Putnam, Inc.

McLemore, S. Dale, from S. Dale McLemore, *Racial and Ethnic Relations in America, 5/e,* copyright © 1998 by Allyn & Bacon. Reprinted with permission.

Miller, John J., from *The New York Times* 5/26/98. Used with permission.

Mosconi, Angela, and Susan Edelman, used with permission of the *New York Post.*

Mukerjee, Bharati, copyright © 1996 by Bharati Mukherjee. Originally published in *The New York Times.* Reprinted by permission of the author.

Novak, Michael, "Faith in Search of Votes," *The New York Times Magazine,* vb3/31/98, p. 37.

Novak, Michael, second edition published as *Unmeltable Ethnics: Politics & Culture in American Life* by Transaction Books: New Brunswick, NJ, 1996 with a new introduction and new materials by the author.

Omi, Michael and Howard Winant, copyright 1986 from *Racial Formation in the United States* by Michael Omi and Howard Winant. Reproduced by permission of Routledge, Inc., part ot the Taylor & Francis Group.

Peyser, Andrea, used with permission of the *New York Post.*

Pharr, Suzanne, "A Match Made in Heaven," *The Progressive* 8/906, pp. 28–29.

Pilon, Roger, used with the permission of the Cato Institute.

Rorty, Richard, used with the permission of Dr. Richard Rorty.

Rose, Mike, reprinted and abridged with the permission of The Free Press, A Division of Simon & Schuster, Inc. "Entering the Conversation" from *Lives on the Boundary: The Struggles and Achievements of America's Underprepared* by Mike Rose. Copyright © 1989 by Mike Rose.

Sabo, Don, used with permission of Don Sabo, Ph.D.

Santiago, Esmeralada, from *When I Was Puerto Rican* by Esmeralda Santiago. Copyright © 1993 by Esmeralda Santiago. Reprinted by permission of Perseus Books Publishers, a member of Perseus Books, L.L.C.

Segell, Michael, from *Standup Guy: Manhood After Feminism* by Michael Segell, copyright © 2000 for specified excerpt from pages 118–136.

Shalit, Wendy, "Among Gender Benders," from *Commentary* magazine 1/99, pp. 54–56.

Steele, Shelby, used with permission of the author.

Sullivan, Andrew, from *Virtually Normal,* by Andrew Sullivan, Copyright © 1995 by Andrew Sullivan. Used by permission of Alfred A. Knopf, a division of Random House, Inc.

Takaki, Ronald, used with permission of Professor Ronald Takaki, University of California at Berkeley.

Tatum, Beverly, from *Why Are All The Black Kids Sitting Together In The Cafeteria?* by Beverly Daniel Tatum. Copyright © 1997 by Beverly Daniel Tatum. Reprinted by permission of Basic Books, a member of Perseus Books, L.L.C.

Walljasper, Jay, "A Fair Share in Suburbia" reprinted with permission from the January 25, 1999 issue of *The Nation.*

Watson, Tom, "The American Way of Golf," *The New York Times,* 6/17/91. Used with permission.

Weinstein, Michael M. from *The New York Times,* 2/18/00. Used with permission.

West, Daniel and Joan M. West, reprinted with permission of Sherman Alexie, Dennis West, Joan M. West and Cineaste magazine.

Wills, Gary, reprinted with permission from The New York of Books. Copyright © 2000, NYREV, Inc.

Wilson, William Julius, from *The New York Times,* 8/18/96. Used with permission.

INDEX